DISCARDED

CLASSICS IN PSYCHOLOGY

CLASSICS IN PSYCHOLOGY

Advisory Editors
HOWARD GARDNER
AND
JUDITH KRIEGER GARDNER

Editorial Board
Wayne Dennis
Paul A. Kolers
Sheldon H. White

MENTAL SCIENCE

BY

ALEXANDER BAIN, M.A

ARNO PRESS
A New York Times Company
New York ★ 1973

Reprint Edition 1973 by Arno Press Inc.

Reprinted from a copy in
The University of Illinois Library

Classics in Psychology
ISBN for complete set: 0-405-05130-1
See last pages of this volume for titles.

Manufactured in the United States of America

Library of Congress Cataloging in Publication Data

Bain, Alexander, 1818-1903.
   Mental science; a compendium of psychology.

   (Classics in psychology)
   Reprint of the 1868 ed. published by D. Appleton,
New York.
   1. Psychology. I. Title. II. Series.
[DNLM: BF B162m 1868F]
BF131.B2 1973   150   73-2958
ISBN 0-405-05132-8

A NOTE ABOUT THE AUTHOR

ALEXANDER BAIN, Scottish psychologist, philosopher, and educator, was born in Aberdeen in 1818. He studied at a university in Aberdeen, then, for twenty years, remained a free-lance teacher in London and Scotland. While in London he became a friend of John Stuart Mill and absorbed the ideas of empiricism and associationism prominent in the British philosophy of that period. He also produced a systematic psychology in two parts: *The Senses and the Intellect* (1855) and *The Emotions and the Will* (1859). These works, which run well over a thousand pages, are generally considered the most complete and authoritative statement of the British school of associationism. As their author, Bain stands at the crossroads of psychology and philosophy, drawing on what was most enduring in the philosophical tradition of Mill, and anticipating the empirical applications of German and British experimenters.

Following the publication of his *magnum opus,* Bain finally was appointed to a chair at Aberdeen in 1860. There he worked on questions of the relationship between mind and body and abridged his psychological treatise into a more readable text, *Mental Science.* He also founded the influential journal, *Mind.* Bain continued to revise and update his works until his death in 1903, at the age of 85.

MENTAL SCIENCE:

A COMPENDIUM OF PSYCHOLOGY,

AND THE

HISTORY OF PHILOSOPHY.

DESIGNED AS A

TEXT-BOOK FOR HIGH-SCHOOLS AND COLLEGES.

BY

ALEXANDER BAIN, M. A.,

PROFESSOR OF LOGIC AND MENTAL PHILOSOPHY IN THE UNIVERSITY OF ABERDEEN,
AUTHOR OF "THE SENSES AND THE INTELLECT," "THE EMOTIONS
OF THE WILL," ETC., ETC.

NEW YORK:
D. APPLETON AND COMPANY,
90, 92 & 94 GRAND STREET.
1868.

ENTERED, according to Act of Congress, in the year 1868, by
D. APPLETON & CO.,
In the Clerk's Office of the District Court of the United States for the Southern District of New York.

AUTHOR'S PREFACE.

The present treatise contains a Systematic Exposition of Mind, and a History of the leading Questions in Mental Philosophy.

The Exposition of Mind is, for the most part, an abridgment of my two volumes on the subject. I have singled out, and put in conspicuous type, the leading positions; and have given a sufficient number of examples to make them understood. It is not to be expected that the full effect of the larger exposition can be produced in the shorter; still, there may be an occasional advantage in the more succinct presentation of complicated doctrines.

As regards the controverted Questions, I have entered fully into the history of opinion, so as to exhibit the different views, both formerly, and at present, entertained on each. Nominalism and Realism, the Origin of Knowledge in the mind, External Perception, Beauty, and Freewill, are the chief subjects thus treated.

Aberdeen, *April*, 1868.

INTRODUCTORY NOTICE TO THE AMERICAN EDITION.

The author of the present volume, Mr. Alexander Bain, is Professor of Logic, Mental Philosophy, and English Literature, in the University of Aberdeen, in Scotland, and is also Examiner in Logic and Moral Philosophy in the University of London. His contributions to the Science of Mind have given him a high reputation in Europe both as an original inquirer and as an authoritative expositor of the most advanced views; and as this is his first work upon these subjects which has been republished in this country, a few words respecting its claims and the author's position will be appropriate in this place.

It is now generally admitted that, as regards its capability of progress, expansion, and the improvement of its methods, Mental Science forms no exception to the other branches of growing knowledge. Those who are familiar with the recent progress of thought understand that the later advances of Physiology have brought that subject into very close relation with questions of Mind. So important are the data thus contributed, and so intimate the mutual dependence of these subjects, that it is no longer possible to study Mind, in the true scientific spirit, without taking into account its material accompaniments. The method hitherto employed of studying mental phenomena by introspection is not superseded, but it has undergone an important extension. No system of Mental Philosophy can ever dispense with the necessity of observing and analyzing the processes of thought and feeling as they are revealed in consciousness; but it is equally certain that any system which stops with this, and neglects the living organism by which thought and feeling are manifested and conditioned, can no longer command the approval of those who seek a full and scientific acquaintance with the subject. This inclusion of its physiological factors, with the consequent widening of its sphere, not only brings the subject of Mental Philosophy into harmonious relation with the other sciences, and gives to its method more precision and completeness, but it also leads to certain practical advantages of much importance.

The old system, which occupied itself with inquiries concerning mind as an isolated abstraction, threw but little light upon the real psychical mechanism and workings of human nature. In this respect it was narrow and deficient, and, failing to reach practical ends, it became obnoxious to the charge of 'fruitlessness.' Indeed, its adherents, so far from denying this imputation, have actually attempted to turn it into a merit. Holding to the ancient doctrine that all quest of knowledge for its mere vulgar uses is degrading, they maintain that the object of mental studies is not so much the establishment of truth for the sake of the benefits which may be derived from it, as the intellectual interest and pleasure of its pursuit; and the claims of metaphysical studies are therefore made to rest chiefly on their alleged value as an educational gymnastic. This was well enough so long as all knowledge was in an imperfect state, and all studies fruitless of application—so long, for example, as physics pursued by a false method remained barren of valuable results. But when the clew to the understanding of Nature was once seized, and science after science arose, clear, positive, and demonstrable, followed by results so practical, beneficent, and universal as to give a new impulse to civilization, it was impossible that the old aims of study should not undergo profound revision, and their practical bearings upon human welfare rise to a higher appreciation. Metaphysics alone has refused to change, and, clinging to its old method, has stood as a landmark of the past, stationary in the midst of progress, vacant of benign influence, while all other knowledges were blossoming and fruiting in the useful service of society. It was, therefore, natural that this study, challenged by the spirit of the age, should decline in interest as it has done, and fall under the protection of tradition.

But that the study of mind in its larger aspects, that is, the actual study of man as a thinking, feeling, and active being, must issue in the noblest applications, is beyond all rational question. In the whole circle of human interests there is no need so vital and urgent as for a better understanding of the laws of mind and character. We may dispense with this kind of information or with that, but the acquirement of true ideas concerning human nature, the springs of its action, the modes of its working, and the conditions and limits of its improvement, is indispensable for all. Parents need it for the training of their children; teachers in the instruction of their pupils; employers in their intercourse with the employed; physicians in treating their patients; clergymen in the management of their congregations; judges and juries in the administration of justice, and statesmen in legislating for the people. In short, whoever lives in social relations requires this knowledge for better and higher guidance in the whole sphere of life. The extension of the subject of Mental Philosophy so as to include the physiological elements and conditions, and help to a better understanding of the constitution of man, is therefore an important step in the direction of our greatest needs. Human nature is no longer to be dealt with by the student in fragments. but as a vital whole. In place of the abstraction mind, is substituted the living being, compounded of mind and body, to be contemplated, like any other object of science, as actually presented to our observation and in our experience. This enlargement of the domain of mental studies, while it is but a part of the general evolution of knowledge, relieves the subject of the reproach of emptiness, and places it at the head of all the sciences in the scale of direct and comprehensive utility. The study of Mind has always ranked as the noblest and most elevating of intellectual pursuits; but its questions can certainly lose nothing in interest or dignity, as it is more and more clearly perceived that they involve the highest concernments of humanity.

Nor are the benefits here claimed by any means still prospective; much has already been done. The labors of various eminent men of the present and past generation, such as Sir Charles Bell, Marshall Hall, Sir Benjamin Brodie, Drs. Laycock and Carpenter, Sir Henry Holland, Herbert Spencer, and others, have resulted in the establishment of a body of facts and principles in mental physiology which has variously influenced the popular works upon mental philosophy from Abercrombie to the present time. But while the authors here enumerated have been mainly occupied with the physiological elucidations, there was still wanting the thinker who, taking up the whole subject in an impartial spirit, and giving due weight to what is valuable in both the old statement and the new, should incorporate all the needed elements into a harmonious, comprehensive, and unitary scheme of Mental Science.

Professor Bain has proved to be the man for this undertaking. He has a distinguished place among the original cultivators of mental science in the aspect here considered. Thirteen years ago he brought out an elaborate work on "The Senses and the Intellect," of which the third edition is now in press. This was followed by "The

Emotions and the Will," completing a systematic exposition of the mind. His views were afterward still further developed and applied in a treatise on "The Study of Character." In these works, while following out the scheme of psychology as laid down by Reid, Stewart, Brown, James Mill, and Sir William Hamilton, the author pushed to a still higher point the analysis and generalization of the mental phenomena, and presented a large stock of original examples and applications. He was the first to introduce into psychology a full handling of all the known physiological accompaniments of the mind, and to show how valuable are the lights which can be derived from them. His works have now the leading place in the teaching of mental philosophy in Great Britain; and the estimate placed upon them by competent judges is exemplified by the following quotations. Mr. John Stuart Mill, in an able analysis of "The Senses and the Intellect," in the *Edinburgh Review*, remarked:

"Bain has stepped beyond all his predecessors, and has produced an exposition of the mind, of the school of Locke and Hartley, equally remarkable in what it has successfully done, and in what it has wisely refrained from—an exposition which deserves to take rank as the foremost of its class, and as marking the most advanced point which the à *posteriori* psychology has reached. . . . ."

"Belonging essentially to the association school, he has not only, with great clearness and copiousness, illustrated, popularized, and enforced by fresh arguments all which that school had already done toward the explanation of the phenomena of mind, but he has added so largely to it, that those who have the highest appreciation and the warmest admiration of his predecessors, are likely to be the most struck with the great advance which this treatise constitutes over what those predecessors had done, and the improved position in which it places their psychological theory. Mr. Bain possesses, indeed, a union of qualifications peculiarly fitting him for what, in the language of Dr. Brown, may be called the physical investigation of mind. With analytic powers comparable to those of his most distinguished predecessors, he combines a range of appropriate knowledge still wider than theirs; having made a more accurate study than perhaps any previous psychologist of the whole round of the physical sciences, on which the mental depend both for their methods, and for the necessary material substratum of their theories; while those sciences, also, are themselves in a far higher state of advancement than in any former age. This is especially true of the science most nearly allied, both in subject and method, with psychological investigations, the science of Physiology; which Hartley, Brown, and Mill had unquestionably studied, and knew perhaps as well as it was known by any one at the time when they studied it, but in a superficial manner compared with Mr. Bain; the science having in the mean while assumed almost a new aspect, from the important discoveries which have been made in all its branches, and especially in the functions of the nervous system, since even the latest of those authors wrote."

Professor Masson, of the University of Edinburgh, in his late work entitled "Recent British Philosophy," speaking of Mr. Bain's treatise, says: "It is, perhaps, the richest natural history of the Human Mind in the language—the most fully mapped out and the most abundant in happy detail and illustration."

The works here so decisively commended by the highest authorities have not been republished in this country; they are besides expensive to import, and are too voluminous for popular use. The present volume is an abstract of them, and presents in a compressed and lucid form the views which are there more extensively elaborated. It is not only the best but it is the *only* manual of Mental Philosophy yet produced which combines a clear exposition of the laws of feeling and thought, with a full statement of their physiological connections so far as known, together with a succinct historical review of the progress of opinion upon controverted questions in the domain of Mind. It was prepared by the author at the solicitation of many who wished a statement of his views in a form convenient for general use, and of gentlemen engaged in teaching, who desired a work for their classes which should represent the present state of thought upon the subject: and as the educational want which it meets in England is equally urgent here, it has been republished in the belief that it will be appreciated by the public and welcomed by our best instructors.   E. L. Y.

NEW YORK, *June*, 1868.

TABLE OF CONTENTS.

INTRODUCTION.

CHAP. I.

DEFINITION AND DIVISIONS OF MIND.

		PAGE
1.	Human Knowledge falls under two departments	1
2.	The Object department marked by Extension; the Subject, by the absence of this property	ib.
3.	Subject Experience—Mind proper—has three functions, Feeling, Will, and Thought. Other classifications of Mind	2
4.	Order of arrangement for exposition	3
5.	Concomitance of Mind and a Material Organism	4

CHAP. II.

THE NERVOUS SYSTEM AND ITS FUNCTIONS.

1. The Brain is the principal organ of Mind. Proofs ... 5
2. The Nervous System consists of a Central mass, and ramifying Nerves ... ib.
3. The nervous substance made up of white and of grey matter. The *fibres* and the *corpuscles* ... 6
4. The Central nerves, or cerebro-spinal axis composed of parts. I. The SPINAL CORD; the Reflex Movements. II. The BRAIN. Parts of the Brain: (1) Medulla Oblongata, (2) Pons Varolii, (3) Cerebral Hemispheres, (4) Cerebellum; their several functions ... 7
5. The nerves are divided into Cerebral and Spinal ... 11
6. The function of a nerve is to transmit influence ... ib.
7. Incarrying and outcarrying nerves ... 12

BOOK I.

MOVEMENT, SENSE, AND INSTINCT.

CHAP. I.

MOVEMENT AND THE MUSCULAR FEELINGS.

1. Muscular Feelings compared with Sensations. The muscular system ... 13
2. Spontaneous Activity of the system. Proofs and illustrations 14

CONTENTS.

THE MUSCULAR FEELINGS.

		PAGE
3.	Three classes of feelings connected with muscle	17

Feelings of Muscular Exercise.

4.	The *dead strain*, or action without movement. Systematic Description: PHYSICAL Side; MENTAL Side. Plan of describing the Feelings generally, *Note*	18
5.	Examples of the dead strain	22
6.	Exertion *with movement*	ib.
7.	Slow movements; allied to repose and passivity	ib.
8.	Waxing and waning movements	23
9.	Quick movements; their exciting character	ib.
10.	Passive movements: the stimulus of riding	24

Discriminative or Intellectual Sensibility of Muscle.

11.	With every feeling, we have consciousness of *degree*	ib.
12.	Consciousness of Exertion, or Expended Force. The Mechanical property of matter	ib.
13.	Consciousness of degrees of Continuance of exertion, either as dead strain or as movement. Time. Space	25
14.	Consciousness of the Velocity of Movement	26

CHAP. II.

SENSATION.

| 1. | Sensation defined | 27 |
| 2. | Sensations classified. Defects of the enumeration of the Five Senses. Omission of Organic Sensations | ib. |

SENSATIONS OF ORGANIC LIFE.

Organic Muscular Feelings.

| 3. | Pains of injury of muscle. Fatigue and Repose | 28 |

Organic Sensations of Nerve.

| 4. | Acute Diseases of the nerves, nervous Fatigue, Healthy nerves, Stimulants | 30 |

Organic Feelings of the Circulation and Nutrition.

| 5. | Thirst, Inanition, arrested circulation, good and ill health | 31 |

Feelings of Respiration.

| 6. | Suffocation, Closeness, Exhilaration of change to pure air | 32 |

Feelings of Heat and Cold.

| 7. | Pain of Chillness, Pleasure of transition to warmth | 33 |

Sensations of the Alimentary Canal.

| 8. | Classification of the kinds of Food | |
| 9. | Feelings of Digestion: Relish and Repletion, Hunger, Nausea, Dyspepsia | 34 |

CONTENTS.

SENSE OF TASTE.

		PAGE
1.	Objects of Taste: chiefly the materials of Food	36
2.	The Tongue	ib.
3.	Sensations of Taste	37
4.	Tastes in Sympathy with the Stomach: Relishes and Disgusts	ib.
5.	Tastes proper: Sweet and Bitter	38
6.	Tastes involving Touch: Saline, Alkaline, Sour, Astringent, Fiery, Acrid	ib.

SENSE OF SMELL.

1.	Smell related to the Lungs	39
2.	Objects of Smell: gaseous or volatile bodies	ib.
3.	Development of odours, by heat, light, and moisture	ib.
4.	Diffusion of odours	40
5.	The Nose	ib.
6.	Mode of action of odours a process of oxidation	ib.
7.	Sensations of Smell: in sympathy with the lungs are Fresh and Close odours	41
8.	Proper olfactory sensibility: Fragrant odours and the opposite	ib.
9.	Odours involving tactile sensibility: Pungency	42

SENSE OF TOUCH.

1.	Touch an intellectual Sense. The Objects, solid bodies	43
2.	Sensitive surface the Skin, interior of the mouth, and nostrils	ib.
3.	Action simple pressure	ib.
4.	Sensations: (Emotional) Soft Touch, Pungent Touch, Temperature, Tickling and acute pains	44
5.	Intellectual Sensations: Plurality of Points—Weber's experiments, Pressure	45
6.	Combinations of Touch with Muscular Feeling: Resistance, Hardness and Softness, Roughness and Smoothness, Extension or the Co-existing in Space	47

SENSE OF HEARING.

1.	Objects of Hearing—material bodies in a state of tremor	51
2.	The Ear	ib.
3.	The mode of action in hearing	52
4.	Sensations of Sound: General Emotional effects—Sweetness, Intensity, Volume	ib.
5.	Musical Sounds: Pitch, Waxing and Waning, Harmony and Discord	54
6.	Intellectual Sensations: Clearness, Timbre, Articulate sounds, Distance and Direction	55

SENSE OF SIGHT.

1.	Objects of Sight	56
2.	The Eye	ib.
3.	Mode of action, in the first place an optical effect	59
4.	Binocular Vision. Seeing objects erect by an inverted image	60
5.	Sensations of Sight (Optical): Light, Colour, Lustre	ib.
6.	Sensations involving the Movements of the Eye: Visible Movement, Visible Form, Apparent Size, Distance, Volume, Visible Situation	62

CHAP. III.

THE APPETITES.

The Appetites defined. Sleep, Exercise and Repose, Thirst, Hunger, Sex ... 67

CHAP. IV.

THE INSTINCTS.

Instinct defined. Instincts classified ... 68

THE PRIMITIVE COMBINED MOVEMENTS.

1. The Locomotive Rhythm ... 69
2. Its Analysis ... ib.
3. Primitive Associated movements ... 70
4. Harmony of Pace in the movements ... ib.

THE INSTINCTIVE PLAY OF FEELING.

1. Union of Mind and Body shown in the Expression of Feeling ib.
2. Physical Accompaniments of the Feelings: Movements of the Face ... 71
3. Voice and Respiratory Muscles ... 72
4. Muscles of the Body generally ... 73
5. Organic Effects: Lachrymal Organs, Sexual Organs, Digestion, Cutaneous changes, Heart, Lacteal Gland in Women ... ib.
6. General principle connecting Pleasure and Pain with bodily functions. Proofs of the Principle. Laughter and Sobbing 75
7. Operation of Stimulants ... 78
8. Law of Self-conservation ... 79

THE INSTINCTIVE GERMS OF THE WILL.

1. Voluntary power, a bundle of acquisitions ... ib.
2. Primitive foundations of the Will. I.—Spontaneity ... ib.
3. II.—Law of Self-conservation ... 80
4. Accident brings about coincidences between feelings and appropriate movements ... ib.
5. III.--The coincidences are confirmed by a process of association 81

BOOK II.

THE INTELLECT.

1. The intellectual functions commonly expressed by Memory, Reason, Imagination, &c. ... 82
2. The primary attributes of Intellect—*Difference, Agreement, Retentiveness* ... ib.
3. Applications of a Knowledge of the Intellectual Powers ... 84

CONTENTS. ix

CHAP. I.

RETENTIVENESS—LAW OF CONTIGUITY.

	PAGE.
1. Retentiveness mostly comprehended under the Law of Contiguity	85
2. Statement of the Law	ib.

MOVEMENTS.

3. Spontaneous and Instinctive actions strengthened by exercise	86
4. Conjoined or Aggregated Movements	ib.
5. Successions of Movements	87
6. Intervention of Sensations in trains of Movement	ib.
7. Conditions governing the rate of Acquisition generally	ib.
8. Circumstances favouring the adhesion of Movements	88
9. All acquirements suppose Physical Vigour	89

IDEAL FEELINGS OF MOVEMENT.—THE SEAT OF IDEAS.

10. Association of Ideas of Movement	ib.
11. The seat of Ideas the same as of Sensations or Actualities	ib.
12. The tendency of Ideas to become Actualities a source of activity distinct from the Will	90
13. The principle applied to explain Sympathy	91
14. Points common to the Idea and to the Actuality	92
15. Ideas of Movement may be associated	ib.
16. The rate of adhesion follows the law of Actual Movement	ib.
17. Movement is mentally known as expended energy in special muscles	ib.

SENSATIONS OF THE SAME SENSE.

18. In all the senses, different sensations are associated together	93
19. Separate ideas become self-sustaining by repetition	ib.
20. Association of Sensations of Touch	94
21. Law of the Rate of Acquirement in Touch	ib.
22. The acquirements of Touch most numerous in the blind	95
23. Associations of Sounds; Musical and Articulate Sounds	ib.
24. Associations of Sights: Forms and Coloured surfaces	97

SENSATIONS OF DIFFERENT SENSES.

25. Movements with Sensations. Muscular Ideas with Sensations; Architecture. Sensations with Sensations	98
26. Law of the Rate of such acquirements	100
27. Localization of the Bodily Feelings	101
28. Our body is an object fact with subject associations	102
29. Associations makes differences in sensations alike in quality	ib.

ASSOCIATES WITH PLEASURE AND PAIN.

30. Pleasure and Pain can persist and be reproduced ideally	ib.
31. Law of the association	103
32. The Special Emotions converted into Affections	104
33. Association of emotions with indifferent objects: Ritual	ib.
34. The interest of Ends transferred to the Means: Money, Formalities, Truth	105
35. Influence of association in Fine Art. Alison's Theory	106

		PAGE
36. The Language of the Feelings has to be acquired		107
37. The Signs of Happiness are cheering to behold		ib.
38. Memories of Pleasure and Pain		108
39. Association has a share in the Moral Sentiment		ib.

ASSOCIATIONS OF VOLITION.

40. Contiguous association of actions and states of feeling ... 109

NATURAL OBJECTS.

41. Our ideas of external nature are associations of sensible qualities ib.
42. The Naturalist mind represents disinterested association ... 110
43. In minds generally, the feelings sway the recollections of nature ib.

NATURAL AND HABITUAL CONJUNCTIONS.

44. Association of things habitually conjoined in our view ... ib.
45. Maps, Diagrams, and Pictorial Representations ... 111

SUCCESSIONS.

46. Successions of Cycle, Evolution, Cause and Effect ... ib.

MECHANICAL ACQUISITIONS.

47. Summary of conditions of Mechanical Acquirement ... 114
48. Proper duration of exercises ... 115

ACQUISITIONS OF LANGUAGE.

49. Oral Language involves the Voice and the Ear ... 116
50. Language a case of heterogeneous adhesion ... ib.
51. Language includes fixed trains of words ... 117
52. Operation of Special Interest in lingual acquisitions ... ib.
53. Elocution involves an Ear for Cadence ... 118
54. Written language appeals to the sense of Visible Form ... ib.
55. Short methods of acquiring language ... ib.
56. Verbal adhesiveness an aid to the memory of expressed Knowledge ... 119

RETENTIVENESS IN SCIENCE.

57. Knowledge, as Science, is clothed in artificial symbols ... ib.
58. The Object Sciences are Concrete or Abstract ... ib.
59. The Subject Sciences are grounded on self-consciousness ... 120
60. Circumstances favouring acquirements in mental Science ... ib.
61. Supposed faculty of Self-Consciousness ... 121

BUSINESS, OR PRACTICAL LIFE.

62. Acquirements in the higher branches of Industry ... 122

ACQUISITIONS IN THE FINE ARTS.

63. Fine Art constructions give refined pleasure ... ib.
64. Conditions of Acquisition in Fine Art ... 123

HISTORY AND NARRATIVE.

65. History the succession of events as narrated ... ib.
66. Transactions witnessed impress themselves as Sensations and Actions ... 124
67. Events narrated have the aid of the Verbal Memory ... ib.

CONTENTS.

OUR PAST LIFE.

68. The complex current of each one's existence 124

CONCLUDING OBSERVATIONS ON RETENTIVENESS.

69. Existence of a Retentive faculty for things generally. Superior plasticity of early years; Limitation of acquirements; Temporary adhesiveness 125

CHAP. II.

AGREEMENT—LAW OF SIMILARITY.

1. Statement of the Law 127
2. Similarity, in one mode, implied under Contiguity 128
3. Impediments to the revival of the past through similarity ... ib.

FEEBLENESS OF IMPRESSION.

4. Impediment of Feebleness or Faintness. By what peculiarities overcome. Conditions of reproduction by Similarity ... 129

SIMILARITY IN DIVERSITY—SENSATIONS.

5. Impediment of Diversity. Special condition for this case ... 130
6. Movements and Feelings of Movement identified 131
7. Sensations of Organic Life 132
8. Tastes. Identification ending in Classification 133
9. Touch. Effects generalized and classified 134
10. Hearing. Articulate language identified under diversity of utterance and cadence. Diversity of Meaning ... ... ib.
11. Sight. Colours, Forms, and their combinations 136
12. Effects common to the Senses generally 137

CONTIGUOUS AGGREGATES—CONJUNCTIONS.

13. Objects affecting a Plurality of Senses 138
14. Aggregates of associated Properties and Uses. The Steam Engine. Davy's discovery of the composition of the alkalies. Botany and Zoology ... ... ib.

PHENOMENA OF SUCCESSION.

15. Successions identified under diversities. Cycle, Evolution, Cause and Effect. Newton's discovery of gravitation 141

REASONING AND SCIENCE IN GENERAL.

16. Generalizing power of the mind gives birth to: I.—Definition; II.—Induction; III.—Deduction. Reasoning by Analogy 143
17. Scope of the Reasoning Faculty 146

BUSINESS AND PRACTICE.

18. Discoveries in Practice due, in part, to Similarity ... ... ib.

ILLUSTRATIVE COMPARISONS AND LITERARY ART.

19. Figures of Similitude abound in all great works of literary genius. Bunyan, Shakespeare, Bacon, Milton 149

THE FINE ARTS IN GENERAL.

20. Similarity exemplified in certain of the Fine Arts 149

SIMILARITY IN ACQUISITION AND MEMORY.

21. Labour of Acquisition saved by the tracing of similarities ... 150

CHAP. III.
COMPOUND ASSOCIATION.

1. Associations may combine their force. Statement of the Law 151

COMPOSITION OF CONTIGUITIES.

2. Conjunctions: Local associations; Persons; Uses and Properties. Successions: Language 152

COMPOSITION OF SIMILARITIES.

3. This case sufficiently expressed under the Law of Similarity ... 154

MIXED CONTIGUITY AND SIMILARITY.

4. Great discoveries of similarity remembered partly by contiguity 155
5. Aid to Similarity by the *proximity* of the things desired ... ib.
6. Mnemonic devices 156

THE ELEMENT OF FEELING.

7. Influence of the Feelings on the trains of thought ... ... ib.

INFLUENCE OF VOLITION.

8. The influence of the Will indirect. Modes of its operation ... 157

OBSTRUCTIVE ASSOCIATIONS.

9. Exemplified in the conflict of the Artistic and the Scientific points of view 159

ASSOCIATION OF CONTRAST.

10. Contrast may be analyzed into Relativity, Contiguity, Similarity, and the influence of Emotion 160

CHAP. IV.
CONSTRUCTIVE ASSOCIATION.

1. Processes of Original Creation 161

MECHANICAL CONSTRUCTIVENESS.

2. Movements combined into new groupings. Three conditions of the Constructive Process generally 162

VERBAL CONSTRUCTIVENESS.

3. Learning to Articulate 163
4. Construction of Sentences 164
5. Higher Combinations of language ... ... ib.

CONTENTS. xiii

FEELINGS OF MOVEMENT.

6. Constructing new muscular ideas. Hitting a mark. Architectural fitness ... 165

CONSTRUCTIVENESS IN THE SENSATIONS.

7. Organic Life; unknown forms of pleasure and pain. The higher senses. Visual constructiveness ... 166

CONSTRUCTION OF NEW EMOTIONS.

8. The Simpler Emotions must be experienced. Change of degree. Transfer to new objects ... 168

CONCRETING THE ABSTRACT.

9. Construction, from abstract elements, of images in the Concrete 169

REALIZING OF REPRESENTATION OR DESCRIPTION.

10. Verbal descriptions, or other Representations, realized ... *ib.*

CONSTRUCTIVENESS IN SCIENCE.

11. Definitions, Inductions, Deductions, and Experimental discoveries involve constructiveness ... 170

PRACTICAL CONSTRUCTIONS.

12. Mechanical Invention. Administrative contrivances. Judgment; adapting one's views to others. Oratory ... 171

CONSTRUCTIVENESS UNDER FEELING.

13. Certain constructions satisfy some present emotion:—Emotional character appears in literary composition. Bias. The Myth 172
14. Fine Art constructions adapted to Æsthetic feelings ... 173
15. IMAGINATION best exemplified under Fine Art constructiveness. Its elements are, (1) Concreteness, (2) Originality, (3) the presence of Emotion. Fancy. Ideality ... 174

CHAP. V.

ABSTRACTION—THE ABSTRACT IDEA.

NOMINALISM AND REALISM.

1. First stage of Abstraction to compare, identify, and *classify* ... 176
2. Abstraction means attending to points of agreement and neglecting points of difference. Question how far this mental separation is possible ... *ib.*
3. In one view, to abstract is to refer to a class ... 177
4. Cases where we seem to form a pure abstraction:—(1) Material separation; (2) Lineal Diagrams; (3) Verbal Definition . 178
5. The only generality, having separate existence, is the Name ... 179
6. Realism and Conceptualism ... 180
7. Natural tendency to ascribe separate existence to abstractions *ib.*

CHAP. VI.

THE ORIGIN OF KNOWLEDGE.

EXPERIENCE AND INTUITION.

		PAGE
1.	Question as to the existence of Intuitive or Innate truths	181
2.	Importance attached to the Intuitive origin of knowledge	ib.
3.	Characters ascribed to Innate principles—NECESSITY and UNIVERSALITY	182
4.	Objection to the doctrine of Intuition—it presumes on the finality of some one Analysis of the mind	ib.
5.	Innate ideas improbable	184
6.	Innate general ideas would require innate particulars	ib.
7.	The character of Necessity has nothing to do with Innate origin	ib.
8.	Concessions of the supporters of Innate principles	186
9.	The controversy turns at present on the Axioms of Mathematics and the Law of Causation	ib.
	Criterion of the 'inconceivability of the opposites'	ib.

CHAP. VII.

OF EXTERNAL PERCEPTION.

1. Two separate questions:—the Theory of Vision, and the Perception of the External and Material World ... 188

THEORY OF VISION.

2. Two views of our Perception of Distance by sight ... ib.
3. The native sensibility of the eye includes (1) Light and Colour, (2) Visible Figure and Visible Magnitude ... 189
4. The visible signs of variation of Distance from the eye ... ib.
5. The import of Distance is something beyond the ocular sensations 190
6. Experience associates the visible signs of Distance with the movements that give the meaning of Distance ... 191
7. Distance an inference. Experiments of Wheatstone ... ib.
8. The perception of Distance illustrated by the Stereoscope ... 192
9. Admission by Berkeley's opponents that the instinctive perception is *aided* by associations ... 193
10. Objection to the theory of Acquired Perception, that we are not conscious of tactual or locomotive reminiscences ... 194
11. Farther objection that the early experience of children is insufficient to form the supposed associations ... ib.
12. Observations on persons born blind and made to see ... 195
13. Instinctive Perceptions of the Lower Animals ... ib.
14. Observations on infants ... 196
15. Hypothesis of *hereditary* transmission of the perception ... 197

PERCEPTION OF A MATERIAL WORLD.

1. All Perception or Knowledge implies mind ... ib.
2. The Perception of Matter a distinct attitude of the consciousness 198
3. The common view of material perception self-contradictory ... ib.

CONTENTS.

	PAGE.
4. Analysis of Perception: I.—The putting forth of Muscular Energy, as opposed to Passive Feeling	198
5. II.—Uniform connexion of Definite Feelings with Definite Energies	199
6. Our own body is a part of our Object experience	200
7. III.—Object—the common to all; Subject—the special to each	201
8. Giving separate existence to the Object a species of Realism ...	202

THEORIES OF THE MATERIAL WORLD.

BERKELEY. Classification of the objects of knowledge:—(1) Ideas imprinted on the senses; (2) Ideas of passions of the mind; (3) Ideas of memory and imagination. Peculiarity of using *Idea* for Sensation. The first class exist in a mind, no less than the others. The vulgar opinion a contradiction. Distinction of Primary and Secondary Qualities of no avail. Supposed substratum—*matter*. The reality of things not abolished. *Spirit* is something apart from ideas ... ... *ib.*

HUME. Summary of his philosophical doctrines generally. The popular belief is that the images on the senses *are* the external objects. Philosophy teaches that nothing can be present to the mind but a perception. The dispute is one as to fact. By Perception we cannot know either *continued* or *distinct* existence. We attain these by the mind's tendency to go on, even where objects fail. We have no idea of substance. There is no such thing as *self* in the abstract. Mind is a bundle of conceptions 205

REID. Reclaimed against Idealism on the ground of Common Sense. His statements confused and contradictory; some point to *mediate* perception, others to *immediate* perception. According to J. S. Mill, his leaning was to the first ... 207

STEWART substantially at one with Reid. BROWN 208

HAMILTON. Classifies the Theories of Perception. His own called Natural Realism, or Immediate Perception. Involves a self-contradiction. His so-called ultimate analysis involves complex notions ... ... *ib.*

FERRIER. His fundamental position. He iterates the essential implication of Object and Subject. Exposes the self-contradictions of the prevailing views. Regards Perception as an ultimate fact 210

MANSEL. Criticism of Berkeley. Analysis of Perception ... 211

BAILEY. Makes Perception a simple, indivisible, ultimate fact 212

J. S. MILL. Advances a Psychological Theory of the Belief in a Material World. Postulates (1) Expectation, and (2) the Laws of Association. Substance, Matter, or the External World, is a *Permanent Possibility* of sensation. Distinction of Primary and Secondary Qualities. Application to the permanence of Mind ... ... *ib.*

BOOK III.

THE EMOTIONS.

CHAP. I.

FEELING IN GENERAL.

	PAGE.
1. The Special Emotions are secondary and derived, and involve the Intellect	215
2. Feeling in general defined	ib.
3. Twofold aspect of Feeling—Physical and Mental	216
4. Physical aspect of RELATIVITY	ib.
5. Law of DIFFUSION	ib.

CHARACTERS OF FEELING.

6. The Characters of Feeling fall under four classes	217

Emotional Characters of Feeling.

7. Every feeling has its characteristic PHYSICAL side	ib.
8. MENTAL side: *Quality* (Pleasure and Pain), *Degree*, *Speciality*	ib.

Volitional characters of Feeling.

9. The voluntary actions a clue to the Feelings	218

Intellectual characters of Feeling.

10. The Ideal persistence of feelings extends their sphere	ib.

Mixed characters of Feeling.

11. Will combined with Ideal persistence makes Forethought	219
12. Desire	ib.
13. It is the property of every feeling to occupy the mind	ib.
14. The influence in Belief is a mixed character	220

THE INTERPRETATION AND ESTIMATE OF FEELING.

15. (1) The Expression indicates the feelings of others	221
16. (2) The Conduct pursued indicates pleasure and pain	ib.
17. (3) The Course of the Thoughts bears the impress of the Feelings	222
18. The influence of Belief a test of strength of feeling	ib.
19. The several indications mutually check each other	ib.
20. Each person may describe their own feelings: Some standard or common measure must be agreed upon	223
21. The criteria of feeling applied to estimate happiness and misery	ib.

THE DEVELOPMENT OF FEELING.

22. An outburst of feeling passes through a certain course	224
23. Alternation and periodicity of emotional states	ib.
24. Ends to be served by the analysis of the Feelings	225

CHAP. II.

THE EMOTIONS AND THEIR CLASSIFICATION.

	PAGE.
1. The Emotions are secondary, derived, or compound feelings	226
2. PLURALITY of Sensations, in mutual harmony, or in mutual conflict	ib.
3. TRANSFER of feelings to new objects	ib.
4. COALESCENCE of separate feelings into an aggregate or whole	ib.
5. Principle of classifying the Emotions	ib.
6. Detailed Classification	227

CHAP. III.

EMOTIONS OF RELATIVITY: NOVELTY.—WONDER.—LIBERTY.

1. Objects of NOVELTY. PHYSICAL circumstance	229
2. MENTAL characters	ib.
3. Pain of Monotony. SPECIES of Novelty	ib.
4. VARIETY, a minor form of Novelty	230
5. SURPRISE; includes an element of Conflict	ib.
6. WONDER. Its relation to the Sublime	231
7. RESTRAINT and LIBERTY, referable to Conflict and Relativity	ib.
8. LIBERTY the correlative of Restraint*	ib.

CHAP. IV.

EMOTION OF TERROR.

1. TERROR defined—The apprehension of coming evil	232
2. PHYSICAL side, a *loss* and a *transfer* of nervous energy	ib.
3. MENTALLY, Terror is a form of massive pain	234
4. SPECIES of Terror. (1) The case of the lower animals. (2) Fear in children. (3) Slavish Terror. (4) Forebodings of disaster generally. (5) Superstition. (6) Distrust of our Faculties in new operations. (7) Fear of Death	235
5. Counteractives of Terror: the sources of Courage	238
6. Re-action from Terror cheering and hilarious	ib.
7. Uses of Terror, in Government, and in Education	ib.
8. The employment of Fear in Fine Art must be qualified	ib.

CHAP. V.

TENDER EMOTION.

1. TENDERNESS. Its OBJECTS are sentient beings. The exciting causes include Pleasures and Pains and local stimulants	239
2. The PHYSICAL side involves (1) Touch, (2) the Lachrymal Organs, and (3) the movements of the Pharynx	240

CONTENTS.

3. Link of sequence, physical and mental, between the stimulants and the manifestations ... 241
4. MENTAL side :—Simple characters of the emotion ... 242
5. Mixed characters: Desire; Control of the Thoughts ... ib.

SPECIES OF THE TENDER EMOTION.

6. Tenderness is vented mainly on human beings ... 243

The Family Group.

7. Mother and Offspring. Paternal relationship ... ib.
8. Relationship of the Sexes; grounds of mutual affinity ... 244

The Benevolent Affections.

9. The main constituent of Benevolence is Sympathy ... ib.
10. The Pleasures of Benevolence analyzed ... ib.
11. Compassion, or Pity ... 245
12. Gratitude founded on Sympathy, and ruled by Justice ... ib.
13. Benevolence and Gratitude in the equal relationships ... 246
14. The spectacle of Generosity stimulates Tenderness ... ib.
15. The Lower Animals are fit subjects of tender feeling ... ib.
16. Form of Tenderness in connexion with Inanimate things ... ib.

Sorrow.

17. Sorrow is pain from the loss of objects of affection; Tenderness a means of consolation ... 247
18. Social and Moral bearings of Tenderness ... ib.

Admiration and Esteem.

19. Admiration is awakened by excellence; and is allied to Love ... ib.
20. Esteem respects the performance of essential Duties ... 248

Veneration—the Religious Sentiment.

21. The Religious Sentiment contains Wonder, Love and Awe.—Veneration, Reverence ... ib.

CHAP VI.

EMOTIONS OF SELF.

1. SELF intended to refer to two allied groups of feelings ... 250

SELF-GRATULATION AND SELF-ESTEEM.

2. The feeling arising from excellent or amiable qualities beheld in self ... ib.
3. PHYSICAL side ... 251
4. MENTAL side :—A mode of Tender Feeling ... ib.
5. SPECIFIC FORMS: Self-complacency, Self-esteem and Self-conceit, Self-respect and Pride, Self-pity, Emulation, Envy ... 252
6. Pains of the Emotion: Humility and Modesty, Humiliation and Self-abasement, Self-reproach ... 253

LOVE OF APPROBATION.

7. Involves, with self-gratulation, the workings of Sympathy ... 254

CONTENTS. xix

8. SPECIES of the feeling: mere Approbation, Admiration and Praise, Flattery and Adulation, Glory, Reputation or Fame, Honour; the rules of Polite society ... 255
9. Pains of Disapprobation: Remorse; Shame ... *ib.*
10. Self-complacency and the Love of Admiration as motives ... 256

CHAP. VII.

EMOTION OF POWER.

1. Depends on a sense of *superior* might or energy, on comparison *ib.*
2. PHYSICAL side: an increase of Power; Laughter ... 257
3. MENTAL side: an elating or intoxicating pleasure ... 258
4. SPECIES: Making a Sensation; control of Large Operations; Command or Authority; Wealth; Persuasion; Spiritual ascendancy; Knowledge; love of Influence; Criticism; Contempt and Derision; Ambition ... 259
5. Pains of Impotence. Jealousy of Power ... 260

CHAP. VIII.

IRASCIBLE EMOTION.

1. Arising in pain, and occasioning pleasure in inflicting pain ... *ib.*
2. The OBJECTS are persons, the authors of pain or injury ... *ib.*
3. PHYSICAL manifestations: (1) Excitement; (2) Activity; (3) Organic effects; (4) Expression or Attitude; (5) Exultation of Revenge ... 261
4. MENTAL side: the *pleasure of malevolence* ... *ib.*
5. Ingredients of Anger: (1) an *effect* sought to vent activity; (2) fascination in the sight of *suffering;* (3) pleasure of *power;* (4) prevention of farther pain *by inducing fear* ... 262
6. SPECIES of Anger: manifestations in the Lower Animals; forms in Infancy and Childhood; Sudden anger; Deliberate Anger —Revenge; Hatred; Antipathy; Warfare; grades of offence. Pleasure of Malevolence called in question. Righteous Indignation; Noble Rage ... 263
7. Interest evoked by Sympathy with irascible feeling ... 266
8. Justice involves sympathetic Resentment ... *ib.*
9. Punishment by law gratifies and moderates resentful passion ... 267

CHAP. IX.

EMOTIONS OF ACTION—PURSUIT.

1. The attitude of PURSUIT induced on voluntary activity ... *ib.*
2. PHYSICAL side: (1) intent occupation of the Senses; (2) harmonizing Muscular Activity ... 268
3. MENTAL side: (1) interest of an end, heightened by its approach; (2) engrossment in Object regards, remission of Subject regards ... *ib.*

xx   CONTENTS.

		PAGE.
4.	Chance, or Uncertainty, contributes to the engrossment	269
5.	The excitement of Pursuit is seen in the Lower Animals	270
6.	Field Sports	ib.
7.	Contests	ib.
8.	The occupations of Industry give scope for Plot-interest	271
9.	The Sympathetic Relationships contain Pursuit	ib.
10.	The search after Knowledge	272
11.	The position of the Spectator contains the interest of Pursuit	ib.
12.	The Literature of Plot, or Story	ib.
13.	Form of *pain*, the prolongation of the suspense	273
14.	Pains of activity generally	ib.

CHAP. X.

EMOTIONS OF INTELLECT.

1.	Pleasures and pains attending Intellectual operations	ib.
2.	Feelings in the working of Contiguity	274
3.	Pain of Contradiction or Inconsistency	ib.
4.	Pleasure of Similarity, an exhilarating surprise; relief from an intellectual burden	ib.
5.	New identities of Science increase the range of intellectual comprehension	275
6.	Discoveries of Practice gives the pleasure of increased power	ib.
7.	Illustrative Comparisons remit intellectual toil	276

CHAP. XI.

SYMPATHY.

1.	SYMPATHY is entering into, and acting out, the feelings of others	ib.
2.	It supposes (1) our remembered experience, (2) a connexion between the Expression of feeling and the Feelings themselves	277
3.	Sympathy an assumption of the physical displays of feeling, followed by the rise of the mental state	ib.
4.	Circumstances favouring Sympathy	278
5.	Completion of Sympathy—vicarious action	279
6.	Sympathy with pleasure and pain	280
7.	Sympathy supports men's feelings and opinions	ib.
8.	Moulding of men's sentiments and views	ib.
9.	Sympathy an indirect source of pleasure to the sympathizer	281
10.	Sympathy cannot subsist upon extreme self-abnegation	282
11.	Knowledge is indispensable to large sympathies	ib.
12.	IMITATION closely allied to sympathy. The Imitative aptitudes	ib.

CHAP. XII.

IDEAL EMOTION.

1.	The persistence of Feeling makes the life in the Ideal	283
2.	Ideal Emotion is affected by Organic states	284
3.	There may be a Temperament for Emotion	ib.

CONTENTS.

	PAGE.
4. Some Constitutions are adapted for Special Emotions	285
5. Mental Agencies:—(1) the presence of some Kindred emotion; (2) Intellectual forces	286
6. Feeling in the Actual often thwarted by the accompaniments	287
7. Application of the facts to account for the power of Ideal Emotion	288
8. Ideal Emotion is connected with Desire	289

CHAP. XIII.

ÆSTHETIC EMOTIONS.

1. These are the pleasures aimed at in the Fine Arts ... *ib.*
2. Distinguishing features of Fine Art pleasures:—(1) Pleasure is their end; (2) Disagreeables are excluded; (3) the Enjoyment is not monopolized ... 290
3. The Eye and the Ear are the æsthetic senses ... 291
4. Muscular and Sensual elements may be presented in *idea* ... *ib.*
5. Beauty not one quality, but a Circle of Effects ... 292
6. Emotions of Art in detail: I.—The simple pleasurable sensations of the Ear and the Eye ... *ib.*
7. II.—Co-operation of the Intellect with the Senses ... 293
8. III.—The Special Emotions ... *ib.*
9. IV.—HARMONY a preponderating Element in Art ... 294
10. The pleasures of Sound and their Harmonies:—Music ... *ib.*
11. Pleasurable Sensations of Sight, and their Harmonies:—Light and Shade; Colours; Proportions; Straight and Curved Forms; Symmetry; Visible Movements ... 296
12. Complex Harmonies ... 298
13. FITNESS as a source of Beauty: Support; Order ... 299
14. UNITY in Diversity ... 300
15. It is a principle in Art, to leave something to Desire ... *ib.*
16. The Feeling of Beauty has great latitude ... *ib.*
17. The SUBLIME:—its definition; Human energy; Inanimate things; Support; Natural agencies; Space; Time. Connexion with Terror ... 301
18. Beauty and Sublimity of Natural Objects; Human Beauty ... 302

THEORIES OF THE BEAUTIFUL.

SOKRATES. Holds the Beautiful and the useful to be the same 304
PLATO. Discusses opposing theories; connects Beauty with the theory of Ideas ... *ib.*
ARISTOTLE. Notices orderly arrangement and a certain size ... 305
AUGUSTIN. Unity in a comprehensive design ... *ib.*
SHAFTESBURY. The Beautiful and the Good both perceived by the same internal sense ... *ib.*
ADDISON. HUTCHESON. DIDEROT ... *ib.*
PÈRE BUFFIER. Beauty is the *type* of each species ... *ib.*
Sir JOSHUA REYNOLDS. Agrees in the main with Buffier ... 306
HOGARTH. Fitness, Variety, Uniformity, Simplicity, Intricacy, Magnitude. The line of Beauty and of Grace ... *ib.*
BURKE. Beauty causes an agreeable relaxation of the fibres. Smoothness ... 307

ALISON. Beauty is (1) the production of some Simple Emotion; (2) a peculiar exercise of the Imagination. The sensible qualities are not beautiful of themselves, but as the signs of associated emotions or affections ... 308
JEFFREY. Adopts substantially the theory of Alison ... 312
DUGALD STEWART. Asserts, against Alison and Jeffrey, the intrinsic pleasures of Colour. Explains the Sublime by Height and its associations ... 313
RUSKIN. Attributes of Infinity, Unity, Repose, Symmetry, Moderation. His asceticism ... 314

THE LUDICROUS.

1. The causes of Laughter ... 315
2. Incongruity not always ludicrous ... *ib.*
3. The Ludicrous caused by the Degradation of some person or interest. Theories of Laughter: Aristotle, Quintilian, Hobbes, Campbell, Kant ... *ib.*
4. The pleasure of degradation referable (1) to the sentiment of Power, or (2) to the release from Constraint ... 317

BOOK IV.
THE WILL.

CHAP. I.
PRIMITIVE ELEMENTS OF VOLITION.

1. The Primitive Elements—Spontaneity and Self-conservation ... 318

SPONTANEITY OF MOVEMENT.

2. Spontaneity illustrated ... *ib.*
3. Muscular groups or Regions ... 319
4. The members commanded separately by the will should have at the outset an Isolated spontaneity ... *ib.*
5. Circumstances accounting for the higher degrees of the spontaneous discharge ... 220

LINK OF FEELING OF ACTION—SELF-CONSERVATION.

6. A link has to be formed between actions and feelings ... 322
7. Self-conservation has two branches. First, Emotional Expression *ib.*
8. Secondly, the concurrence of Activity with Pleasure, and the obverse ... 323

CHAP. II.
GROWTH OF VOLUNTARY POWER.

1. Conversion of the primitive elements into the mature volition ... 325

CONTENTS. xxiii

2. Process of acquirement stated. The coincidence of a movement with a pleasure, at first accidental, is maintained by the link of Self-conservation, and finally associated by Contiguity. Exemplified in detail, in the Muscular Feelings and the Sensations ... 325
3. Second stage, the uniting of movements with Intermediate Ends 332
4. Movements transferred from one connexion to another ... 333
5. Volition made *general*. The Word of Command ... ib.
6. Imitation ... 334
7. Acting on the Wish to move ... 336
8. Association of movements with the idea of the Effect to be produced ... 337

CHAP. III.

CONTROL OF FEELINGS AND THOUGHTS.

1. All voluntary control is through the muscles ... 338

CONTROL OF THE FEELINGS.

2. The power of the Will confined to the muscular accompaniments 339
3. The voluntary command of the muscles is adequate to suppress the movements under emotion ... 340

COMMAND OF THE THOUGHTS.

4. The medium is the control of Attention ... 341
5. The will has power over muscular movements in *idea* ... 342
6. Command of the thoughts may be acquired ... ib.
7. Enters into Constructive Association ... 343
8. Command of the Thoughts a means of controlling the Feelings 344
9. Power of the Feelings to influence the Thoughts ... 345

CHAP. IV.

MOTIVES, OR ENDS.

1. Actual pleasures and pains, as Motives ... 346
2. Prospective pleasures and pains. Circumstances of ideal persistence 347
3. The Means of pleasure and pain:—Money, Bodily Strength, Knowledge, Formalities, Virtues ... 349
4. The Will biased by Fixed Ideas ... 351

CHAP. V.

THE CONFLICT OF MOTIVES.

1. Conflict of concurring pleasures and pains ... 354
2. Spontaneity may oppose the motives to the Will ... ib.
3. Exhaustion a bar to the influence of Motives ... 355
4. Opposition of two Motives in the Actual ... ib.
5. Conflict between the Actual and the Ideal ... 357
6. Intermediate Ends in conflict ... 358
7. The Persistence of Ideas makes the Impassioned Ends ... 359

CHAP. VI.

DELIBERATION.—RESOLUTION.—EFFORT.

PAGE.

1. DELIBERATION a voluntary suspense, prompted by the evils of hasty action 360
2. The Deliberative process conforms to the theory of the Will ... 362
3. RESOLUTION is postponed action 363
4. A strong motive, with insufficiency in the active organs, makes the state called EFFORT 365
5. Deliberation, Resolution, and Effort, are accidents, and not essentials of the will. Herschel on the sense of Effort, *note* *ib.*

CHAP. VII.

DESIRE.

1. Desire is a motive to act—without the ability 366
2. In Desire, there is a state of conflict ... ... *ib.*
3. Modes of escape from the unrest of Desire:—*Forced quiescence* ... 367
4. *Ideal or imaginary action* 368
5. Provocatives of Desire:—(1) the wants of the system; (2) the experience of pleasure 369
6. Feelings named from the state of Desire:—Avarice, Ambition, Curiosity 370
7. In Desire, there may be the disturbance of the Fixed Idea ... *ib.*
8. Desire not a necessary prelude to volition 371

CHAP. VIII.

BELIEF.

1. Belief, while involving the Intellect and the Feelings, is essentially related to *activity*, or the Will ... ... *ib.*
2. We are said to believe what we act upon. Apparent exceptions:—(1) action against our beliefs; (2) believing where there is no occasion to act; (3) belief determined by feeling; (4) belief apparently an intellectual process 372
3. Belief attaches to the pursuit of *intermediate* ends 375
4. The intellectual element is an Association of Means and Ends ... 376
5. Mental foundations of Belief:—(1) our Activity—Spontaneous and Voluntary; we believe whatever is uncontradicted ... *ib.*
6. (2) Intellectual Association is an aid to Belief 380
7. (3) Operation of the Feelings in Belief ... ... *ib.*
8. Belief in the order of the World varies with the three elements 382
9. Belief is opposed, not by Disbelief, but by DOUBT 384
10. HOPE and DESPONDENCY are phases of Belief ... ... *ib.*

CHAP. IX.

THE MORAL HABITS.

		PAGE.
1.	The Moral Habits are related to Feelings and Volitions	385
2.	The Moral Acquirements follow the laws of Retentiveness	ib.
3.	Special conditions:—(1) an Initiative, and (2) a Graduated Exposure in cases of conflict	386
4.	Habits in the control of Sense and Appetite:—Temperance. Command of Attention	ib.
5.	Habits under the Special Emotions:—(1) Emotional susceptibility on the whole; (2) the Emotions singly	387
6.	Habits modifying the Activity, or the Will:—Invigoration, and power of Endurance	390
7.	Control of the Intellectual trains made habitual	391

CHAP. X.

PRUDENCE.—DUTY.—MORAL INABILITY.

1. Influences on the side of PRUDENCE ... 392
2. Influences on the side of DUTY;—Sympathy, coupled with Prudential motives ... 393
3. Strengthening adjuncts common to Prudence and to Duty ... 395
4. MORAL INABILITY is the insufficiency of ordinary motives, but not of all motives ... ib.

CHAP. XI.

LIBERTY AND NECESSITY.

1. The exposition of the Will has proceeded upon uniformity of sequence between motive and action. This uniformity denied on various grounds: Sokrates ... 396
2. The perplexity of the question is owing to the inaptness of the words—Freedom and Necessity ... 398
3. Meanings of Choice, Deliberation, Self-determination, Moral Agency, Responsibility. Responsibility for Belief. Is a man the author of his character? ... 400

HISTORY OF THE FREE-WILL CONTROVERSY.

PLATO. ARISTOTLE. THE STOICS. THE EPICUREANS. ... 406
NEO-PLATONISTS:—PLOTINUS. JUSTIN MARTYR. TERTULLIAN. 407
AUGUSTIN. Doctrine of Predestination. Free-will with him does not mean independence of motives ... 408
AQUINAS. Follows Augustin in the doctrines of original sin, irresistible grace and predestination. Modes of meeting the difficulties ... 409
CALVIN. Accepted, in their rigour, the views of Augustin ... 410
PELAGIUS and ARMINIUS ... ib.
HOBBES. Voluntary action follows the last Appetite. Deliberation. Intention or Inclination. Liberty is freedom of compulsion from within. Nothing begins with itself ... 411

	PAGE.

DESCARTES. We are conscious of Freedom. Liberty is not indifference. God's perfection requires pre-determination ... 412
LOCKE. Liberty opposed, not to necessity, but to coercion. A man is free if his actions follow mental antecedents—pleasures and pains. All motives are resolved into *uneasiness* ... 413
SPINOZA. Free-will inconsistent with the nature of God. Question of evil ... 414
COLLINS. Defends the Necessitarian doctrine ... *ib.*
LEIBNITZ. Necessity is hypothetical or absolute. Hypothetical necessity does not derogate from liberty. Different kinds of Fatalism. Motives are dispositions ... 415
SAMUEL CLARKE. Asserts that the mind has a self-moving faculty ... 416
JONATHAN EDWARDS. Vindicates Philosophical Necessity. The will is determined by the strongest motive. Self-determination is inconsistent and inconceivable. Liberty of Indifference untenable. Every event must have a cause; this is contradicted by free-will. Fore-knowledge supposes infallible sequence. Morality does not require liberty. Necessity does not involve bad consequences ... 417
PRICE. Took up Clarke's view of self-motion ... 420
PRIESTLEY. Controverted Price. Denied that consciousness is in favour of freedom. Reconciled necessity with accountability. Permission of evil means appointing it. Actions must be ultimately traced to the Deity. Materialism leads to necessity ... 421
REID. Liberty defined. Arguments in support of Free-will. Refutation of Necessity ... 422
HAMILTON. Defends Free-will on his Law of the Conditioned. Liberty and Necessity are both inconceivable. Freedom is a datum of consciousness, and is involved in duty ... 425
J. S. MILL. Law of Cause and Effect established by Experience. The testimony of Consciousness. Accountability. Necessity is not Fatalism. Influence of Motives ... 426

APPENDIX.

A.—*History of Nominalism and Realism.* PAGE.

The controversy on Universals first obtained its place through Sokrates and Plato. Earliest germs in the doctrines of Parmenides and of Heracleitus 1
SOKRATES. His manner of life, and method Search for the meanings of universal terms 2
PLATO. Theory of Ideas (in *Kratylus*). *Timæus;* Distinction of the Transient and the Permanent, the one perceived by Sense, the other by Intelligence; the intelligent or cogitable element—the Ideas, prior in time and in order. *Phædrus:* Pre-existence of the Ideas. *Phædon:* Sense erroneous and can give only Opinion; it is only the Cogitant mind, disengaging itself from the body, that attains the contemplation of Universals, the only eternal realities. *Republic:* iteration of the contrast between Sensible Particulars and Cogitable Universals; Idea of the Good. *Theætetus:* the Particulars, although distinct from, yet participate in, the Universals, and thus become partially existent and cognizable. In these views is given the first statement of REALISM. In the dialogues—*Sophistes* and *Parmenides*—Plato, in his usual dialectical manner, sets forth the objections to the theory of Ideas: these objections are no where answered by him 4
ARISTOTLE. Enters his protest against separating Universals from Particulars. Advances a series of objections against the Platonic Ideas. The Sensible Particular alone has full reality. The Universals exist as predicates, or concomitants, of the Particulars. The Categories 13
THE STOICS. Their alteration of the Categories 21
PLOTINUS. Falls back upon Platonism. The Cogitables are the only realities. The Idea of the Good the highest of all ... 22
PORPHYRY. Vindication of the Categories. His doubts as to the separate existence of Genera and Species ... ... *ib.*
SCOTUS ERIGENA. A Christian Platonist with Aristotelian ideas. Maintained that reality exists only in the Cogitable or Incorporeal Universal. The first start of Scholastic Realism 23
ANSELM and ROSCELLIN. Debated the question as bearing on the Trinity. Rise of designations Nominalist and Realist. ABAELARD. AQUINAS. Supports the Aristotelian doctrine, with a qualification as to the ideas in the Divine Mind. DUNS SCOTUS 24
OCKHAM. Associated with the downfall of Scholasticism. Universals have no existence but in the mind. Nominalism from his time in the ascendant. After Descartes, the question fell into a second rank 25
HOBBES. The most outspoken representative of extreme Nominalism 26
LOCKE. General terms the signs of general ideas 27
BERKELEY. Denies the power of conceiving any property in the abstract 28
HUME. Abstract ideas are in themselves individual ... ... *ib.*
REID. General names must imply general conceptions. We may disjoin, in our conception, attributes inseparable in nature 29
STEWART. Abstraction as exemplified in Geometry and Algebra *ib.*

	PAGE
BROWN. A general word designates certain particulars, together with the fact of their resemblance	30
HAMILTON. Considers both parties misled by the ambiguity of the terms. Expresses Nominalism with exactness, but admits a form of Conceptualism	31
JAMES MILL. A general term is associated with a *multitude* of particulars; the idea complex and indistinct, but not unintelligible	ib.
BAILEY. The mental conceptions the same for proper names and for general names	32

B.—*The Origin of Knowledge—Experience and Intuition.*

PLATO. The doctrine of *Reminiscence*	33
ARISTOTLE. Did not regard the notions of Cause, Substance, &c. as Intuitions. Common Sense belongs to the region of Opinion, and not to Science or Cognition; and includes the provinces of Rhetoric and Dialectic—the matters generally received among men. The *Topica*. The principles of Science: some special to the several sciences; others common to all sciences—the First Philosophy or Ontology. Demonstration must end in principles that are indemonstrable. These highest principles are not intuitive; they are the growth of the higher human faculties; their truth is ascertained by Induction. Relation to Intellect or Nous. Principles of the First Philosophy—the Maxim of Contradiction, and the Maxim of Excluded Middle. His vindication of those maxims consists in an appeal to Induction	ib.
THE SCHOOLMEN. Opposing views were held. The question became prominent at the close of the scholastic period.	49
DESCARTES. First position—Thought implies Existence. The idea of Perfection involves a perfect Deity. The veracity of God warrants the Existence of Matter. Mind a thinking substance, Body an extended substance. His Deductive system founded on self-evident truths. Examples of Intuitions	ib.
ARNAULD. Distinguishes between Image and Idea. There are simple ideas not arising from Sense	51
CUDWORTH. Sense and Cognition. Ideas of Cognition ...	52
HERBERT OF CHERBURY. What is accepted by all men must be true. The Common Notions are Instinctive. Their characters	ib.
LOCKE. His replies to the arguments for Innate Ideas:—Argument from Universality. That the propositions, as soon as heard, are assented to. Opposing considerations:—The maxims are not known to children; they appear least in savages, and in the illiterate. Examination of some alleged innate ideas	53
LEIBNITZ. Charges Locke with overlooking the distinction between truths of fact and *necessary* truths. The Intellect itself is innate. Examples of necessary principles. Particular experiences cannot impart universality. The mode of pre-existence of the innate ideas	56
KANT. His position as between the opposing schools. Maintained the existence of à *priori* or Innate Principles. Examples from Mathematics. The native elements are *Forms*, experience supplying the Matter. I.—Forms of Intuition—Space and Time. II.—Categories of the Understanding—Unity, Plurality, Universality, Reality, Negation, Limitation, Substantiality, Causality, Reciprocal action, Possibility, Existence, Necessity. III.—Ideas of the Reason—the Soul, the World, God	58

CONTENTS.   xxix

	PAGE.
BUFFIER. His anticipation of Reid. Defines Common Sense. Enumeration of First Truths	62
REID. Common Sense is the judgment of sound minds generally. Principles of Contingent Truth. The Principles of Necessary Truth:—Grammar, Logic, Mathematics, Taste, Morals, Metaphysics, &c.	63
STEWART. Theory of Axioms, Definitions, and Mathematical Demonstration	65
HAMILTON. Common Sense another name for the final appeal to Consciousness. Criteria of the principles of Common Sense. Meanings of Necessity. Law of the Conditioned. Applied to Causality and to Substance	67
J. S. MILL. The nature of the certainty of mathematical truths. Reply to the arguments in favour of the à priori foundation of the mathematical axioms. Discussion of the test of inconceivableness of the opposites. Logical basis of Arithmetic and Algebra. Examination of Mr. Spencer's theory of the axioms	69
MANSEL. Different kinds of Necessity:—Mathematical necessity: the axioms of Geometry; Arithmetic. Metaphysical Necessity. Substance; Causality. Logical Necessity. Moral Necessity	73

C.—*On Happiness.*

Enumeration of primary Pleasures and Pains. Important distinctions among pleasures and pains. Happiness as affected by the principle of RELATIVITY. HEALTH. ACTIVITY, or Occupation. KNOWLEDGE. EDUCATION. INDIVIDUALITY. WEALTH. VIRTUE, or Duty. RELIGION. Formation of a Plan of Life, or METHOD	78

D.—*Classifications of the Mind.*

THE INTELLECTUAL POWERS. Aquinas. Reid. Stewart. Brown. Hamilton, Bailey	88
THE EMOTIONS. Reid. Stewart. Brown. Hamilton. Spencer. Kant. Herbert. Schleidler	89
THE LAWS OF ASSOCIATION. Aristotle. Ludovicus Vives. Hobbes. Locke. Hume. Gerard. Beattie. Hartley. James Mill. Stewart. Brown. Hamilton	91

E.—*Meanings of Certain Terms.*

CONSCIOUSNESS.—As mental life on the whole. As the subjective life more especially. View that Consciousness, as a whole, is based on knowing	93
SENSATION. Expresses various contrasting phenomena	94
PRESENTATION and REPRESENTATION	95
PERSONAL IDENTITY. Identity in living beings involves unbroken continuity. Two views of Personal Identity: (1) a Persistent Substance underlying consciousness; (2) the Sequence of conscious states. Nature of our belief in Memory	96
SUBSTANCE. Every property of a thing may be called an Attribute, and the question arises what is the Substance? Two alternatives:—(1) an unknowable substratum; (2) the reservation of the fundamental or essential property, as the Substance. Substance of Matter: of Mind. The total of any concrete may be held as the subject of the various individual attributes. The questions of Substance and Personal Identity in great part the same	98

INTRODUCTION.

CHAPTER I.

DEFINITION AND DIVISIONS OF MIND.

1. HUMAN Knowledge, Experience, or Consciousness, falls under two great departments; popularly, they are called Matter and Mind; philosophers, farther, employ the terms External World and Internal World, Not-Self or Non-Ego and Self or Ego; but the names Object and Subject are to be preferred.

The experience or consciousness of a tree, a river, a constellation, illustrates what is meant by Object. The experience of a pleasure, a pain, a volition, a thought, comes under the head of Subject.

There is nothing that we can know, or conceive of, but is included under one or other of these two great departments. They comprehend the entire universe as ascertainable by us.

2. The department of the Object, or Object-World, is exactly circumscribed by one property, Extension. The world of Subject—experience is devoid of this property.

A tree or a river is said to possess extended magnitude. A pleasure has no length, breadth, or thickness; it is in no respect an extended thing. A thought or idea may refer to extended magnitudes, but it cannot be said to have extension in itself. Neither can we say that an act of the will, a desire, a belief, occupy dimensions in space. Hence all that comes within the sphere of the Subject is spoken of as the Unextended.

3. Thus, if Mind, as commonly happens, is put for the

sum total of Subject-experiences, we may define it negatively by a single fact—the absence of Extension. But, as Object-experience is also in a sense mental, the only account of Mind strictly admissible in scientific Psychology consists in specifying three properties or functions—Feeling, Will or Volition, and Thought or Intellect—through which all our experience, as well Objective as Subjective, is built up. This positive enumeration is what must stand for a definition.

FEELING includes all our pleasures and pains, and certain modes of excitement, or of consciousness simply, that are neutral or indifferent as regards pleasure and pain. The pleasures of warmth, food, music; the pains of fatigue, poverty, remorse; the excitement of hurry and surprise, the supporting of a light weight, the touch of a table, the sound of a dog barking in the distance—are Feelings. The two leading divisions of the feelings are commonly given as Sensations and Emotions.

WILL or VOLITION comprises all the actions of human beings in so far as impelled or guided by Feelings. Eating, walking, building, sowing, speaking—are actions performed with some *end* in view; and ends are comprised in the gaining of pleasure or the avoiding of pain. Actions not prompted by feelings are not voluntary. Such are the powers of nature—wind, gravity, electricity, &c.; so also the organic functions of breathing, circulation, and the movements of the intestines.

THOUGHT, INTELLECT, Intelligence or Cognition includes the powers known as Perception, Memory, Conception, Abstraction, Reason, Judgment, and Imagination. It is analyzed, as will be seen, into three functions, called Discrimination or Consciousness of Difference, Similarity or Consciousness of Agreement, and Retentiveness or Memory.

The mind can seldom operate exclusively in any one of these three modes. A Feeling is apt to be accompanied more or less by Will and by Thought. When we are pleased, our will is moved for continuance or increase of the pleasure (Will); we at the same time discriminate and identify the pleasure, and have it impressed on the memory (Thought). (Hamilton's Lectures on Metaphysics, vol. i. p. 188.)

Thus the Definition is also a Division of the Mind; that is, a classification of its leading or fundamental attributes.

We may advert to some of the previous modes of defining and

dividing the Mind. Reid says, 'By the *mind* of a man, we understand that in him which thinks, remembers, reasons, wills:' a definition by means of a division at once defective and redundant; the defect lies in the absence of Feeling; the redundancy in the addition of 'remember' and 'reason' to the comprehensive word 'think.'.

Reid's formal classification in expounding the mind is into *Intellectual Powers* and *Active Powers*. The submerged department of Feeling will be found partly mixed up with the Intellectual Powers, wherein are included the Senses and the Emotions of Taste, and partly treated of among the Active Powers, which comprise the exposition of the benevolent and the malevolent affections.

Dr. Thomas Brown, displeased with the mode of applying the term 'Active' in the above division, went into the other extreme, and brought forward a classification where Feeling seems entirely to overlie the region of Volition. He divides mental states into *external affections* and *internal affections*. By external affections he means the feelings we have by the Senses, in other words Sensation. The internal affections he subdivides into *intellectual states of mind* and *emotions*. His division, therefore, is tantamount to Sensation, Emotion, and Intellect. All the phenomena commonly recognized as of an active or volitional character he classes as a part of Emotion.

Sir William Hamilton, in remarking on the arrangement followed in the writings of Professor Dugald Stewart, states his own view as follows:—' If we take the Mental to the exclusion of Material phœnomena, that is, the phœnomena manifested through the medium of Self-consciousness or Reflection, they naturally divide themselves into three categories or primary genera;—the phœnomena of *Knowledge* or *Cognition*,—the phœnomena of *Feeling* or of *Pleasure and Pain*,—and the phœnomena of *Conation* or of *Will and Desire*.' Intelligence, Feeling, and Will are thus distinctively set forth.

4. It is not practicable to discuss the powers of the mind in the exact order of the three leading attributes.

Feeling and Volition each involve certain primary elements, and also certain secondary or complex elements due to the operation of the Intellect upon the primary. For example, Sensation is a primary department of feeling, and always precedes the Intellect; while the Emotions, which are secondary and derived, follow the exposition of the Intellectual powers. The Will is to a great extent the product of the Retentive function of Intelligence; it is also dependent throughout on the Feelings; hence it is placed last in the course of the exposition; only, at an early stage, some notice is taken of its primary constituents.

The arrangement is as follows:—

First, Feeling and Volition in the germ, together with the full detail of Sensation, which contains a department of Feeling, and exemplifies one of the Intellectual functions—Discrimination. The convenient title is MOVEMENT, SENSE and INSTINCT.

Secondly, The INTELLECT.

Thirdly, The EMOTIONS, completing the department of Feeling.

Fourthly, The WILL.

5. Although Subject and Object (Mind and Matter) are the most widely opposed facts of our experience, yet there is, in nature, a concomitance or connexion between Mind and a definite Material organism for every individual.

The nature and extent of this connexion will appear as we proceed; and, afterwards, the phraseology of the proposition will be rendered more exact. Each mind is known, by direct or immediate knowledge, only to itself. Other minds are known to us solely through the material organism.

The physical organs related to the mental processes are:— I. The Brain and Nerves; II. The Organs of Movement, or the Muscles; III. The Organs of Sense; IV. The Viscera, including the Alimentary Canal, the Lungs, the Heart, &c. The greatest intimacy of relationship is with the Brain and Nerves.

It has always been a matter of difficulty to express the nature of this concomitance, and hence a certain mystery has attached to the union of mind and body. The difficulty is owing to the fact that we are apt to insist on some kind of local or space relationship between the Extended and the Unextended. When we think of connexion, it is almost always of connexion in space; as in supposing one thing placed in the interior of another. This last figure is often applied to the present case. Mind is said to be *internal* to, or within, the body. Descartes localized mind in the pineal gland; the schoolmen debated whether the mind is all in the whole body, or all in every part. Such expressions are unsuitable to the case. The connexion is one of *dependence*, but not properly of local union.

CHAPTER II.

THE NERVOUS SYSTEM AND ITS FUNCTIONS.

(*Summary of Results.*)

1. THE Brain is the principal, although not the sole, organ of mind; and its leading functions are mental.

The proofs of this position are these:—
(1) The physical pain of excessive mental excitement is localized in the head. In extreme muscular fatigue, pain is felt in the muscles; irritation of the lungs is referred to the chest, indigestion to the stomach; and when mental exercise brings on acute irritation, the local seat is the head.

(2) Injury or disease of the brain affects the mental powers. A blow on the head destroys consciousness; physical alterations of the nervous substance (as seen after death) are connected with loss of speech, loss of memory, insanity, or some other mental deprivation or derangement.

(3) The products of nervous waste are more abundant after mental excitement. These products, eliminated mainly by the kidneys, are the alkaline phosphates, combined in the triple phosphate of ammonia and magnesia. Phosphorus is a characteristic ingredient of the nervous substance.

(4) There is a general connexion between size of brain and mental energy. In the animal series, intelligence increases with the development of the brain. The human brain greatly exceeds the animal brain; and the most advanced races of men have the largest brains. Men distinguished for mental force have, as a general rule, brains of an unusual size. The average weight of the brain is 48 oz.; the brain of Cuvier weighed 64 oz. Idiots commonly have small brains.

(5) By specific experiments on the brain and nerves, it is shown that they are indispensable to the mental functions.

2. The Nervous System, as a whole, is composed of a *central mass,* or lump, and a system of branching or ramifying threads, designated the *nerves*.

The *central* mass, or lump, is called the cerebro-spinal axis, or centre, because contained in the head and backbone, being a large roundish lump (in the head), united to a slender column or rod (in the spine).

The *nerves* are the silvery threads proceeding from the central lump, and ramifying to all parts of the body. As there is a circle of action between the brain and the bodily organs, one-half of the nerves carry influence outwards, the other half inwards.

3. The nervous substance is composed of two elements, described as the *white* matter and the *grey* matter.

The white matter is made up of minute *fibres*. The grey matter contains fibres, together with small bodies, termed *cells*, or *corpuscles*.

By slicing through a brain, we may observe the two kinds of substance. The interior mass is a pale, waxy white; the circumference shows an irregular cake of ashy grey colour.

Microscopically viewed, the two elements of the nerve substance are (1) *fibres*, and (2) little bodies called *cells* or *corpuscles*. The white matter is made up of fibres; the grey matter contains cells intermingled with fibres.

One remarkable peculiarity of the nerve fibres is their exceeding minuteness. Their thickness ranges from the $\frac{1}{1500}$th, the $\frac{1}{3000}$th, $\frac{1}{15,000}$th, $\frac{1}{30,000}$th, to the $\frac{1}{100,000}$th of an inch. In a rod of nervous matter, an inch thick, there might be, from ten to one hundred millions of fibres. Such minuteness and corresponding multiplication of fibres must be viewed with reference to the variety and complicacy of the mental functions.

A second fact is their position. This is always a completed connexion between the extremities of the body and the cells of the grey matter, or else between one cell and another of the central lump; there are no loose ends. The fibres are thus a connecting or conducting material.

The *cells* or *corpuscles* are rounded, pear shaped, or irregular little bodies, and give origin each to two or more fibres. They are on a corresponding scale of minuteness. They range as high as the $\frac{1}{300}$th of an inch, and as low as the $\frac{1}{12,000}$th. A little cube of grey matter, a quarter of an inch in the side, might contain one hundred thousand cells.

These corpuscles are richly supplied with blood (so are the nerve fibres), and are supposed to be Centres of nervous energy or influence, or, at all events, parts where the nervous energy is re-inforced. Hence the masses of grey matter are spoken of as constituting the Nerve Centres.

A second function attaching to the corpuscles supplies a key to the plan of the brain. They are Grand Junctions or Crossings, where the fibres extend and multiply their connexions. The fibres coming from all parts of the body, enter sooner or later into the corpuscles of the grey substance, and, through these, establish forward and lateral communications with other fibres, which communications are required for grouping and co-ordinating sensations and movements in the exercise of our mental functions.

4. The Central nervous mass, or Cerebro-Spinal Axis, is composed of parts, which may be separately viewed, and to which belong separate functions.

I. The SPINAL CORD is the rod or column of nervous substance enclosed in the back-bone. It is chiefly made up of white matter, but contains a core of grey substance.

The Spinal Cord is supposed to terminate at the edge of the hole in the skull where the column enters to join the brain. At this point, it is expanded both in width and in depth, and receives additions of grey matter. The expanded portion, about $1\frac{1}{4}$ inch in length, is called the *medulla oblongata*, and is a body of great importance, being the centre of important nerves.

The functions of the Spinal Cord are known to be these—

First, It is the main Trunk of all the nerves distributed to the body generally (the head excepted). Its destruction or severance at any part puts an end to all communication with the members supplied with nerves below the point of severance; whence follow paralysis and loss of feeling.

Secondly, It has the functions of a Centre; in other words, it completes a circle of nervous action, so that certain movements, in answer to stimulants, can be kept up by means of it alone. This property is allied with the inside core of grey matter. A decapitated frog will draw up and throw out its limbs when the skin is pinched or irritated.

Taking together the Spinal Cord and the Medulla Oblongata, we find that by their means a certain class of living actions are maintained, called *automatic*, and also *reflex* actions. These are involuntary actions; they are maintained without any feeling, intention, or volition, on our part. They are enumerated as follows:—

(1) Movements connected with the process of *Digestion*.

The first operation upon the food in the mouth—the chewing or masticating—is voluntary, and requires the co-operation of the brain. When the morsel passes from the tongue into the bag of the throat, it is forced down the gullet by a series of contractions and movements which are involuntary; we have no feeling of them, and no control over them. The contact of the food with the surface of the alimentary tube impresses certain nerves distributed there; influence is conveyed to a nervous centre (in some part below the brain, probably the medulla oblongata, together with the sympathetic ganglia), and the response is manifested in the contracting of the muscular fibres of the alimentary tube.

(2) The movements connected with *Respiration*. The breathing action is sustained by a power withdrawn from our will, although voluntary muscles are made use of. In taking in breath, the lungs are expanded by the muscles of the chest; in expiration, the chest is compressed, and the air forced out, by the abdominal muscles. The medulla oblongata is the centre for sustaining this process.

The acts of *coughing* and *sneezing* are reflex acts, operated through the lungs. The irritation of the very sensitive surfaces of the throat and bronchial tubes, and of the lining membrane of the nose, originates, through the medulla oblongata, a powerful discharge of nervous force to the expiratory muscles, and the air is forced out with explosive violence. *Sucking* in infants is a purely reflex act.

(3) Certain reflex movements are connected with the *Eyes*. The act of *winking* is stimulated by the contact of the eye with the inner surface of the upper eyelid, and serves to distribute the tears, or eye-wash, and clean the ball. There is also a reflex action of the light in opening and closing the pupil of the eye.

(4) There is a tendency, of a purely reflex nature, to move the muscles of any part, by a stimulus specially applied to that part. In the decapitated frog, the pinching of a foot leads to the retractation of that foot. An object placed in the open hand of any one asleep, stimulates the closure of the hand. Touching the cheek of a child makes it laugh. In tasting anything, the sensation, while awakening a general expression of feeling, more especially excites the muscles of the mouth. The same applies to smell; a bad odour produces a contortion of the nose. In these effects of the more special senses, the influence may not be limited to the spinal cord, but it illustrates the kind of reflex action referred to, an action which the cord

FUNCTIONS OF THE CEREBRUM.

is capable of sustaining. This whole class has sometimes been called *sensori-motor* actions.

(5) The effect denominated the tension, tone, or *tonicity* of the muscles. It is a fact, that in the profoundest slumber there is still a certain degree of contraction in the muscles; only after death are they wholly relaxed. Now, experiments seem to show that this remaining contraction is maintained through the agency of the spinal cord; it disappears with the destruction of the cord.

II. The BRAIN, or Encephalon, is the rounded or oval lump of nervous matter filling the cavity of the skull. It is a complex mass, but there are certain recognized divisions, with probable difference of function.

Commencing from below, and continuous with the Spinal cord, is the *Medulla Oblongata*, which has been already noticed.

Next is the *Pons Varolii*, or ring-like protuberance, so called because it embraces like a ring the main stem of the brain, continued upwards from the medulla oblongata. It contains white, or fibrous matter, running partly up and down, and partly in a transverse direction, with diffused grey matter. As regards the white portion, it serves as a track of communication from below upwards, and from one half of the cerebellum (which adjoins it) to the other half. As regards the grey matter, it must perform some of the functions of a centre, in reflecting and multiplying nervous communications. No more special explanation can be given of its functions.

The *Cerebral Hemispheres*, sometimes called the brain proper, constitute the highest and by far the largest part of the human brain. This mass is egg-shaped, but with a flattened base; the big end of the egg being behind. There is a complete division into two halves, right and left, by a deep fissure all round, leaving only a connecting band of white matter. The surface is not plain, but moulded into numerous smooth and tortuous eminences, called convolutions, which are separated by furrows of considerable, though variable depth. The convoluted surface consists of a cake of grey matter, somewhat less than half an inch thick, and very much extended by the convoluted arrangement. Inside of this cake, the hemispheres are made up of white matter, with the exception of certain small enclosed masses, which contain considerable portions of grey matter.

These last-named bodies, called the *lesser grey centres* of the brain, are regarded as the medium of connexion between the hemispheres above, and the great stem below. Probably in them occurs that multiplication of fibres, necessary to the enormous expansion of the white matter of the hemispheres. Two of these bodies are usually named together, the *corpora striata* and *thalami optici*, as being closely conjoined in the heart of the white substance of the hemispheres; through them most of the ascending fibres of the main stem spread out into the hemispheres. They contain a large amount of grey matter. A third mass, the *corpora quadrigemina*, or quadruple bodies, is more detached, and lies behind, between the cerebrum and the cerebellum. This centre is closely connected with the optic nerve, and has important functions relating to vision. In the lower vertebrata (as fishes), it assumes very large proportions as compared with the rest of the brain. Resting on the middle cleft of the four eminences, is a small conical body, called the *pineal gland*, curious as being supposed, by Descartes, to be the seat of the soul.

The functions of the Hemispheres of the Brain, including the enclosed Ganglia, comprehend all, or nearly all, that is comprised in mind. When they are destroyed, or seriously injured, sensation, emotion, volition, and intelligence are suspended. Movements are still possible, but there is no evidence that they are accompanied with consciousness, in other words, with feeling and intelligence; they are without purpose, or volition.

It would be interesting, if we could assign distinct mental functions to different parts of this large and complicated organ; if we could find certain convolutions related to specific feelings, or to specific intellectual gifts and acquirements. This Phrenology attempted, but with doubtful success. Yet, it is most reasonable to suppose that, the brain being constituted on a uniform plan, the same parts serve the same functions in different individuals.

The *Cerebellum, little brain*, or *after-brain*, lies behind and beneath the convoluted hemispheres. It is a nearly wedge-shaped body, divided into two halves, with connecting white matter. Like the hemispheres, its outer surface is a thin cake of grey matter, extended, not by the convoluted arrangement, but by being folded into plates or laminæ. The connexions of the cerebellum are, beneath, with a detached branch of the great stem, and above with the hemispheres, through the corpora quadrigemina; the two halves are united laterally by the pons varolii.

The functions of the Cerebellum are still under discussion. Certain experiments, made by Flourens, were interpreted as

FUNCTIONS OF THE CEREBELLUM.

showing that it is the centre of rhythmical and combined movements, such as the locomotive movements—walking, flying, swimming, &c. Its destruction in pigeons took away the power of standing, flying, walking, leaping, without seeming to destroy the cardinal functions of the mind, the powers of sensation and volition. The inference has been denied by Brown-Séquard, who affirms that the same inability of guiding and combining the movements follows the destruction or irritation of other parts of the base of the brain. The two sets of observations are not inconsistent; for, as the nervous action has to traverse a certain course or circuit, it may be suspended by destroying any part of the line. What seems to be established by the observations is, that there is a separate locality concerned in joining movements into harmonious or combined groups for executing the voluntary determinations.

THE NERVES.

5. The nerves are the branching or ramifying cords, proceeding from the centres, and distributed to all parts of the body.

They have been locally divided into *spinal* and *cerebral*, according as they emerge from the Spinal Cord, or directly from the Brain. This is chiefly a matter of local convenience; those nerves supplying the head and face, emerge at once from the brain, through openings in the skull; the rest descend in the spinal cord, and are given off, at openings between the vertebræ, higher or lower, according to their ultimate destination.

The mode of emergence from the spinal cord is peculiar. At the interstices of the vertebræ, a couple of branches emerge, for the two sides of the body. Each member of the couple is composed of two portions, or roots, an anterior and a posterior root, which at a little distance unite in a common stem. It is observed, however, that the posterior root has a little swelling or ganglion, containing grey substance, there being nothing to correspond in the anterior root.

6. The general function of the nerves is to transmit influence from one part of the system to another.

The nerves are supposed to originate nothing; they are exclusively employed in carrying or conveying energy of their own kind. In the final result, this energy stimulates muscles into action, and without it no muscle ever operates. But in the circles of thought, a great many nerve currents go their rounds, without stimulating muscles.

7. The circuit of nervous action supposes two classes of nerves, the incarrying and the outcarrying. These are usually combined in the same trunk nerve. They appear in separation, in the double roots of the spinal nerves.

The nervous influence does not proceed indiscriminately to and fro, in the same fibres; one class is employed for conveying influence inwards, in sensation, and the other class for conveying influence outwards, in volition. At the emergence of the spinal nerves, the classes are distinct. It was the discovery of Bell, that the posterior roots, distinguished by the little ganglionic swellings, are nerves purely of sensation; the anterior roots, nerves purely of movement. It would be a point of great interest, if these pure nerves could be traced upwards into the nerve centres, so as to show which centres received sensory fibres, and which motory; this would be the first clue to a genuine Phrenology.

The Cerebral Nerves are nearly all pure nerves. They were formerly divided into nine pairs, but there are, in reality, twelve pairs.

The *first* pair is the olfactory, or nerve of Smell. The *second* is the *optic*, or nerve of Sight. The *third, fourth,* and *sixth* pairs are distributed to the muscles of the eye, and therefore determine its movements. The *fifth* pair is double, containing a motor branch to the muscles of the jaws, and a sensory branch connected with the sensibility of the face, and containing the nerve of Taste. The *seventh* pair is motor, and supplies the muscles of the face. The *eighth* is the nerve of Hearing. The *ninth* supplies sensory fibres to the tongue and throat (being a second nerve of Taste), and motor fibres to the muscles of the throat or pharynx. The *tenth*, called *pneumo-gastric*, supplies the larynx, the lungs, the liver, and the stomach, and is the medium of a large amount of sensibility. The *eleventh*, called *spinal accessory*, is motor. The *twelfth* pair (hypo-glossal) is the motor nerve of the tongue.

BOOK I.

MOVEMENT, SENSE, AND INSTINCT.

CHAPTER I.

MOVEMENT, AND THE MUSCULAR FEELINGS.

1. THE Muscular Feelings agree with the sensations of the senses in being primary sources of feeling and of knowledge, localized in a peculiar set of organs; their characteristic difference is summed up in the consciousness of active energy.

The most fundamental contrast existing among the feelings of the human mind, is the contrast of Active and Passive. The exercise of rowing a boat gives a feeling of activity or energy; in a warm bath, the consciousness is of the passive kind. The contrast would appear to be embodied in the nervous system; the outcarrying nerves, together with the nerve centres whence they immediately proceed, being associated with the feelings of activity; the incarrying nerves and their allied centres with sensation or passivity.

Not only should the muscular feelings form a class apart from the sensations, on the ground now stated, but it is farther believed that their consideration should precede the account of the senses. The reasons are—that movement precedes sensation, and is at the outset independent of any stimulus from without; and that action is a more intimate and inseparable property of our constitution than any of our sensations, and in fact enters as a component part into every one of the senses, giving them the character of compounds, while itself is a simple and elementary property.

Of the Muscular System.—The movements of the body are performed by means of the substance called muscle, or flesh: a substance composed of very fine fibres, collected into separate masses, of great variety of form, each mass being a muscle. The peculiar property of the muscular substance is *contractility*, or the forcible shrinking of the fibres under a stimulus, whereby the muscle is shortened, and the attached bones drawn together in consequence. As an example, we may mention the muscle of the calf of the leg, a broad round mass of flesh, ending above and below in the strong white fibrous substance, known as tendon, by which it is connected with the bones; the upper tendon with the bone of the leg, the lower with the heel; its contraction draws the heel towards the leg, straightening the line of leg and foot, and thus compelling the body to rise.

The ultimate fibres of the muscles, the fibrils or fibrillæ (less than the ten-thousandth of an inch in diameter), are found to consist of rows of rectangular particles; in the contraction of the muscle, these particles become shorter and thicker. The fibrils are made into bundles, about $\frac{1}{400}$ of an inch in thickness, called fibres; and the fibres are made up into larger bundles, or threads, which are visible to the eye, as the strings composing flesh.

The contraction of the muscle requires the agency of the nerves, distributed copiously to the fibres. A farther condition of contractile power is a supply of arterial blood. The oxidation of the substances found in the blood is the ultimate source of muscular power; the oxygen, taken into the lungs, and the food, taken into the stomach, are the raw material of all the forces of the system.

2. For the most part, our movements are stimulated through our senses, as when a flash of light or a loud sound makes us start; but it is a fact of great importance, that movements arise without the stimulation of sensible objects, through some energy of the nerve centres themselves, or some stimulus purely internal. This may be called the Spontaneous Activity of the system.

Spontaneous Activity is the explanation of many appearances, and is an essential element of the will, on the theory maintained in this work. The following facts are adduced as both proving and illustrating the doctrine:—

(1) The muscles never undergo an entire relaxation during life. Even in profound slumber, they possess a certain degree of tension, or rigidity. This state is called their 'tonicity,' or tonic contraction. It is excited through the medium of the nerves. The cutting of the nerves, or the destruction of the nerve centres, renders the muscles flaccid. The inference is, that at all times a stream of nervous energy flows to the muscles, irrespective of stimulation from without.

(2) The permanent closure of the muscles called sphinc-

ters, is an effect of the same nature. The lower extremity of the alimentary canal is kept close by a self-acting muscle; if the connexion with the nerve centres is destroyed, this muscle is relaxed.

(3) The operation of the *involuntary* muscles, as in breathing, the heart, and the movements of the intestine, shows that there is a provision for keeping up movements, independent of the stimulus of the senses. These muscles never cease to ply. The only stimulation that could be assigned in their case is the contact of the materials propelled—the air in the lungs, the blood in the blood-vessels, the food in the stomach and bowels; but even these contacts would fail to account for the first beginning of the movements. By what influence do we draw our first breath? Still, what is contended for is, not the absence of internal organic influences, but the absence of agents operating on the external senses.

(4) In wakening from sleep, movement often precedes sensation. Most commonly the first symptom of awakening is a general commotion of the frame, a number of spontaneous movements—the stretching of the limbs, the opening of the eyes, the expansion of the features—to which succeeds the revived sensibility to outward things. No decided facts have ever been adduced to show that a stimulation of the senses invariably precedes the wakening movements. We are therefore led to believe that the re-animation of the system consists in a rush of nervous power to the moving organs, at the same time that the susceptibility of the senses is renewed.

(5) The movements of infancy, of young animals generally, and of animals distinguished for activity, are strongly in point. The mobility of infants is very great, and the same feature characterizes childhood and youth. We may attribute it in part to the acute sensations and emotions of early years. But this is not the whole explanation. When the senses are in no ways solicited, the youthful mobility is strongly manifested; it seems chiefly to follow the physical circumstances of rest and nutrition, and is, as might be expected, most vehement after confinement or restraint.

The activity of young animals in general, and of animals specially active (as the insect tribe), are most adequately represented on the present hypothesis. When the kitten plays with a worsted ball, we always attribute the overflowing fulness of moving energy to the creature's own inward stimulus, to which the ball merely serves for a pretext. So an active young hound, refreshed by sleep, or kept in confinement, pants for being let loose, not because of anything that attracts his view or kindles up his ear, but because a rush of activity courses through his members, rendering him uneasy till the confined energy has found vent in a chase or a run. We are at no loss to distinguish this kind of activity from that awakened by sensation or emotion, and the distinction is accordingly recognized in the modes of interpreting the movements and feelings of animals. When a rider speaks of his horse as 'fresh,' he implies that the natural activity is undischarged, and pressing for vent; the excitement caused by mixing in a chase or in a battle, is a totally different thing from the spontaneous vehemence of a full-fed and under-worked animal.

(6) The activity of morbid excitement may next be quoted. Under a peculiar state of the nervous system, movements arise without any stimulation, or in undue proportion to the stimulants applied. This shows incontestably, that the condition of the nerve centres may be such as to originate activity, without any concurrence of sensible agencies ; now if there be an unhealthy spontaneity, there may also be a healthy mode, as in the freshness of the young and vigorous animal. There are occasions when it is impossible to be still ; the internal fires are generating force, which we cannot repress. Certain drugs, as strychnine, induce this excessive spontaneity, in the shape of strong convulsive erections and movements of the body.

(7) Activity and Sensibility are not developed in equal proportions in individual character; more frequently they stand in an inverse proportion to each other. The strong, active, restless temperament is usually the least sensitive, the least open to the varying solicitations of the senses. This energetic temperament is manifestly the result of a constitutional, self-prompting force. There is, in many individuals, a love of activity for its own sake, a search after occasions for putting forth energy ; we may instance, the restless adventurer, the indefatigable traveller, the devotee of business, the lover of political bustle. The activity of the more susceptible natures is prompted by the feelings, and ceases when they are gratified ; as when a man like Wilberforce is stimulated to redress some flagrant wrong, and otherwise leads an inactive career.

The Spontaneity of the system is shown in all the regions of muscular activity. Foremost of our muscular groupings is the *Locomotive Apparatus*, which includes the limbs, together with the trunk ; in energetic promptings, these organs are the readiest means of discharging the surplus activity ; the excited animal walks, runs, flies, or gesticulates. The organs of *Mastication* form a second grouping. The *Vocal Organs* are an isolated group of great interest. The utterance of the voice is, on many occasions, plainly due to mere freshness of the organs. The morning song of the bird bursts out spontaneously, although also liable to the influence of infection, and other external causes. Among the smaller organs, we may mention the *Tongue*, so remarkable for flexibility; its spontaneous movements occur in the play of infancy, and are of importance in the beginnings of articulation.

We might illustrate the spontaneous, as contrasted with the stimulated discharge, in the special aptitudes of animals. As the battery of the torpedo becomes charged by the mere course of nutrition, and requires to be periodically relieved by being poured upon some object or other, so we may suppose that the jaws of the tiger, the fangs of the serpent, the spinning apparatus of the spider, require at intervals to have some objects to spend themselves upon. It is said that the constructiveness of the bee and the beaver incontinently manifests itself, even where there is no end to be gained.

The spontaneous activity necessarily rises and falls with the vigour and state of nutrition of the system; being abundant in states of good health, and deficient during fatigue, hunger, and sickness.

THE MUSCULAR FEELINGS.

3. There are three classes of these:—

First, Feelings connected with the *organic condition of the muscles*, as those arising from hurts, wounds, diseases, fatigue, rest, nutriment.

Most of these affections the muscles have in common with the other tissues of the body; and the appropriate place for expounding them will be under a subsequent head. It is our purpose, at this stage, to exhibit prominently the *active* side of our nature, in its contrast to the *passive* or receptive side.

Secondly, Feelings connected with *muscular action*, including all the pleasures and pains of *exercise*. These are states peculiar to muscular activity.

18 MOVEMENT AND THE MUSCULAR FEELINGS.

Thirdly, The *discriminative sensibility of muscle*, or the consciousness that arises during the varying tension of the moving organs.

These are mental states of a neutral kind as regards pleasure and pain, but all-important as the basis of Intellect. The muscular feelings, like the sensations, have two characters; one in the region of Feeling strictly so called, and decisively shown in pleasure and pain; the other in the region of Intellect, and manifested in discrimination, or the consciousness of difference. The two aspects may be illustrated, in the sense of sight, by comparing the rainbow or a bonfire with a man's name or an arithmetical number.

I. *Of the Feelings of Muscular Exercise.**

4. These are feelings proper and peculiar to the muscular system; they cannot be produced in any other connexion.

The first and simplest case is the *dead strain,* or exertion without movement.

PHYSICAL SIDE.—The physical circumstances of muscular

---

* There are many things to be said with reference to Feeling in general; but I consider it inexpedient to introduce the whole of the generalities before giving a certain number of examples in the concrete. Accordingly, I prefer to proceed at once with the Muscular Feelings and Sensations in the detail, and to expound the general laws and properties of Feeling in a chapter introductory to the Emotions. All that is necessary, in the meantime, is to understand the plan followed in the description of the feelings; and, with this view, a few explanatory observations are here offered.

All feelings have a PHYSICAL SIDE, or relation to our bodily organs; the sensations, for example, arise on the stimulation of a special organ of sense; and both sensations and emotions have a characteristic outward display, or expression, which indicates their existence to a spectator. I include in the description of each feeling whatever is known of its physical accompaniments.

The feeling proper, or the MENTAL SIDE, has its relationships exhausted under the three fundamental attributes of Mind—Feeling, Volition, and Intellect. As Feeling. it is pleasurable, painful, or neutral—its Quality; it has Degree, as regards Intensity, or as regards Quantity; and it may have Special characteristics besides. Farther, all feelings that are either pleasurable or painful are motives to the Will; this is their Volitional property. Lastly, when we look to the susceptibility of being discriminated, compared, and remembered, we are dealing with Intellectual properties, in which feelings are not necessarily identical, because agreeing in other things.

tension, so far as known, are these. There is a shrinking or contracting of the length of the muscle, through the shortening and widening of the ultimate particles that make up each fibril. To induce the contraction, there is required a nerve current from the brain, by the outgoing or motor nerves. Equally essential is the presence of blood : in which oxidation is going on, in proportion to the muscular energy produced.

There are numerous indirect and remote consequences of muscular exertion. The increased consumption of oxygen and the production of carbonic acid give more work to the lungs, augmenting the breathing action. From the same causes, there is a quickening also of the heart and circulation; to which follows a rise of animal heat throughout the body. Partly from the accumulation of waste products, and partly from the augmented flow of blood, and the increased temperature, there is an augmentation in the eliminating function of

The plan in its completeness may be represented thus:—
PHYSICAL SIDE.
    Bodily Origin. (For Sensations chiefly).
    Bodily Diffusion, expression, or embodiment.
MENTAL SIDE.
    Characters as *Feeling*.
        Quality, *i. e.*, Pleasure, Pain, Indifference.
        Degree.
            As regards Intensity or acuteness.
            As regards Quantity, mass, or volume.
        Special characteristics.
    Volitional characters.
        Mode of influencing the Will, or Motives to Action.
    Intellectual characters.
        Susceptibility to Discrimination and to Agreement.
        Degree of Retainability, that is Ideal Persistence and Recoverability.

It is to be remarked that, as a general rule, pleasures agree in their physical expression, or embodiment, and also in their mode of operating on the will, namely, for their continuance, increase, or renewal. In like manner, pains have a common expression, and a common influence in promoting action for their removal, abatement, or avoidance. Hence the fact, that a state is pleasurable or painful, carries with it these two other facts as a matter of course.

Again, as regards the Intellect; Discrimination, Agreement, and Retainability are to a certain extent proportional to the *degree* of the feeling, or the strength of the impression. This being the case, the statement of the degree involves the probable nature of the properties connected with the Intellect. Hence, in most cases, it is unnecessary to carry the delineation through all the particulars of the table. It is only when a feeling possesses any peculiarities rendering it an exception to the general laws of coincidence now mentioned, that the full description is called for. Two or three examples of the complete detail will be given.

the skin. Moreover, the great demand for blood in the muscles causes it to be withdrawn from other organs, such as the brain and the stomach; thus diminishing mental excitement, and interrupting for the time the digestive processes. Provided sufficient food is supplied, the entire effect of exercise is favourable to the animal processes; the increased functions of the lungs, heart, and skin are good for the system generally; the temporary withdrawal of blood from the brain, and from the stomach, prepares the way for its going back with renewed efficiency. Mankind have always known that muscular exercise, in proper time and quantity, improves health.*

The Expression or outward embodiment of muscular exertion is determined by the muscles engaged, and by the tendency of the rest to chime in with them, through a general law of the system. In so far as not completely pre-occupied in this way, the features and other organs of expression are affected according as the mental state is pleasurable or the reverse.

MENTAL SIDE.—Of *Feeling* proper, the first point is Quality. Observation shows that this is pleasurable, indifferent, or painful, according to the condition of the system. The first outburst of muscular vigour in a healthy frame, after rest and nourishment, is highly pleasurable. The intensity of the pleasure gradually subsides into indifference; and, if the exercise is prolonged beyond a certain time, pain ensues. In ordinary manual labour there may be, at commencing in the morning and after meals, a certain amount of pleasure caused by the exercise; but it is probable that during the greater part of a workman's day, the feeling of exertion is in most cases indifferent. If we confine ourselves to the discharge of surplus energy in muscular exertion, there can be no doubt that this is a considerable source of pleasure in the average of human beings, and doubtless also in the animal tribes. The fact is shown in the love of exercise for its own sake, or apart from the ends of productive industry, and the

---

* The muscles receive principally motor, or outcarrying nerves; they are not, however, destitute of sensory or incarrying fibres. It is an inference supported by many facts, and accepted by the generality of physiologists, that the feeling of exertion accompanies the outgoing nerve current, and does not arise, as a sensation, by the sensory fibres. The other feelings of muscle being of a more passive kind, and are allied to sensation, and seem to be connected with the ingoing currents by the sensitive fibres. See the whole question argued at length, ' *Senses and Intellect*,' p. 92, 2nd edit.

preservation of health. In the case of active sports and amusements, there are additional sources of pleasurable excitement, but the delight in the mere bodily exertion would still be reckoned one ingredient in the mixture.

As to the Degree of this pleasure, it is *massive* rather than *acute*. The sensibility of muscle under the dead strain is not very great, and becomes considerable only by multiplication or extent, as when a number of large muscles are powerfully engaged.

We estimate pleasures directly, by comparing them in our consciousness, as when we decide which of two apples is the sweetest, and prefer one picture to another. We estimate them indirectly, by the amount of pain that they can subdue, as in restoring cheerfulness under a shock of suffering. Bodily exercise has a great soothing power, but not exclusively from its being a source of pleasure. It has the physical effect of deriving blood from the brain, so as to calm excitement, and a farther effect to be next noticed.

The third point in the description of a mental state, considered as Feeling, is its Speciality, apart from quality and degree. Now, we have already remarked that there is a generic difference of nature between muscular feeling proper and sensation proper. This radical distinction in kind is familiar to each person's experience, and is designated by such phrases as 'the sense of power,' 'the feeling of energy put forth,' 'the sense of resistance,' &c. It has the peculiarity of determining an attitude of mind hostile to passive feeling, and to self-consciousness in every form; in proportion as it is manifested we are indifferent as regards pleasure and pain; pleasure may be stimulated, but will not be felt. This attitude of indifference, coupled with the consciousness of energy, is the ultimate meaning of what is called the *Object*, as opposed to the *Subject*,—the *not-me*, as opposed to the *me*. Even the pleasure of exercise and the pain of fatigue during exercise are not steady, but fitful and transitory feelings. It is only at intervals that we remit the putting forth of effort, and subjectively attend to the resulting pleasure or pain.

There are thus two modes of mental indifference, or mental life with the absence of pleasure or pain. The one is the state of neutral emotion, as in mere surprise, and may be called subjective indifference. The other is the objective attitude, under which all emotion is for the moment submerged.

The *Volitional* property of the pleasure, or the pain, of muscular exercise falls under the general law of the will. As pleasure, and in proportion to the degree, it works for its own continuance or increase. Owing to the existence of the spontaneous discharge, the stimulus of pleasure is not necessary to begin activity, but is a co-operating cause for maintaining it when once begun.

In the *Intellectual* point of view, a feeling is considered as to Discrimination (together with Agreement) and as to Retainability in the memory. These properties are so important as to constitute a distinct branch of the subject. I shall merely allude here to one small part of the case, namely, our recollection of states of muscular exercise regarded as pleasure, so as to render them an object of desire and pursuit when they are not actually present. This is a truly intellectual property of feeling. In so far as active amusements and sports, and occupations largely involving muscular exercise, are a fixed object of passionate pursuit, to that extent they abide in thought, or stand high in one of their intellectual aspects.

5. As examples of the dead strain, we may mention the supporting of a weight, the holding on as a drag, the exertion of force, or the encounter of resistance in pressing, squeezing, wrestling, &c. A certain amount of accompanying movement does not alter the character of the situation; as, for example, in slowly dragging a heavy vehicle.

6. Exertion *with movement.*

Movement developes a new mode of sensibility, which is more apparent as the force expended is small; a circumstance rendering it likely that the special effect is associated with the passive sensibility of muscle.

PHYSICALLY, all that we know of the fact of movement is the perpetual change of the muscular tension; there is a constantly varying and alternately remitted strain, instead of the pouring forth of energy in a fixed attitude.

MENTALLY, the characters differ according as the movements are *slow* or *quick.*

7. And first of *slow* movements.

Under a loitering, sauntering walk, drawling tones of speech, solemn gestures, and dawdling occupation, there is a voluminous pleasurable feeling, with little energy expended. The two facts are mutually implicated. The sense of expended energy is wanting, and the attention is disengaged for the passive sensibility of the muscles; so that, in fact, with the show of activity there is the substance of passivity. The state is closely allied to muscular repose, or the reaction from great muscular expenditure, and to the approach of sleep. Slow movements are of a soothing tendency; they quiet the irritated nerves, and prepare the way for complete repose. They have a close alliance with the emotions of awe, solemnity, and veneration; hence the funeral pace, the slow enunciation of devotional exercises, the long-drawn tones of organ music, are appropriated to religious worship.

8. Movements *gradually increasing or diminishing* give rise to a still greater degree of pleasurable feeling. The gradual dying away of a motion is pleasurable and graceful in every sort of activity—in gesture, in the dance, in speech, and in visible movements. It is this peculiarity that seems to constitute the beauty of curved lines and rounded forms. We may explain it on the great law of the mind that connects all sensibility with change of impression; in these rising and falling movements, there is unceasing variation of effect.

9. Next as to *quick* movements.

Movements of great rapidity, whether the energy expended be great or little, have a tendency to excite the nervous system; they are in that respect a kind of stimulant, like a loud noise, or the glare of light. All the mental functions are quickened in consequence. It depends on circumstances, whether this effect is pleasurable or the opposite. If the nervous system is fresh and vigorous, the stimulation is agreeable, and may end in a kind of intoxication; in a jaded condition of the nerves, the effect is apt to be acutely painful and distressing. Under excitement, there may be a third situation, wherein fatigue passes off in favour of a delirious pleasure, for which the system has afterwards to pay the cost by a protracted depression. The ecstatic worship of antiquity, which consisted in wild and furious dances in honour of Bacchus and of Demeter, brought on a peculiar frenzy of intense enjoyment; and something of the same kind still happens among the Orientals, and in a less degree with the lovers of dancing everywhere. The physical circumstance may be presumed to be a great excess of blood to the brain, the result of the protracted stimulation.

It appears thus, that movement, in the extreme phases of slowness and quickness, and not involving much exertion, does not represent the main fact of the consciousness of muscular energy, but certain incidental peculiarities allied more to the passive, than to the active, side of our mental constitution. If great energy is to be put forth under these modes of movement, their incidental character will be subordinated to the proper consciousness of expended muscular force.

10. A third situation connected with muscular exercise is improperly expressed by *passive* movements.

Riding in a vehicle is the commonest instance; carriage exercise is both pleasurable and wholesome. There is a gentle muscular stimulus, such as accompanies slow and varying movements, which results in voluminous passive sensibility. To this Dr. Arnott adds the circumstance, that the shaking of the body propels the blood; and, as it can move only one way, the circulation is quickened. The fresh air also counts in the effect. Another mental influence is derived from the shifting scene; the eye is regaled with novelty, without the labour of moving to obtain it.

For the sensuous luxury of motion, the Americans have devised the rocking chair, an extension of the children's hobby-horse and swing.

II. *Of the Discriminative or Intellectual Sensibility of Muscle.*

11. Along with every feeling, we have a consciousness of degree.

To be affected *more* or *less*, is a consequence of being affected at all. Even our pleasures and pains are discriminated according to their intensity. To regard any feeling as differing from another in quantity, or otherwise, is the first condition of intelligence, or thought; it is the feature of distinctness, character, or individuality, as opposed to blank sameness or monotony. Not to distinguish one colour from another is a form of blindness; to be more than ordinarily discriminative is to have a high intellectual endowment. The discriminations in the muscular feeling are of great moment.

12. First, with respect to the *degree* of Exertion, or Expended Force, movement being left out of the account.

We here go back upon the feeling of muscular exercise, considered not as giving pleasure or pain, which are subjective states, but as making up our object attitude, under which our consciousness is merely of the degree of expended energy. This state is the sense or feeling of Resistance, and is our conception of Body, and our measure of Force, Momentum,

Inertia, or the Mechanical property of matter. No feeling of the human mind is more fundamental, more constant, or more worked up into complex products, than this. When a weight is put into the hand, we are aware of an expenditure of force; when the amount is increased, we are conscious of increased expenditure. The delicacy of our discrimination is the smallness of the addition or the subtraction that will alter our consciousness. An ordinary person can discriminate between 39 and 40 ounces.

The feeling of graduated resistance is brought out in encountering or checking a body in motion, as in stopping a carriage or in obstructing another person's progress. It is also manifested in putting forth power to move resisting bodies, as in rowing a boat, digging the ground, or other manual exertion; likewise in bearing burdens. We have it present to us, in supporting our own body. Our varying experience in all these forms, consists of a varying muscular consciousness, a series of modes of expended energy, which the memory can retain, and which we can associate with other mental states, as with the sensations of colour, of sound, of contact, &c. We connect one degree of resistance with a small, and another with a large, optical impression, as in comparing a pebble with a paving stone.

The delicate discrimination of degrees of muscular expenditure serves us in many manual operations; for example, in graduating a blow, in throwing a missile to a mark, and in forming plastic substances to a certain consistency.

We have a consciousness of distinctness, remarkable in its kind, between exertions made by different muscles; for example, in the two hands. It is not the same to us that a pound weight is put into either hand; if it were so, we should be in the proverbial situation of not knowing the right hand from the left.

13. Secondly, a muscular exertion may vary in *continuance;* and this variation is felt by us as different from variation in the intensity of the effect.

A dead strain of unvarying amount being supposed, we are differently affected according to its duration. If we make a push lasting a quarter of a minute, and, after an interval, renew it for half a minute, there is a difference in the consciousness of the two efforts. The endurance implies an increased expenditure of power in a certain mode, and we are distinctly aware of such an increase. We know also that it is not the same as an increase in the intensity of the strain. The two modes of increase are not only discriminated as regards degree, they are also felt to be different modes. The one is our feeling and measure of Resistance or Force, the other stands for a measure of Time. All impressions made on the mind, whether those of muscular energy, or those of the ordinary senses, are felt differently according as they endure for a longer or a shorter time.

The estimate of continuance thus attaches to dead resistance, but not to that alone. When we put forth power to move, as in pulling an oar, or in lifting a weight, we are aware of different degrees of continuance of the movement. Moreover, we do not confound movement with dead strain; we are distinctively affected by the two modes of exercising force; supposing the total amount of power expended the same, the consciousness of each is characteristic.

Now Continuance of Movement expresses a different fact from continuance of dead strain. It is the sweep of the organ through space, and is, therefore, the measure of space or extension. It is the first step, the elementary sensibility, in our knowledge of space. Other experiences must be combined in this great fundamental notion, but here we have the primary ingredient.

The simplest form of muscular continuance is the sweep of a limb in one direction, nearly corresponding with linear extension (the spontaneous sweep of the arm is not a straight line). A greater complication of movement is involved in superficial extension; and a greater still, in cubical extension. But in the last resort, linear, superficial, and solid extension are to us nothing but the consciousness of continued and complicated movements, which we can associate in different groups, and remember among our intellectual acquisitions. A square foot of surface is embodied in one muscular grouping, a circle of three feet in diameter in another, a nine inch cube in a third; these muscular groupings may be tactual, visual, or locomotive, one or all, as will be afterwards seen.

14. Thirdly, as regards movements, the *speed* may vary; and we are characteristically conscious of the variation.

It is probable that the peculiar difference of character, above adverted to, between slow and quick movements, is an element in our discrimination of change of speed. When we increase the rate of movement of the arm, we are aware not merely that more virtue has gone out of us, but also that the mode is not the same as an increased strain or an increased continuance. This is a valuable addition to our means of muscular discrimination. It enables us, in the first place, to be directly cognizant of the important attribute of speed or velocity of movement, whether in ourselves or in bodies without us. It supplies, in the next place, a farther means of measuring extension, checking and supplementing that derived from the continuance of a uniform movement. A greater velocity, under one amount of continuance, is equivalent to a less velocity with a greater continuance.

CHAPTER II.

SENSATION.

1. A SENSATION is defined as the mental impression, feeling, or conscious state, resulting from the action of external things on some part of the body, called on that account sensitive.

Such are the feelings caused by tastes, smells, sounds, or sights. They are distinguished from the feelings of energy expended from within (the muscular), and from the emotions, as fear and anger, which do not arise immediately from the stimulus of a sensitive surface.

2. The Sensations are classified according to their bodily Organs; hence the division into Five Senses.

Distinctness of *organ* is accompanied with distinctness of *agent*, and of *feeling*, or consciousness. Light, as an agency, is distinct from sound, and the consciousness under each is characteristic; we should never confound a sight with a sound.

The common enumeration of the Five Senses is defective.

When the senses are regarded principally as sources of knowledge, or the basis of intellect, the five commonly given are tolerably comprehensive; but when we advert to sensation, in the aspect of pleasure and pain, there are serious omissions. Hunger, thirst, repletion, suffocation, warmth, and the variety of states designated by physical comfort and discomfort, are left out; yet these possess the characteristics of sensation as above defined, having a local organ or seat, a definite agency, and a characteristic mode of consciousness.

The omission is best supplied by constituting a group of Organic Sensations, or Sensations of Organic Life.

In the Senses as thus made up, it is useful to remark a division into two classes, according to their importance in the operations of the Intellect. If we examine the Sensations of Organic Life, Taste, and Smell, we shall find that as regards pleasure and pain, or in the point of view of Feeling, they are of great consequence, but that they contribute little of the permanent forms and imagery employed in our Intellectual processes. This last function is mainly served by Touch, Hearing, and Sight, which may therefore be called the Intellectual Senses by pre-eminence. They are not, however, thereby prevented from serving the other function also, or from entering into the pleasures and pains of our emotional life.

SENSATIONS OF ORGANIC LIFE.

Like the senses generally, these will be classified according to Locality or Seat.

Organic Muscular Feelings.

3. The passive feelings, or sensations proper, connected with Muscle, are chiefly the pains of injury, and the pains and pleasures of fatigue and repose.

When a muscle is cut, lacerated, or otherwise injured, or when seized with spasm, there is a feeling of acute pain. We shall describe this state in full, as typifying, once for all, the class of acute physical pains.

PHYSICAL SIDE.—The Bodily Origin is some destruction or injury of the muscular fibres, such as to irritate violently the imbedded nerves.

The Bodily Diffusion, or Expression, is various and interesting to study. The *features* are violently contorted, and assume certain characteristic appearances; the *voice* is excited to sharp utterances; the *whole body* is agitated. In short, movements are stimulated, intense according to the pain.

The accompaniment of sobbing shows that the involuntary muscles and the glands may also be affected; which is confirmed by closely observing the changes in the heart and the lungs, the effects on digestion, on the skin, &c.; all which changes are of the nature of depression and derangement.

MENTAL SIDE.—As *Feelings*, these states are indicated by the name. In Quality, they are painful; in Degree, acute or intense. As respects Specialities of character, we find a certain number of discriminative names; pains are racking, burning, shooting, pricking, smarting, aching, stunning; distinctions of importance in pathology.

Violent pains are apt to rouse certain of the special emotions, as grief, terror, rage; the selection depending less upon the nature of the pain than on the temper and circumstances of the individual.

The *Volitional* character of an acute pain would be, according to the law of the Will, to stimulate efforts for relief and avoidance. Such is the fact, but with an important qualification. The operation of the will demands a certain remaining vigour in the active organs; now, pain soon exhausts the strength; hence the will is paralyzed by long continuance of the irritation. A temporary smart quickens the energies, a continued agony crushes them.

Part of the expression of a sufferer is made up of postures and efforts of a voluntary kind, prompted with a view to relief; these vary with the locality and the nature of the attack.

The *Intellectual* quality of acute physical pains is complicated. Intensity of excitement is favourable to impressiveness; while in extreme degrees, the intellectual functions are paralyzed. These two considerations allowed for, the discrimination and the persistence of organic states are at the bottom of the scale of feelings. They are very inadequately remembered.

People differ greatly in their effective recollection of pains, no less than in the memory for language or for scenery; and the consequences are notable. First, the recollection of pain is the essential feature of preventive or precautionary volition, that is, Prudence. Secondly, it constitutes the basis of fellow-feeling, or sympathy. The Socratic doctrine that knowledge is virtue, might be transmuted into a profound and important truth, if knowledge were interpreted as the effective recollection of good and evil. Virtue has its sources in the retentive property of the Intellect; but the subject matter of the recollection is not knowledge, but feelings.

The special muscular pain of *cramp*, or spasm, may be separately noticed. Physically, it is the violent contraction of some portion of a muscle, through an irritation of the motor nerves. The best mode of relief is to give way to the contraction, by relaxing the muscle to the utmost. Mentally, this is the species of pain named racking; it arises from violent muscular distension. The pains of the uterus in childbirth are of this nature. Distressing spasms occur in the muscular fibres of the stomach and intestine.

The pains of excessive *fatigue* are among the acute pains of muscle. Like spasm, they have a peculiar character, connecting them with the muscle, and not with any other tissue.

The state of *muscular repose* after ordinary fatigue is one of our pleasurable feelings. There is a complication of physical circumstances attending it. The blood previously accumulated in the muscular tissue, is now returning to the other important organs, the brain, the stomach, &c.; while the muscles are remitted from further action. Both causes concur to yield pleasure, not acute, but massive. The other organic accompaniments cannot disguise the muscle's own sensibility to the condition of repose; the feeling is one that has a certain reflexion of energy :—

Even in our ashes glow their wonted fires.

There is, in rest after exercise, a close kinship to sleep; as if a part of the fact were already realized. These pleasures are the reward of bodily toil and hard exercise.

We may include under the present head what little is to be said on the Bones and Ligaments, whose sensibility is exclusively manifested in the shape of pain from injury or disease. The diseases and lacerations of the periosteum are intensely painful; a blow on the shin is acute and prostrating. The ligaments are painful when wrenched, although not when cut. The tendonous part of the muscles seems to share in the pain of over-fatigue. The joints are the seat of painful diseases, as gout, if not also rheumatism.

Organic Sensations of Nerve.

4. Besides being the medium of all sensibility, the nerves are the seat of a special class of feelings related to the Organic condition of the Nervous tissue. In this class, we may include acute affections of the nerves; the de-

pression arising from nervous fatigue and exhaustion; and the exhilaration of freshness and of stimulants.

(1) *Diseases* and *injuries* of the nerves are productive of intense suffering, as in tic-doleureux and the other neuralgic affections. It is enough to class these among acute pains. Their specific character, as feelings, is somewhat different from the acute pains of muscle, or of the other tissues, but language hardly suffices to mark the difference.

(2) *Nervous fatigue* or *exhaustion*, caused by over-exertion of mind, and even of body, by deficiency of rest or nutriment, and by intense or prolonged suffering, may induce neuralgic affections, but more commonly ends in general depression. This state is known to every one. Technically, we may designate it as pain, not acute, but massive; the amount is known by comparison, and by the pleasure swallowed up in neutralizing it. Weakness, ennui, heaviness, insupportable dullness, the sense as of an atmosphere of lead, the blackness of darkness,—are names for this general condition. An accumulation of pains and privations will produce the misery of depression, while the nerves are fresh and healthy, as in the punishment of the young offender; and, on the other hand, a morbid change in the nerve substance will cause the state in any one surrounded with delights, and shielded from hardship.

(3) It is implied in what is now said, that the *healthy condition of the nerves* is of itself a cause of exhilaration. This is the unspeakable blessing of perfect health, the result of a good constitution well preserved by the circumstances of a happy lot.

This mental condition is, for a short time, equalled, and even surpassed, by the perilous help of *stimulating drugs*, whose nature it is to operate directly on the substance of the nerves.

Organic Feelings of the Circulation and Nutrition.

5. Although it is difficult to isolate the separate organic influences, in their agency on the mind, we are entitled to presume that feelings of exhilaration and of depression are connected with the Circulation of the Blood and the Nourishment of the Tissues.

The formidable states, *thirst* and *inanition*, arise from deficiency in the blood in the first instance; but a derangement of the organs generally must be assumed to account f their virulence.

Thirst is not purely localized in the stomach; and Inanition is different from Hunger. Both conditions, mentally viewed, are modes of suffering, not so acute as acute pains proper, but yet much more so than mere dejection, and at the same time large in mass or volume. . There is present the depressing state of exhaustion, coupled with the acute irritation of deranged organs.

A feeling purely connected with the Circulation is what arises from long confinement to one posture, sitting or lying. The circulation in the skin being arrested, an uneasy feeling results, which prompts to changes of posture; it causes great discomfort to the bed-ridden patient, as well as being a source of new disease; an efficient remedy for both has been found in Dr. Arnott's water bed.

Part of the consciousness of good or ill health must depend on the contact of the blood with the nerve tissue; it being hardly possible to assign the proportions severally due to the nerve's own condition, and to that nutritive contact, although the facts have to be distinguished in the analysis of the mind. The sleek, fat, full-blooded temperament has its peculiar mental tone, attributable to the circulation and nutrition rather than to the quality of the nerves.

Feelings of Respiration.

6. The interchange of oxygen with carbonic acid takes place at the surface of the lungs, and any variation in the rate of this interchange is accompanied with sensibility. The extreme form of pain is Suffocation; the opposite state is a grateful Freshness or exhilaration.

Oxygen is our aerial food; our vital forces are measured by the amount of it consumed in oxidizing our food proper. The first requisite in the process is that the oxygen be abundantly inhaled by the lungs. The hindrance of the inhalation is painful, the furtherance pleasurable. A settled pace is neutral.

The characteristic sensibility of the lungs is manifested in *suffocation*. Its causes are the want of air, as from drowning, from certain irritating gases, such as chlorine or sulphurous acid, from asthma and other diseases. The insupportable sensation ensuing on want of breath hardly resembles any other

SENSATION OF PURE AIR. 33

feeling. It has a certain element of the racking pain, as of muscles drawn opposite ways; but it is something more than muscular, and must be set down at present as a unique result, of a unique process.

Short of suffocation, there may be a temporary lowering of the respiratory vigour, the effect of which is mere depression of tone, without characteristic accompaniment. On entering a crowded room, the depression is instantly felt; it may approach, or amount to, fainting.

The transition to a purer atmosphere gives the exhilaration, described as buoyancy and freshness; but we can scarcely determine how much of this is due to the better oxidation of the blood throughout the system, and how much to a stimulation of the surface of the lungs. The extreme case of suffocation must be held as proving a special lung-sensibility; whence we are to presume that part of the sensation of changes in the air is localized in the lungs.

Neither the continuation of the same state of the air, nor a very gradual change, is accompanied with sensation, a fact exemplifying the most universal condition of the production of consciousness, namely, change of impression from one state to another.

Feelings of Heat and Cold.

7. Changes of Temperature give rise to feeling, in all parts of the body, although the greatest sensitiveness is in the skin.

The operation of cold and heat is on the organic functions. The capillary circulation is first affected; the vessels being contracted by cold, and expanded by heat. The contraction of the vessels stops the supply of blood, and diminishes the nutrition of the parts, causing organic depression and discomfort. At the same time, however, a reflex stimulus to the lungs quickens the breathing action, and additional oxygen is taken in; so that, indirectly, the vital forces are increased, and the temporary and local depression may be more than atoned for. We may thus account for the bracing effects of cold applied within certain limits. Heat is in every respect the obverse.

The sensation of Cold is, as a rule, painful, and may be either acute or massive; nowhere is this distinction in the two modes of Degree so clearly marked. An *acute* cold acts like a cut or a bruise, and is sufficiently characterized among acute physical pains; the destruction of the tissue and the irritation of the nerve is the same as in a scald. The *massive* feeling of cold, expressed by chillness, may amount to extreme wretchedness.

The sensation of Warmth, on emerging from cold, is one of the greatest of physical enjoyments. It may be acute, as in drinking warm liquid, or massive, as in the bath, or other warm surrounding. Of passive physical pleasure, it is perhaps the typical form; the other modes may be, and constantly are, illustrated by comparison with it; as are also the genial passive emotions—love, beauty, &c.

The principle above alluded to,—namely, change of impression as a condition of consciousness, is also prominently exemplified in heat and cold; an even temperature gives no sensation.

Sensations of the Alimentary Canal.

8. These sensations, although closely allied to Taste, are not to be confounded with it.

The *objects* of the sense are the materials taken into the body as food and drink.

Food is variously classified. Water is the liquid basis, or vehicle. The solids are divided into Saccharine substances, including starch and sugar; Oily substances, as the various fats and oils, including alcohol; Albuminous substances (which contain nitrogen), as albumen, the fibre of meat, caseine (from cheese), gelatine, &c. These last are requisite in renewing the tissues, which nearly all contain nitrogen; while the others serve the more exclusive function of producing force, (as muscular power, nervous power, and animal heat,) by slow combustion or oxidation, which is also the destination of the largest part of the albuminous food.

9. Omitting the physiology of Digestion, we may enumerate, as follows, the chief feelings due to Alimentary states—Relish and Repletion, Hunger, Nausea, and the Pains of Deranged Digestion.

Relish and Repletion are the pleasurable states of eating. Varying with the digestive power of the system, and with the quality of the food, these feelings are, in ordinary circumstances, an important part of human pleasure. The first stage is represented by Relish, a pleasurable sensation, both acute and of considerable amount. The volitional energy inspired by it, in all animals, is the most remarkable testimony to its intensity as pleasure. The acute stage of relish is succeeded by the more voluminous pleasure of Repletion, whose seat is in the surface of the stomach, the part engaged in the digestion of the food; a massive exhilaration, closely allied to agreeable warmth, and to the elation of stimulants.

The physical concomitants of Hunger are a collapsed condition of the stomach, and a deficiency of nutritive material in the system. Of the feeling itself, the first stages are mere depression or uneasiness; next come on gnawing pains referred to the region of the stomach, and in part muscular; these are followed by sensations of a more massive character, derived from the system at large, and indicating the stage of inanition or starvation.

Nausea and Disgust express a mode of powerful feeling characteristic of digestion, as suffocation is of the lungs. The feeling is associated with the act of vomiting; the wretchedness of it in extreme cases, as sea-sickness, is insufferable. The sensation is unique. The healthy routine of comfortable digestion is exchanged for a depression great in mass, and aggravated by acute nervous suffering. The memory of this state is an active recoil from whatever causes it; hence disgust is a term for the most intense repugnance and loathing.

The pains of Deranged Digestion are numerous. Some are extremely acute, as spasm in any part of the intestine. Many forms of indigestion are known simply as inducing a depressed tone, or interfering with the exhilaration of healthy meals. Sluggishness of the bowels is attended with massive depression; the re-action brings a corresponding buoyancy.

Under the present head may be classed the feelings connected with the sexual organs, the mammary glands in woman, and the lachrymal gland and sac. These are the result of organic processes in the first instance; but they enter into complicated alliances, to be afterwards noticed, with our special emotions.

There still remain the important organic functions of the Skin, which are attended with pleasurable and painful sensibilities. They will be noticed under the sense of Touch.

In the Muscular Feelings, together with the Organic Sensations now enumerated, arises that large body of our sensibility denominated physical Comfort and Discomfort.

SENSE OF TASTE.

1. The sense of Taste, attached to the entrance of the alimentary canal, is a source of pleasure and pain, and a means of discrimination, in taking food.

The *Objects* of Taste are chiefly the materials of food.

Of mineral bodies, water is without taste. But most liquid substances, and most solids that can be liquified or dissolved, have taste; vinegar, common salt, alum, are familiar instances.

Nearly all vegetable and animal products, in like manner, are characterized by taste. A few substances are insipid, as white of egg, starch, gum; but the greater part exhibit well marked tastes; sweet, as sugar; bitter, as quinine, morphine, strychnine, gentian, quassia, soot, &c.; sour, as acids generally; pungent, as mustard, pepper, peppermint; fiery, as alcohol.

2. The *Organ* of Taste is the tongue, and the seat of sensibility is its upper surface.

The upper surface of the tongue is seen to be covered with little projections called papillæ. They are of three kinds, distinguished by size and form. The smallest and most numerous are conical or tapering, and cover the greatest part of the tongue, disappearing towards the base. The middle-sized are little rounded eminences scattered over the middle and fore part of the tongue, being most numerous towards the point. The large-sized are eight to fifteen in number, situated on the back of the tongue, and arranged in two rows at an angle like the letter V. The papillæ contain capillary blood vessels and filaments of nerve, and are the seat of the sensibility of the tongue.

Two different nerves supply the tongue; branches of the nerve called *glosso-pharyngeal* (tongue and throat nerve) are distributed to the back part; twigs of the *fifth pair* (nerve of touch of the face) go to the fore-part. The effect, as will be seen, is a two-fold sensibility; taste proper attaches to the first named nerve, the glosso-pharyngeal; bitter is tasted chiefly at the back of the tongue. Taken as a whole, the sensibility of the tongue is distributed over the whole upper side, but less in the middle part and most in the base, sides, and tip. The relish of food increases from the tip to the back, which is an inducement to keep the morsel moving backwards till it is finally swallowed.

The indispensable condition of taste is solubility. Also the tongue must not be in a dry or parched condition. The sensibility is increased by a moderate pressure; and is deadened by cold.

No explanation has yet been given of the mode of action on the nerves during taste. It is probably of a chemical nature, resulting from the combination of the dissolved food with a secretion from the blood-vessels of the papillæ.

3. The *Sensations* of Taste fall under a three-fold division: (1) those in direct sympathy with the Stomach, as Relish; (2) Taste proper, and (3) Touch.

As to the first, there is an obvious continuity of structure in the Tongue and Alimentary canal, a common character of surface as regards mucous membrane, glands, and papillæ. Moreover, apart from taste proper, the feeling in the tongue indicates at once whether a substance will agree or disagree with the stomach; the tongue is in fact the stomach begun. And farther, what we call relish is distinct from taste; butter and cooked flesh are relishes; salt and quinine are tastes; the one varies with the condition of the stomach, being in some states converted into nausea, as in sea-sickness; the other remains under all variations of the digestive power.

4. The Tastes in sympathy with the Stomach are *Relishes* and *Disgusts.*

Relishes, as already explained, are the agreeable feelings arising from the kinds of food called savoury, as animal food, and the richer kinds of vegetables. Sugar is both a relish and a taste. As a feeling of pleasure, a relish is more acute and less massive than the digestive sensations, but less acute and more massive than mere sweetness of taste. The speciality of the feeling is the alliance with digestion. What possesses relish may be hard to digest, but will not be nauseous in the stomach. The strength of this feeling is farther measured by its volitional urgency, or spur to the act of eating. The intellectual persistence is not high.

Relishes imply their opposite, *disgusts*, in which the stomachic sympathy is equally apparent, and which may be similarly characterized with reference to the corresponding digestive sensation.

5. Taste proper comprehends *Sweet* and *Bitter* tastes.

Sweetness is typified in the taste of sugar, to whose presence is owing the sweetness of fruits and articles of food generally. This sensation may be called the proper pleasure of taste, or the enjoyment derivable through a favourable stimulus of the gustatory nerves. In Degree it is acute; in Speciality we recognize it as possessing a character, indescribable in language, but not confounded with the pleasure of any other sense. Its volitional character accords with its nature as pleasure. It is more intellectual than Organic sensations generally, or than Relish; we can discriminate its degrees better, and remember it better. Taste may be the lowest of the five senses, as regards intellectual properties, but it is above the highest of the organic group.

Bitter tastes are exemplified in quinine, gentian, bitter aloes, and soot. This, and not sourness, is the opposite of sweet; it is the proper pain of taste, the state arising by irritating, or unfavourably stimulating, the gustatory nerve. The characteristics are the same, with obverse allowance, as for sweetness.

6. In the third class of tastes, there is present an element arising through the nerves of Touch. Pungency is their prevailing character. They include the *saline, alkaline, sour* or *acid, astringent, fiery, acrid.*

The *saline* taste is typified in common salt. It is neither sweet nor bitter, but simply pungent or biting; and, in all probability, the sensation is felt through the nerves of the fifth pair. In some salts, the pungency is combined with taste proper; Epsom salts would be termed partly saline, and still more decidedly bitter.

The *alkaline* taste, as in soda, potash, or ammonia, is a more energetic pungency, or more violent irritation of the nerves; the pungency amounting to acute pain, as the action becomes destructive of the tissue.

The *sour* or *acid* taste is the most familiar form of pungency, as in vinegar. The pain of an acid resembles a scald rather than a bitter taste. The pleasure derivable from it is such as belongs to pungency, and must observe the same limits.

The *astringent* is a mild form of pungency; it is exemplified by alum. The action in this case has manifestly departed from pure taste, and become a mere mechanical irritation of the nerves of touch. Astringent substances cause a kind of shrinking or contraction of the surface; an effect imitated by the drying up of a solution of salt on the skin. What is called a 'rough' taste, as tannin, is a form of astringency.

The *fiery* taste of mustard, alcohol, camphor, and volatile oils, is of the same generic character, although more or less mixed with taste proper. The *acrid* combines the fiery with the bitter.

SENSE OF SMELL.

1. The Sense of Smell, placed at the entrance of the lungs, is a source of pleasure and pain, and a means of discrimination as regards the air taken into the lungs.

This sense is also in close proximity to the organ of Taste, with which smell frequently co-operates.

2. The *Objects* of smell are gaseous or volatile bodies, the greater number of such being odorous.

The chief inodorous gases are the elements of the atmosphere, that is, nitrogen, oxygen, vapour of water, and carbonic acid (in the small amount contained in the air). Carbonic oxide, sulphurous acid, chlorine, iodine, the nitrous gases, ammonia, sulphuretted and phosphuretted hydrogen, and the vapour of acids generally, are odorous. The newly discovered *ozone*, is named from the odour it gives. Some minerals give forth odorous effluvia, as the garlic odour of arsenic, and the odour of a piece of quartz when broken. The vegetable kingdom is rich in odours; many plants are distinguished by this single property. Animal odours are also numerous.

The pleasant odours, chemically considered, are hydrocarbons; they are composed chiefly of hydrogen and carbon. Such are alcohol and the ethers, eau de Cologne, attar of roses, and the perfumes generally. Of the repulsive and disagreeable odours, one class contain sulphur, as sulphuretted hydrogen. The worst-smelling substances yet discovered have arsenic for their base. Such are the *kakodyle* series of compounds discovered by Bunsen, from the study of a substance long known as 'liquor of Cadet.' The pungent odours are typified by ammonia; nicotine, the element of the snuffs, is an analogous compound.

3. The *development* of odours is favoured by Heat, and by Light. The action of Moisture is not uniform.

Heat operates by its volatilizing power, and by promoting decomposition. Light is a chemical influence. Moisture may dissolve solid matters and prepare the way for their being volatilized.

4. The gaseous property, called *diffusion,* determines peculiar manifestations in odours.

Some odours are light, and therefore diffuse rapidly, and rise high; as sulphuretted hydrogen. The aromatic and spice odours, by their intensity and diffusibility combined, are smelt at great distances; the Spice Islands of the Indian Archipelago are recognized far out at sea. The animal effluvia are mostly dense gases; they are slowly diffused and do not rise high in the air. In scenting, a pointer dog keeps his nose close to the ground. Unwholesome effluvia, very strong on the ground, are unperceived at the height of a few feet. In tropical swamps, safety is obtained by sleeping at a height above the ground.

5. The *Organ* of Smell is the nose, and the place of sensibility is the membrane that lines the interior and the complicated cavities branching out from it.

The nose is lined throughout with a mucous membrane; and the complicated bones adjoining it, give extension of surface to that membrane, whereby the sensibility is magnified. It is also an important fact, in the Anatomy of the organ, that the proper nerve of smell, called olfactory, is most copiously distributed in the interior recesses, and not at all near the entrance of the nostrils; to which part, twigs of the fifth pair are distributed, conferring upon it a tactile sensibility.

6. The *mode of action* of odours appears to be a process of oxidation.

The facts in favour of that view were pointed out by Graham. Odorous substances in general are such as oxygen can readily act upon; for example, sulphurous hydrogen, and the perfumes. Again, gases that have no smell are not acted on by oxygen at common temperatures; the pure marsh gas, carburetted hydrogen, which has no smell, has been obtained from deep mines, where it has been in contact with oxygen for geological ages. It is farther determined that unless a stream of oxygen passes through the nose, there is no smell.

7. The *Sensations* of Smell are, first, those in sympathy with the Lungs; secondly, those of Smell proper; thirdly, those involving excitation of nerves of Touch.

Those in sympathy with the Lungs may be described by the contrasting terms—*fresh* and *close* odours.

Fresh odours are the feelings of exhilaration from the quickened action of the lungs. Certain odorous substances have that quickening efficacy, as eau de Cologne, lavender, peppermint, and many, but not all, perfumes; the spirit used in dissolving the essences being not unfrequently the source of the stimulus. These are the substances used for reviving the system depressed by the atmosphere of a crowd. Freshness may, or may not, be joined with fragrance; the odour of a tanyard is stimulating to the lungs; the smell of a cow is fresh and sweet. Musk is probably stimulating.

Close or suffocating odours arise from a depressed action of the lungs. The effluvia of crowds, and of vegetable and animal decay, the deficiency of oxygen, and the accumulation of carbonic acid, however caused, lower the powers of life, and are accompanied with a depressing sensation, which should properly be called a sensation of the lungs, but which we connect also with smell. The smell of a pastry-cook's kitchen is close and yet sweet.

Certain odours, as sulphuretted hydrogen, are *nauseous* or disgusting, which implies a sympathy with the stomach, although in what mode, or through what nerves, is not clear.

8. Connected with proper olfactory sensibility are *fragrant* odours and their opposites.

For *sweet* or *fragrant* odours we refer to the rose, the violet, the orange, the jasmine, &c. In them we have the proper pleasure of the organ of smell; the enjoyment derivable through the olfactory nerves. It is acute or massive, according to the concentration or diffusion of the material; compare an essence, as lavender, or rosemary, with a bed of mignonette or a field of clover. A certain degree of what is termed refinement attaches to the pleasures of pure smell; the stimulus is so gentle that it can be endured for a length of time without palling.

The opposite of sweetness is given in the expressive name *stink*; a milder substitute is *malodour*. The smell of assafœtida is an example; some of our repulsive odours are in part disgusting, and do not represent pure olfactory pain. Valerian, rag-wort, and the scum of stagnant marsh (squeezed in the fingers) give forth malodours. Whenever the olfactory nerves are painfully irritated, this is the character of the pain. Amid many distinguishable varieties of bad smell, there is a common type of sensation.

9. Through excitation of the nerves of touch we derive the *pungent* odours.

Ammonia (as in smelling salts), nicotine, mustard, acetic acid, give rise to a sharp stinging sensation, for which the best name is *pungency*. It is most probably a mechanical irritation of the nerves of the fifth pair; habitual snuff-takers lose the pure olfactory sensibility. The general effect, named pungency, is a mode of nervous and mental excitement; within limits, it gives pleasure. A loud sound, a flash of light, a hurried pace, have a rousing effect, pleasurable, if the nerves are fresh and unoccupied, painful otherwise.

The *ethereal* odours, as alcohol and the aroma of wines, are partly fresh and sweet, and partly pungent.

There are odours that we may call *acrid*, combining pungency with ill smell, as the odour of coal-gas works.

The sensual appetites are, in many cases, fired by odours. The smell of flesh excites the carnivorous appetite; which may be due partly to association, and partly to that sympathy of smell with digestion, shown in the nauseous odours. Sexual excitement, in some animals, is induced by smell, as by many other sensations. There is here a general law, that one great pleasure fires the other pleasurable sensibilities. (See TENDER EMOTION.)

Some sapid bodies are also odorous. In the act of expiration accompanying mastication, especially the instant after swallowing, the odorous particles are carried into the cavities of the nose, and affect the sense of smell. This is *flavour*. Cinnamon has no taste, but only a flavour; that is, an odour brought out during mastication.

Viewing Smell in the Intellectual point of view, once for all, we find it considerably in advance of Organic Sensibility, if not of Taste also. The power of discrimination exercised by smell is very great; we derive much instruction and guidance by means of it. Yet higher in this respect is its development in many animals, as the ruminants, certain of the pachydermatous animals, and, above all, the carnivorous quadrupeds. The scent of the dog seems miraculous.

The power of recollection is usually in proportion to the

THE SKIN. 43

aptitude for discrimination; and in regard to smells, the power of recollecting is considerable. We can, by an effort, restore to mind the sweetness of a rose, the pungency of smelling salts, or the bouquet of an essence.

SENSE OF TOUCH.

1. As an intellectual, or knowledge-giving sense, Touch ranks decidedly above Taste and Smell.

The *Objects* of Touch are principally solid substances.

Gases do not affect the touch, unless blown with great violence. Liquids give little or no feeling, except heat or cold. A certain firmness of surface is necessary, such as constitutes solidity.

2. The sensitive *Organ* is the skin, or common integument of the body, together with the interior of the mouth, the tongue, and the nostrils.

The parts of the skin are its two layers—cuticle and true skin; the papillæ; the hairs and the nails; the two species of glands—the one yielding sweat, the other an oily secretion; with blood vessels and nerves.

The *cuticle* is the protective covering of the skin, being itself insensible; it varies in thickness from the $\frac{1}{240}$ to the $\frac{1}{12}$ of an inch; being thickest on the soles of the feet, and on the palms of the hands. The *true skin* lying underneath, and containing the papillæ, nerves, and blood-vessels, is the sentient structure. It is marked in various places by furrows, also affecting the cuticle, as may be seen in the skin of the hand. The *papillæ* are small conical projections, besetting the whole surface of the skin, but largest and closest on the palm of the hand and fingers, and on the sole of the foot. Their height on the hand is from $\frac{1}{200}$ to $\frac{1}{100}$ of an inch. Into them blood-vessels enter, and also nerves; and they are the medium of the tactile sensibility of the skin. The two sets of *glands* concern the skin as a great purifying organ. Very small *muscular fibres* have been discovered in the skin; they are easily affected by cold, and their contraction makes the shivering of the skin.

3. The *action* in Touch is simple pressure.

The contact of a firm body compresses the skin, and, through it, the nerve filaments embedded in the papillæ.

4. The *Sensations* of Touch may be arranged under the following heads :—the Emotional, and the Intellectual sensations of Touch proper ; and the sensations combining Touch and Muscularity.

The first class includes *soft Touches, pungent smarts, temperature,* and some others.

Soft Touches. In these we suppose the gentle contact of some extended surface with the skin, as the under clothing, or the bed clothes. From such contact, results a pleasurable sensation, of little acuteness, but of considerable mass, when a large surface is affected. In most instances of pleasurable contact, there is warmth combined with touch, as in the embrace of two creatures of the warm blooded species, or in the contact of one part of the body with another. We become insensible to the habitual contact of our clothing, on the general principle of Relativity ; but the transition to, or from, the naked state makes us aware of our sensibility to touch.

The mixed sensation of contact and warmth is strongly manifested in the clinging of the young to the mother, both in the human species and in the inferior tribes. The warm contact is maintained with great energy of will. It also determines many of the peculiar modes of expression in human beings ; as the putting of the finger or the hand to the mouth and face, either as mere sensuous luxury, or as a solace in pain. In luxurious repose, a soft warm contact is desiderated for the hands.

Pungent and painful sensations of Touch. A sharp, intense, smarting contact with the skin, produces, up to a certain point, an agreeable pungency or excitement ; beyond that, an acute pain of the physical class. This is precisely analogous to the effects of pungency spoken of under the foregoing Senses. Mere sensation, as such, is pleasurable within limits, when the nerves are fresh. Excitement is joyful to the unexpended nervous vigour ; and this is gained by pungency.

The acute pains of the skin are illustrated in the discipline of the whip ; a form of pain supposed to have both volitional efficiency at the moment, and intellectual persistency for the future.

Sensations of Temperature. We included the feelings of heat and cold among organic sensations. They are, in the vast majority of instances, connected with the skin, of whose sensibility they are a large and important item. The effect of changes of temperature on the nerves may still be mechanical, seeing that the direct influence of such changes is to expand or contract the tissue. Some have supposed special nerves of heat and cold, but without good evidence. The pleasures and pains from this source have been sufficiently characterized.

The intellectual aspect of the sense of Temperature deserves mention. The power of discrimination has been estimated by Weber, and is found the same at high and at low temperatures; we can distinguish 14° from 14°.4 Reaumur, as well as 30° from 30°.4; this amounts to discerning a difference of about 1° Fahrenheit. The order of sensitiveness of the parts is as follows;—tip of the tongue, eyelids, lips, neck, trunk: this is nearly, but not exactly, the order of sensitiveness to tactile sensation.

Other painful sensations of the skin. The organic sensibility of the skin gives rise to a variation of sensations; its healthy condition is an element in our physical comfort, and obversely. Long compression of the same part, by checking the circulation and affecting the nerves, occasions a massive uneasiness. Fretting, chafing, pulling the hairs, tearing open the nails, bring on acute pains.

Another peculiar sensation of the skin is Tickling. On this, Weber remarks, that the lips, the walls of the nasal openings, and the face generally, when touched with a feather, give the peculiar sensation of tickling, which continues till the part is rubbed by the hand. In the nose, the irritation leads at last to sneezing. The excitation extends to the ducts of the glands, which pour out their contents, and increase the irritation. The violent sensation produced by bodies in contact with the eye, is of the nature of tickling accompanied by flow from the glands, and readily passing into pain. Why some places are liable to this sensation and others not, it is difficult to explain. The possession of delicate tactual discrimination is not necessary to the effect.

5. The Intellectual sensations of Touch proper are *Plurality of points* and *Pressure*.

Plurality of points. One great feature in the intellectual superiority of Touch, is the separateness of the sensations on different parts of the skin. The points of a two-pronged fork resting on the hand are noted as giving a double sensation; whereas in smell, there is no sense of plurality; there may be a sense of increase or diminution of degrees, but the whole effect is one and continuous.

Very remarkable inequalities in the degree of this discrimination are observable on comparing different parts of the body. The experiments for determining these (first instituted by Weber) consists in placing the two points of a pair of compasses, blunted with sealing wax, at different distances asunder, and in various directions, upon different parts of the body. It is then found that the smallest distance, for giving the sense of double contact, varies from the thirty-sixth of an inch to three inches. In Weber's observations the range was the twenty-fourth of an inch to two and a half inches. The part most sensitive is the tip of the tongue; according to Weber, the smallest interval of doubleness is $\frac{1}{24}$ of an inch.

The interval of plurality varies according to the following circumstances. (1) It is greater across than along any of the limbs; across the middle of the arm or fore-arm it is two inches, along the arm, three. (2) It is greater when the surfaces vary in structure, as the inner and outer surface of the lips. (3) If one of the points is pressed forcibly, the other ceases to be distinguished. (4) Two points, at a great distance apart, on a surface of greater sensibility, are judged to be more widely apart. This will be shown by drawing compasses over the different parts; they will seem to widen in the most sensitive organs. The tongue exaggerates holes in the teeth. (5) By moving the points, instead of keeping them still, the sensitiveness is greater; an interval felt single at rest, may feel double under motion. In the tactile discrimination of a surface, we usually move the hand.

Whenever two points produce a double sensation, we may imagine that one point lies on the area supplied by one distinct nerve, while the other point lies on the area of a second nerve. There is a certain stage of subdivision or branching of the nerves of touch, beyond which the impressions are fused into one on reaching the cerebrum. How many ultimate nerve fibres are contained in each unit nerve, we cannot pretend to guess; but on the skin of the back, the middle of the thigh, and the middle of the fore-arm, an area of three inches diameter, or between six and seven square inches, is supplied by the filaments of a single unit. On the point of the finger, the units are so multiplied, that each supplies no more than a space whose diameter is the tenth of an inch. Such units correspond to the entire body of the olfactory or gustatory nerve; for these nerves give but one undivided impression for the whole affected. If we had two different organs of smell, and two distinct olfactory nerves, we should then probably have a feeling of doubleness or repetition of smells, like the sense of two points on the skin.

Sensation of Pressure. When a contact amounts to a certain energy of compression, we have a sensation passing beyond mere touch. Muscular resistance apart, there is a feeling induced by the compression of the deep-seated parts together with the skin. It is a neutral feeling, unless carried to the pitch of acute pain; but as we are intellectually conscious of its various degrees, it is a help to our perception of mechanical forces.

The discrimination of pressure is obtained free from the muscular discrimination, by supporting the hand on a table, and putting weights upon it. In this way, Weber found that the tips of the fingers could discriminate between 20 oz. and 19·2 oz.; and the forearm 20 oz. from 18·7 oz. This discrimination does not increase in proportion to the abundance of the nervous filaments supplied to the part.

6. The third class of Sensations of Touch are those combining touch with muscular feeling. They include *resistance, weight,* and *pressure; hardness* and *softness; roughness* and *smoothness;* and the various modes of *Extension.*

Resistance, Weight, and Pressure. These, as already shown, are primarily connected with muscular energy; a greater weight induces a greater muscular expenditure. We have just seen, however, that the compression of the skin and subjacent parts is also a clue to the same property. But the muscular discrimination surpasses the tactile at least in a threefold degree : and what is of more consequence, the muscular or active consciousness is what constitutes to us the property of weight, pressure, or force. The feeling of compression of the hand or limb is of itself a subjective sensation, and might be confounded with mere subjective pains, as in hurts. The feeling of expended energy is unambiguous and decisive ; it means to us the objective fact of mechanical force, the fundamental consciousness that we call matter.

Hardness and Softness. We appreciate these qualities also by the combined sensibility to pressure. The degree of resistance to change of form is the degree of hardness. The nice discrimination of this property enters into various manual processes, as the art of the pastry-cook, the builder, the sculptor, &c. We must still consider it as mainly residing in the muscular tissue, which, according to its nervous endowments, may be unequally developed among individuals, in respect of discrimination. *Elasticity* is a mere variety of hardness and softness ; it means the varying resistance, together with the rebound of the body compressed.

Roughness and Smoothness are referable, in the first instance, to the sense of plurality of points. The finger resting on the face of a brush gives the feeling of a plurality of pricks, and we can judge whether these are few and scattered, or whether they are numerous and close, up to the point where they become too close for the sensibility of the part. We can thus discriminate between a coarse pile and finer one. But by moving the finger, according to a principle already laid down, we increase the power of discrimination. A third means is the organic sensibility to chafing, which is greater as a surface is rougher; this brings in the peculiarity of sharpness or bluntness of the asperities; it applies accurately to the operation of polishing, where the purpose is to do away with all asperities. In discerning the qualities of woven textures, softness and smoothness are taken together; and there are great individual differences of tactual delicacy, natural or acquired, in that discernment. The fineness of a powder, and the beat of a pulse, are judged of almost exclusively by skin sensibility.

These tactile sensations, whose importance consists in the intellectual property of discrimination, have also a corresponding retentiveness. We can recall and compare ideas of touch, we can imagine or construct new ones, although with less facility and vividness than in the case of sights. With the blind, whose external world is a world of touch, this memory attains a much higher compass.

Extension, Form, &c.—It has been already laid down that Extension, the most general property of the object world, is based on our consciousness of muscular energy, and not on any mode of passive sensation. Still, our two senses—Touch and sight, play an important part in the development of the notion, which is highly complex, and not a simple or elementary feeling, like mere resistance.

The purely muscular part of the feeling or idea of Extension is unresisted movement, as in the sweep of the arm, or the forward movement of the body, in free space. It has been seen that we have a discrimination of the duration and the pace of these unobstructed movements. But the power of measuring degrees and of making comparisons is aided by touch (and by sight), and that in various ways. (1) In the first place, Touch (or the mixed sensation of touch and resistance) supplies definite marks to indicate the beginning and the end of the sweep, as in estimating the width of a doorway by the hand, or the dimensions of a room by walking across it. Extension is the antithesis of resistance or obstructed movement, and is felt by the presence of its contrast, and this involves contact or touch. The only real notion that we can ever form of extension, as empty space, is a sweep between two resistances; infinite space, where the points, or termini, of resistance are done away with, is therefore an incompetent, irrelevant, impossible conception; it does not comply with the conditions indispensable to the notion. (2) In the second place, when the hand is moved over a surface, the feeling of continuance of movement is accompanied with a continuance of tactile sensation, and the estimate of the two jointly is more exact than of one singly. A feeling of the subject (touch proper) is superadded to a feeling of the object (expended energy, as movement) and deepens the impress of that sensibility without constituting itself the objective basis. (3) In the third place, movement in vacuo is unable to indicate the vital difference between succession and co-existence—time and space. Now, co-existence in space is implied in our matured*idea of extension. But this co-existence is the result of a peculiar experience, and to that experience the senses must contribute. When we move the hand over a fixed surface, we have, together with feelings of movement, a *succession* of feelings of touch; if the surface is a variable one, as when a blind man reads with the hand, the sensations are constantly changing, and are recognized as a definite series. Repeat the movement, and the series is repeated; invert the movement, and the series appears in an inverted order. Now this continuance of a fixed serial order marks something different from mere continuing movement by itself, which gives no element of fixity or persistence. A person looking on while a procession passes by, is differently affected from another person walking up and down by the side of the same body standing still. Such is the difference between time and space, as appreciated by combined movement and sensation. Time or succession is the simpler fact; co-existence, or extension in space, is a complex fact; and the serial fixedness of sensations is one element of the complication.

Extension is recognized by us as linear, superficial, or solid; the difference being one of complexity. Linear extension nearly corresponds to a simple sweep of the arm; the straight direction, however, demands a muscular adjustment. Superficial extension, as in a pane of glass, involves cross movements in addition. Cubical extension is merely a higher stage of complication. We are capable not only of the muscular groupings requisite for these three grades of extension, but of discriminating one grouping from another; a short line from a longer, an oblong from a square, and so on; and we are farther capable of retaining or laying up abiding impressions corresponding to each. We can retain, and recall, the muscular movements, groupings, and adjustments, determined in our tactual examination of a one foot cube; such a cube means to us (sight apart) a series of touches imbedded in a series of muscular feelings.

Our having two hands, and five fingers in each, gives us another, and shorter, clue to surface and solidity. The outspread hand with its plurality of touches is a means of distinguishing surface, enhanced by the use of both hands. In like manner, solidity can be perceived by the clench of one hand on two surfaces, or still better, by combining both hands. The sense of solidity gained by combining the hands is parallel to the solid effect in vision from the two eyes.

Size, Distance, Direction, Situation, and Form, are merely modes of Extension; they are all muscular experiences aided by sense. Size or magnitude is merely another name for extension. Distance is extension between two points. Direction, mathematically taken, is measurement of distance from some standard of reference. The primitive reference is to our own body; and direction consists in the specific movements of the different members—the putting forth of the right arm or the left, the throwing the hand or body forwards or backwards, up or down. Situation is distance and direction combined. Form is the successive positions of the outline; we acquire definite movements corresponding to the different forms—a straight line, a circle, an oval, a sphere, a cube, and embody our recollection of these in ideal movements or muscular feelings, with tactile accompaniments.

Thus, in the knowledge of Extension, and its modes, through touch and locomotion, there is already a vast and complicated mass of acquirements, involving a large number of muscles and an immense apparatus of connecting nerves.

The observations made on persons born blind have furnished a means of judging how far touch can substitute sight, both in mechanical and in intellectual operations. These observations have shown, that there is nothing essential to the highest intellectual processes of science and thought, that may not be attained in the absence of sight. The integrity of the moving apparatus of the frame renders it possible to acquire the fundamental notions of space, magnitude, figure, force, and movement, and through these to comprehend the great leading facts of creation, as taught in mathematical, mechanical, or physical science.

SENSE OF HEARING.

1. The *Objects* of hearing are material bodies in a state of tremour or vibration, from being struck; which tremour affects the air, and thence the ear.

Hard and elastic textures are the most sonorous. The metals rank first; next, are woods, stones, and earthy bodies. Liquids and gases sound feebly, unless impinged by solids. The howling and the rustling of the wind are its play upon the earth's surface, like the Æolian harp. In the cataract, water impinges water; and, in the thunder, air is struck by air.

2. The Ear, the *Organ* of hearing, is divisible into (1) the External ear, (2) the Tympanum or Middle ear, and (3) the Labyrinth, or Internal ear.

The two first divisions are appendages or accessories of the third, which contains the sentient surface.

The Outer ear includes the wing of the ear—augmenting the sound by reflexion, and the passage of the ear, which is closed at the inner end by the membrane of the tympanum.

The Middle ear, or Tympanum, is a narrow irregular cavity, extending to the labyrinth, and communicating with the throat, through the Eustachian tube. It contains a chain of small bones, stretching from the inner side of the membrane of the tympanum to an opening in the labyrinth; there are also certain very minute muscles attached to these bones. The inner wall of the tympanum, which is the outer wall of the labyrinth, is an even surface of bone, but chiefly noted for two openings—the oval and the round—both closed with membrane. It is to the oval opening that the inner end of the chain of bones, the stirrup bone, is applied. Of the muscles, the largest is attached to the outer bone of the chain (the malleus), and is called *tensor tympani*, because its action is to draw inwards, and tighten, the tympanum. Two or three other muscles are named, but their action is doubtful.

The Internal ear, or Labyrinth, contained in the petrous or hard portion of the temporal bone, is made up of two structures, the bony and the membranous labyrinth. The bony labyrinth presents externally a spiral shell called the cochlea, and three projecting rings called the semicircular canals. The interior is hollow, and filled with a clear liquid secreted from a thin lining membrane. It contains a membranous structure, corresponding in shape to the tortuosities of the bony labyrinth, hence called the membranous labyrinth; this structure encloses a liquid secretion, and supports the ramifications of the auditory nerve.

3. The *mode of action,* in hearing, is the ultimate compression of the filaments of the nerve of hearing, by the compression of the liquid contents of the labyrinth. The ear is thus a very delicate organ of touch.

The waves of sound, entering the outer ear, strike the membrane of the tympanum, and make it vibrate. These vibrations are communicated to the chain of bones; and the last of the chain—the stirrup bone, gives a corresponding series of beats to the tight membrane of the oval opening, the result of which is a series of condensations of the liquid contents, and compressions of the auditory nerve; these compressions propagated to the brain are connected with the sensation of sound. An experimental imitation of the mechanism has shown that the arrangement answers well for delicate hearing; the surface best adapted for receiving aerial beats is a stretched membrane; which membrane imparts these most advantageously to a solid rod; and between a solid rod and the auditory nerve the most suitable medium is a liquid. The intensity and the rapidity of the nerve compressions are exactly in accordance with the aerial waves. Our greatest difficulty is to understand how a single rod can be the medium of a large volume or plurality of sounds; we must suppose them taken in succession by an extraordinary rapidity of the vibrating action. Attempts have been made to allocate the different degrees of pitch to different parts of the labyrinth, and thence to distinct nervous filaments.

It has not been completely ascertained on what occasions, and with what effect, the tensor tympani muscle is brought into play. It was observed by Wollaston, that when the membrane is stretched the ear is less affected by *grave* sounds, as thunder or cannon, and more sensitive to shrill sounds, as the rattling of carriages or the creaking of paper. Hence the action of the tensor tympani muscle would be protective against painfully grave sounds, and obversely.

4. The *Sensations* of Sound may be divided into three heads:—(1) The General Emotional effects of sound; (2) Musical sounds; and (3) the Intellectual sensations.

The General effects of sound may be considered under

EMOTIONAL SENSATIONS OF SOUND.

Quality (pleasant and painful), *Intensity*, and *Volume* or *Quantity*.

Sweetness. The terms sweet, rich, mellow, silvery, are applied to the pleasing sensations of sound, pure and simple. Certain materials, instruments, and voices, by their mere tone, please and charm the ear; while some are indifferent, and others have a grating, harsh effect. The structural peculiarities connected with these differences are still a matter of conjecture. From the analogy of touch, we may suppose that a gentle stimulation of the nerves of hearing is pleasurable, and the admixture of violent impulses painful. Another circumstance is assigned by Helmholtz—namely, purity or singleness of tone, instead of discordant variety.

The character of sweet sounds generally is acute pleasure, as we might expect from an organ small and sensitive. While the emotional and volitional peculiarities are sufficiently implied in this designation, a remark must be made on the intellectual property of the pleasures of sound. We are now approaching, if we have not reached, the top of the scale in this respect; the pleasures of hearing, taken as a whole, are more endurable, more persistent, and more easily revived in idea, than any other sensible pleasures, except sights.

Intensity, Loudness. Any sound, not too loud, may be agreeable solely as stimulus, without giving the acute pleasure above described. A certain pitch of loudness amounts to pungency of sensation, mere excitement, which is grateful under the circumstances already noticed, namely, unexhausted nervous irritability. A certain coarse pleasure is given to robust natures and to children by loud noise, as by any other kind of exciting stimulus. Beyond these limits, loudness of sound passes into acute pain, and is a cause of nervous exhaustion ; as in the screeching of a parrot-menagerie, the shrill barking of dogs, the screaming of infants, the railway whistle. The mental discomposure is greater when they are *sudden* and unexpected.

Volume or *Quantity*. Acute as is the general character of hearing as a sense, we may have effects that are by comparison voluminous. This happens when the sound comes from a sounding mass of large surface or extent ; for example, the shout of a great multitude, the waves of the many-sounding sea, the thunder, or the wind. The multiplication of sound is more agreeable than the augmented intensity ; the stimulus is increased without adding to the nervous fatigue. Apart from intrinsic sweetness and music, the greatest pleasures of sound are derived from voluminous effects.

5. Musical Sounds involve the properties of *Pitch, Waxing* and *Waning, Harmony* and *Discord.*

Pitch, or *Tone.* This is the fundamental property of musical sounds.

By pitch is meant the acuteness or graveness of the sound, as determined by the ear; and this is found to depend on the rapidity of vibration of the sounding body, or the number of vibrations performed in a given time. Most ears can mark a difference between two sounds differing in acuteness or pitch; those that cannot do so, to a minute degree, are incapable of music. The gravest sound audible to the human ear is stated, by the generality of experimenters, at 20 vibrations per second; the limit of acuteness is various for different individuals, the highest estimate is 73,000 vibrations in the second. The cry of a bat is so acute as to pass out of the hearing of many persons. The extreme audible range would amount to between nine and ten octaves.

A musical note is sweeter than an unmusical sound emanating from the same source. The explanation may be partly its purity, and partly its containing already an element of harmony, in the equal timing of the beats.

Waxing and *Waning* of sound. The charm of this peculiar effect, resembling the waxing and waning of movements (p. 23), is well known. 'That music hath a dying fall.' The moaning of the wind exemplifies it. The skilful singer knows how to turn it to account. In some kinds of pathetic oratory, it degenerates into the whine or sing-song.

Harmony and *Discord..* When a plurality of sounds concur, there may be harmony, discord, or mere indifference.

Harmony is known to arise from the proportions of the rates of vibration of musical sounds; 1 to 2 (octave), 2 to 3 (fifth), 3 to 4 (fourth), and so on, up to a certain point, when the harmony fades away into discord. The harmonious adjustment of sounds in succession (melody), and in concurrence (harmony proper), is musical composition, to which are added other effects of Time, Emphasis, &c. The pleasures of harmony are well known, but they somewhat transcend the simple sensations, and trench upon the sphere of the higher emotions, under which some farther notice will be taken of them.

6. The more Intellectual sensations of sound are principally those connected with perceiving *Articulateness,*

INTELLECTUAL SENSATIONS OF SOUND. 55

Distance, and *Direction.* Reference may also be made to *Clearness* and *Timbre.*

Clearness. This is another name for purity, and implies that a sound should stand out distinct, instead of being choked and encumbered with confusing ingredients. Both the pleasure of music, and the perception of meaning, are involved in the clearness of the sounds. We have already surmised that the primitive sweetness of sounds may be involved with their purity, and so with their clearness; silver and glass are remarkable for both the sweetness and the purity of their tones.

Timbre, Complexion, or *Quality.* Different materials, instruments, and voices, although uttering the same note, with the same intensity, yet affect the ear differently, so as to be recognized as distinct. This is called the *timbre* or speciality of the instrument. Certain experiments made by Helmholtz profess to explain this difference, and, along with it, the difference of vowel quality in articulate sounds.

Articulate sounds. The discrimination of these is the foundation of speech.

The consonants in general are distinguished through the characteristic shock given by them severally to the ear. The hissing sound of s, the burring of r, the hum of m, are well marked modes of producing variety of effect. We can understand how each should impart a different kind of shock to the nerve of hearing. So we can see a reason for distinguishing the abrupt sounds p, t, k, from the continuous or vocal sounds b, d, and g, and from the same sounds with the nasal accompaniment m, n, ng. It is not quite so easy to explain the distinction of shock between the labials, dentals, and gutturals; still, if we compare p (labial), with k (guttural), we can suppose that the stroke that gives the k is in some way harder than the other.

Much greater difficulty attaches to the vowel sounds, which differ only in the mode of opening the mouth while the sound is emitted. Helmholtz lays it down, as the result of numerous experiments, that vowel sounds contain, besides the ground-tone, a number of upper-tones, or by-tones, with double, triple, &c., the number of vibrations of the ground-tone; and are distinguished, or have their peculiar character, according to the nature of the accompaniments in each case. Willis and Cagniard-Latour contrived modes of producing vowel sounds artificially; and Helmholtz, by making specific combinations of various simple tones, imitated all the vowel articulations.

When the ground-tone is heard alone, the sound has the character of *u* (full). The *o* has, along with the ground-tone, the next octave audibly combined. The *a* (ah) is characterized by the marked presence of the very high octaves.

56 SENSE OF HEARING.

Distance. This is judged of entirely by intensity, and is ascertainable only for known sounds. The same sound is feebler as it is remote, and we infer accordingly. Where we have no opportunities of comparing a sound at different known distances, our judgment is at fault, as with the thunder, and with the roar of cannon. It being an effect of distance to make sounds fade away into a feeble hum, if we encounter a sound whose natural quality is feeble, as the humming of the bee, we are ready to imagine it more distant than it is.

Direction. We have no primitive sense of direction; it is an acquired perception, based on our discrimination of the intensity and the clearness of sounds. In certain positions of the head, the same sound is stronger than in others; the direction most favourable being no doubt the straightest, or the line of the passage of the outer ear.

Let us consider first the case of listening with a single ear. When the turning of the head makes a sound less loud and distinct, we conclude that it has passed out of the direct line of the ear, or a direction at right angles to that side of the head. When another movement brings it into greater distinctness, we conclude that it was at first away from that direction.

The combined action of the two ears materially aids the perception. The concurrence of the greatest possible effect on the right ear with the least on the left ear, is a token that the sound is on our right hand; an equal effect on both ears shows it to be before or behind. At best, the sense of direction of sounds is not delicate. We cannot easily find out a skylark in the air from its note; nor can we tell the precise spot of a noise in a large apartment.

SENSE OF SIGHT.

1. The *Objects* of Sight are nearly all material bodies.

Bodies at a certain high temperature are self-luminous; as flame, red-hot iron, &c.; the celestial lights being supposed analagous. Other bodies, as the greater number of terrestrial surfaces, the moon and the planets, are visible only by reflexion from such as are self-luminous.

2. The *Organ* of Sight, the Eye, is a compound optical lens in communication with a sensitive surface.

COATS OF THE EYE-BALL.

Besides the structures composing the globe of the eye, there are various important accessory parts. The *eye-brows* are thick arched ridges, surmounting the orbit, and acted on by muscles, so as to constitute part of the expression of the face. The *eye-lids* are the two thin moveable folds that screen the eye; the upper is the larger and more moveable, having a muscle for the purpose. The length of the opening varies in different persons, and gives the appearance of a large or a small eye. The lids are close to the ball at the outer angle; but a small red body (lachrymal caruncle) intervenes at the inner angle; and near this body the lachrymal ducts pierce both eye-lids. The *lachrymal apparatus* consists of (1) the gland for secreting the tears at the upper corner of the outer side of the orbit; (2) the two canals for receiving the fluid in the inner side of the orbit; and (3) the sac, with the duct continued from it, through which the tears pass to the nose. The tears are secreted by the lachrymal gland, and poured out from the eye-lids upon the eye-ball; the washings afterwards running into the lachrymal sac, and thence away by the nose.

The globe or ball of the eye is placed in the fore-part of the cavity of the orbit; it is fixed there by the optic nerve behind, and by the muscles with the eye-lids in front, but with freedom to change its position. The form of the ball is round but irregular, as if a small piece were cut off from a larger ball, and a segment of a smaller laid on; the smaller segment is the projecting transparent part seen in front. Except under certain influences, the two eyes look nearly in the same direction; otherwise expressed by saying, their axes are nearly parallel.

The eye-ball consists of three investing membranes, making up the shell, and of three transparent masses, called its humours, which constitute it an optic lense. External to it in front, is a thin transparent membrane called the *conjunctiva*, a mere appendage arising out of the continuation of the lining mucous membrane of the eye-lids. The red streaks in the white of the eye are its blood-vessels.

The outer investing membrane or tunic is called the *sclerotic*, and is a strong, opaque, unyielding fibrous structure; on it depend the shape and the firmness of the ball. It extends over the whole of the larger sphere to the junction of the smaller in front. Its continuation, or substitute, in the clear bulging part of the eye is the *cornea*, which is equally firm, but transparent. The sclerotic is about four-fifths of the shell; the cornea, one-fifth.

Next the sclerotic is the *choroid* coat, a membrane of a black or deep brown colour, lining the chamber of the eye up to the union of the sclerotic and cornea. It is composed of various layers. Outside are two layers of capillary blood-vessels, veins and arteries. Inside is the layer containing the black pigment, which it is the object of the numerous blood-vessels to supply. The pigment is enclosed in cells, about the thousandth of an inch in diameter, and closely packed together.

The *retina*, or the nervous coat, lies upon the choroid, but does not extend so far forward. It is transparent, with a reddish colour, owing to its blood-vessels. In its centre is a small, oval, yellow spot, $\frac{1}{17}$ inch long, $\frac{1}{70}$ inch wide; the centre of this is a thinner portion of the retina called the central hole. The retina consists of various layers. Beginning at the fore part, in contact with the back lense of the eye, we find a transparent membrane called the *limiting membrane*, not more than $\frac{1}{30,000}$ inch in thickness. Next are *the ramifications of the optic nerve*, fine meshes of nerve fibres, exceedingly minute; the average diameter not more than $\frac{1}{30,000}$ inch, while some are less than $\frac{1}{100,000}$ inch. Behind this is a layer of *nerve cells*, resembling the cells of the grey matter of the brain. Next is a *granular* layer, of fine grains or nuclei, with exceedingly minute filaments perpendicular to the retina. Lastly, comes the *bacillar* layer, made up of closely-packed perpendicular rods, transparent and colourless, about $\frac{1}{1000}$ inch long, and $\frac{1}{30,000}$ thick. Interspersed with these are larger rods called cones, $\frac{1}{2500}$ of an inch in diameter. By these larger and smaller rods, is effected the junction of the retina with the choroid; six or eight of the cones, and a large number of the smaller rods grouped round them, enter each pigment cell. The rods are themselves in connexion with the nerve fibres and nerve cells of the retina, through the fine perpendicular filaments. All the elements of the retina are most abundant and close in the yellow spot or its vicinity, where vision is most distinct.

To complete the account of the investing membranes of the eye, we must allude to certain structures continuous with the choroid coat, at the junction of the sclerotic with the cornea. Three distinct bands are found here; a series of dark radiated folds, called the *ciliary processes;* a band or ligament connecting the choroid with the iris, called the *ciliary ligament;* and, behind the ciliary ligament, and covering the outside of the ciliary processes, the *ciliary muscle*, a muscle of great importance. The *iris* is the round curtain in front of the eye, with a central hole the pupil, for the admission of light. It is attached all round at the junction of the sclerotic and cornea, and may be considered a modified prolongation of the choroid. The anterior surface is coloured and marked by lines, indicating a fibrous structure. The fibres are muscular, and of two classes, circular and radiating; their contraction diminishes or widens the pupil of the eye, according to the intensity of the light.

Next as to the Humours, or lenses of the eye. The *aqueous* humour, in front, is a clear watery liquid lying under the cornea, and bounded by the next humour, the crystalline lens, and its attachments to the ciliary process. The *vitreous* humour, behind, occupies the whole posterior chamber of the eye, about two-thirds of the whole. It is a clear thin fluid enclosed in membrane, which radiates into the interior like the partitions of an orange, without reaching the central line where the rays of light traverse

MUSCLES OF THE EYE.

the eye. In shape, it has the convexity of the eye behind; while there is a deep cup-shaped depression for receiving the crystalline lens in front. The *crystalline lens* is a transparent solid lens, in form double convex, but more rounded behind than before. It is suspended between the two other humours by the membrane of the vitreous humour, attaching it to the ciliary processes.

The eye is moved by six muscles, four *recti*, or *straight*, and two called *oblique*. The four recti muscles arise from the bony socket in which the eye is placed, around the opening where the optic nerve enters from the brain; and are all inserted in the anterior external surface of the eyeball, their attachments being respectively on the upper, under, outer, and inner edges of the sclerotic. The superior oblique, or trochlear, muscle arises close by the origin of the superior straight muscle, and passes forward to a loop of cartilage; its tendon passes through the loop, and is reflected back, and inserted on the upper posterior surface of the eyeball. The inferior oblique muscle arises from the internal inferior angle of the fore part of the orbit, and is inserted into the external inferior surface of the eyeball, behind the middle of the ball.

The sweep of the eye in all directions arises from the movements of these muscles singly, or in combination. Most, if not all, the movements might be caused by the four straight muscles, but the others come into play, whenever they are able to facilitate any desired movement.

3. The *mode of action* of the eye involves, in the first place, an optical effect.

When the eye is directed to any object, as a tree, the rays of light, entering the pupil, are so refracted by the combined operation of the humours, as to form an inverted image on the back of the eye, where the transparent retina adjoins the choroid coat. The precise mode of stimulating the nervous filaments of the retina is not understood; but we must presume that the pigment cells of the choroid play an important part, being themselves acted on by the light.

The image must be formed, by the due convergence of the rays, exactly on the retina, and not before or behind. When an object is looked at too near, the convergence of the rays is behind the retina, and not upon it. The limits of distance, for very distinct vision, may be stated at from five to ten inches for the majority of persons.

There is a natural barrier to the power of minute vision; we can distinguish very minute lines and points, but there is a degree of minuteness that cannot be discerned. This limit is the limit of the fineness of the meshes of the retina about the yellow spot. It would seem necessary that every separate nerve, filament, and nerve cell should take a distinct impression.

There is a certain power of adjustment of the eye-ball to render vision distinct at varying distances. If an object is seen clearly at six inches off, all objects nearer and farther will seem indistinct; the convergence of their rays will be behind or before the retina. But, by a change in the eye-ball, more distant objects will become distinct, the near becoming indistinct. The ciliary muscle is the means of effecting this change; for near vision it contracts, and, in contracting, compresses the vitreous humour, and pushes forward the crystalline lens, pressing more upon the edges than on the middle, and thus increasing its curvature; the optical result is a more rapid convergence of the rays of light, whereby the image is advanced from behind the retina to an exact coincidence with the retina. For distant vision, the muscle relaxes, and the elasticity of the parts restores the shape of the lens. This adjustment suits a range of from four inches to three feet.

4. The two eyes, instead of presenting two perfectly distinct pictures of the same thing, conspire to render the single picture more complete. This is Binocular vision.

When both eyes are fixed on a near object, as a cubical box, held within a few inches of the face, each sees a different aspect of it; the dissimilarity is greater the nearer it is, and becomes less as it is more remote, there being a certain distance where the two pictures seem identical. Such explanation as can be given of this fact belongs to a later stage; but it is here mentioned as involving a farther adjustment to distance, namely, the convergence of the two eyes for near distances, their parallelism for great distances.

From misapprehending the process of vision, a difficulty has been started as to our seeing objects erect by means of an inverted image in the retina. The solution is found in the remark that the estimate of up and down is not optical but muscular; up is what we raise the eyes or the head to see.

5. The *Sensations* of Sight are partly Optical, the effect of light on the retina; and partly Muscular, from the action of the six muscles. We can scarcely have a sensation without both kinds.

The Optical sensations are *Light, Colour,* and *Lustre.*

Light. The effect of mere light, without colour, may be exemplified in the diffused solar radiance. This is a Pleasure,

SENSATION OF LIGHT.

acute, or voluminous, according as the source is a dazzling point, or a moderate and wide-spread illumination. The Speciality of the pleasure is the endurability without fatigue, in which respect, sight ranks highest of all the senses, and the same cause renders it the most intellectual. The influence, although powerful for pleasure, is yet so gentle, that it can be sustained in presence and recalled in absence to a distinguishing degree. Whence, as a procuring cause of human and animal pleasure, light occupies a high position; there being a corresponding misery in privation.

The intense pleasure of the first exposure after confinement can last only a short time; but the influence, in a modified degree, remains much longer. After excess, a peculiar depression is felt, accompanied with morbid wakefulness and craving for shade. One of the cruellest of tortures was the barbarian device of cutting off the eye-lids, and exposing the eyes to the glare of the sun.

As regards Volition, the pleasures of light observe the general rule of prompting us to act for their continuance and increase. But this does not express the whole fact. There is a well-known fascination in the glare of light, a power to detain the gaze of the eye even after the point of pleasure has been passed. We have here a disturbance of the proper function of the will, of which there are other examples, to be afterwards pointed out.

The Intellectual property of the sensations of sight has been already adduced as their speciality. They admit of being discriminated and remembered to a degree beyond any other sense, being approached only by hearing. It is possible that a well-endowed ear may be more discriminative and tenacious of sounds, than a feebly-endowed eye of sights, but, by the general consent, sight is placed above hearing in regard to intellectual attributes.

By the Law of Relativity, the pleasures of light demand remission and alternation; hence the art of distributing light and shade. The quantity received, on the whole, may be too much, as in sunny climates, or too little, as in the regions of prevailing fogs.

Colour. This is an additional effect of light, serving to extend the optical pleasures, as well as the knowledge, of mankind. The pure white ray is decomposable into certain primary colours, and the presentation of these separately and successively, in the proportions that constitute the solar beam, imparts a new pleasurable excitement, having all the attributes of the pleasure of mere light. There is no absolute beauty in any single colour; when we give a preference to red, or blue, or yellow, it is owing to a deficiency as regards that colour, in the general scene. As a rule, the balance of colour, in our experience, is usually in favour of the blue end of the spectrum, and hence red, and its compounds, are a refreshing alternation.

Lustre. Some surfaces are said to have lustre, glitter, or brilliancy. This is a complex effect of light. A colour seen through a transparent covering is lustrous, as the pebbles in a clear rivulet. There is also a lustrous effect in a jet black surface, if it reflects the light. This luminous reflection, superadded to the proper visibility of the surface, is the cause of lustre. Transparent surfaces reflect light, like a mirror, as well as transmit the colour beneath; and this multiplication of luminous effects adds to the pleasure. The many-sided sparkle of the cut crystal, or gem, is a favourite mode of giving brilliancy; the broken glitter is more agreeable than a continuous sheet of illumination.

The highest beauty of visible objects is obtained by lustre. The precious gems are recommended by it. The finer woods yield it by polish and varnish. The painter's colours are naturally dead, and he superadds the transparent film. This property redeems the privation of colour, as in the lustrous black. The green leaf is often adorned by it, through the addition of moisture. Possibly much of the refreshing influence of greenness in vegetation is due to lustrous greenness. Animal tissues present the effect in a high degree. Ivory, mother of pearl, bone, silk, and wool, are of the class of brilliant or glittering substances. The human skin is a combination of richness of colouring with lustre. The hair is beautiful in a great measure from its brilliancy. The finest example is the eye; the deep black of the choroid, and the colours of the iris, are liquified by the transparency of the humours.

6. The sensations involving the Muscular Movements of the eye are *visible movement, visible form, apparent size, distance, volume,* and *situation.*

Visible Movement. The least complicated example of the muscular feelings of sight is the following a moving object, as a light carried across a room. The eye rotates, as the light moves, and the mental effect is a complex sensation of light and movement. If the flame moves to the right, the right muscles contract; if to the left, the left muscles; and so on; there being different muscles, or combinations of muscles, engaged

VISIBLE MOVEMENT.

for every different direction. Instead of following a straight course, the light may change its direction to a bend or a curve. This varies the muscular combinations, and their relative pace of contraction; whence results a distinguishable mode of consciousness.

Thus it is, that one and the same optical effect, as a candle-flame or a spark, may be imbedded in a great variety of muscular effects, every one of which is distinguished from the rest, and characteristically remembered. The embodiment must be contained in the numerous nerve centres and nerve communications related to the muscles of the eye.

As with the muscles generally, we can distinguish; by the muscles of the eye, longer or shorter *continuance* of movement. We can thus estimate, in the first place, duration; and, in the second (under certain conditions), visual or apparent extension. In like manner, we are conscious of degrees of speed or *velocity* of movement, which also serves as an indirect measure of visible extension. The kind of muscular sensibility that, from the nature of the case, cannot belong to the eye, is the feeling of Resistance or dead strain, there being nothing to constitute a resisting obstacle to the rotation of the ball, except its own very small inertia. Hence the eye, with all its wide-ranging and close-searching capabilities, cannot be said to contribute to the fundamental consciousness of the object universe, the feeling of resistance.

The various pleasures of movement, formerly recited, appertain to moving spectacle. The massive, languid feeling of slow movements, the excitement of a rapid pace, the pleasures of waxing and waning movements (the beauty of the curve), can be realized through vision.

Among the permanent imagery of the intellect, recalled, combined, and finally dwelt upon, we are to include visible movements. The familiar motions of natural objects—running streams, waving boughs, &c.; the characteristic movements of animals, the movements and gestures of human beings, the moving machinery and processes of industry—are distinguished and remembered by us, and form part of our intellectual furniture.

Visible Form. This supposes objects in stillness, surveyed in outline by the eye, and introduces us to co-existence in Space, as contrasted with succession in Time. With regard to the mere fact of muscular movement, it is the same thing for the eye to trace the outline of the rainbow, as to follow the flight of a bird, or a rocket. But, as in the case of Touch, already considered, the accessary circumstances make a radical difference, and amount to the contrast of succession with co-existence. The points of distinction are these:—(1) In following the outline of the rainbow, we are not constrained to any one pace of movement, as with a bird, or a projectile. (2) The optical impression is not one, but a series, which may be a repetition of the same, as the rainbow, or different as the landscape. (3) We may repeat the movement, and find the same series, in the same order. (4) We can, by an inverted movement, obtain the series in an inverted order. These two experiences—repetition and inversion—stamp a peculiar character of fixity of expectation, which belongs to our idea of the extended and co-existing in space, as opposed to passing movement. (5) As regards sight in particular when compared with touch, the power of the eye to embrace at one glance a wide prospect, although minutely perceiving only a small portion, confirms the same broad distinction, between the starry sky and the transitory flight of a meteor. When a series of sensations can be *simultaneously* grasped, although with unequal distinctness, this gives, in a peculiar manner, the notion of plurality of existence, as opposed to continued single existence.

The course moved over by the eye in scanning an outline, leaves a characteristic muscular trace, corresponding to the visible form. Thus we have Linear forms—straight, crooked, curved, in all varieties of curvature; Superficial forms and outlines—round, square, oval, &c. The visible objects of the world are thus distinguished, identified and retained in the mind as experiences of optical sensation embedded in ocular movements; and we have a class of related feelings, pleasureable and otherwise, the same as with visible movements. Our intellectual stores comprise a great multitude of visible forms.

Apparent Size. The apparent size or visible magnitude embraces two facts, an optical and a muscular. The optical fact is the extent of the retina covered by the image, called by Wheatstone the *retinal magnitude;* the muscular fact is the muscular sweep of the eye requisite to compass it. These two estimates coincide; they are both reducible to angular extent, or the proportion of the surface to an entire sphere. The apparent diameter of the sun, and of the full moon, is half a degree, or $\frac{1}{720}$ of the circumference of the circle of the sky. This combined estimate, by means of two very sensitive organs—the retina and the ocular muscles, renders our estimate of apparent size remarkably delicate; being, in fact, the universal basis of all accurate estimate of quantity. In measuring other properties of bodies, as real magnitude, weight, heat, &c., we reduce each case to a comparison of two visible magnitudes; such are the tests of a three-foot rule, a balance, a thermometer.

The fluctuations of apparent size in the same thing—a remote building for example—are appreciated with corresponding delicacy; and when we come to know that these fluctuations are caused by change of real distance, we use them as our most delicate indication of degrees of remoteness.

The celestial bodies are conceived by us solely under their apparent or visible size. Terrestrial objects all vary in visible size, and are pictured by the mind under a more or less perfect estimate of *real* size.

Distance, or *varying remoteness*. We have as yet supposed visible movement and form in only two dimensions, or as extending horizontally and vertically. The circumstance of varying remoteness, necessary to volume, or three dimensions, demands a separate handling. We must leave out, at this stage, the knowledge of *real* distance, as well as real magnitude.

There are two adaptations, or adjustments, of the eyes for distance; a change in the ball for near distances, and a convergence or divergence of the two eyes for a wider range. Both changes are muscular; they are accompanied with a consciousness of activity, or the contraction of muscles. The change made, in each eye-ball, for a nearer distance is a conscious change; the return from that is also conscious. The gradual convergence or divergence of the two eyes is accompanied with a discriminative muscular consciousness. We can thus, by muscularity, discriminate (although not as yet knowing the whole meaning of) bodies moving away from the eye, or approaching nearer it. An object moving across the field of view is distinguished from the same object retreating or advancing; distinct muscles being brought into play. We may, likewise, have the emotional effects of slow, quick, or waning movements, by change of distance from the eye. As a general rule, there is a relief in passing from a near view to a distant.

We have seen, under the previous head, that variation of optical size accompanies variation of distance, and is the most delicate test of all. To this we have to add the *binocular dissimilarity*, which is at the maximum for near distances, and is nothing for great remoteness. There are thus *four* separate circumstances engaged in making us aware of any alteration of the distance of objects from the eye. A fifth will be stated afterwards. The importance of this powerful combination will appear at an after stage, when the visual perceptions of real distance and real size are under consideration.

Visible Movements and Visible Forms in three dimensions: Volume. Applying the discrimination of Distance to visible movements and visible forms, we can take cognizance of these in all the three dimensions of space. A ship, instead of simply crossing the field of view, partly crosses and partly moves off; in which case, we combine the lateral movements of the eye with the various adjustments and effects of distance; we distinguish the appearance of movement without alteration of distance, from alteration of distance without lateral movement, and from other combinations of the two.

So with visible forms in three dimensions, as the vista of a street. In examining this object, we move the eyes and the head right and left, up and down; and also make conspicuous adjustments for distance, finding that these are the remedy for the picture's being confused in certain parts. The feeling of the picture is thus a compound of lateral movements, adjustments, and changes of optical magnitude in the things observed.

In every solid form, as a book, a table, a house, this alteration of adjustment enters into the movements of the eye in tracing out the form. Visible solidity, or volume, is thus a highly complex perception, involving optical impressions, with a series of muscular movements, lateral and adjusting. Each different solid combines these in a characteristic way; cube, oblong, sphere, cylinder, human figure—are all distinguished and remembered as distinct.

Visible Situation. Visible situation is made up of the elements now described. It is the visible interval between one thing and some other thing or things, measured either laterally, or in visible remoteness. The situation of a human figure, with reference to a pillar, is right or left, up or down, near or far, and at definite visible intervals.

CHAPTER III.

THE APPETITES.

The Appetites are a select class of Sensations; they may be defined as *the uneasy feelings produced by the recurring wants or necessities of the organic system.*

Appetite involves volition or action; now volition demands a motive or stimulus; and the stimulus of Appetite is some sensation. All sensations, however, that operate on the will are not appetites. The commonly recognized appetites grow out of the periodic or recurring wants of the organic system; they are *Sleep, Exercise, Repose, Thirst, Hunger, Sex.*

Sleep. The two conditions, namely, periodic recurrence, and organic necessity, are well exemplified in sleep. The natural course of the system brings on sleep, without our willing it; and its character as an appetite, or craving, appears when it is resisted. A massive form of uneasiness is then felt; the will is urged to remove this uneasiness, and to obtain the corresponding voluminous pleasure of falling asleep; which volitional urgency is the appetite.

Exercise and *Repose.* Within the waking state, there is an alternation of exercise and repose, essential to a sound organic condition; and this is accompanied with cravings. After rest, the refreshed organs start into exercise; the withholding of this causes physical discomfort, which is the motive to burst forth into activity. Mere spontaneity sets us on; any obstruction urges the will to take steps for its removal; this is the working of appetite. Similar observations apply to Repose.

The alternation of exercise with repose is sought throughout all our activities, bodily and mental. In the use of our different organs, whether muscles or senses, in the employment of the brain in intellectual functions, there is a point where the tendency to repose sets in, and where resistance occasions appetite.

Thirst, Inanition, Hunger. The cravings under these states show the twofold operation of Appetite—the massive uneasiness of privation, and the equally massive pleasure of gratification, whose combined motive power makes the strength of the volition or appetite. Besides these general cravings growing up under deficiency of nourishment, we are said to have artificial cravings, for special foods, condiments, and stimulants, that we have found agreeable, and have become accustomed to: for example, sweets, alcoholic drinks, tea, tobacco, &c.

The craving for *pure air*, after closeness and confinement, strictly conforms to the general definition of appetite.

Sex. The appetite that brings the sexes together is founded on peculiar secretions, periodically arising in the system after puberty, and creating an uneasiness until discharged or absorbed. The organic necessity here is of a less imperious kind, and the motive power lies most in the delight of gratification.

The habitual *routine* of life, if in any way crossed, is a species of appetite. Uneasiness is caused by any thwarting circumstance, while the compliance may be, of itself, either pleasurable or indifferent.

CHAPTER IV.

THE INSTINCTS.

THE account now given of the sensations is a sufficient preparation for entering on the Intellect. Nevertheless, it is convenient to comprise, in the present book, a view of the instinctive arrangements related both to Feeling and to Volition; for upon these also are based many intellectual growths.

Instinct is defined as untaught ability. It is the name given to what can be done prior to experience or education; as sucking in the child, walking on all fours by the newly-dropped calf, pecking by the bird just emerged from its shell, the maternal attentions of animals generally.

In all the three regions of mind—Feeling, Volition, and Intellect—there is of necessity a certain primordial structure, the foundation of all our powers. There are also certain arrangements, not usually included in mind, that yet are in close alliance and continuity with mental actions—as, for

LOCOMOTIVE RHYTHM.

example, swallowing the food. The following subjects are exhaustive of the department:—
1. The *Reflex Actions.*
2. The *Combined and Harmonious Movements.*
3. The *Primitive Manifestations of Feeling.*
4. The *Germs of Volition.*

The Reflex Actions have already been described under the functions of the Spinal Cord and Medulla Oblongata.

THE PRIMITIVE COMBINED MOVEMENTS.

1. Of the primitive arrangements for Combining Movements in Aggregation, or in Succession, the most Prominent example is the *locomotive rhythm.*

In the inferior quadrupeds, this is manifestly instinctive. The calf, the foal, the lamb, can walk the day they are dropped. Although human beings are unable to walk for many months after birth, there are reasons for the fact, in the unconsolidated state of the bones, in the immature condition of the human infant generally, and in the special difficulty of maintaining the erect posture. It is still probable that man has an instinctive tendency to alternate the movements of the lower limbs. The analogy of the quadrupeds is in favour of this view, and it is a matter of observation that infants in the arms are disposed to throw out their limbs in alternation.

2. The Locomotive Rhythm may be analyzed into three distinct combinations.

First, it involves the *reciprocation* of each limb separately; or the tendency to vibrate to and fro, by the alternate stimulus of the two opposing sets of muscles. In walking, the flexor and the extensor muscles have to be contracted by turns; the pendulous movement being also partly aided by gravity. It may easily be supposed that the nervous connexion of these opposing sets of muscles is made on a general plan throughout the body; as no continuous exertion is possible without replacing each member in the position that it starts from. On this assumption, the swing of all the organs would be the result of a primitive arrangement.

Secondly. There must be an *alternate* movement of corresponding limbs. The right and left members must move, not together, but by turns. For this, too, there is needed a primitive nervous arrangement availing itself of the commissural nervous connexions of the two sides of the body. The effect is not exclusively confined to the limbs; the arms and the entire trunk join in the alternation. We shall see presently that there are important exceptions.

Thirdly. The locomotion of quadrupeds involves a farther arrangement for alternating the fore and hind limbs. In reptiles, worms, &c., there is a progressive contraction from one end of the body to the other. The successive segments of the body are united in their action by an appropriate nervous connexion. It is hardly to be expected that any trace of this should appear in man, so rare are the occasions for it. Still, we may remark the great readiness to alternate arms and legs, in climbing, and in rowing a boat.

3. We find in the human system examples of primitive *associated* movements.

The chief example is furnished by the *two eyes*. We cannot, if we would, prevent them from moving together. The only interference with this tendency is the act of converging them in the adjustment for distance.

There is also in the eyes an associated action between the iris and the inward movement of the eyeball for near vision. In near vision, the iris is always contracted.

The association of the two sides of the body, in common movements, extends to the eyelids and the features, although there is a possibility of disassociating these, or of distorting the face. We find also a considerable proneness to move the arms together, as may be seen plainly in children.

4. The different moving members tend to *harmony of pace*.

Any one organ quickly moved imparts quickness to the rest of the movements; rapid speech induces rapid gesticulation; the spectacle of hurried action has an exciting effect. So, by inducing a slow pace on any member, we impart a quieting influence throughout: slow speech is accompanied with languid gestures. This principle indicates a medium whereby our actions are brought under control.

THE INSTINCTIVE PLAY OF FEELING.

1. The union of mind and body is specially shown in the Instinctive play or Expression of the Feelings.

It is one of the oldest and most familiar experiences of the human race, that the several feelings have characteristic bodily accompaniments. Joy, sorrow, fear, anger, pride, have each their distinct manifestations, sometimes called their natural language, the same in all ages and in all peoples. This points to certain primitive or instinctive connexions between the mental and the bodily processes.

2. The bodily accompaniments of the Feelings are of two classes—Movements, and Organic effects. The *Face* and features are most susceptible to movement under feeling; hence the face is by pre-eminence the index to the mind.

The movements of the Face have been analyzed by Sir Charles Bell.

The muscles of the face, by means of which its expression is governed, are arranged round the three centres,—the mouth, the nose, the eyes.

The expression of the EYES is due chiefly to the movements of the eyebrow, under the action of two muscles. The one *(occipito-frontalis)* is the broad thin muscle of the scalp, and extends down the forehead to the eyebrows; its action being to raise them in cheerful expression. The other muscle *(corrugator of the eyebrows)* passes across from one eyebrow to the other, and, when in action, knits the brows as in frowning; indirectly it lowers them in opposition to the scalp muscle.

Expression in a smaller degree attaches to the movements of the eyelids. The lids are closed by the orbicular muscle, or sphincter of the eyes. They are opened by the elevating muscle of the upper eyelid *(levator palpebræ)*; the rapid action of which under strong emotion gives the effect of a flash of the eye.

The NOSE is moved by three small muscles and one large. The *pyramidal* is a small muscle lying on the nasal bone, or upper half of the nose, and appears to be a continuation of the scalp muscle; it wrinkles the skin at the root of the nose. The *compressor* of the nose is a thin small muscle running transverse, on the lower part of the nose, but, instead of compressing the nose as the name indicates, it expands the nostril, by raising the cartilages. The *depressor* of the wing of the nose is a small flat muscle lying deep in the upper lip; according to its name it would be opposed to the preceding.

No very conspicuous manifestation is due to any one of these three muscles; the expansion of the nostril by the second is perhaps the most marked effect. The most notable expression attaches to the *common elevator of the lip and nose*. This muscle lies along the side and wing of the nose, extending from the orbit of the eye to the upper lip. It raises the wing of the nose and the upper lip together; it is thoroughly under the command of the will, and produces a very marked contortion of feature, wrinkling the nose and raising the upper lip. In expressing disgust at a bad smell, it is readily brought into play, and is thence used in expressing repugnance generally.

The MOUTH is moved by one orbicular muscle, and by eight pairs radiating from it round the face. The orbicular *(orbicularis oris)* is composed of concentric fibres surrounding the opening of the mouth, but not continued from one lip to another.

The eight radiating pairs may be enumerated in order from above, round to beneath, as follows:—

(1) The *proper elevator of the upper lip* extends from the lower border of the orbit of the eye to the upper lip, lying close to the border of the common elevator of lip and nose. When the lip is raised without raising the nose, which is not a very easy act, this muscle is the instrument. (2) The *elevator of the angle of the mouth* lies beneath the preceding, and partly concealed by it. (3, 4) The *zygomatics* are two narrow bands of muscular fibres, extending obliquely from the cheek bone to the angle of the mouth, one being larger and longer than the other. In combination with the elevator of the angle of the mouth, they serve to retract the mouth, and curve it upwards in smiling. (5) The *buccinator* (or cheek muscle) is a thin, flat, broad muscle, occupying the interval between the jaws. It is used in masticating the food; it would also conspire with the zygomatics in drawing out the mouth in the pleasing expression. Proceeding to the lower region of the face, we have (6) the *depressor of the angle of the mouth*, extending from the angle of the mouth to the lower jaw, and acting according to its name. (7) The *depressor of the lower lip* is a small square muscle, lying partly underneath, and partly inside, the preceding. (8) The *elevator of the lower lip* arises from a slight pit below the teeth sockets of the lower jaw, and thence *descends* to the lower part of the integument of the chin, so as to raise the lower lip. The combined action of this muscle and the depressor of the angle (6) is to curve the mouth downward, and pout the lower lip, a very marked expression of pain and displeasure.

3. The Voice and the Respiratory muscles concur with the face in the expression of feeling.

The proper organ of voice is the Larynx, with its vocal cords. Certain muscles operate in tightening, relaxing, and approximating the cords; to produce sound, they must be tightened and drawn together. But the exertion of the Laryngeal muscles is only a part of the case. The chest must act in a manner different from ordinary breathing, and force air more quickly through the air passages; while, in articulate utterance, the tongue and mouth have to co-operate. All these parts are actuated under feeling. In joy or exultation, and in anger, energetic shouts are emitted; in fear, the voice trembles; in acute pain, it gives forth sharp cries; in sorrow, there is a languid drawling note.

Irrespective of the play of the voice, the respiratory muscles are affected under emotion. In laughter, the diaphragm is convulsed; in depressing emotion, the sigh shows that it is partially paralyzed.

4. The muscles of the Body generally may be stimulated under strong feeling.

Any great mental excitement is accompanied with agitation of the whole body; the concurring nervous wave requires the larger organs to discharge itself upon.

5. States of feeling have also Organic accompaniments, or influences on the viscera and the processes of secretion, excretion, &c.

Probably no organ is exempted from participating in the embodiment of the feelings.

(1) The *Lachrymal Gland* and *Sac*. The effusion of tears from the gland is steady and constant during waking hours. States of emotion,—tenderness, grief, excessive joy—cause the liquid to be secreted and poured out in large quantities, so as to moisten the eye, and overflow upon the cheek. By such outpouring, a relief is often experienced under oppressive pain, the physical circumstance being apparently the discharging of the congested vessels of the brain. A strong sensibility undoubtedly lodges in the lachrymal organ, the proof of a high cerebral connexion. The ordinary and healthy flow of this secretion, when conscious, is connected with a comfortable and genial feeling; in the convulsive sob, not only is the quantity profuse, but the quality would appear to be changed to a strong brine.

(2) The *Sexual Organs*. These organs are both sources of feeling when directly acted on, and the recipients of influence from the brain under many states of feeling otherwise arising. They are a striking illustration of the fact that our emotions are not governed by the brain alone, but by that in conjunction with the other organs of the body. No cerebral change is known to arise with puberty; nevertheless, a grand extension of the emotional susceptibilities takes place at that season. Although the sexual organs may not receive their appropriate stimulation from without, the mere circumstance of their full development, as an additional echo to the nervous waves diffused from the cerebrum, alters the whole tone of the feelings of the mind, like the addition of a new range of pipes to a wind instrument. It is the contribution of a *resonant* as well as a sensitive part.

(3) The *Digestive Organs*. These have been already fully described; and their influence upon the mind has also been dwelt upon.

In the present connexion, we have to advert more particularly to the reciprocal influence of the mind upon them. It may be doubted if any considerable emotion passes over us without telling upon the processes of digestion, either to quicken or to depress them. All the depressing and perturbing passions are known to take away appetite, to arrest the healthy action of the stomach, liver, bowels, &c. A hilarious excitement within limits, stimulates those functions; although joy may be so intense as to produce the perturbing effect; in which case, however, it may be noted that the genuine charm or fascination is apt to give place to mere tumultuous passion.

The influence of the feelings in Digestion is seen in a most palpable form in the process of salivation. In Fear, the mouth is parched by the suppression of the flow of the saliva: a precise analogy to what takes place with the gastric juice in the stomach.

An equally signal example in the same connexion is the choking sensation in the throat during a paroxysm of grief. The muscles of the pharynx, which are, as it were, the beginning of the muscular coat of the alimentary canal, are spasmodically contracted, instead of alternating in their due rhythm. The remarkable sensibility of this part during various emotions, is to be considered as only a higher degree of the sensibility of the intestine generally. The sum of the whole effect is considerable in mass, although wanting in acuteness. In pleasurable emotion even, a titillation of the throat is sometimes perceptible.

(4) The *Skin*. The cutaneous perspiration is liable to be acted on during strong feelings. The cold sweat from fear or depressing passion, is a sudden discharge from the sudorific glands of the skin. We know, from the altered odour of the insensible or gaseous perspiration during strong excitement, how amenable the functions of the skin are to this cause. It may be presumed, on the other hand, that pleasurable elation exerts a genial influence on all those functions.

A precisely similar line of remarks would apply to the *Kidneys*.

(5) The *Heart*. The propulsive power of the heart's action varies with mental states as well with physical health and vigour. Some feelings are stimulants, and add to the power, while great pains, fright, and depression may reduce the action to any extent. Müller remarks, that the disturbance of the heart is a proof of the *great range* of an emotional wave; or its extending beyond the sphere of the cerebral nerves to parts affected by the sympathetic nerve.

(6) The *Lacteal Gland* in women. Besides the five organs now enumerated as common to the two sexes, we must reckon the speciality of women, namely, the Secretion of the Milk. As in all the others, this secretion is genial, comfortable, and healthy, during some states of mind, while depressing passions check and poison it. Being an additional seat of sensibility, and an additional resonance to the diffused wave of feeling, this organ might be expected to render the female temperament a degree more emotional than

the male, especially after child-bearing has brought it into full play.

6. The connexion of feelings with physical states may be summed up, for one large class of the facts, in the following principle :—*States of pleasure are concomitant with an increase, and states of pain with an abatement, of some, or all, of the vital functions.*

The proofs of this principle turn upon the consideration, first, of the Agents, and secondly, of the Manifestations of feeling.

(1) Taking the simple feelings, as already described, and beginning with the muscular, we remark that muscular exercise, when pleasurable, is the outpouring of exuberant energy. Muscular fatigue is the result of exhaustion. The pleasure of repose after fatigue is probably connected with the reflux of the blood from the muscles to other organs, as the brain, the stomach, &c. Muscular activity subsides, and organic activity takes its place; and there are other reasons for believing, that our pleasurable tone is more dependent upon the organic than upon the muscular vigour.

The extensive and important group of feelings denominated Sensations of Organic Life, attest with singular explicitness the truth of the principle. The organic pleasures—from Respiration, Digestion, &c.—are associated with the vitalizing agencies; the organic pains, which include the catalogue of diseases and physical injuries, point to the reverse. The apparent exceptions are an interesting study. Thus, Cold may be both painful and wholesome. The explanation seems to be that cold for the time depresses the functions of the skin, and is thus a medium of pain, while it invigorates the muscles, the nerves, and the lungs, and through these eventually the digestion. And the instance illustrates the superior sensitiveness of the skin, as compared with these other organs; whence we see that though our pleasures are connected with high vitality, they are not equally connected with *all* the vital functions. This remark may enable us to dispose of the other exception, namely, the concurrence of bodily diseases with painlessness, and even with comfort and elation of mind. In such cases, the disease may attach to insensitive organs and functions. Mere muscular weakness is not in itself uncomfortable; the heart may be radically deranged without pain; and there may be forms of disease of the lungs, liver, kidneys, &c., that do not affect the sensitive nerves. But skin disease, insufficient warmth, indigestion, and certain other forms of derangement, together with wounds and sores, are attended with unfailing pain and misery.

Thus, as regards the muscular feelings, and the sensations of the organic group, the induction may be held as proved, with the qualification now stated. When, however, we proceed to the five senses, we are not struck with the same concurrence. In the pleasures of Taste, Smell, Touch, Hearing, Sight, there may be, and undoubtedly is, a certain increase of vital power, as in the influence of light, or 'the cheerful day,' yet the increase of general vitality is not in the same rate as the pleasure. In short, the induction fails at this point; and some other principle is needed to complete the desired explanation.

(2) Let us view the *manifestations* under the opposing states of pleasure and pain. This will comprehend the theory of Expression, of which we have seen the particulars.

Here the general fact is, that under pleasure all the manifestations are lively, vigorous, and abundant, showing that our energies are somehow raised for the time. Under pain, on the contrary, there is a quiescence, collapse, and paralysis of the energies; hurt and disease prostrate the patient; the sick-bed is the place of inactivity.

To quote Bell's analysis of the pleasing and the painful expression of the face:—In joy, the eye-brows are raised, and the mouth dilated, the result being to open and expand the countenance. In painful emotions, the eye-brows are knit by the corrugator muscle, the mouth is drawn together and perhaps depressed at the angles.* Now, in the joyful expression, there is obviously a considerable amount of muscular energy put forth; a number of large muscles are contracted through their whole range. So far the principle holds good. Again, in pain the same muscles are relaxed, but then other muscles are in operation ; so that the difference would seem to be, not difference of energy, but a different direction to the energy. This fact has the air of a paradox, and has been felt as a puzzle. Pleasure and pain are states totally opposed, like plus and minus, credit and debt ; and their physical conditions ought to disclose a like opposition. Perhaps we may reconcile the appearances in the manner following. It is true, that in pain certain muscles operate, but they are muscles of small size ; and, by their contraction, they more thoroughly relax much larger muscles, thus on the whole releasing nervous energy and blood to go to other parts of the system. The slight exertion of the corrugator of the eyebrows completes the relaxation of the far more powerful muscle that elevates them; the contraction of the mouth releases the larger muscles of retractation. Still more apparent is the operation of the flexor muscles of the body; the great preponderance of muscular strength is in the muscles of erection; now, in the crouching and collapsed attitude, these are relaxed more completely through a small exertion of the flexor muscles. Hence the putting forth of power may set free power on the whole; the forced sadness of the countenance making the heart better.

Another exceptional manifestation is the energetic display under acute pain. This, however, is only the operation of another law of the constitution. Any sudden and intense shock is a stimulus to the nerves, and produces a general excitement in consequence. It is well known that, in the case of pain, such excitement is fully paid for by the after-prostration, and that the effect, on the whole, is in accordance with the main principle.

The two great convulsive outbursts—Laughter and Sobbing—supply additional examples.

Laughter is a joyful expression; and, in all its parts, it indicates exalted energy. The great muscle of expiration, the diaphragm, is convulsed; in other words, is made to undergo a series of rapid and violent contractions, showing the presence of a forcible stimulus. The voice concurs in active manifestations; the features are expanded to the full limit of the cheerful expression. Yet, with all this expenditure, there is no subsequent depression, as in acute pains; on the contrary, the organic functions are popularly believed to share in the general exaltation.

In the convulsive outburst of Grief nearly everything is reversed. The expiration is rendered slow—that is, the diaphragm and the other expiratory muscles fail in their office for want of nervous power. The voice acts feebly, and sends out a long-drawn melancholy note. The pharynx, or bag of the throat, is partially paralyzed, and swallowing impeded. The features are relaxed; the whole body droops. (When a robust child cries for a trifling reason, there may be few signs of weakened vitality; but then there is no real grief.) Finally, the lachrymal effusion is supposed to have a relation to the congested state of the blood vessels of the brain, which it partially relieves.

The proofs of the principle in question, derived from the study of the separate manifestations under pleasure and under pain, apply both to sensations and to emotions. They show that, although there may be forms of pleasure, with no such apparent addition to the physical resources, as in the digestive and respiratory processes, yet the existing resources are drawn upon to augment some of the active functions.

This last consideration appears to meet the case of the pleasures of the five senses. Sights and sounds add nothing to the material resources of the body, like food and air, but they render them available for the evolution of nerve force. We are thus conducted to the enunciation of another principle, qualifying and completing the one that we started with.

7. The concomitance of pleasure and increased vitality (with the obverse) is qualified, but not contradicted, by the operation of Stimulants.

Stimulants are of two classes : (1) the ordinary agents of the senses (tastes, odours, touches, &c.) and the emotions (wonder, love, &c.) ; and (2) the stimulating drugs.

(1) As regards three of the senses, Touch, Hearing, and Sight, their natural stimulation by the appropriate agents, is pleasurable within certain limits of intensity, determined by the vigour and freshness of the nervous system. It is pleasant for the ear to be assailed with sound, and the eyes with light, until such time as the organs are fatigued, and the nervous irritability exhausted. In these senses, pain is due mainly to *excess* of stimulus. With reference to Taste and Smell, the case is different ; there are agents specifically pleasurable, and agents specifically painful, in all degrees ; the sweet and bitter in taste, the fragrant and malodorous in smell, are not grounded on mere difference of intensity. We must suppose that certain agents are, in all degrees, favourable to nervous stimulation, and certain other agents unfavourable.

The higher Emotions present no difficulty. Those that are pleasurable, as Wonder, Love, Power, Complacency, Approbation, Knowledge, Harmony, are favourable to vitality, or give healthful stimulus ; the painful emotions, as Fear, Hatred, Impotence, Shame, Discord, are depressing physically as well as mentally.

(2) The stimulating drugs, as alcohol, tea, tobacco, opium, hemp, betel-nut, do but little to enhance vital action, and, in all but their moderate application, greatly waste it. They are therefore the extreme form of stimulation proper ; they draw upon the nervous power, without contributing to it : thereby proving in a still more obtrusive form, that we do not realize all the pleasurable excitement that the physical forces of the

STIMULATION. 79

system can afford, unless we employ agents to irritate or provoke nervous assimilation and activity.

8. The principle of the concomitance of pleasure and vitalizing influences (with the obverse) may be designated the Law of Self-conservation.

If the case were otherwise, the human and animal system would be framed for its own ruin. If pleasure were uniformly connected with lowered vitality, and pain with the opposite, who would care to keep themselves alive? On the other hand, the dangerous licence of the qualifying principle of Stimulation, is the limitation to the principle, and the open door for abuse. We cannot have pleasure without at least one element of activity—nervous assimilation; it is possible, however, that other interests may be suffering without affecting the tone at the moment, although they will fulfil the inexorable law on some future day.

We shall presently have to appeal to the principle of Conservation, in looking out a basis for the will.

THE INSTINCTIVE GERMS OF THE WILL.

1. Our voluntary power, as appearing in mature life, is a bundle of acquisitions.

The hungry man, seeing food before him, puts forth his hand, lifts a morsel to his mouth, chews, masticates, and swallows it. The infant can do nothing of all that; there is no link of connexion established in its mind between the state of hunger and the movements for gratifying it. A fly lights upon the face of a child, producing a tickling irritation; but the movement for brushing it away is not within the infant's powers. It is by a course of acquirement, that the local feeling of irritation in any part is associated with the movement of the hand towards that part. Such associations are necessarily very numerous; the will is a machinery of detail.

The acquirement must rest on certain primitive foundations; these alone are to be considered at the present stage.

2. I.—One of the foundations of voluntary power is given in the spontaneity of muscular action.

We have already adduced the evidence for the spontaneity of the muscular discharge. In it, we have a source of movements of all the active organs; each member is disposed to pass into action merely through the stimulus of the central energy. The locomotion, the voice, the features, the jaws, and tongue are all exerted by turns, when their nervous centres are in a fresh and nourished condition.

Still spontaneity does not amount to will. Its impulses are random and purposeless; the movements of the will are select and pointed to an end; spontaneity fails, when the will is most wanted—that is, when the system is exhausted and needs refreshment.

3. II.—Another foundation of voluntary power is to be sought for in the great law of Self-conservation.

In the fact that pleasure is accompanied with heightened energy, and pain with lowered energy, there is a beginning of voluntary control, although only a beginning. Under certain circumstances, this concurrence does what the will is expected to do, namely, secures pleasure and alleviates pain. Should a present movement coincide with a present pleasure, the pleasure, through its accompaniment of increased energy, would tend to maintain and increase the movement; as when already the sucking infant experiences the relish and nutritive stimulus of the mother's milk; or when mastication already begun is yielding the pleasurable relish of the food. The process is a roundabout one; for, by the law of conservation, all that is gained at first is increase of vital energy in the organs generally—organic functions and muscles alike: the special movement in question merely participating in the general rise of power.

Again, to illustrate from the side of pain. If a present movement coincides with a present pain (not a stimulating smart), the concomitant of the pain is lowered vital energy, which lowering extends to the movement supposed, and arrests it; as when an animal moving up to a fire encounters the scalding heat, with its depressing influence, and thereupon has its locomotion suspended.

In the cases now supposed, the influence of self-conservation is tantamount to the action of the will at any stage: the deficiency is, that mere conservation will not, any more than spontaneity, determine the right movement to arise from the dormant condition. To get at this is the real difficulty of the problem.

4. The coincidence of a pleasure with the movements proper to maintain or increase it, must be at first accidental.

Nothing but chance can be assigned as the means of first

bringing together pleasure and movement. Spontaneity induces a variety of movements: should any one of these coincide with a moment of pleasurable feeling, it would be rendered more energetic by the accompanying outburst of energy. The newly-dropped animal, on touching the warm body of the mother, is physically elated through the pleasure of the contact, and increases the movement that keeps it up. When after an hour's fumbling, it gets the teat into its mouth, there is a new burst of pleasure and concomitant vitality. The stimulus of the sucking (itself an untaught or reflex process) still farther inspires the energies to continue the movement once begun. But previous to the accidents that brought on these encounters, the animal could not of its own accord hit upon the appropriate actions. The human infant cannot find its way to the breast; it can only suck when placed there.

5. III.—When the same movement coincides more than once with a state of pleasure, the Retentive power of the mind begins an association between the two.

After a few returns of the favourable accident that first brought together the movement and the pleasure (or relief from pain), the two are connected by an associating link, and the rise of the pleasure is then apt to be attended with the movement for retaining and increasing it. After a number of concurrences of the relish of food with the masticating process, the morsel of food in the mouth directly prompts the jaws to operate.

This part of our education will be again touched on, under the Intellect, and more fully in the detailed explanation of the growth of the Will.

BOOK II.

THE INTELLECT.

---

1. THE functions of Intellect, Intelligence, or Thought, are known by such names as Memory, Judgment, Abstraction, Reason, Imagination.

These last designations were adopted by Reid, Stewart, and others, as providing a division of the powers of the Intellect. But, strictly looked at, the division is bad; the parts do not mutually exclude each other. The real subdivision of the intellectual functions is that formerly given, and now repeated.

2. The primary attributes of Intellect are (1) Consciousness of *Difference*, (2) Consciousness of *Agreement*, and (3) *Retentiveness*. Every properly intellectual function involves one or more of these attributes and nothing else.

(1) Discrimination or Feeling of *Difference* is an essential of intelligence. If we were not distinctively affected by different things, as by heat and cold, red and blue, we should not be affected at all. The beginning of knowledge, or ideas, is the discrimination of one thing from another. Where we are most discriminative, as in our higher senses, we are most intellectual. Even with reference to our pleasures and pains, we perform an intellectual operation when we recognize them as differing in degree.

This function of the Intellect has been already apparent in the Feelings of Movement and the Sensations. The very fact of distinguishing the Senses, and their Sensations, supposes the exercise of discrimination. No separate chapter is required for the farther elucidation of this fact. There are

DISCRIMINATION.—AGREEMENT.—RETENTIVENESS. 83

higher cases of discrimination, as when a banker detects a forged bank note, or a lawyer sees a flaw in a deed, but these are involved in the intellectual acquisitions, or the Retentive power of the mind.

The fundamental property of Discrimination is also expressed as the Law of Relativity, more than once already alluded to. As we can neither feel, nor know, without a transition or change of state,—every feeling, and every cognition, must be viewed as in relation to some other feeling, or cognition. The sensation of heat has no absolute character; there is in it a transition from a previous state of cold, and the sensation is wholly relative to that state. It is known, with regard to the feelings generally, that they subsist upon comparison; the pleasure of good health is relative to ill health; wealth supposes comparative indigence. Also, as regards knowledge, everything known, is known in contrast to something else; 'up' implies 'down;' 'black' presumes 'white,' or other colours. There cannot be a single or absolute cognition.

(2) The conscious state arising from *Agreement* in the midst of difference, is equally marked and equally fundamental. Supposing us to experience, for the first time, a certain sensation, as redness; and after being engaged with other sensations, to encounter redness again; we are struck with the feeling of identity or recognition; the old state is recalled at the instance of the new, by the fact of agreement, and we have the sensation of red, together with a new and peculiar consciousness, the consciousness of agreement in diversity. As the diversity is greater, the shock of agreement is more lively.

All knowledge finally resolves itself into Differences and Agreements. To define anything, as a circle, is to state its agreements with some things (genus) and its difference from other things (differentia).

The identifying process implied under Agreement, is a great means of mental resuscitation or Reproduction, and hence is spoken of as the Associating, or Reproductive principle of Similarity. A considerable space will be devoted to the exposition of the principle in this view.

(3) The attribute named *Retentiveness* has two aspects or degrees.

First, The persistence or continuance of the mental agitation, after the agent is withdrawn. When the ear is struck by the sound of a bell, there is a mental awakening, termed the sensation of sound; and the silencing of the bell does not silence the mental excitement; there is a continuing, though feebler consciousness, which is the memory or idea of the sound.

Secondly, There is a further and higher power,—the recovering, under the form of ideas, past and dormant impressions, without the originals, and by mere mental agencies. It is possible, at an after time, to be put in mind of sounds formerly heard, without a repetition of the sensible effect. This is true memory, and is a power unknown except in connexion with the animal organism. The previously-named property is paralleled by the waves of a pool struck by a stone, or by any other example of the law of mechanical persistence. But the distinct recovery of effects that have been obliterated from the actual view, and the accumulation, in one organism, of thousands of these recoverable effects, may be affirmed to be the unique function of creatures endowed with a brain and nervous system.

As the principal medium of this recovery is the presence of some fact or circumstance formerly co-existing with, or in any way contiguous to, the effect remembered,—as when we recall a thing by first knowing its name,—the Retentive property has been designated *Contiguous* Association.

It is not meant that the three attributes now specified can work in separation, or could exist in separation. On the contrary, they are implicated to such a degree that the suspension of one would destroy the others. Discrimination could not exist without Retentiveness; there would be nothing to retain without Discrimination; and no progress in retention without Agreement. Yet, notwithstanding this mutual implication in their working, the three processes are logically distinct; each means something quite apart from the others. It is as in the combination of extension and colour in material bodies; the properties are inseparable and yet distinct.

The exhaustive discussion of the Intellectual powers turns chiefly upon the two last-named attributes, Agreement and Retentiveness; but, as the most interesting applications of Agreement lie among remembered or acquired products, it is better to commence with the Retentive or plastic property. Next will be given the exposition of Agreement or Similarity. A third chapter will be devoted to the cases of Complicated mental reproduction. And lastly, some account will be taken of the process of forming original constructions, or what is termed the Creative or Inventive faculty of the mind.

3. Certain important uses are served by an accurate, or scientific, knowledge of the Intellectual Powers.

First, There is a natural curiosity to discover the Laws that govern the stream of our Thoughts. All the workings of nature are interesting, and not least so should be the workings of our own minds.

Secondly, The statement and the explanation of the differences of Intellectual Character must proceed upon a knowledge of the attributes and laws of our intelligence.

Thirdly, The art of Education is grounded on a precise knowledge of the retentive or plastic power of the mind. The arts of Reasoning and Invention, if such there be, naturally connect themselves with the laws of the faculties involved.

Fourthly, Many important disputes turn upon the determination of what parts of our intelligence are primitive, and what acquired. Such is the subject of Innate Ideas generally; also the questions raised by Berkeley—namely, the Theory of Vision, and the doctrine of External Perception.

CHAPTER I.

RETENTIVENESS—LAW OF CONTIGUITY.

1. WITH few exceptions, the facts of Retentiveness may be comprehended under the principle called the Law of Contiguity, or Contiguous Adhesion.

Retentiveness is the comprehensive name for Memory, Habit, and the Acquired powers in general. The principle of Contiguity has been described under various names, as Hamilton's law of 'Redintegration;' the 'Association of Ideas,' including Order in Time, Order in Place, Cause and Effect. The principle may be stated thus:—

2. Actions, Sensations, and States of Feeling, occurring together, or in close succession, tend to grow together, or cohere, in such a way that when any of them is afterwards presented to the mind, the others are apt to be brought up in idea.

The detail of examples will bring out the various circumstances regulating the rate of growth of the cohesive link. Generally, as is well known, a certain continuance, or repetition, is necessary to make a firm connexion.

MOVEMENTS.

We commence with the association of movements and states of muscular activity. Our acquisitions are known to comprehend a great many aggregates and sequences of movements, united with unfailing certainty. We shall see, however, that the chief aggregates of this kind include sensations also, and that the case of pure association of movement is not frequent, although both possible and occasionally realized.

3. It is likely that our Spontaneous and Instinctive actions are invigorated by exercise.

The various actions occurring in the round of Spontaneous discharges, are likely to become more vigorous, and more ready, after they have arisen a number of times; while Instinctive actions, as walking on all-fours, or sucking, &c., are also improved by repetition.

In the growth of the Will, which involves spontaneous actions, something is gained by the greater facility of beginning any movement after a certain frequency of occurrence. The hands, the voice, the tongue, the mouth, exercise their powers at first in mere aimless expenditure of force; by which they are prepared for starting forth to be linked with special feelings and occasions.

4. Movements, frequently Conjoined, become associated, or grouped, so as to arise in the aggregate, at one bidding.

Suppose the power of walking attained, and also the power of rotating the limbs. One may then be taught to combine the walking pace with the turning of the toes outward. Two volitions are at first requisite for this act; but, after a time, the rotation of the limb is combined with the act of walking, and unless we wish to dissociate the two, they go together as a matter of course; the one resolution brings on the combined movement.

Children attempting to walk, must learn to keep their balance. This depends on properly aggregated movements; the lifting of the right foot has to be associated with the movements for making the whole body incline to the left, and obversely. The art of walking includes other aggregates; the lifting of one foot is accompanied with a rising upon the other, and with a bending forward of the whole body. The education in walking consists in making these aggregates so secure,

ACQUISITIONS OF MOVEMENTS.

that the one movement shall not fail to carry with it the collaterals.

Articulate speech largely exemplifies the aggregation of muscular movements and positions. A concurrence of the chest, larynx, tongue, and mouth, in a definite group of exertions, is requisite for each alphabetic letter. These groupings, at first impossible, are, after a time, cemented with all the firmness of the strongest instinct.

5. We acquire also Successions of Movements.

In all manual operations, there occur successions of movements so firmly associated, that when we will to do the first, the rest follow mechanically and unconsciously. In eating, the act of opening the mouth mechanically follows the raising of the morsel. In loading a gun, the sportsman does not need to put forth a distinct volition to each movement of the hands.

6. It is rare to find an association of movements as such, or without the intervention of sensations.

In most mechanical trains, the sense of the effect of one movement usually precedes the next, and makes a link in the association. Thus, in loading a gun, the feeling that the cartridge is sent home, precedes, as an essential link, the withdrawing of the ramrod. There is, in such instances, a complex train of feelings and movements.

A deaf person speaking would appear to illustrate the sequence of pure movement; but, even in that case, there is a feeling of muscular expenditure. Such a feeling can never be absent until the very last stage of habit is reached, the stage when the mind is entirely unconscious of the movements gone through. A great practical importance attaches to this final consummation. It is the point where actions take place, with the least effort or expenditure of the forces of the brain. The class of actions so performed have been named *secondary automatic*, as resembling the automatic or reflex actions— breathing, &c.

Although the learning of successions of movements nearly always involves the medium of sensation, in the first instance, yet we must assume that there is a power, in the system, for associating together movements as such, and that special circumstances favour this acquisition.

7. There are certain conditions that govern the pace of acquisition generally. These are (1) Repetition or Con-

tinuance, (2) Concentration of Mind, and (3) the Natural Adhesiveness of the individual constitution.

(1) In order to every acquisition, a certain Continuance, *repetition*, or practice is needed, varying according to circumstances. By repetition, we make up for natural weakness or other defects, as in the extra drill of the awkward squad.

(2) Mental *concentration* will make a great difference in the pace of acquisition. When the whole of the attention is given to the work in hand, the cohesive growth is comparatively rapid. Distraction, diversion, remission are hostile to progress.

Concentration, as a voluntary act, depends on the motives. If the work is pleasant in act or in prospect, and if no other pleasure interferes, the whole mind is gained. This is concentration from the side of Pleasure. Whatever we have a strong liking for, we learn with ease. Our Tastes are thus a leading element in our acquisitions.

But concentration may be determined by Pain. The work itself being distasteful in comparison of something else, the mind revolts from it, until some strong pain is set up in the path; the lesson may not be liked, but the consequences of engaging the mind elsewhere may be sufficiently painful to neutralize the pleasure.

Another influence of pain is as mere Excitement, which intensifies the mental processes, and impresses on the memory whatever objects are present to the mind, giving to things disagreeable a persistence in opposition to the will.

(3) All the facts show that constitutions differ as to power of Adhesiveness, under exactly the same circumstances. In every class of learners, on every subject, there are the greatest inequalities. This Natural Adhesiveness usually shows itself in special departments—aptitude for languages, for science, for music, &c.; but it also shows itself in a more general form, or as applied to things generally. Hence part of it may be attributed to an endowment of the system, as a whole; while part depends on local endowments, as, for example, the musical ear.

8. The circumstances favouring the adhesion of movements in particular may be supposed to be (1) Muscular vigour, (2) The Active Temperament, and (3) Muscular Delicacy.

(1) Mere *muscular vigour*, by favouring the performance

CONDITIONS OF RETENTIVENESS.

of mechanical exercises, or the energy and persistence of muscular practice, cannot but contribute to progress in the mechanical arts.

(2) Of equal, if not of greater importance is the nervous peculiarity that prompts to muscular activity, determining a profuse and various *spontaneity* of the bodily movements.

(3) In the muscular system, as in the special senses, there may be degrees of *delicacy*, shown in nicety of muscular discrimination. This may be hypothetically connected with a higher organization of the ganglia of the active side of the brain—the motor centres whence the motor nerves immediately emanate. Whenever the test of discrimination shows superior muscular endowment, we are entitled to presume a greater degree of muscular retentiveness. The analogy of the senses is strong on this point, and will be referred to afterwards; the best case being the ear for music.

9. Acquirement in every form demands a certain Physical Vigour.

The freshness and vigour of the general system may be looked upon as essential to the plastic operation. Fatigue, exhaustion, indifferent nourishment, derogate from the powers of the learner. The greater physical vigour of early years is one, among other reasons, why youth is the season of improvement.

The mental concentration, or exercise of the Attention, necessary to new acquirements, is costly and exhausting.

IDEAL FEELINGS OF MOVEMENT.—THE SEAT OF IDEAS.

10. The Ideas of Movement may be associated together.

We may have ideas, or recollections and imaginations, of our various activities. We may rehearse, in the thoughts, the movements of a dance, or the manipulation of a sailing boat.

11. In regard to Ideas generally, it is probable, if not certain, that the renewed feeling, or idea, occupies the same parts, and in the same manner, as the original or actual feeling.

It was vaguely surmised, in former times, that the memory of things consisted in storing up images in a certain part of the brain, distinct from the places originally affected; that, in actually seeing a building, one portion of the brain is exercised, and, in remembering it, a different portion. The facts are opposed to such a conclusion.

In very lively recollection, we find a tendency to repeat the actual movements. Thus, in mentally recalling a verbal train, we seem to repeat, on the tongue, the very words; the recollection consists of a suppressed articulation. A mere addition to the force or vehemence of the idea, or the withdrawal of the restraint of the will, would make us speak out what we speak inwardly. Now, the tendency of the idea of an action to become the action, shows that the idea is already the fact in a weaker form. But if so, it must be performing the same nervous rounds, or occupying the same circles of the brain, in both states.

The same doctrine must equally apply to the Sensations of the Senses, and will derive illustration from them. The mere idea of a nauseous taste can excite the reality even to the production of vomiting. The sight of a person about to pass a sharp instrument over glass excites the well-known sensation in the teeth. The sight of food makes the saliva begin to flow. In the mesmeric experiments, this effect is carried still farther; the patient, through the suggested idea of intoxication, simulates the reality. Persons of weak nerves have been made ill actually, by being falsely told that they looked ill.

So it is with the special Emotions and passions. The thought or recollection of anger brings on the same expression of countenance, the same gestures, as the real passion. The memory of a fright is the fright re-induced, in a weaker shape.

To this doctrine it may be objected, that the loss of eyesight would be the loss of memory of visible things; that Milton's imagination must have been destroyed when he became blind. The answer is, that the inner circles of the brain must ever be the chief part of the agency both in sensations and in ideas. The destruction of the organ of sense, while rendering sensation impossible, can be but a small check upon the inward activity; it cuts off merely the extremity of the course described by the nerve currents. Moreover, the decay of the optic sensibility does not impair the activity of the *muscles* of the eye, wherein are embodied the perceptions of visible motion, form, extension, &c., which are one half, and not the least important half, of the picture.

12. The tendency in all Ideas to become Actualities, according to their intensity, is a source of active impulses distinct from the ordinary motives of the Will.

TENDENCIES OF IDEAS TO BECOME ACTUALITIES.

The Will is under the two influences—pleasure and pain; being urged *to* the one and *from* the other. But an idea strongly possessed may induce us to act out that idea, even although it leads to pain rather than to pleasure. The mesmeric sleep shows the extreme instance; in ordinary sleep, also, we are withdrawn from the correcting influence of actualities, and follow out whatever fancy crosses the view. In the waking state, we do not, as a rule, act out our ideas; they are seldom strong enough to neutralize the operation of the will. Still the power exists, and is, on occasions, fully manifested.

As an unequivocal instance of the power of an idea to generate its actuality, we may quote the infection of special forms of crime, and even of self-destruction. The impression made on susceptible minds by some notorious example is often carried out to the full, in spite of the deterring action of the usual motives of the will.

The fascination of a precipice is also in point. The spectator, seeing himself near precipitation, has the act of falling so forcibly suggested, that he has to put forth an effort of will to resist the suggestion.

Temptation to do something forbidden often comes of merely suggesting the idea, which is then a power to act itself out. In this way, ambition is inflamed, so as to master the sober calculation of future happiness.

The operation of an idea strongly possessed is especially prominent in the outgoings of Fear. It is the peculiarity of this passion to impress the mind unduly with its object, to magnify evil possibilities, and so to exaggerate the idea of escape, that one cannot be restrained from acting it out.

13. In the workings of Sympathy, there seems to be the carrying out of an Idea, apart from the usual operation of the will.

If the will be defined the pursuit of pleasure and the abstinence from pain, then disinterested conduct, involving frequently self-sacrifice, must spring from some other part of our nature. Now, as we are able, by means of our own experience, to form ideas of other men's pains and pleasures, we are disposed, according to the principle in question, to act these out, even although we forfeit a certain amount of pleasure, or incur a certain amount of pain. We conceive the pain of another man's hunger, and act out the idea by procuring for him food, even at some cost to ourselves.

14. It is a consequence of the doctrine as to the seat of revived feelings, that the Idea and the Actuality must have a great deal in common.

Memory and Imagination may be described in the language used for sensation, with certain allowances. A person vividly recollecting a former transaction, exclaims, 'I now see before me.' Next, the delicacy of the senses is likely to be reproduced in the recollection and in the imagination. Also, for the purposes of the will, in pursuit or in avoidance, the idea operates like the actuality. Farther, the same exhaustion of brain, and in the same parts, follows prolonged exercise in sensation and in thought.

15. Feelings of Movement may be associated together.

Since we can repeat mentally the steps of any complicated action, as a dance, we may, in consequence of this mental repetition, strengthen the cohesion of the train of movements. Practically, the process is seen at work in our vocal acquirements. We can acquire trains of language, without repeating aloud, although perhaps not quite so well. Children have often to learn their lessons by conning them in a whisper, which is the next stage to a mere idea. So, in meditating a discourse, and fixing it in the memory, without writing, as was the practice of Robert Hall, an adhesion takes place between ideal movements of articulation.

16. The Growth of Associations among Ideal movements must be supposed to follow the law of associations among the corresponding Actual movements.

The centres where the connexions are formed being the same, the only difference will be the feebler impetus of nerve action in the case of the ideal movements. Under great excitement, this difference will not exist, and the adhesion may be equally good in both.

Hence in any part of the system, where the adhesiveness of actual movements is good, that of ideal movements will be good also; and all the circumstances and endowments favouring one will favour both.

17. A movement, whether real or ideal, is Mentally known as a definite Expenditure of Energy in some Special muscle or muscles.

We must first discriminate degrees of expenditure, and next associate the different modes or degrees into grouped situations. A delicate discrimination is thus the condition of all retentiveness, as it marks out clearly the distinctive features of what is to be retained. To this we must add, as above remarked, that nice discrimination is to be regarded as indicating a superior organization in the centres of muscular activity—a higher multiplication of the nervous elements, whence arises a corresponding superiority in the plastic power, or Retentiveness.

SENSATIONS OF THE SAME SENSE.

18. Throughout all the Senses, the associating process connects sensations that happen frequently together.

In the inferior senses, the examples are neither numerous nor interesting. We may have a series of Organic pains, representing the course of an attack of illness, and remembered by the patient. We might also have a train of ideas of Taste, the first recalling to the mind all the rest; but there are few occasions for acquiring such trains. As regards Smell, there might be a succession of odours, regularly encountered in going in a particular track, through gardens, &c.; and if such an experience were often repeated, there would be found in the memory a cohering train of ideas of smell; the occurrence of one to the mind would suggest the others.

19. In the same operation that fixes, in the mind, a train of ideas, formed from sensations, the individual ideas become Self-sustaining.

In order that the first member of an often repeated train of tastes or odours should recall the next, each must be so far impressed or engrained that it can subsist of itself, without the original, to a greater or less degree of vividness. Before the taste of bread recalls the taste and relish of butter, usually conjoined, we must have tasted butter often enough to be able to retain some idea, more or less adequate, of that particular taste. This is equally a consequence of the retentive process of the mind, and follows all the laws governing the rate of adhesive growth.

The simplest sensation that we can have is a complex fact, as far as concerns being retained. A coherence must be effected in the mechanism of the brain, to enable a touch, or sound, or an idea of light, to possess a mental persistence; and the greater the degree of this coherence, in consequence of repetition and the other means of retentiveness, the better will be the mental conception.

20. The cohesive grouping of Sensations of the same sense appears largely in Touch.

In Touch, we have great variety of sensations; the purely emotional,—as soft touches and pungent touches; and those entering into ·intellectual perceptions,—as the feelings of roughness, weight, size, form, &c. Associations are formed among the different modes of these sensations; resulting in our tactual notions of familiar things. The child accustomed to handle a muff, forms an association between its softness, its elasticity, and its warmth to the touch; to these are added the muscular elements of size and form. If this aggregate has been definitely·connected in one group, by familiarity with the same thing, the experience of one of the qualities would recall the whole aggregate. The soft touch would make the mind expect everything else. So it is that we acquire distinctive notions of all the objects we are accustomed to handle; the lady knows her fan in the dark, the workman knows the tool he wants by the first contact; we each know whether we touch the poker or the hearth brush, a cinder or an ivory ball, a pen or a piece of string, a book or the cat, the table or the mantel-shelf. Every one of these familiar things is a definite grouping by plastic association between different modes of touch, some purely tactile, and others muscular.

Of course, one definite touch will not recall the whole of the tactile qualities of a specific object, unless there has been an exclusive association. When the cold touch of polished marble has been associated with many different forms, it will not recall any one in particular. The hand placed on a wooden surface tells nothing, because so many known things have the same touch; either a plurality of different objects will be recalled, or some one will be singled out by other links of association, or there will be no revival at all.

21. In considering the Rate of Acquirement among associations of Touch we must take into account, besides the general conditions of acquirement, the special character of the sense.

Touch being a two-fold sense, we must refer to the constituents in separation.

The purely tactile sensibility, the passive element of touch, is, in the scale of intellect, superior to Taste and Smell, inferior to Hearing and Sight. This comparative superiority and inferiority must be supposed to attach equally to the discriminative power, and to the retentiveness (we have assumed these two properties to rise and fall together).

The other element of Touch is Muscularity; the weight, hardness, size, and form of things, are tested and remembered principally by the muscles of the hand and the arm.

The intellectual character of the muscular feelings is probably not the same for all muscles; hence each set would have to be independently judged. We know that the muscles of the eye excel in delicacy of discrimination and retentiveness; they would not otherwise be on a par with the optical sensibility. Probably the muscles of the voice and articulation come next, and, after these, the hand and the arm; the difference being no doubt related to the comparative supply of nerves, and the expansion of the corresponding centres.

There may be great individual differences of character in respect of tactual endowment. These are principally indicated by degrees of delicacy in the manual arts.

Both in the tactual and in the muscular element, any superior delicacy will tell upon the worker in plastic material. The muscular precision of the hand and the arm is a guarantee for nicety of execution in every species of manipulation—with the surgeon and the artist, no less than the common artizan.

22. It is only in the Blind, that we can appreciate the natural delicacy, or intellectual susceptibility, of the sense of Touch.

None but the blind are accustomed to think of outward objects as ideas of Touch; in the minds of others, the visible ideas preponderate, and constitute the chief material of recollection. A blind workman remembers and discriminates his tools by their tactile ideas. The trains of associations that determine the order and array of surrounding things are, to the blind, trains of ideas of touch.

23. The associations among Sounds include, besides many casual connexions, the two great departments of Musical and Articulate Sounds.

Any two sounds heard together, or in close succession, for a number of times, would mutually reproduce each other in idea. When a sound is made in front of an echoing wall, we anticipate the echo.

In Musical training, the individual notes are rendered self-sustaining, and are at the same associated in musical successions. One note sounded brings on the idea of another that has usually followed it. When a sufficient number are given to determine an air, the remaining notes rise to the mind. The education of an accomplished musician is composed of many hundreds of these successions.

Besides the general conditions of acquirement, we must refer, in this case, to the quality termed the musical ear. Although the ear is improvable by cultivation, the basis of all great musical skill is a primitive endowment. There must be, from the beginning, a comparatively nice discrimination of musical tones, for which we may assume the physical basis of extensive auditory centres. A bad ear will not distinguish one note from the next above it or below it on the scale. A good ear will discriminate the minute fraction of a note.

It must be taken for granted, until the contrary is shown, that the delicate feeling of Agreement follows Discrimination; and that Retentiveness will follow both. Once for all, therefore, we may assume that delicacy of Discrimination is to be accepted as the criterion of all the three intellectual properties. Hence, when a sense has an unusual degree of discriminative power, there will also be an unusual retentiveness for its sensations. Not in music alone, therefore, but in everything, good memory will accompany acute feeling of difference.

Articulate sounds are made coherent on the same principle as musical sounds. We are familiarized with each distinct articulation, and are, at the same time, occupied with combining them into groups in the complex sounds of words and trains of words. In the minds of the uneducated, these connexions exist by hundreds; in a cultivated mind, they count by thousands.

The good articulate ear may be, to some extent, a modification of the musical ear. In so far as the letters are distinguished by being combinations of musical tones, the two sensibilities must be the same. But this applies only to the vowels; the consonants are discriminated by other kinds of effect. It would not be in accordance with fact to say, that a good musical ear infers a good articulate ear.

The successions of sounds, both musical and articulate, possess the quality termed Cadence or Accent. The ear remembers the cadences familiar to it, and reproduces them in vocal imitation. The brogue or accent of a province is impressed on the young ear; a large variety of cadences enters into the more elaborate training of the elocutionist. The ear for cadence may be somewhat different from, although containing points in common with, the musical and articulate ears.

24. Cohering aggregates and trains of Sight are, by pre-eminence, the material of thought, memory, and imagination.

Sensations of sight are composed of visual spectra and muscular feelings—passive feelings mixed with active.

While the separate colours and shades are acquiring ideal persistence, they are becoming associated together in aggregates and trains. We cannot produce cases of association of colours alone, or without muscular elements, but there are many instances where colour is the predominating fact. The splendours of sunrise and sunset, the succession of tints of the sky, exemplify the preponderance of colour. The variegated landscape is an aggregate of coloured masses, which may be associated in great part optically. The aspect of a city, with its streets, houses, shops, is many-coloured, and must be remembered chiefly by the help of associated colours.

On the other hand, in objects with little colour, and with sharp outlines, the muscular element predominates, as in a building or an interior, in machinery, and, most of all, in the forms and diagrams of Geometry, Architecture, Engineering, &c.

We shall illustrate the adhesiveness, first, in *Forms;* secondly, in *Coloured Surfaces.*

When the eye follows a circular form, as a ring, the effect is principally muscular. The adhesion resides in the active centres connected with the muscles of the eye. By these, we hold the figures of Geometry, the symbols of the sciences generally, outline plans of mechanical structures, the characteristic forms of all special objects. In the Fine Arts of Sculpture and Architecture, form is predominant.

There is probably a special endowment for the retention of visible forms, whose natural locality would be the active centres of vision. It would show itself in the rapid and extensive acquirement of unmeaning symbols, written characters, and skeleton outlines, as in maps and diagrams. The Chinese language is probably the extreme instance of the acquisition of forms. The memory for maps is also a trying instance. These cases require the strongest disinterested adhesion.

In the case of Scientific forms, there may enter the scientific interest, determining special concentration of mind. Such forms are comparatively few in number, but intensely important.

In regard to Artistic forms, the Artistic interest is a

prompting to mental concentration; only such as enter into Art would be specially retained. Curves, for their beauty, and certain geometric forms, for their symmetry, would be laid hold of; those that have no interest except as symbols would be disregarded.

In *Coloured Surfaces*, we suppose the colour to be the chief fact; for, although Form can never be absent, the optical adhesiveness is the essential consideration. Such are, in addition to natural scenes and prospects, highly decorated interiors, pictures, assemblies of people, the human face and figure, animals, plants, and minerals.

The endowment for discriminating and remembering Colour may well be supposed to be special and distinct. Phrenology is justified in supposing a special organ of colour. The centres in relation with the optic nerve are probably far more expanded and richer in nervous elements, in some constitutions than in others. A special retentiveness for colour is a great determining fact of character. It not only constitutes a facility in remembering scenes, pictures, and coloured objects, thus entering into the faculty of the painter and the poet: it also leads to a liking for the concrete surface of the world with all its emotions and interests, and to a disliking or revulsion from the bare and naked symbols, forms, and abstractions of science.

SENSATIONS OF DIFFERENT SENSES.

25. Our education involves various connexions among Movements, Feelings of Movement, and the Sensations of the different senses.

In the complication of actual things, the same object may operate upon several senses at once. A bell is ideally retained as a combination of touch, sound, and sight. An orange can affect all the senses.

Movements with Sensations. Our movements are extensively associated with sensations. Our various actions are instigated by sensible signs, as names or other signals; the child's early education comprises the obedience to direction or command. Animals also can take on the same acquisition. The notes of the bugle, and the signals at sea, are associated with definite movements.

Our locomotive and other movements are incessantly attended with changes of our visible environment, and become associated with these changes accordingly. Every step forward alters the visual magnitude of all objects before the eyes;

and of such as are near, in a very palpable degree. This is a principal part of our acquired perceptions of distance. (See Chap. VII.)

It was already remarked, under Associations of Movement, that there are few associations of mere movement; the sense of the effect generally intervenes and accompanies the exertion. A man digging does not mechanically put in the spade and turn it up; he, at the same time, sees and feels the results; the sight and the feeling co-operate in directing and guiding each movement, and in introducing the one that follows.

Muscular Ideas with Sensations. We may associate Ideas of Force and Movement, resulting from muscular expenditure, with Sensations. There are some interesting examples in point. We connect the weight and inertia of different kinds of material, with the visible appearance, and other sensible properties. On looking at a block of stone, at an iron bar, or a log of wood, we form a certain ideal estimate of the comparative weights, or of the muscular expenditure requisite to move, or support the several masses. This association is gained partly by our direct experience, and partly by seeing the muscular exertions of other persons; it becomes at last one of the powerful associations that enter into our ideas of external things. It is at the basis of our Architectural tastes and demands. When we see a mass of stone supported on a pedestal, we form at once an estimate of the sufficiency or insufficiency of the support, and are affected pleasantly or unpleasantly according to the estimate. By a rapid process of association, almost like an instinct, we imagine the pressure of a block of any given size; an idea of its gravitating energy is constructed out of our own experiences; and a similar idea is formed of the strength of the rope that is to hoist it up, and the waggon that is to transport it. The same feeling determines our sense of Architectural proportions; these being very different in the case of wood, of stone, and of iron; and would be modified into another shape still, if gold were the material employed. From want of familiarity with gold in masses, we should be greatly at fault in connecting the visible appearance of a block with its weight and inertia.

Sensations with Sensations. We may have as many groups of combinations as there are possible unions among our senses. Organic sensations may be associated with Tastes, Smells, Touches, Sounds, Sights; Tastes with Smells, &c.; Smells with Touches, and so on. The more interesting cases occur under the three higher senses.

Touches are associated with Sounds, when the ring of a substance suggests its surface to the touch, and *vice versâ*, as in discriminating stone, wood, glass, pottery, cloth, &c.

Touches are associated with Sights, on a very great scale. We connect with the visible appearance of every substance that we may have frequently handled, its feeling to the touch, as soft, hard, rough, smooth, as well as the tactile form and tactile magnitude.

This is the association that Berkeley principally founded upon, in explaining the acquired perceptions of Sight (see Chap. VII.). The fact itself is not to be disputed; we do acquire associations of singular firmness between visible surfaces and their tactile sensations; the cold, hard smoothness of polished marble, the roughness of the fracture of a piece of cast iron or steel, the clamminess of a lump of clay, are suggested rapidly and vividly in the case of all familiar things. And if such be the case with the strictly tactile properties (where no one contends for an instinctive conjunction), we need not wonder at the rapid and vivid suggestion of tangible resistance and magnitude. Still, as will be seen, there are other experiences required to constitute our associations of real distance with its visible signs.

Sounds are associated with Sights, on a still greater scale. Every characteristic sound emanating from an object of characteristic visible appearance, is firmly associated with that appearance. We associate the sound not merely with the sounding object, but with the distance and position of the object. (See *Hearing*, p. 56.) So that we may be said to hear distance as well as to see it; by both senses, we are made aware of the locomotive effort that would be required to traverse the interval between one distance and another.

We connect every object with its sound when struck; every instrument with its note; every animal with its cries; every human being with their voice, and even with their cough or sneeze.

Our mother tongue is, in great part, a series of associations between sounds (as names) and visible objects. The extension to written language embraces the further associations between the audible sounds and the printed characters.

26. In the association of different senses, it is to be presumed that the rapidity of the adhesive growth will vary with the adhesive quality of each of the senses.

In the absence of anything to the contrary, we must suppose that when sights and sounds are associated, the progress will depend upon the adhesiveness in sight by itself, and in sound by itself. The mother tongue will be learned with more rapidity, according as the articulate ear is good, and according as the visible associations within themselves are good. No other consideration can be assigned from our present knowledge. It does not seem that any barrier is presented to the union of sensations of different senses; the process is as easy and rapid between two, as in the sphere of one.

27. The Localization of our Bodily Feelings is an acquired perception.

Previous to experience, we do not know the locality of any bodily sensation—for example, a pressure on the shoulder or the toe. But our own body is to us an object of sense; we can see it, and move the hand over it. It is also a seat of subjective sensibilities; it undergoes changes attended with pleasure, and with pain. When we see the hand touching a part, we couple the objective or pictorial aspect with a special tactile feeling; if the hand is transferred to another part, the altered pictorial aspect is connected with the new contact. This is the beginning of our local associations with the parts of the body, and is the means of enabling us to assign the locality of any part that is occasioning a subjective feeling.

Some explanation is necessary here. How should the same pressure, causing the same feeling, be recognized sometimes in one spot, and sometimes in another? The quality of a sensation may be the same in two cases, yet we may learn to localize them differently. On this point, we can only assert the fact, and surmise, that it is physically supported by the independence of the nerves distributed over the different parts; an independence already assumed for the feeling of plurality of contacts, as described under Touch. The nerves of touch in the right forefinger are so far distinct from the nerves of the left forefinger, that a separate track or line of association can be formed between each and the movements that determine us to look to the right or to the left. We seem to have qualitative sameness of sensation with artificial or associated difference.

We are best able to localize the feelings connected with the surface, because its changes are accessible to observation. The deep-seated parts can be got at, only when they are brought into some relation with the surface; as when pressure on the stomach or the liver modifies a feeling supposed to be connected with the part; or as when local treatment soothes an irritation.

28. Our body occupies, as it were, a position between the subject mind and the object world at large. Attention to our body is an object state, but with strong subject associations.

By gazing on things external to our body, we are in a truly object attitude; by gazing on any part of the skin, we bring up subject feelings. By imagining the local appearances of a pain, we may almost realize it physically. This is one of the connexions of idea and reality, occurring in an exaggerated form under the mesmeric sleep. Mr. Braid used the fact to induce healthy actions on diseased organs. It is scarcely possible to gaze intently for a long time on any part of the body without inducing subjective feelings in reference to it; and these carry with them actual changes in the part.

29. Associated differences in sensations alike in quality may occur, not only in Touch, but also in Sight, and in Muscular Movements.

The foregoing remarks apply to Touch. The same is true of Sight. A sensation of light may be qualitatively the same as another; but, by arising through different parts of the retina, they are recognized as different; they become associated with different movements. If two twins are so alike that we cannot distinguish them, some variation is made in their dress to prevent confusion. In the same way, sensations through different parts of the retina are made distinct by their alliances. One requires an upward motion to place it in the centre of vision, another a downward; one a larger, and another a smaller sweep, to attain the same position.

As regards the muscles likewise, we have to assume a sense of difference, not due to quality, but to local seat. It may be the same as regards the feeling itself, whether we raise the right arm or the left; but the two feelings enter into distinct alliances with other feelings not the same.

ASSOCIATES WITH PLEASURE AND PAIN.

30. By means of contiguous association, states of Pleasure and Pain can, to some extent, persist, or be reproduced, without the original stimulus.

The extending of association to states of pleasure and pain, or states of feeling, or emotion generally, must render it a great power as regards our happiness. By a reference to the facts, we can ascertain how far the principle operates in this direction. A familiar example is furnished by our likings for objects and places, after long connexion with them.

The pleasures of the Senses are usually reflected by things that are their causes, or by certain regular accompaniments. Thus we connect the enjoyment of exercise with our instruments of sport or gymnastic; the pleasures of repose with an easy chair, a sofa, or a bed; and the pleasure of riding with a horse and carriage. The sight of food, and its preparation, recalls something of the delight of eating; the scantily indulged child is fascinated by the mere view of the pastry-cook's window. The representation of fragrant flowers gives an agreeable recollection of the fragrance.

The pains of the Senses could be still more decisively appealed to. All objects that have severely pained us are painful to encounter. It takes a certain effort, to overcome the repugnance to the instruments of a severe surgical operation.

It cannot be contended that such associated pleasures and pains are individually of any great force, as compared with the originals; the fractional value of each echo is but small. But a total result, very far from insignificant, may be gained, by accumulating around us a great many things associated with our pleasures, and reflecting a number of our happy moments. The sportsman's trophies, the traveller's curiosities, the naturalist's collections made by himself, the student's prizes, the engineer's models, are able to revive an occasional glow of foregone excitement.

31. The law of this association may be assumed to accord with the case of different senses (§ 26). We have already assumed that there may be a good, or a bad, memory for pleasure as such, and for pain as such; while, in regard to special modes of pleasure and pain, as in the several senses, the retentiveness will vary with the goodness of the sense in other respects.

We have formerly seen that a full and accurate memory for pleasure and for pain is the intellectual basis, both of prudence as regards self, and of sympathy as regards others. This may be a general feature of the character, applicable to pleasures and pains as such. Still, we must suppose the general power greatly modified according to the class or local origin. A high endowment for colour will naturally include the retentiveness for the pleasures and the pains of colour. So, the circumstances that direct attention upon any sense will impress, not only its intellectual elements, but its pleasures and pains.

The revival of a foregone pleasure by force of memory must be measured by the amount of change it makes on the present condition of the mind, as otherwise occasioned. In a happy mood, we are liable to happy recollections, and repel the opposite; but in this case, the pleasurable state represents the present influence, and not the past.

32. The Special Emotions, by being directed habitually on the same object, become Affections.

After the feeling of Love or Tenderness has been often aroused in connexion with the same person, a habitual or customary regard is induced, of greater power than the original attraction. The memories of the past then add their power to heighten the present impression. This influence, however, is chiefly manifested in neutralizing the deadening influence of familiarity. The recollected warmth of past moments keeps up a glow, when the present stimulation has lost its influence. Past associations of tender feeling will even overcome causes of positive dislike.

So, Anger repeated generates hatred. Fear may take on a habitual, and thence more aggravated form. The Egotistic passions are notably strengthened, after having often run in the same channel without opposition. The religious sentiment is converted into an affection, by being made frequently to arise in connexion with the object of worship.

33. The Emotions may spread themselves over collateral and indifferent objects.

We have here a more testing case of association. The accidental connexions with the objects of our love, anger, fear, egotism, suffice to recall the feelings, and have a value on that account. Hence tokens of friendship, relics, places, acquire a deep hold of our affections.

This is carried to the utmost in religion. Holy places, symbols, rites, formalities, language, reflect and magnify the feelings towards the main object of worship; and the difficulty ever has been to keep them from wholly usurping, by their sensuous facilities, the place of the unseen Deity.

Human authority avails itself of such associations, in order to extend its influence. Official robes and symbols, a ceremonial of obeisance and deference, solemnities in the investiture to office, forms observed in degrading and punishing, have the effect of diffusing the respect for authority in civil society. The Romans, who were the greatest inventors in the substance of law, were also the most attentive to its forms; such attention being partly the cause, and partly the effect, of their great regard to authority in the worst of times.

Those formalities that have an intrinsic expressiveness, as bending, prostration, passing under the yoke, are necessarily more impressive than what is intrinsically unmeaning.

34. Association transfers the interest of an End of pursuit to the Means.

The familiar example of this is *money*. Allied in the first instance with the delights that it obtains, and the relief from numerous pains, it becomes at last an object of affection in itself, and is preferred, in its unemployed state, to all purchasable gratifications.

The circumstances that favour the transference are such as these:—Money is a tangible, measurable, permanent possession; the pleasures obtained by it being often fugitive, are apt to leave a feeling of regret, as if they had cost too much. The mind easily learns to derive more satisfaction from the permanent possibility, than from the perishing actuality; especially such minds as are more susceptible to fear for the future than to present enjoyment.

The influence of early penury and privation in disposing to avarice is of itself an example of associated feeling, as well as a contributing cause to the love of money unspent.

The accessions of distinction and power, attached to the possession of wealth, necessarily enrich the agreeable associaciations connected with it.

The feeling of Property, in its full comprehension, contains a mass of blended sentiment, and of piled-up associations, that can scarcely be tracked out in their detail. The things that serve so many of the primary uses of life, become also the subject of mingled pride and affection. Property in land has charms of its own; it is an impressive object to the eye and to the mind, and involves both present influence, and the memory of ancient privileges. The possession of a spot of land is the most powerful of all known motives to industry.

Another example of means converted into ends by transferred feeling is the attachment to *forms* of business, as book-keeping, legal and technical formalities, even after they have ceased to answer their ends. This is an element in the conservation of laws and formalities whose spirit has evaporated.

The regard to *truth* is, and ought to be, an all-powerful sentiment, from its being entwined in a thousand ways with the welfare of human society. We are not to be surprised, if an element of such importance as a means, should be often regarded as an absolute end, to be pursued irrespective of consequences, whether near or remote.

35. Many objects of Fine Art derive their charm from associations.

Fine Art contains effects intrinsically pleasing, as sweet and harmonious sounds; colours and their harmonies; curved lines; proportions in general.

Other effects are due to association with pleasing qualities. Thus, the hues and complexion of health are not the most pleasing colours intrinsically. There is nothing in breadth of chest, development of muscle, size of bone, to give a primitive delight in connexion with the manly figure; but the connexion of these qualities with physical power gives them an adventitious charm. A large cranial development would not be interesting in itself; viewed as disproportion, it might be even unpleasing But as indicating mental power it is agreeable to behold.

The lustre of a polished surface is intrinsically pleasing; there is a farther pleasure when it is connected with ease in machinery, or with cleanliness in household management.

The celebrated theory of Alison consisted in attributing all the pleasures of Beauty, to associations with primary modes of the agreeable; which primary modes, would of course not themselves be admitted into the æsthetic circle. The following out of this theory led the author to collect examples of borrowed or associated emotions, although in many of his instances, primitive effects could be assigned.

The following are some of his illustrations for the Sublime. 'All sounds are in general SUBLIME, which are associated with ideas of great Power or Might; the Noise of a Torrent; the Fall of a Cataract; the Uproar of a Tempest; the Explosion of Gunpowder; the Dashing of the Waves, &c.' Most of these sounds, however, produce a strong effect by their intensity and volume, without regard to what they suggest. More in point are the following. 'That the Notes or Cries of some animals are Sublime, every one knows: the Roar of the Lion, the Growling of Bears, the Howling of Wolves, the Scream of the Eagle. In all these cases, those are the notes of animals remarkable for their strength, and formidable for their ferocity.' As illustrations of Beauty, he gives the following:—' The Bleating of a Lamb is beautiful in a fine day in spring; the Lowing of a Cow at a distance, amid the scenery of a pastoral landscape in summer. The Call of a Goat among rocks is strikingly beautiful, as expressing wildness and independence. The Hum of the Beetle is beautiful on a fine summer evening, as appearing to suit the stillness and repose of that pleasing season. The twitter of the swallow is beautiful in the morning, and seems to be expressive of the cheerfulness of that time.'

36. The Language of the Feelings, both in their natural manifestations, and in their verbal expression, has to be acquired.

The meaning of the smile and the frown is learnt in infancy by observing what circumstances they go along with. The various modifications of the features, tones, and gestures for pleasure, pain, love, anger, fear, wonder, are connected with known occasions that show what they mean. Animals understand this language. There is a certain intrinsic efficacy in some modes of expression, as when soft and gentle tones are used for affection, and harsh, emphatic utterances for anger; but the play of the features has no original meaning, it must be understood by experience.

Verbal expression greatly enlarges the compass of the language of the feelings. Every emotion has its characteristic forms of speech, expressing its shades with very great delicacy. Poets, who have to depict and excite the emotions, require an unusual command of these forms, and of all the images and associated circumstances that have the power to resuscitate the varieties of feeling.

37. The Signs of Happiness in others have a cheering effect on ourselves.

It is a part of our pleasures to see happy beings around us, and especially those that have the power of expressing their feelings in a lively manner. Children and animals, in their happy moods, impart a certain tone of gaiety to a spectator. On the other hand, the wretched, the downcast, and the querulous, are apt to chill and depress those in their company. There is a satisfaction in merely beholding, or even in imagining, the appearances and accompaniments of superior happiness, which probably accounts in part for the disposition to do homage to the wealthy, the powerful, the renowned, and the successful among mankind.

38. The happiness of our later life is in great part made up of the pleasurable memories of early years.

The early period of life, so favourable to acquirement generally, is adapted to the storing up of pleasures and pains. The same pleasure, happening in youth and in middle age, will not be equally remembered as a cheering association in advanced life. The joys of early years have thus an additional value. A pinched, severe, and ascetic bringing-up will sensibly depress the tone of the whole future life; scarcely any amount of subsequent good fortune will suffice to redeem the waste.

39. In the Moral Sentiment, association counts for a share, although the extent of the influence is variously estimated.

It is only in accordance with all the other facts of associated feelings, that if a certain kind of conduct, say theft, or evil speaking, is constantly made the subject of punishment, censure, or disapprobation, an associative growth will be formed between the conduct and the infliction of pain; and the individual will recoil from it with all the repugnance acquired during this conjunction between it and painful feelings. The general principle is confirmed by the actual facts; those that have received a careful moral education are almost as superior, in their moral conduct, to the offspring of dissolute parents, as the educated man is to the uneducated in any other respect.

The conditions of progress in these moral acquirements are worthy of being specified. The natural and predisposing endowments are the good retentiveness for pleasure and pain generally, constituting the natural gift of Prudence, and the tendency to enter into the pleasures and pains of others (called Sympathy). To these must be added, as a negative condition, the moderate degree of the counter impulses (which will be specified in another place). General retentiveness would apply to this acquirement. Repetition, or assiduous iteration, must co-operate under circumstances favourable to the impressiveness of the lesson: which circumstances vary according as the associations are intended to be chiefly of fear, or of love. Moreover, for moral discipline as for everything else, a certain portion of the life and the thoughts must be left free from other pressing cares and acquisitions.

The association between objects and feelings also enables feelings to bring up their associated objects. This bond, however, rarely operates singly; an emotion, as love, anger, or fear, is not usually associated with one object in particular; when it is so, it is able to suggest the object. Most generally, the association with feeling is one determining link among others, in a compound association.

ASSOCIATIONS OF VOLITION.

40. In Volition, there is involved a process of contiguous association between specific actions and states of feeling.

This is the third element in the growth of the Will, as already described; Spontaneity and Self-conservation being the two other elements. The law of Self-conservation would determine the continuance of an action that feeds a pleasure, and the abatement of an action concurring with pain; but does not enable us to begin a specific movement that would bring pleasure or remove pain. This is believed to be at first a fortuitous concurrence, made to adhere after a certain amount of repetition.

When the mature will is regarded in its whole compass, it contains a wide range of successive growths, the earliest being attended with the greatest difficulties. These will be traced, once for all, in the department of the Will.

NATURAL OBJECTS.

41. Our permanent Recollections, or Ideas, of the Concrete objects of external nature, consist of associated sensible qualities.

The concrete combinations that we call natural objects, in most instances, affect a plurality of senses. The distant starry sphere, reveals itself only to sight; but all terrestrial things, in some form or other, appeal to several senses. A piece of quartz, besides being seen, has a characteristic touch; an orange has taste and odour in addition.

The present case, therefore, merely applies the association of a plurality of senses to the individual things making up the object world (the conjunctions or groupings of things will be viewed separately). The complete image of a mineral, plant, or animal, is the enduring association of all its sensible impressions, the lead being taken by sight.

The conditions of rapid and abundant acquirement in this region of things are,—the adhesiveness of the senses, and chiefly of sight, and the circumstances that determine attention or concentration of mind.

42. The Naturalist mind represents the maximum of disinterested associations.

The purpose of the Naturalist is, not selective, but exhaustive; whatever be the department that he applies himself to, he notices every species belonging to it. In order to lighten the load of detail, and for other reasons, he studies classification and orderly method; but, notwithstanding the utmost economy, his mind must retain a vast number of the sensible aggregates constituting the specific objects of the natural world. He must possess a high degree of sensible, and especially visual, retentiveness; his turn of mind must be objective, or towards the exercise of the senses; and his life must be largely engrossed by the exercise of observation. He must not have any strong emotional likings, of the nature of preference; having to give an account of everything that exists, because it exists, his main delight should be to attain impartiality and exhaustive completeness; he should be especially charmed by the arts of classification and method adapted to this end.

43. In minds generally, the associations of natural objects are generally ruled by the feelings.

Next to frequency, or familiarity of encounter, and often before it, in point of associating efficacy, is the interest awakened in objects either by their striking qualities, or by their uses in the economy of life. The one is the artistic preference, and the other the industrial. The gems, the more attractive flowers, shrubs, and trees, the animals distinguished for their imposing qualities, are singled out for recollection, in preference to the indifferent specimens of each kind. And still more universally stimulating to the attention is the influence of our wants, uses and conveniences, our occupations and pursuits.

NATURAL AND HABITUAL CONJUNCTIONS.

44. The things habitually or frequently conjoined in our experience are conjoined in our recollection.

The things about us that maintain fixed places and relations become connected in idea, as they are in reality; and the mind thus reflects the habitual environment. The house we live in, with its furniture and arrangements, the street, town, or rural scene that we encounter daily, by their incessant iteration, cohere into abiding recollections, any one part easily bringing all the rest to the mind's view. Our knowledge of such familiar objects is made up of the connexion of each with its associated objects. Our knowledge of a man or woman includes the external circumstances constantly conjoined with him or her—locality, family, and occupation. The conditions favouring the adhesiveness are Repetition and special Interest in what is near ourselves.

For the easy retention of the variegated imagery of the world, the prime requisite is powerful retentiveness for Colour. This gives to the mind a pictorial character, a grasp of the Concrete of nature, with all the emotional interests thence arising. It is required by the Naturalist, and is indispensable to the Painter and to the Poet. Also, in large operations, involving the external world, as in the military art, engineering, the laying out of towns, plantations and gardens, the visual endowment is the predominating circumstance; while the optical, or colour element, is still more important than the element of form.

45. Among aggregates or conjunctions, may be included Maps, Diagrams, and Pictorial Representations.

These artificial conjunctions are a large part of our higher knowledge; they bring to view, by a medium of representation, what we have no access to, in the reality. The retentiveness for them follows the same laws, and is influenced by the same conditions. According as they depend upon light and shade and colour, on the one hand, or upon outline form, on the other, they exercise the optical, or the muscular adhesiveness of the sight. When the complicacy is great, as in a map, or a drawing, the varieties of light and colour are the main fact; in mere skeleton diagrams, visible form is the principal. The special interest varies according to circumstances. To the mind of Dr. Arnold, a map had intense fascination; it was suggestive of the multifarious human interest of his recollections of history.

SUCCESSIONS.

46. The phenomena of the world may be divided into the Co-existing and the Successive, although, so far as the mind is concerned, the generic fact is Succession.

If we except such cases as—complex and coinciding muscular movements, the concurrence of sensations, through different senses, at the same moment, and our mixed or blended emotions,—our mental perceptions are all successive; we must shift the attention from point to point in viewing a landscape, and must make a corresponding series of jumps, even in the recollection. Co-existence, as we have seen, is an artificial growth, formed from a certain peculiar class of mental successions. The subjective mind, in its power of attention, is single and confined; it overtakes the object world, only by movement in time.

Still, after Co-existence has been established as something distinct, we recognize, as its contrast, phenomena of Succession. All such phenomena, if by their uniformity or regularity, they are iterated to the view, give rise to a corresponding association in our ideas.

Successions of Cycle. The successions that perform a cycle, as day and night, the moon's phases, the seasons of the year, the routine of occupations and professions—are engrained on our recollection, and make part of our expectation of the future.

Successions of Evolution. These are chiefly exemplified in living beings. It is the very nature of organized life to evolve itself through a series of changes; and this series, which is characteristic for different species, enters into our knowledge of living beings. To know a plant we must know it at every stage. A certain number of observations made upon each kind gives coherence in the mind to the successive aspects. Wherever we have any special interest, as in farming, gardening, rearing stock, we become acquainted with every phase in the order of development. The evolution of the human being is impressed in our mind by repetition, and by the quickening stimulus of our interest in humanity. Evolution farther applies to the course of disease, to any long operation, as a process of law, and to the history of nations. When there is a slight uncertainty in the issue, the additional interest of plot may be roused.

Apart from the special interest in the unwinding of the future, the associations of evolution are, in principle, not materially different from the associations of still life. As regards both Cycles and Evolutions, the laws or conditions of adhesion are the same as has been repeatedly stated above, in connexion with the aspects of the outer world. A more definite peculiarity belongs to the successions next to be named.

Cause and Effect. Leaving out of view, for the present, strict scientific causation, we may advert to what is commonly regarded as cause and effect, namely, a sudden and impressive change; as when a blow is followed by a noise and a fracture. A large part of our knowledge of nature is made up of these successions.

According to the general principle of Relativity, or Change, we are impressed in proportion to the intensity and the suddenness of any effect. So marked and powerful are some effects, that one experience is remembered for life. The explosion of gunpowder, the cutting away of a support to some heavy body, the extinction of a life,—are so pungent and exciting, that a second occurrence is unnecessary to stamp the fact on the memory. The order of nature, in so far as composed of these more sudden effects, is rapidly learnt.

The associations of things with their *uses*, or practical applications, involves the stimulus of cause and effect, together with the farther interest of utility. A lever in itself is an unexciting visible object; in operation, it produces the excitement of change, and the gratification arising from a useful end. Furniture, tools, and implements generally, are, in their ideas, aggregates of visible appearance and tangible qualities, together with their superadded appearances when in use.

The scientific properties of objects, brought out by experiment, or observed in the course of nature, often involve the most startling effects, and are thereby quickly impressed upon the mind. The distinguishing property of oxygen, to support combustion, is for ever remembered by means of the experiment of combustion in the pure gas. The properties of a salt that affect the senses strongly, are learnt at once. The decomposition of light by the prism is one of those startling appearances that the stupidest person will remember through the mere force of the sensation.

The Effects produced by our own agency are additionally impressive. The antecedent in this case is our expended energy, whose familiarity makes it the type of all causation. There is nothing so well remembered by us, as the results of our own actions; we possess the cause in ourselves, and there is occasionally added the charm of pride or complacency. Hence, in studying natural processes, we succeed best by making the observations and experiments for ourselves.

The most impressive part of our knowledge of living beings —men and animals—consists in seeing them, now as acting, and now as acted on. The effects that they produce upon outward things, and the effects that outward agents produce upon them, are remembered by us under the stimulus of movement and change. There is a highly complex interest in watching the movements of our fellow men ; the mere excitement of change and effect is a part of the case; our sympathies, antipathies, fears, admiration, and other emotions, lend impressiveness to the display. Thus, what may be called the *object* part of our knowledge of human nature, depends, in the first place, on our visible or pictorial retentiveness, and, in the next place, on our susceptibility to the various feelings awakened by the manifestations of humanity.

MECHANICAL ACQUISITIONS.

We have now touched on the chief classes of things associated under Contiguity. To give the principles in another light, we will allude to the recognized departments of acquisition.

Under Mechanical Acquisitions, we include the whole of handicraft industry and skill, as well as the use of the bodily members in the more obvious and universal actions of daily life. Whether for self-preservation and bodily comfort, for industry, or for sport and recreation, we have to be educated into a number of bodily aptitudes.

47. In Mechanical Acquirements, the conditions are : (1) The endowments of the Active Organs ; (2) the delicacy of the Sense concerned ; and (3) the special Interest.

(1) The endowments of the Active Organs are, first, mere muscular vigour and strength, which we must assume as a requisite, if only as bringing about persistency in exertion. Secondly, we may assume as a separate fact, involving the nerve centres, great Spontaneity, or the disposition to put forth muscular activity, which does not always go along with muscular development. Thirdly, and most vital of all, is the still deeper peculiarity shown in the Perception of Graduated Muscular expenditure and the retentiveness for muscular groupings.

The first and second elements by themselves would determine the Active Temperament—the disposition and avidity for bodily occupation, and the consequent readiness to apply to all pursuits giving scope to this prompting. The third peculiarity would most specifically contribute to the rapidity of acquirement in the skilled exercise of the bodily organs.

(2) The delicacy of the special Sense concerned in the art,

CONDITIONS OF MECHANICAL ACQUIREMENTS.

is of equal, if not of greater, importance. If it is to produce effects of tactile delicacy,—as in surface polish, or soft consistency,—a nice touch is requisite; if the work is judged by colour, the optical part of sight is demanded; if to produce musical or articulate effects, the ear is involved.

No amount of flexibility or compass of the active organ will enable us to rise above our discrimination of the effect produced; and an inferior flexibility will be greatly extended by the effort to comply with a delicate perception. Moreover, the associations of mechanical skill are, as has been seen, a mixture of grouped muscular movements and situations with sensible impressions; and the importance of the sensible part has been shown by the failure of the other connexions on its being withdrawn.

(3) The special Interest in the work may flow from various sources. The possession of the active endowments is an inducement to exercise them, and all exercise within the scope of one's powers is agreeable; while superiority is still more agreeable. Then, as regards the Sense : a sensibility highly developed, say for colour, is a source of pleasure, as well as of discrimination. Besides these modes of interest, growing out of the possession of the natural aptitudes, there may be adventitious sources. It not unfrequently happens that a charm attaches to something not within the compass of our aptitudes. We may have sufficient musical ear to enjoy music, but not to acquire the musical art; and the same with colour. We then have a sort of admiration for a power that gives us a pleasure, and that we do not possess. Finally, whatever circumstances give an artificial value to mechanical acquirements, incline our devotion to them, and so facilitate our progress.

48. In the conduct of mechanical training, regard is to be had to the vigour and freshness of the system ; and the exercises must be continued long enough to bring the energies into full play.

The physical vigour and freshness, both of the moving organs, and of the senses, being a prime requisite, mechanical drill is most effectual in the early hours of the day, and after the refreshment of meals. The exercise should be continued long enough to draw the circulation and the nervous agency copiously towards the organs exercised; at the outset of an operation, there is both a stiffness of the parts and a feeling of fatigue, both transitory; the blood as yet has not found its way to the members engaged. When, at a later stage, genuine fatigue comes on, the exercise should cease; the cohesive power is then at a minimum. In the army, recruits are drilled three times a-day—early morning, after breakfast, and after dinner—for an hour and a half to two hours each time. The apprentice at a trade learns by fits and snatches, and mixes up the performance of work with the acquisition of new powers. The pains special to the learner are of two sorts—fatigue of the attention, and the exhaustion caused by repeated trials and failures.

ACQUISITIONS IN LANGUAGE.

49. First, Oral Language. This acquisition involves an active endowment—Articulation by the Voice; and a sense—the Ear.

The beginnings of articulation belong to the early stage of the voluntary acquirements. The child must first arrive at the power of articulating single letters and syllables; these are then united into words; and words are conjoined into sentences.

As in the case of the Active organs for mechanical acquisition generally, we must assume as the conditions of articulate cohesiveness, (1) the muscular vigour of the larynx and associated members, (2) the vocal spontaneity, and (3) most important of all, the special discrimination and retentiveness attaching to the vocal movements, connected, we may suppose, with the high organization of the allied motor centres.

Next, is the delicacy of the Ear for Articulate Effects, implying both discrimination and retentiveness, the first being accepted as a criterion of the second. This endowment may be looked upon as related to the special nerve centres of hearing (on the passive or ingoing side of the brain).

When these two natural endowments stand high, the acquisition of words and of verbal sequences will proceed with proportionate rapidity. If there be a good general adhesiveness in addition, the progress will be still greater. Moreover, language is the acquisition of words, not by themselves, but in association with things. Hence, the next condition :—

50. As language is an association of names with objects or meanings, we must include, as a condition, the law of heterogeneous adhesion.

That is to say, we are to look to the goodness of the associations *(inter se)* of speech on the one hand, and of the objects named on the other, as formerly explained. We learn much sooner the names of things that impress us, than of those that do not. Each man's vocabulary is made up, by preference, of the names of the objects that interest himself; the Naturalist knows more names of his own department than of other departments.

51. Besides the mere vocabulary, Language includes a great number of definite arrangements of words, with a view to its various ends, and subject to grammatical and other laws.

We have not only to name things, but to make affirmations about them, and, in other ways to unite or compose consecutive statements. These forms may be exceedingly numerous and varied for the same meaning or purpose. Their ready acquisition is almost exclusively governed by the circumstances of pure verbal adhesion. The fluent orator, the diffuse and illustrative writer, the poet, must excel in mere verbal abundance, irrespective of the limits of the subject matter.

52. While the acquisition of language must depend, in the first instance, upon the opportunities of hearing and speaking, the effect of Repetition is greatly modified by special interest.

Of the mass of language that passes through the ear, only a selection is retained, and that selection, although partly depending on iteration, is also greatly dependent on our interest in the subjects, and our liking for special modes of describing the same subject.

A man's vocabulary will show who he has kept company with, what books he has studied, what departments he knows; it will show farther his predominating tastes, emotions, or likings. We see in Milton, for example, his peculiar erudition, and also his strong fascination for whatever was large, lofty, vast, powerful, or sublime. In Shakespeare, the adhesiveness for language as such, was so great, that it seemed to include every species of terms in nearly equal proportions. Only a very narrow examination enables us to detect his preferences, or his lines of study, and veins of more special interest.

Many terms and forms of language are permanently engrained by some purely accidental concentration of the mind, or awakening of attention. Thus, when we happen to have felt very much the want of a word, before being told it, the impression is a durable one. Any interesting circumstance attending the utterance of a phrase stamps it for ever. The emphasis of a great orator, or actor, will impress his peculiarity of language.

53. As regards Elocution, the powers of the voice are subservient to the Ear for Cadence.

The Ear for Cadence is probably a sense partaking both of the musical and the articulate ear. Either of these alone, in the greatest perfection, with the other deficient, would not suffice for the actor or the elocutionist. The fine sense of cadence stores the mind with many strains or melodies of utterance, which the orator reproduces in his oral delivery, choosing, if need be, the words that give most scope to the melody.

The purest exercise of verbal adhesiveness is seen in vocal mimicry, which demands the endowments of voice, articulate ear, and ear for cadence, with little besides.

54. Written language appeals to the sense of Arbitrary Visible Forms.

Written symbols depend for their adhesiveness on the muscular endowment of the eye and its related nerve centres. A well-known aid to verbal memory is to write with one's own hand what has to be remembered. The effect of this is not simply to add a new line of adhesion, the arm and finger recollections—although we might remember by these—but to impress the forms upon the eye, through the concentrated attention of the act of copying.

55. Short modes of acquiring languages have been often sought; but there are no rules special to language. Any undue stimulus of the attention to one thing is at the expense of something else.

Health, regularity, method, the absence of distractions, are the conditions favourable to all acquisition; granting these, each mind has a certain amount of adhesive aptitude, which may be distributed in one way or in another, but cannot be added to. A language involves a certain definite number of adhesive growths, drawing upon the adhesive capability to a proportionate degree. What is spent upon that must be taken from something else. It will afterwards be seen, that acquisition is economized by the detection of similarities; and this has a special application to the study of languages that are cognate to one another. It is now the custom for good teachers of the classical, as well as of the continental, tongues, to lay open the deeper affinities with our own, so as thereby to promote the memory of the vocables.

56. A good verbal adhesiveness is of value in the memory of knowledge or information conveyed in language.

The repetition of speeches, poetry, &c., by rote is an exercise of the verbal memory. Sir Walter Scott had this power, although doubtless it was greatest where the subject inspired his feelings. Macaulay was distinguished by his verbal memory. Such men, by their memory for words, remembered also the information attached to the words. In the extreme cases of this endowment, the memory of an exposition or discourse is consistent with a total ignorance of the meaning.

RETENTIVENESS IN SCIENCE.

57. Knowledge, as Science, is liable, in a greater or less degree, to be clothed in artificial and uninteresting symbols, in which guise it has to be held in the mind.

Familiar and matter-of-fact knowledge may be embraced under the sensible and concrete forms of nature: the rising of the sun is a phenomenon of visible succession. But in Astronomy, the gorgeous march of the heavenly bodies appears as a mass of algebraical calculations.

58. Sciences are divided into Object Sciences—those of external nature, and Subject Sciences, or those relating to mind.

The Object Sciences range between the most Concrete, as Natural History, and the most Abstract, as Mathematics.

In the more Concrete and Experimental Sciences, as the Natural History group (Mineralogy, Botany, Zoology, &c.), Geography, Anatomy, Chemistry, Heat, Electricity,—the actual appearances to the senses constitute a large part of the subject matter; hence in them, the Concrete mind (whose starting point is Colour) will be at home. The number or detail of the visible aspects is such as to need this endowment. Still, as sciences, they involve generalization and general notions, and cannot be divorced from the arbitrary symbolism or machinery suited to the high generalities; hence they may be regarded as the mixed type of Science. The pure type is seen in the next class.

The Abstract Sciences are Mathematics, the mathematical parts of Natural Philosophy, much of Chemistry and Physiology, and the more technical parts of the other Concrete Sciences. These, when in character, are represented to the mind by numbers, by line diagrams, by symbols and signs, most frequently adopted from the alphabet, but united in unfamiliar and repulsive combinations; while many of the generalities are expressed in ordinary language, but in the most abstract terms of language.

As mere sense presentation, this machinery is laid hold of by the eye for form reposing on the muscular retentiveness of vision. It is, as it were, a variety of written language, also named orally so as to obtain a concurring hold on the ear. The interest of colour is set aside; the forms have no æsthetic charm. The motive that quickens the natural adhesiveness of the eye for forms, must be some extraneous interest.

That interest is the interest of Truth in its comprehensiveness or generality. This is the inducement to lay up in the mind uninteresting forms, and to endure the labour attendant on abstract notions and reasonings.

59. The Subject Sciences, those of Mind proper, are grounded on self-consciousness, or introspective attention.

Although the science of mind includes many phenomena of an Object character,—namely, the bodily manifestations of mind, and the actions of living beings, as prompted by their feelings,—yet the essential properties of mind are known only in each one's self-consciousness.

There being no special medium of observation for the phenomena of mind, like the eye, the ear, or the touch, for the departments of the object world, we must follow a different course in endeavouring to assign the special attitude for discriminating and retaining the self-conscious states generally.

60. The special circumstances favouring the accumulation of knowledge in regard to mental, or subject states, are the Absence, or moderate pressure, of Object regards, and Interest in the department.

As we cannot appeal to a positive endowment, a mental eye, analogous to the bodily eye for colour, we may suppose that the waking consciousness, being divided between Object and Subject regards, may in each person incline more

CONDITIONS OF SUBJECTIVE ACQUIREMENTS.

to one than to the other. Given a certain native power of intellect, the direction taken by it, will determine the intellectual character. If the Object regards are exclusive or overpowering, the knowledge of the Subject, as such, will be at its lowest ebb.

The circumstances favouring the Objective attention can be assigned, with great probability, and their remission would therefore account for the Subjective attention. These objective circumstances are, first, great spontaneous muscular activity in all its forms, and next, a high development of the senses most allied with object properties, as sight, touch, and hearing. Where the forces of the system are profusely determined towards bodily energies, the character is rendered pre-eminently objective; whereas, not only persons differently constituted, but the same persons under advancing years, illness, and confinement of the energies, are thrown more upon self-consciousness, and exhibit the consequences of this attitude, in greater knowledge of the feelings, more sympathy with others, and an ethical or moralizing tendency. Again, as regards the Object senses, a strong susceptibility to colour, or to music, or to tactile properties, operates in the direction of the object regards; if these sensibilities are only average, or below average, in a mind of great general powers, a large share of attention will be given to subject states. On the other extreme, great organic sensibility inclines the regards to the subject-self.

61. In order to indicate the medium, or organ, of mental study, Reid and Stewart designated a faculty for that purpose, under the name 'Consciousness.' Hamilton spoke of the same power as the 'Presentative Faculty' for Self.

'Reflexion' had been previously used by Locke, to mean the source of our knowledge of the Subject world; the name, however, was not well chosen. The word 'Consciousness' is preferable; but if consciousness be comprehensively applied to the Object as well as to the Subject regards, the qualified form 'Self-consciousness' is still more suitable; it is also justified by common usage.

Hamilton calls the first source of our knowledge of facts, the faculty of Presentation. The Senses are the Presentative medium for the object world; Self-consciousness is the Presentation of the subject world.

BUSINESS, OR PRACTICAL LIFE.

62. The Education of the higher Industry, as opposed to mere handicraft, varies with the different departments. Among the elements involved, we may specify (1) an acquaintance with Material forms and properties, (2) certain technical Formalities akin to science, and (3) a practical knowledge of Human beings.

(1) The knowledge of a certain class of natural properties is involved in the various industrial arts,—in Agriculture, Manufactures, and Commerce. This is not essentially distinct from scientific knowledge, although differently selected and circumscribed. The scientific attribute, generality, is not so much aimed at, as precision or certainty in the particular applications. The steel-worker must have a minute acquaintance with the properties of steel; the cotton-spinner must know all the shades and varieties of the material.

(2) The formalities of book-keeping, and the modes of reckoning money transactions, are of the nature of arbitrary forms, like Arithmetic and Mathematics.

(3) In many practical departments, as statesmanship, oratory, teaching, &c., human beings are the material, and the knowledge of them, in the practical shape, is a prime requisite. The same knowledge is of avail to the employer of workmen, and to the trader who has to negotiate in the market with other human beings.

The comprehensive Interest in the present case is worldly means, which is a far higher spur to attention than truth. There are special likings for special avocations, owing to the incidents of each suiting different individualities. Another biassing circumstance is the greater honour attached to certain professions.

There is a close relation, in point of mental aptitude, between the higher walks of material Industry and the Concrete or Experimental Sciences; and between the formal departments, as Law and Mathematics. The management of human beings would depend upon the aptitude for the subject sciences.

ACQUISITIONS IN THE FINE ARTS.

63. Fine Art constructions are intended to give a certain species of pleasure, named the pleasure of Beauty, Taste, or Æsthetic emotion.

CONDITIONS OF FINE ART ACQUIREMENTS.

The usually recognized Fine Arts are Architecture, Sculpture, Painting, Poetry, Dramatic display, Refined Address, Dancing, Music. Their common end is refined pleasure, although their means or instrumentality is different. They are divided between the Eye and the Ear, the two higher senses. Poetry and Acting combine both.

64. The most general conditions of acquisition in Fine Art are (1) Mechanical Aptitude, (2) Adhesiveness for the Subject-matter of the Art, and (3) Artistic sensibility.

(1) In those Arts where the artist is a mechanical workman, he requires corresponding Active endowments. The singer, the actor, the orator, need powers of voice (strength, spontaneity, and the condition that determines alike discrimination and retentiveness): the actor and orator are farther in want of corresponding powers of feature and gesture. The instrumental performer of music, the painter, and the sculptor, are workers with the hand. The architect and poet are exempted from the present condition.

(2) An adhesiveness for the Subject or Material of the Art is of consequence as storing the mind with available recollections and forms. The painter and poet should have extensive memories for the pictorial in nature, as mere visible display, without regard to beauty in the first instance. The poet should have, in addition, a mind well stored with vocables, and their melodious and metrical combinations. The actor should have an eye and memory for gestures. The musician would derive advantage from an adhesiveness for sounds as such.

(3) The Artistic feeling is the guide to the employment of these powers and resources, and the motive for concentrating attention upon such objects as gratify it. The Artist must have a special and distinguishing sensibility for the proper effects of his art; proportions in Architecture, fine curves and groupings in Sculpture, colour harmonies in Painting, melody in Music, and so on. To have a large command of material, without artistic selection is to fail in the proper sphere of art; a pictorial mind, without æsthetic feeling, might make a naturalist or a geographer, but not a painter or a poet. The profuse command of original conceptions was apparent in Bacon, but not a poet's delicacy in applying them.

HISTORY AND NARRATIVE.

65. The successions of events and transactions in human life, remembered and related, make History.

The adhesion for witnessed or narrated events is often looked upon as a characteristic exhibition of memory. Bacon, in dividing human knowledge, according to our faculties, assigned History to Memory, Philosophy to Reason, Poetry to Imagination.

66. Transactions witnessed impress themselves as Sensations, principally of Sight and of Sound, and as Actions, when the spectator is also an agent.

A pageant, ceremony, or other pictorial display commends itself to the pictorial memory. Most active demonstrations are accompanied, more or less, with effects of sound; human agency is usually attended with the exercise of speech.

Historical transactions have an interest with human beings generally, although with some more than others. Hence the memory for witnessed events, being the result of a stimulated attention, is usually good.

Sometimes a single transaction is, in its minutest details, remembered for life. This is owing partly to the length of time occupied in attending to it, partly to the interest excited, and partly to the frequent mental repetition and verbal narration afterwards.

67. Transactions narrated obtain the aid of the Verbal memory.

A narrative is a complex stream of imagery and language. In so far as we can realize the picture of the events, we connect the succession pictorially; in so far as we remember the flow of words, we retain it verbally. Probably, in most cases, the memory is formed now by one bond, now by another; different minds portioning out the recollection differently between the two.

OUR PAST LIFE.

68. The complex current of each one's existence is made up of all our Actions, Sensations, Emotions, Thoughts, as they happened.

Our own actions are retained in various shapes.

(1) Inasmuch as they produce a constantly altered spectacle about us, they form alliances with our sensations. A walk in the country, although a fact of energy or activity, is remembered as a series of pictorial aspects. The same is true of our executed work; an artist's finished picture is the embodiment of his labour for a length of time, and the easiest form of remembering it.

(2) If we remember actions as such, and apart from the correlative changes of sensible appearance, it is as *ideal movements*, for which we have a certain adhesiveness, varying no doubt with the motor endowments as a whole. If we remember an action sufficiently to do it again, we remember it also ideally. We remember our verbal utterances, partly as connected threads of vocal exertion. Still, we rarely depend on this single thread. A surgeon may remember how he operated for stone, by his memory of hand movements; but the sensible results of the different stages impress him much more.

The memory of our feelings or emotions, in their pure subject character, as in pleasure and pain, comes under the proper adhesiveness of the subject states. Allusion has been made to the permanent recollection of states of pleasure and pain, as a thing variable in individuals, and of great importance in its practical results. It was also remarked that no law can be laid down as governing this department, no special endowment of sensibility pointed out, except the negation of extreme object regards, in a mind of good general retentiveness.

CONCLUDING OBSERVATIONS ON RETENTIVENESS.

69. (1) There is some difficulty in establishing what we have named general Retentiveness, seeing that so much depends on the special organ, and on the interest excited. Still, when we encounter a person distinguished as a *learner* generally, with a strong bent for acquisition in all departments—bodily skill, languages, sciences, fine arts—we seem justified in representing the case as an example of adhesive power on the whole, and not as an aggregate of local superiorities. The renowned 'admirable Crichton' is a historical example of the class. And we find many men that are almost equally good in language and in science, in business and in fine art. Moreover, the superiority of man over the lower animals is general and pervasive, and better expressed by a general retentiveness than by the sum of special and local distinctions.

(2) There can be no question as to the superior retentiveness or plasticity of early years. We cannot state with precision the comparative adhesiveness of different ages, but from the time that the organs are fully under command, onward through life, there appears to be a steady decrease. The formation of bodily habits seems to be favoured not solely by nervous conditions, at their maximum in youth, but by mus-

cular conditions also; the growing stage of the muscles being the stage of easiest adaptation to new movements.

As regards the mental peculiarities, the earliest periods are most susceptible to Moral impressions; also to Physical habits, such as bodily carriage, the mechanical part of language (pronunciation), or the use of the hand as in drawing. After these, come the Verbal memory, and the exercise of the senses in Observation, with the corresponding pictorial recollections. The Generalizing, Abstracting, and Scientific faculties are much later; Arithmetic, Grammar, Geometry, Physical Science, &c., begin to be possible from about the tenth year onwards. Up to fourteen or sixteen, the concrete side of education must prevail with the vast majority, although, by that time, a good many abstract elements should be mastered, more especially mathematics and grammar. The basis of every aptitude, not of a high scientific kind, should be laid before sixteen.

(3) The limitation of the acquirements possible to each person has been repeatedly noticed. There are reasons for believing that this limitation has for its physical counterpart the limited number of the nervous elements. Each distinct mode of consciousness, each distinct adhesive grouping, would appear to appropriate a distinct track of nervous communications, involving a definite number of fibres and of cells or corpuscles; and numerous as are the component fibres and cells of the brain (they must be counted by millions) they are still limited; one brain possesses more than another, but all have their limitations.

It is hardly correct to speak of improving the Memory as a whole. We may, by devotion to a particular subject, make great acquisitions in that subject; or we may, by habits of attention to a certain class of things, remember those things better than others; but the plasticity on the whole, although susceptible of being economized, is scarcely susceptible of being increased. No doubt by leaving the other powers of the mind in abeyance—those entering into Reason, Imagination, &c.—and by not wasting ourselves in the excitement of the feelings, we may determine a certain additional portion of the collective mental energies to plastic acquisition; but this is still to divert power, not to create it.

(4) There is a *temporary adhesiveness*, serving many of the occasions of daily life. When we have to follow a direction, to convey a message, to answer a question, to put a fact on record, a few minutes' retention is all that is necessary. In such instances, we fulfil the requirements before the present impression has died away.

The next grade of adhesiveness is represented by the superior readiness and liveliness of recollection for things that have occurred within a few hours or a few days, or perhaps months. It is the difference between days, or weeks, and years of interval. The things are supposed to have gone completely out of mind, to have been overlaid by many newer impressions; still we find that nearness in time makes a great difference; that as our impressions go into the far past, without being renewed, they tend to decay; that, after a few years, extinction has come over a great many that were good for a few months, especially such as were formed late in life.

What is called *cramming* is a case of temporary adhesiveness. But the reproach implied in this name attaches more to the circumstance that the acquisitions are made by an undue pressure and excitement of the brain, which can be only temporary, and ends in an exhaustion of the plastic forces. An even pace of acquirement, within the limits of the strength, is the true economy in the long run.

CHAPTER II.

AGREEMENT—LAW OF SIMILARITY.

1. THE statement of this law is as follows:—
   Present Actions, Sensations, Thoughts, or Emotions tend to revive their LIKE among previously occurring states.

Contiguity joins together things that occur together, or that are, by any circumstance, presented to the mind at *the same time*; as when we associate heat with light, a falling body with a concussion. But, in addition to this link of reproductive connexion, we find that one thing will, by virtue of similarity, recall another separated from it in time, as when a portrait brings up the original.

The second fundamental property of Intellect, termed Consciousness of Agreement, or Similarity, is thus a great power of mental reproduction, or a means of recovering past mental states. It was recognized by Aristotle as one of the links in the succession of our thoughts.

2. *Similarity, in one form, is implied under Contiguity. When a contiguous bond is confirmed by repeated exercises, each new impression must recall the total of the past.*

In order that we may, by repetition, attain an enduring idea of the winding of a river, seen from the same point, each new view must reinstate the effect of the previous; which is a species of the attraction of similarity. In such a case, however, the similarity amounts to identity, and is never failing in its operation. There is no need to mention what can with certainty be counted on; hence this condition of the success of contiguous association was tacitly assumed. The cases that demand our attention are those where the similarity does not amount to identity, and where it may fail to operate: the circumstances leading to the failure or the success are then a matter of distinct enquiry.

3. *The impediments to the sure revival of the Past, through the bond of similarity, are Faintness and Diversity.*

There are cases where a present impression is too Feeble to strike into the old-established track of the same impression, and to make it alive again; as when we are unable to identify a faint colour, or to recognize a visible object in twilight dimness. This forms one department of difficult and doubtful re-instatement. The most numerous and interesting cases, however, come under the head of Diversity, or likeness accompanied by unlikeness; as when an air is played with new variations, or on strange instruments. It will then depend upon various circumstances, whether or not we shall be struck with the similarity.

It will appear, as we proceed, that there are the greatest individual differences, in respect of the power of re-instating a past experience through similarity, under the obstructions caused by faintness and diversity. This power would seem to follow laws of its own, and not to rise or fall in the proportion of the Contiguous adhesiveness. As with Contiguity, however, so here we find that the facts tally best with the assumption of a General Power of attraction for Similars, modified by the Local endowments of the Senses. Each intellect would seem to be gifted with a certain degree of Similarity on the whole, or for things generally; such general power being consistent with special differences, according to the same local peculiarities as we have allowed for in Contiguity. These will be made to appear in the illustration of the workings of

Similarity, first under the disadvantage of Faintness, and secondly, and at greater length, under the obstruction of Diversity.

FEEBLENESS OF IMPRESSION.

4. Under a certain degree of Faintness, a present impression will be unable to recall the past, even although the resemblance amounts to identity.

When a present impression is very faint or feeble, it is the same as no impression at all. Nevertheless, we are interested in considering the instances, of not unfrequent occurrence, where a faint impression is recognized by one man and not by another. Suppose a taste. In the case of a very feeble brine, many persons might consider the water quite fresh; others again would discern the taste of the salt; that is to say, the present impression of salt would recall the previous collective impression of the taste of salt, and with that the name and characters, or the full knowledge of salt; in other words, would *identify* the substance.

(1) Let us reflect on the mental peculiarity that may be supposed to cause the difference. In the first place, we must admit that *the natural delicacy of the sense* of Taste might vary. We know that all the senses are subject to individual variations of natural acuteness; the readiest test of the comparative acuteness being the power of Discrimination, which power also implies a delicate sense of Agreement, as well as a special force of Retentiveness. In the same way, a delicate sense of smell, as in the dog, would show itself in identifying very faint odours; a good ear would make out fainter impressions of sound; an eye for colour would recognize a faint shade of yellow in what to another eye would seem the absence of colour.

(2) In the second place, through familiarity, or other cause, *the previous impression might be more deeply engrained* in one mind than in another; as a consequence of which, it would start out on a slighter touch of present stimulus. We should expect this to happen from the very nature of the case, and we know, by abundance of familiar facts, that it does happen. The sailor identifies a ship in the offing, and determines its build, sooner than a landsman. According as our familiarity with spoken language increases, we identify the faintest whisper, or most indistinct utterance. It matters not by what means the previous impression has been rendered deep and strong,—whether by mere iteration, or by the influence of feeling.

(3) A third possible source of inequality, in recognizing a faint impression, is the habit of attending to the particular class of impressions. This may be otherwise described, as *the acquired delicacy of the sense;* by repeated acts of attention or concentration of mind, on any one sense, or any one region of things, a habitual concentration is determined, augmenting, by so much, the natural delicacy of the sense. Hence all professional habits of regarding some particular objects, render the individuals susceptible to the feeblest impression of any one of those objects.

It need not be made the subject of a separate head, that the undistracted condition of the mind at the time, necessarily favours the power of making out the identity. A full concentration of the observing powers is supposed in order to do justice to the case; the concentration may, or may not, be aided by motives of special interest, or by circumstances that excite the nervous energy beyond its ordinary pitch.

These three conditions, differing in origin or source, have one common effect, namely, to give greater strength or intensity to the previous impression. They may be considered as exhausting the local and special aids to the restoration of a past state by Similarity, under the disadvantage of feebleness in the present or actual stimulus. If we assume, in addition, a General Power of Similarity, greater in some minds than in others, we seem to exhaust the means of accounting for superior power of identification in the case of Feebleness.

For the sake of clearness, let us repeat the four conditions in a summary statement.

I. General Powers of Similarity. This is the deep and pervasive aptitude, the intellectual gift, good for all classes of impressions.

II. Special and Local Circumstances.

(1) Natural delicacy or acuteness of Sense.

(2) The depth or intensity of the previous impression.

(3) Acquired delicacy, or habitual attention, to a particular class of things.

All these considerations are no less applicable to the means of conquering the obstruction of Diversity; they must, however, for that case, be supplemented by a fourth special circumstance, to be presently mentioned.

SIMILARITY IN DIVERSITY—SENSATIONS.

5. Movements, Feelings of Movement, and Sensations

generally, are revived in idea, by the force of partial similarity, or likeness in difference.

When a portrait brings to our mind the original, it is by virtue of similarity; the differences between painted canvass and a living man or woman do not blind us to the points of likeness. Increase the diversity, however, by dress, attitude, and by idealizing the features, and the remaining likeness may be insufficient to recall the original; the diverse circumstances carry the mind away from the points of similarity.

As regards Diversity, therefore, the distinctive feature is the influence of the points of dissimilarity. These, by the general law, have a tendency to call up *their* like; and hence a struggle of opposing influences. A person that we have seen only in ordinary costume is painted in military or official uniform. Viewing the picture, we may be instigated, by similarity, in various directions. As a portrait, the picture may suggest other portraits, the reviving stroke of similarity operating upon the painter's execution. Or the military dress may suggest some soldier by profession. Lastly, the portrait may recall its original by the resemblance of the face. Three persons looking at the same portrait may thus be moved in three different lines of mental resuscitation; and to each one there will be an attraction of likeness in diversity; the points of diversity, by their own independent attractions, operating as a hindrance to the similarity. Whichever point brings on the recall is the likeness; the others are the unlikenesses; and in their efforts to recall their own similitudes, they count for so much dead weight against the successful identity.

It is thus apparent that the circumstance special to the obstruction caused by Diversity, is the striving of the separate features, each for itself, to strike the recall. Hence, besides the three special circumstances contributing to resuscitation, under Faintness, we must now add a fourth—namely, (4) *a low or inferior susceptibility to the points of diversity.*

6. *Movements and Feelings of Movement.* Before proceeding to the Sensations proper, we may advert to the one case of movement that furnishes interesting examples of Similarity, namely, Articulate movements, or Speech. Any train of words presently uttered is liable to recall previous trains containing salient identities, although in the midst of difference. In using a particular phrase, or in telling an anecdote, we are liable to be made aware that we are repeating our-

selves. We may trace similarities still farther removed from identity. In uttering the expression 'rights of property,' we may be led to remember a famous saying, that 'property has its duties as well as its rights.' Coincidences of phraseology in authors are thus recalled. Pronouncing Campbell's lines—

> —— we linger to survey
> The promis'd joys of life's unmeasured way,

we can hardly fail to recall, if we have previously read, Pope's—

> —— we tremble to survey
> The growing labours of the lengthened way.

Verbal similitudes form one powerful link in the resuscitations necessary for continuous address or composition. They are favoured by all the special circumstances above laid down— the verbal or articulate susceptibility, natural and acquired, the previous familiarity, and the low susceptibility to the differences between the new and old, which differences may be sometimes in the words, but as often in the sense; the consequence being that a regard to meaning or sense is often a bar to verbal similitudes being struck, especially those, like epigrams or puns, that play upon similarities in the form of the word, amidst the greatest discordancies of meaning.

7. *Sensations of Organic Life.* Among the organic sensations, there are many cases of the repetition of a feeling with new admixtures, and variety of circumstances, all tending to thwart the reviving or identifying operation. The same organic depression may have totally different antecedents and collaterals. A shock of grief, a glut of pleasure, a fit of overwork, an accidental loss of two or three nights' rest, may all end in the very same kind of headache, stupor, or feeling of discomfort; but the great difference in the antecedents may prevent our identifying the occasions. The derangement caused by grief is more likely to recall a previous occasion of a similar grief, than to suggest a time of overdone enjoyment; the sameness in organic state is, in the case of such a parallel, nullified by the repulsion of opposites in the accompanying circumstances; a state of grief does not permit a time of pleasure to be recalled and dwelt upon; the loss of a parent at home is not compatible with the remembrance of a long night of gaiety abroad. Hence we do not identify the supposed state of organic depression with all the previous recurrences of the same state; unless, indeed, a scientific education has made us aware of the sameness of the physical effects resulting from the most dissimilar causes.

IDENTIFICATION OF TASTES—CLASSIFICATION. 133

8. *Taste.* A taste may be disguised by mixture with other tastes. Each of the various ingredients tends to recall its like, but under more or less obstruction from the others. Three or four salts might be dissolved together, to their mutual confusion of taste; the one actually identified would be probably the most familiar. Sugar, common salt, alcohol, would be discerned in preference to less common tastes or relishes.

In the different wines, there is a common effect, partly of organic sensation, and partly of taste; and this is identified in the midst of much diversity. If a person were to encounter at intervals all the different juices of the grape, in all countries,—the varieties, or diversities, would obscure the sameness; the common taste of alcohol would hardly emerge under the accessories—sweetness, sourness, tartness, and the rest; the mind would, at first, fail to identify a sweet and a sour liquid as agreeing in alcoholic pungency. Such an identification, however, would sooner or later be effected; and it is important to mark the consequences, as representing one of the fruits of the operation of similarity. The discovery of this important point of community in substances so widely scattered, and so various in their concrete totalities, was what Plato called seeing 'the one in the many'—the discovery of a *class;* it was rising to the unity of nature in the midst of her diversity. Such discoveries have a twofold value; they ease the intellectual grasp; and they enlarge our practical resources.

We can carry the identification, in the instance supposed, still farther. When the fermentation of malt was discovered, new liquids were obtained; and the distillation of malt and various sugary substances added others. The same identifying stroke, obstructed for a time by differences, would trace a community in the wine group, the malt liquors, and the distilled liquors; the range of community is now extended; 'the one' is found in a larger 'many.' The class is henceforth widened to alcoholic drinks; the intellect embraces all by a single effort; the needs of practical life, as regards this one property, are gratified by a more abundant choice.

The identification may stretch yet farther. The common fact of stimulating the nervous system, and imparting elation to the mental tone, may be detected in other substances, as in the so-called stimulants—opium, tobacco, tea, hemp, &c. There are differences to break through, before arriving at this point; the power of Similarity may need to be aided by favouring conditions, such as familiarity with the substances to be identified; still, the differences would not long hold out against the felt agreement of wine, coffee, tobacco, and opium.

A separate illustration for *Smell* is needless.

9. *Touch.* The plurality of effects in tangible objects affords scope for recognizing agreement in difference. More especially does the combination of the tactile with muscular sensibility allow of great variety of impressions.

We identify a wooden surface in every variety of form; we identify the spherical shape in variety of surface, and of size; we identify silken, woollen, linen, fabrics by the touch, although the texture may be coarse or fine. We identify viscid and powdery substances by their peculiar consistency, although the specimens may be disguised by unlike accompaniments.

In this way we generalize and *classify* effects of touch, and the substances that produce them, however different in other points. The classified sensations of Touch, as described above (see *Touch*), namely, soft touch, pungent touch, plurality of points, hardness, resistance, tactile form, &c., all suppose this operation of identifying the same effect, in the midst of diverse accompaniments. Until we have made some progress in identification, we cannot be said to *know* these various effects; we do not separate them from the concretes where they first appear. If hardness were always accompanied with a fixed degree of warmth, we should know only the joint sensation, which we should recognize as one and not as two. It is by identifying the common effect of hardness, under variety of temperature, that we possess the idea of hardness by itself. Such is an example of the operation of Similarity in the very beginnings of our cognitive separation of nature's concretes.

10. *Hearing.* The still greater complexity of effects of Sound affords ample scope for seeing the like in the unlike. Thus, the *pitch* of a note may be overlaid by varying intensity, by difference of voice or instrument, and so on. In such a case, only the good ear will recognize it: the natural and acquired delicacy of the sense of pitch is tested by identifying a note heard amidst distracting accompaniments.

The *articulate* property of sound may be disguised beyond the power of ordinary identification. When a person talks with indistinct utterance, or with an unaccustomed voice, pronunciation and accent, the points of difference overpower the articulate agreement; failing to identify the articulate characters, we fail to understand the speaker. This is a testing case for the local aids to similarity, namely, the good articulate ear, and the indifference or low sensibility to effects of cadence, which are felt by the ear for elocution or oratory. A provincial brogue, unfamiliar to us, always renders a speaker more or less unintelligible; in other words, the diversity of accent drowns the community of articulation. We might have, as a converse instance, the ear for cadence so acute as to identify a very disguised provincialism of accent.

In listening to a continuous *musical* piece or air, we identify the piece, or we do not. A bad ear, and little previous familiarity, would account for the failure; the obstruction being increased by a strong susceptibility for instrumental and other particularities apart from the character of the piece. Also, we may identify the key, although the piece be new; we may identify the style of the composer; or we may trace a certain ethical character—the gay, the solemn, the pathetic, the melancholy.

Continuous spoken address is diversified by cadence, as already remarked, and by all the arts of elocution, as well as by the visible accompaniments of gesture. The hearer may incline, by preference, to one class of effects, being comparatively insensitive to the others; and the course of the identification will alter accordingly. Our easy understanding of every-day speech is owing to the uniformity of all the accompaniments of voice, pronunciation, cadence, and gesticulation; if these accompaniments are altered, as when we listen to strangers, or foreigners, the diversity clouds the perception of the articulate sameness.

Our memory for language spoken is a mixture of articulate and auditory recollections; the ear counting for more than the voice. The occasions for tracing similarity in diversity, among verbal trains, are innumerable. When another person is speaking, we are affected through the ear, and are reminded of previously heard sayings, more or less similar according to the circumstances. We detect resembling phrases, and styles, in different speakers; we are reminded of past occasions when the same forms were used by the same or by other persons. We generalize mannerisms and peculiarities in each person that we are accustomed to listen to, and assign characteristics in accordance therewith.

The great diversifying accompaniment in language is the meaning or subject matter. A mind intently regarding the sense will be less apt to dwell upon the phraseology; the suggestiveness will be for meaning and not for words. And, conversely, a small regard to meaning, and an acute appreciation of words, will make the mind keenly alive to similarities of phrase in spite of disparity of sense.

11. *Sight.* We identify *colours* under difference of shade; which leads to the classifying of colours, as blues, yellows, reds, &c. When a colour is intermediate, or on the margin between two principal colours, we may identify it with either the one or other, according to the circumstances. We generalize the peculiar effect of lustre, as seen in many different situations,—in the pebbly brook, the coating of varnish, the brilliant surface of jet black, the polished marble, the human eye. It requires a higher stretch of Similarity to identify with those the sparkle of solar reflection from broken surfaces.

Combinations of Colour with visible Form and Size, are identified now on one feature, now on another. We identify a common colour, or shade of colour, through all changes of form and magnitude; such identification being our notion, or idea, of that colour. A deep susceptibility to colour will make us perceive delicate agreements, as well as differences, and enlarge our fund of these distinct notions of shades of colour. It is by consciousness of agreement, that we recognize a colour according to its precise shade, and not merely according to its generic class—red, blue, orange, &c.

To identify visible *forms* in the midst of differences of colour and dimensions, is to classify and generalize the forms of natural bodies. We discern a common effect in all the bodies called round, or oval, or triangular. We identify less symmetrical forms that recur in nature and in art—the egg-shape, heart-shape, pear-shape, &c. The resemblances are generally obvious; sometimes they are obscure, as in many of the descriptive comparisons in Botany and in Anatomy. Deep identities of form would be soonest arrived at by minds little sensitive to colours.

Under arbitrary and symbolical forms, we have the case of deciphering handwriting. The perception of alphabetical identity is sometimes difficult; and the difficulty is aggravated if there be great symmetry or proportion in other respects. An *elegant* indistinct hand is often the most illegible of any. The best decipherer would be a person susceptible to the alphabetic distinctions, and wholly unsusceptible to regularity and symmetry.

Visible forms, linked together, enter into our recollections of Language. We may trace similarities of phrase through the eye, as well as through the ear. The suggestive force of a sentence uttered is greatly increased by writing it down and exhibiting it to the eye.

So, visible forms artistically pleasing are identified on that ground, by the artist, although there should not be either mathematical symmetry or literal agreement. The strong sense of the mathematical, the regular, or the literal, might be a hindrance to artistic invention generally.

A scene of nature is to the eye a mixed and complicated effect, suggesting to different minds different comparisons, according to susceptibility and to previous experience. The same is true of any varied spectacle, as a pageant or procession. We have only to ring the changes on the several circumstances, positive and negative, that favour a particular recall, to exhaust all the varieties of individual characters. The mental preference for form, or for colour, for symmetrical forms, for artistic effects, will each operate characteristically upon the course of the identification.

Under Sight, finally, we may mention *visible movements*. Notwithstanding diversity of accompanying circumstances, we trace identity, and form classes, among rectilineal movements, circular movements, elliptical movements, pendulums, waves, waterfalls, and so on. The more complex movements of animals are reduced to identical modes—the walk, gallop, trot, shamble, of quadrupeds; also the peculiar flight of different species of birds. The gait of human beings is a part of their character, and is identified in the midst of other differences. Once more, a visible movement is identified with a resembling form in still life, as the rainbow with a projectile; a falling body with a crushing weight.

12. *Effects common to the Senses generally.* Although there is a generic and fundamental difference of feeling between one sense and another, as between touch and smell, hearing and sight, yet we identify many common effects. Thus the characteristic called 'pungency' applies to tastes and to smells alike, and is not inappropriate when describing Touch, Hearing, or Sight. In all the senses, we identify the pleasing and the painful, and the different modes of acute and massive. The feeling of warmth is identified with effects of vision; mention is made of *warm* colours. By a farther stretch, we speak of warm emotions, a cold nature, a bitter repentance, a sweet disposition. These last, however, pass into the region of metaphor and poetry, where resemblances are purposely multiplied on slight pretexts.

CONTIGUOUS AGGREGATES—CONJUNCTIONS.

13. First, Objects affecting a Plurality of Senses.

Two things may agree to the touch, and differ to the sight; or agree to the sight, and differ to the taste or smell. Nevertheless, the difference need not necessarily blind us to the similarities. We identify the heavy metals on the point of weight, although they are unlike in appearance; we identify the metallic lustre, amid variety of colour, weight, and other differences, including in one case the difference of liquid and solid. Still, if some one feature of diversity were very alluring, as the glitter of the diamond, we should not proceed to identify the crystalline form, or the specific gravity, until our admiration of the more startling quality were exhausted.

14. Secondly, Aggregates of associated properties and uses.

No one object in nature discloses the whole of its characteristics as it appears in stillness and isolation. A flint is not fully known, until we manipulate it, for hardness, brittleness, and the rest. Our knowledge of each object is therefore a compound of its permanent aspects, and of its possible aspects, under certain operations. A hammer is not completely known till it is seen in action; a weather-cock must be observed turning with the wind.

In such cases, likeness may be accompanied with great diversity. Things widely different in their mere sensuous appearance may be identical in their uses; and things widely different in their uses may be identical in their appearance. Take the first case—diversity in appearance, with identity in use. A rope is in appearance very unlike two bevelled tooth wheels working into one another, but it may serve the same end of communicating movement from one revolving axle to another.

A still more remarkable instance of diversity of appearance, in company with identity of use, is seen in the Prime Movers. It is easy to identify human force with animal force; a difference so small could be got over by the most ordinary intellect in search of a mechanical power. A waterfall is a much less obvious comparison; it would demand a considerable stretch of identifying faculty concentrating itself on the point of mechanical force. Still farther removed in sensuous aspects is the power of the wind. It is not recorded under what circumstances the human mind extended its grasp to these less apparent sources of motive power; but we happen to be fully acquainted with the discovery of the greatest of them all; and can produce it as a highly illustrative example of the workings of Similarity in Diversity. To the common eye, steam, or vapour, suggested nothing but fleecy tenuity; it seemed the farthest remove from anything that could exert moving power. Doubtless, the forcing up of the lid of a boiling kettle was a familiar fact, but this fact did not suggest as a parallel the other sources of moving power; the likeness was shrouded by too many circumstances of unlikeness. The special conditions of such an identification, in the mind of Watt, were his previous studies of mechanical properties, the habit of directing his mind to these on all occasions, and the negative peculiarity of indifference to mere sensuous aspects as such. To these, we must probably add the general power of Similarity in an unusual degree; an assumption necessary when we consider the number of successful fetches made by him, as compared with other men of like education, pursuits, and habits.

In the class of Mineral bodies, we have the concurrence of many attributes in each individual, some sensible and permanent, others experimental and occasional. If we take the group of metals, we find a certain number easily identified; the differences, although considerable, do not overpower the marked sameness in appearance and in specific gravity. But when Sir Humphrey Davy suggested that metals were locked up in soda, potash, and lime, the identification was opposed by everything in the sensible appearance; it proceeded upon associated properties, and remote relationships, appreciated only by the intellect. An identity had already been struck, and a class formed, among the bodies termed salts; it was also known that many of these are composed of an acid and the oxide of a metal; such are sulphate of *oxide of iron,* nitrate of *oxide of silver ;* others consist of an acid and an alkali, as sulphate of *soda,* nitrate of *potash.* Thus, the neutral salts, as a whole, being so far analogous as to suggest a like constitution, while an oxide of a metal and an alkali served an identical function in neutralizing the acid, the thought came across the mind of Davy, that *the alkalies are oxides of metals ;* a flash of insight that he had the skill and good fortune to verify. This was hunting out nature's similarities in the deepest thickets of concealment.

The progress of science in the Vegetable world would

reveal the operation of the principle before us, in striking out deep identities in superficial diversities. In the first classifications of plants, the more obvious feature of size took hold of the attention; the Trees of the Forest, were marked off from the Shrubs, and the Flowers. The great step made by Linnæus, consisted in tracing identity in less conspicuous parts of the plant, the organs of fructification; under which the largest trees and the smallest shrubs were brought together.

Botany presents other examples. Thus, Goethe saw in the flower the form of the entire plant; the circular arrangement of the petals of the corolla was paralleled by the corkscrew arrangement of the leaves round the stem. So, Oken, in the leaf, identified the plant; the branchings of the veins of a leaf are, in fact, a miniature of the entire vegetable, with its parent stem, branches and ramifications.

In the Animal Kingdom, we might quote many deep fetches of Similarity. The first superficial classification of animals according to their element,—animals of the land, the water, and the air, has since been traversed by other classifications founded on deep community of structure; the bat has been detached from birds, and the seal, whale, and porpoise from fishes. More pointed still, as illustrating the power of a few select minds to detect similarities unapparent to the multitude, is the discovery of the deep identities in the vertebrate skeleton, termed homologies. The first suggestion of them is attributed to Oken, a man remarkable for this species of intellectual penetration. Walking one day in a forest, he came on the blanched skull of a deer. He took it up, and while examining the anatomical arrangements, there flashed upon him the identity between it and the back bone; the skull, he said, was four vertebræ distorted by the expanded cerebral mass and the development of the face. It is strange that this similarity should not have been first struck out in the case of the fishes, where the deviation of the head from the spine is smallest. To see it in the quadruped, was to work at a far greater disadvantage. But Oken was a man, not merely gifted with large powers of analogical discovery, or, as one should say, general Power of Similarity; he was, by the bent of his mind, an analogy-hunter; he studiously set himself to look at things in diverse aspects, so as to detect new analogies. No man ever suggested so many identities of that peculiar class; although only a small number, perhaps not above half a dozen, have been found to hold upon farther examination.

The homologies of the vetebrate series of animals, whose discovery and exposition enter into Comparative Anatomy, consist in showing the deep correspondence of parts superficially unlike; the upper arm of man, the fore leg of the quadruped, the wing of the bird, the anterior fin of the fish.

SUCCESSIONS.

15. The natural successions have been already considered under Cycle, Evolution, and Cause and Effect. In all of them, there is scope for Identification in the midst of difference.

Cycle. The chief natural phenomena of cycle, the day and the year, are too obviously alike not to be identified; the differences are insignificant as compared with the agreements. In the rising and setting of the stars, there is a point of similarity that may have been long unobserved, the constancy of angle in the same latitude, the angle being the co-latitude of the place. Besides being an unobvious fact, there are two disguising unlikenesses in the rising and setting of the stars in the same place; namely, the height reached by them, and the change of the time of rising throughout the year. The cycles of the planets would be easy to trace in the superior planets, not so in Mercury and Venus.

The cycles of human affairs are sometimes apparent, but often obscure. Writers on the Philosophy of History have remarked a sort of vibratory tendency in human societies, or a transition between two extremes, as from asceticism to licence, from severity of taste to laxity, from conservation to innovation.

Evolution. The successions of Evolution are typified, and principally constituted, by the growth of living beings. Each plant and animal, in the course of its existence, presents a series of phases, and, as respects these, we discover a similarity in different individuals and species. The department, called Comparative Embryology, traces identities in the midst of wide diversities. Again, the mental evolution of human beings is a subject of interesting comparison.

Cause and Effect. Causation is the name for the total productive forces of the world, and, as these are comparatively few in number, but wide in their distribution, and often disguised in their operation, the ingenuity of man has long been exercised in detecting the hidden similarities. An example will show the nature of the difficulties and the means of conquering them. The burning of coal, and the rusting of iron, show to the eye nothing in common except the fact of change. No mere force of Similarity, however aided by the ordinary favouring conditions, positive and negative, could have detected the deep community of these two phenomena. Other phenomena had to be interposed, having relations to both, in order to disclose the likeness. The experiments of Priestley upon the red oxide were the intermediate link. Mercury, when burned, becomes heavier, being converted into a red powder, by taking up material from the air, which can be again driven off by heat, so as to reproduce the metallic substance. Thus, while the act of combustion of the mercury has a strict resemblance to the burning of coal, the resulting change on the substance could suggest the rusting of iron, the only difference being the time occupied. By such intermediate comparisons, the general law of oxidation has been gradually traced through all its entanglements.

If not the greatest known stretch of identifying genius, the example most illustrious from its circumstances was the discovery of universal gravitation. Here the appearances were, in the highest degree, unfavourable to identification. Who could see anything in common between the grand and silent march of the moon and the planets round the heavens, and the fall of unsupported bodies to the ground? A preparatory process was necessary on both sides. Newton, by studying the planetary motions as a case of the composition of forces, resolved them each into two; a tendency in a straight line through space, and a tendency to the sun as a centre. He thus had clearly before him the fact, that there was an attraction of the planets to the sun, and of the moon to the earth. This was the preparation on one side. On the other side, he meditated on the various phenomena of falling bodies, and, putting away as irrelevant the accidental circumstances and interests that engross the common mind, he saw in these bodies a common tendency of the nature of attraction to the earth's surface, or rather ·the earth's centre. Viewed in this light, the phenomenon was closely assimilated to the great effect of Solar attraction, which he had previously isolated; and we are not to be surprised that, in some happy moment, the two flashed together in his mind. Even after the preparatory shapings on both sides, the stroke of identification was a remarkable fetch of similarity; the attendant disparities were still great and imposing; and we must suppose that the mind of Newton was distinguished no less by the negative condition of inattention to the vulgar and sensuous aspects, than by absorption in the purely dynamical aspect, of the phenomena.

REASONING AND SCIENCE IN GENERAL.

16. The Generalizing power of the mind, already seen to be a mode of Similarity, culminates in Science, and is designated under the names Abstraction and Reasoning.

The example just quoted, and others previously given, exhibit Similarity at work in scientific discovery. Still, it is desirable to give a more complete view of the relations of science to the identifying faculty. The chief scientific processes are these four—Observation, Definition, Induction, Deduction; the first is the source of the individual facts, and depends on the senses; the three last relate to the generalities, and are all dependent on the intellectual force of Similarity.

I. *Classification*, *Abstraction*, *Generalization of Notions or Concepts*, *General Names*, DEFINITION. These designations all refer to the one operation of identifying a number of things on some point, or property, which property is finally embodied in language by the process called Definition. The start is given by an identifying operation, a perception of likeness or community in many things otherwise diverse. In watching the heavenly bodies, the early astronomers discovered a few that moved steadily through the fixed stars, and made the circle of the heavens in longer or shorter periods. The bodies identified and brought together on this common ground, made a *class*, as distinguished from a mere confused aggregate. The mind, reflecting on the things so classified, attends to their similarity, and endeavours to leave out of view the points of dissimilarity; this is the long-disputed process of *abstraction;* the common attribute or attributes is called the *abstract idea*, the *notion*, or the *concept*. When a name is applied to the things compared, because of their agreement or community, it is a *general name*, as 'planet.' And when we are further desirous of settling, by the help of language, the precise nature and limits of the common attribute, the result is a *definition*. A planet would now be defined as 'a body circulating around the sun as its centre, in an orbit nearly circular.' (On ABSTRACTION, see Chap. v.)

II. *Conjoined properties generalized*, *General Affirmations*, *Propositions*, *Judgments*, *Laws of Nature*, INDUCTION. In Abstraction, a *single* isolated property, or a collection of properties treated as a unity, is identified and generalized; under Induction, a conjunction, union, or concurrence of *two* distinct properties is identified. A proposition contains two notions bound together by a copula. 'Heat' is the name of one general property or notion; 'expansion' is the name of a second notion; the proposition 'heat expands bodies,' is a proposition uniting the two properties in an inductive generality, or a law of nature. Here, too, the prime requisite is the identifying stroke of Similarity. One present instance of the concurrence of heat with increase of bulk, may recall by similarity other instances; the mind, awakened by the flash of identity, takes note of the concurrence, looks out for other cases in point, and ventures (rightly or wrongly) to affirm a general law of nature, connecting the two properties.

All the difficulties and the facilities connected with the working of Similarity may be found attending these inductive generalizations. There is one noticeable circumstance special to the case. That two things or two properties affect us together, excites no attention at first; we are so familiar with such unions that we take little note of the fact. It is, however, a point of some importance to know whether two things, occurring together, do so merely by accident, or by virtue of some fixed attachment keeping them always together; for, in the first case, the coincidence is of no moment, while in the last case, it is something that we may count on and anticipate in the future. Now, the real problem of inductive generalization consists in eliminating the regular and constant concurrences from the casual and inconstant. It is the identifying stroke of Similarity that is the means of rousing us to the constant concurrences; these repeat themselves while other things come and go, and the repetition is the prompting to suspect an alliance, and not merely a coincidence.

The favouring conditions of mind for scientific induction are the conditions, positive and negative, of the scientific intellect on the whole. General Power of Similarity being supposed, the special circumstances are, susceptibility to symbols and forms; the previous familiarity with the subject matter; the scientific interest; and the absence of the purely sensuous and concrete regards. Such are unquestionably the intellectual features of the greatest scientific geniuses, the men whose lives are a series of discoveries.

Some conjunctions are obvious; as light and heat with the sun's rays. Others are less obvious, but yet discernible, without any artificial medium; such are the signs of weather, seasons and crops, the pointing of the loadstone to the north, many of the causes of agreeable and disagreeable sensation and of good and ill health, the influences of national prosperity. A third class demand artificial media and aids, as Kepler's laws, and the law of refraction of light, which could not have been discovered without the intervention of numerical and geometrical relations.

III. DEDUCTION, *Deductive Inference, Ratiocination, Application or Extension of Inductions, Syllogism.* When an Inductive generality has been established, the application of it to new cases is called Deduction. Kepler's laws were framed upon the six planets; they have been deductively applied to all that have since been discovered. The law of gravity was deductively applied to explain the tides.

Deduction also is a process of identification, by the force of Similarity. The new case must *resemble* the old, otherwise there can be no legitimate application of the law. Newton, by an inductive identification, detected, among transparent bodies, a conjunction between combustibility and high refracting power; the oils and resins bend light much more than water or glass. He then, by a farther stroke of identification, bethought himself of the diamond, the most refracting of all known substances; the deductive application of the law would lead to the inference that it was composed of some highly combustible element; which afterwards was found to be the case.

The Deductive process appears under two aspects; a principle may be given, and its application to facts sought for; or a fact may be given, and its principle sought for. In both, the discovery is made by the force of Similarity. When the law of definite proportions was first promulgated, an unbounded range of applications lay before the chemist; which was the carrying out of the principle deductively.

Reasoning by *Analogy.* This is a mode of reasoning that bears upon its name the process of Similarity; the fact, however, being that in it the similarity is imperfect, and the conclusion so much the less cogent. When we examine a sample of wheat, the production of the same soil, and infer that the rest will correspond to the sample, we make a rigid induction; there being an identity of nature in the material or kind. But when we reason from wheat to the other cereals, the similarity is accompanied with diversities, and the reasoning is then precarious and only probable; such is reasoning by Analogy. Thus, there is an analogy, not an identity, between waves of water and waves of air as in sound; between electricity and the nerve force; between the functions, bodily and mental, of men and of the inferior animals; between the family and the state; between the growth of a living being and the growth of a nation. These analogies are struck out by the intellectual power of Similarity; they are useful when no closer parallelism can be drawn.

17. The scientific processes, named Induction and Deduction, correspond to what is called the REASON, or the Reasoning faculty of the mind.

The name Reason is used in a narrow sense, corresponding to Deduction, and also in a wider sense, comprising both Deduction and Induction. To express the scientific faculty in its fulness, the process called Abstraction would have to be taken along with Reason in the wider sense. What is variously termed by Hamilton the Elaborative or Discursive Faculty, Comparison, the Faculty of Relations, Thought (in a peculiar narrow sense), includes the aggregate of processes now described as entering into the operations of science. It has just been seen, that the working of Similarity renders an adequate account of the principal feature in all these operations, although, to complete the explanation, there still remains a circumstance to be brought forward under the head of the Constructive operations of the Intellect.

BUSINESS AND PRACTICE.

18. Of Practical discoveries, some are due to observation and trial; others are the extension or application of known devices, through the perception of Similarity.

The first discovery of a lever, a pump, or a boat, could be made only by a stumbling and tentative method; accident alone could disclose the advantage of these implements. But the extension, to new cases, of machinery once discovered, proceeds on the identifying stroke of Similarity, sometimes in the midst of great dissimilarity. Among early nations, we find few indications of discoveries by this last method; the mechanical knowledge of the Egyptians, or of the Chinese, would seem to be all of tentative or experimental origin. In modern invention, however, we can trace the workings of great intellectual force of Similarity. It is eminent in the career of Watt. His 'governor balls' is a wonderful stroke of intellectual grasp; it was not a mechanical tentative; it was not even the extension of a device already in existence. The similarity lay deeper; he wanted to institute a connexion between the increase or diminution of a rapid rotatory movement and the opening and shutting of a valve; and he was so fortunate as to recall the situation of bodies flying off by centrifugal force, where the distance from the centre varies slightly according to the change of speed. No other apposite parallel has ever been suggested for the same situation; and the device once thought of has been carried out into many different applications. His suggestion of the lobster-jointed pipe, for conveying water across the bottom of the Clyde, was another pure fetch of similarity.

The device of carving a mould and impressing it upon any number of separate things, goes back to a high antiquity; as we see in coins. One of its many extensions is the art of Printing.

The common water pump, discovered by experiment, was transmuted into the air pump. The water-wheel is the prototype of the ship's paddle. The screw-propeller is an extension of the vanes of the windmill.

In the administration and the forms of business, something must first be devised by trials, or suggested by accident; the further extension is a purely intellectual process. The organization of masses of men to act together began, doubtless, in the necessities of war; repeated trials showed that there must be a chief or superior head, with subordinate grades of command. The machinery once suggested is extended to all other organizations of large bodies, as for public works, manufactures, &c.

The arts of book-keeping, including the employment of printed forms and schedules, have been gradually made to permeate all departments of business.

The art of *Persuasion* is greatly dependent on the attractive force of Similarity. The orator has to make out an identity between his end and the views, opinions, and motive forces of his hearers; and such identity may be very much clogged and disguised. If he has to address an assembly of men of wealth, he must reconcile his aims with the rights and interests of property. Now, all reconciliation proceeds on the perception of points of agreement, real or supposed; hence a mind fertile in discoveries of identification is so far fitted for the task of persuasion. Burke's speeches abound in these strokes of discernment.

ILLUSTRATIVE COMPARISONS AND LITERARY ART.

19. A large department of invention, more especially in Literature, consists in striking out similitudes, among things different in kind, yet serving to illustrate each other.

Of the Figures of Speech, one extensive class is denominated Figures of Similarity, including the Simile, Metaphor, Personification, Allegory, &c. These are called Figures, because they proceed upon some likeness of form in difference of subject. When we compare the act of eating in a man and in a dog, the comparison is real, literal, a comparison in kind; when we talk of digesting and ruminating knowledge, the comparison is illustrative or figurative. Since the origin of literature, many thousands of such comparisons have been struck out; every great literary genius has contributed to the stock; the profusion of Shakespeare being probably unmatched.

These illustrative comparisons are of two kinds, depending, for their invention, on different mental conditions. Of the first kind are those that render an obscure subject clearer, as when we compare the heart to a force pump, the lungs to a bellows, and business routine to a beaten track. The expositor of difficult subjects and doctrines avails himself, as far as his intellectual reach will go, of such illustrative similitudes. They are numerous in Plato. Among the moderns, Bacon is conspicuous for both the number and felicity of his illustrations. Some have become household words. His 'Essay on Delays' may be referred to, as exemplifying his profuse employment of similes.

The invention of such similes is a pure intellectual effort of Similarity. They suppose previous acquaintance with the regions whence they are drawn, an acquaintance terminating in deep or vivid impressions, enhanced by a sensibility for the material of them.

The other class comprehends those serving for ornament, or emotional effect; as when one man is extolled as god-like, another compared to the brutes. Here the likeness involves a common emotion, with or without intellectual similitude. For their invention, a deep emotional susceptibility must be combined with the force of intellect. He that would command similitudes illustrative of a pathetic situation, must have often been pathetically moved in actually contemplating the original objects of comparison.

An unlearned genius like Bunyan knows the commoner appearances of nature, the experience of the mind open to every one, the more familiar aspects of society and manners, and the compass of religious doctrine. Out of these materials, Bunyan drew his similes and his allegories; being favoured by a special susceptibility to the concrete world of sense, by strong emotions superadding an element of interest to a greater or less number of objects, and, we must suppose also, by large general power of Similarity.

Shakespeare, without being learned, had more reading than Bunyan. Still his resources were to a great degree personal observation, and common things. His glances around him impressed the things on his mind with a force out of all proportion to the attention that he could have given them. Natural scenery, natural objects, human character, his own mind, society and its usages, were absorbed by him, as material for his identifying and constructive faculty. He had a moderate knowledge of books, which extended his sphere of allusion to foreign scenes, and to the incidents and personalities of the ancient world; and his study of the subject of one play gave him a stock of allusive references to be employed incidentally in the others.

Bacon had an eye for the concrete world about him, but his mental attention was divided between this and book study in philosophy, scholarship, politics, and law. His sphere of similitudes has a corresponding compass.

Milton also had the concrete eye for the real world, a poet's interest in nature, and a vein of emotion that gave special impressiveness to whatever was large, vast, unbounded, mysterious in its immensity. He likewise had very great stores of reading, and had absorbed the scenes and pictures of remote countries and times.

Literary comparisons being expressed in language, are very much subject to verbal conditions. The associations with words concur to bring some forward, and to keep others back. A great poet needs verbal profusion, as well as pictorial suggestiveness.

THE FINE ARTS IN GENERAL.

20. The intellectual power of tracing similarity in diversity is most conspicuous in Poetry and the Literary Art. It may enter, in some degree, into Painting, Sculpture, Architecture, and Design. But, as regards the

effusive arts—Music, Elocution, Stage-display, Dancing, and the graces of Demeanour—the mental endowment even of the greatest genius has but little that is purely intellectual; the elements are—Sensibility, and the compass and power of the Organs engaged.

What has been said under the foregoing head is sufficient for the Poetical Art. In Painting, it is conceivable and likely that the resources of the artist should be aided by a far-reaching power of Similarity; in recalling scenes to select from, and combine, he draws upon his past experience, brought up by the force of likeness in unlikeness; although his final appropriation must be governed entirely by his sense of artistic effect. An artist may have great intellectual forces, with only a moderate sensibility to the refinements of composition; in other words, great profusion and little taste. It would be easy to produce literary artists of this character; and perhaps we may regard Michael Angelo, as a parallel in Painting.

In the other class of Fine Arts, typified by Music, it seems unsuitable to appeal to an unusual force of the identifying faculty. The fine Sensibility is the great requisite; second to which is the endowment of the Active Organ concerned. A great musician depends principally on delicate ear for pitch; an elocutionist on the ear for cadence; an actor superadds the eye for gesture and pictorial elements.

SIMILARITY IN ACQUISITION AND MEMORY.

21. To whatever extent new acquisitions are the repetition of old, there is an intellectual saving. Now, it being necessary that the old should be recovered to the view, any superiority in the identifying faculty will be apparent in diminishing the labour of acquirement.

It is of some importance to remark, that our more complicated acquisitions are a kind of patchwork. The memory of a scene in nature is the tacking together of previous memories. If a pleader, after once reading a brief, can remember its contents, the reason is that only a small part is new. In geometry, one demonstration is so like another, that after a certain familiarity with the matter of demonstrations, the fresh cost to the memory, in each, is very small.

It is obvious, then, that by a greater reach of the identifying power, the means and resources of this piecing operation may be extended. The scientific man whose penetrating glance can recognize the smallest identity between something fresh and something already known, recovers that portion of the past for present use; while he that is unable to bring about the recovery, must learn the whole anew. This is a genuine and often realized distinction between one intellect and another. A mind like Bacon's, studying Law, would make tenfold strides, as compared with one of average endowment.

The value of method, order, uniformity of plan, in aiding memory, is wholly explicable on the principle of making one acquisition serve for a great many occasions. When things are always put in the same places, we have only to form one local tie in our memory of each; whereas, if tools and utensils are put away at random, there must be either a distinct local adhesion, or the trouble of a search as often as any one is used.

CHAPTER III.

COMPOUND ASSOCIATION.

1. Associations, separately too weak, may, conjointly, be strong enough to revive a past experience.

Hitherto we have assumed the links of association to be single or individual; we must now consider the very frequent case of the union of several bonds of contiguity or similarity. The facts brought up in the course of the illustration will show that, here as elsewhere, union is strength.

The combinations may be of Contiguity solely, or of mixed Contiguity and Similarity. Besides these purely intellectual bonds, an Emotion may contribute to the recall; and we have farther to ascertain what influence may be exercised by the will or Volition.

The general law may be stated thus :—

> Past actions, sensations, thoughts, or emotions, are recalled more easily, when associated either through contiguity or similarity, with more than one present object or impression.

COMPOSITION OF CONTIGUITIES.

2. In the Composition of Contiguities, we may distinguish Conjunctions and Successions.

Conjunctions. Most things affect the mind by a plurality of impressions. So simple an object as a star, is an aggregate of light, visible magnitude, and visible form; a diamond is a greater aggregate; a human being is more complicated still. A link of association with any one of the component parts of these aggregates may be strong enough to recall the whole; this would be single-handed contiguity. Or, a plurality of links, individually unequal to the recall, might compass it by their united force. A diamond might be suggested to the mind, partly by some circumstance that recalled its brilliancy, partly by an alliance with its hardness.

It is, however, when we pass beyond isolated objects to the aggregates made up by the various relationships of things, that we find the greatest scope for plurality of associations; as in the connexions with locality, with persons, with uses, and with properties.

Local associations play a great part in memory, both in single sufficiency, and in partnership with others. All things, with a fixed or usual locality, become connected in the mind with that locality. But a great many of these bonds are individually too feeble; we cannot, by thinking of the interior of a house, recall the whole of its furniture and contents. Nevertheless, local connexions may eke out other ties also insufficient of themselves. We may not be able to remember a mineral specimen by its being a certain ore of iron; but some local association in a museum or cabinet may complete the recall of its visible aspect. It often happens to us to meet persons in the street, whom we have formerly seen, but cannot tell who they are; something brings to mind the place of our former meeting, which, although of itself unable to effect the recall, in co-operation with the other, may be found adequate. Abercrombie relates that, walking in the street one day, he met a lady whose face was familiar, but whose name and connexions he could not remember. Some time after, he passed a cottage, to which he had been taken six months before, to see a gentleman who had met with an accident on the road, and had been taken there insensible. He then remembered that the lady was the wife of that patient. The local association completed the defective link in his memory.

MULTIPLE ASSOCIATIONS WITH PERSONS. 153

The connexions with *persons* frequently unite with other contiguous links. Objects become associated with their owners, makers, inventors, with all persons concerned in their use, or frequenting their locality. Many of those associations are imperfect in themselves, but capable of adding something to other associating bonds. A doctrine may be recalled partly by its subject, and partly by its being a doctrine of Aristotle or of Locke. The buildings rendered famous by great men may be remembered through this bond, in conjunction with locality.

We may adduce the converse case, the recall of persons by multiple associations. The relations of human beings are so numerous as to give frequent occasion to their being remembered by the union of many bonds. Persons are associated with their name; with locality, habitation, and places of resort; with blood and lineage, a very powerful mental tie, in consequence of the strength of the family feelings; with associates and friends; with occupation, pursuits, amusements; with property and possessions; with rank and position; with the many attributes that make up character and reputation; with a particular age; with the time they have lived in; with the vicissitudes and incidents that mark the course of their life. Desiring to recall the names of the Cabinet Ministers, we might think of them first as enumerated in a list; if we failed to remember any one or more, we should then recall the departments of state, next the leading men in the Lords and in the Commons, and so on, till everyone was brought up to mind.

The connexion with *uses* and properties is a frequent means of association, both single, and in combination. In recalling some great exhibition of works of industry, we assist the local alliances with the associations of use; we go over mentally the implements of Agriculture, Mining, Engineering, War; wearing apparel, furniture, &c. So with regard to the natural properties of things—the physical and chemical properties of a salt, the distinguishing marks of a vegetable species, the anatomy of an animal. Iron, nickel, and cobalt are remembered in part by their magnetic properties; the simple bodies in chemistry are associated with the idea of simplicity; the oxides with their containing oxygen.

Successions. Among the various kinds of succession adverted to, under Contiguity, there may be cases of combination. The memory of any series of events may be assisted by collateral and concurring series, or by conjunctions, such as above described. In the grand succession of our total experience in the Order of Time, many intermediate links that fail us, when exclusively relied on, are yet able to count in combined action. Our historical recollections are almost always composite; the main thread is helped by collateral currents, conjunctions, and associations; and we are so well aware of this, that, whenever we are at a loss, we make an express search for such additional aids. To remember any considerable series of events, say in English history, we should have to avail ourselves of concurring associations with persons, places, striking incidents, casual conjunctions. Thinking of the 16th century, we remember the two great monarchs between whose reigns it was almost equally divided; with their personalities many of the events are associated so strongly as to be recalled by that single link; others less strongly, and recoverable only in combination with a different link, as the date or order of time. Localities and local objects—the metropolis, the Tower, Tilbury fort, the monasteries—contribute additional ties, some sufficient in themselves, the rest useful in raising other links to the point of sufficiency.

Language. The coherence of names, and of trains of language, is a very large fraction of our total acquisitions. We are often aided here by composite links. When unable to recall a name, we fall back upon the circumstances of last hearing it, or on some other known bond of connexion.

Many of our recollections are a mixture of language with our conceptions of things. A discourse heard impresses us partly as a train of words, partly as a train of thoughts, images, and feelings; the remembrance of it is therefore of a compound nature. The learner in any subject, as Geometry, depends partly on his verbal memory, partly on his memory for the actual conceptions, the lines, angles, circles, &c. A pictorial description is held by verbal associations in conjunction with the hold of the purely pictorial elements. In all such cases, defects in the one train may be supplied from the other.

COMPOSITION OF SIMILARITIES.

3. The case of plurality of points of likeness contributing to the recall of something past, is sufficiently represented under the Law of Similarity.

It is merely a case of greater resemblance, the effect of which is to augment the chances of recall. If a thought, resembling in the subject some one previously known, has also a resemblance in the language, the operation of similarity in restoring the fact is so much the more certain. If we are reading a work which has imitated, or borrowed from, some other work that we have known, the similarity does not strike at first, but as we go on, the increasing number of resembling points brings on the flash of recognition. Wherever we have any means of increasing the similarity, and reducing the diversity, between what is present and what is out of mind, we necessarily provoke the reviving encounter.

MIXED CONTIGUITY AND SIMILARITY.

4. Things first brought together by the stroke of Similarity are afterwards retained by the help of Contiguity.

A man of inventive reach of mind brings up a new simile, or achieves a great identification in science. The two remote things thus brought together may then be made coherent by contiguous association; the recall at first due to genius is afterwards caused by memory. It is thus that we remember the fetches of great poets, and the scientific generalities that are the triumphs of modern discovery.

There is, however, an intermediate stage, wherein great strokes of Similarity may not have become matter of pure memory by Contiguity, but are recovered partly by the force of the similarity, and partly by the aid of a nascent, but incomplete, contiguous association. It is by this mixed or united hold, that a second-rate mind can appropriate and use the inventions of original minds, before they have become so hackneyed and common as to be in everybody's memory. It is in the same way that we can retain scientific truths, through our own perception of their generalizing sweep, when once they have been brought to our view. No man could take hold of any large amount of scientific doctrines, without seeing for himself the similarities that they involve, besides his memory of the statements of them. We can, after Newton, compare Terrestrial with Celestial gravity, and keep in mind his law by the force of the similarity that makes one recall the other; we are also assisted by the contiguous junction of the two facts in the wording of the law.

5. The reviving stroke of Similarity may be aided by the *proximity* of the things desired.

A poet living in the country falls readily upon rural

images. The books that we have lately read are the most likely to furnish parallels to any present subject. Hence, an important rule for assisting invention—namely, to refresh our minds with the subjects where we expect to find the identities that we are in quest of. A natural philosopher is in need of certain mathematical formulæ, but is unable to discover those that are suitable; his resource is to renew his mathematical studies for a time, thereby coming into closer mental proximity with the whole range of the department. Gibbon tells us that he replenished his resources of sarcasm, by perusing annually Pascal's Provincial Letters. So a poet might prepare himself for composing in the Spenserian stanza, by familiarizing himself with the Faerie Queen, and the other models. In whatever point a writer either feels intellectual weakness, or desires to be unusually strong, he should keep close companionship with the highest examples of the quality. If he aspires to elevated diction, his flight will be aided by frequent recurrence to Æschylus and Milton.

6. The bond of similarity is sometimes artificially employed as a help to Memory.

The art of Mnemonics, or artificial memory, among other devices, uses a combination of similarity and contiguity. One of the simplest examples is the use of alliteration; the sequence of words 'life and liberty' is better remembered than 'life and freedom.' The effect would also arise from the arrangement of a series of leading names in the alphabetical order of their commencing letters. Verse is a mnemonic aid; knowing the metrical form that a saying must assume, we have already a certain hold of it by similarity, which will in part make up for the weakness of the contiguous bond.

Another mnemonic art, applicable to the learning of a string of words, as the exceptions to a rule in grammar, is to arrange them so as to have a connexion of meaning. Thus, in English, there are certain verbs that are followed by other verbs in the infinitive without the use of the preposition 'to.' For remembering these more easily, we might cast them thus:—feel, hear, see (senses), will, shall, may, can, do, have (auxiliaries), let, bid, make, dare, durst, must, need (different forms of permission and compulsion).

THE ELEMENT OF FEELING.

7. The link of Feeling may enter powerfully into composite association.

EMOTIONAL CONTROL OF THE THOUGHTS.

The association of objects and feelings has been already noticed (CONTIGUITY, § 30). The consequences, which are numerous and far-reaching, will be still farther traced in the description of the higher emotions.

A present feeling is a power in the mind, retaining and reviving the objects that are in harmony with it, and repelling such as are discordant, or merely indifferent. In an affectionate mood, the thoughts and images partake of love and tenderness. The habitual egotist has a facility in recalling facts for his own glorification.

When a number of things are equally open to be suggested by the intellectual bonds, the emotional state gives the preference. The thoughts of persons of intense feelings, and of small intellectual power, have the monotonous stamp of the prevailing emotion; such are fond and weak-minded mothers, exclusive devotees to business, and enthusiastic temperaments in general. The plausibility of characters in fiction or romance is made to depend on this circumstance. All the thoughts and expressions of a Shylock bear the cast of the feelings attributed to him.

INFLUENCE OF VOLITION.

8. The influence of the Will in intellectual production is indirect.

No mere urgency of motive can make a feeble bond stronger. If one's life were to depend upon an effort of memory beyond the pitch of the formed adhesion, it would be of little avail.

(1) A powerful Motive, by exciting the system, may exalt the intensity of the mental processes.

Any great pain to be avoided, or pleasure to be commanded, is accompanied with an increased nervous action, under which all the powers are enhanced, including the forces of revival by contiguity and similarity. The effect of increased cerebral action is seen in the extreme case of the delirium of fever, during which long-forgotten trains have sometimes been revived with minute fidelity. The greatest stretches of invention usually require a more than ordinary cerebral excitement, sometimes worked up by physical stimulants, but commonly arising in the voluntary effort.

(2) The Will operates under the form of Attention, or mental concentration upon special objects present to the view.

It is probable that a greater force of attention, directed upon what is present, will in some degree quicken the power to revive the associated past. In difficult recollection, we assume this to be the case; anxious to recall the name of a distant hill, we gaze upon the hill for some time, thinking thereby to add to the chance of the recovery. We can do the same with a mere mental image: the will fixes the mental attention as well as the bodily—a fact very much in favour of the doctrine as to the seat of revived impressions. If we come to a stand in repeating a discourse, we dwell strongly upon the last remembered words; if a local association snaps, we concentrate the mind upon the part next the break.

(3) The Will prompts the search after collateral links.

It has been seen, that, by uniting several links, each too weak of itself, we may form a compound that will be sufficient. Now, by a voluntary act, we can go off in search of these collateral bonds. Not remembering in the order of time, all the chief events of a given century, we can, by mere voluntary determination, pass to other links, as persons, places, and notable circumstances.

The power of the Will over the trains of thought; through these indirect means, may be considerable. We may not at once determine what thoughts shall arise, but, of those that have arisen, we can determine the attention upon some rather than upon others; the withdrawal of the attention from any one will nullify its power of farther reproduction. We thus refrain from pursuing trains not available for the purpose in hand. If we are building up a geological speculation, we confine our local recollections to geological features.

It may be remarked as frequently occurring, that although there are present to the mind one or more objects, each richly associated with mental trains, yet there is nothing actually suggested. The inertness may be owing to various causes, highly illustrative of the workings of the intellect. It may arise from mere exhaustion, indolence, or inactivity. The condition of the mind and brain in respect of activity, is very variable, and very much within our control. Or, again, the forces of the mind may have got into a set track or attitude, opposing a certain resistance to the assumption of any other trains of thought; as when some one subject engrosses our attention, so that even during a break in the actual current of the thoughts, other subjects are not entertained. And, farther, when numerous solicitations on different sides are nearly equally balanced, the result is a kind of intellectual suspense; when an object is associated equally with many outgoing trains, as the sun, or the sea, no start is made till some concurring links point to one definite movement. If the sea is stormy and we are contemplating a sea voyage, we are led off into all the trains of recollection of our seafaring experience.

OBSTRUCTIVE ASSOCIATIONS.

9. The power to assist includes the power to resist. Any agency that is helpful when with us, is obstructive when against us. This is fully applicable to the case of concurring associations.

It often happens that we fail to remember a name, from having the mind pre-occupied with a wrong syllable. So when things are lost; should we accidentally be prepossessed with some mistaken locality, or some erroneous supposition, we have not the full benefit of our power of recollection in the matter; at some other time, when the wrong prepossession has left us, our memory may be quite adequate to the recall.

The history of science would furnish many instances of discoveries kept back by the force of a prejudice or pre-occupation, some false bent or cue once getting hold of men's minds. Several of the glimpses of Aristotle in Psychology were nearer the truth than the views that long prevailed after him; not so much from his superior genius, as from his not being involved in the mazes of an ultra-spiritualistic philosophy. It is remarked of Priestley, that though he began his researches in Chemistry with little knowledge of what had been already done, he entered on the subject *free from the prejudices that warped the judgment and limited the view* of the educated chemists.

Obstructive associations may be traced, on a grand scale, in the conflict of different modes of viewing the objects and occurrences of the world. There is a standing hostility between the Artistic and the Scientific modes of looking at things, and an opposition less marked between the Scientific, or the Theoretical, and the Practical points of view. The artistic mind is obstructed by the presence of considerations of scientific truth; and the scientific mind, bent on being artistic, walks encumbered, and with diminished energy. Poetic fiction is never so brilliant as when the poet is untrammeled by a regard to truth.

A good instance of the obstructiveness of incompatible ideas is found in the effort of guessing riddles and conundrums. These usually turn upon the equivocal meanings of words. Now a mind that makes use of language to pass to the serious import or genuine meanings, is disqualified from following out the play of equivocation, not because the requisite associations do not exist, but because these are overborne by others inimical to the whole proceeding.

ASSOCIATION OF CONTRAST.

10. It being known as a fact, that objects, on many occasions, recall their contraries; Contrast, or Contrariety, has been admitted among the forces that revive past thoughts. The influence may be analyzed as follows :—

(1) Contrast is a phase of the primary function of mind, named Discrimination or Relativity.

If every state of feeling and of knowledge implies a transition, and is therefore a double or two-sided fact, our knowledge is essentially a cognition of contraries. Heat means, not an absolute state, but the shock of a transition from cold; the recent cold is as essential to the fact as the present heat. When we think of heat, we have a tacit reference to cold; when we think of 'up,' we have a tacit reference to 'down.' To pass into the contrary cognition in these cases, is merely to reverse the order of the couple, to make cold the explicit, and heat the implicit element.

(2) Contrasts are frequently suggested by Contiguity.

A great number of the more usual contrasts acquire a farther connexion through the habitual transitions of thought and speech. Our memory contains numerous associated couples,—up and down, great and small, rich and poor, true and false, life and death.

When we come to understand the value of contrast as a Rhetorical device both for intensifying the expression of feeling, and for clearness in expounding doctrine, we acquire the habit of introducing contrasts on all important occasions.

(3) The mutual suggestion of contraries may be partly due to Similarity.

There is an old maxim that contraries must have a ground of likeness. This is true of all contraries up to the highest contrast of all (Object and Subject). Matter and Space are in the genus Extension (the Object): Intellect and Feeling are both under Mind, the subject; blue and red are in the class colour. Thus, while the highest opposition can be suggested only by Relativity or pure Contrast, the lower kinds introduce an element of similarity in their generic agreement. Wealth may suggest poverty, partly by the opposition, and partly by leading us to think of the generic subject—human conditions.

It is by the mutual attraction of similars, that we are made alive to contradictions. We hear a certain affirmation; the sameness of subject recalls a previous affirmation of an opposite tenor. The announcement that a certain rock is of a sedimentary origin, brings to our mind by similarity the idea of the same rock, coupled with the assertion of its igneous origin.

(4) Many Contrasts are stamped on the mind through Emotion.

Apart from the influence of the shock of change, necessary to consciousness in any degree, the mind may be quickened by strong special emotions. When any quality is in excess, as heat, cold, exercise, rest, we are urged to think of the opposite as a desired relief. The disappointment of our expectations may take the form of a shock of contrast; looking for favour, we may encounter contumely; a journey for health may confirm our malady.

The contrasts of Poetry and Art are transitions for heightening an effect.

The moralist delights in pourtraying the contrasts in human conditions—the pride of prosperity with the chances of misfortune and the certainty of the last end.

CHAPTER IV.

CONSTRUCTIVE ASSOCIATION.

1. By means of association, the mind has the power to form Combinations, or aggregates, different from anything actually experienced.

The processes named Imagination, Creation, Constructiveness, have not been taken account of in the preceding exposition. In Similarity, we had before us a power tending to originality and invention; but the genius of the mechanical inventor, the man of science, the poet, the painter, the musician, implies something more complex. In the steam-engine, in the science of geometry, in Paradise Lost, we find something beyond the grandest fetches of Similarity.

Nevertheless, the intellectual powers already described are sufficient for these creations; the addition consists of a stimulus and guidance supplied by the Feelings and the Will. This will appear from the examples.

MECHANICAL CONSTRUCTIVENESS.

2. In Mechanical Acquisition, we have often to combine movements into new groupings. An exercise of volition, directed to the movements separately, brings them together in the first instance.

In learning to dance, the separate positions are first acquired; when the will can command these, the pupil is directed to combine them into the steps and figures; these at last become coherent by the plastic force of Contiguity. It is the same with military drill, and with education in the manual arts; the learner is first able to command certain elementary movements, and then unites them, in time and order, as directed.

Sometimes the process is to dissociate and suppress movements, as in endeavouring to walk without swinging the arms. The instrumentality is the same. One effort of volition determines the complex movement; another is directed to the members to be arrested; and the required act is the result of the differential operation.

When a complex act has to be performed, made up of timed and ordered movements, successive attempts are needed to make them fall into their places. Thus, in learning to swim, we throw out the limbs, by separate volitions, but cannot at first attain to the exact rhythm of the swimmer. After a time, we make the effort that happily combines every movement in the proper order. The difficulty is at an end: we then keep up the successful conjunction, and fall into it, at pleasure, ever afterwards.

These constructions of our mechanical or muscular energies, exemplify the three conditions or essentials of the Constructive process of the Intellect.

(1) There must be a command of the separate elements.

CONDITIONS OF THE CONSTRUCTIVE PROCESS. 163

The more thorough and complete this command, the easier is the work of uniting them into new combinations.

(2) There must be an *idea*, plan, or conception, of the desired combinations; some mental delineation of it, such as to make us aware when we have succeeded. This idea may be a model for imitation, as the fugleman of a company at drill; or it may be a conception of the effect to be produced, as in laying out grounds. In other cases, it is a verbal combination or description, as when we are told to conceive a gold mountain.

(3) There is a series of *tentatives*, or a process of trial and error. The distinct volitions are put in exercise to bring on the separate movements, but these do not at first chime in to the joint result; the sense of failure determines another trial, and then another, until some one prove successful. The moment of success is attended with a certain satisfaction, or elation, under which arises a re-inforced prompting to maintain the fortunate combination; and the circumstances are then, in the highest degree, favourable for the beginning of a permanent association.

VERBAL CONSTRUCTIVENESS.

3. Verbal constructiveness is exemplified, first, in learning to Articulate.

A certain power of uttering the elementary articulations—the vowels, consonants, and simpler syllables—being presupposed, it is desired to combine these into words, under the spur of imitation. The ear supplies the type to be conformed to; the will urges various tentatives; there is a sense of these being unconformable to the type, which invites renewal, until conformity is attained. The child can pronounce the syllables *may*, *ree*, in separation; it hears *Mary*, with the wish to say the word; the first endeavours are sensibly wrong; they are renewed, and, at some favourable conjuncture, the two syllables fall exactly together in the right order. The ear is satisfied and delighted, and a gush of nervous influence accompanies the satisfaction, which goes a good way to cement the connexion; every succeeding endeavour involves fewer stumbles, and the association is at last completed.

The child's initial difficulties in this acquirement are owing to the imperfect command of the elementary sounds. The voice is not at first formed to them, and the voluntary link that arouses them is for a long time wanting.

4. The combining of words into Sentences is a farther exercise of constructiveness.

To imitate literally a sentence heard, is substantially the same effort as now described. A farther advance is exemplified, when the child constructs new sentences to suit new meanings. From the combination 'good boy,' and the separate name 'Tom,' coupled with an approving sentiment towards Tom, the will is prompted to dissociate and recombine the form, 'Tom,' so as to make 'good Tom.' The idea or type in the mind is to convey some expression having the same force towards the new subject, as the old form has towards 'boy;' there must be a feeling, from analogy, that 'good Tom' answers the end; and accordingly, when this is struck out, there follows the throb of successful endeavour. As before, the more or less easy attainment of the end depends on the familiarity with the constituents. When a considerable variety of sentences have been mastered, the process of dropping out and taking in, to answer new meanings, is performed with the utmost rapidity.

5. The highest Combinations of Language fulfil the same conditions.

It is necessary, first, to lay up in the memory a certain store of names (allied to things), and of formed combinations of these into affirmations, clauses, sentences, and connected portions of discourse, with meanings attached. This acquired store contains the material of new compositions; the more abundant and the more familiar the verbal sequences at command, and the nearer they approach to our requirements, the less troublesome will be the work of composition. A meaning has to be expressed, partly, but not wholly, coinciding with expressed meanings already laid up in the memory; the nearest of these previous forms are recalled by the associating forces; we operate upon them by combination, by excision, and by substitution, until our mind is satisfied that the resulting verbal construction embraces the subject proposed.

The compliance with other conditions, besides the signifying of a meaning, demands greater resources to start from, or else more numerous tentatives. Not to mention the forms of grammar, which are comparatively easy to satisfy when the stored up arrangements have been grammatical, there may be in the mind certain ideals of perspicuity, of terseness, of elegance, of melody, of cadence, all which have to be complied

CONSTRUCTIVENESS IN LANGUAGE. 165

with by the method of tentatives. It is then requisite to compose many sentences to the same meaning, in order to choose one that combines the other requisites. But in order to embody each one of those high demands, we must have already, in the memory, numerous forms adapted to each; forms of perspicuous statement, of brevity, of elegance, of melody. We should also have a very decided feeling of the result when attained.

To take the example of Versification. The power of verse-making supposes a memory largely stored with verses. A given meaning has to be expressed in verse. The prose mind, following the lead of meaning, would first light upon a prose form, and, on that as a basis, would proceed to make the accommodations needed for verse. The true poet, however, is he that 'lisped in numbers, for the numbers came;' his first basis of operations is a metrical form; this is shaped and modified to comply with the signification, yet never departing from metre.

FEELINGS OF MOVEMENT.

6. We may, by help of experience, create new combinations in the Ideas or Feelings of Force and Movement.

The most important muscular feelings, for the purposes of the intellect, are our numerous impressions of resistance, pressure, movement, embodied in the various muscles and muscular groupings. Through the hand and arm, we have engrained impressions or ideas of different degrees of weight and resistance—one pound, four pounds, twenty pounds. It is possible to construct intermediate grades or varieties of quantity. Given the idea of a one pound weight, and the idea of a double or a treble, we can, by an effort of construction, form some approximate idea of two pounds or three pounds. The main condition is still the vividness of our hold of the constituent notions. The greatest difficulty lies in knowing when we have succeeded, it not being in our power to say exactly that the constructed impression corresponds to the double or the triple of the original.

The graduation of our muscular efforts to a certain end, as hitting a mark, or striking a measured blow, supposes the power of interpolating shades of muscular consciousness. The feelings of Architectural fitness are an excellent example of the same constructiveness. From our experience of the weight and the tenacity of small pieces of stone, we take upon ourselves to judge what bulk of support is needed, in a column, for masses altogether beyond our means of direct estimate.

It is by a vague effort of constructiveness, applied to our muscular acquirements, that we conceive untraversed distances, as the remote Alpine summits, the moon and the stars. We increase numerically known exertions of our own—that is, combine them with notions of multiplied quantity, and thereby obtain representations, doubtless feeble and inadequate, of these vast distances.

The *emotional* feelings of movement fall under the analogy of the emotions generally, which are given in a separate head.

CONSTRUCTIVENESS IN THE SENSATIONS.

7. In the Sensations of the Senses, whether Emotional or Intellectual, there is large scope for original constructions.

In the lower senses, as those of Organic Life, Taste, and Smell, the principal effect is emotional, and is attended by the circumstances special to the feelings. We may, by a great effort, conceive new forms of organic pain or pleasure, provided they are resolvable into elements known to us. If it be true, that the pains of parturition are of the nature of spasm, or cramp, they may to some extent be conceived through that experience. The pain of gout may be realized through the knowledge of other modes of acute inflammatory pain. Many modes of acute pain are comparable to scalding heat.

So with the pleasurable organic feelings. We all know what exhilaration is, and can conceive the general fact with varieties of mode. We may thence be made to conceive the exciting effect of some unknown stimulant, as opium or Indian hemp.

The obstacle in such a case is the low intellectual persistence of these feelings; we cannot, without considerable striving, recover an organic state under a present state of an alien character. Even the familiar pleasures of eating are not easy to revive ideally in their absence. The constructive exertion is fruitless, if the elements have no abiding hold of the mind.

Tastes, as being more intellectually persistent than organic states, are more constructible. From the experience of relishes, sweets, bitters, &c., we might conceive a complex taste never known, a new mixture of relish and bitterness, of sweet and sour. So with Smells. We might endeavour to conceive assafœtida from garlic, or an oriental spice-grove from our own flowers and perfumes.

In the higher senses, the examples are abundant. In Touch, Hearing, and Sight, the pleasures and pains, as being more intellectually persistent, are more constructible, than the feelings of the lower senses; while the sensations whose character is knowledge, and not feeling, are pre-eminently disposed to the combining operation.

We have a large experience of Touches, soft, pungent, hard, rough, smooth, and may often be called upon, to realize new varieties. Many minerals have specialities of touch; for example, asbestos. If we had never touched cork, we should have to combine mentally the several elements, namely, a special kind of soft touch, warmth, and lightness.

The textile bodies have specialities of touch; and from the experience of a certain number we are qualified to conceive others, if resolvable into the known. The blind must frequently perform this operation.

In the sense of Touch, considered as including muscular exertion, there is scope for constructing grades of tactual size and form, as well as pressure and resistance.

In the sense of Hearing, there is frequent occasion for constructiveness. We may be asked to conceive unheard sounds, as the muttering of an earthquake, the crash of a falling house, the shout of a battalion in a bayonet charge. The describer, in these cases, must assign some sounds known to us, such as, if combined and intensified, would approach the reality. An ear retentive for sounds generally, and a special familiarity with those to be combined, would be conditions of success.

In Sight, constructiveness is facilitated by the intellectual quality of the sense. Given a dead colour, we could conceive it made brilliant or lustrous. It is a more doubtful matter whether we could make the construction supposed by Hume, namely, to interpose an unexperienced shade of colour. Inasmuch as all the varieties of colour are reducible to three primary colours, there should be a possibility of picturing new shades. Hobbes's example, a mountain of gold, typifies a comparatively easy class of constructions, the alteration of colour in a given form; such are a white crow, a room when painted, a sketch when the colours are laid in, London built of the stone of Edinburgh, or of Paris. Here we have to dismiss or dissociate one element, and introduce another, an operation that may be very much thwarted or aided by the feelings: the colour most agreeable in itself will cling to us by preference. Another class involves the putting together of new shapes, as the mermaid, the dragon, the chimæra, Milton's pictures of Sin and Death.

The ready hold of the elements to be combined is still the grand condition of success. Also, in order to possess ourselves permanently of a new image, by means of construction, we must continue or repeat the effort, as for any other desired remembrance.

CONSTRUCTION OF NEW EMOTIONS.

8. Examples may be taken from the higher Emotions.

The more simple Emotions, as Wonder, Fear, Love, Power, must be known by experience. Even although we be able to resolve into simpler elements, Self-complacency, Anger, the Intellectual Emotions, the Artistic and the Moral Feelings, yet some experience should be had of them as compounds, in order to enlarge the constructive basis.

The simplest exercise of construction would be to change the degree of an emotion; as in entering into the feelings of another person, habitually more or less courageous, loving, self-complacent, irascible, than one's-self. We should then have to multiply or diminish our known states of feeling, together with their collaterals and consequences. We should not merely endeavour to intensify our conception of courage, for example; we should also deal with its occasions, its expression, and its results, which also, being multiplied, would support the attempt to magnify the proper emotion. As a considerable aid, we might go back to the occasion when our own feeling was accidentally stimulated to an intense degree.

Any one feebly constituted in the emotions generally would be disqualified from realizing a temperament of the opposite stamp, unless by a very intense exertion. So it would be with a person of weak volition endeavouring to conceive a man of energy. There is a natural repugnance to the very attempt to pass so far out of one's own bounds; whence the maxim—to know a man we must love him.

A still more frequent exercise is to transfer a familiar emotion to a new object. This is the way that we enter into other men's tastes, and likings, their fears, hatreds, and antipathies. We have the feelings in ourselves, and we can by an effort of construction suppose them to invest other objects. Ambition is at bottom the same, whether for temporal power or for spiritual power; for official command, or for intellectual and moral sway. The sentiment of worship is generically alike, whatever be the objects of worship; still, a considerable effort would be necessary for a Christian to enter into the manner of feeling of a Pagan, or for a Calvinist to sympathize with a Romanist.

The authors of Poetry and Romance have to unfold the workings of characters far removed from their own, which involves emotional constructiveness. In such cases, it is desirable to check the imaginative adaptation, by actual observation of individuals nearly approaching to the type in view. This is the usual course of novelists, when pourtraying a character far removed from their own. Goethe's 'Fair Saint,' in Wilhelm Meister, was depicted from acquaintance with a real person.

CONCRETING THE ABSTRACT.

9. The forming, out of abstract elements, images in the Concrete, is an application of constructiveness.

We may join together size, form, and colour into a concrete visible image; as when we are told to fancy to ourselves a golden ingot of given dimensions. So we may conceive a building from its plans, elevations, and known material. The facility in such cases, depends, for the most part, upon the ideal hold of colour. When there is great complication of form, something depends on the muscular retentiveness of the eye.

Another case is the conceiving of a country from a map, the actual dimensions and the colours being also given. The mind must endeavour to regain as vividly as possible the memories most nearly corresponding to the prescribed elements, and by a voluntary act hold them in the view till they fuse into a concrete. Or, we may start from a well-remembered concrete, and strike out and insert portions, till it suit the elements given.

It is substantially the same operation to picture to ourselves minerals, plants, and animals, from their descriptions, with or without the aid of drawings.

REALIZING OF REPRESENTATION OR DESCRIPTION.

10. To realize Verbal descriptions, or other Representations of things not experienced, is a constructive process.

This is but the continuation of the foregoing cases. Language, pictures, sculptured forms, models, and diagrams are modes of indicating the elements, whose mental combination will give the idea of the object intended. It is a part of the Rhetorical Art, to show how to describe things so as to give the utmost aid to the mind in conceiving them.

The realizing of things, not personally experienced, but brought before us in description or other indication, is the chief meaning of the act of Conceiving, or Conception, sometimes treated as one of the intellectual faculties. It passes above memory, as being an exercise of Constructiveness, and falls below Imagination proper, as containing no exercise of originality or invention.

CONSTRUCTIVENESS IN SCIENCE.

11. The Abstractions, Inductions, Deductions, and Experimental Discoveries of Science, already included under similarity, also involve constructiveness.

To begin with Abstraction. We may represent a form by an outline diagram as in Euclid. But this, as giving a definite size, colour, and material, is not an abstraction. The most perfect type of the abstract idea is the verbal definition, which is a construction of language adapted to exclude whatever does not belong to the generalized attribute. The definition, 'a line is length without breadth,' is a verbal construction, intended to give what belongs to the line in the abstract. So with the definitions of science generally; inertia, polarity, heat, cell, animal, mind, and so on. They are, on the part of the first framers, exercises of original construction, proceeding tentatively till a form of words is arrived at, conformable to all the individuals to be included in the generality.

Induction presents no new peculiarity. All inductions have at last to be shaped and tied down by precise language, expressing neither more nor less than is common to the facts comprehended in each. Sometimes an induction is made up of numerical and geometrical elements, as the laws of Kepler, and Snell's law of Sines. These involve, in the first instance, discoveries of Similarity.

The Deductive Sciences are made up of a vast machinery, exemplifying, in a remarkable degree, the creative or constructive, as opposed to the merely reproductive, processes of the mind. Nature does not provide cubic equations, chemical formulæ, or syllogistic schemes. These are built up by slow degrees, out of elementary symbols, and the constructions are governed and checked by the ends to be served.

The discoveries of Experimental Science are a more palpable and obvious case of constructiveness, being mostly material operations. The first inventor of an instrument, as the air-pump, may have certain previous instruments to proceed upon, as the common water-pump, the instruments for enclosing air, &c.; these he tentatively modifies and adapts till the new end is answered.

PRACTICAL CONSTRUCTIONS.

12. In all the departments of Practice, there are examples of constructive arrangement.

The discoveries and devices of the mechanical arts consist in machinery adapted to ends. They may be described in the terms above applied to the Experimental discoveries of science.

The mere transfer, by a stroke of Similarity, of a machinery already in use to a new case, constitutes one department of practical invention; as in the extension of the wheel and pinion to all kinds of machinery. But a very great number of advances in machinery are absolutely new creations, as in the first invention of the mechanic powers, the pump, the melting of metals, the devices of surgery. There must be a certain amount of accident to begin with; but the accidents must fall into the hands of men prepared, by a peculiar cast of mind, for turning them to account. The main qualities of the inventive genius for practice are—intellectual attainments in the subject matter of the discoveries, activity of temperament applied to the making of experiments, and a charm or fascination for the subject. Such men as Kepler, Hooke, Priestley, James Watt, Sir William Herschell, combined the intellectual, active, and emotional constituents of great inventors in the arts. To resources of knowledge, they added an equally indispensable gift,—compounded of activity and emotional interest—namely, unwearied groping and experimentation. Mere handicraft skill is also an element in mechanical constructiveness.

The like qualities belong to the contrivers of business arrangements, of social organization, law, and administration. Sometimes, a mere fetch of Similarity is enough, but oftener there is a long series of tentatives, ending in a construction suitable to the object sought. The organization of an army, the keeping of public accounts, the management of a large factory, are the result of innumerable trials checked by felt similarity to the ends.

The quality of mind named Judgment, has a meaning with reference to constructiveness, being a clear sense of the purpose to be served, and of the fitness of any construction for that purpose. Judgment is often put in contrast to genius, or intellectual fertility; it does not provide the suggestions, but tests them. There are various obstacles to the exercise of a severe judgment of the fitness of means to ends;—impatience of the labour of repeated constructions, self-conceit, and a feeble sense of the importance of the objects to be gained. Wellington is, by common consent, held to have been a man of pre-eminent judgment, at least in military affairs.

The adapting of one's views and plans to the opinions of others, as in party leadership, is a case containing all the elements of constructiveness. According to the number of conditions to be fulfilled, the operation is the more protracted, the mental conflict more severe, and the greater the demand for variety of suggestions, the product of associating forces working on previous knowledge. Long experience, by accumulating constructions already formed, diminishes the labour in suiting the new cases.

The imitating of a model is an instance of constructiveness. The model has to be changed in certain particulars to suit the case in hand; as when one Act of Parliament is framed upon another. The facility of the construction depends on having fully present to the mind the model and the subject to be shaped according to it. If both the one and the other are perfectly familiar, the combination emerges easily and almost unconsciously.

In Oratory, there is a perpetual series of constructions; it is rare to repeat the same form of words. The speaker has before him, as *disjecta membra*, a certain meaning to be expressed, and sentences expressing approximations to that meaning; he has also an ideal of cadence, taste, and other requisites. Possessing a full mastery of all these elements, he puts them together in the required shape, with a rapidity that causes astonishment. The repartees of a ready wit are surprising from the quickness of the combining operation. Still more remarkable, in this respect, are the Italian Improvisatori; their facility must be due to their abundance of ready formed combinations.

CONSTRUCTIVENESS UNDER FEELING.

13. It is the nature of certain constructions to satisfy some immediate feeling or emotion—as Fear, Love, Anger, Beauty, Moral Sentiment.

We are supposed to be strongly occupied with an emotion, and to impart its tinge to the constructions of the thoughts.

Under Compound Association, notice was taken of the agency of the feelings in mere reminiscence; the same agency is farther displayed in new constructions. In strong Fear, we construct imaginations of danger; in general elation of mind, all our pictures take a sanguine form. The warm enthusiastic temperament of Wordsworth and of Shelley pourtrays nature in gorgeous hues. All images brought up by intellectual resuscitation are shaped and adapted till they conform to the reigning emotion.

The exemplifications of this kind of constructiveness are numerous. In literary compositions, we detect the emotional nature of the writers, as well as their knowledge and habits of thought; the warm geniality of Shakespeare, the lofty pride of Milton, the mildness of Addison, the gloomy scorn of Swift.

Bias, or the influence of the Feelings in truth and falsehood, means the shaping of facts and doctrines to suit a sentiment. Properly speaking, this influence is completed by a constructive operation, the taking out and putting in of parts and particulars till the feeling is conformed to. It is thus that many theories of philosophy have been framed to suit the dignity of nature, or rather the sentiment of the dignified in the mind of the theorizer.

The Myth is a construction so far governed by feeling as to give evidence only of feeling and not of fact. Such are the Grecian legends referring to the divine and heroic descent or the several tribes; and the legends of saints and remarkable persons in more recent times.

The natural craving of the mind for something beyond fact and reality, is the motive for ideal and hyperbolical creations. The intellectual processes supply the material; various constructions are attempted and rejected, until the feeling is complied with.

14. The Constructions of the FINE ARTS generally are framed to suit the Æsthetic Feelings, or Taste, of the artist.

What these feelings are will be shown in detail afterwards. They are different from the feelings that guide us in scientific and in practical constructions, from none of which can a motive (ultimately grounded on feeling) be absent.

For example, there is no requirement in art more constant

than the satisfying of the feeling of Harmony. Take the case of Poetry. The images must harmonize with the sentiments; the characters, besides being consistent with themselves, must be placed in suitable scenes and situations; the language must be intrinsically melodious, and also in keeping with the subject-matter. The composition has to be modified in submission to this all-pervading requirement. The tentatives may be numerous and protracted, but the elements of success are now apparent. There should be a command of language for selection. The feeling of harmony should be strong and delicate, and should be already embodied in numerous familiar examples. With abundant material and a decisive sense of the effect, the execution is a series of trials, continued till the result fully accords with the sensibility of the artist.

A humourist has in his mind a certain subject, as Knight Errantry, and a certain feeling called humour, and with this feeling he possesses many instances of combinations for gratifying it. Out of the career of the Knight Errant, he singles out passages, susceptible of being combined into ludicrous images, as for example, the extravagances of the pursuit; he heightens these, excludes any sobering or redeeming features, and also contrives situations for giving them in their most ludicrous form; and at last produces a construction successfully appealing to the emotion that he starts with.

15. IMAGINATION will be found most characteristically exemplified in Fine Art Constructiveness. The principal elements of Imagination are (1) Concreteness, (2) Originality or Invention, and (3) the presence of an Emotion.

(1) Imagination has for its objects the *concrete*, the real or the actual, as opposed to abstractions and generalities, which are the matter of science, and occasionally of the practical arts. The full colouring of reality is supposed to enter into our imagination of a scene in nature, or of a transaction in history. To imagine the landing of Julius Cæsar in Britain, is to be impressed with the visible aspect of the scene, in the same way—although without the vividness, accuracy, or completeness—as an actual spectator would remember it. Sensation, Memory, Conception, Imagination, alike deal with the fulness of the actual world, as opposed to mere abstractions.

(2) Imagination farther points to some Originality, Novelty, Inventiveness, or Creativeness, on the part of the mind imagining, and is not a mere reproduction of previous forms. It ranks as a Constructive process, thus rising above both

memory and conception. The name is occasionally used in the sense of Realizing a Description, or Conceiving what is represented to us through language; but this usage is undesirable, as confounding two very different operations, while the inferior exercise is sufficiently denoted by other words. The prevailing employment of the term Imagination, is to express originality; by a powerful imagination we mean a wide compass of creative effort, as in the highest productions of poetry or the other Fine Arts. The word in its best application, is identical with Fine Art Constructiveness, as will farther appear under the subsequent head.

(3) Imagination is subject to some present *emotion* of the mind. This needs explanation. All constructions are for some end, which must be a feeling in the last resort. A pump is constructed to gratify the feeling of thirst, and other wants, all resolvable into feelings. A geometrical diagram is intended to give some satisfaction immediate or remote.

The feelings or emotions ruling the constructions of Imagination are, first, the Æsthetic Emotions, or those of Fine Art. A construction that gratifies these is not included either in Science or in Practice. The Paradise Lost is a work of Imagination; Euclid's Elements, and the Chinese Wall, are not works of Imagination. When a work of Utility is shaped, decorated, or adorned, to gratify æsthetic sensibility, it combines Imagination with practical constructiveness.

Secondly, Imagination is allowed to be used for expressing the *bias* given by present emotions to the constructions for Truth, or for Utility, as when we distort facts through our fears, likings, antipathies, or our artistic feelings. The perverting influence of the feelings, either in matters of knowledge, or in matters of practice, is often described as intruding Imagination into the province of Reason, although Reason itself must work for ends, and these ends must centre in feelings. There are feelings that are the legitimate goal of the reason; and there are others that are not legitimate; and to give way to these last (which are either æsthetic feelings, or in close alliance with them), is to fall under the sway of Imagination.

The name FANCY, a corruption of phantasy (from the Greek *phantasia*, which had nearly the meaning of 'idea' in modern times, as opposed to sensation and actuality), is applied to those creations that are farthest removed from nature, fact, or sober reality. The pictures of Fairy land, and the supernatural, are creatures of the fancy. The light, sportive vein of Art, as contrasted with the thoughtful, grave, and serious, is called fanciful. 'Comus,' as compared with 'Paradise Lost,' is a work of fancy.

IDEALITY, or the Ideal, is another name for Imagination. It notes more particularly the tendency to soar above the limits of the actual, and to combine scenes where our aspirations and desires may find gratification, if only in idea; there being nothing to satisfy us in the world of reality.

CHAPTER V.*

ABSTRACTION—THE ABSTRACT IDEA.

NOMINALISM AND REALISM.

1. THE first stage in Abstraction is to identify and compare a number of objects possessing similarity in diversity; as stars, mountains, horses, men, pleasures. Such objects constitute a Class.

Until we have been struck with the resemblance of various things that also differ, we do not make a beginning in abstraction. We feel identity among the stars in spite of their variety. There is something common to the state named pleasure, amid much disparity. The things thus identified make a class, and the operation is called *classifying*.

2. We are able to attend to the points of agreement of resembling things, and to neglect the points of difference; as when we think of the light of the heavenly bodies, or the roundness of round bodies. This power is named Abstraction.

It is a fact that we can direct our attention, or our thoughts, to the points of agreement of bodies that agree. We can think of the light of the heavenly bodies, and make assertions, and draw inferences respecting it. So we can think of the roundness of spherical bodies, and discard the consideration of their colour and size. In such an object as the full moon, we can concentrate our regards upon its luminous

* The four preceding chapters complete the systematic view of the Intellect; the three following embrace the leading controversies.

character, wherein it agrees with one class of objects; or upon its figure, wherein it agrees with another class of objects. We can think of the taste of a strawberry, either as agreeing with other tastes, or as agreeing with pleasures generally.

In the case of concrete objects operating upon different senses, we can readily concentrate attention upon the properties of a single sense. Notwithstanding the solicitations of a plurality of senses at once, we can be absorbed with one; we can be all eye, although also affected with sounds, and all ear, although also affected with sights; the mental attention may flow in one exclusive channel of sense. We may likewise, to some extent, give a dominant attention to the active or to the passive feelings of a sense. Thus, in sight, we can be more engaged with the muscular than with the optical elements, and *vice versa;* but we cannot entirely separate the two.

The special difficulty of abstraction occurs in the indivisible sensations of a sense; every sound has a plurality of characters, intensity, volume, pitch, &c.; to these we can give a separate attention, only by the method described in the next paragraph.

3. Every Concrete thing falls into as many classes as it has attributes; to refer it to one of these classes, and to think of the corresponding attribute, are one mental operation.

When a concrete thing before the view recalls others agreeing in a certain point, our attention is awake upon that point; when the moon recalls other luminous bodies, we are thinking of its light; when it recalls other round bodies, we are thinking of its roundness. The two operations are not different but identical.

On this supposition, to abstract, or to think of a property in the abstract, is to classify under some one head. To abstract the property of transparency from water, is to recall, at the instance of water, window glass, crystal, air, &c.; to abstract its liquidity, is to recall milk, vinegar, melted butter, mercury, &c.; to abstract its weight is to bring it into comparison with other kinds of gravitating matter.

Hence abstraction does not properly consist in the mental separation of one property of a thing from the other properties—as in thinking of the roundness of the moon apart from its luminosity and apparent dimension. Such a separation is impracticable; no one can think of a circle without colour and a definite size. All the purposes of the abstract idea are served by conceiving a concrete thing in company with others resembling it in the attribute in question; and by affirming nothing, of the one concrete, but what is true of all those others.

When we think of the moon in comparison with a circle drawn on paper, and make that the subject of a proposition, we affirm only what is common to these two things; we refrain from affirming colour, size, or position; we confine ourselves to what is involved in the community of form.

In abstract reasoning, therefore, we are not so much engaged with any single thing, as with a class of things. When we are discussing government, we commonly have in view a number of governments, alternately thought of; if we notice in any one government a certain feature, we run over the rest in our mind, to see if the same feature is present in all. There is no such thing as an idea of government in the abstract; there is only possible a comparison of governments in the concrete; the abstraction is the likeness or community of the individuals. To be a good abstract reasoner, one should possess an ample range of concrete instances.

4. There are various cases, where we seem to approach to a pure Abstract Idea.

(1) In some instances, we can perform a material separation of one property from others. Thus the sweetness of wine depends upon its sugar; the stimulating property is due to alcohol; the bouquet to a certain ether. Now, all these elements can be presented in separation. This, however, is not abstraction; every one of the substances is a concrete thing, having many other properties besides the one noted. Sugar is not mere sweetness; nor is alcohol a stimulant in the abstract.

(2) In the Lineal Diagrams of Geometry, the substance is attenuated to a bare form; solidity is absent, and no more colour is left than is necessary to the outline of the figure. Still, the object is concrete. The colour of the line is essential to its purpose; and there is a definite size. When studying the circle from a diagram, we must take heed of affirming anything that is not common to other round things. One way of observing the precaution is to keep before the view a plurality of round objects, differing in colour and in size; each is then checked by the others. It is the principle of sound generalization to affirm nothing of a class but what is true of all its recognized members.

There may be indistinctness, or a want of vividness, in our conceptions of concrete things; we may fail in realizing the richness of colouring and the minute tracery of an object; we may think of the form under a dim, hazy colour, far below the original; still this is not abstraction; the colour and the form are not divorced in the mind.

(3) The verbal expression of what is common to a class appears to give a separate existence to the generality. The description, 'A line is length without breadth,' may be called an abstract idea of a line. Still, the meaning of the words 'length' and 'breadth' is inconceivable, without the aid of individual concrete things possessing length and breadth. Length is a name for one or more things agreeing in the property so called; and the property is nothing but this agreement. When, therefore, an abstraction is defined by a verbal reference to other abstractions, the effect is to transfer the attention from one class of concrete things to some other classes of concrete things. 'A triangle is a figure bounded by three right lines,' directs us to contemplate the concretes implied under 'boundary,' under 'three,' and under 'right line.'

After arriving at the verbal definition, we are able to reason of a class by reference to a *single* individual. When told that 'a line is length without breadth,' we are cautioned against viewing the line before us, in a diagram, under any other view but its length. A certain width is necessary to our seeing or conceiving the line, but we take warning from the definition not to affirm or include any proposition as to width. We contract a habitual precaution on this head, which enables us to work correctly upon one specimen, instead of needing the check of various differing specimens. Thus, while nothing can dispense with the presence of a concrete example, it is possible to work without a plurality of examples; and what enables us to do so is the restraint imposed by the verbal definition.

5. The only generality possessing separate existence is the Name; and the proper force of a general name is to signify agreement among the concrete things denoted by it.

When a certain number of things affects the mind with similarity in difference, it is of importance to make the fact known; which is done by the use of a common name. The things called fires have a community of effect, and the application of one word to all, shows that to be the case; and shows nothing else. Every name that we find applied to a plurality of objects is a declaration of agreement (in a given manner) among such objects; man, horse, river, just. To this view of the nature of general, or abstract ideas, is given the designation 'Nominalism.'

6. General Ideas, separated from particulars, have no counterpart Reality (as implied in Realism), and no Mental existence (as affirmed in Conceptualism).

Because we have a name 'round,' or 'circle,' signifying that certain things impress us alike, although also differing, it does not follow that there exists in nature a thing, of pure roundness, with no other property conjoined; a circle, of no material, no colour, and no size. All nature's circles are circles in the concrete, each one embodied along with other material attributes; a certain colour and size being inseparable from the form. This is the denial of Realism.

Neither can we have even a mental Conception of any property abstracted from all others; we cannot conceive a circle, except of some colour and some size; we cannot conceive justice, except by thinking of just actions.

7. There is a strong tendency in the mind to ascribe separate existence to abstractions; the motive resides in the Feelings, and is favoured by the operation of Language.

The ascribing of separate existence to abstractions is seen more particularly in early philosophy; as in the Indeterminate of Anaximander, the Numbers of Pythagoras, the One and the Absolute of the Eleates, the Nous or Mind of Anaxagoras—offered as the primal source, or first cause of all existing things. To account in some way or other for all that we see around us, has been an intense craving of mankind; and one mode of satisfying it is to construct fictitious agencies, such as those above named.

The facility that language affords to Realism depends on the circumstance that we are apt to expect every word to have a thing corresponding. What is true of concrete names, as Sun, Earth, England, we suppose to be true of general names, as space, heat, attraction; we naturally regard these as something more than mere comparisons of particulars.

Time is a pure abstraction; it has no existence except in concrete duration. Things enduring are what we know; until we have become aware of a certain number of these, we have no notion of time. Yet, owing to the sublime effect produced by the things that have great duration, we contract an association with the name for this property in general, and speak of Time as if it were a real and separate existence.

The existence of a supposed External and Independent material world, is the crowning instance of an abstraction converted into a separate entity. (For an account of the controversy of Nominalism and Realism, see APPENDIX A.)

CHAPTER VI.

THE ORIGIN OF KNOWLEDGE.

EXPERIENCE AND INTUITION.

1. THE question has been raised, with reference to a certain small and select portion of our knowledge, whether it is derived from Experience like the larger portion, or whether it is Intuitive.

While the great mass of our knowledge is obviously attained in the course of our experience of the world, it is contended by some philosophers that certain elements exist in the mind at birth; as, for example, our ideas of Space, Time, and Cause; the Axioms of Mathematics; the distinction of right and wrong; the ideas of God and Immortality.

These inborn elements have received many other names; as Innate ideas, Instinctive truths, notions and truths *a priori*, First Principles, Common Sense, primary Beliefs, Transcendental notions and truths, truths of the Reason.

2. It is considered that the assigning of a purely mental origin to certain ideas, both accounts for what is otherwise inexplicable, and confers an Authority, higher than experience, upon some important principles, speculative and practical.

There are certain peculiarities, it is maintained, belonging to such notions and principles as those above specified, that mere experience and acquisition cannot account for.

Again, the ante-natal origin of an idea is believed to give it a character of certainty, authority, dignity, such as cannot be affirmed of anything obtained in the course of experience.

Thus Kant, in remarking on the notion of Cause, said the question respecting it was,—'Whether this notion were excogitated by the mind *a priori*, and thus possessed an intrinsic truth, independent of all experience, and consequently *a more extensive applicability*, one not limited merely to objects of actual experience.' A superior and more commanding sweep is thus accorded to the notions originating in the mind.

3. In more explicit terms, the characters ascribed to the Intuitive or Innate principles, whereby they transcend, or rise above, other principles, are mainly these two— NECESSITY and UNIVERSALITY.

The *necessary*, or what must be true, is opposed to the *contingent*, which may or may not be true. That the whole is greater than its part, and that every effect must have a cause, are said to be necessary; that unsupported bodies fall to the ground is contingent, the fact might have been otherwise.

Universality follows necessity; what must be true cannot but be universally true.

4. The first objection to the doctrine of Innate ideas and principles, is that it presumes on the finality of some one Analysis of the Mind.

Nothing is to be held innate that can be shown to arise from experience and education. Language is not innate; we can account for any one's power of speech by instruction, following upon the articulate capacity, the sense of hearing, and the admitted powers of the intellect.

To affirm that the notions of Space and Time are intuitive, is to affirm that by no possibility shall mental philosophers ever be able to account for them by the operation of our perceptive faculties. Now, although the analysis of the mind at any one time should not be able to explain the rise of these notions, we are not, for that reason, justified in saying that they are never to be explained.

Although, strictly speaking, we are not entitled to call any notion ultimate, and underivable, any more than chemists are entitled to call a substance absolutely simple, yet there are certain appearances indicating that a fact, whether material or mental, is either simple or the reverse. The so-called elementary bodies,—oxygen, nitrogen, carbon, and the metals, are probably simple, because none of the powerful decomposing agencies now possessed have been able to decompose them. A newly-discovered saline body or crystal would be

INTUITION SUPPOSES ONE ANALYSIS FINAL. 183

considered compound, because such bodies are susceptible of decomposition.

So in the Mind, it is not probable that we shall ever be able to analyze the sensation of Colour; it is an effect arising on the presentation of what is called a visible body, and is not resolvable into any other effect. In like manner, the feeling of Resistance, or Expended Energy, has all the appearance of being a simple fact or experience of the mind. It enters into many mental states, but we cannot show that any other mental state enters into it. On the other hand, there are good reasons for thinking that our notion or idea of a pebble is a compound, being made up of resistance, touch, visible form, and visible colour; we can identify the presence of all these elements in the notion, which is the only proof we have of its being a complex and not a simple notion.

The question then is, may not our notion of Space, or Extension, be derived from the Muscular feelings or Sensations, co-operating with the Intellectual powers? Can we identify all that there is in the notion with these elements of sensible experience, intellectually combined? Is the analysis of Space given in previous chapters (pp. 26, 48, 63), sufficient to account for it? If not, what element is there that cannot be identified with Muscular feeling, and Sensation, under the intellectual properties of Difference, Agreement and Retentiveness? It is now allowed, (by Hamilton, for example,) that we have an *empirical* knowledge of extension; why may not this be the whole?

In the final appeal, the sufficiency of an analysis rests upon each person's feelings of identity, or difference, in comparing the thing to be analyzed with the elements affirmed to enter into it. If any man is conscious that his notion of Space contains nothing but what is supplied by muscular and sensible experience, operated on by the intellect, he has all the evidence that the case admits of.

Even granting that our present analysis of Space is unable to resolve it into elements of post-natal experience, we are not, therefore, to hold the matter closed for ever. The power of analysis is progressive; and the most that any one is entitled to say, is, that, as yet, Space has not been resolved—that it contains an element that is unique, and not identified with any mode of consciousness gained in our experience of the world.

The notion of Time, in the same way, may be held as either resolvable into muscular and sensible impressions, associated and generalized, or as not so resolvable at present. But no one is entitled to affirm it as absolutely simple and underived, or that Analysis has reached the last term, in respect of this notion.

In point of fact, the analysis of the feeling of Time seems the easiest of all. Every muscular feeling, sensation, and emotion, is different according to the degree of its endurance; we discriminate the greater from the less persistence of any state of consciousness. This discriminated persistence is the attribute of Time. We usually measure Time by some mode of our muscular sensibility, as motion; but we may measure it upon any kind of consciousness; we being differently affected by the unequal continuance of every mental condition.

5. The existence of Innate ideas has an Improbability corresponding to the amount of our dependence on experience for our knowledge.

The unquestionable rule being that our knowledge is gained through Movement and Sense (Intellectual functions co-operating), the burden lies with the advocate of innate truth to make good any exceptions to the rule.

The difficulties in the way of such an attempt are formidable. We cannot interrogate the new-born child; we have no means of testing its knowledge, until a large store of ideas has been acquired. It is different with the powers of action; we can see that a child is able to suck at birth, and to perfom various movements and gesticulations. But there is no evidence that it possesses any kind of knowledge or ideas.

6. On the theory of Nominalism, innate general ideas would involve innate particulars.

If an abstraction, or generality, be nothing but a host of particulars identified and compared, the abstraction is nothing without the particulars. Space has meaning in reference to extended things, and to nothing besides. If we are born with a pre-existing idea of space, we must have pre-existing ideas of concrete extended objects, which we compare and classify as extended. But the same objects would also be susceptible of classifications according to other properties, as colour, so that we should also possess innate ideas of colour.

7. The characteristic of Necessity, rightly understood, does not point to an Innate origin.

A proper necessary truth is one where the subject implies

the predicate; it is a truth of Implication. What is called the Law of Identity—whatever is, is, A is A—is given as an example of a necessary truth. That a thing is what it is, we may pronounce necessary in the highest sense; we cannot without self-contradiction, say otherwise. Now, there is no apparent reason why our ordinary faculties would fail to teach us this necessity, or why there must be innate forms provided expressly for the purpose. The difficulty would be to avoid recognizing such a necessity. Were it admissible that a thing could both be and not be, our faculties would be stultified and rendered nugatory. That we should abide by a declaration once made, is indispensable to all understanding between man and man. The law of necessity, in this sense, is not a law of things, but an unavoidable accompaniment of the use of speech. To deny it, is intellectual suicide.

Another so-called necessary truth is the Law of Contradiction. A thing cannot both be and not be. This is merely the law of Identity in another form. For example, if it be affirmed, 'This room is hot;' the inference is necessary that it is not cold. Such an inference, however, according to the principle of Relativity, is no new fact; it is the same fact stated from the other side; hot and not-cold express the same thing. There is no march of information in these necessary truths; the necessity lies in a thing being exactly what it is; in an affirmation being still true, although perhaps differently expressed, or looked at from another side.

Again, when we say 'all men are mortal,' the inference is necessary, that one man, in particular, or some men, are mortal. The necessity lies in the fact that the inference merely repeats the proposition, only not to the same extent. 'All men' is an abbreviation for, this man, the other, and the other; and when we apply the proposition, 'all men are mortal' to the case of this man, we do nothing but abide by our affirmation. When we have maintained a principle in one shape, we are understood to be ready to maintain it in any other equivalent shape—to be consistent with ourselves. This we should be equally inclined to, on any supposition as as to the origin of our ideas.

These necessary truths have, from their very nature, the highest possible 'Universality.' That 'whatever is, is;' that 'if all matter gravitate, some matter gravitates,'—are true at all times and places, on the same grounds as they are true now. The obligation of consistency cannot be dispensed with at any conceivable place, or any conceivable time. If nature had omitted to supply the supposed innate tendency to recognize such Universality, we should still recognize it, from a feeling of the utter helplessness that its denial would plunge us into.

There is, besides, in the active tendency of the mind, a strong disposition to extend to all places and times whatever is true in the present (see BELIEF). So powerful, indeed, is this impulse, that it constantly leads us too far, and needs to be checked and reduced within limits. We are induced to generalize to the utmost whatever we find in our limited experience; we believe that our present feelings will always continue. Instead of requiring an intuitive preparation to bring us up to the mark of Universality, we are constantly urged, through the operation of our active tendencies, to over-universality; and it would have been well for us to have been endowed with some innate caution in this respect.

8. The concessions made by the supporters of Innate Principles are almost fatal to the evidence of these principles, and to their value as authority.

It is allowed that experience is the occasion of our being conscious of our intuitive knowledge. We have no idea of Space, till we encounter extended things, nor of time, till we experience continuing or successive things. The innate element is always found in the embrace of an element of sense-perception. This circumstance casts the greatest uncertainty upon the whole speculation. It is scarcely possible to say how much is due to experience, and how much to intuition. May not the exactness, the purity, the certainty of an innate principle be impaired by its alliance with the inferior element of actual sensation?

9. In the present position of the controversy in question, the chief alleged Innate (speculative) Principles are the Axioms of Mathematics, and the Law of Causation.

The axioms of Mathematics have been variously stated. There are good reasons for regarding as axioms, in the proper sense of the word, these two. 'Things equal to the same thing are equal to one another;' and 'The sums of equals are equal.' It may be maintained that on these two axioms, together with the definitions, the whole fabric of mathematics can be raised.

Neither of these two axioms is necessary, in the sense of Implication. When we affirm that 'things equal to the

AXIOMS OF MATHEMATICS.

same thing are equal to one another,' we do not affirm an identical proposition; the subject is not involved in the predicate. Equality is properly defined as *immediate* coincidence (things that, being applied to one another, coincide, are equal). Now, the axiom affirms *mediate* coincidence, or coincidence through some third thing; and however obvious we may suppose the truth affirmed, it is not an identical proposition; it connects together two facts, differing not in language only, but in nature; it declares *mediate* coincidence to be as good as *immediate* coincidence; that where we cannot bring two things together for direct comparison, we may presume them to be equal, if they can be indirectly compared with some third thing. There would be no self-contradiction in denying this axiom.

The same line of observation is applicable to the second axiom; 'the sums of equals are equal.' It is not an identical proposition; it joins together two distinct properties—equality (by coincidence) and equality by the medium of the sum of equalities.

Neither of these axioms is intuitive, any more than necessary. They both flow from our actual experience; they are abundantly confirmed by repeated trials; and would, to all appearance, be as strongly believed as they are, by virtue of the extent and variety of the confirmations of them. Such is the view taken by those that impugn innate principles, and contend for the origin, in experience, of all our ideas whatsoever.

Some of the axioms of Euclid are necessary, in the strict sense. 'Things that, being applied to one another, coincide, are equal,' is not an axiom, but a definition—namely, the definition of equality. 'The whole is greater than its part,' is a corollary from a definition, the definition of whole and part; from the very nature of whole and part, the whole must be greater than any one part. This is a necessary, because an identical, proposition. 'That two straight lines cannot enclose a space,' (Kant's stock instance) is, in reality, a corollary from the definition of straight lines, and is therefore necessary indeed, but is an implicated or identical statement. To contradict it, is to contradict the very definition.

That every Effect not only has, but *must have*, a Cause, is alleged to be a truth at once necessary and intuitive. Experience, it is said, cannot show that every change has a cause, still less that it must have a cause.

As the word 'effect' is a correlative term, implying a cause, we must substitute the word 'event,' in order to represent the question fairly; 'Every event must be preceded by some other event,' would then be the statement of the law. This assertion is obviously not necessary in the sense of Implication; it is not an identical proposition; the opposite is not self-contradictory. It has all the appearance of an induction from facts.

The upholders of the innate origin of Causation refer to another criterion of the necessary and the intuitive—*the inconceivability of the opposite.* They contend that we cannot conceive an absolute beginning; we are obliged to think of every event as growing out of some previous event. Consequently, they say, there cannot be a creation out of nothing.

As an assertion of fact, this is easily met by denial. There is nothing to prevent us from conceiving an isolated event. Any difficulty that we might have, in conceiving something to arise out of nothing, is due to our experience being all the other way. The more we are instructed in the facts of the world, the more are we made aware that every event is chained to some other event; this begets in us a habit of conceiving events as so enchained; if it were not for this habit, there would be no serious obstacle to our conceiving the opposite state of things. (For the historical view of the opinions on the subject of this chapter, see APPENDIX B.)

CHAPTER VII.

OF EXTERNAL PERCEPTION.

1. THE relations of the Mind to the External, Material, or Extended World, give rise to two distinct, although connected questions—the Theory of Vision, and the Perception of the External and Material World.

Logically, as well as historically, these questions are connected; in both of them, Berkeley endeavoured to subvert what had been the received opinions up to his time.

THEORY OF VISION.

2. Berkeley's Theory of Vision professes to account for our perceiving Distance by sight. One explanation

refers the perception to Instinct, the other to Experience, or education.

The instinctive theory prevailed before Berkeley; the other view was introduced by him, and has been generally, though not universally, received by scientific men.

We find ourselves able, as far back as we can remember, to perceive by sight the comparative distances of objects, and to assign their real magnitudes; whence it would seem that the perception comes to us by nature, and not by education. In opposition to such an inference, Berkeley held that Distance is not seen, but felt by touch, and that we learn to connect our tactile experiences with the accompanying visible signs. In the same way we judge, by the eye, of the real magnitudes of things, after we have both seen and handled them.

Berkeley's arguments were greatly enfeebled by the imperfect views prevailing in his time, regarding our active or muscular sensibility. We shall, in the following summary, present the full force of the arguments as they stand now.

3. The native sensibility of the eye includes (1) Light and Colour, and their various shades, (2) Visible Figure, and Visible (or retinal) Magnitude.

The optical sensibility of the eye is for light and colour. The muscular sensibility is for visible forms and visible magnitudes, and their degrees. It is interesting to note that the judgment of visible size is the most delicate and accurate of all the judgments of the mind. Every accurate standard of comparison is in the last resort an appeal to visible magnitude, as the balance, the thermometer, &c.

Visible magnitude corresponds to the extent of the image upon the retina, and hence is called, by Wheatstone, Retinal magnitude.

4. The visible appearances or signs connected with variation of distance from the eye are these: (1) The feeling of muscular tension in the interior of the eye-ball. (2) The feeling of convergence or divergence of the two eyes. (3) The varying dissimilarity of the pictures presented to the two eyes. (4) The greater clearness of near objects, and the haziness of distant. (5) The variation of retinal magnitude.

(1) It has been seen (*Sight*) that to adjust the eye to a near object (a few inches), there is a muscular strain in the eye-ball.

(2) Another sign of nearness is the convergence of the two eyes, which is relaxed more and more as the object is removed; at great distances the eyes being parallel.

(3) For near distances, the pictures seen by the two eyes are dissimilar; as the distance increases, they are less so, and at great distances they are exactly similar. Such identity is, therefore, a sign of great distance.

(4) Incidental to distance, when very great, is a certain haziness, which is so far a constant fact, that painters make use of it in their perspective.

(5) When an object retreats from the eye, its visible or retinal magnitude steadily diminishes, and we are very sensitive to this diminution. If one human figure is seen at six feet distance, and another at twelve, nearly behind the first; the one has four times the retinal magnitude of the other; and this disparity strikes the mind more forcibly, perhaps, than all the other signs put together.

5. The meaning, or import, of Distance, is something beyond the experience of the eye.

The meaning of distance may be illustrated thus. If a ball is held before the eyes, first at six inches, and then at twelve, the optical changes will be as above described. But conjoined with visible changes is a definite movement of the arm, of which we are conscious. This introduces a new sensibility into the case; and when we say that the ball has been removed to the greater distance, one (and the more important) meaning of the fact is, that the hand and arm would have to be moved to carry it to its new position, or to touch it there.

Such is an example of the meaning of distance for near objects. Another measure is introduced for distant objects. To compare six feet with twelve feet, we must move the whole body in locomotion, and estimate, from our muscular sensibility, the difference between one locomotive exercise and another. To come up to one object, we move two paces, to another four, and so on. To change one visible appearance, or retinal magnitude, to another, we put forth a definite locomotion, which is not merely our measure or estimate *practically* of the interval between the two appearances, but the *sole meaning* or import of distance. If any one denies this, let him say what meaning is left, if all that is signified by locomotion of the whole body, or any part of it, be wholly withdrawn.

But if Distance has no meaning apart from the move-

OPPORTUNITIES FOR ASSOCIATING DISTANCE. 191

ments of other organs than the eye, the question then is, has nature gifted us at birth with the power of learning through one sense the experience of another sense? Do we smell sounds, or hear touches, or taste colours? Such conjunctions may not be impossible, but they are unusual; and the burden of proof lies upon the affirmer.

6. The experience of early infancy and childhood is incessantly forming the Associations between the visible signs of distance and the movements that constitute the meaning of distance (together with real magnitude).

The infant in the nurse's arms is perpetually experiencing the visible changes consequent on its being carried about; and as soon as it is aware of the fact of its being moved or carried (an unavoidable muscular consciousness), it connects this experience with the startling changes of visible magnitude in the things before its eyes. The visible appearance of the wall of a room is doubled, tripled, or quadrupled, while the child is carried from one end of the room to another. There would be no possibility of avoiding the association of the two facts. After a time, the momentary visible magnitude of the familiar wall would be connected with the amount of locomotion necessary to increase the magnitude to its maximum, or reduce it to its minimum; which would be a perception of distance begun. When the child attains to its own powers of locomotion, experiments are greatly increased in number and in variety; in a single day, the child might cross a room several scores of times, and every time the optical changes would be felt in connexion with its movements. A few weeks or months of this experience could not but engrain a vast number of associations of visible change with degrees of locomotion. The child would at the same time be handling things, taking their measures with the arms; walking round tables and chairs, estimating their real magnitudes by experimental muscular exertions, and connecting these real magnitudes with optical adjustments and changes. There are thus abundant opportunities of attaining the required connexions of real distances and real sizes with visible signs; every instant of the active life of the child is furnishing additional confirmations; and the final result is likely to be a firm and indissoluble alliance between visible signs and the multifarious locomotive and other experience accompanying them.

7. According to the experiments of Wheatstone, the order of dependence among our visual perceptions is as

follows :—The Inclination of the Axes of the eyes, in company with a given Retinal picture, suggests the *magnitude first;* and from the true magnitude thus known and the retinal magnitude, we infer the *distance*.

It was the prevalent opinion, that the feeling of the degree of convergence of the axes at once suggests distance; and that the distance thus suggested, taken along with the visible or retinal magnitude, gives the true magnitude. Wheatstone, on the contrary, concludes from his experiments that the first suggestion made is real magnitude (as experienced by touch and locomotion), and that, by combining this with the visible magnitude, the suggestion of distance follows. A block of stone is first judged to be, in size, a foot in the side; we then know from its *visible* or retinal size, whether the distance be ten feet, or fifty; there being, as already remarked, no more delicate means of discrimination than by differences of retinal size.

These experiments are important, as showing that Distance is not even the first inference, but the last, and implicates with it a prior inference of true Magnitude; all which increases the difficulty of supposing the perception of distance to be instinctive.

8. The perception of Distance is farther illustrated by the Stereoscope.

This great invention of Wheatstone's has given an impetus to the study of what is termed Binocular vision, or the concurrence of the two eyes in the single picture. The connexion of *solid effect*,—in other words, the perception of *distance*,—with double vision, is rendered very striking. It is shown, that the dissimilarity of the two pictures is a sign of distance, bound up in inseparable association with the fact.

To account for our seeing an object single with two eyes, the following considerations are offered.

(1) The picture of the object is received by *one eye;* the other merely extending its compass, and giving the dissimilarity of aspect that is a sign of the distance. It is a mistake in fact, to suppose that each eye sees a full and entire picture, independent of the other; one eye takes the lead and receives the picture, the other supplying the additions. Supposing the right eye to be the leader, if we shut that eye, the picture will be observed to shift its ground to the right; in fact, an entirely new picture is now formed by the left eye alone,—a

picture that is never allowed to be formed when both eyes are open. It is as in Touch, where we may employ both hands, but we attend chiefly to one, using the other as an extension of the contact.

(2) Equally pertinent is the consideration that, in vision, what the mind conceives is, not the optical effect actually presented at the moment, but a *compound or accumulated effect*, the result of all our past experience of vision in connexion with the various movements that enable us to estimate real size and distance. As in reading, our mental picture is not confined to a visible word, but involves the feeling of articulation and the melody on the ear, together with the suggested meanings,—so, in vision, the mind supplies far more than the sense receives. In looking at an extended prospect, we see distinctly only the part in the line of the eye; all the rest is to the vision indistinct and vague. Nevertheless, the mind supplies from memory a clear picture of the other parts. Also, in looking down a vista, the adjustment of the eyes permits only one portion to be clearly seen, the rest being necessarily confused; but the mind easily gives the correct picture throughout, so that the indistinctness demonstrably attaching to the optical image does not cloud the mental perception.

9. It is admitted by the opponents of Berkeley, that the instinctive perception must be *aided* by certain acquirements or associations.

The concession is made that, 'although the eye possessed the most perfect power of perceiving distance, *it could not possibly convey an idea of the amount of walking necessary to pass over it.*' This, as Mr. J. S. Mill remarks, is to surrender the whole question. The author of the remark parries the conclusion, by saying that there is no more in it than the difference between hearing musical tones and the power of distinguishing them accurately. But the perception of any quality must involve the perception of its degree; we could not be said to perceive weight, unless we could distinguish between a greater and a less; very nice shades of difference might not be felt without education; but not to feel any amount of difference is not to feel at all. The loose remark is made, 'we first roughly estimate the difference by the eye—this we correct by measurement.' But a rough estimate is still an estimate of more or less, a sense of difference.

The question still returns, What is the meaning or import of Distance? One meaning of vital importance practically, is the greater or less locomotion or other movement required to traverse it. Subtract that meaning, which is said by all not to be instinctive, and what meaning remains? Until the two contending parties agree upon this, it is vain to argue the question. Nevertheless, we shall now present a summary of the chief arguments on the side of instinctive perception.

10. I.—In perceiving distance, we are not conscious of tactual feelings or locomotive reminiscences; what we see is a visible quality, and nothing more.

If distance is merely the suggestion of touch, &c., we ought to be conscious of a tactile state, a state of locomotive, or other muscular, effort. It is denied that we have any such consciousness. We never, it is said, see resistance or hardness, which are the real tactile qualities.

The supporters of Berkeley meet this allegation by saying, that we are conscious of associated qualities in being conscious of distance. Even as to the more strictly tactile properties of resistance and hardness, we are distinctly conscious of these in looking at a stone wall; we do not see them in the eye, but their visible signs so strongly suggest them, that they are inseparable from the act of vision.

Mr. Mill, remarking on his own experience, says, that in judging the distance of an object, the idea suggested to his mind 'is commonly that of the length of time, or the quantity of motion, that would be requisite for reaching to the object if near, or walking up to it if at a distance.'

It thus appears that opposite allegations can be made as to the interpretation of individual consciousness, which renders this argument indecisive on either side; as in all assertions referring to the subjective world, each one must judge for themselves.

11. II.—The early experience or education of children is inadequate to produce the requisite strength of association.

It is affirmed that the opportunities are wanting for uniting the visual signs with the tactual and other effects; that the constant association requisite does not take place; that the visible experience is sufficiently frequent, but the tactual and locomotive experience rare. 'We see a house at the distance of forty yards, a mountain at ten miles; but how often do we estimate the distance by any other sense?' For every separate adjustment of the eye, corresponding to all grades of distance, we ought to have made innumerable experiments of touch or locomotion.

But to all this it is replied, first, that the infant is making the experimental connexions as often as it is moved from place to place, no matter how. And, secondly, it being admitted that we originally see distance only in the 'rough,' and without discrimination of degree, and have to learn by experience all the separate stages, it seems no great additional demand on our education to acquire the rough estimate as well, implying as it does so much less than the numerous associations that distinguish degrees.

It is farther urged against the doctrine of acquirement, that the associated things should be able to reproduce one another reciprocally. Tactual and locomotive perceptions ought to suggest their visual signs as efficiently as the inverse operation; that is, in putting forth our hand in the dark to touch a thing, there ought to flash upon us the visible remembrance of its distance; which, it is alleged, is not the case. So, walking a few steps in the dark should give us the visual sensations corresponding to the interval passed over.

It may be replied, that we have in both cases a visual estimate of distance, just as accurate as our estimate of movement or locomotion from visible signs. When we walk six paces in the dark, retreating from a wall, we can then, and do, think of the visual distance of the wall at six yards; every pace that we take suggests the retreating figure of the wall; and if our estimate is not perfectly accurate, neither is our estimate of real distance, judged by its signs, always accurate.

12. III.—Observations made upon persons born blind, and after a lapse of years made to see, are affirmed to be in favour of the instinctive origin of the perceptions.

The first and best known of these cases, a youth couched by Cheselden (*Phil. Trans.* 1728), has, until lately, been considered as confirmatory of Berkeley's doctrine. But the recent opponents of Berkeley have endeavoured to give it a different turn, as well as to explain the other cases in their view. It is admitted, however, that the observers were not sufficiently aware of the points to be noted in order to settle this question. Two patients are quoted by Mr. Bailey, who could distinguish by the unassisted eye whether an object was brought nearer or carried farther from them. But in neither case, were the circumstances of the experiment such as to prove the fact.

Cheselden's patient said that 'all objects seemed to touch his eyes,' which is not compatible with his seeing things at a distance, and some things farther off than others. A similar remark was made by other patients, and although laborious attempts are made to explain away the effect of the observation (see Abbot's 'Sight and Touch,' chap. x.), the necessity of such attempts is fatal to the decisiveness of such cases as proofs of intuitive perception.

13. IV.—The case of the lower animals is adduced as presenting an instinct such as is contended for, which would at least show that the fact is one within the compass of nature.

The power of many animals to direct their movements, almost immediately after birth, seems established by a large mass of concurrent observations. For example, 'the moment the chicken has broken the shell, it will dart at and catch a spider. Sir Joseph Banks said he had seen a chicken catch at a fly whilst the shell stuck in its tail.' Many similar facts have been related over and over again by veracious witnesses. Such powers obviously imply an intuitive measure of distance, and a farther instinctive power of directing the movements in exact accordance therewith. On these facts, it is open to the adherents of Berkeley's theory to make the following comments.

(1) There does not exist a body of careful and adequate observations upon the early movements of animals. It is not enough that even a competent observer makes an occasional observation of this nature; it is essential that a course of many hundred observations should be made on each separate species, varying the circumstances, in every possible way, so as to ascertain the usual order of proceeding in the species generally, and all the conditions and limitations of the aptitudes alleged. We know enough to pronounce such facts as the above, respecting the chick, to be extreme and exceptional instances; usually a certain time (two or three days) elapses ere the chick can peck at seeds of corn; and the nature of its operations during that interval, as well as the character of the first attempts, should receive the most careful scrutiny by different observers. There is satisfactory evidence that these animals do possess, at a remarkably early period, a power of precise adjustment of their moving organs to external objects; but it is not proved that this power is complete at the instant of birth in any single species.

(2) As regards the bearing upon the Theory of Vision in man, these observations have the fatal weakness of proving too much. They prove that animals have not only the power of seeing distance, but the power of appreciating its exact amount, and the still farther power of graduating their own movements in exact correspondence with the distance measured. They include both the gift that we are alleged to have by nature, and two other aptitudes that in us are acquired. This enormous disparity reduces the force of the analogy to almost nothing. A natural endowment that goes the length of a precise muscular adjustment adapted to each varying distance, so far transcends the utmost that can be affirmed of our primitive stock of visual perceptions, as to amount to a new and distinct attribute, presupposing a totally different organization.

14. V.—The observations on infants are held as favouring the instinctive perception of distance.

It is not alleged that infants at birth exhibit any symptoms of this knowledge, like the animals just quoted, but that they show it before they have developed the powers of touch and locomotion requisite for actual distances. The infant is said to have the power of bringing its hand accurately to its mouth about the eleventh week, while the power of touching and handling has made very little progress at the end of six months. Yet, by this time, the child knows the difference between a friend and a stranger, and throws itself out in the direction of the one, and turns away from the other; it also knows when it is moved towards the object it likes, and makes no attempt to seize a thing until it is brought quite close. Of course, locomotion has not yet begun.

We have given by anticipation the only answer to these facts, supposing them accurately stated (which is doubtful). The earliest associations of visible appearances with actual trials of distance and real magnitude are not made by the hand, or by the child's own locomotion, but by its movements as carried from place to place; and until some one can show that it can have no adequate consciousness of these movements, at the same time that it is conscious of the changes of the retinal magnitude of the things about it, the Berkleian theory is not affected by the facts in question.

15. It has been suggested, as a third alternative in this dispute, that there may be a *hereditary* or transmitted experience of the connexion between the visible signs and the locomotive measure of distance.

This view belongs to what is called the Development hypothesis. If there be such a thing as the transmission of acquired powers to posterity, it may operate in the present instance. Facts are adduced (by Darwin, Spencer, and others) to show that this transmission is possible, although the utmost extent of it would appear to be but small for one or a few generations. Still, it is argued that, if there be any experience likely to impress itself on the organization permanently, it would be an experience so incessant as the connexion of the visible signs with the locomotive estimate of distance.

It may be remarked, with reference to this hypothesis, that, whatever be the case with certain of the lower animals, the hereditary transmission has not operated to confer the instinct upon man (unless the opposition to Berkeley be successful, which is not admitted). Hereditary experience may have predisposed the nervous system to fall in more rapidly into the connexions required. This is what no Berkeleian is in a position to deny, while it might ease the difficulty suggested by the great strength and maturity of the acquisitions at the earliest period of our recollections.

PERCEPTION OF A MATERIAL WORLD.

1. All Perception or Knowledge implies mind.

To perceive is an act of mind; whatever we may suppose the thing perceived to be, we cannot abstract it from the percipient mind. To perceive a tree is a mental act; the tree is known *as perceived*, and not in any other way. There is no such thing known as a tree wholly detached from perception; and we can speak only of what we know.

2. The Perception of Matter points to a fundamental distinction in our experience. We are in one condition, or attitude, of mind when surveying a tree or a mountain, and in a totally different condition or attitude when luxuriating in warmth, or when suffering from toothache.

The difference here indicated is the greatest contrast within our experience. It is expressed by Matter and Mind (in a narrow sense), External and Internal, Object and Subject.

3. The distinction between the attitude of material perception and the subjective consciousness has been commonly stated, by supposing a material world, in the first instance, detached from perception, and, afterwards, coming into perception, by operating upon the mind. This view involves a contradiction.

The prevailing doctrine is that a tree is something in itself apart from all perception; that, by its luminous emanations, it impresses our mind and is then perceived; the perception being an effect, and the unperceived tree the cause. But the tree is known only through perception; what it may be anterior to, or independent of, perception, we cannot tell; we can think of it as perceived, but not as unperceived. There is a manifest contradiction in the supposition; we are required at the same moment to perceive the thing and not to perceive it. We know the touch of iron, but we cannot know the touch apart from the touch.

4. Assuming the Perception of Matter to be a fact that cannot be disengaged from the mind, we may analyze the distinction between it and the modes of subjective consciousness, into three main particulars.

I.—The perception of Matter, or the Object consciousness, is connected with the putting forth of Muscular Energy, as opposed to Passive Feeling.

The fundamental properties of the material or object world are Force or Resistance, and Extension,—the Mechanical and the Mathematical properties. These have sometimes been called the *primary qualities* of matter. The modes of Extension are called, by Hamilton, primary qualities, and the modes of Resistance or Force, *secundo-primary*.

Now, it has been formerly seen (MUSCULAR FEELINGS) that, in experiencing resistance, and in perceiving extension, our moving energies are called into play. The exertion of our

PERCEPTION OF MATTER CONNECTED WITH ENERGY. 199

own muscular power is the fact constituting the property called resistance. Of matter as independent of our feeling of resistance, we can have no conception; the rising up of this feeling within us amounts to everything that we mean by resisting matter. We are not at liberty to say, without incurring contradiction, that our feeling of expended energy is one thing, and a resisting material world another and a different thing; that other and different thing is by us wholly unthinkable.

On the other hand, in purely *passive* feeling, as in those of our sensations that do not call forth our muscular energies, we are not perceiving matter, we are in a state of subject consciousness. The feeling of warmth, as in the bath, is an example. If we deliver ourselves wholly to the pleasure of the warmth, we are in a truly subject attitude, we are in noways cognizant of a material world. All our senses may yield similar experiences, if we resign ourselves to their purely sensible or passive side; if we are absorbed with a relish without moving the masticating organs, or with an odour, without snuffing it, or moving up to it. In pure soft touch, we approach to the subject attitude; but there are few exercises of touch entirely separated from muscular effect. On the same conditions, sounds might be a purely subject experience. Lastly, it is just possible, although difficult, to make light a subject experience; mere formless radiance would be an approach to it; the recognition of form or boundary introduces an object property, embodied in ocular movements.

The qualities of matter affecting our senses on their purely passive side—their special or characteristic sensibility—are called the *secondary* qualities of matter—Taste, Odour, Touch proper (soft touch, &c.), Sound, and Colour.

The distinction of Primary and Secondary qualities is made chiefly with reference to Perception. The primary, on the common theory, are those of pure and independent matter, matter *per se;* the secondary are tinged or coloured by the percipient mind.

We have thus, in putting forth energy, a mode of consciousness belonging to the object side; and in passive feeling, a mode of consciousness belonging to the subject side.

5. II.—Our object experience farther consists of the uniform connexion of Definite Feelings with Definite Energies.

The effect that we call the interior of a room is, in the final analysis, a regular series of feelings of sense, related to definite muscular energies. A movement, one pace forward, makes a distinct and definite change in the ocular impressions; a step backwards exactly restores the previous impression. A movement to one side gives rise to another definite change, and so on. The coincidences are perfectly uniform in their occurrence. Again, in moving down a street, we undergo a series of sensible feelings, in accordance with our movements; we reverse the movements, and encounter the feelings in the reverse order. We repeat the experiment, with the same results. All our so-called sensations are in this way related to movements. Our sensations of light vary with our movements, and (allowance being made for other known changes) always in the same way with the same amount of movement. We open the eye and light is felt; we close it, and light ceases. This gives to light its object character. Sound, by itself, would be purely subjective; but a sound steadily increasing with one movement, and steadily decreasing with another, is treated as objective.

On the other hand, what, in opposition to sensations, we call, the flow of *ideas*,—the truly mental or subjective life—has no connexion with our movements. We may remain still and think of the different views of a room, of a street, of a prospect, in any order. This is a total contrast to the other experience; mankind are justified in using very decided language to express so great a difference; they are not, however, justified in using language to affirm that, in the object perception, there are unperceived existences giving the cue to our actual perceptions.

Thus, then, what we call Sensation, Actuality, Objectivity, is an unlimited series of associations of definite movements with definite feelings; the Idea, Ideality, Subjectivity, is a flow of feelings without dependence on muscular or active energy. In this property also, we see that it is still our energetic or active side that constitutes the basis of the object experience, the object consciousness.

6. Our own body is a part of our Object experience.

It is in our own body that Object and Subject come together in that intimate alliance known as the union of mind and body. Still, the body is object to the mind, and is viewed in the same manner as other parts of the objective aggregate.

When we speak of an *external* world, the comparison is

strict only in comparing our body with the things that surround it. External and Internal are not strictly applicable to express the totality of the object as compared with the totality of the subject. The terms 'alliance,' 'union,' 'association,' are less unsuitable; they do not commit us to the impropriety of specifically locating the Unextended.

7. III.—In regard to the Object properties, all minds are affected alike: in regard to the Subject properties, there is no constant agreement.

By communicating with others, we find that, in regard to the feelings that definitely vary with definite energies, what happens to one happens to all. Two persons walking down the same street, have the same changes of sensation, at each step. Whoever performs the definite series of movements called ascending a mountain, will be conscious of the same sensitive changes, the same series of ocular effects. Other persons as well as we experience light in the act of opening the eyes, in definite circumstances.

On the other hand, although on the same mountain top the optical experience of all beholders is the same, they may differ in many other feelings,—in the sense of fatigue, in the sense of hunger, in the æsthetic enjoyment. They will also differ in the flow and succession of their ideas; no two will have the same train of thoughts. These are subjective elements of the mind. For although they also are affected by movements, and are under a strict law of succession of their own, yet there is no exact uniformity as to the time, degree, and manner of their showing themselves. Now, the object world is limited to points of strict and rigorous community, where the effect is the same to all minds.

This rigorous uniformity belongs only to the so-called primary qualities, Extension and Resistance; visible form and visible magnitude, tangible form and tangible magnitude, and degrees of force or resistance, are the points where beings are constituted alike. They are not constituted strictly alike as regards Colour (witness Colour-blindness), Sound, Touch proper, Smell, Taste, still less Organic Sensation. They are constituted, however, very nearly alike in the higher senses; there is little difference in regard to colour; hence the popular notion of the independent external world is a *coloured world*, but it ought to be only an Extended, Shaped, and Resisting world. Colour is a secondary quality, varied by the varieties of the subject; and should therefore be withdrawn from rigorous object existence, as not being strictly common to all. Still we join it to the object properties, by reason of its being definitely varied with definite movements in each person, although it may not be precisely the same experience in all persons.

8. When, in order to distinguish what is common to all from what is special to each, we ascribe separate and independent existence to the common element, the Object, we not only forget that the object qualities are still modes of conscious experience, but are guilty besides of converting an abstraction into reality—the error of Realism.

In the perception of Extension, Shape, Resistance, and to a certain extent Colour, we all agree; and it is important to express the agreement. But it does not follow, that the agreeing properties subsist apart, and in isolation; any more than that roundness exists as a separate entity, or detached from all round things. We are conscious of object qualities only in their union with subject qualities; we may, by the exercise called Abstraction, think of the object qualities by themselves, but we cannot thereby confer upon them an existence aloof from all subject qualities.

THEORIES OF THE MATERIAL WORLD.

BERKELEY. The so-called Ideal Theory of Berkeley is given in his work entitled 'The Principles of Human Knowledge,' and is farther defended and elucidated in 'Three Dialogues between Hylas and Philonous.'

The Introduction to the 'Principles of Human Knowledge' is occupied with an onslaught on the doctrine of Abstract Ideas. The author felt that the common theory of the material world is a remnant of Realism, and incompatible with thorough-going Nominalism.

The objects of human knowledge, he goes on to say, are ideas of one or other of these three classes :—(1) Ideas actually imprinted on the senses, (2) ideas arrived at by attending to the passions and operations of the mind—as pleasure, pain, sweetness, love, conscience, &c., and (3) ideas formed by memory or by imagination reviving and combining the two other classes.

It is necessary to remark on this peculiar use of the word 'idea,' to express what we commonly call 'sensations' and 'things,' that Berkeley does not thereby mean to assimilate the perception of a tree to the idea that we form of a tree when remembered; he only intends to say that sensation, or perception, is a *mental* fact or product, a phase or aspect of mind, and cannot have any existence apart from mind. He has, however, taken a word, hitherto employed only in the *subject* sphere, and generalized it to express both the object and the subject, marking the difference by specific designations, as if we should say, *object* ideas (sensations, things, objects), and *subject* ideas (feelings, passions, thoughts, &c.).

Sight, he continues, gives ideas of colour; touch gives hardness and softness; smelling furnishes odours. Moreover, there may be *concurrences* of these; a certain colour, taste, smell, figure, may go together, and have one name, *apple*.

Besides these three kinds of ideas, countless in their detail, there is a something that knows or perceives them, and exercises the various functions called, willing, imagining, remembering. This is *mind, spirit, soul, myself;* a something different from the ideas that constitute knowledge.

Now, with regard to ideas of the second and third classes,— ideas of our thoughts and passions, and ideas of memory and imagination—it is allowed by everybody that *these exist only in the mind*.

To Berkeley, it is equally evident that ideas of the *first class*— sensations of the senses—cannot exist otherwise than *in* a mind perceiving them. The table I write on exists; that is, I see or feel it; if I were out of my study, I should say it existed, meaning if I return I shall perceive it; or if any other persons are now there, they will perceive it. In short, with regard to outward things generally, they exist as perceived; the *esse* is *percipi*.

To suppose otherwise (the vulgar opinion), is a contradiction. Sensible objects are the things perceived by sense; but whatever we perceive is our own ideas or sensations; it is self-contradictory to say that anything exists unperceived. It is only a nice abstraction that enables us to suppose things unperceived; the things we see and feel are so many sensations, notions, ideas, impressions of sense, and it is no more possible to divide them from the act of perception, than to divide a thing from itself. The choir of heaven, the furniture of the earth, all the things that compose the mighty frame of the world, have no existence without a mind; they subsist either in the minds of created spirits, or, failing these, in the mind of some eternal spirit. There is no other *substance* but spirit, that which perceives; it is a perceiving substance that alone furnishes the substratum of colour, figure, and other sensible qualities.

He next supposes some one to allege, that although ideas are in the mind, yet something like them, something that they are *copies* of, may exist in an unthinking substance. The reply is, an idea is like only to an idea. Either the supposed originals are perceived, and then they are only ideas; or they are not perceived, in which case, colour is declared to resemble something invisible.

The distinction between Primary and Secondary Qualities is of no avail. Extension, Figure, and Motion are still ideas of the mind; neither they nor their archetypes can exist in an unperceiving substance. It being admitted that the secondary qualities exist in the mind alone, and yet are inseparably united with the primary qualities, (extension is always coloured), it follows that these primary qualities can have no separate existence. Again, the properties called *great* and *small*, *slow* and *swift*, are entirely relative; they change with the position of the perceiving organs. Therefore the absolute, and independent extension, must neither be great nor small, which would amount to nothing. So the qualities *Number* and *Unity* are creatures of the mind. In short, whatever goes to prove that tastes and colours exist only in the mind, proves the same as to Extension, Figure, and Motion.

He then examines the received opinion that extension is a mode of the substratum *matter*, and finds the expression devoid of meaning.

Granting the possibility of solid, figured, movable substances, existing without the mind, how can we ever know this? Is it not possible that we might be affected with all the ideas we have now, though no bodies exist without that resemble them? Moreover, the assumed existence of such bodies is no help in explaining the rise of our ideas, seeing that we are unable to comprehend how body can act on spirit. In short, if there were external bodies, it is impossible that we should know it; and if there were not, we should still have the same reason for believing it.

He points out (although with insufficient Psychology) the difference between ideas of sensation, and ideas of reflection or memory: the ideas of sense do not depend on our will (we open our eyes and cannot resist the consequences). Moreover, these ideas of sense are more strong, lively, and distinct, than the others; they have a steadiness, order, and coherence, unlike the ideas influenced by our own will; the set rules of their coherence constitute the laws of nature, the knowledge of which is our practical foresight.

To the objection that the *reality* of things is abolished or removed by his theory, he merely repeats his main position in varied terms. There are spiritual substances or minds having the power of exciting ideas in themselves at pleasure; but ideas so arising are faint, weak, and unsteady. There is another class of ideas, those perceived by sense; which are impressed according to certain rules or laws of nature; and to them, the idea of reality is attached in a more peculiar meaning. He, therefore, removes no reality as understood by the vulgar, but only a philosophic fiction.

It may seem very harsh, he further remarks, to say that we eat and drink and are clothed by *ideas*. But so is any deviation from familiar language. Underneath the language is a question of fact. To use the terms 'object of sense,' 'thing,' is to assume the error he is combating.

He then notices other objections; such as the supposed perpetual annihilation and creation involved in the theory; the notion, that to regard extension as a purely mental fact is to make the mind extended; the consent of mankind to the view he is opposing; the superfluity of the curious organization of plants and animals on his system, &c. His answers bring out nothing new. He repeats his attacks on abstract ideas, in the leading instances of Time, Space, and Motion; and combats the doctrine of mathematicians as to the Infinite Divisibility of lines.

He is strenuous in maintaining the existence of *spirit* apart from ideas; spirit is the support and substratum of ideas, and cannot be itself an idea. The supposition that spirit can be known after the manner of an idea, or sensation, is a root of scepticism. He considers the Deity the immediate cause of all our sensations, and that the theory of the world is simplified by reducing everything to his direct agency; while atheism is deprived of its greatest support—the independent existence of matter.

All the ingenuity of a century and half, has failed to see a way out of the contradiction exposed by Berkeley; although he has not always guarded his own positions. It is to be regretted that he could not find some other name than *idea*, for expressing our object consciousness. In spite of all his attempts to distinguish ideas of sensation from the commonly understood ideas, he laboured under a heavy disadvantage in running counter to the associations of familiar language. He laid himself open to refutation by something more severe than a 'grin,' or a nickname—Idealist.

HUME. Hume is noted for having embraced the views of Berkeley, with the exception of that relating to a separate soul or spirit. He thus reduced all existence to perceptions and ideas.

Hume's philosophy is given at greatest length in the 'Treatise on Human Nature.' The application of his philosophical principles to Material Perception, is found in Part IV. His subsequent work, entitled, 'An Enquiry concerning Human Understanding,' is prefaced by a note, desiring that this work, and not the Treatise on Human Nature, may be taken as representing his philosophical sentiments and principles. On referring to the 'Enquiry,' we find that the handling of the doctrine of perception is compressed into one very short chapter (Sect. xii.), entitled, 'Of the Academical or Sceptical Philosophy.' It does not appear, however, that the author's views on this doctrine underwent any change; or that any injustice would be done to him by referring to the more expanded treatment of Perception in the 'Human Nature.' His fundamental views of the mind are the same in both treatises. His resolution of all our Intellectual elements into Impressions and Ideas, differing only in vividness or intensity; his thoroughgoing Nominalism; his repudiation of any nexus in Cause and Effect beyond mere experience of their conjunction; his explanation of Belief by the greater vividness of the object; his reference of the belief in nature's uniformity to Custom; his refusal to admit anything that cannot be referred to a primary impression on the mind through the senses,—are cardinal doctrines of his philosophy from first to last.

In the later work, his remarks on Perception are in the following strain:—Men are prompted by a strong instinct of their nature to suppose the very images, presented by their senses, to *be* the external objects; not to *represent* them. On the other hand, philosophy so-called teaches that nothing can be present to the mind but an image or perception, that the senses are only the inlets, and do not constitute immediate intercourse between the mind and external objects. Thus philosophy has obviously departed from the dictates of nature, and has been deprived of that support, while exposing itself to the cavils of the sceptic, who asks, how it is that the perceptions of the mind must needs be caused by external objects (different, though resembling), and not from some energy of the mind itself, or through some unknown spirit or other cause? Can there be anything more inexplicable than that body should operate upon mind, the two being so different, and even so contrary in their nature? It is a question of *fact*, whether the perceptions of the senses be produced by external objects resembling them. How shall this question be determined? By experience surely; but in such a matter experience must be silent. The mind has nothing present to it but the perceptions, and cannot reach any experience of their connexion with objects.

He then remarks on the distinction between the secondary and primary qualities, with a view of showing that, as regards the independent existence of their objects, the two classes are on the same level.

If we turn to the Treatise on Human Nature, we find the subject of Sense Perception handled with great fulness of detail (Part IV. Sect. 2). Hume argues that, by the senses, we cannot know either *continued* or *distinct* existence. He then enquires how we came by the belief in the continued existence of the objects of the senses, and ascribes it to the *coherence* and *constancy* of our impressions respecting them. He observes that the mind once set agoing in a particular track, has a tendency to go on, even when objects fail it; and, through this tendency, we transmute interrupted existence into continued existence. He accounts, on his general theory of belief (following vividness of impression) for our believing in this imagined continuity. *Continued* existence, when once recognized, easily conducts us to *distinct* or *independent* existence; both being equally grounded on imagination, and not on reality.

In Sect. v., he treats of the Immateriality of the Soul, in which he represents the question, 'Whether our perceptions inhere in a material or in an immaterial substance?' as one wholly devoid of meaning. We have no perfect idea of anything but a perception. A substance is entirely different from a perception. We have therefore no idea of a substance. 'The doctrine of the immateriality, simplicity, and indivisibility of a thinking substance is a true atheism, and will serve to justify all those sentiments for which Spinoza is so universally infamous.'

In the chapter (Sect. vi.) on Personal Identity, he denies the existence of *self* in the abstract; there is nothing to give us the impression of a perennial and invariable self. 'When I enter,' he says, 'most intimately into what I call *myself*, I always stumble on some particular perception or other, of heat or cold, light or shade, love or hatred, pain or pleasure.' Mind is nothing but a bundle of conceptions, in a perpetual flux and movement. He goes on to explain by what tendencies of the mind the fiction of a pure, absolute self is set up, and what is the real nature of what we call 'personal identity.'

Such is a brief indication of the celebrated scepticism of Hume. It is, however, to be remarked of him, in contrast to Berkeley, that he often expresses himself as if his theory was at variance with the experience of mankind. As he was a man fond of literary effects, as well as of speculation, we do not always know when he is earnest; but he speaks as if the belief that fire warms and water refreshes, was the revolt of nature against his scepticism. It is no wonder that others have supposed him to deny both the existence of matter and the existence of mind, although, in point of fact, he denies neither, but only a certain theoretic mode of looking at and expressing the phenomena admitted by all. The outcry against him and Berkeley proves that a rose under another name does not always smell as sweet.

REID. Reid reclaimed against Berkeley and Hume, on the ground of what he called Common Sense. 'To what purpose,' he says, 'is it for philosophy to decide against common sense in this or in any other matter? The belief of a material world is older, and of more authority, than any principles of philosophy.' 'That we have clear and distinct conceptions of extension, figure, and motion, and other attributes of body, *which are neither sensations, nor like any* sensation, is a fact of which we may be as certain as that we have sensations.' In general, it may be said, that Reid declaims, rather than reasons on the question; and Hamilton, who equally repudiates the ideal theory, and appeals to consciousness in favour of the prevailing opinion, finds Reid 'often at fault, often confused, and sometimes even contradictory.' In his edition of Reid (Note C, p. 820), Hamilton draws up two classes of statements on the part of Reid, pointing to two opposing doctrines, one called 'the doctrine of *mediate perception*,' which Hamilton disavows, and the other called '*immediate perception*,' which Hamilton adopts.

The doctrine of mediate conception, or representative conception, is the most glaring form of the doctrine of the separate existence of matter; its self-contradictory character is exposed by no one more vigorously than by Hamilton. He finds Reid slipping into it, in saying that the primary qualities, Extension, &c., are suggested to us through the secondary: the secondary are the *signs*, on occasion of which we are made to 'conceive' the primary. But, says Hamilton, if the primary qualities are suggested conceptions, our knowledge of the external world is wholly subjective or ideal. Equally unguarded is the expression that, 'if sensation be produced, the perception *follows*, even when there is no object.' So, to localize sensation (a pain in the toe, for instance) *in the brain* is conformable to mediate or representative perception. Reid's use of the terms 'notion' and 'conception' likewise favours the same view. Also, in calling imagination of the past an *immediate* knowledge, Reid is on dangerous ground: such *immediate* knowledge, applied to perception, is really a mediate knowledge. Again, the doctrine of Reid and Stewart, that perception of *distant* objects is possible, if sifted, leads to representationism. Once more, Reid's calling perception an *inference* is of the same tendency. Finally, he ought not to separate, as he does, our *belief* of an external world from our cognition of it.

On the other hand, Hamilton adduces statements conformable to Real or Immediate presentation. These chiefly consist in repeating the common opinion of mankind, that whatever is perceived exists. Mr. J. S. Mill, in opposition to Hamilton, maintains that Reid throughout adhered to the doctrine of Representation, or mediate perception, and quotes numerous passages, where he iterates the view that the sensations are merely *signs*, and that the objects themselves are the things signified. What he did not maintain was, that the sign *resembled* the original; which is a crude form of representative perception.

STEWART followed Reid so closely on the subject of Perception, that a separate account of his opinions is unnecessary. BROWN is noted for the virulence of his attack upon Reid's claims to have vindicated Common Sense against Idealism. The attack has been reviewed by Hamilton, who in his turn is reviewed by Mr. J. S. Mill. Mr. Mill's reading of Brown is that he is substantially at one with Reid. 'He (Brown) thought that certain sensations, irresistibly, and by a law of our nature, suggest, without any process of reasoning, and without the intervention of any *tertium quid*, the notion of something external, and an invincible belief in its real existence. Brown differed from Reid (and also from Hamilton) in denying an intuitive perception of the Primary Qualities of bodies.

HAMILTON. Hamilton has distinguished himself both as the historian and critic of the Theories of Perception, and as the propounder of a theory of his own, different alike from Berkeley and from Reid.

He has endeavoured to give an exhaustive classification of all the possible theories. [See Edition of Reid, Note C, and Lectures.]

As his scheme is a theoretical rather than a historical one, it comprehends doctrines that have probably never been held. The first great division is into Presentation and Representation; or into those that consider what is presented to the mind as the whole fact, and those that consider that there is some other fact not presented to the mind. The first class—the Presentationists—

is divided into the Natural Realists or Natural Dualists, who accept the common sense view that the object of perception is something material, extended, and external [Hamilton's own opinion], and the Idealists, who consider that nothing exists beyond ideas of the mind. He gives various refined subdivisions of this class, which must of course take in Berkeley and Hume. Hume's extreme doctrine, he calls (in the Lectures) Nihilism, and expressively describes it as 'a consciousness of various bundles of baseless appearances.' The second great class—the Representationists—has many supposed varieties; but the main example of it is designated by the phrase 'Cosmothetic Idealism'; meaning that an External World is supposed apart from our mental perception, as the inconceivable and incomprehensible cause of that perception. The mental fact or perception is thus not ultimate, but vicarious, and intermediate,—the means of suggesting or introducing something else. This view Hamilton, in common with Berkeley, Hume, and Ferrier, holds to be untenable, and absurd.

His own doctrine—Natural Realism—by which he proposes to vindicate the common sense view, and yet avoid the difficulties of the Representative scheme, contains the following allegations :—

1. In the act of sensible perception, I am conscious of two things—of *myself* the *perceiving subject*, and of *an external reality* in relation with my sense as the *object perceived*.

2. I am conscious of knowing each not mediately in something else, as *represented*, but immediately, as *existing*.

3. The two are known together, but in mutual contrast; they are one in knowledge, but opposed in existence.

4. In their mutual relation, each is equally dependent, and equally independent.

5. We are percipient of nothing but what is in proximate contact, in immediate relation with our organs of sense; in short, with the rays of light on the retina (Reid, p. 814). From which it follows as an inference, that when different persons look at the sun, each sees a separate object.

In the hostile criticisms of Mr. Samuel Bailey, and Mr. Mill, this last position has been singled out as the author's greatest contradiction both of fact and of himself. It may be remarked, however, that in his more fundamental positions, there is an insurmountable contradiction. By his hypothesis of *immediate* perception, he has escaped the difficulties of the Representationist, to fall into others equally serious. If we are to interpret terms according to their meaning, how are we to reconcile *immediate knowledge*, and an *external reality?* A reality external to us must be removed from us, if by never so little interval; and it is impossible to understand how the mind can be cognizant of a thing detached from itself. Then, how can the two things be *equally dependent* and *equally independent*. This is admissible as an epigram, but must be resolvable by a double sense of the words. In no sense can we reconcile independent existence with the dependence necessary to knowledge.

There is another criticism applicable to these positions. Hamilton justly lays it down as the condition of a fact of consciousness, or fundamental truth, that it must be *ultimate* and *simple;* in other words, the terms of the fact must refer to ultimate elements of our experience. Apply this test to the terms 'external,' 'independent,' and 'reality;' and we shall have to admit that these are not simple or ultimate notions, but complex and derived. It is inadmissible, therefore, to regard any proposition involving them as an ultimate fact of consciousness.

FERRIER. Ferrier's system is occupied with illustrating under every imaginable variety of expression, from the rigour of geometrical forms to the richest colours of poetry, the necessary implication of the object and the subject,—the impossibility and the self-contradiction of an independent material world. His first proposition in the 'Institutes,' is perhaps not the most satisfactory in its wording, but viewed by the light of those that follow, its meaning becomes clear:—' Along with whatever our intelligence knows, it must as the ground or condition of its knowledge, have some cognizance of self.' This he conceives the most fundamental expression of the fact that our knowledge of the world is a mental modification; a something held in the grasp of mind, not something totally apart from mind.

He proceeds, in his second proposition, to say that—' The object of knowledge, whatever it may be, is always something more than is naturally or usually regarded as the object. It always is, and must be, the object with the addition of one's self,—object *plus* subject; thing, or thought, *mecum.* Self is an integral and essential part of every object of cognition'—a various wording of the general doctrine. So is Prop. III. 'The objective part of the object of knowledge, though distinguishable, is not separable in cognition from the subjective part, or the ego; but the objective part and the subjective part do together constitute the unit or minimum of knowledge.' Still more pointed in the statement, though still the same in substance, is Prop. IV.:—
' Matter *per se,* the whole material universe by itself, is of necessity absolutely unknowable.' After this, it is little else than tautology (justifiable in the circumstances) to add in Prop. V.:—' All the qualities of matter *by themselves* are of necessity absolutely unknowable.' His other propositions still repeat the main idea, but with reference to the explication of the various terms of philosophy —Universal and Particular, Ego and non-Ego, Sense and Intellect, Presentation and Representation, Phenomenon, Substance, Relative, Absolute, Contingent.

The questionable expression in the first and fundamental proposition, is the phrase ' have some cognizance of itself,' which suggests a more specific effect of self-consciousness than the author really means. His other propositions are content with the more general and safe affirmation, that, in knowledge, self must be present as an essential part of the fact. It is not necessary, and it appears scarcely accurate, to say that the mind, while cognizing an object, must at the same time be cognizing self. The cognition of self points to the study of the subject mind, in which there is a remission of the object regards.

Besides his 'Institutes of Metaphysic,' Ferrier has several dissertations on the same question, now brought together in a posthumous publication. The burden of them all is the same; his effort still is to expose the self-contradiction of the prevailing theory. He is almost exclusively occupied in clearing the ground; and when we seek his own positive views we find only a few brief indications.

In the first place, he contends that Perception is a simple, ultimate, indivisible fact: 'the absolutely elementary in cognition, the *ne plus ultra* of thought. It has no pedigree. It admits of no analysis. It is not a relation constituted by the coalescence of an objective and a subjective element. It is not a state or modification of the human mind. It is not an effect which can be distinguished from its cause. It is positively the FIRST, with no forerunner.' (Lectures and Remains, ii. 411.)

Secondly, as the ultimate support of our Perception and Matter, he follows Berkeley in assigning the direct agency of the Deity. He puts the question, 'Is the Perception of matter a modification of the human mind, or is it not?' and replies, 'that in his belief it is not.' He thus repudiates 'subjective idealism, and cares not what other idealism he is charged with.'

MANSEL. Mr. Mansel maintains (1) that being in itself, or substance without attributes, is not only unknowable but contrary to the nature of things. (2) That Berkeley's denial of the existence of matter (in the sense of the unknown support of qualities) is not in any way contrary to common sense. (3) But when Berkeley went so far as to assert the *non-existence* of matter, he went as far beyond the evidence as his opponents did in maintaining its existence. [Berkeley might, however, deny it on the ground that it was a self-contradictory and fictitious entity of the imagination.] (4) It is possible to take an intermediate course, to admit that we have no right to assert the existence of any other kind of matter than what is presented in consciousness; but to deny Berkeley's other position, that we are conscious only of our own ideas. 'If, in any mode of consciousness whatever, an external object is *directly presented* as existing in relation to me, that object, though composed of sensible qualities only, is given as a material substance, existing as a distinct reality, and not merely as a mode of my own mind.' This is very much the language of Hamilton's Natural Realism; and, like it, treats the adult consciousness as expressing the natural or primitive consciousness. (5) He maintains with Berkeley, and against Hume, that a personal *self* is directly presented in intuition, together with its several affections.

(6) He, moreover, analyzes the fact of external perception, and specifies resistance to locomotive energy, as the mode of consciousness which directly *tells us* of the existence of an external world.

He would not admit that this consciousness *is* the external world. (Metaphysics, pp. 329, 346.)

BAILEY. Mr. Samuel Bailey has devoted a large portion of his 'Letters on the Human Mind' to the problem before us. He criticises Locke, Berkeley, Hume, Reid, Brown, Stewart, Kant, and Hamilton. His own view is, that 'the perception of external things through the organs of sense is a direct mental fact or phenomenon of consciousness not susceptible of being resolved into anything else.' 'It is vain attempting to trace any mental event between the percipient and the thing perceived; vain trying to express the fact more simply or fully than by saying, we perceive the object.' In short, perception is a simple, indivisible, ultimate experience of the human mind.

A conclusion to the same effect is enunciated by Ferrier, although he and Mr. Bailey would probably not accord on anything else as regards this problem.

The absolute simplicity of this experience is as doubtful in itself, as it is at variance with the common belief. There are experiences of the mind that we pronounce, with great confidence, to be simple (although always reserving the possibility of future resolution), as our feeling of muscular energy, our sensation of sweetness in taste, our sensation of white light. But these cases of unequivocal simplicity are few in number, and difficult to state in their absolute purity; and all of them are, indeed, crusted over with a numerous body of associations. But when we turn to the fact called perception, we cannot help being struck with the *appearance*, at least, of complexity. There is seemingly a combination of a perceiving mind, a mode of activity of that mind, and a something to be perceived—nothing less than the whole extended universe. To make out this seemingly threefold concurrence to be an indivisible fact, would at least demand a justifying explanation. It is true that most of the attempts to analyze it have only brought their authors into contradictions; and that there may be wisdom as well as safety in renouncing the task. Still, no one can answer for the whole future of philosophy; no one can affirm that a fact, having so much the appearance of complexity as this, shall never be made to yield to analysis.

J. S. MILL. In his 'Examination of Sir W. Hamilton's Philosophy,' Mr. Mill, after criticising Hamilton's mode of handling Perception, advances what he calls 'The Psychological Theory of the Belief in an External World.'

The theory postulates certain truths, proved by experience, and generally admitted, although not adequately felt by the school of Hamilton.

The first truth is that the human mind is capable of *Expectation*; in other words, after experiencing actual sensations, we can conceive Possible sensations.

He next postulates the Laws of Association. After briefly stating these laws, and alluding to the power of repetition in making the bond of Contiguity more secure, he points out that, in certain circumstances of unbroken and iterated conjunction, there may arise an Inseparable, or Indissoluble, association between two things, so that we shall be practically unable to conceive the things in separation; as in the acquired perceptions of sight.

Setting out from these premises, the theory maintains that there are associations naturally, and even necessarily, generated by the order of our sensations, and of our reminiscences of sensation, such as would give rise to the belief of an external world, and make it seem an intuition.

Mr. Mill asks, ' What is the meaning of a thing being external to us, and not a part of our thoughts ? ' and replies that there is meant something that exists when we are not thinking of it, that existed before we had thought of it, and would exist if we were annihilated; and further, that there exist things that have never acted on our senses, and things never perceived by any one. Now, such a belief is within the compass of the known laws of association. ' I see a piece of white paper on a table. I go into another room, and though I have ceased to see the paper, I am persuaded that it is still there. I have not now the sensation, but I believe that when I place myself in the same circumstances, I shall have it again, at any moment.' Thus, together with a small and limited portion of actual sensation, there is always a vast compass of *possible sensation*. These possibilities are to us the external world; the present sensations are fugitive, the possible sensations are Permanent. To this wide region of Permanent Possibility of sensation, a name is given—Substance, Matter, the External World; and although the thing thus named is related to, and based upon, our actual sensations, yet ' from a familiar tendency of the mind,' the different name comes to be considered the name of a different thing.

These certified or guaranteed possibilities of sensation, have another peculiarity ; they refer to sensations not single, but Grouped. A material substance is the rallying point of a great and indefinite number and variety of sensations : and when a few of these are present, the remaining number are conceived by us as Present Possibilities. As this happens in turn to all the sensations, the group as a whole presents itself to the mind as Permanent, in contrast to the temporary and passing individual sensations. The present sensation of a piece of money is but one of a vast aggregate of possible sensations that we might have in connexion with it.

Again, we recognize a fixed Order of our sensations ; an Order of succession, giving rise to the idea of Cause and Effect, through the fixity of the sequence. But this order is not realized so much in actual sensations, as in the groups or possibilities of sensation. We find the possibilities to be regular, when the actualities are not ; the fire goes out and puts an end to one particular possibility of warmth and light. There is a constant set of possible sensations forming the background to every actual sensation at any moment.

Now, when this point is reached, the Permanent Possibilities have assumed such an unlikeness of aspect, and such a difference of position to us, from the mere actualities, that it would be contrary to all our experience of the human mind, if they were not conceived to be something intrinsically and generically distinct from the present feelings. The sensations cease; the possibilities remain; they are independent of our will, our presence, and everything belonging to us.

Moreover, we find other sentient beings recognizing, in common with ourselves, the Permanent Possibilities. They may not have the same actual sensations, but they have always the same possible sensations. This puts the final seal to our conception of the groups of possibilities as the fundamental Reality in Nature.

The idea of Externality is derived solely from the notion that experience gives of the Permanent Possibilities. Our sensations we carry with us, and they never exist where we are not; but, when we change our place, we do not change the Permanent Possibilities of Sensation. When we have ceased to feel, they will remain to others.

The distinction of Primary and Secondary Qualities corresponds to the greater permanence of one class of sensations. The sensations of the Primary Qualities—Extension, Weight, &c., are constant, and the same at all times to all persons; those of the Secondary qualities are only occasional; they vary in the same person, and are different to different persons.

As regards MIND, Mr. Mill holds that we have no conception of Mind in itself, as distinguished from its conscious manifestations. The notion that we form of Mind, as a unity, is still derived from the attribute of Permanence. It is a Permanent Possibility of sensation, and also of thoughts, emotions and volitions. Its states differ from matter in not occurring in groups; and still farther, in not being shared by other sentient beings.

BOOK III.

THE EMOTIONS.

CHAPTER I.

FEELING IN GENERAL.

1. Of the two great divisions of the Feelings — Sensations (with muscular feelings), and Emotions — the second has now to be entered upon. As a preparation, it is expedient to resume the characters of Feeling in general.

This survey might have preceded the consideration of the lower department of the Feelings; but, in exposition, there is often an advantage gained by deferring the higher generalities until some of the particulars have been given.

The Muscular Feelings and Sensations are the primary Feelings, those arising out of the immediate operation of external agents, with the minimum of intellectual processes and growths. The Special Emotions are secondary or derived, and involve the intellect.

2. Positively, Feeling comprehends pleasures and pains, and states of excitement that are neither. Negatively, it is opposed to Volition and to Intellect.

If Feeling were confined to pleasure and pain (as Hamilton assumes), it would have all the precision of our experience of those two states. But certain modes of consciousness, neither pleasurable nor painful, embraced by the word 'excitement,' are accounted feelings. This leaves a vague and uncertain margin in the boundary of the Feelings.

There are only three ultimate modes of mind—Feeling, Volition, and Intellect. Volition is action under Feeling; its *differentia*, therefore, is active energy for an end, which is a distinctive and well-defined property. Intellect has three constituents, — discrimination, similarity, retentiveness,—all clearly definable. The precision attaching to Volition and to Intellect gives a precise *negative* definition to Feeling. Thus, any mental state not being Action for an End, and not regarded as Discrimination, Agreement, or Retentiveness, must be viewed as Feeling.

3. Feeling has a two-fold aspect—Physical and Mental.

The PHYSICAL aspect involves all the organs recognized as connected with mental operations—the Brain, Muscles, Senses, and Secreting organs.

The manner of working of these organs, under states of feeling, is summed up in two great laws—Relativity and Diffusion.

The details already given in a former Book (I.) will render sufficient a brief statement of these laws.

4. The principle of RELATIVITY, in its purely *physical* aspect, means that, in order to Feeling, there must be some change in the mode or intensity of the cerebral and other processes.

The proofs in favour of the principle of Relativity embrace at once its physical and its mental sides. It is scarcely possible to separate, in language, the two sides; our most familiar names having a reference to both aspects. An *impression* suggests a physical as well as a mental phenomenon.

5. The Law of DIFFUSION is thus expressed :—' According as an impression is accompanied with Feeling, the aroused currents *diffuse* themselves freely over the brain, leading to a general agitation of the moving organs, as well as affecting the viscera.'

This law is implied in the details already given as to the expression or embodiment of the feelings. Every feeling, in proportion to its strength, is accompanied with movements, and with changes in the organic functions. If a feeling has no such apparent accompaniments, we conclude, either that it is weak, or that there is an effort of voluntary (and, it may be, habitual) suppression.

The physical groundwork of the great distinction of PLEASURE and PAIN, is fully explained in Book I., chap. IV. (p. 75).

CHARACTERS OF FEELING.

6. The characters of Feeling are (1) those of Feeling proper (Emotional); (2) those referring to the Will (Volitional); (3) those bearing upon Thought (Intellectual); and (4) certain mixed properties, including Forethought, Desire, and Belief.

Emotional Characters of Feeling.

7. Every feeling has its characteristic PHYSICAL side.

As regards the Senses, a distinct *origin* or agency can be assigned, as well as a *diffused* wave of effects, the expression or outward embodiment of the state. In the Emotions, the physical origin is less definable, there being a supposed coalition of sensations with one another and with ideas; the diffusion or expression is, therefore, the principal fact. For the opposite states of pleasure and pain, and for the leading emotions, as wonder, fear, love, &c., the outward expression is remarkably characteristic.

8. On the MENTAL side, we recognize *Quality* (Pleasure, Pain, Indifference); *Degree,* in the two modes of Intensity and Quantity; and *Speciality.*

Quality. This expresses the fundamental distinction of Pleasure and Pain, involving the sum of all human interest, the ends of all pursuit. Happiness and Misery are the names of aggregates, or totals of pleasures and pains. Each one's happiness may be defined as the surplus centre when the total of pain is subtracted from the total of pleasure.

We may have feeling without either pleasure or pain. Surprise is a familiar instance. Some surprises give us delight, others cause suffering; but many do neither. A painful emotion may be deprived of its pain, and yet leave us in a state of excitement; and still oftener, a pleasurable emotion may cease as delight, but not as feeling. The name excitement applies to many such states. There may be a certain amount of pleasure or of pain, but we are conscious of a still greater amount of mere agitation or excitement.

Degree. The degree or strength of a feeling admits of the two distinct modes, named Intensity or acuteness, and Quantity or mass. The prick of a pin is an acute pain; the depression of general fatigue is massive. The physical fact, in acuteness, is the intense stimulation of a small surface, in massive feeling, the gentler stimulation of a wide surface.

Acute pleasures and pains stimulate the will, and impress the intellect, perhaps more strongly than an equivalent stimulation of the massive kind. Hence their efficacy as motives. In punishment, acute pains have the advantage of being much dreaded, while they do not endanger health.

Massive pleasures have the power of soothing morbid activity, and of inducing the tender emotion. Massive pains are recognized under such names as depression, gloom, melancholy, despair. Their amount is known by the pleasure that they can neutralize. They debilitate and weaken the tone of the system, and are not favourable to voluntary exertion, although their motive force ought to be great. They are powerful to induce abstinence from the actions that give rise to them.

For *Speciality*, see examples under the Senses.

Volitional Characters of Feeling.

9. The Will is moved by the feelings; pleasure causing pursuit, pain avoidance. Hence the voluntary actions are a farther clue to the states of feeling. There is no direct volitional stimulus given by neutral excitement.

As the energy of pursuit or avoidance is in proportion to the degree of the pleasure or pain, other things being the same, we possess both an additional character of those feelings, and an important indication of their presence and amount in human beings.

The neutral feelings govern the actions only through the *fixed idea*, by which a disturbing force is brought to bear on the operations of the will, as influenced by pleasure and pain.

Intellectual Characters of Feeling.

10. A Feeling viewed with reference to any one of the three properties—Discrimination, Agreement, Retentiveness—assumes an intellectual aspect, and is on the eve of becoming a state of intellect proper. Still, as there belongs to all feelings a certain degree of ideal persistence and recoverability, and as importance attaches to this Retentive property, we may recognize it as their intellectual attribute.

Feelings have a different value according as, on the one hand, they pass away and are forgotten; or as, on the other, they are easily recovered, at after times, by mental instigation solely. The violent shocks of physical pain, as in organic sensations, are not easily remembered. The pleasures and pains of the higher senses are more retainable; and the feelings connected with some of the special emotions, as Tender Feeling, Pride, &c., are perhaps still better remembered. One of the meanings of *refinement* as applied to pleasures is the being more easily sustained in the ideal state; in this meaning, the intellectual senses impart more refined pleasures than Taste or Smell.

Farther applications of the Retentiveness of Feeling will be given under the next head.

Mixed Characters of Feeling.

11. The consideration of Feeling, under the intellectual attribute of Retentiveness or Ideal permanence, brings into view the nature of Forethought or Prudence.

A feeling in the actual, as Hunger, prompts the will according to its strength or degree; the same feeling, in anticipation, has power according as the force of the actual cleaves to it in the ideal, which depends on the Retentiveness of the mind for past states of the feeling. A feeling, however strong in the actual, if feebly remembered, will have no power to stimulate efforts of pursuit or avoidance. According as the remembrance of a pleasure approaches the vividness of actuality, is the energy of the will on its account sustained in absence; the pursuit is thus steady, although the fruition is only occasional.

12. The state of Desire grows out of the retentiveness of the mind for pleasure and pain.

Desire is a mixed property. A pleasure is present to the mind as an idea; the idea, however falls short of the original; the consciousness of this inferiority is painful, and urges us to realize the full actuality.

13. It is the property of every feeling to Occupy the mind—to fix the attention upon the cause or object of the feeling, and to exclude other objects.

This applies alike to pleasures, to pains, and to neutral excitement; with modifications due to the characteristics of the three modes of feeling.

Pleasure, as such, detains the mental regards; the charm of a spectacle or a piece of music is all-engrossing. Hence the pleasing emotions are what most strongly possess the attention and repel all attempts at diversion. If we were to look to this case solely, we might suppose that the engrossment was due to the pleasure as such.

It is, however, a fact that painful feelings have a power to detain and engross the mind. This is contrary to the working of pain as such, which is to repel whatever causes it; we shut the ears to discord, and turn the eyes away from a dizzying sight. But the mere fact of our being excited by a painful idea retains it in the mind: we cannot banish it, although we will to do so; the very attempt often increases the mental excitement, which is to increase its permanence. Thus, a painful excitement, as excitement, or feeling, detains the mind, while, *as pain*, it would seek to remove our attention from the cause, and allay the state of feeling.

We can now understand the characteristic attribute of Neutral feelings. As feeling, they detain and occupy the mind, although without the aid of pleasure, or the opposition due to pain. The detention is due simply to the strength of the excitement as such. A surprise makes us attend to the circumstance causing it; it is a power to prevent us from attending to, or thinking of, other things. It controls our thoughts for the time that it lasts, directing them towards the matters connected with it, and away from all unconnected things.

14. The influence of the feelings on Belief is of a mixed nature.

That influence can be understood from what has just been said. Pleasure, as such, influences belief. In the first place, it influences the Will in action or pursuit, which carries belief with it; he that is fond of sport is urged to follow it, and believes (in opposition to evidence) that no harm or risk will attend it. In the next place, pleasure detains the mind upon the favourite objects, and excludes all considerations of a hostile kind: this is the influence upon the thoughts, even when no voluntary action is instigated; any opinion that is agreeable to us gains possession of our thoughts, and is a hostile power against the suggestion of views running counter to it.

Pain, as such, would make us revolt from the objects and thoughts that induce it, and would make us disbelieve in those objects and thoughts; a narrative of great atrocity would, through that circumstance, induce to disbelief. But through the excitement of mind that it causes, it keeps our attention morbidly fixed on all its circumstances, and by the very intensity of the feeling, and in spite of the pain, favours our reception and belief of the particulars alleged.

Neutral Excitement, as such, and in proportion to its strength, by detaining the thoughts, and excluding others, is a power on the side of belief. We are to a certain extent disposed to believe whatever we are made strongly to conceive and feel.

Thus all the feelings of the mind are influential in swaying the beliefs, in thwarting the reason, and in perverting the judgment in matters of truth and falsehood.

THE INTERPRETATION AND ESTIMATE OF FEELING.

15. For a knowledge of the feelings of others, we must trust to external signs, interpreted by our own consciousness. The signs are (1) the Expression, (2) the Conduct, and (3) the indications of the Course of the Thoughts.

(1) The outward Expression or Embodiment is a key to the nature and the amount of the feeling.

This arises out of the fact that different feelings express themselves differently, and that the stronger the feeling the stronger the expression.

In interpreting the signs of feeling furnished by the features, voice, gestures, &c., we have to observe certain precautions. In the first place, the same outward expression may not correspond in all persons to the same degree of feeling. Some temperaments are naturally demonstrative, others are wanting in demonstration. One man may be in the practice of giving way to the outburst of feeling, another may habitually suppress, or moderate, the external display. Even in the same person, the vigour of the demonstrations will vary with the strength and freshness of the organs; the young are more lively than the old, without being necessarily more affected. The practical inference is that we should make allowance for temperament (if it can be ascertained) and for the state of bodily vigour, before concluding that the most vociferous and demonstrative person feels most.

16. (2) The Conduct pursued is an indication of the strength of the feelings, especially as regards pleasure and pain.

This is the law of the Will. According to the degree of a pleasure is the urgency to pursue it; according to the degree of a pain, is the urgency to avoid it. We infer strength of taste or liking on the one hand, and strength of disliking on the other, from the motive force of each in pursuit and avoidance. The criterion of conduct is probably more to be trusted than the criterion of demonstrativeness; the combination of the two makes a still greater approach to accuracy.

The exceptions to this test, are the exceptions to the Will. In a very energetic temperament, strength of action does not imply strength of feeling; allowance must be made for the vigour of mere spontaneity. Again, the fixed idea may be a disturbing element, as in Fear. Lastly, habits of acting once formed, cease to represent the power of a present feeling.

17. (3) The Course of the Thoughts may bear the impress of Feeling, and give evidence of its kind and degree.

We have seen that the feelings detain the mind with their objects, and, in proportion to their strength, exclude other objects. There is no stronger proof of affection, than the constant occupation of the thoughts with a beloved object. Vanity is attested in the same unmistakeable way. The inability to banish a painful subject is an evidence of the intensity of the pain, since it overcomes the force of the will, as well as confines the intellectual trains to one channel.

The counteractive to this test is the natural and acquired amount of the intellectual forces, which offer a certain strength of resistance to the detention of the mind on one class of ideas. A man of high intellectual endowments may have strong feelings, without being possessed by them to the same degree as a feebler intellect. Moreover, it is a part of self-control to check the influence of emotion in this, as well as in other points where it exercises a mastery.

18. The influence on Belief is a decisive test of the strength of a feeling.

This is the practical outcome of the volitional and intellectual power combined. When one is carried away by some ideal, in despite of facts and evidence, the cause is a strong emotion. Such is the influence of love or of antipathy.

19. The liabilities to error of these several tests, taken separately, are to a great degree counteracted when they are taken together.

The demonstrative temperament exaggerates the expression of feeling, but the test of conduct will apply a correction. The man of natural energy may seem to have strong likings for the things that he pursues, or dislikings for what he avoids; but the course of his thoughts and the strength of his beliefs, failing to confirm the inference, will set his character in its true light.

20. We attain an insight into the feelings of others by their own description of them. Each man can compare his own feelings, and state their relative degree. The thing required is a standard, or common measure, between one person and another.

If by means of the various tests already indicated, one man can obtain the assurance that, in some point, he feels exactly as another does, a common measure is established between them; by reference to which they can make known to each other the intensity of their feelings generally. Two persons comparing notes, as to expression, conduct, and the course of thought, may arrive at the conclusion that in the enjoyment of music, they are on a par; they are then able (approximately) to estimate one another's feelings as to all other things.

21. The criteria of feeling may be applied in estimating the Happiness or the Misery of our fellow-beings.

As the estimate of our own happiness or misery is the guide to our actions as regards ourselves, the estimate of the happiness or misery of our fellows is the basis of our sympathies, our duties, and our entire conduct towards them. It is the immediate foundation of Ethics and of Politics, and the final consideration in all knowledge, science, and art.

It is remarked by Paley, with reference to the amount of happiness belonging to different pursuits and modes of life, that there is 'a presumption in favour of those conditions of life in which men appear most *cheerful* and *contented*. For though the apparent happiness of mankind be not always a true measure of their real happiness, it is the best measure we have.' For a rough estimate, cheerfulness and contentment are good indications; both, however, are liable to mislead. Cheerfulness, in the demonstrative temperament of a Frenchman or an Italian, would not mean the same thing as in an Englishman. A still greater uncertainty would belong to the other criterion—contentment; for that state is a proof, not so much of happiness, as of training. Many are content with little;

others, with a large fund of happiness, remain dissatisfied; as regards these, therefore, it is not true that discontent is a sign of unhappiness. Contentment is a virtue of great importance to society generally; still, it does not indicate the possession of happiness by the subject of it.

Men's happiness can be measured only by the degree and the continuance of their enjoyments, as compared with the degree and the continuance of their pains. We have to apply the various tests, in the course of a sufficient observation, to determine these points. If we can farther interrogate each one as to their own feelings and experience, we shall come still closer to the truth.

An easier mode of approximating to the estimate in question, and one far more accurate than Paley's two tests (although not suitable to some of his opinions), is to consider each man's share of the usual sources of pleasure, and his exemptions from the usual sources of pain. The so-called good things of life—Health, Wealth, Friends, Honours, Power, opportunities of gratification, a smooth career—so unequally possessed by mankind, are a rough measure of happiness. The estimate may, however, be made more exact by close individual observation and the application of the tests.

THE DEVELOPMENT OF FEELING.

22. An outburst of feeling passes through the stages of rise, culmination, and subsidence.

What we call a state of feeling, or emotion, is a transitory outburst from a permanent condition approaching to indifference. There is every variety of mode as respects both degree and duration. A feeble stimulus can be continued longer than a powerful one; while every intense display must be rendered short by exhaustion.

Practically, the moment of culmination of feeling, or passion, is the moment of perilous decisions and fatal mistakes.

23. The emotional states are prone to alternation and periodicity.

The Appetites are marked by regularity of recurrence depending on bodily causes. In the pleasurable feelings generally, the great alternation is from exercise, on the one hand, to remission or repose on the other. This is a prime condition of the maintenance of a flow of pleasure. Each sensibility is roused in turn, and remitted when the point of exhaustion is reached.

ENDS OF THE ANALYSIS OF THE FEELINGS.

Habit determines a more specific alternation. Sensibilities accustomed to be gratified at periodic intervals, acquire the force of appetites.

24. It is proper, in conclusion, to set forth the ends to be served by the analysis of the Feelings.

(1) Here, as elsewhere, there is scope for gratifying enlightened curiosity, by the reference of various and complicated phenomena to general laws.

(2) The chief foundations of Ethics are to be found in the nature of the human feelings. The question of the Moral Sense is a question as to the simple or compound character of a feeling.

(3) The wide department of Æsthetics, in like manner, supposes a knowledge of the laws and varieties of feeling. The Poetical and Literary Art, for example, is amenable to improvement, according as the human emotions are more exactly studied. The science of Rhetoric, for the time being, contains the application of the science of mind in general, and of the feelings in particular, to literary composition.

(4) The theory of Human Happiness reposes immediately on the knowledge of the human feelings. This must ever be the point of convergence of all the sciences, but it is the science of the feelings that gives the line of direction.

(5) The Interpretation of Human Character, the understanding of men and their motives, will grow with the improved knowledge of the feelings. Not merely the emotional character as such, and the conduct, or voluntary actions, whose motives are the feelings, but also much of what seems purely intellectual tendencies, may derive elucidation from the present subject. The intellectual forces are, in all men to some extent, and in many men to a great extent, swayed by emotion. In particular, the man of Imagination, in the proper sense of the word, the poet or artist, is determined, in his productions, as much by feeling as by intellect.

CHAPTER II.

THE EMOTIONS AND THEIR CLASSIFICATION.

1. THE Emotions, as compared with the Sensations, are secondary, derived, or compound feelings.

The Muscular Feelings and the Sensations are assumed to be the primary or fundamental sensibilities. The concurrence, or combination, of these, in various ways, originates new states that acquire a permanent and generic form, wherein the simple elements cease to be apparent.

2. Sensations, and their ideas, may coalesce to form new feelings, or emotions.

First, The simplest case is a *plurality* of sensations, whether of the same sense, or of different senses, in MUTUAL HARMONY or in MUTUAL CONFLICT.

Harmony is a source of pleasure, Discord of pain. We may reasonably assume, as the physical basis of the situation, that, in the one case, the nerve currents conspire to a common effect, and, in the other case, run into wasting conflict.

Examples will arise in the subsequent detail. The element of Harmony is prominent in the Fine Art Emotions. Consistency and Inconsistency in truth and falsehood are feelings related to the exercise of the Intellect. There is a species of Harmony in the workings of Sympathy.

3. Secondly, There may be, as a consequence of the Law of Contiguity, a *transfer* of feelings to things that do not originally excite them, as in the cases already illustrated (Contiguity, § 33).

4. Thirdly, There may be a *coalescence* of separate feelings into one aggregate or whole, as in Property, Beauty, Justice, and the Moral Sentiment.

These examples nearly all illustrate both transfer and coalescence.

5. We cannot, in classifying the emotions, comply with the rules of logical division. The nature of the case admits of but one method—to proceed from the simpler to the more complex.

GENERA OF EMOTION.

There are several well-marked and important genera of emotion, which must find a place under every classification, although there may be different views as to the best order to take them in; as, for example, Love, Anger, Fear, Wonder; which are all comparatively simple. Others have a high degree of complexity; such, in my opinion, are Beauty and the Moral Sentiment.

The treatment of the various kinds of Emotions must essentially consist in defining and describing each with precision, in assigning the derivation, if possible, and in tracing out the most usual forms and varieties. In the description, we shall apply the Natural History method, already exemplified in the Sensations.

6. The arrangement is as follows:—

I. While the *Law of Relativity* is essential to Feeling in every form, there are certain Emotional states of a very general kind, developed by the mere intensity of the transition; such are NOVELTY, SURPRISE, and WONDER.

There are also certain pleasurable feelings that are the rebound from very general modes of pain, and which are, therefore, more peculiarly connected with Relativity; as LIBERTY with reference to RESTRAINT, and POWER as the rebound from IMPOTENCE.

In none of the feelings, can we leave out of view this great condition of mental life; but, in a certain number of instances, the emotional state exists only as a transition between *opposites:* the pleasure supposes a previous pain, and the pain a previous pleasure.

II. The emotion of TERROR, or Fear, may receive an early consideration.

III. The TENDER EMOTION, or LOVE, is a well-marked and far-reaching susceptibility of our nature, and a leading source of our pleasures. We may append to it the emotions of ADMIRATION, REVERENCE, and ESTEEM.

IV. When we see in ourselves the qualities that excite love or admiration in others, we are affected by a pleasurable emotion, named SELF-COMPLACENCY, Self-gratulation, Self-esteem. This will be shown to be a derivative of the Tender Emotion.

A still further effect of the same pleasurable kind is produced on us by the admiration or esteem of others, the names for which are APPROBATION, Praise, Reputation, Glory, and the like.

V. The elation of superior POWER is a very marked and widely ramifying genus of pleasurable emotion, being an emotion of pure Relativity or Comparison; the correlative is the pain of IMPOTENCE.

VI. ANGER or the IRASCIBLE EMOTION is the pleasurable emotion of *malevolence.*

The foregoing comprise the best marked of our simpler emotions. For although they are all more or less of a compound nature, yet there is, in each, something characteristic and peculiar, imparting a generic distinctness, and obtaining a separate recognition throughout the human race.

VII. There are certain Emotional situations arising under the action of Will. Besides the pleasures and pains of Exercise, and the gratification of succeeding in an End, with the opposite mortification of missing what is laboured for, there is, in the attitude of PURSUIT, a peculiar state of mind, so far agreeable in itself, that factitious occupations are instituted to bring it into play. When I use the term PLOT-INTEREST, the character of the situation alluded to will be suggested with tolerable distinctness.

VIII. The exercise of the INTELLECT also is attended with states of Emotion. More especially, under the Law of Similarity, the identification of Like in the midst of unlike is the cause of agreeable surprise; while Inconsistency or Contradiction is an occasion of pain.

IX. The foregoing classes possess each a certain unity and distinctness as respects their origin in the human constitution. The next class is one that has been very commonly regarded as a unity in the investigations of philosophers. I mean the emotions of FINE ART, expressed by the single term Beauty, or the Beautiful. There is doubtless a certain individuality in the feeling that mankind have agreed to designate by the common phrase, 'the feeling of beauty,' but this community of character implies little more than a refined pleasure. If we take the productions of Fine Art, and examine the sources of the delight that they give us, we shall find a very great variety of species, notwithstanding the generic likeness implied in classifying them together. Many of our simple sensations, and many of the feelings belonging to the different heads just enumerated, are brought into play by artistic compositions.

X. The MORAL SENSE in man, like the sense of beauty, has been very generally looked upon as one and indivisible; a position exceedingly open to question. The subject will be fully considered, in the part of this volume devoted to Ethics.

CHAPTER III.

EMOTIONS OF RELATIVITY: NOVELTY.—WONDER.—LIBERTY.

1. The OBJECTS of the emotion of Novelty are well understood.

The PHYSICAL circumstance may be inferred to be a change in the locality of nervous action, extending also to the allied organs—the muscles and the senses.

That pleasure should arise from varying the parts and organs stimulated, is a necessary consequence of the fact that stimulation is pleasurable.

2. The EMOTION is, in Quality, pleasurable; in Degree, various, according to the stimulation, which may be acute or massive. It has no Speciality.

The pleasure is, in fact, the primitive charm of all sensation, before it has been dulled by continuance and satiety. It has the vagueness of character belonging to mere organic stimulation.

3. The corresponding pain is Monotony, tedium, ennui.

This arises from some parts of the system being unduly drawn upon, while others have their stimulation withheld. Its ordinary modes are generally known; the extreme and agonizing degrees are made use of in punishment.

Monotony is often aggravated by the pain of excessive Subjectivity, or self-consciousness. The absence of objective attractions leaves the mind in the subjective condition, which, when long continued, gives the sense of intolerable ennui. To be confined in the dark, or without occupation, is to be made the victim of subjective tedium.

Under the SPECIES of Novelty, we may indicate, first, the simple Sensations, as encountered in early life. Such of these as are in their nature pleasing, are, in the first experience, pre-eminently so. The general exhilaration designated by the word Freshness, is due, among other causes, to novelty of sensation.

The primary sensations are speedily gone through, and fall into the ordinary routine of pleasures, which, by being remitted or alternated, continue to afford a certain measure of delight. The charm of novelty then belongs only to new and varied combinations, and in that form it may be sustained, although with decreasing force, to the end of life. New scenes, new objects, new persons, and new aspects of life, constitute the attractions of travel. Novelty in incidents and events, is furnished by the transactions of life, and by the pages of story. Inventions in the Arts, and discoveries in Science, have the initial charm of novelty, as well as the interest of permanent utility. In Fine Art, whose end is pleasure, the powerful effects of novelty are earnestly invoked; pleasurable surprises are expected of the artist in every department; beauty must be enhanced by originality; while the passion for change, uncontrolled, leads in the end to decadence. Last of all, in Fashion, novelty is supreme. Throughout the whole, but one rule prevails; other things the same, the greater the novelty, the greater the pleasure.

4. Next to Novelty is VARIETY, alternation, or change.

The longer any stimulant has been remitted, the greater the impression on its renewal. Variety is a minor form of novelty.

Our happiness depends materially on the wise remission and variation of objects of delight. Mere change of pleasures will produce, within limits, a continuance of the pleasurable wave. Still, it is likely that periods of absolute indifference and quiet, if not of painful privation, should intervene, in order to maintain the highest zest of enjoyment.

5. SURPRISE is a breach of expectation, and in addition to mere Relativity, includes an element of Conflict.

In Surprise, we are said to be startled. There is a shock of contradiction, which is always exciting. The excitement may be pleasurable, painful, or neutral, according to the case. As pure conflict, it would be a source of pain; as a pungent stimulus, when the nerves are fresh, it may be pleasurable. Frequently, it is neither, being our typical instance of neutral emotion.

The circumstances of the surprise may farther affect its character. When the occurrence is something better than we expected, there is an access of pleasure; when worse, of pain.

6. WONDER, or the Marvellous, is felt on the view of what rises above, or what falls beneath, our expectations. In the one case, it is an elating emotion, of a kindred with the Sublime; on the other, it tends to depression, or else to contempt.

The pleasing side of Wonder is due to what greatly transcends use and wont. It is an emotion of pure relativity.

If we exclude the side of Littleness and Contempt, everything included in Wonder has its foundation either in pure Surprise, on the one hand, which is the shock of contradiction, or in the admiration of what is great or Sublime, on the other. The full account of this last emotion belongs to a much later stage of the exposition.

7. The opposing couple—RESTRAINT and LIBERTY—are wholly referable to Conflict, combined with Relativity.

Restraint is a case of conflicting impulses, and induces the depression due to conflict. It may have every variety of degree, being in all cases painful. The active spontaneity repressed by confinement; the free vent of emotional diffusion arrested by dread of punishment; the voluntary movements opposed; the wishes thwarted,—are cases of intestine conflict, and of suffering. The pain induced has a speciality through its connexion with the active organs. In the more acute struggles, it is characterized as a 'racking' pain.

There is a stimulating effect in opposition or conflict. Physically, we may suppose, that the sudden check to the nervous currents develops new activity in the brain: while, mentally, it is a fact of pregnant application, that hostility, not overpowering, rouses the energies to more than ordinary efforts. This is seen in every species of contest. Even the intellectual powers attain a more commanding success in the ardour of polemics.

Under continued restraint, the system at length adapts itself to the situation. The taming down of impulses by steady suppression is one of the effects of habit, exemplified in moral discipline. (See MORAL HABITS.)

8. LIBERTY is the correlative of Restraint. It is the joyous outburst of feeling on the release from a foregone bondage, or on the cessation of a conflict.

The liberation must occur while the restraint is still painful; after the system has thoroughly accommodated it self, there is no reaction, and no flush of joyous elation. This fact has been remarked in those that have grown old in servitude, or have undergone long imprisonment. So in minds long fettered by subscription to creeds, even the desire of freedom is extinct.

The character of the emotion of Liberty is an undefined elation, or intoxication, great according to the suddenness and the extent of the release, as well as the previous galling of the chain. Like all other feelings of relativity, it can be renewed only by a renewal of the pain of restraint, and, therefore, is not an absolute addition to the sum of happiness, except to those already in bondage.

A condition so familiar to every human being needs little farther to be said in the way of example or illustration. We may remark, however, that Liberty has an incalculable value, as including the scope given to individuals to seek their own happiness in their own way.

The emotions of Power and Impotence are, to some extent, coincident with the foregoing, but have a far wider range. In consequence of their superior complication and great importance, they are discussed in a separate chapter.

We have included, in the present chapter, feelings of a very elementary and very general kind, subsisting purely by the contrast of opposites. We might give a very wide illustration to the general principle, by adverting to the painful depression of burdens, labours, toils, present and prospective; and to the joyous rebound upon the occasions of their mitigation or abatement.

CHAPTER IV.

EMOTION OF TERROR.

1. The emotion of Terror originates in the apprehension of coming evil. Its characters are—a peculiar form of pain or misery; the prostration of the active energies; and the excessive hold of the related ideas on the mind.

First, as to the OBJECT, or cause—the apprehension of coming evil:—

It does not appear that a present pain, without anticipation, induces the state of fear. A person may have received a severe blow, but if it is done and past, although the smart remains, there is a total absence of terror. A present infliction, as the beginning or *foretaste* of more to come, is pre-eminently a cause of the feeling.

Sometimes the apprehension is of *certain* evil, as when some painful operation has to be gone through. The mere idea of pain is depressing, but the certainty of its approach gives a new character to the suffering. This situation, although, in one view, the most terrible, is yet the most favourable to an effort of courageous endurance; we are most ready to make an exertion, when we are sure it will be wanted.

A second case is *uncertain*, but possible or probable, calamity, as in the chances of a storm, a severe illness, an equal contest for a great stake. This is a state of varying probabilities and fluctuating estimate. The distraction may be harassing in the extreme.

Any *new* uncertainty is especially a cause of terror. We become habituated to a frequent danger, and realize the full force of apprehension only when the evil is one previously unknown. Such are—the terror caused by epidemics, the apprehensions from an unexperienced illness, the feeling of a recruit under fire.

2. Terror, on the PHYSICAL side, shows both a *loss* and a *transfer* of nervous energy. Power is suddenly and extensively withdrawn from the Organic processes, to be concentrated on certain Intellectual processes, and on the bodily Movements.

The appearances may be distributed between effects of *relaxation* and effects of *tension*.

The *relaxation* is seen, as regards the Muscles, in the dropping of the jaw, in the collapse overtaking all organs not specially excited, in tremblings of the lips and other parts, and in the loosening of the sphincters.

Next as regards the Organic Processes and Viscera. The Digestion is everywhere weakened; the flow of saliva is checked, the gastric secretion arrested (appetite failing), the bowels deranged. The Expiration is enfeebled. The heart and Circulation are disturbed; there is either a flushing of the face, or a deadly pallor. The skin shows symptoms of derangement—the cold sweat, the altered odour of the perspiration, the creeping action that lifts the hair. The kidneys are directly or indirectly affected. The sexual organs feel the depressing influence. The secretion of milk in the mother's breasts is vitiated.

The increased *tension* is shown in the stare of the eye and the raising of the scalp (by the occipito-frontalis muscle), in the inflation of the nostril, the shrill cry, the violent movements of protection or flight. The stare of the eye is to be taken as an exaggerated fixing of the attention on the dreaded object; and there concurs with it an equally intense occupation of the thoughts in the same exclusive direction. Whatever movements of expression, or of volition, are suggested by these thoughts, have a similar intensity.

That such a physical condition should be accompanied with great depression is a consequence of the theory of pleasure and pain. The prostration affects the most sensitive processes, the organic ; the increase of energy is in the movements, which have comparatively little sensibility.

3. Mentally, Terror is a form of massive pain.

The depression of a severe fright is known to be, for the time, overwhelming. If we apply the test of the submergence of pleasure, we shall reckon it one of the most formidable visitations of human suffering. Of its Speciality, we can only say that the great depression is accompanied with great excitement.

As regards *Volition*, the pain would operate like any other pain to seek relief. It has been formerly remarked, that the generic tendency of all pain is to quench activity ; and this is more especially true when fear accompanies the pain. Hence, as a deterring instrument, and especially in subduing active opposition, terror is a great addition to mere pain; nothing so effectually tames the haughty spirit into submission. Its defective side (even if we overlook the misery) is shown, if we endeavour, by means of it, to induce great and persevering exertions, the discharge of multifarious duties ; the waste of power being incompatible with anything arduous. Slave labour is notoriously unproductive.

With regard to the *Intellect*, the characters of the emotion are very marked. The concentration of energy in the perceptions and the allied intellectual trains, gives an extraordinary impressiveness to the objects and circumstances of the feeling. In a house believed to be haunted, every sound is listened to with avidity ; every breath of wind is interpreted as the approach of the dreaded spirit. Hence, for securing attention to a limited subject, the feeling is highly efficacious.

Terror, in its intellectual excitement, affords the extreme instance of the fixed idea, or the persistence of an image or intellectual train, against the forces of the will and the intellect combined. An impending danger monopolizes the thoughts. The protracted forms of fear expressed by anxiety, watchfulness, care,—engross the intellect, to the exclusion of liberalizing studies.

The influence of Fear on Belief, follows from its other characters. The tendency is to give way to the suggestions of danger, and to bar out all considerations on the other side.

4. The following are the chief SPECIES of Terror.

(1) The case of the Lower Animals.

In them, we have manifest traces of timidity, as an addition to mere pain. In the deterring smart of the whip, there might be nothing beyond the effect of pain on the will; while the threat of it is still pain in the idea. The evidence of fear is seen in the exaggerated activity inspired by trifling causes; the surrender of great advantages to small risks. Still more is the state shown in the dread of what has never done any harm : the dread of the human presence, in so many animals; the dread of other animals before experience of their disposition; and the liability to be disturbed by slight commotions, noises, and strange appearances.

(2) Fear in Children.

The mental system in infancy is highly susceptible, not merely to pain, but to shocks and surprises. Any great excitement has a perturbing effect allied to fear. After the child has contracted a familiarity with the persons and things around it, it manifests unequivocal fear on the occurrence of any thing very strange. The grasp of an unknown person often gives a fright. This early experience very much resembles the manifestations habitual to the inferior animals. At the more advanced stage, where known evils are to be encountered, if the child knows that it has to go through something painful, the feeling is of the usual or typical kind, modified only by the feebleness of the counteractives, and the consequent vehemence of the manifestations.

(3) Slavish Terror.

Slavish terror takes its rise under a superior unlimited in power, capricious in conduct, or extreme in severity. The possibility of some great infliction is itself necessarily a cause of terror. The uncertainty that one knows not how to meet, or provide against, is still more unhinging. It is not possible to preserve composure under a capricious rule, except by being in a state of preparation for the very worst. The

Stoical prescriptions of Epictetus, himself a slave, are in harmony with such a situation. Another circumstance tending to beget slavish fear is the conscious neglect of duty on the part of the inferior, he at the same time being unprepared calmly to face the consequences. The state of slavery is a state of terror from the power and arbitrary dispositions of the master; the free-born servant has mainly to fear the effects of his own remissness.

(4) Forebodings of disaster generally.

The usual form of Fear may be expressed as the Foreboding of evil or disaster, more or less certain. No human being is wholly exempt from this condition; it is a standing dish in the banquet of life. There is a possibility of encountering evil with the minimum of fear, of bearing the pain by itself, without the unhinging apprehensions; a lofty ideal realized only by a favoured few.

The term *Anxiety* generally implies an element of fear, although it may be used when there is nothing intended but the rational and measured avoidance of pain, which is the true antithesis of fear. *Suspicion* expresses the influence of the fears on Belief. It is a state wherein trifling incidents are read as the certain index of great calamities. More especially, it points to exaggerated estimates of the motives and intentions of other men. To be suspicious is a part of the general temper of timidity. *Panic* is an outburst of terror affecting a multitude in common, and heightened by sympathy or infection. It has ruined many armies, otherwise equipped for victory. It renders a populace utterly uncontrollable in great emergencies.

Like any other emotion, there may be a permanent association between the state of Fear and the objects that have often called it forth, or have been connected with it. The mother is in habitual trepidation about a sick, or wayward, or incapable child. Even when there is no cause for alarm, a shade of terror is apt to be present. This has been called an Affection of Fear, as we have an Affection of Love, and an Affection of Anger (Hatred). The solicitude of a woman about her person and appearance, or of a man of genius for his fame, is an affection of fear. The same fact is expressed by Anxiety and Care.

(5) The Terrors of Superstition.

Our position in the world contains the sources of fear. The vast powers of nature dispose of our lives and happiness with irresistible might and awful aspect. Ages had elapsed ere the knowledge of law and uniformity, prevailing among those powers, had been arrived at by the human intellect. The profound ignorance of primitive man was the soil wherein his early conceptions and theories sprang up; and the fear inseparable from ignorance gave them their character. The essence of superstition is expressed by the definition of fear. An altogether exaggerated estimate of things, the ascription of evil agency to the most harmless objects, and false apprehensions everywhere, are among the attributes of the superstitious man.

(6) The Distrust of our Faculties in new operations.

In all untried situations, in the exercise of imperfect powers, and in the commencement of enterprises where we but partly see our way, we are liable to the quakings of terror. This is one of the miseries of early years. In great posts, where every movement affects the happiness of multitudes, the sensitive mind will always have a certain amount of apprehension.

One remarkable form of this distrust is the being Abashed before a strange face, a new company, or a great multitude. This is a reproduction, in manhood, of childish fear, but the circumstances are somewhat altered. After we have seen something of the world, we are aware of the possibilities of evil that lie in the compass of every human being; every new encounter is attended with dread, until experience gives assurance; we are apt to regard every man an enemy till we prove him a friend.

It might be a question as regards shyness before strangers, whether the more instinctive form of dread, shown in early infancy, does not cling to us in later years, requiring a hardening process to dispel it. If anything seemed to imply such a weakness, it would be the awful sensation of first appearing, as a speaker or performer, before a large assembly. Probably, however, there is enough in the evil possibilities of the case to account for the excessive perturbation of most persons so situated.

The world's censure may be looked at merely as so much pain, and estimated accordingly, or it may be accompanied with the agitation of fear. Being somewhat uncertain and capricious, as well as potent for evil, it is liable to this aggravation of its severity.

(7) The Fear of Death.

In the fear of Death, we have two elements. The extinction of life's pleasures, interests, and hopes, is looked forward to with apprehension according to the zest for these: in the young and vigorous, the misery of the prospect is extreme; a youthful culprit sentenced to execution is heart-rending in his tones of anguish. The other element is the dread Unknown, which operates variously according to a man's temper, conscience, and education.

5. Terror is farther illustrated by its Counteractives and Opposites—the sources of Courage.

These are:—(1) Physical vigour of constitution; which resists the withdrawal of the blood from the organic functions. (2) The Active or Energetic Temperament; or the presence, in large quantity, of what the shock of fear tends to destroy. (3) The Sanguine Temperament; which, being a copious fund of emotional vigour, shown in natural buoyancy, fulness of animal spirits, manifestations of warm sociability, and the like, is also the antithesis of depressing agencies—whether mere pain, or the aggravations of fear. (4) Force of Will; arising from the power of the motives to equanimity. (5) Intellectual Force; which refuses to be overpowered by the fixed idea of an object of fright, and so serves to counterbalance the state of dread. (6) In so far as terror is grounded on Ignorance, the remedy is Knowledge. The victories gained over superstition, in the later ages, have been due to the more exact acquaintance with nature. Pericles, instructed in Astronomy under Anaxagoras, rescued his army from the panic of an eclipse, by a familiar illustration of its true cause.

6. The Reaction, or Relief, from Terror, like any other rebound from a depressing condition, is cheering or hilarious.

This is the source of the cheerfulness of the state of confidence, security, assurance; a pleasure purely relative to the depression of fear.

7. The uses of Terror in government, and in Education, are easily understood.

The discipline of pain, if reinforced by terror, is still more efficacious in subduing obduracy of mind. Pride, independence, self-reliance, are incompatible with the perturbation of fear.

8. The employment of the passion of Fear in Art demands explanation.

The essence of Fear is misery, and the essence of Art is pleasure. But incidental to Fear, is a certain amount of excitement, which may be so regulated as to have the pungency without the pain of the emotion. Mere sympathetic terrors, and still more such as are wholly fictitious, attain this happy medium. There is, nevertheless, a limit; which has been overstepped both by Shakespeare and by Walter Scott.

A slight fear, with speedy relief, may be stimulating at all times. To robust constitutions, even serious danger is welcomed for its excitement.

CHAPTER V.

TENDER EMOTION.

1. TENDERNESS is a pleasurable emotion, variously stimulated, whose effect is to draw human beings into mutual embrace.

The OBJECTS, or causes of tenderness, are chiefly found in connexion with human beings and other sentient creatures; towards whom alone it can be properly manifested.

The exciting causes or stimulants of the feeling are, more particularly, the following,—

First, the massive, or voluminous Pleasures. Under this head, we have already included slow movements, repose after exercise, repletion, agreeable warmth, soft contacts, gentle and voluminous sounds, mild sunshine. Such pleasures are known to soothe or calm down the activity, as opposed to the acute and pungent pleasures; they also incite tender feeling.

In the next place, very great pleasures incline to the tender outburst. Under the agitation of joy, an affectionate warmth is manifested, demanding a response. Occasions of rejoicing are celebrated by social gatherings and hospitality.

Thirdly, Pains are among the causes of tenderness. This seems a contradiction and a paradox; but in reality it is consistent with all the characters of the feeling. There would be no marvel in calling a pleasure to our aid on occasion of pain: the marvel is that, at that moment, the system is prepared to yield an assuagement merely because there is a want. It has to be explained why this emotion in particular should be so ready to burst out in times of suffering. We can best understand its occurring in connexion with pains of the affections.

Fourthly, There are certain more local and special causes that deserve to be mentioned, as farther illustrating the feeling and its physical embodiments. The touch of the breast, the neck, the mouth, and the hand, and the movements of the upper members, are allied to this feeling; as the contact and the movements of the inferior parts of the body are concerned in sexual excitement. The reason is to be found in the vicinity of the organic functions peculiar to each of the feelings. Farther, there are certain special stimulants in the higher senses. In Hearing, the high and mellow note, occurring sometimes in the wail of grief, and adopted in pathetic address, has a touching efficacy. By virtue of this coincidence, too early in its date to be the result of mere association, (and probably a mode of voluminous sensation), there is a power in the outburst of grief to affect others with tenderness. The 'dying fall' is pathetic, as a mode of soft and pleasurable feeling. Finally, in Sight, the sensations of lustre have a like efficacy. The influence of the clear drop, appearing on the moistened eye, and inducing the secretion in the eye of the beholder, is probably more than mere lustre; it adds the stimulus to self-consciousness, and possibly an effect of association besides.

The alliance of tenderness with inaction renders it the emotion of weakness; whence the experience or the view of weakness very readily suggests it. The helplessness of infancy, of age, of sickness, of destitution, calls it forth. Even among inanimate things, slender and fragile forms, after being personified, are sources of tender feeling, and are thence considered objects of beauty. In Burke's theory of the Beautiful, this was made the central feature.

2. The PHYSICAL side of the Tender Emotion specially involves (1) Touch, (2) the Lachrymal Organs, and (3) the movements of the Pharynx.

(1) The soft extended contact, the source of a voluminous sensation of touch, as a physical fact, is both the beginning and the end of the tender feeling. One might suspect a glandular, as well as a purely tactile, effect in this contact; not only is the skin a vast secreting organ, but there is something in the feeling strongly analogous to the organic or visceral sensi-

PHYSICAL ACCOMPANIMENTS OF TENDERNESS. 241

bilities. The remark is farther confirmed by the consideration of the next accompaniment.

(2) The Lachrymal Organs—Gland and Sac—are specifically affected under the tender feeling. We must assume two stages or degrees of this action ; a gentle, healthy flow, accompanied with genial sensibility, and, in the case of great stimulation, a violent, profuse flow, from excessive action and congestion of the brain, under pain or extreme joy.

(3) The movements of the Pharynx, or bag of the throat, the muscular cavity where the food is swallowed, are susceptible to the tender feeling. In violent grief, these muscles are convulsed, so as to be unable to swallow; in the gentler degrees, they are the seat of a sensibility characteristic of the emotion. Considering that these muscles are but the commencement of the muscular fibres of the alimentary canal, we may presume, from analogy, that the alimentary canal as a whole is affected under the feeling. The phrase 'bowels of compassion' would point to this conclusion.

In women, we must add, as an adjunct of tender feeling, the mammary secretion, an eminent addition to the sources of the feeling in organic sensibility.

3. The link of sequence, physical and mental, between the stimulants of tender feeling and the manifestations, is to be sought in the common character of the two sets of phenomena.

It would be in accordance with the Law of Self-conservation, that a pleasurable wave should extend itself, by reflexion from all the sources of the same emotion. If the warm embrace is a cause of the feeling, the feeling, otherwise suggested, would seek its increase and consummation in the embrace, as well as in the other responsive tokens of tenderness—the smile, the glance, the tones, the sympathies of other beings.

The same principle is seen in the diffusive manifestations of feeling generally. Joyful emotion prompts to the musical outburst that would, of itself, be an inspiration of joy.

When pain is a stimulant, the motive still is to have recourse to something pleasurable. This is not the only resort on an occasion of pain. In some states, Anger, or the pleasure of malevolence, is called to aid; the circumstances being natural vigour, an irascible habit, and the absence of genial sympathies. When tenderness is invoked, the circumstances are usually extreme weakness, the tender disposition, or the connexion of the pain with some tender relationship.

4. On the MENTAL side, Tenderness is a feeling, in quality pleasurable, in degree massive and not acute. Its remarkable speciality (which may be a consequence of the foregoing properties) is its connexion with tranquillity and repose.

It is the character of a voluminous excitement to affect lightly a large surface, being thus a more enduring and sustainable source of pleasure. This is pre-eminently the nature of the Tender Feeling, and constitutes its great value in human life. It is a tranquillizer under morbid excitement, a soothing power in pain, and a means of enjoyment when the forces of the system are at the lowest ebb, or in abeyance for the time.

As regards *Volition*, the tender feeling prompts to efforts for its own fruition, like other pleasures, according to their degree. Its tranquillizing influence upon morbid excitement is the substitution of a new state, such as, from its occupying the mind strongly and agreeably, is a power to displace other states.

The *Intellectual* peculiarity of tenderness follows from the others. Being easily sustained, it has in a high degree the property of persistence, and recoverability in idea.

The readiness to form permanent associations, under the law of Contiguity, is a further extension of the intellectual property. The feeling is one superadded to proper sensuous charm, as terror is an addition to mere pain; but when often excited in connexion with an object of sense, it is kindled at the mere mention or suggestion of that object; such habitual or associated Tenderness being the meaning of Affection.

5. The *mixed* characters of the feeling farther illustrate its main feature.

The operation upon the Will in pursuit, corresponding to the degree of the pleasure and the retentiveness combined, is shown in the energies put forth in favour of objects of affection and tender regard.

As Desire, this emotion maintains its consistency. In an easily sustainable feeling, the mere idea contains a large amount of the pleasure; 'the imagination of the feast' is in some degree satisfying. Love is often satisfied with objects purely ideal.

MATERNAL RELATIONSHIP.

The Control of the Attention and the Trains of thought, even in the ordinary degrees of the feeling, would naturally be great, while, in the intenser forms, it is apt to be overwhelming. The same can be said of the allied effect on Belief; the partialities of love, affection, and friendship, are counted upon as laws of human nature.

SPECIES OF THE TENDER EMOTION.

6. It is the nature of the Emotion to vent itself mainly on human beings.

A human person combines the stimulants beyond any other object. The sensuous exterior, the voice and movements purposely attuned, largely arouse the feeling, while the response supposes another personality.

The companionable animals are within the compass of the feeling.

The Family Group.

7. The relation of Mother and Offspring deserves to rank first.

The infant, as a sensuous object, has all the properties that stimulate the feeling. The skin soft and pure, the eye fresh and clear, the outline rounded; the diminutive size and helplessness; the interest of the comparison showing so much likeness to the full-grown individual; the action so different and yet so similar,—render the child an impressive object of tenderness to every one. And in the case of the mother, there is superadded a powerful element of regard, arising out of the original relation to herself, and the special engagement of her energies in supporting the infant's existence. Such a combination of self-interest and the associations of a strong solicitude would, under any circumstances, stamp an object on the mind; a house, or a garden, so situated grows upon the feelings of the possessor. When, however, the object is a human being of the age most fitted to act on the tender susceptibilities, we can easily understand how this relationship becomes the crowning instance of intense personal regard.

The full explanation of maternal love involves the fact of Sympathy, which is distinct from proper Tender feeling, although fusing with it.

The Paternal relationship contains many of the same elements. There is less of personal contact, but the ideal feelings are no less strong, while the influence of contrast and the sentiment of protectorship may be even greater.

8. The relationship of the Sexes, founded in the procreative constitution, is one of Tenderness.

The pleasure connected with the intercourse of the sexes is itself a stimulant of tenderness. There is, besides, that difference of personal conformation, which makes the one sex a variety as it were to the other, possessing a distinct order of attractions. There can be no doubt of the extensive working of this principle, which puts a limit to the influence of the most perfect forms, and the highest excellence. The merits that we carry about with us are apt to pall upon our taste, and the objects that interest us must be something different, even although inferior. The greatest affinities grow out of the stronger contrasts; with this important explanation, that the contrast must not be of hostile qualities, but of *supplemental* ones. The one person must not love what the other hates, but the two must mutually supply each other's felt deficiencies. Affections grounded on disparity, so qualified, exist between individuals of the same sex. The Platonic friendship was manifested chiefly between men of different ages, and in the relation of master and pupil. But in the two sexes there is a standing contrast, the foundation of a more universal interest. The ideal beauty arising from conformation is on the side of the woman: the interest of the masculine presence lies more in the associations of power.

The Benevolent Affections.

9. In Benevolence, the main constituent is Sympathy, which is not to be confounded with Tenderness.

It will be seen more fully afterwards, that, in Sympathy, the essential point is to become possessed of the pains and pleasures of another being. Now, the tender feeling, or love, greatly aids this occupation of mind with the feelings of others, but is not the sole agent concerned. Another power, of a more intellectual kind, is demanded.

10. Sympathy not being necessarily a source of pleasure, the Pleasures of Benevolence are incidental and indirect.

The following considerations are to be taken into account, in resolving this matter.

In the first place, love or tender feeling, is by its nature pleasurable, but does not necessarily cause us to seek the good of the object farther than is needful to gratify ourselves in the indulgence of the feeling. It is as purely self-seeking as any other pleasure, and makes no enquiry concerning the feelings of the beloved personality.

In the second place, in a region of the mind quite apart from the tender emotion, arises the principle of Sympathy, or the prompting to take on the pleasures and pains of other beings, and act on them as if they were our own. Instead of being a source of pleasure to us, the primary operation of sympathy is to make us surrender pleasure and to incur pains.

Thirdly, The engagement of the mind by objects of affection gives them, in preference to others, the benefit of our sympathy; and hence we are specially impelled to work for advancing their pleasures and alleviating their pains. It does not follow that we are made happier by the circumstance; on the contrary, we may be involved in painful and heavy labours.

Fourthly, The *reciprocation* of sympathy and good offices is a great increase of pleasure on both sides; being, indeed, under favourable circumstances, one of the greatest sources of human delight.

Fifthly, It is the express aim of a well-constituted society, if possible, never to let good offices pass unreciprocated. If the immediate object of them cannot or will not reciprocate in full, as when we relieve the destitute or the worthless, others bestow upon us approbation and praise. Of course, if benevolent actions, instead of being a tax, were self-rewarding, such acknowledgment would have no relevance.

Sixthly, There is a pleasure in the sight of happy beings, and we naturally feel a certain elation in being instrumental to this agreeable effect.

11. Compassion, or Pity, means Sympathy with distress, and usually supposes an infusion of Tender Feeling.

The effective aid to a sufferer springs from sympathy proper, and may be accompanied, or not, with tender manifestations. Many persons, little given to the melting mood, are highly sympathetic in the way of doing services. Others bestow sympathy, in the form of mere tender effusion, with perhaps little else. To be full of this last kind of sympathy is the proper meaning of Sentimentality.

12. The receipt of favours inspires Gratitude; of which the foundation is sympathy, and the ruling principle, the complex idea of Justice.

Pleasure conferred upon us, by another human being, immediately prompts the tender response. With whatever power of sympathy we possess, we enter into the pleasures and pains of the person that has thus engaged our regards. The highest form of gratitude, which leads us to reciprocate benefits and make acknowledgments, in some proportion to the benefits conferred, is an application of the principle of Justice.

13. In the Equal relationships of life, there is room for the mutual play of Benevolence and Gratitude.

In brotherhood, friendship, co-membership of the same society, occasional inequalities give room for mutual good offices. In the tenderness thus developed, there is a bond of attraction to counterwork the rivalries and repellant egotisms of mankind.

14. The operation of Sympathy renders the mere spectacle of Generosity a stimulant of Tender Feeling.

This is one great producing cause of the fictitious tenderness made use of in Fine Art. Sympathy interests us in other beings; their pains and pleasures become to a certain extent ours; and the benefits imparted to them can raise a tender wave in us. The more striking manifestations of generosity, as when an injured person or an enemy renders good for evil, are touching even to the unconcerned spectator.

15. The Lower Animals are subjects of tender feeling, and of mutual attachment.

Their total dependence forbids rivalry; while their sensuous charms, vivacity, their contrast to ourselves, and their services, are able to evoke tenderness and affection.

The reciprocal attachment of animals to men, so much greater than they can maintain to their own species, shows that the sense of favours received is able to work in them the genuine tender sentiment. All that the feeling can amount to, in the absence of the totally distinct aptitude of sympathy, is seen in them, very much as it appears in early human infancy.

16. There is a form of tenderness manifested towards Inanimate things.

By associated pleasurable emotion, we come to experience towards our various possessions, and local surroundings, a certain warmth of the nature of an attachment. It is from their original power to give pleasure, that these things work upon the springs of tenderness; but, as they are unsuited to its proper consummation, the indulgence of the feeling is imaginary or fictitious. The personifying impulse here comes to our aid; and, by going through some of the forms, we experience the reality, of tender regard.

Sorrow.

17. Sorrow is pain from the loss of objects of affection; the tender feeling becoming a means of consolation.

Affection supposes a habitual reference to another person, an intertwining of thoughts, interests, pleasures, and conduct, extensive in proportion to the intimacy of the relationship. To be deprived of such a one, is to lose a main stay of existence; on the principle of Self-conservation the loss is misery. The giving way of anything that we have been accustomed to depend upon, leaves us in a state of helplessness and wretchedness, till we go through the process of building up new supports.

The lower animals are capable of sorrow. The dog will sometimes pine and die of absence from his master: being unable to endure the privation, or to reconstitute a bond of attachment.

It is, however, the characteristic of the tender feeling to flow readily, on the prompting of such occasions, and to supply, in its almost inexhaustible fulness, a large measure of consolation. This is the genial and healing side of sorrow. It is a satisfaction not afforded, in the same degree, by other losses,—by failure in worldly aspirations, by the baulking of revenge, or by the incurring of an ill name.

18. The Social and Moral bearings of tenderness are important, although the best part of the effect is due to the co-operation of Sympathy.

Anything tending to give us pleasure in other beings makes us court society, and accommodate ourselves to others. The cultivation of the modes and expression of tenderness belongs to the arts of civilized man.

Admiration and Esteem.

19. *Admiration* is the response to pleasurable feeling aroused by Excellence or superiority; a feeling closely allied to love.

The occasions of admiration are various and complicated, and will be resumed under the Sublime (ÆSTHETIC EMOTIONS).

What we notice here is that the feeling is one readily passing into tenderness; the reason being not solely that it is a pleasure, but also that it supposes another sentient being to receive the admiring expression.

The frequent transition from Admiration to Love shows the community of the two feelings: an admiration without some portion of kindly regard is an exceptional and artificial state, which it takes a certain effort of mind to entertain; as in contemplating an Alcibiades or a Marlborough.

20. *Esteem* refers to the performance of essential Duties, whose neglect is attended with evil.

Our Esteem is moved by useful, rather than by shining, qualities. As we are painfully aware of the consequences of individual remissness in the duties and conduct of life, there is a cheering re-action in witnessing the opposite conduct. It is a rebound from pain not unmixed with apprehension, and being connected with persons, it falls into the strain of tender feeling. We esteem the prudent man, the just man, the self-sufficing or independent man; and our agreeable sentiment has its spring in the possible evils from the absence of these qualities, and is greater as our sense of those evils is greater.

Both Admiration and Esteem are accompanied with Deference, a mode of gratitude to the persons that have evoked those sentiments.

Veneration—the Religious Sentiment.

21. The *Religious Sentiment* is constituted by the Tender Emotion, together with Fear, and the Sentiment of the Sublime.

We must premise that the generic feature of Religion is Government, or authority; the specific difference is the authority of a Supernatural rule. It may thus be distinguished from mere Poetic Emotions, which are so largely incorporated with it.

The composition of the feeling is expressed in the familiar conjunction—'wonder, love, and awe.'

(1) The vastness of the presiding power of the world, in so far as it can be brought home, is a source of the elation of the Sublime. The great difficulty here is in connexion with the unseen and spiritual essence, which requires the sensuous grandeurs of the actual world, and the highest stretch of poetic diction, as aids to bring it within the compass of imagination.

(2) Our position of weakness, dependence, and uncertainty, brings us under the dominion of Fear. This feeling varies with our own conscious misdeeds, as compared with the exactions of the supreme Governor. The secondary uses of Religion, in the hands of the politician, are supposed to be favoured by the terror-inspiring severity of the creed; a weapon fraught with dangers. The autocrat of Russia was unable to induce even his soldiers to dispense with the Lenten fasting, during the ravages of cholera.

In almost all views of Religion, the Sense of Dependence is given as the central fact.

(3) Love or Tender Emotion enters into the feeling, according as the Deity is viewed in a benign aspect. There is a certain incompatibility between tenderness and fear; indeed, in any close relation between governor and governed, a perfect mutual affection is rare and exceptional; the putting forth of authority chills tenderness.

A great and beneficent being might be conceived, and is conceived, by many, as bestowing favours without imposing restraints, or inflicting punishments. It is to such a being that tender and adoring sentiment might arise in purity, or without the admixture of fear. The benefactor is in that case separated from the ruler, and the essential character of Religion is no longer present.

Veneration, in the terrestrial and human acceptation, is a sentiment displayed, not so much to active and present authority, as to power that is now passing or past. It mingles with the conception of greatness the pathos of mortality and decay. It is the tribute to the memory of the departed, and is sometimes expressed by rites of a semi-religious character. The followers of Confucius in China, who have no religion, in the proper sense of the term, join in the periodical observances of the Chinese in honour of their departed ancestry.

Reverence is a name for high admiration and deferential regard, without implying authority. We may express reverence and feel deference to a politician, a philanthropist, or a man of learning or science.

CHAPTER VI.

EMOTIONS OF SELF.

1. The term 'Self' is not used here in any of its wide acceptations, but is a brief title for comprehending two allied groups of Feelings—the one expressed by the names Self-gratulation, Self-complacency, Self-esteem, Pride; the other by Love of Approbation, Vanity, Desire of Fame, or Glory.

The comprehensive words Selfishness, Self-seeking, Egotism, imply the collective interests of the individual, as excluding, or simply as not including, the interests of others. There are, therefore, many forms of egotism besides what are to be now treated of. For example, the love of Power (not here included) is at the extreme pole of Egotism; being scarcely, if at all compatible, with a regard to others. Many feelings are in themselves purely egotistic, but their enjoyment is not complete without a social alliance, such as Tenderness and Sexual feeling; these are sympathetic by accident, if not by design.

SELF-GRATULATION AND SELF-ESTEEM.

2. This is the feeling experienced when we behold in ourselves the qualities that, seen in others, call forth admiration, reverence, love, or esteem.

Admiration, as above stated, combines the elation of the sublime with tenderness, and is, in favourable circumstances, highly pleasurable. Any fresh display of excellence, of a kind that we are able to appreciate, fills us with delight, part of which may be set down to the indulgence of the admiring sentiment.

In the present case, we have to consider what change is effected, when we ourselves are the admired personality. The pleasure, in such circumstances, is usually much greater. The question arises, is it the same sentiment, with assignable modifications, or is it a new feeling of the mind?

3. The PHYSICAL side of the feeling presents an expression of marked pleasure, serene and placid, such as might accompany tender feeling.

There is nothing in this expression to give a clue to the ultimate analysis of the feeling, although quite consistent with the view to be given of it from the mental side.

4. On the MENTAL side, we may consider self-complacency as a mode of tender feeling, with self for the object; the pleasure caused by it, is the pleasure of admiring an object of tender affection.

Let us suppose, first, the case of admiration drawn forth to a beloved person, as when a parent is called to witness the merits, virtues, or charms of a child. There is here obviously a double current of pleasurable excitement; the admiration wakens the affection into active exercise, and the aroused affection quickens the admiration. It is not to be believed that the pleasure of admiring one that we are interested in, from other causes, should be only the same as towards a person wholly indifferent.

Now, there are various facts to show, that every human being is disposed to contract a habitual self-tenderness, so as to become, each to one's self, an object of affection.

It is towards other personalities that we have the full and primary experience of the tender feeling, but if it can extend in any form to inanimate things, much more should it arise towards our own personality. When, besides the enjoyment of pleasures, and the pursuit of ends, we direct our attention upon self as the subject of all those pleasures and pursuits, we may be affected with a superadded tender feeling, which will in time grow into an affection. The attentions and care of the mother to the child greatly contribute to the strength of her affection; the sickly child is often the most beloved. A similar round of attentions and care, consciously bestowed on self, have a similar tendency; we may in this way, if we indulge ourselves in self-consciousness, become the object of self-tenderness, growing into self-affection (a feeling not to be confounded with what is commonly called *self-love*).

It is possible for the regards to take a direction so exclusively outward, to be so far absorbed with other personalities, and purely external concerns, as not to become habitual towards self. In such a situation, the self-complacent sentiment would be dried up; the sight of excellence in certain other persons might have a warm and pleasing efficacy, while in self it would awaken but a feeble response. Such a total absence of self-gratulation may be rare, because the self-conscious tendency can hardly be nullified by any outward attractions; yet there are wide variations of degree in the feeling, as there are great differences in the choice of objects of tender concern.

If such be the derivation of the sentiment, its characters are plain. It is a pleasure of great amount, allied to the passive side of our being, and possessing all the recommendations of the tender feeling. It may subsist in a condition of weakness and prostration; it is easily sustained and recovered in the ideal form; if based on a large emotional nature, it may afford a copious well-spring of enjoyment.

It has the same high intellectual efficiency as the original form of tenderness; directing the attention, controlling the thoughts, and inducing beliefs in conformity with itself.

5. The more usual SPECIFIC FORMS of the feeling have received names in common language.

Self-complacency expresses the act of deriving pleasure from mentally revolving one's own merits, excellencies, productions, and imposing adjuncts. It also disposes us to court the sympathy and attention of others, by verbal recitals to the same effect.

Self-esteem and Self-conceit imply a settled opinion of our own merits, followed up with what is implied in esteem, namely, preference to others, on a comparison. This preference is shown most conspicuously in the feature of Self-confidence; which may be a sober and correct estimate of our own powers, but may also be an estimate heightened by self-tenderness or affection. In some characters, of great natural abundance of energy, active or emotional, the feeling is so well sustained as to dispense with the confirmation of other men's opinions. This is the respectable, but unamiable, quality of Self-sufficingness.

Self-respect and Pride suggest the feeling as a motive to conduct. Having formed a high estimate of self in certain respects, we are restrained from lowering that estimate by inconsistent conduct. The skilled workman has a pride in not sending out an inferior production. The man of upright dealings, if he is consciously proud of his own integrity, has an additional motive for strictness in acting up to it. It is the sense of honour, viewed as self-honour; and may co-exist with regard to the sentiments of others.

Self-pity—being sorry for one's self—is a genuine manifestation of the feeling before us. It is unmistakeable as a mode of tender feeling, and yet it ends in self; being a strong confirmation of the foregoing analysis.

Emulation, and the feeling of Superiority, express the emotion, as it arises in the act of measuring ourselves with others. All excellence requires a comparison, open or implied; when the comparison is openly made, and when we are distinctly aware of our advantage over another person, and enjoy the pleasure of that situation, the feeling is called sense of Superiority, and the impulse to gain it, Emulation. Envy is the feeling of inferiority, with a malevolent sentiment towards the rival.

6. There are well-marked forms of Pain, in obverse correspondence to the pleasures now described.

Most amiable and estimable, on this side, is the virtue named Humility and Modesty, which, without supposing self-depreciation, implies that, for the sake of others, we abstain from indulging self-complacent sentiment. It is a species of *generosity*, in renouncing a portion of self-esteem, to allow a greater share of esteem to others.

The sense of positive Worthlessness or Demerit is the genuine pain of self-tenderness, and is denoted by the names Humiliation and Self-abasement. It is not often that human beings can be made to feel this state; the regard to self is too strong to allow it a place. When it does gain a footing in the mind, the anguish and prostration are great in proportion to the joy of the opposite state. It is analogous to the discovery (also slow to be made) of demerit in objects of affection, which operates as a shock of revulsion and distress, of the severest kind. Just as the pleasures of tender feeling diffuse themselves over the life, by their ideal self-subsistence, so do the pains of worthlessness in one's own eyes, if they have once taken possession of the mind.

Self-abasement, the consequence of a sense of demerit, is also the first step towards relief; supposing, as it does, that the person has renounced all pretensions to merit, and acquiesced in the penalties of guilt. The penitential state begins with conscious worthlessness, and proceeds to regain the lost position by new endeavours.

Self-reproach is another name applicable to the loss of one's good opinion of self.

LOVE OF APPROBATION.

7. The feeling of being approved, admired, praised by others, is a heightened form of self-gratulation, due to the workings of sympathy.

The operation of sympathy will be minutely traced in a subsequent chapter. It is enough here to assume, that the coinciding expression of another person sustains and strengthens us in our own sentiments and opinions; there being assignable circumstances that vary the influence exerted by the sympathizer.

When we are affected with any emotion, the sympathy of another person may increase both the intensity of the feeling, and the power of sustaining it; in either way, adding to the pleasure of whatever is pleasurable. Our admiration of a work of genius is more prolonged, has a brighter and more enduring glow, when a sympathizing companion shares in it.

Again, as regards our strength of assurance in our opinions or convictions, we are greatly assisted by the concurrence of other persons. A conviction may be doubled or tripled in force, when repeated by one whom we greatly respect.

Now, both the circumstances named are present in the case of our being commended by others. Our self-complacency is made to burn brighter, and our estimate of self is made more secure, when another voice chimes in unison with our own.

It is also to be noticed, that a compliment from another person is an occasion for bringing our own self-complacency into action. As our various emotions show themselves only in occasional outbursts from long tracks of dormancy, we are dependent on the occurrence of the suitable stimulants. Now, as regards self-complacency, one stimulant is some fresh performance of our own; another is a tribute from some one else. Novelty in the stimulation is the condition of a copious outpouring of any emotion, pleasurable or otherwise.

To the intrinsic pleasure of Approbation, and the corresponding pain of Disapprobation, we must add the associations of other benefits attending the one, and of evils attending the other. Approbation suggests a wide circle of possible good, or the relief from possible calamities, which must greatly enhance the cheering influence exerted by it on the mind. As influences of Joy on the one hand, and of Depression on the other, the manifested opinions of our fellow-beings occupy a high place among the agencies that control our happiness.

8. The following are SPECIES, or modes, of the feeling of being admired.

Mere Approbation is the lowest, and the most general, form of expressing a good opinion. It may intimate little more than a rescue from disapprobation, the setting our mind at ease, when we might be under some doubt; as in giving satisfaction to a master or superior. The pleasure in this case is a measure of our dread of disapprobation and its consequences.

Admiration, and Praise, mean something higher and more stirring to self-complacency. Flattery and Adulation are excess, if not untruth, in the paying of compliments. Glory expresses a high and ostentatious form of praise; the general multitude being roused to join in the acclaim. Reputation or Fame is supposed to reach beyond the narrow circle of an individual life, and to agitate remote countries, and distant ages; an effort of imagination being necessary to realize the pleasure. Future Fame is not altogether empty; the applause bestowed on the dead resounds in the ears of the living. Honour is the according of elevated position, and is shown by forms of compliment, and tokens of respect.

The rules of Polite society include the bestowal of compliment with delicacy. On the one hand, the careful avoidance of whatever is calculated to wound the sense of self-importance, and, on the other hand, the full and ready recognition of all merit or excellence, are the arts of a refined age, for increasing the pleasures of society and the zest of life.

9. The varieties of Disapprobation represent the painful side of the susceptibility to opinion.

Disapprobation, Censure, Dispraise, Abuse, Libel, Reproach, Vituperation, Scorn, Infamy, are some of the names for the infliction of pain by the hostile judgments of others. If we are ourselves conscious of demerit, they add to the load of depression; if we are not conscious of any evil desert, they still weigh upon us, in proportion as we should be elated by their opposites. As signifying the farther evils associated with ill opinion on the part of society, the intense disapprobation of our fellow-men, uncounteracted, is able to make life unendurable.

The pain of Remorse is completed by the union of self-reproach with the reproach of those around us. Many that have little sensibility to the first, acutely realize the last. The feeling of Shame is entirely resolvable into disapprobation, either openly expressed, or known to be entertained.

10. Self-complacency and the Love of Admiration are motives to personal excellence and public spirit.

Egotistic in their roots, the tendency of these feelings may be highly social. Indeed, so much of social good conduct is plainly stimulated by the rewards and punishments of public opinion, that some ethical speculators have been unable to discern any purely disinterested impulses in the conduct of men.

The unsocial side of these emotions is manifested in the intense competition for a luxury of limited amount. The disposable admiration of mankind is too little for the claims upon it.

CHAPTER VII.

EMOTION OF POWER.

1. THE Emotion of POWER is distinct from both the pleasure of Exercise and the satisfaction of gaining our Ends. It is due to a sense of *superior* might or energy, on a comparative trial.

We have already seen what are the pleasures connected with muscular Exercise, when there is surplus vigour to discharge. There may also be a certain gratification in intellectual exercise, as exercise, under the same condition of abounding energy in the intellectual organs.

In the active pursuit of an End, there is necessarily some pleasure to be gathered, or pain to be got rid of. When our exertion secures our ends, it brings us whatever satisfaction belongs to those ends.

Neither of these gratifications is the pleasure of Power; which arises only when a comparison is made between two persons, or between two efforts of the same person, and when the one is found *superior* to the other.

The sentiment of superior Power is felt in the development of the bodily and mental frame. The growing youth is pleased at the increase of his strength; every new advance, in knowledge, in the conquest of difficulties, gives a thrill of satisfaction, founded essentially on comparison. The conscious decline of our faculties in old age is the inverse fact.

A second mode of comparison has regard to the greater productiveness of our efforts; as when we obtain better tools, or work upon a more hopeful material. The teacher is cheered by a promising pupil. An advanced grade of command gives the same feeling.

The third mode is comparison with others. In a contest, or competition, the successful combatant has the gratification of superior power. According to the number and the greatness of the men that we have distanced in the race, is our sense of superiority. Like all other relative states, the emotion cannot be kept up at the highest pitch without new advances. Long continuance in an elevated position dulls the mere sense of elevation (without derogating from the other advantages); in proportion as the remembrance of the inferior state dies away, so does the joy of the present superiority. The man that has been in a high position all his life, feels his greatness only as he enters into the state of those beneath him; if he does not choose to take this trouble, he will have little conscious elation from his own pre-eminence.

2. The PHYSICAL side of the emotion of Power shows an erect lofty bearing, and a flush of physical energy, as if from a sudden increase of nervous power; a frequent accompaniment is the outburst of Laughter.

Erectness of carriage and demeanour is looked upon as the fitting expression of superior might; while collapse or prostration is significant of inferiority. If we advert to the moment of a fresh victory, we shall see the proofs of increased vital power in the exuberance and excitement, and in the disposition for new labours. We are accustomed to contrast the spirits of men beating with the spirits of men beaten.

There are various causes of the outburst of Laughter, but none more certain than a sudden stroke of superiority, or the *éclat* of a telling effect. The evidence is furnished in the undisguised manifestations of childish glee, in the sports of youth, and in the hilarious outbursts of every stage of life.

The physical invigoration arising from a sense of superior power is in conformity with the general law of Self-conservation. Conscious impotence is a position of restraint, a conflict of the forces; to escape from it is the cessation of a struggle, the redemption of vital energy.

The bearing on the Will is a consequence of the special alliance of the state with our activity. By it we are disposed to energy not merely through its stimulus as pleasure, but also through its direct influence on the active side of our constitution. This can be best understood by contrast with the passive tone under tender emotion.

3. On the MENTAL side, the feeling of Power is, in Quality, pleasurable; in Degree, both acute and massive; in Speciality, it connects itself with our active states.

The gratification of superior Power falls under the comprehensive class of elating, or intoxicating pleasures, due to a rebound, or relief from previous depression. It is most nearly allied to Liberty. In both, the active forces are supposed to have been in a state of wasting conflict, from which they are suddenly rescued.

Intellectually, this pleasure is not of the highest order, if we are to judge from the cost of sustaining it. Being an acute thrill, it may impress the intellect in one way, namely, in the fact of its having been present; but we do not easily repeat the pleasure ideally, in the absence of the original stimulation. Hence its mere memory would give comparatively little satisfaction, while it might contain the sting and prompting of desire. In this respect also, it is contrasted with tenderness. As a present feeling, it has power to occupy the mind, to control the thoughts, and to enthrall the beliefs.

4. Next, as to the SPECIFIC FORMS of the emotion.

What is vulgarly called 'making a sensation,' is highly illustrative of the rebounding elation of conscious Power. This is the infantile occasion of hilarity and mirth. Any act that gives a strong impression, that awakens the attention, or arrests or quickens the movements of others, reflects the power of the agent, and stimulates the joyous outburst. To cause a shock of fright, or disgust, or anger (not dangerous), is highly impressive, and the actor's comparison of his own power with the prostration of the sufferer occasions a burst of the joyous elation of power; laughter being a never-failing token of the pleasure.

The control of Large Operations reflects by comparison the sense of superior efficiency. This is the position of the man in extensive business, the employer of numerous operatives, all working for his behoof. Such a one not merely reaps a more abundant produce, but also luxuriates in a wide control.

The exercise of Command or Authority, in all its multitudinous varieties, is attended with the delight of power. It

SPECIES OF THE EMOTION.

appears in the headship of a family; in early ages, a position of uncontrolled despotism. It is incident to all the relations of master and servant. In some forms of employment, as in military service, it is, for certain reasons of expediency, made very impressive; the contrast between the airs of the superior and the deferential attitude of the inferior, is purposely exaggerated. In the departments of the state, great powers have to be entrusted to individuals, who thereupon feel their own superiority, and make others feel their inferiority.

The pleasure of Wealth, especially in large amount, involves to a high degree the sentiment of power. Riches buys the command of many men's services, and gives, unemployed, the feeling of ideal power.

By force of Persuasion, eloquence, counsel, or intellectual ascendancy, any one may have the consciousness of power, without the authority of office. The leader of assemblies, or of parties in the state, enjoys the sentiment in this form.

The luxury of power attaches to Spiritual ascendancy. In the ministry of religion, a man is conscious of an authority superior to all temporal rule. The preacher is apt to suppose, that his most ordinary composition is raised, by a supernatural afflatus, to an efficacy far beyond the choicest language employed by other men.

Even superior Knowledge gives a position of conscious power, although the farthest removed from the influence of force or constraint. In proportion as a man possesses information of great practical moment, such as others do not possess, he is raised to an eminence of pride and power.

The love of Influence, Interference, and Control, is so extensive and salient as to be a great fact in the constitution of society, a leading cause of social phenomena. It prompts to Intolerance, and the suppression of individuality. Many are found willing to submit to restraints themselves, provided they can impose the same upon their unwilling neighbours.

In the disposition to intrude into other people's affairs, and to give opinions favourable or unfavourable on the conduct of mankind generally, there is still the same lurking consciousness of power. More openly and avowedly, it shows itself in the various modes of conveying Disapprobation, whether extorted by the just sense of demerit, or set on for the pleasure of raising ourselves by judging and depreciating others. Contempt, Derision, Scorn, Contumely, measure the greatness of the person expressing them, against the degradation and insignificance of the person subjected to them.

The feeling of Power is likely to abound in the active or energetic temperament, to which it is closely allied. In the form of Ambition, it takes possession of such minds; who have their crowning satisfaction in becoming the masters of mankind. We need only to refer to the class of men that successively held the throne of Imperial Rome.

The present emotion will now be seen to be widely different from the feelings considered in the foregoing chapter, although fusing readily with these. Men have often sought power at the sacrifice of reputation; and have enjoyed ascendancy accompanied with universal hatred.

5. The pains of Impotence are in all respects the opposite of the pleasurable sentiment of Power.

Being subject to other men's wills, and rendered small by the comparison; being beaten in a conflict; being dependent on others; being treated with contumely and contempt; being frustrated in our designs,—all bring home the depressing sense of littleness. A great exertion with a trifling result is the occasion of ridicule and contempt.

Belonging to the exercise of power is a form of Jealousy. Any one detracting from our sense of superiority, influence, command, mastership,—stings us to the quick; and the resentment aroused, to which is given this formidable designation, shows the intensity of our feelings.

CHAPTER VIII.

IRASCIBLE EMOTION.

1. THE Irascible Emotion, or Anger, arising in pain, is marked by pleasure derived from the infliction of pain.

The unmistakeable fact of Anger is that pointed out by Aristotle, the desire to put some one to pain.

2. The OBJECTS of the feeling are persons, the authors of pain, or injury.

Inanimate objects may produce pain in us, together with some of the accompaniments of anger, as for example, the rousing of the energies to re-act upon the cause of the pain;

but, without clothing them in personality, we cannot feel proper anger towards these. The old Arcadians, when unsuccessful in the chase, showed their resentment by pricking the wooden statue of Pan, their Deity.

3. The PHYSICAL manifestations of Anger, over and above the embodiment of the antecedent pain, are (1) general Excitement; (2) an outburst of Activity; (3) Deranged Organic functions; (4) a characteristic Expression and Attitude of Body; and (5), in the completed act of Revenge, a burst of exultation.

(1) A general Excitement of the system follows any shock, especially if sudden and acute, yet not crushing. The direction that the excitement takes depends on other things.

(2) In Anger, the excitement reaches the centres of Activity and rouses them to an unusual pitch, sometimes to frenzy bordering on delirium. Herein lies the contrast to Fear, which draws off power from the active organs, and excites the centres of sensibility and thought.

(3) The derangement of the Organic functions is probably due solely to the withdrawal of blood and nervous power; it does not assume any constant form. The popular notion as to 'bile' being secreted in greater abundance, is no farther true than as implying loss of tone in the digestive organs.

(4) The Expression of Feature and the Attitude of Body are in keeping with strong active determination, bred by pain.

(5) In the stage of consummated Retaliation, the joyful and exulting expression mingles with the whole, and gives a peculiar set to the features, a complication of all the impulses.

4. On the MENTAL side, Anger contains an impulse knowingly to inflict suffering upon another sentient being, and a positive gratification in the fact of suffering inflicted.

The first and obvious effect of an injury is to rouse us to resist it. We may do more; we may, for our more effectual protection, disarm and disable the person that has injured us. All this is volition, and not anger. Under the angry feeling we proceed farther, and inflict pain upon the author of the injury, knowing it to be such, and deriving satisfaction in proportion to the certainty and the amount of the pain. This positive *pleasure of malevolence* is the fact to be resolved.

5. In the ultimate analysis of Anger, we seem to trace these ingredients :—(1) In a state of frenzied excitement, some *effect* is sought to give vent to the activity. (2) The sight of *bodily infliction and suffering* seems to be a mode of sensuous and sensual pleasure. (3) The pleasure of *power* is pandered to. (4) There is a satisfaction in preventing farther pain to ourselves, *by inducing fear* of us, or of consequences, in any one manifesting harmful purposes.

(1) When the state of active excitement is induced, something must be done to give it scope or vent. To be full of energy, and have nothing for it to execute, is an unsatisfactory state to be in. Some change or effect produced on inanimate things, wholly irrelevant to the occasion, gives a certain measure of relief. Kicking away a chair, upsetting a table, tearing down a bell-rope, are the actions of a man under a mere frenzied or maniacal excitement. The rending of the clothes, among the Jews, would seem intended to signify a great shock and agitation, with frenzied excitement.

(2) In the spectacle of bodily infliction and suffering, there seems to be a positive fascination. In the absence of countervailing sympathies, the writhings of pain furnish a new variety of the sensuous and sensual stimulation arising from our contact with living beings. In the lower races, the delight from witnessing suffering is intense.

(3) In putting another to pain, there is a glut of the emotion of power or superiority. The felt difference or contrast between the position of inflicting pain, and the being subjected to it, is a startling evidence of superior power and a source of joy and exultation. The childish delight in making an effect, or a sensation, is at its utmost, when some person or animal is victimized and shows signs of pain.

Were it not for our sympathies, our fears, and our conscientious feelings generally, this delight would be universal; we should omit no chance of gratifying it. Now, when another person puts us to pain, or causes us injury, the immediate effect is to suspend the feelings of sympathy, respect, and obligation, and to open the way for the other gratifications. It is putting the injurer under the ban of the empire—making him an outlaw; the sacredness of his person is torn away, and he is surrendered to the sway of the passions that find their delight in suffering. It is rare in a civilized community to victimize the harmless and innocent; let, however, any man or animal, by their bearing or ill conduct, furnish a pretext for suspending *habeas corpus* in their case, and a multitude will be ready to join in their destruction.

(4) In retaliating upon the author of an injury, to the point of effectually deterring from a renewal of the offence, we deliver ourselves from a cause of fear; which is to enjoy the reaction and relief from a depressing agency. We have this satisfaction in destroying wild beasts; in punishing a gang of robbers; in routing and disarming an aggressive power.

Considered as a pleasurable gratification, the feeling will vary according to the element that we suppose to prevail. If the chief fact be the glut of sensuality and of power, the feeling is one of great and acute pleasure, and might be described in part by the language already given with reference to the emotion of power.

6. The various aspects and SPECIES of Anger may next be reviewed.

In the Lower Animals, certain manifestations pass for modes of irascibility. The beasts of prey destroy and devour their victims, with all the frantic excitement of wrath; while some herbivorous animals, as the bull and the stag, fight one another to the death. All animals possessing courage and energy repel attacks and invasion by positive inflictions; the poisonous reptiles and insects, when molested, discharge their venom.

The vehemence in the destruction of prey is nothing more than volition under the stimulus of hunger. So in resisting attacks, the animal is awakened to put forth its active endowment, whatever that may be. It is not easy to fix the point where something more than the exertion of energy is concerned. An ordinary development of intelligence in discerning the means to ends, would enable an animal to see, in the destruction of a rival, a step to the satisfying of its own sensual appetites. It is possible that an effect of association might convert this means into an end in itself, like the miser's love of money; so that even an animal without special wants, in the abundance of surplus energy, might manifest its destructive propensity uncalled for. In bull-fighting and cock-fighting, the active energies are under express stimulation from without, and the fury manifested has all the frenzied excitement of rage. Still, it is not necessary to assume anything beyond a mere rudiment of the proper pleasure of power. The victorious animal may have sufficient recollection of its own chequered experiences to enter somewhat into the position of being vanquished, and to feel the difference between that and success; and exactly as this intellectual and emotional comparison is within the compass of its powers, will it feel the glut of its own superiority. If we are unable to assign to any but the highest animals such an intellectual range as this, we cannot credit animals generally with the developed form of anger.

By the study of Infancy and Childhood, we may expect to see the gradual unfolding of the passion. The earliest experiences of pain in the infant lead to a more or less energetic excitement of grief. After the development of distinct likings and dislikings, with the accompanying voluntary determinations, any strong repugnance will lead to a burst of energetic avoidance; following the law of the will. There will likewise be the manifestation of beating off a rival claimant, as means to an end. Then comes the stage above supposed to be traceable in the higher animals, the sense of one's own present energy, in comparison with the understood pain and humiliation of another. Only the human intellect can fully attain such an elevation; but when it is attained, the pleasure of power has come to birth, and, therewith, genuine anger. The child is not long out of the arms when it reaches this point, and it proceeds rapidly to perfect the acquisition. Side by side with the sense of power over others, will also be shown the venting of active excitement on things inanimate.

In the irascible feeling, as seen in maturity, it has been usual to make a distinction between Sudden and Deliberate Anger. The Sudden form of Anger is the least complicated, and shows the natural and habitual disposition. Excitable temperaments, not trained to suppression, are those liable to the sudden outburst.

In Deliberate Anger, or Revenge, the mind considers all the circumstances of the injury, as well as the measure and the consequences of retaliation. There is implied, in Revenge, the need of retaliation to satisfy the feelings of the offended person. According to the amount of the injury, and to the exacting disposition of the injured party, is the demand for vengeance. When men have been injured on matters that they are deeply alive to,—plundered, cheated, reviled, deprived of their rights,—their resentment attests the magnitude of their sufferings, the value that they set upon their own inviolability. The ordinary measure of revenge, in civilized life, is in some proportion to the fancied injury; the barbarian exceeds all proportions, and gluts himself with the satisfaction of vengeance. What are we to expect from him that can take unmingled delight in the sufferings of an unoffending fellow-being?

The affection grounded on anger is called Hatred. The sense of some one wrong never satisfied, a supposed harmful disposition on the part of another, an obstructive position maintained,—keep up the resentful flame, till it has become an affection, or a habit. Sometimes a mere aversion or dislike is cherished into hatred. Rivalry, superiority in circumstances, the exercise of power or authority, are frequent causes. A familiar example is seen in Party spirit. Men banded together in sects or parties, generally entertain a permanent animosity to their rival sects. It is in this form of the affection that Anger becomes a paramount element of one's life, like Tender Affection, Habitual Anxiety, or Cultivated Taste. Modified by accidental causes, sometimes intensified by special provocation, sometimes neutralized by temporary occasions of sympathy, it is one of the moral forces of the human being, imparting pleasure and pain, controlling the attention and thoughts, and swaying the convictions.

The formidable manifestation named Antipathy, is stronger than Hatred. It owes part of its intensity to an infusion of Fear. The violent antipathies towards certain animals, as the poisonous reptile, are in a great measure due to fear. Others offend sensibilities of the æsthetic kind, as when they are associated with filth and disgust.

Even towards human beings, the state of Antipathy may arise without the provocation of injury, as in the antipathies of race, of caste, and of creed. The natural or artificial repugnance thus occasioned will inspire, no less than vengeance, a disposition to inflict harm, and to exult over calamity.

The state of Warfare, Hostility, Combat, brings before us the irascible feeling in its highest activity. The elements present are too obvious to require detail. The potency of opposition, as a stimulant of the active powers, has already been adverted to. A frenzied active excitement is the characteristic fact of hostility, as of anger. Fighting and rage are not two things, but the same thing.

The different grades and varieties of offence make corresponding differences in the spirit and manner of retaliation. In the case of Involuntary harm, the wrathful impulse is transitory, unless it be from avoidable carelessness, which is treated as a fault demanding reparation. It is common for persons, without intending harm, to proceed with their own objects, giving no heed to the feelings or interests of others; as in tobacco smoking. Lastly, there is the case of malicious design, which necessarily provokes, to the full, the resentful energy of the sufferer.

Seeing that the wrathful feelings originate in pain, and lead to the risks of a counter resentment, some Ethical writers have contended against the reality of a Pleasure of Malevolence. But these attendant pains are only a part of the case. It is true that when the sympathies and tender feelings are highly developed, the exercise of resentment may be more painful on the whole than pleasurable; in this case, however, it is suppressed; a benevolent mind seldom gives way to revenge. The burden of proof lies upon whoever would maintain that mankind deliberately and energetically aim at a present pain. The fact is known to occur under certain modes of excitement, and possibly, therefore, in the irascible excitement. We have already noticed the influence of fear, in thwarting the ordinary course of the will. But revenge is far too common, too persistent in its exercise, both in hot blood and in cool, to be an insane fixed idea, working nothing but pain. The whole human race cannot be under a mistake on this head. The Homeric sentiment would be echoed by the millions of every age,—Revenge is sweeter than honey.

When resentment comes to the aid of the moral feelings, as revenge for criminality and wrong, it is termed 'Righteous Indignation.' A positive and undeniable pleasure attends the retributive vengeance that overtakes wrong-doers and the tyrants and oppressors of mankind. The designation 'Noble Rage' points to a more artistic effect, being the display of anger in striking attitudes, and magniloquent diction, as in a hero of romance—the Achilles of Homer, the Satan of Paradise Lost.

7. The working of Sympathy gives a great expansion to the irascible feeling; to whatever degree we enter into the injuries of others, we also participate in their Revenge.

Inasmuch as the occurrence of injury is a wide-spread fact, it makes a considerable part of our interest as spectators of actual life. We receive a shock, more or less painful, when a great wrong is perpetrated before our eyes; and have a corresponding pleasure in the retaliation. The historian can sometimes gratify us by the spectacle of retribution for flagrant wrongs; the romancist, having the events at command, allows few failures.

8. In the Sentiment of Justice, when analyzed, there

may be traced an element of resentful passion; and the idea of Justice, when matured, guides and limits revenge.

A main prompting to Justice, in the first instance, is sympathetic resentment. But in the fully developed idea of the Just, there is a regard to the value of one man as compared with another, according to the reasonings and conventions of the time.

9. The infliction of Punishment, by law, although gratifying to the sympathetic resentment of the community, is understood to be designed principally for the prevention of injury.

The design of punishing offenders by Law is to secure the public safety. Incidental to this is the gratification of resentment; which, however, is still to be in subjection to the principal end. Mr J. S. Mill remarks that there is a legitimate satisfaction due to our feelings of indignation and resentment, inasmuch as these are on the whole salutary and worthy of cultivation, although still as means to an end.*

CHAPTER IX.

EMOTIONS OF ACTION—PURSUIT.

1. In voluntary activity three modes of feeling have now been considered:—(1) the pleasures and pains of exercise; (2) the satisfaction of the end (or the pain of missing it); and (3) the pleasure of superior (and pain of inferior) power.

---

* 'The benefits which criminal law produces are twofold. In the first place, it prevents crime by terror; in the second place, it regulates, sanctions, and provides a legitimate satisfaction for the passion of revenge. I shall not insist on the importance of this second advantage, but shall content myself with referring those who deny that it is one, to the works of the two greatest English moralists, each of whom was the champion of one of the two great schools of thought upon that subject—Butler and Bentham. The criminal law stands to the passion of revenge in much the same relation as marriage to the sexual appetite.' (J. F. Stephen's Criminal Law, Chap. IV., p. 98.)

There remains the mental attitude under a gradually approaching end, a condition of suspense, termed Pursuit and Plot-interest.

In working to some end, as the ascent of a mountain, or in watching any consummation drawing near, as a race, we are in a peculiar state of arrested attention, which, as an agreeable effect, is often desired for itself.

2. On the PHYSICAL side, the situation of pursuit is marked by (1) the intent occupation of some one of the senses upon an object, and (2) the general attitude or activity harmonizing with this; there being, on the whole, an energetic muscular strain.

When the pursuit is something visible, we are 'all eye,' as in witnessing a contest; if the end is indicated by sound, as in listening to a narrative, we are all ear. If we are spectators or listeners merely, the general attitude shows muscular tension; if we are agents, we are sustained in our activity by the approach of the end.

3. On the MENTAL side, Pursuit supposes (1) a motive in the interest of an end, heightened by its steady approach; (2) the state of engrossment in object regards, with remission of subject regards.

Some end is needed to stimulate the voluntary energies; and, by the Law of Self-conservation, the gradual approach towards the consummating of the end heightens the energies, and intensifies the pursuit.

Now, all muscular exertion is objective (p. 21); it throws us upon the object attitude, and takes us out of the subject attitude. Whatever promotes muscular exertion, both as to the intensity of the strain, and the number and the importance of the muscles engaged, renders us objective in our regards, and withdraws us from the subject side. More especially are we put in the object position by the energetic action of the external senses, so extensively and closely allied with the cerebral activity. Hence, whatever keeps up an intent and unremitted muscular strain, involving the higher senses, is an occasion of extreme objectivity; and this is the essential character of pursuit and plot-interest.

The value of the situation is relative to the circumstance that we are apt to be too much thrown upon the subject consciousness; which, although essential to enjoyment (for perfect objectivity is perfect indifference) is also the condition of our being alive to suffering, and of our dwelling upon our pleasures till they exhaust us and pass into the pains of ennui. Subjectivity is apparently more costly to the nervous system; the objective attitude, if not unduly strained, can be longest endured. As far as actual pleasure is concerned, it is time lost; but an unremitted pleasurable consciousness is beyond human nature; tracts of objective indifference seem as necessary to enduring life, as the total cessation of consciousness for one-third of our time. These objective tracts are found in our periods of activity, and especially the activity of the bodily organs; but they occur most advantageously when the activity is bringing us near to an interesting goal of pursuit.

It is the nature of the waking mind to alternate from object to subject states, the one giving as it were a refreshing variety to the other. A highly exciting stimulus, as a stage performance, keeps us in the objective attitude, but not in unbroken persistence or perfect purity; were it not for our frequent lapses into subjectivity, we should slip out of the primary motive, and submerge the whole of the enjoyment. The transitions are performed with great rapidity; the same attitude may not last above two or three seconds; while, the longer we are kept in the object strain, the sweeter is the relapse to the subject consciousness, supposing it to be pleasurable.

4. Chance, or Uncertainty, within limits, contributes to the engrossment of Pursuit.

Absolute certainty of attainment, being as good as possession, does not constitute a stimulus to plot-interest; in looking forward to the payment of an assured debt, there is no excitement. But a certain degree of doubt, with possibility of failure, gives so much of the state of terror as excites the perceptive organs to the look-out; in which situation, the steady approach of the decisive termination, either cheers us, by removing the fear, or increases the strength of the gaze, by deepening the doubt.

The most favourable operation of uncertainty is when there is before us a prospect of something good, such that the attainment is a gain, while failure only leaves us as we were. There is not, in this case, the depressing terror of impending calamity, but merely the agitation consequent on our hopes being raised, and yet not assured. Still, if the stake be high, the fear of losing it will deprive the situation of the favourable stimulus of plot-interest. It is by combining a small amount of uncertainty with a moderate stake, that we best realize the proper charm of pursuit.

As in all other things, Novelty gives zest to pursuit. A new game, a new player, a different arrangement of parties, will freshen the thoughts, and re-animate the dubiousness of the issue.

5. The excitement of Pursuit is seen in the Lower Animals.

An animal chasing its prey puts forth its energies according to the strength of its appetite. The excitement, however, manifestly becomes greater near the close, when the victim is gradually gained upon, and all but seized. We have here the essentials of the situation; and the feelings of the animal may be presumed to correspond with its accelerated movement, and intensified expression.

6. As regards human experience, we may first take notice of Field Sports.

In these, the end is, to most men, highly grateful; being the triumph of skill and force in the capture of some animal gifted with powers of eluding the pursuer. The pursuit is long and uncertain; the attention is on the alert, and at the critical moments screwed up to a pitch of intensity. To succeed in bringing down the victim after a hot and ardent pursuit, is to relapse from an objective engrossment, into a subjective flash of successful achievement and gratified power.

The circumstances of the different sports are various, and easily assigned. The most difficult to account for, perhaps, is the interest of Angling; there being so many fruitless throws against one success. We need to suppose that the Angler has an emotional temperament more copious and self-sustaining than most other men. In the Chase, there are additional excitements of a fiery sort, to make it the acme of the sporting life. The more dangerous sports of hunting the tiger, the elephant, the boar, are ecstasy to the genuine sportsman.

7. The excitement of pursuit is incident to Contests.

The combatant in an equal, or nearly equal contest, has a stake and an uncertainty that engages his powers and engrosses his attention to the highest pitch. His objectivity is strained to the uttermost limits, and if he succeeds, he gains the joys of triumph, after being forcibly withdrawn from self-consciousness.

The excitement of contests has, in all ages, been a favourite recreation. The programme of the Olympic games was a series of contests. Gladiatorial shows, Tournaments, Races, have had their thousands of votaries. Even the encounters of the intellect—in disputation, oratory, wit,—attract and detain a numerous host of spectators.

In many of the common games, skill and strength are disturbed by Chance, which opens up to each player greater possibilities, and therefore quickens the intensity of the object regards. In Cards and Dice, although long-continued play eliminates chance, yet, for a single game, hazard is nearly supreme.

8. The occupations of Industry involve, more or less, the suspense of Plot-interest.

Wherever our voluntary energies are engaged, a certain attention is fastened on the end, which has a suspensive or arrestive effect. Hence all industry is, to some degree, anti-subjective, or calculated to take a man out of himself. The prisoner's ennui does not attain its extreme pressure unless he is debarred from occupation. But, where there is great monotony in the execution, together with certainty, as well as absence of novelty, in the result,—for example, in turning a wheel, or unloading a ship,—there is little to stretch the gaze, or arrest the attention. The exciting occupations are those that involve high and doubtful prospects, as war, stock-jobbing, and the more hazardous species of commerce. In Agriculture, the seasons supply a succession of ends, with the interest of suspense, often attended with pain and disappointment, but still of a kind to sustain the objective outlook.

In every piece of work that has its beginning, middle, and end, there is an alleviation of tedium by measuring the steps gained, and watching the remainder as it dwindles to nothing.

9. In the Sympathetic Relationships, there is the additional interest of plot.

The gratifying of the tender feelings being an end in life, the progress towards it necessarily inspires the forward look, and the suspensive attitude, from which the relapses into subjective consciousness are exciting by alternation. All the successes, the epochs and turning points in the career of an object of affection, a child or a friend, give periods of intent occupation, taking one out of self, and out of one's own pleasures. Still, we are seldom losers by the objective attitude; we are made the more alive to the subjective relapses; and, if pleasure be awaiting us, it is all the greater for the diversion.

10. The search after Knowledge is attended with plot.

The feeling of knowledge attained being one of the satisfactions of life, the gradual approach to some interesting disclosure, or some great discovery, enlivens the forward look and the attitude of suspense. The sense of difficulty to be solved, of darkness to be illuminated, awakens curiosity and search; and the near prospect of the result has the same effect as in every other engaging pursuit. The art of the teacher and expositor lies first in awakening desire, by a distinct statement of the end to be gained, and then in carrying the pupil forward by sensible stages to the consummation; the attitude of suspense is identical with earnest attention.

11. The position of the Spectator contains the essential part of the interest of pursuit.

Any chase, contest, or pursuit, of a kind to interest us as actors, commands our sympathy as spectators; and the moments of nearing the termination and settling the issue inspire our rapt attention. As with sympathy generally, this circumstance gives a great additional scope to our interest and our feelings. Contests are peculiarly fitted to arrest the gaze of the spectator; and they have accordingly been adopted into the public amusements of all times. The daily business of the world, as, for example, the large affairs of nations, by affecting us either personally, or sympathetically, usually contain a stake, a greater or less uncertainty, and a final clearing up preceded by a state of suspense. We may also witness with interest, the steps and issues of great (or even small) industrial undertakings, provided their consummation is calculated to give us pleasure, and is attained through a progress from uncertainty.

12. The Literature of Plot, or Story, is the express cultivation of the attitude of suspense.

A narrative will give the same sympathetic interest as a spectacle. An interesting stake, at first remote and uncertain, is brought nearer by degrees; and whenever it is visibly approaching to the decision, the hearer assumes the rapt attitude that takes him out of the subject sphere. Events going on around us, and past history for the first time made known, command the elements of the situation, and thence derive much of their power of detaining the mind. But, whereas real events, although containing the circumstance of suspense, often disappoint expectation, the composer of fiction and romance studies how to work up the interest to the highest pitch. The entire narration in an epic poem, or romance, is conceived to an agreeable end, which is suspended by intermediate actions, and thrown into pleasing uncertainty; while minor plots engage the attention and divert the pressure of the main plot.

13. The form of *pain*, incident to pursuit, is the too great prolongation of the suspense.

There is a pain in the crossing of our wishes as to the catastrophe. There is also the suffering caused by a high and serious risk. But the form of pain special to the attitude of suspense, is the prolongation or adjournment of the issue. This is merely one of the many forms of the pain of Conflict; the mind is wrought up to a certain attitude of expectation, to be baulked or disappointed.

14. The more general pains accompanying activity are connected in various ways with the labour or difficulty of execution.

Excessive muscular efforts produce the pains of muscle. Baffled attempts, from want of strength or skill, have the dispiriting effect of all thwarted aims, according to the law of Conflict.

CHAPTER X.

EMOTIONS OF INTELLECT.

1. THE operations of the Intellect may be attended with various forms of pleasure and pain.

As mere exercise, the Intellectual trains may give pleasure in a fresh condition of the system, and be attended by nervous fatigue when long continued.

2. The working of Contiguity, as in ordinary memory, does not yield any emotional excitement. Laboured recollection brings the usual pain of difficulty or Conflict.

We derive no emotion from repeating the alphabet or the multiplication table. The pleasures and pains of memory are due to the things remembered, and not to the exercise of remembering.

Laboured recollection is a case of baffled endeavours, and brings the distress, more or less acute or massive, of that form of Conflict. Of a similar nature are all the pains, both of difficult intellectual comprehension, and of difficult constructiveness. The successive checks sustained by the thinking powers, in a work of thought, have the same painful character, as checks to the muscular powers in a manual enterprise. The student labouring long in vain to understand a problem, the poet dissatisfied with his verses, the man of speculation puzzled and defeated, the military commander undecided as to his tactics, all experience the pains of distraction and conflict.

3. To complete the painful side of Intellectual exercise, reaction from which is the main source of intellectual pleasure, we may add the pain of Contradiction or Inconsistency.

Contradiction or Inconsistency is one of the most obvious forms of Conflict, and, in proportion to its hold on the mind, gives all the characteristic pain of conflict. When our immediate interests are concerned, the contradiction is felt in thwarting some end of pursuit; as when we receive contradictory opinions respecting the character of an ailment, or the conduct of a law suit. On subjects that concern others and not ourselves, the pain of the contradiction depends on the strength of the sympathies. With regard to truth generally, or matters of science and erudition, where the applications to practice are not immediately apparent, contradictions produce no impression on the mass of men; they are felt only by the more cultured intellects, who are accustomed to contemplate all the bearings of true knowledge, and who have thereby contracted a strong sense of its value.

4. The pleasure attending strokes of Similarity in diversity may be described generally as an agreeable or exhilarating Surprise. Yet, the largest part of the pleasure is the sudden and unexpected relief from an intellectual burden.

There can be no novelty or freshness in the trains of Contiguity; but the operation of Similarity in bringing together, for the first time, things hitherto widely apart, makes a flash of novelty and change, the prime condition of emotional effect. The Greeks that conquered India, under Alexander, must have been surprised at finding in that remote region words belonging to their own language.

It is not, however, the flash of novelty from an original conjunction of ideas, a new intellectual situation, that fills up the charm of original identities; it is their effect in alleviating or removing the intellectual burdens and toils above described as the pains of intellect. When, by a happy stroke of Similarity, the difficulties of comprehension and of constructiveness, just alluded to, are cleared away, there is a joyous reaction and elation of the kind common to all forms of relief from conflict and oppression of the faculties. The instances will be given under separate heads.

5. New identities in Science—whether classifications, inductions, or deductions—increase the number of facts comprehended by one intellectual effort.

This has been abundantly seen in the exposition of Similarity. Every great generalization, as Gravity, the Atomic theory, the Correlation of Force, enables us to include in one statement an innumerable host of particulars. To any one previously endeavouring to grasp the details, by separate acts of attention, the generalizing stroke that sums all up in a single expression, brings a toilsome march to a glorious and sudden termination. The pleasure is determined by the previous pain, by the sense of difficulty overcome, and by the position of command attained, after being conscious of the former position of grovelling inferiority.

Sometimes a new discovery operates to solve a contradiction or anomaly, in which case the result is equally an elation of relief from intellectual pain in the form of distraction or conflict.

6. Great discoveries of Practice, besides contributing to knowledge, give the elation consequent on the enlargement of human power.

Such discoveries as the steam-engine, which have the effect of either diminishing human toil, or increasing its productiveness, minister directly to the sentiment of increased power, as well as of increased resources for all purchasable enjoyments. In this point of view, the pleasure is not so much in the intellect, as in the results upon our other sensibilities.

The strongest part of the sentiment that attaches us to Truth is due to the urgency of practical ends. The True is something that we can rely upon in the pursuit of our various interests. Whether it be in firing a deadly shot, or in escaping a deadly pestilence, truth is the same as precision, accuracy, certainty, in adjusting the means to the end. The emotion of Truth is a feeling of Relativity or comparison, a rebound or deliverance from the miseries of practical error.

7. Illustrative Comparisons are another mode of remitting intellectual toil.

The happy comparisons or analogies that illuminate the obscure conceptions of science, are pleasing from the same general cause, the lightening of intellectual labour. The celebrated simile of the Cave, in Plato's Republic (see APPENDIX A), is considered to assist us in viewing the difficult question relating to the nature of Knowledge.

The comparisons of poetry introduce another element, not strictly of the nature of intellectual pleasure, namely, the harmony of the feelings. Possibly the ultimate foundation of the pleasure of harmony is the same, but the difference between the strictly intellectual form, and what enters into Fine Art, is such as to constitute two species in the classification of the emotions.

CHAPTER XI.

SYMPATHY.

1. SYMPATHY is to enter into the feelings of another, and to act them out, as if they were our own.

Notice has already been taken of the disposition to assume the feelings of others, to become alive to their pleasures and pains, to act vicariously under the motive power of those pleasures and pains. We have seen that Pity is tender emotion conjoined with sympathy.

2. Sympathy supposes (1) one's own remembered experience of pleasure and pain, and (2) a connexion in the mind between the outward signs or expression of the various feelings and the feelings themselves.

(1) The good retentiveness or memory for our states of pleasure and pain, the intellectual basis of Prudence, is also the basis of Sympathy. We cannot sympathize beyond our experience, nor up to that experience, without some power of recalling it to mind. The child is unable to enter into the joys and griefs of the grown-up person; the humble day-labourer can have no fellow-feeling with the cares of the rich, the great, the idle; the man without family ties fails to realize the feelings of the domestic circle.

(2) The various feelings have outward signs or symptoms, learned for the most part by observation. Noting how we ourselves are outwardly affected under our various feelings, we infer the same feelings when we see the same outward display in others. The smile, the laugh, the shout of joy, conjoined in our own experience with the feeling of delight, when witnessed in some one else, are to us an indication and proof of that person's being mentally affected, as we remember ourselves to have been, when moved to the same manifestations.

It matters little, so far as concerns *reading* the emotions, whether the knowledge of the signs of feeling is wholly acquired, or partly acquired and partly instinctive. There are certain signs of feeling that appear to have a primitive efficacy to excite the feeling; as, for example, the moistened eye, and the soft wail of grief. But sympathy is something more than a mere scientific inference that another person has come under a state of tenderness, of fear, or of rage; it is the being forcibly possessed for the time by the very same feeling. In this view, there must be a certain energy of expressiveness, or suggestiveness, in the signs of feeling, which is favoured by the combination of primitive with acquired connexion.

As examples of the energetic and catching modes of expression, we may mention the sound of clearing the throat, the yawn, laughter, sobbing. Such emotions as Wonder, Fear, Tenderness, Admiration, Anger, are highly infectious, when powerfully manifested.

3. Sympathy is a species of involuntary imitation, or assumption, of the displays of feeling enacted in our presence; which is followed by the rise of the feelings themselves.

We are supposed to give way to the manifestations of another's feelings, to imitate those manifestations, and as a consequence to be affected with the mental state conjoined therewith. Even when we do not repeat the displays of feeling to the full, we have the idea of them, that is, their embodiment in the nervous currents, to which attaches the corresponding state of mind. We come under the influence of every pronounced expression of feeling, and if the circumstances be favourable, reproduce it in ourselves, and follow out its determinations, the same as if it grew wholly out of ourselves. It is thus that we are affected by an orator, or an actor, or by the enthusiasm of a multitude.

4. The following are the chief circumstances favourable to Sympathy.

(1) Our being disengaged at the time, or free from any intense occupation, or prepossession. The existing bent of the feelings and thoughts has always a certain hold or persistence, and is a force to be overcome by any new impression.

(2) Our familiarity with the mode of feeling represented to us. Each one has certain predominant modes of feeling; and these being the most readily excited, we can sympathize best with the persons affected by them. The mother easily feels for a mother. And obversely, where there is total disparity of nature or pursuits, there can be comparatively little sympathy. The timid man cannot enter into the composure of the resolute man; the cold nature will not understand the pains of the ardent lover.

(3) Our relation to the person determines our sympathy; affection, esteem, reverence, attract our attention and observation, and make us succumb to the influence of the manifested feelings. On the other hand, hatred or dislike removes us almost from the possibility of fellow-feeling; the name 'antipathy' is the derivative formed for the negation of sympathy. Still, it must be distinctly understood, that love is not indispensable to sympathy, properly so called; and that aversion may not wholly extinguish it.

(4) The energy or intensity of the language, tones, and gestures, necessarily determines the strength of the impression and the prompting to sympathy.

(5) The clearness or distinctness of the expression is of great importance in inducing the state on the beholder. This is the advantage of persons gifted with the demonstrative constitution; it is the talent of the actor and the elocutionist,

and the groundwork of an interesting demeanour in society. When the remark is made, that to make others feel, we need only to feel ourselves, the power of adequate expression is also implied.

(6) There is in some minds, more than in others, a susceptibility to the displays of other men's feelings, as opposed to the self-engrossed and egotistic promptings. It is a branch or species of the receptive or susceptible temperament, the constitution more strongly endowed on the side of the senses, and less strongly in the centres of activity. To this natural difference we may add differences in education and the course of the habits, which may confirm the sympathetic impulses on the one hand, or the egotistic impulses on the other.

5. The climax or completion of Sympathy is the determination to act for another person exactly as for self.

It is not enough that we become affected nearly as others are affected, through the medium of their manifestations of feeling, to which we surrender ourselves; sympathy farther supposes that we act vicariously in removing the pain, or in promoting the pleasure, that we thus share in. The precise nature of this impulse, or its foundation in our mental system, is a matter of some subtlety. I have already (CONTIGUITY, § 13) expressed the opinion that it springs not from pure volition, but from the agency of the *fixed idea*. That mere volition is not the whole case, may be seen at once by considering, that the short and easy method of getting rid of a sympathetic pain, is to turn away from the original, as we frequently do when we are unable or indisposed to render assistance. But the fact that we cannot always or easily do this, shows the persisting tendency of an idea once admitted, and the influence it has to work itself out into action, irrespective of the operation of the will in fleeing pain and grasping pleasure. The sight of another person enduring hunger, cold, fatigue, revives in us some recollection of these states, which are painful even in idea. We could, and often do, save ourselves this pain by at once averting the view, and looking out for another object of attention; but the operation is one of some difficulty; we feel that there is a power to seize and detain us, independent of the will, a power in the expression of pain to awaken our own ideas of pain; and these ideas once awakened keep their hold, and prompt us to act for relieving the original subject, whose pain we have unwittingly borrowed or assumed.

6. Men in general can sympathize with pleasure and pain as such; but in the kinds and varieties of these, our sympathies are limited.

The mere fact that any one is in pain awakens our sympathy; but, unless the causes and attendant circumstances also come home to us, the sympathy is neither persistent nor deep. Pains that have never afflicted us, that we know nothing of, that are, in our opinion, justly or needlessly incurred, are dismissed from our thoughts as soon as we are informed of the facts. The tears shed by Alexander, at the end of his conquests, probably failed to stimulate one responsive drop in the most sensitive mind that ever heard his story.

7. The Sympathy of others lends support to our own feelings and opinions.

When any feeling belonging to ourselves is echoed by the expression of another person, we are supported and strengthened by the coincidence. In the case of a pleasurable feeling, the pleasure is increased; self-complacency, tender affection, the sentiment of power, are all enhanced by the reflexion from others. It seems as if the cost of maintaining the pleasurable tone were diminished to us; we can sustain it longer, and with augmented intensity. In the case of a painful feeling, as fear, remorse, impotence, the concurrence of another person has the same deepening effect; to increase our pains, however, is not usually considered a part of sympathy. A sympathizing friend endeavours to counterwork depressing agencies. Still, the principle is the same throughout; the expressed feelings of a second person are a power in our mind for the time; they impress themselves upon us, more or less, according to the various circumstances and conditions that give effect to personal influence. The strength and earnestness of the language used, its expressiveness and grace, our affection, admiration, or esteem of the sympathizer, and our own susceptibility to impressions from without, are the chief circumstances that rule the effect. The sympathy of persons of commanding influence, and especially the concurring sympathies of a large number, may increase in a tenfold degree the pleasure of the original, or self-born feeling.

8. Through the infection of sympathy, each individual is a power to mould the sentiments and views of others.

This is merely stating the previous proposition in a form suited to make it a text for the influence of society at large on the opinions of its members. If all individualities were equally pronounced and equally balanced, the mutual action would result in an 'as you were;' but as there is usually a preponderance of certain sentiments, opinions, and views, the effect is to compress individuality into uniformity in most societies. Few persons have the strength of innate impulse to resist the feelings of a majority powerfully expressed; hence the uniformity, conservatism, and hereditary continuance of creeds, sentiments, opinions, that have once obtained an ascendancy. Even when men form independent judgments, they abstain from expressing them, rather than renounce the support that social sympathy gives to the individual.

9. Sympathy is, indirectly, a source of pleasure to the sympathizer.

If the view here taken be correct, the disposition to sympathize with, and to act for, others does not mainly depend on the motives to the will—the pursuit of pleasure, and the revulsion from pain. Hence the sacrifice of self that it leads to is strictly and properly a sacrifice, a surrender or giving up of advantages without consideration of recompense or return. This position is indispensable to the vindication of disinterested action as a fact of the human mind. The direct, proper, immediate result of sympathy is loss, pain, sacrifice to the sympathizer.

Indirectly, however, the giving of sympathy, as well as the receiving of it, may be a source of pleasure. What brings this about is reciprocity. The person benefited, or others in his stead, may make up, by sympathy and good offices returned, for all the sacrifice. And it is one of the remarkable facts of sympathy, the reason of which has been fully given, that the giving and receiving of good offices, and the interchange of accordant feelings, make up a large source of pleasure, and form one of the chief characteristics of civilized man. Even with considerably less than a full reciprocation, the sympathizing and benevolent man may be recompensed for his self-surrender; but there is no evidence that

—— in virtuous actions,
The undertaker finds a full reward,
Although conferred upon unthankful men.

What gives plausibility to this doctrine is that society at large labours to make up, by benefits and by approbation, for individual unthankfulness or inability. Failing this world, the future life is considered as making good all deficiencies.

10. Sympathy cannot exist upon the extreme of self-abnegation; the regard to the pleasures and pains of others is based on the regard to our own.

Without pleasures and pains of our own, we are ignorant of the corresponding experience of our fellows. But this is not all. We must retain a sufficient amount of the self-regarding element to consider happiness an object worth striving for. We learn to value good things first for self; we then transfer this estimate to the objects of our sympathy. Should we cease to evince any interest in our own personal welfare, or treat our own happiness with indifference, we practically lay down the position that happiness is nothing; the consequence being to render philanthropy absurd and unmeaning.

11. A wide range of Knowledge of human beings is requisite for large sympathies.

The carrying out of sympathy, in a career of kind and beneficent action, wants a full knowledge of the sensitive points of others. To note and to keep in remembrance the likings and dislikings, the interests and the needs, of all persons that we are well disposed to, will occupy a considerable share of our thoughts and intelligence; while uniformly to respect all these, in our conduct, involves sympathetic self-renunciation in a like eminent degree.

12. IMITATION, voluntary and involuntary, from its resemblance to sympathy, is elucidated by a parallel exposition.

In their tendencies and results, sympathy and imitation differ, but in their foundations they have much in common. There is an acquired power, one of the departments of our voluntary education, by which we move our own members to the lead of another person; as when under a master or a fugleman. The nearest approach to proper sympathy is a case of involuntary imitation, whereby we contract the gestures, tones, phraseology, and general demeanour of those around us. In all these points, the activity displayed by others is not merely a guide that we may avail ourselves of if we please, it is a power that we succumb to; the child is assimilated to the manners prevailing around it, before it receives any express instruction.

The conditions of imitation are (1) the Spontaneity of the active members, and (2) the Sense of the Effect, that is, of the conformity with the original. As regards the second condition, there is real pleasure in sensibly coinciding with movements witnessed and tones heard; and a certain painful feeling of discord, so long as the coincidence is not attained. In the case of children, who look up with deference and admiration to the superior powers of their elders, successful imitation has an intense charm; it is to them an advance in the scale of being. Many of the amusements of children are imitative; it is their delight to dramatize imposing avocations, to play the soldier, the judge, or the schoolmaster.

There is also exemplified with reference to Imitation, the same antithesis or contrast of characters; the susceptible or impressionable on the one hand, as against the self-moved, self-originating, on the other. The physical basis of the distinction may be supposed to lie in the distinctive endowment of the sensory and motor centres; at all events, the greater susceptibility to impressions received, represents the most general condition, alike of sympathy and of imitation.

The imitator or Mimic must possess facility in the special organs employed, as the voice, the features, the gestures. This is a mode of spontaneity in those organs, with the farther gift of variety, flexibility, or compass. But still more requisite is the extreme susceptibility of sense to the effects to be imitated. The thorough and entire absorption of these effects by the mind is the guide to the employment of the active organs to reproduce them. The case is exactly parallel to artistic ability—a combination of flexibility of organ with sensibility to the special effect. Indeed, as regards a certain number of the Fine Arts,—Poetry, Painting, Sculpture,—the Artist's vocation is in great part to imitate. And although Imitation is supposed to bend to artistic purpose, yet one of the pleasing effects of art is the fidelity of the imitation itself; and a considerable school of Art subordinates ideal beauty to this exactness of reproduction.

CHAPTER XII.

IDEAL EMOTION.

1. THE fact that Feeling or Emotion persists after the original stimulus is withdrawn, and is revived by purely mental forces, makes the life in the IDEAL.

Much of our pleasure and pain is of this ideal kind; being due not to a present stimulus, but to the remembrance of past states, either literally recalled, or shaped into imaginations and forecastings of the future. Recollected approbation or censure, the pleasures of affection towards the absent, the memory of a well spent life, are ideal feelings capable of great intensity.

2. I.—The purely Physical organs and processes affect the self-subsistence of Emotion.

Enough has been said on the organic processes (*Sensations of Organic Life*) to show their influence on mental states. In the vigour of youth, of health, of nourishment, the mind is buoyant of its own accord. Joyous emotion is then persistent and strong; ideal pleasure, the mere recollections of moments of delight, will possess a high intensity, by the support given to it, under the existing corporeal vigour. In this state of things, the excited brain, attracting to itself the abundant nourishment, maintains a high pitch of activity, and a like pitch of emotional fervour, whatever be the emotion suggested at the time. So, in holiday times, all ideal states of genial emotion—self-complacency, affection, the sense of power—are more than ordinarily intense and prolonged.

We may add, likewise, as a purely corporeal cause, the agency of the stimulating drugs, which, by quickening the brain, disposes a higher degree of emotion. Thus, alcohol stimulates both the tender emotion, and the sense of power, to a notable and ludicrous degree.

In states of corporeal elation, any pleasing emotion, suggested by its proper agent, burns brighter; a compliment is more acutely felt. For the same reason, the recall of pleasure by mental suggestion, would be more effective.

In the powerful and active brain, mental manifestations in general are stronger and more continuing; although there is, in most cases, a preference for some one mode of activity—Feeling, Will, or Intellect.

3. II.—The Temperament may be specially adapted for Emotion.

There is a physical foundation for this also, an endowment of Brain and other organs,—apparently the glandular or secreting organs; but whether we speculate on the physical side or not, we must recognize the mental fact. Some persons maintain with ease a persistent flow of comparatively strong emotion; others can attain to this only for short intervals. The strength of the system inclines *to* Feeling, and *away* from Will and from Intellect; such persons, unless largely endowed on the whole, are defective either in activity or in intellect. In them, however, emotion is fervid whether actual or ideal; the recollection of pleasure counts as present pleasure.

The emotional temperament may not make all emotions equally strong; we must allow for specific differences. But when we find such leading emotions as Wonder, Tender Feeling, Self-complacency, Power, and all the feelings of rebound, in exuberant fulness, we may express the fact by a general tendency, or temperament, for emotion.

The Emotional Temperament is framed for pleasurable emotion; it is a mode of strength, of elation, and buoyancy. It does not, therefore, magnify pain as it does pleasure; on the contrary, it has resources to submerge, and to forget, the painful feelings. The memory for pains, the ideal life of pain, except in so far as it ministers to prudential forethought, and vicarious sympathies, is a weakness, a defect of the constitution; showing itself in times of physical weakness, and conquered by physical renovation.

4. III.—There may be constitutions endowed for Special Emotions.

It is not to be assumed that the emotions all rise and fall together. Besides the general temperament for emotion, there are constitutions either endowed or educated for the separate emotions. To ascertain which of them may in this way be developed singly, is one use of an ultimate analysis of the feelings.

Reverting to the fundamental distinction between the ingoing or sensitive side of our nature, and the outgoing or active side, we have reason for believing that the two sides as a whole are unequally developed in individuals. Now, as there are emotions belonging to the sensitive or passive side —Tenderness, for example—and emotions allied to the active side, as Power, we may expect specific developments corresponding to these emotions. A constitutional Tenderness is a common manifestation, even without supposing a large emotional temperament on the whole. The persons so endowed will be distinguished for cherishing affection; and, when there are not enough of real objects, the feeling will be manifested in ideal forms.

So the sentiment of Power may be inordinately developed

in particular persons; and being so, it will sustain itself, in the absence of real occasions, by persistence in the ideal. The memory, the anticipation, the imagination of great power may give more delight than strong present gratifications of sense; something of this is implied in the toils of ambition, in the ascetic self-denial that procures an ascendancy over the minds of men.

The derived emotions, as Complacency, Irascibility, Love of Knowledge, will follow the strength of their constituent elements; they also may attain great self-sustaining force, or ideal persistence. The feelings of Revenge, Antipathy, or Hatred, may burn with almost unremitted glow in a human being; the real occasions of it are few, but the system is able to maintain the tremor over a large portion of the waking life.

In cases of remarkable development of special emotions, cultivation or habit has usually been superadded to nature. Any strong natural bent becomes stronger by asserting itself, and acquiring the confirmation of habit; besides which, education and influence from without may create a strong feeling out of one not strong originally.

5. IV.—Of Mental agencies, in the support of ideal emotion, two may be signalized :—(1) The presence of some Kindred emotion, and (2) the Intellectual forces.

(1) It is obvious that a present emotion, of an allied or congenial kind, must facilitate the blazing forth of an ideal feeling. The emotion of Religious reverence is fed and supported by a ritual adapted to stimulate the constituent feelings —sublimity, fear, and tenderness.

Present sensations of pleasure enable us to support dreams of ideal pleasure. The excitement of music inflames the ideal emotions and pleasures of the listener; whether love, complacency, glory, wealth, ambition : the mental tremor is transferred to a new subject.

(2) The chief intellectual force is Contiguity, or the presence of objects strongly associated with the feeling, as when the tender feeling towards the absent or the departed is maintained by relics, tokens, or other suggestive circumstances.

Our favourite emotions are kindled by the view of corresponding situations in the lives of other men. Biography is most charming when it brings before us careers and occupations like our own. The young man entering political life is excited by the lives of statesmen : the retired politician can resuscitate his emotions from the same source.

An element of Belief is an addition to the power of an Ideal Feeling. This is the emotion of Hope, which is ideality coupled with belief. There are various ways of inducing belief, some being identical with causes already mentioned; such as the various sources of mental elation. But belief may be aided by purely intellectual forces; in which case it has still the same efficacy.

The foregoing considerations bring before us certain collateral aids to feeling, whether actual or ideal. They enable us to account for the exceptions to the general rule, affirming the superiority of the present or actual, over the remembered or ideal. But before making that application, we must have before us the following additional circumstance.

6. V.—A Feeling generated in the Actual is liable to be thwarted by the accompaniments of the situation.

The reality of a success, or a step in life, is more powerful to excite joyous emotion than the dream or idea of it. The presence of a friend, or beloved object, is a happiness far beyond the thought of them in absence. Still, there are disadvantages incidental even to this highest form, of perfect fruition. The reality comes in the course of events, without reference to our preparation of mind for enjoying it to the full. And, what is more, it seldom comes in purity; it is a concrete situation, and usually has some adjuncts of a detracting, not to say a painful, nature. The hero of a triumph is perhaps 'old, and cannot enjoy it; solitary, and cannot impart it.' Something is present to mar the splendour of every great success; and even moderate good fortune may not be free from taint. The beloved object in actual presence is a concrete human being, and not an angelic abstraction.

Now, in the Ideal, the case is altered. In the first place, we do not idealize unless mentally prepared for it; we unconsciously choose our own time, and consult our emotional fitness; in fact, it is because we are emotionally capable of indulging in a certain reverie of ambition, love, brilliant prospects, that we fall into it.

And, in the next place, the Ideal drops out of view the disagreeable adjuncts of the reality. If we imagine the delight of attaining some object of pursuit, an office, a fortune, an alliance, we do not at the same time imagine the alloying drawbacks. The predominance of a feeling, by the law of its nature, excludes all disagreeables. Nothing but a severe discipline, partaking of the highest rigour of prudential forethought, qualifies a man to body forth the concrete situation when he anticipates some great pleasure. Cæsar toiled through many a weary march, in all weathers, to obtain his Triumph; but he probably did not forecast the mixture of base elements with his joyful emotions on that day.

It is not meant, that the detracting elements in every concrete situation entirely do away with the delights of attaining what we struggle for. Moreover, the after recollection of these bespattered joys, in suitable moods, will again take the form of ideal purity. The married woman whose lot is fortunate and temperament cheerful, will remember her wedding day without the worry, the heat, and the headache, which a faithful diary would have included in the narrative.

7. The circumstances now given account for the play and predominance of Ideal Emotion.

All other things being the same, a feeling in the Actual would surpass a feeling in the Ideal: the present enjoyment of a good bargain, a piece of music, an evening's conversation, is much stronger than the remembrance or imagination of that enjoyment. Still, in numerous instances, from the operation of the causes enumerated, one feeling in the ideal may be far stronger than another in the actual. The emotions that predominate in the mind may be quite different from what the occasions of life would of themselves give support to.

(1) In what is called day-dreaming, we have a large field of examples. Anything occurring to fire one of the strong emotions, in circumstances otherwise favourable, takes the attention and the thoughts away from other things to fasten them upon the objects of the feeling. The youth inflamed with the story of great achievements, and bold adventures, forgets his home and his father's house, and dreams of an ideal history of the same exciting character. The intellect ministers to the emotion, which without the creation of appropriate circumstances, would not be self-supporting. When love is the inflaming passion, there is the same obliviousness to the stimulation of things present; the life is wholly ideal.

This is one acceptation of the phrase 'pleasures of the Imagination.' They are the pleasures ideally sustained, to which the intellect supplies imagery and circumstances, and in that capacity is termed Imagination. The phrase has another meaning in Addison's celebrated Essays, namely, the Pleasures derived from works of Art, in which case ideality is only an incident. In looking at a picture or a statue, we have something that may be called real, and present, although undoubtedly a principal design of works of art is to suggest ideal emotions. Ideality is an almost 'inseparable accident' of Art.

(2) In our Ethical appreciation of conduct we are influenced by ideal emotions. Disliking, as we do in practice, severe restraints, and ascetic exercises, we admire them in idea from the great fascination of the sentiment of power. The superiority to pleasure is a fine ideal of moral strength, and we consecrate it in theoretical morality, however little we may care to practise it.

(3) The Religious sentiment implies a certain class of emotions incompletely gratified by the realities of the present life. Minds exactly adapted to what this world can supply—the 'worldly-minded,' are the contrast of the 'religiously-minded.' The feelings of Sublimity, Love and Fear, in such strength as to transcend the limited sphere of the individual lot, are easily led into the regions of the unknown and the supernatural.

8. Ideal Emotion is more or less connected with Desire.

When a pleasure exists only as the faded memory of a previous pleasure, there accompanies it the consciousness of a painful inferiority, with a motive to the will to seek the full reality. This is Desire. If the reality is irrecoverable, the state is called Regret. Should the ideal feeling be so aided by vividness of recollection, or by collateral supports, as to approach the fulness of a real experience, we accept it as a sufficing enjoyment, and have no desire. In the excitement of conversation, we recall delightful memories with such force as to fill up a satisfying cup of pleasure.

CHAPTER XIII.

ÆSTHETIC EMOTIONS.

1. THE Æsthetic Emotions—indicated by the names, Beauty, Sublimity, the Ludicrous—are a class of pleasurable feelings, sought to be gratified by the compositions of Fine Art.

In the perplexity attending the question as to the Beautiful, a clue ought to be found in the compositions of Fine Art. Such compositions aim at pleasure, but of a peculiar kind, qualified by the eulogistic terms 'refined,' 'elevating,' 'ennobling.' A contrast is made between the Agreeable and the Beautiful; between Utility and Beauty; Industry and Fine Art.

2. The productions of Fine Art appear to be distinguished by these characteristics :—(1) They have *pleasure for their immediate end ;* (2) they have *no disagreeable accompaniments ;* (3) their enjoyment is *not restricted to one or a few persons.*

(1) We assume, for the present, that the immediate end of Fine Art is Pleasure; whereas the immediate end of eating and drinking is to ward off pain, disease, death.

(2) In Fine Art, everything disagreeable is meant to be excluded. This is one element of refinement; the loathsome accompaniments of our sensual pleasures mar their purity.

(3) The objects of Fine Art, and all objects called æsthetic, are such as may be enjoyed by a great number; some indeed are open to the whole human race. They are exempt from the fatal taint of rivalry and contest attaching to other agreeables; they draw men together in mutual sympathy; and are thus eminently social and humanizing. A picture or a statue can be seen by millions; a great poem reaches all that understand its language; a fine melody may spread pleasure over the habitable globe. The sunset and the stars are veiled only from the prisoner and the blind.

It will now be seen why many agreeable and valuable things, the ends of industry, can be distinguished from Fine Art. Food, clothing, houses, medicine, law, armies, are all useful, but not necessarily (although sometimes incidentally) beautiful. Even Science, although remarkable for the absence of monopoly (3), is not æsthetic; its immediate end is not pleasure (1), although remotely it brings pleasures and avoids pains; and it is too much associated with disagreeable toil in the acquisition (2).

Wealth is obviously excluded from the æsthetic class. So also is the delight of Power, which is not only a monopolist pleasure, but one that implies, in others, the opposite state of impotence or dependence. The pleasure of Affection is also confined in its scope; being, however, less confined, and less hostile to the interests of others, than power.

3. The Eye and the Ear are the æsthetic senses.

The Muscular feelings, the Organic sensibilities, the sensations of Taste, Smell, and Touch, cannot be multiplied or extended like the effects of light and sound; their objects are engrossed, if not consumed, by the present user. The consideration of monopoly would be decisive against the whole class, while many have other disqualifications. But pleasures awakened through the eye and the ear, in consequence of the diffusion of light and of sound, can be enjoyed by countless numbers. There is a faint approach to this wide participation in the case of odours; but the difference, although only in degree, is so great as to make a sufficient line of demarcation for our present purpose.

4. The Muscular and the Sensual elements can be brought into Art by being presented in the *idea*. The same may be said of Wealth, Power, Dignity and Affection.

A painter or a poet may depict a feast, and the picture may be viewed with pleasure. The disqualifying circumstances are not present in ideal delights. So Wealth, Power, Dignity, Affection, as seen or imagined in others, are not exclusive. In point of fact, mankind derive much real pleasure from sympathizing with these objects. They constitute much of the interest of surrounding life, and of the historical past; and they are freely adopted into the compositions of the artist.

It may be objected here, that to permit, without reserve, the ideal presentation of sensual delights, merely because of its being a diffused and not a monopolized pleasure, is to give to Art an unbounded licence of grossness; the very supposition proving that the domain of Art is not sufficiently circumscribed by the three facts above stated. The reply is, that the subjects of Fine Art are limited by considerations that are very various in different countries and times, and are hardly reducible to any rule. The pourtraying of sensual pleasures is objected to on moral and prudential grounds, as overstimulating men to pursue the reality; but there is no fixed line universally agreed upon. It is evidently within the *spirit* of Fine Art, as implied in the conditions above given, to cultivate directly and indirectly the sources of pleasure *that all can share in*, that provoke sympathy, instead of rivalry. Hence tales that inflame either the ambition or the sensuality of the human mind, in their consequences, inspire what are termed the *baser* passions, properly definable as the passions involving rivalry and hostility, because their objects are such as the few enjoy, to the exclusion of the many.

It is in the same spirit that Art is considered to occupy its proper province when inspiring sympathy and benign emotions, and lulling angry and hateful passion. Hence it allies itself with Morality, being in fact almost identified with the persuasive part of Morality, as opposed to the obligatory or compulsory sanction.

5. The source of Beauty is not to be sought in any single quality, but in a Circle of Effects.

The search after some common property applicable to all things named beautiful is now abandoned. Every theorist admits a plurality of causes. The common attribute resides only in the emotion, and even that may vary considerably without passing the limits of the name.

Among terms used to express æsthetic qualities—Sublimity, Beauty, Grace, Picturesqueness, Harmony, Melody, Proportion, Keeping, Order, Fitness, Unity, Wit, and Humour—there are a number of synonyms; but a real distinction is marked by the names Sublimity, Beauty, the Ludicrous (with Humour). The most comprehensive of the three designations is Beauty; the problem of what are the characteristics of Fine Art is chiefly attached to it. Sublimity and the Ludicrous, which also enter into æsthetic compositions, have certain distinctive features, and are considered apart.

The objects described in these various phrases may occur spontaneously in nature; as, for example, wild and impressive scenery: they may spring up incidental to other effects, as when the contests of nations, carried on for self-protection or supremacy, produce grand and stirring spectacles to the unconcerned beholders, and to after ages; or when the structures, designed for pure utility, rise to grandeur from their mere magnitude, as a ship of war, or a vast building: and lastly, they may be expressly produced for their own sake, in which case we have a class of Fine Arts, a profession of Artists, and an education of people generally in elegance and Taste.

6. The objects and emotions of Fine Art, so far as brought out in the previous exposition of the mind, may be resumed as follows:—

I.—The simple sensations of the Ear and the Eye.

The pleasurable sensations of sound and of sight come within the domain of Fine Art. This view, maintained by Knight in his Essay on Taste, is strongly opposed by Jeffrey, who denies that there are any intrinsic pleasures due to these sensations. On such a point, the appeal must be made to the experience of mankind. We have, in discussing these senses, classified and enumerated their sensations, affirming the intrinsically pleasurable character of a large part of them; as, for example, voluminous sounds, waxing and waning sounds, mere light, colour, and lustre. If these are admitted to be pleasurable for their own sake (and not for the sake of certain suggested emotions), their pretensions to be employed in Art are based on their complying with the criteria of the Artistic emotions. The pleasures arising from them are sometimes called *sensuous*, as contrasted with the narrow or monopolist pleasures of the other senses, called *sensual*.

7. II.—Intellect, co-operating with the Senses, furnishes materials of Art.

Muscular exercise and repose *seen* or *contemplated*, as in the spectacle of games, would be regarded as an æsthetic pleasure. The pleasures of the monopolist senses, when presented in idea by the painter or the poet, attain the refinement of art.

The sensations of bodily health and vigour are in themselves exclusive and sensual; in their idea, as when we contemplate the outward marks of health, they are artistic. The actual enjoyment of warmth or coolness is sensual, the suggestion of these in a picture is refined and artistical. Pleasant odours are frequently described in poetry. The feeling of soft warm touch ideally excited is a feeling of art.

The intervention of language (an intellectual device) is a means of overcoming the disagreeable adjuncts of our senses, and of rendering the sensual pleasures less adverse to artistic handling. There are ways of alluding to the offensive processes of organic life, that deprive them of half their evil, by removing all their grossness. This is the purpose of the Rhetorical figure, called Euphemism; it is a mode of refinement describable as the purification of pleasure.

8. III.—The Special Emotions, either in their actuality, or in idea, enter largely into Fine Arts.

This has been already pointed out. The first class, the Emotions of Relativity—Wonder, Surprise, Novelty—are sought in Art, as in other pleasures not artistic. The emotion of Fear is of itself painful, and would be excluded by the artist, but for its incidentally contributing to artistic pleasure. Tender emotion in actuality is too narrow, but in idea it is very largely made use of as a pleasure of Art; the objects that inspire tender emotion, that rouse ideal affection, are universally denominated beautiful. According to Burke, tenderness is almost identified with beauty: and in the Association theory of Alison and Jeffrey, the power to suggest the warm human affections is placed above all other causes; the feminine exterior being considered beautiful as bodying forth the graces and amiability of the character. The egotistic group of emotions—Self-complacency, Love of Approbation, Power, Irascibility—even ideally viewed, are adverse to the spirit of Art, unless we can sympathize with the occasions of them, in which case their manifestation gives us pleasure. The situation of Pursuit, in idea, is eminently artistic; plot-interest enters into most kinds of poetry. The Emotions of Intellect would be æsthetic, from their broad and liberalizing character, and from their not containing, either directly or indirectly, the element of rivalry; but the province of Truth and Science, in which they appear, is, for the most part, too arduous to be a source of unmixed pleasure.

9. IV.—HARMONY is an especial source of artistic pleasure.

It was noted (CLASSIFICATION OF EMOTIONS, § 2), that emotional states are produced from sensations, through Harmony and Conflict; Harmony giving pleasure, and Conflict pain. It is in the works of Fine Art, that the pleasures of Harmony are most extensively cultivated. The illustration of this position in detail would cover a large part of the field of Æsthetics. The law that determines the pleasure of Harmony and the pain of Conflict, is a branch or application of a higher law, the law of Self-conservation; in harmony, we may suppose that the nerve currents are mutually supporting; in conflict, that there is opposition and loss of power.

10. The pleasurable Sensations of SOUND, and their Harmonies, constitute a department of Fine Art.

In Music, we have, first, all the pleasing varieties of simple sound—sweet sounds, voluminous sounds, waxing and waning sounds; and next, the combinations of sound in Melody and in Harmony, according to laws of proportion, now arithmetically determined.

The musical note is a sound of uniform Pitch, or of a constant number of beats per second. In this uniformity, there is a source of pleasure; it contains the element of harmony. The regularity of the beats is more agreeable than irregularity.

The same fact enters into a musical air or melody, and reappears in the harmonies and proportions of visible objects.

Harmony is the concurrence of two or more sounds related, as to number of vibrations and beats, in a simple ratio. The Octave is the most perfect harmony, the numbers being as two to one. In this concord, every second beat of the higher note coincides with every beat of the lower; and, between these coinciding and double beats, there is a solitary beat. The intervals, therefore, are equal, but the beats unequal; a double and a single alternating. This is the first departure from uniformity towards variety, and the effect is more acceptable, probably on that ground. In the concord of a Fifth, every third vibration of the higher note coincides with every second of the lower; and between these two coincidences, there are three single beats (two in one note and one in the other) at intervals varying as $1, \frac{1}{2}, \frac{1}{2}, 1$ respectively. In the concord of a Fourth, every fourth vibration of the higher note coincides with every third of the lower; and between the two coincidences, there are five single beats (three in one note and two in the other), at intervals of $1, \frac{1}{3}, \frac{2}{3}, \frac{2}{3}, \frac{1}{3}, 1$. In these two last mentioned concords, there is a mixture of different sets of equal intervals; the coinciding or double beat, and the single beats recurring in the same order of unequal but proportioned intervals.

The element of Time, in music, is probably the same effect on the larger scale. Besides allowing harmonies to be arranged, the observance of time in the succession of notes is a kind of concord between what is past and what is to come—a harmony of expectation—and the violation of it is a jar or discord, and is painful according to the sensitiveness of the ear.

The varying Emphasis of music, properly regulated, adds to the pleasure, on the law of Relativity, or alternation and remission, as in light and shade. According as sounds are sharp and loud, is it necessary that they be remitted and varied. The gradations of pitch have respect to variety, as well as to harmony and melody. Since a work of Art aims at giving pleasure to the utmost, it courts variety in every form, only not to produce discords, or to miss harmonies.

Cadence is an effect common to music and to speaking, and refers, in the first instance, to the close or fall of the melody. An abrupt termination is unpleasing, partly from breach of expectation, and partly because, on the principle of relativity, the sudden cessation of a stimulus gives a shock analogous to the sudden commencement. Cadence farther includes, by a natural extension, the variation of emphasis and pitch; the gentle commencement, the gradual rise to a height or climax, and the ending fall; there being a series of lesser rises and falls throughout the piece. Alternation or variety is the sole guide to this effect, which enters alike into musical performance, and into oratorical pronunciation.

There is, in Music, a superadded effect, namely, the imitation of emotional expression, by which various emotions may be directly stimulated, as Tenderness, Devotion, the Exultation of Power.

This imitation is effected by varying the sounds themselves, but still more through the pace, or comparative rapidity and emphasis of the notes; the very same rule governing music and poetry.

11. The pleasurable Sensations of SIGHT, with their Harmonies, are a distinct source of the Beautiful in Art.

Mere light is pleasant in proper limits and alternation; whence the art of Light and Shade. The employment of colour is regulated by harmony; there is a mutual balance of the colours, according to the proportions of the solar spectrum. Red, yellow, and blue are accounted the primary colours. The eye, exposed for some time to one colour, as red, desiderates some other colour, and is most of all delighted with the complementary colour; thus red harmonizes with green (formed out of yellow and blue); blue with orange or gold (a mixture of red and yellow); yellow with violet (red and blue). Colour Harmony is the maximum of stimulation of the optic nerve, with the minimum of exhaustion.

The influence of Lustre has been already described. It is the outburst of sparkles of light on a ground of comparative sombreness.

In the muscular susceptibility of sight, the elementary pleasurable effect is the waxing and waning motion, and the Curve Line, the two being in character the same. This has always been a conspicuous part of the beauty of Form.

The Harmonies of Sight are exemplified by movements, as the Dance, where also there is observance of Time.

In still life, there are harmonies of Space. In arranging objects in a row, equality of intervals has a pleasing effect, on the principle already quoted. The equality may be combined with variety, by introducing larger breaks, also at equal intervals, which gives subordinate gradations, with a unity in the whole.

The subdivision of lines or spaces should be in simple proportions, as halves, thirds, fourths; these simple ratios constitute the beauty of oblong and triangular figures, and the proportions of rooms and buildings. An oblong, having the length three times the width, is more agreeable to the observant eye than if no ratio were discernible. A room, whose length, width, and height follow simple ratios, as 4 to 3, or 3 to 2, is well proportioned. Equality of angles, in angular figures, is preferable to inequality; and the angles of 30°, 45°, or 60°, being simple divisions of the quadrant, are more agreeable than angles that are incommensurate.

In Straight Forms, the laws of proportion determine beauty, subject to considerations of Fitness, to be presently noticed. In Curved Forms, the primitive charm of the curve line may be combined with proportions and with pleasing associations. The circle, and the oval, contain an element of proportion. Besides these effects, there is in the curved outline the suggestion of ease and *abandon*. The mechanical members of the human body, being chiefly levers fixed at the end, naturally describe curves with their extremities; it is only after a painful discipline that they can draw straight lines. Hence straightness, in certain circumstances, is suggestive of restraint, and curvature of ease. The beauty of the straight form, when it is beautiful, will arise partly from proportion, and partly from the obvious utility of order in arrangement. The straight furrows of a ploughed field are agreeable, if our mind is occupied with the ploughman's labour, not on the side of its arduousness, but on the side of its power and skill.

In the dimension of up and down, form or outline is interwoven with the paramount consideration of sustaining things against the force of gravity; in other words, we have to deal with Pressure and Support. The evils of loss of support are so numerous, so pressing, so serious, that adequacy on this score is one of our incessant solicitudes, a real 'affection of Fear.' The mere suggestion of a possible catastrophe from weakness of support is a painful idea; and the existence of such pains renders the appearances of adequate support a kind of joyful relief. When a great mass has to be supported, we gaze with satisfaction upon the firmness of the foundations, the width of the base, the tenacity of the columns or other supports. The pyramid and the well-buttressed wall are objects that we can think of with comfort, when more than usually oppressed with examples of flimsiness and insecurity.

Sufficiency of apparent support does not exhaust the interest of the counteraction of gravity. Next to doing work adequately, is doing it with the least expenditure of means or labour. It gratifies the feeling of Power, and is an aspect of the Sublime, to see great effects produced with the appearance of Ease on the part of the agent. The pyramid, although satisfactory in one point of view, is apt to appear as gross, heavy, clumsy, if used merely to support its own mass. We obtain a superadded gratification, when we see an object raised aloft without such expenditure of material and such width of base. In these respects, the obelisk is a refinement on the pyramid. The column is a still greater refinement; for in a row of columns, we discern a satisfactory, and yet light, support to a superincumbent mass. Another modification of support for smaller heights is the pilaster, which is diminished near the bottom, and also near the top, retaining breadth of base, and a resisting thickness in the middle; there being an opportunity also for the curved outline. Vases, drinking cups, wine glasses, and other table ware, combine adequate with easy support, while availing themselves of proportions and the curved form. The tree, with its spreading roots and ample base, its slender and yet adequate stem, supporting a voluminous foliage, is an example of support that never ceases to afford gratification.

The beauty of Symmetry is in some cases due to proportion, and in others to adequacy of support. When the two sides of a human face are not alike, there is a breach of proportion; a wasted limb is both disproportioned and inadequate for support.

The beauties of Visible Movement might be expanded in a similar detail. The curve movement is a beauty—that is, a refined pleasure in itself. Upward movements, being against gravity, suggest power; so also rapid projectile movements, as the cannon ball. The spectacle of a dance combines a number of effects already recognized.

12. In the Fine Arts, there are Complex Harmonies; as when Sound, Colour, Movement, Form, are in keeping with each other, and with the intention of the work as a whole.

There is no intrinsic suitability of a sound to a colour, or of a colour to a form; a voluminous sound is not more in harmony with red than with blue. But the moods of mind generated by sensation may have a certain community; at one time, the prevailing key may be pungent excitement, at another time, voluminous pleasure. Through this community, glare and sparkle chime in with rapid movements; sombre light and shade with slow movements. There is the same adaptation of musical measures to the state of the mind as determined by spectacle, or by emotion. The dying fall in music harmonizes with the waxing and waning movement, or the curved line.

13. A wide department of the Beautiful is expressed under the FITNESS of means to ends.

This has been already brought into view in the discussion of Support, which is the fitness of machinery to a mechanical end, namely, the counteraction of gravity. On account of the pleasure thus obtained, we erect structures that have no other end than to suggest fitness. In all kinds of mechanism, where power is exerted to produce results, there is a like feeling. When anything is to be done, we are sympathetically pained in discovering the means to be inadequate; and being often subject to such pains, there is a grateful reaction in contemplating a work where the power is ample for its end. There is a farther satisfaction in seeing ends accomplished with the least expenditure of means. The appearances of great labour, effort, or difficulty, are unpleasant; a man bending beneath a load, a horse sticking in the mud, give a depressing idea of weakness. The noise of friction in machinery, and the sight of roughness and rust, suggestive of friction, are calculated to pain our sensibilities. On the other hand, all the indications of comparative ease in the performance of work, even although illusory, are a grateful rebound of sympathetic power. The gentle breeze moving a ship, or a windmill, gives us this illusory gratification. Clean, bright tools are associated with ease and efficiency in doing their work.

The beauties of ORDER may consist of mere proportion, but they are still oftener the effects conducive to the attainment of ends. In a well kept house, or shop, everything is in its place; there are fit tools and facilities for whatever is to be done; all the appearances are suggestive of such fitness and facility: although it may happen that the reality and the appearance are opposed. The arts of cleanliness, in the first instance, are aimed at the removal of things injurious and loathsome; going a step farther, they impart whiteness of surface, lustre and brilliancy, which are æsthetic qualities. The neat, tidy, and trim, may be referred to Order; even when going beyond what is necessary for useful ends, neatness suggests a mind alive to the orderly, which is a means to the useful.

14. The feeling of UNITY in Diversity, considered as a part of Beauty, owes its charm principally to Order, and to Intellectual relief.

The mind, overburdened with a multitude of details, seeks relief in order and in unity of plan. The successful reduction of a distracting host of particulars to simple and general heads, as happens through great discoveries of generalization, gives the thrill of a great intellectual relief. In all works abounding in detail, we crave for some comprehensive plan, enabling us to seize the whole, while we survey the parts. A poem, a history, a dissertation in science, a lecture, needs to have a discernible principle of order or unity throughout.

15. It is a principle of Art, founded in the nature of the feelings, to leave something to Desire.

To leave something to the Imagination is better than to express the whole. What is merely suggested is conceived in an ideal form and colouring. Thus, in a landscape, a winding river disappears from the sight; the distant hazy mountains are realms for the fancy to play in. Breaks are left in a story, such as the reader may fill up. The proportioning and adjusting of the expressed and the suggested, would depend on the principles of Ideal Emotion.

16. Under so great a variety of exciting causes, a certain latitude must be allowed in characterizing the feeling of Beauty.

Experience proves, that all these different effects are not merely modes of pleasure, but congenial in their mixture. The common character of the emotion may be expressed as refined pleasure. Even when not great in degree, it has the advantage of durability. The many confluent streams of pleasure run into a general ocean of the pleasurable, where their specialities are scarcely distinguishable.

When Beauty is spoken of in a narrow sense, as excluding Sublimity, it points to the more purely passive delights, exemplified in sensuous pleasures, harmonies, tender emotion. Burke's identification of delicacy (as in the drooping flower) with beauty, hits the passive delights, as contrasted with the active. The boundary is not a rigid one. Much of the beauty of fitness appeals to the sentiment of power, the basis of the Sublime.

THE SUBLIME. 301

17. The SUBLIME is the sympathetic sentiment of superior Power in its highest degrees.

The objects of sublimity are, for the most part, such aspects and appearances as betoken great might, energy, or vastness, and are thereby capable of imparting sympathetically the elation of superior power.

Human might or energy is the literal sublime, and the point of departure for sublimity in other things. Superior bodily strength, as indicated either by the size and form of the members, or by actual exertion, lifts the beholder's mind above its ordinary level, and imparts a certain degree of grateful elation. The same may be said of other modes of superior power. Greatness of intellect, as in the master minds of the human race, is interesting as an object of mere contemplation. Moral energy, as heroic endurance and self-denial, has inspired admiration in all times. Great practical skill in the various departments of active life awakens the same admiring and elevating sentiment. The spectacle of power in organized multitudes is still more imposing, and reflects an undue importance on the one man that happens to be at the head.

The Sublime of Inanimate things is derived or borrowed, by a fictitious process, from the literal sublimity of beings formed like ourselves. So great is our enjoyment of the feeling of superior power, that we take delight in referring the forces of dead matter to a conscious mind; in other words, personification. Starting from some known estimate, as in the physical force of an average man to move one hundred-weight, we have a kind of sympathetic elation in seeing many hundredweights raised with ease by water or steam power. When the spectacle is common, we become indifferent to it; and we are re-awakened only by something different or superior.

The Sublime of Support is of frequent occurrence. It applies to the raising of heavy weights; to the upward projection of bodies; and to the sustaining of great masses at an elevation above the surface, as piles of building, and mountains. All these effects imply great upheaving power, equivalent to human force many times multiplied. The more upright or precipitous the elevated mass, the greater the apparent power put forth in sustaining it. Sublimity is thus connected with *height*; from which it derives its name.

The Sublime of Active Energy, or power visibly at work, is seen in thunder, wind, waves, cataracts, rivers, volcanoes, steam power, ordnance, accumulated animal or human force. Movement in the actual is more impressive than the quiescent results of movement.

The Sublime of Space, or of Largeness of Dimensions, is partly owing to the circumstance that objects of great power are correspondingly large. The ocean is voluminous. As regards empty space, great extent implies energy to traverse it, or mass to occupy it.

An Extended Prospect is sublime from the number of its contained objects, each possessing a certain element of impressiveness. There is also a sense of intellectual range or grasp, as compared with the confinement of a narrow spot; which is one of the many modes of the elation of superior power.

The Great in Time or Duration is Sublime; not mere duration in the abstract, but the sequence of known transactions and events, stretching over many ages. In this too, there is an intellectual elevation, and a form of superior might. The far past, and the distant future, to a mind that can people the interval, arouse the feeling of the sublime. The relics of ancient nations, the antiquities of the geological ages, inspire a sublimity, tinged with melancholy and pathos, from the retrospect of desolation and decay.

There is an incidental connexion of the Sublime with Terror. Properly, the two states of mind are hostile and mutually destructive; the one raises the feeling of energy, the other depresses it. In so far as a sublime object gives us the sense of personal, or of sympathetic danger, its sublimity is frustrated. The two effects were confounded by Burke in his Theory of the Sublime.

18. The foregoing principles might be tested and exemplified by a survey of Natural Objects. It is sufficient to advert to Human Beauty.

The Mineral world has its æsthetic qualities, chiefly colour and form. In Vegetable nature, there are numerous effects, partly of colour and form, partly of support, and partly of quasi-human expression. The beauties of scenery—of mountains, rocks, valleys, rivers, plains—are referable, without much difficulty, to the constituent elements above indicated. The Animal Kingdom contains many objects of æsthetic interest, as well as many of an opposite kind. The approach to humanity is the special circumstance; the suggestion of feeling is no longer fictitious, but real; and the interest is little removed from the human.

As regards Humanity, there are first the graces of the Exterior. The effects of colour and brilliancy,—in the skin, the eyes, the hair, the teeth,—are intrinsically agreeable. The Figure is more contested. The proportions of the whole are suited for sufficient, and yet light support; while the modifications of foot and limb are adapted for forward movement. The curvature of the outline is continuous and varying (in the ideal feminine figure), passing through points of contrary flexure, from convex to concave, and, again resuming the convex.

The beauties of the Head and Face involve the most difficult considerations. In so far as concerns the symmetry of the two halves, and the curved outlines, we have intelligible grounds; but the proportional sizes of the face, features, and head, are determined by no general principles. We must here accept from our customary specimens a certain standard of mouth, nose, forehead, &c., and refine upon that by bringing in laws of proportion, curvature, and the susceptibility to agreeable expression. This is the only tenable mean between the unguarded theory of Buffier and Reynolds, who referred all beauty to custom, and the attempts to explain everything by proportion and expression. A Negro or a Mongol sculptor would be not only justified, but necessitated, to assume an ideal type different from the Greek, although he might still introduce general æsthetic considerations, that is to say, proportions, curves, fitness, and expression, so as not to be the imitator of any one actual specimen, or even of the most common variety. The same applies to the beauties seen in animals. The prevailing features of the species are assumed, and certain considerations either of universal beauty, or of capricious adoption, are allowed to have weight in determining the most beautiful type.

The graces of Movement, as such, are quite explicable. In the primitive effects of movement are included the curve line and the 'dying fall.' The movements, as well as attitudes, of a graceful form, can hardly be other than graceful.

The suggestion of Tender and of Sexual Feeling is connected with Colour, with Form, and with Movements. The tints of the face and of the surface generally are associated with the soft warm contact. By a link of connexion, partly natural (the result of a general law), the rounded and tapering form is suggestive of the living embrace; lending an interest to the hard cold marble of the statuary. The movements that excite the same train of feelings are known and obvious.

On all theories of Beauty, much is allowed to the Expression of pleasing states of mind. The amiable expression is always cheering to behold; and a cast of features permanently suited to this expression is beautiful.

When we inquire into what constitutes beauty in the human character, or the mental attributes of a human being, we find that the foundation of the whole is self-surrender. This is apparent in the virtues (also called *graces*) of generosity, affection, and modesty or humility; all which imply that the individual gives up a portion of self for others.

THEORIES OF THE BEAUTIFUL.

It is usual to carry back the history of the question of Beauty to Sokrates and Plato.

The question of Beauty is shortly touched upon, in one of the Sokratic conversations reported in the Memorabilia. SOKRATES holds that the beautiful and the good, or useful, are the same; a dung-basket, if it answers its end, may be a beautiful thing, while a golden shield, not well formed for use, is an ugly thing. (*Memorabilia* III. 8.)

In the Dialogue of PLATO, called *Hippias Major*, there is a discussion on the Beautiful. Various theories are propounded, and to all of them objections, supposed insuperable, are made by the Platonic Sokrates. First, The Suitable, or the Becoming, is said to constitute beauty. To this, it is objected, that the suitable, or becoming, is what causes objects to *appear* beautiful, not what makes them really beautiful. Secondly, The Useful or Profitable. Much is to be said for this view, but on close inspection (says Sokrates) it will not hold. Thus Power, which when employed for useful purposes is beautiful, may be employed for evil, and cannot be beautiful. If you qualify by saying—Power employed for good—you make the good and the beautiful cause and effect, and therefore different things, which is absurd. Thirdly, The beautiful is a particular variety of the Agreeable or Pleasurable, being all those things that give pleasure through *sight* and *hearing*. Sokrates, however, demands why these pleasures should be so much distinguished over other pleasures. He is not satisfied to be told that they are the most innocuous and the best; an answer that (he says) leads to the same absurdity as before; the beautiful being made the cause, the good the effect; and the two thereby accounted different things.

Turning now to the *Republic* (Book VII.), we find a mode of viewing the question, more in accordance with the mystic and transcendental side of Plato. Speaking of the science of Astronomy, he says (in summary):—' The heavenly bodies are the most *beautiful* of all visible bodies, and the most regular of all visible movements, approximating most nearly, though still with a long interval of inferiority, to the *ideal* figures and movements

THEORIES OF BEAUTY—PLATO.

of genuine and self-existent *Forms*—quickness, slowness, number, figure, &c., *as they are in themselves*, not visible to the eye, but conceivable only by reason and intellect. The movements of the heavenly bodies are exemplifications, approaching nearest to the perfection of these ideal movements, but still falling greatly short of them. They are like visible circles or triangles drawn by some very exact artist; which, however beautiful as works of art, are far from answering to the conditions of the *idea* and its definition, and from exhibiting exact equality and proportion.' All this is in accordance with the Ideal theory of Plato. Ideas are not only the pre-existing causes of real things, but the highest and most delightful objects of human contemplation.

It is remarked by Mr. Grote that the Greek τὸ καλόν includes, in addition to the ordinary meanings of beauty, the *fine*, the *honourable*, the *exalted*.

ARISTOTLE alludes to the nature of Beauty, in connexion with Poetry. The beauty of animals, or of any objects composed of parts, involves two things—orderly arrangement and a certain magnitude. Hence an animal may be too small to be beautiful; or it may be too large, when it cannot be surveyed as a whole. The object should have such magnitude as to be easily seen.

Among the lost writings of ST. AUGUSTIN was a large treatise on Beauty; and it appears from incidental allusions in the extant works, that he laid especial stress on Unity, or the relation of the parts of a work to the whole, in one comprehensive and harmonious design.

In SHAFTESBURY's *Characteristics*, the Beautiful and the Good are combined in one lofty conception, and a certain internal sense (the Moral Sense) is assumed as perceiving both alike.

In the celebrated Essays of ADDISON, on *The Pleasures of the Imagination*, the æsthetic effects are resolved into Beauty, Sublimity, and Novelty; but scarcely any attempt is made to pursue the analysis of either Beauty or Sublimity.

HUTCHESON maintains the existence of a distinct internal sense for the perception of Beauty. He still, however, made a resolution of the qualities of beautiful objects into combinations of variety with uniformity; but did not make the obvious inference, that the sense of beauty *is*, therefore, a sense of variety with uniformity. He discarded the considerations of fitness, or the secondary aptitudes of these qualities.

In the article 'Beau,' in the French *Encyclopédie*, the author, DIDEROT, announced the doctrine that 'Beauty consists in the perception of Relations.' This is admitted on all hands to be too wide and too vague.

PÈRE BUFFIER. Père Buffier identified Beauty with the *type* of each species; it is the form at once most common and most rare. Among faces, there is but one beautiful form, the others being not beautiful. But while only a few are modelled after the ugly forms, a great many are modelled after the beautiful form. Beauty, while itself rare, is the model to which the greater number conform. Among fifty noses we may find ten well-made, all after the same model; whereas out of the other forty, not above two or three will be found of the same shape. Handsome people have a greater family likeness than ugly people. A monster is what has least in common with the human figure; beauty is what has most in common. The true proportion of parts is the most common proportion. From this it might be concluded that beauty is simply what we are most accustomed to, and therefore arbitrary —a conclusion that Buffier does not dispute. At least, hitherto, he thinks, the essential character of beauty has not been discovered. If there be a true beauty, it must be that which is most common to all nations.

Sir Joshua Reynolds, in his theory of beauty, has followed Père Buffier. The deformed is what is *uncommon*; beauty is what is above 'all singular forms, local customs, particularities, and details of every kind.' He gives, however, a turn to the doctrine, in meeting the objection that there are distinct forms of beauty in the same species, as those represented by the Hercules, the Gladiator, and the Apollo. He observes that each of these is a representation, not of an individual, but of a class, within the class *man*, and is the central idea of its class. Not any one gives the ideal beauty of the species man; 'for perfect beauty in any species must combine all the characters which are beautiful in that species.'

Hogarth, in his *Analysis of Beauty*, enumerates six elements as variously entering into beautiful compositions. (1) *Fitness* of the parts to the design for which the object was formed. Twisted columns are elegant; but, as they convey an idea of weakness, they displease when required to bear a great weight. Hogarth resolves *proportion* (which some consider an independent source of beauty) into fitness. The proportions of the parts are determined by the purpose of the whole. (2) *Variety*, if it do not degenerate into confusion, is a distinct element of beauty. The gradual lessening of the pyramid is a kind of variety. (3) *Uniformity* or *symmetry* is a source of beauty only when rendered necessary by the requirements of fitness. The pleasure arising from the symmetry of the two sides of the body, is really produced by the knowledge that the correspondence is intentional and for use. Painters always avoid regularity, and prefer to take a building at an angle rather than in front. Uniformity is often necessary to give stability. (4) *Simplicity* (as opposed to complexity), when joined with variety, is pleasing, because it enables the eye to enjoy the variety with ease; but, without variety, it is wholly insipid. Compositions in sculpture are generally kept within the boundary of a cone or pyramid, on account of the simplicity or variety of those figures. (5) *Intricacy* is pleasing because the unravelling of it gives the interest of pursuit. Waving and serpentine lines are 'beautiful, because they 'lead the eye a wanton kind of chase.' (6) *Magnitude* contributes to raise our admiration.

Hogarth's best known views refer to the beautiful in Lines.

THEORIES OF BEAUTY—BURKE.

Waving lines are more beautiful than straight lines, because they are more varied; and among waving lines, there is but one entitled to be called the Line of Beauty, the others bulging too much, and so being gross and clumsy, or straightening too much, and thereby becoming lean and poor. But the most beautiful line is the serpentine line, called, by Hogarth, the Line of Grace. This is the line drawn once round, from the base to the apex, of a long, slender cone. As contrasted with straight lines, the lines of beauty and grace possess an intrinsic power of pleasing. Hogarth produced numerous instances of the beauty of those forms, and inferred that objects were beautiful according as they could be admitted into composition. This doctrine, although denied by Alison, contains a portion of the truth.

BURKE's theory, contained in his *Essay on the Sublime and Beautiful*, is couched in a material phraseology. He says that beautiful objects have the tendency to produce *an agreeable relaxation of the fibres*. Thus, '*smooth* things are relaxing; *sweet* things, which are the *smooth* of taste, are relaxing too; and *sweet smells*, which bear a great affinity to *sweet tastes*, relax very remarkably.' 'We often apply the quality of *sweetness* metaphorically to *visual* objects;' and following out this *remarkable analogy of the senses*, he purposes 'to call *sweetness the beautiful of the taste.*'

His theory leads him to put an especial stress on the beauty of *smoothness*, a quality so essential to beauty, he says, that he cannot recollect anything beautiful but what is smooth. 'In trees and flowers, smooth leaves are beautiful; smooth slopes of earth in gardens; smooth streams in landscapes; smooth coats of birds and beasts in animal beauty; in fine women, smooth skins; and, in several sorts of ornamental furniture, smooth and polished surfaces.' The one-sidedness of this view was obvious enough. Smoothness is one element of beauty, in certain circumstances, and for obvious reasons. The smoothness and the softness of the animal body are connected with the pleasure of touch. The smoothness of polished surfaces is the condition of their brilliancy; an effect enhanced by sharp angles, although Burke alleges that he does not find any *natural* object that is angular, and at the same time beautiful. The 'smooth, shaven green' of well kept lawns is associated with the fit or the useful; it suggests the industry, attention, or art, bestowed upon it by the opulent and careful owner. The same smoothness and trim regularity, Stewart observes, would not make the same agreeable suggestions in a sheep walk, a deer park, or the neighbourhood of a venerable ruin. Again, in the moss-rose, the opposite of smoothness is beautiful.

It has been remarked by Price (and Dugald Stewart concurs in the remark) 'that Burke's general principles of beauty—smoothness, gradual variation, delicacy of make, tender colours, and such as insensibly melt into each other—*are strictly applicable to female beauty.*' Even in treating of the beauty of Nature, says Stewart, Burke's imagination always delights to repose on her softest and most feminine features; or, to use his own language, on 'such qualities as induce in us a sense of tenderness and affection, or some other passion the most nearly resembling them.'

ALISON'S work on *Taste* was published in 1790. The First Part of it is occupied with an analysis of what we feel when under the emotions of Beauty or Sublimity. He endeavours to show that this effect is something quite different from SENSE, being in fact, not a Simple, but a Complex Emotion, involving (1) the production of some Simple Emotion, or the exercise of some moral affection, and (2) a peculiar exercise of the Imagination.

The author occupies many pages in describing the nature of this peculiar exercise of Imagination, which must go along with the simple pleasure. When any object of sublimity or beauty is presented to the mind, every man is conscious, he says, of a train of thought being awakened analogous in character to the original object; and unless such a train be awakened, there is no æsthetic feeling. He illustrates the position by supposing first the case where something occurs to prevent the outgoing of the imagination, as when the mind is occupied with some incompatible feeling, for example, pain or grief, or a purely intellectual engrossment of attention. So, there may be characters wholly unsuited to this play of imagination, as there are others in whose minds it luxuriates. Again, there are associations that increase the exercise of imagination, and also the emotion of beauty. Such are the local associations of each one's life, and the historic associations whereby the interest of places is enhanced—Runnymede, Agincourt, to an Englishman; also the effect of poetry, music, and works of art in adding to the interest of natural objects and of historic events. The effect called Picturesqueness operates in the same direction, whether the occurrence of picturesque objects in a scene—an old tower in a deep wood—or the picturesque descriptions of poetry.

It is necessary to enquire farther into the distinctive nature of those trains of Imagination; or, wherein they differ from other trains. The author resolves the difference into these two circumstances: 1st, the nature of the Ideas or Conceptions themselves, and 2ndly, the Law of their Succession. On the first head, he remarks, that, while the great mass of our ideas excite no emotion whatever, the ideas of Beauty excite some Affection or Emotion —Gladness, Tenderness, Pity, Melancholy, Admiration, Power, Majesty, Terror; whence they may be termed *ideas of emotion.* On the second head,—the Law of Succession,—the ideas of imagination have an emotional character allied to the original emotion; the emotional keeping is preserved throughout.

The author adds a series of illustrations of the influences that further, or that arrest, the development of Sensibility and Taste, all tending to establish his two positions above given. On these positions, it may be remarked, that they evade, rather than explain, whatever difficulty may be on the subject; and that their value consists in illustrating the really important point that Imagination involves, as a part of its nature, the predominance of some emotion. When he says, that unless the imagination be free to operate, no feeling of beauty will arise in the presence of a beautiful object, he means only that we cannot be awakened to beauty, if the mind is preoccupied by some incompatible state; the possibility of imagination is the possibility of feeling.

He also assumes, without sufficient grounds, that the state of reverie is necessary to the emotion of beauty; that the mind cannot confine its thoughts to the original object, but must wander in quest of other objects capable of kindling the same emotion. Now, although this is a very natural and frequent effect of being once aroused to a strong emotion, there is no absolute necessity for it; nor would the emotion be excluded from the æsthetic class, although the thoughts were to be detained upon the beautiful object.

Such being his general doctrine, Alison applies it to explain the Sublimity and Beauty of the *Material World*. He starts with affirming positively that matter in itself, or as perceived by the senses, is unfit to produce any kind of emotion; the smell of a rose, the colour of scarlet, the taste of a pine-apple, are said to produce agreeable Sensations, but not agreeable Emotions. But the *sensible qualities may form associations with emotions or affections*, and become the *signs* for suggesting these to the mind. The author enumerates various classes of associations so formed. (1) The signs of Useful qualities, or the forms and colours of objects of utility, as a ship, suggest the pleasure of Utility. (2) The marks of Design, Wisdom, or Skill, suggest the emotions corresponding to those qualities. (3) Material appearances,—as the countenance, gesture, or voice of a human being,—suggest the human attributes, Power, Wisdom, Fortitude, Justice, Benevolence, &c., and the pleasurable emotion that their contemplation inspires. (4) There are appearances that suggest mental qualities by metaphorical or personifying resemblance; whence we speak of the Strength of the Oak, the Delicacy of the Myrtle, the Boldness of a Rock, the Modesty of the Violet. So there is some analogy between an ascending path and Ambition, a descending and Decay; between sunshine and Joy, darkness and Sorrow, silence and Tranquillity, morning and Hope, soft colouring and Gentleness of Character, slenderness of form and Delicacy of Mind.

He then discusses the Sublimity and Beauty of Sound. As regards simple sounds, he allows no intrinsically pleasing effect, and attributes all their influence to associations, of which he cites numerous examples. He considers, however, that the leading distinctions of sound,—Loud and Low, Grave and Acute, Long and Short, Increasing and Diminishing,—have general associations, the result of long experience of the conjoined qualities: thus loud sound is connected with Power and Danger, and so on.

Under Compound Sounds, he has to consider Music. He still resolves the pleasure of musical composition into associations. Each musical Key suggests a characteristic emotion, by imitating as nearly as possible the expression of that emotion. He allows that music cannot very specifically set forth any one passion; the assistance of Poetry is requisite to distinguish Ambition, Fortitude, Pity, &c. As to elaborate compositions and harmonies, their superiority over a simple air consists in suggesting the Skill, Invention, or Taste of the composer, and the performer.

The Beauty of *Colours* is also exclusively referred to their associations with a number of pleasing qualities. For example, White, the colour of Day, expresses cheerfulness and gaiety. Blue, the colour of the Heavens in serene weather, expresses serenity of mind; Green, the colour of the Earth in Spring, is associated with the delights of that season. These are general and prevailing associations. Others are more accidental, as Purple, the dress of kings, with royal authority; Red, in this country the uniform of the soldier, with military functions and prowess.

The author gives a more detailed explanation of the Sublimity and Beauty of *Forms*. Denying, as before, all intrinsic pleasure in any one form, he quotes a series of examples of their derived effects. Thus, the forms of bodies dangerous or powerful, as the weapons and insignia of war, are sublime. The forms of Trees are sublime as expressive of strength; still more so the rocks that have stood the storms and convulsions of ages. The sublimest of mechanical arts is Architecture, from the strength and durability of its productions; and the most sublime result of Architecture is the Gothic castle, which has resisted alike the desolations of time and the assaults of war. The sublime of Magnitude generally is referable to strength; while magnitude in height expresses Elevation and Magnanimity; in depth, Danger and Terror; in length, Vastness and Infinity; and in breadth, Stability.

In the Beauty of Forms, account must be taken (1) of angular lines, and (2) of winding or curve lines. The first are chiefly connected with bodies possessing Hardness, Strength, or Durability; the second (seen in the infancy and youth, both of plants and of animals) are expressive of Infancy, Tenderness, and Delicacy; and also the very important circumstance of Ease, as opposed to constraint, being the beauty of the bending river, of the vine wreathing itself about the elm, and so on.

From Simple Forms, he proceeds to Complex, which involve new considerations. In the first place, complex arrangements must have some *general character* [a feeble and inadequate mode of stating the condition of Harmony], in which he quotes largely from landscape Gardening. He applies the same rule to Complex Colours, which are beautiful only by their Expression; the beauty of Dress, for example, being altogether relative to the wearer and the circumstances.

In the next place, Composite Forms afford wide scope for the exhibition of Design, Fitness, and Utility. The beauty of Design he expounds at great length, and with indiscriminate application to the Useful Arts and to the Fine Arts. He descants upon the opposing demands for Uniformity and for Variety, the one a sign of Unity of Design, the other a sign of Elegant, or embellished Design. Beautiful compositions must include both. By *Fitness*, is meant the adaptation of means to Ends, also a source of beauty. He explains Proportion purely by reference to Fitness, and discusses the Orders of Architecture under this view. The beauty of architectural proportions is (1) the expression of Fitness of Support, (2) the expression of Fitness to the Character of the apartment, and (3) the Fitness for the particular purpose of the building. *Utility* also contributes to beauty, as in a clock or watch; this is our satisfaction at the attainment of valuable ends.

He then considers the Sublimity and Beauty of *Motion*, which he resolves into the expression of Power. Great power, able to overcome obstacles, is sublime; gentle, moderate, diminutive power inspires Tenderness, or Affection. Rapid motion, as indicating great power, is sublime; slow motion, by indicating gentle power, is beautiful. Motion in a Straight Line, if rapid, is sublime; if slow, beautiful. Motion in an Angular Line, expresses obstruction and imperfect power, and, considered in itself, is unpleasing, although in the case of Lightning, the impressiveness of the phenomenon redeems it. Motion in Curves is expressive of Ease, of Freedom, of Playfulness, and is beautiful.

The Beauty of the *Human Countenance and Form* is discussed at length. As regards the *Countenance*, the first point is Colour or Complexion. On general grounds, whiteness expresses Purity, Fineness, Gaiety; the dark complexion, Melancholy, Gloom, or Sadness. Clear and uniform colours suggest Perfection and Consistency; mixed and mottled complexions, Confusion and Imperfection. A bright Eye is significant of Happiness; a dim and turbid eye, of Melancholy. Colour has also an efficacy as suggesting Health or Disease; and a farther efficacy in expressing Dispositions of Mind; dark complexions being connected with Strength; fair complexions with Cheerfulness and Delicacy. The variable colours, or the changes of complexion, are still more decisively connected with states of mind; the blush of Modesty, the glow of Indignation, and so on. That there is no intrinsic power in colour seems to be shown by our being at one time pleased, and another time displeased with the same colour, as with the blush of modesty and the blush of guilt.

A like reasoning applied to the Forms of the Countenance, or the Features, points to the conclusion that their beauty depends on the expression of character and passion; we have one set of forms for the beauty of infancy and youth, another set for mature age; and so with the variable expression of states of feeling.

In reference to the *Human Form*, he argues against the principle of Proportion, and rests the beauty first, upon its Fitness as a machine; and secondly, on its Expression of mind and character. The account of Beauty of Attitude and of Gesture, on the same principles, follows and concludes the work. The closing summary is in these words:—' The Beauty and Sublimity which are felt in the various appearances of matter, are finally to be ascribed to their Expression of Mind; or to their being, either directly or indirectly, the signs of those qualities of mind which are fitted, by the constitution of our nature, to affect us with pleasing or interesting emotions.'

JEFFREY, in the article 'Beauty,' in the Encyclopædia Britannica, adopts substantially the theory of Alison. He states the theory thus:—' Our sense of beauty depends entirely on our previous experience of simpler pleasures or emotions, and consists in the *suggestion* of agreeable or interesting sensations with which we had formerly been made familiar by the direct and intelligible agency of our common sensibilities; and that vast variety of objects, to which we give the common name of beautiful, become entitled to that appellation, merely because they all possess the power of recalling or reflecting those sensations of which they have been the accompaniments, or with which they have been associated in our imagination by any other more casual bond of connexion.' He takes exception, however, to Alison's statement that the existence of a *connected train or series* of ideas, is an essential part of the perception of beauty; remarking that the effect of a beautiful object may be instantaneous and immediate, and that a train of ideas of emotion may accompany the perception of ugliness.

In answer to the question—What are the primary affections by whose suggestion we experience the feeling of beauty?—Jeffrey answers, all pleasing sensations and emotions whatsoever, and many that are, in their first incidence, painful. Every feeling agreeable to experience, to recall, or to witness, may become the source of beauty in any external thing that reminds us of that feeling.

It follows that we never can be *interested* in anything but the fortunes of sentient beings; that every present emotion must refer back to some past feeling of some mind. We may be actuated in the first instance by a pure organic stimulus; the pleasure at that stage is not beauty, it becomes so only by recollection, or mental reproduction.

The author gives a variety of examples of his doctrine. Female beauty is explained by being the signs of two sets of qualities; the first, youth and health: the second, innocence, gaiety, sensibility, intelligence, delicacy or vivacity. A common English landscape is beautiful through the picture of human happiness presented to the imagination by a variety of signs. A Highland scene of wild and rugged grandeur has for its leading impressions, romantic seclusion, and primeval simplicity; the sense of the Mighty Power that piled up the cliffs and rent the mountains; the many incidents of the life of former inhabitants; and the contrast of perishable humanity with enduring nature. The beauty of Spring is the renovation of life and joy to all animated beings.

After adducing, in support of the theory, examples of the arbitrary beauties of natural tastes and fashions, he follows Alison in adverting to the influence of similarity or analogy in giving interest to objects; which explains much of the interest of Poetry. He then notices the objection that, if beauty be only a reflexion of love, we should confound the two feelings under one name, and answers first, that beauty really does affect us in a manner not very different from love; secondly, the fact of being *reflected*, and not primitive, gives a character to the feelings in question; and thirdly, there is always present a real and direct perception, imparting a liveliness to the emotion of beauty.

Jeffrey argues strongly against Payne Knight's doctrine of the intrinsic beauty of colours. Even as regards the harmony and composition of colours, so much insisted on by artists and connoisseurs, he suspects no little pedantry and jargon; the laws of colouring will have their effect only with trained judges of the art, and through the force of associations. Apart from association, he will not admit that any distribution of tints or of light or shade bears a part in the effect of picture. He has the same utter scepticism as to the intrinsic pleasure of sounds, or the mere musical arrangement of sounds.

As inferences from the theory, Jeffrey specifies the substantial identity of the Sublime, the Beautiful and the Picturesque; and also the essentially relative nature of Taste. For a man himself, there is no taste that is either bad or false; the only difference is between much and little. The following sentence is a clue to the author's own individuality:—'Some who have cold affections, sluggish imaginations, and no habits of observation, can with difficulty discern beauty in anything; while others, who are full of kindness and sensibility, and who have been accustomed to attend to all the objects around them, feel it almost in everything.'

DUGALD STEWART has devoted to the discussion of Beauty a series of Essays, making a large part of a volume, entitled *Philosophical Essays*, published in 1810. He agrees with the greater part of Alison's views on the influence of association in determining the beauty of Colour, Form, and Motion, but maintains, against Alison, a primitive organic pleasure of colour. As to the curve line, or line of beauty according to Hogarth, he admits only 'that this line seems, from an examination of many of Nature's most pleasing productions, to be one of her most favourite forms.' He gives examples of Order, Fitness, Utility, Symmetry, &c., constituting beauty. He discusses at length the Picturesque, in criticising the theory of Price. With reference to the view that would restrict beauty to mind, and make it exclusively a mental reflexion from primitive effects of matter, he repeats his claim for the intrinsic beauty of objects of sight: the visible object, if not the physical cause, is the occasion of the pleasure; and it is on the eye alone that the organic impression is made. He strongly repudiates any idea or essence of Beauty, any one fact pervading all things called beautiful, as savouring of the exploded theory of general Ideas.

Stewart's theory of the SUBLIME principally takes account of the element of Height, the efficacy of which he traces to a continued exercise of actual power to counteract gravity. To this he adds the associations of Height with the rising and setting of the heavenly bodies, and also with the position assigned by all nations to their Divinities. He supposes that the idea of the Terrible may add to the sublimity, and speaks of the 'silent and pleasing awe' experienced in a Gothic cathedral. The sublimity of Horizontal Extent arises entirely from the association between a commanding prospect and an elevated position; extent of view being, in fact, a measure of height. The sublime of Depth is increased by the awfulness of the situation. The celestial vault owes its sublimity to the idea of architectural support ('this majestical roof'), enhanced by the amplitude of space and the sidereal contents. The Ocean combines unfathomable depth with sympathetic dread, and the power of its waves and waters; there being numerous superadded associations.

Mr. RUSKIN, in his *Modern Painters*, vol. ii., has discussed the principles of Beauty. He puts forward as the leading attributes of what he calls Typical Beauty (opposed to Vital Beauty), Infinity, Unity, Repose, Symmetry, Purity, Moderation. There are superadded, in Vital Beauty, all the considerations relative to function, or the adaptation to ends. The author raises Art to a kind of religion; every one of these attributes is connected with the Deity: Infinity, the Type of Divine Incomprehensibility; Unity, the Type of the Divine Comprehensiveness; Repose, the Type of Divine Permanence; Symmetry, the Type of Divine Justice; Purity, the Type of Divine Energy; Moderation, the Type of Government by Law. It is in detached and incidental observations, rather than in the systematic exposition, that Mr. Ruskin adverts to the ultimate analysis of Beauty. He defends the æsthetic character of the two senses—Sight and Hearing—on the grounds of their permanence and self-sufficiency; and as regards the pleasures of Sight, he takes notice of their unselfishness, to which he adds purity and spirituality. He contests Alison's theory, without being aware that many of his own explanations coincide with that theory. His view of association is that it operates more in adding force to Conscience, than in the sense of beauty. He contends for the intrinsic and even exclusive beauty of curvature in Form; and holds that the value of straight lines is to bring out the beauty of curves by contrast. The curve is a type of infinity. Something analogous belongs to the gradation of shades and colours, which gradation is their infinity.

The general tendency of Mr. Ruskin's speculations in Art is towards a severe asceticism, a kind of moral code, for which his only conceivable justification is the tendency of Art to cultivate pleasures free from the taint of rivalry and selfishness. To make this object perfect, no work of Art should ever inspire even ideal longings for sensual or other monopolist pleasures; an elevation both impossible and futile. Where to draw the line between the

CAUSES OF LAUGHTER.

interesting and the elevated, in the above meaning, must be a matter of opinion.

THE LUDICROUS.

1. The Ludicrous is connected with Laughter.

The outburst, termed Laughter, has many causes. Not to dwell upon purely physical influences,—as cold, tickling, hysteria,—the exuberance of mere animal spirits chooses this among other violent manifestations, from which we may conclude that it is an expression of agreeable feeling. Any great and *sudden* accession of pleasure, in the vehemence of the stimulation, chooses laughter as one outlet; the great intensity of the nervous wave is marked by respiratory convulsions, which are supposed (by Spencer) to check the ingress of oxygen, and thus moderate the excitement. The outburst of Liberty in a young fresh nature, after a time of restraint, manifests itself in wild uproarious mirth and glee. The emotion of Power, suddenly gratified, has a special tendency to induce laughter.

2. The most commonly assigned cause of the Ludicrous is *Incongruity;* but all incongruities are not ludicrous.

Inequality of means to ends, discord, disproportion, falsehood, are incongruous, but not necessarily ludicrous. An idiot ruling a nation is highly incongruous, but not laughable. The incongruity that leads to laughter is a peculiar sort, marked by a quality that deserves to be accounted the generic fact, and not a mere qualification of another fact.

3. The occasion of the Ludicrous is the Degradation of some person or interest possessing dignity, in circumstances that excite no other strong emotion.

When any one suddenly tumbles into the mud, the spectator is disposed to laugh, unless the misery of the situation causes pity instead. Should the victim, by pretentious attire, or pomposity of manner, or from any other reason, inspire contempt or dislike, the laughter is uncontrolled. Putting one into a fright, or into a rage (if not dangerous), giving annoyance by an ill smell, attaching filth in any way, are common modes of laughable degradation. An intoxicated man is ludicrous, if he does not excite pity, or disapprobation.

In the Dunciad, a ludicrous effect is aimed at by describing the flagellation of the criminals in Bridewell as happening after morning service at chapel. To most minds, the ludicrousness of the conjunction would be overborne by another sentiment.

Amid the various theories of Laughter, this pervading fact is more or less recognized. According to Aristotle, Comedy is an illustration of worthless characters, not, indeed, in reference to every vice, but to what is *mean;* the laughable has to do with what is deformed or mean; it must be a deformity or meanness not painful or destructive (so as to produce pity, fear, anger, or other strong feelings). He would have been nearer the mark if he had expressed it as causing something to appear mean that was formerly dignified; for to depict what is already under a settled estimate of meanness, has little power to raise a laugh: it can merely be an occasion of reflecting our own dignity by comparison. Some of Quintilian's expressions are more happy. 'A saying that causes laughter is generally based on false reasoning (some play upon words); has always something low in it; is often purposely sunk into buffoonery; *is never honourable to the subject of it.*' 'Resemblances give great scope for jests, and, especially, resemblance to something *meaner or of less consideration.*' Campbell (*Philosophy of Rhetoric*), in reply to Hobbes, has maintained that laughter is associated with the perception of oddity, and not necessarily with degradation or contempt. He produces instances of the laughable, and challenges any one to find anything contemptuous in them. 'Many,' he says, 'have laughed at the queerness of the comparison in these lines,—

"For rhyme the rudder is of verses,
With which, like ships, they steer their courses."

who never dream't that there was any person or party, practice or opinion, derided in them.' Now, on the contrary, there is an obvious degradation of the poetic art; instead of working under the mysterious and lofty inspiration of the Muse, the poet is made to compose by means of a vulgar mechanical process.

In the theory of Hobbes, 'Laughter is a sudden glory arising from sudden conception of some eminency in ourselves, by comparison with the infirmity of others, or with our own formerly.' In other words, it is an expression of the pleasurable feeling of superior power. Now, there are many cases where this will afford a complete explanation, as in the laugh of victory, ridicule, derision, or contempt, against persons that we ourselves have humiliated. But we can also laugh sympathetically, or where the act of degrading redounds to the glory of some one else, as in the enjoyment of comic literature generally, where we have no part in causing the humiliation that we laugh at. Moreover, laughter can be excited against classes, parties, systems, opinions, institutions, and even inanimate things that by personification have contracted associations of dignity; of which last, the couplet of Hudibras upon sunrise, is a sufficient example. And, farther, the definition of Hobbes is still more unsuitable to Humour, which is counted something genial and loving, and as far removed as may be, from self-glorification and proud exultation at other men's discomfiture. Not, however, that there is not even in the most genial humour, an element of degradation, but that the indignity is disguised, and, as it were, oiled, by some kindly infusion, such as would not consist with the unmitigated glee of triumphant superiority.

Kant makes the ridiculous to arise from the sudden collapse of a long-raised and highly-wrought expectation. He should have added, supposing the person not affected with painful disappointment, anger, fear, or some other intense emotion.

4. The pleasure of degrading something dignified may be referred (1) to the sentiment of Power, direct or sympathetic, or (2) to the release from a state of Constraint.

In the deepest analysis, the two facts are the same; there is in both, a joyful elation of rebound or relief from a state of comparative depression or inferiority. In such cases as have been described, the more obvious reference is to the sentiment of Power or superiority. In another class of cases, we may best describe the result as a release from Constraint.

Under this last view, the Comic is a reaction from the Serious. The dignified, solemn, and stately attributes of things require a certain portion of rigid constraint; and if we are suddenly relieved from this position, the rebound of hilarity ensues, as with children set free from school. The Serious in life is made up of labour, difficulty, hardship and all the necessities of our position, giving rise to the severe and constraining institutions of government, law, morality, education, religion. Whatever strikes awe or terror into men's minds is serious; whatever prostrates, even for a moment, an awe-striking personage, is a delightful relief. A degrading conjunction may have the effect, as when Lucian vulgarizes the gods by mean employment. But then we must have ceased to entertain a genuine homage for the dignities thus prostrated; or we must be willing to forego for a moment our sentiment of regard. The Comic is fed by false or faded dignities; by affectation and hypocrisy; by unmeaning and hollow pomp. Carlyle's Teufelsdröckh was convulsed with laughter once in his life, and the occasion was Richter's suggesting a *cast-iron king*.

The MORAL SENSE is discussed under Ethics, Part I. Chap. III.

BOOK IV.

THE WILL.

CHAPTER I.

PRIMITIVE ELEMENTS OF VOLITION.

1. THE Primitive Elements of the Will have been stated to be (1) the Spontaneity of Movement, and (2) the Link between Action and Feeling, grounded in Self-conservation. In the maturing or growth of the Will, there is an extensive series of Acquisitions, under the law of Retentiveness or Contiguity.

THE SPONTANEITY OF MOVEMENT.

2. Spontaneity expresses the fact that the active organs may pass into movement, apart from the stimulus of Sensation.

This doctrine has been already explained, and supported by a series of proofs (p. 14). The impulse is not stimulation, but a certain condition of the nervous centres and the muscles, connected with natural vigour, nourishment, and rest. The exuberant movements of young and active animals are referable to natural spontaneity, rather than to the excitement of sensation. The movements of delirium and disease have no dependence whatever on sensation, but on the morbid congestion of the nerve centres. In the example of parturition, the uterus is prepared by the growth of muscular fibres, which, on reaching their maturity, contract of their own accord, and expel the fœtus; there is no special stimulation

ISOLATION OF SPONTANEOUS DISCHARGES. 319

at the moment of birth, but merely the ripening of the active mechanism.

3. The muscles are distinguished into local groups, or Regions.

It is convenient to study the operation of spontaneity in the separate groups of muscles.

The Locomotive Apparatus is in every animal the largest muscular department. In vertebrate animals, this involves the limbs, with their numerous muscles, and the trunk of the body, which chimes in with the movements of the extremities. When the central vigour of the system is copious, it overflows in movements of locomotion; the infant can throw out its legs and arms, and swing the trunk and head.

An important group is connected with the movements of the Mouth and Jaw. The Tongue is distinguished for flexibility and for independence, and we may consider its muscles as forming a group. The muscles of the Larynx, or voice, are also grouped. Vocal spontaneity is a well-marked fact; there being numerous occasions when vocal outbursts have no other cause but the exuberant vigour. Other groups are found in the Abdomen and Perinæum.

4. It is necessary for the commencement of voluntary power, that the organs to be commanded separately, should be capable of Isolation from the outset.

The grouping of the muscles is shown by the parts being moved in company, as when the fingers are simultaneously closed or extended. It is necessary, however, that this grouping should not be rigid or absolute, otherwise no separate movement could ever be acquired. Through distinctness of nervous connexions, there must be a possibility of spontaneous impulses affecting one without the others. A remarkable instance of primitive isolation, such as to prepare the way for voluntary command, is seen of the forefinger; the child, from the first, moves it apart, while the three others go together. The isolation of the thumb is less than of the forefinger, and greater than of the other fingers. There is very little isolation of the toes; yet their grouping is not inseparable, as we may see from the instances of acquired power to write and perform other operations by the feet. The limbs are grouped for the locomotive rhythm; but they are also spontaneously moved in separation. The upper limbs, or arms, in man, have a certain tendency to common action, together with tendencies to individual action. The two sides of the face are moved together in a very powerful conjunction, yet not without occasional spontaneous separation, so as to give a starting point for voluntary separation. The chief example of indissoluble union is the two eyes. Also, there is a tendency in the different parts of the face to go together in characteristic expressions—eyebrows, mouth, nose—but not without that occasional isolation through which we can acquire a separate control of each part.

That spontaneous impulses should be directed, in occasional isolation, upon all these various organs, separately controlled in the maturity of the will, is thus the first step in our voluntary education. The spontaneity of the moving system, at the outset, is various and apparently capricious; at one time, it overtakes a large number of muscles, at other times, a smaller number; it does not always unite in the same combinations: and out of this variety, we can snatch the beginnings of isolated control.

In parts where there are no spontaneous movements at the beginning, there can never arise voluntary movements. Such is the case with the two ears, which are rarely commanded by human beings. In them the failure to acquire voluntary control must be ascribed to the immobility of the parts, and not merely to the absence of isolating spontaneity.

5. It is requisite to show in what way the spontaneous discharges may vary in degree, through the wide compass attained by our voluntary energies.

Our command of the voluntary organs involves a great range of gradation, rising to a violent sudden blow, almost like an explosion. In order to account for these violent exertions, by the hypothesis of spontaneity converted into will, we have to show that there may be corresponding energy in the spontaneous discharges.

(1) The Natural vigour of the system, nurtured and pent up, leads to outbursts of very considerable energy. We see this in the daily experience of robust children and youth. The explosiveness of the boy or girl relieved from constraint is of the kind suited to any violent effort. To leap ditches, to throw down barriers, and displace heavy bodies, are what the system, in its mere spontaneity, is adequate to achieve.

(2) The vigour may be greatly increased by Excitement; that is, an unusual flow of blood to the active organs, through what are termed Stimulants. We usually give this name to drugs, such as alcohol, but the most usual and the readiest

stimulation is mere exercise, and especially rapid movements continued for a little time. The exertion of any part determines an increased flow of blood to that part, at the expense of other organs; a quick run makes the circulation course to the muscles, away from the stomach, brain, and other parts. When the accumulation of blood is at its maximum, there is a corresponding energy of the movements.

(3) Stimulation may arise through *mental* causes, as pleasure and pain: it being understood that these are not abstractions, but embodiments. According to the law of Self-conservation, an access of pleasure is an access of vital power, shown in some of the forms of increased activity, muscular movement being one of the most usual. An acute and sudden thrill of pleasure,—as in the overthrow of a rival, the conquering of a difficulty, the view of an imposing spectacle,—is physically accompanied with elation of body; the robust frame dances with joy. The profuse expenditure at that moment is equal to the requirements of a great occasion. He that has overcome one barrier, in the flush of success, is stronger for the next.

The pleasure of exercise, to a fresh and vigorous system, supplies a new stimulus.

(4) Although, by the law of Conservation, pain is accompanied by a lowering of energy, yet in the exceptional form of the acute and pungent smart, not crushing or severe, a painful application may increase the active energies for a time. The nervous currents awakened by a pungent stimulus, as the smart of a whip, find no adequate vent except in muscular activity, and to that they tend.

It is well known that Opposition may act as an efficacious stimulant. An invincible resistance indeed both stops progress, and suspends the motive to proceed; but a small conquerable opposition provokes a reaction, with augmentation of power. The effect is a complex one. Part of it is due to the stimulus of the shock of obstruction, which operates like an acute smart; and part to the flush consequent on a successful struggle. The feelings connected with our desires, and the emotions of pride, humiliation, and anger, complete the influence of the situation.

These various circumstances are adduced as a sufficient explanation of the flexibility and compass of our spontaneity. The rise of one or other of these various stimulations produces, in the first instance, an outburst of active energy; and among the associations constituting the mature will, there are formed links of connexion between strong exertions and the occasions for them. The young horse needs the spur and whip to prepare him for a leap; after a time, the sight of the barrier or the ditch is enough to evoke the additional impetus. One of the aptitudes most signally absent in infancy is the power of increasing the efforts so as to overcome a difficulty.

It should be remarked that although, in our mature volition, we can, on demand, originate a very rapid movement, as in preventing a breakage, we cannot suddenly exert a very great momentum, as in striking a heavy blow. A little time must be allowed to work up the system to a higher pitch of activity. Mere association cannot command, in a moment, a massive expenditure; we must first resort to the stimulants of active power, and chiefly to the exciting agency of a continuing effort, as in making a run before jumping a high bar. Combatants strike their heaviest blows after the fight has lasted for some time.

LINK OF FEELING AND ACTION.

6. As Spontaneity is not necessarily preceded by Feeling, there must be some medium for uniting it with our feelings. The requisite Link is believed to be given under the Law of Self-conservation.

The doctrine connecting pleasure with increased, and pain with diminished, vitality, gives a starting point for the union of action and feeling. A state of pleasure, by its connexion with increased vitality in general, involves increased muscular activity in particular. A shock of pain in lowering the collective forces of the system, saps the individual force of muscular movement.

7. From the one mental root, named Self-conservation, there grow two branches, which diverge widely, and yet occasionally come together. The first branch includes the proper manifestations or Expression of Emotion.

The Emotional manifestations have been already described as consisting in part of movements of all degrees of force or intensity; thus affording at least one connexion between feeling and action. Under pleasure, we put forth a variety of gesticulations; and under pain, we collapse into a more or less passive condition (the exceptional operation of acute pain being left out of account). But these effects of movement, although distinct from spontaneity, are not of a kindred with volition. The movements of expression under pleasure appear to be selected according to a law pointed out by Mr. Herbert Spencer, namely, the natural priority of muscles small in calibre and often exercised, as in the expression of the face, the breathing, the voice, &c.; whereas the movements selected in volition are such as promote pleasure or abate pain.

It is a proper question to consider whether these emotional movements are not of themselves sufficient to account for the beginning of volition, without our having recourse to Spontaneity, or action unpreceded by any feeling. The answer is, first, that spontaneous movements being established as a fact, are already in the field for the purpose. Secondly, in them, and not in the emotional movements, do we most readily obtain the *isolated* promptings that are desiderated in the growth of the will. The emotional wave almost invariably affects a whole group of movements. Still, it is possible that these movements of emotion may occasionally come into the service.

8. The second branch or outgoing of Self-conservation is more directly suited for the growth of Volition. Movements being supposed already begun by Spontaneity (or in other ways), and to concur with pleasure; the effect of the pleasure, on its physical side, is to raise the whole vital energy, these movements included.

It is necessary to show that this (with the obverse) is a law of the constitution, operating all through life, as well as at the commencement of the education of the Will.

It is known that any tasted delight urges us, by an immediate stimulus, to continue the movements that have procured it. Moving from the cold towards an agreeable warmth, our pace is quickened as of its own accord. We do not deliberate and formally resolve to go on; we are at once laid hold of by what seems a primordial link of our mental system, and move to the increasing pleasure. The act of eating is another example. The relish of the food, by an immediate response, adds energy to mastication. Animals and children, who have departed least from the primary cast of nature, conspicuously exhibit the augmented activity following on a tasted pleasure.

An apparent exception to the law occurs in the sedative effect of some pleasures, chiefly such as are massive rather than acute. A voluminous and agreeable warmth soothes down an activity already begun, and inclines us to repose and to sleep. But in such cases, the law is disguised merely, and not suspended. The warmth really promotes the activity suited to its own fruition, as soon as that activity is singled out and connected with the pleasure; which activity consists in maintaining a rigid and quiescent attitude. The occupant of a position of comfortable snugness may seem to be quiescent and passive; let any one, however, attempt to dispossess him, and he will put forth energy in resistance. Still, the fact must be admitted that the voluminous pleasures are quieting and serene; they do not provoke unbounded Desire and pursuit, like the more acute enjoyments, but rather lull to indolence. And the explanation appears to be, that the physical state corresponding to them, is inimical to vehement, intense, or concentrated activity.

Another exception to the rousing efficacy of pleasure is the exhaustion of the strength. All voluntary pursuit supposes a certain freshness of the active organs, as a concurring requisite. In the extremity of fatigue, the most acute pleasure will fail as a motive.

The obverse position is equally well supported by our experience. Allowing for the exception of the acute smart, the ordinary effect, or collateral consequence of pain, is cessation of energy. If any present movement is bringing us pain, there is a self-acting remission or suspension of the damaging career. The mastication is arrested, in the full sway of its power, by a bitter morsel turning up. The most effectual cure of over-action is the inflicting of pain.

Hence, whenever the cessation of a movement at work is the remedy for pain, the evil cures itself by the general tendency of self-conservation. The point is to explain how pain, in opposition to its nature, initiates and maintains a strenuous activity for procuring its abolition. In this case, the operating element may be shown to be, not the pain, but the *relief from pain*. When in a state of suffering, there occurs a moment of remission, that remission has all the elating and quickening effect of pleasure; as regards the agency of the will, pleasure and the remission of pain are the same thing. Relief in fact or in prospect, is the real stimulant to labour for vanquishing pain and misery.

It is an undoubted fact, that in a depressed tone of mind, with no hope or prospect of relief, we are indisposed to active measures of any sort. This represents the proper tendency of pain. The activity begins with some conscious amelioration, and is maintained and increased, as that amelioration increases.

CHAPTER II.

GROWTH OF VOLUNTARY POWER.

1. THE elements of voluntary power being assumed as (1) Spontaneity and (2) Self-conservation, we have to exemplify the connexion of these into the matured will, by a process of education.

The distinctive aptitude of the mature will is to select at once the movements necessary to attain a pleasure or relieve a pain, as when we raise to the nostrils a sweet violet, or move away from something malodorous. There is no such power possessed by us at birth.

2. The process of acquirement may be described generally as follows:—At the outset, there happens a coincidence, purely accidental, between a pleasure and a movement (of Spontaneity) that maintains and increases it; or between a pain and a movement that alleviates or removes it; by the link of Self-conservation, the movement bringing pleasure, or removing pain, is sustained and augmented. Should this happen repeatedly, an adhesive growth takes place, through which the feeling can afterwards command the movement.

To exemplify this position, we will now review, in order, the primitive feelings, and the volitions grafted upon them.

Commencing with the Muscular Feelings, we may remark upon the pleasures of Exercise. Spontaneous movements occurring in a fresh and vigorous system give pleasure; and with the pleasure there is an increased vitality extending to the movements, which are thereby sustained and increased; the pleasure as it were feeding itself. Out of the primitive force of self-conservation, we have the very effect that characterizes the will, namely, movement or action for the attainment of pleasure.

The pains of Fatigue give the obverse instance. The immediate effect of pain being abated energy, the movements will suffer their share of the abatement and come to a stand; a remedy for the evil as effectual as any resolution of the mature will.

These instances do not indicate any progress in our voluntary education. Let us next take the pains of Muscular Restraint, or of Spontaneity held in by obstacles, as when an animal is hedged into a narrow chamber. Various writhings are the natural consequence of the confined energies; at last some one movement takes the animal to an opening, and it bolts out with explosive vehemence. When this experience is repeated several times, an association will be formed between the state of constraint and the definite movements that lead to a release; so that the proper course shall be taken at once, and without the writhings and uncertainties attending the first attempts. As soon as this association is complete, we have a step in the career of voluntary acquirement.

Proceeding next to the Sensations proper, we begin with Organic Life. Among organic acute pains generally, we may single out the instructive case of a painful contact, as with a hot or a sharp instrument. The remedy is to retract the member; and people are apt to suppose, erroneously, that we do this by instinct. Now, it is true that a painful pinch will induce, by a reflex process, a convulsive movement of the part; while, as a part of the emotional wave, there will be a stir over the whole body. But there is no certainty that the reflex movement would be the remedial one; it might be the very opposite. Supposing the limb contracted, the reflex stimulus would probably throw it out; and if the sharp point lay in the way, there might be a much worse injury. The process of education would be this. Some one movement would be found to concur with diminished pain; that movement would be sustained by the general elation of relief; other movements increasing the pain would be sapped and arrested. A single experience of this kind would go for little; a few repetitions of the suitable coincidence would initiate a contiguous association, gradually ripening into a full coherence; and the one single movement of retraction would be chosen on the instant the pain was felt. That may appear an uncertain and bungling way of attaining the power of ridding ourselves of a hot cinder; and the more likely course would seem to be the possession of an instinct under the guise of a reflex action. But if we have an instinct for one class of pains, why have we not the same for others? For example, the pain of cramp in the leg, suggests to us no remedy. Only after many fruitless movements, does there occur the one that alleviates the suffering. The fair interpretation is that we have too little experience of this pain to acquire the proper

VOLITIONAL GROWTHS IN THE SENSATIONS.

mode of dealing with it; while the painful contacts with the skin are so numerous from the beginning of life, that our education is forced on and is early completed.

The Sensations of the Lungs may be referred to. Respiration is a reflex act, under voluntary control. The painful sensation of most frequent occurrence is that arising from deficient or impure air. The primitive effect of pain is the opposite of the remedy; for, instead of collapsing into inactivity, the lungs must be aided by increased breathing energy. How is this attained in the first instance? The only assignable means is some accidental exertion of the respiratory muscles followed by relief, and maintained by the new power accruing to the general system. The infant is in all likelihood unequal to the effort of forced breathing. This is perhaps one of the deficiencies of the uneducated will of childhood, rendering life more precarious at its early stages.

The augmented energy from pure air, suddenly encountered, would directly lead to an augmented respiration. The voluntary acquisition of the command of the lungs would, in this case, be a more apparent offshoot from the primary instinct.

Every sentient creature contracts many volitional habits in connexion with Warmth and Chillness. Animals soon learn to connect the crouching attitude with increased warmth. Other devices are fallen upon, as lying close together, and creeping into holes and shelters. I cannot say how far even the intelligent quadrupeds associate relief from chillness with a quick run. The lesson is one very much opposed to the primary effect of the sensation, which, in its character of massive pain, damps and depresses the energies.

The sensations of the Alimentary Canal are rich in voluntary associations. Sucking is said to be purely reflex in the new-born infant; swallowing is performed by involuntary muscles, and is always reflex. The child put to the nipple commences to suck by a reflex stimulus of voluntary muscles; the act being one of considerable complication, involving a co-operation of the mouth (which has to close round the nipple), the tongue (which applies itself to the opening of the nipple, making an air-tight contact), and the chest (which performs an increased inspiration, determining the flow of the milk when the tongue is pulled away). Being a conscious effect, operated by muscles all voluntary, it comes immediately under the fundamental law we are considering; the stimulus arising from the nourishment heightens the activity, until the point of satiety is reached, when a new and depressing sensibility comes into play, and induces cessation. Two powers, however, are at work; the nourishment received permanently increases the active vigour; the sensation of satiety has to counterwork this, by the temporary depression due to stomachic fulness. Probably at first infants glut the stomach too much before the depression arrests their sucking activity, in the face of the general stimulation brought about by the nourishment; very frequently they are withdrawn from the breast before ceasing of themselves. So far we have a reflex act controlled by the power of self-conservation; the only supposable education is the giving over at the extreme point of satiety. But in the next stage, there is room for voluntary acquirements of a high order. The applying the mouth to the breast under the sensation of hunger is a somewhat complex arrangement; it involves an association with the sight of the breast and the nipple, as well as with movements for approaching it. In fact, we have here a branch of our education in perceiving distance, or in connecting visible magnitudes with approaching and receding movements; an education that doubtless commences in the most interesting cases, and extends itself gradually over the whole sphere of action.

In Mastication, the progress of voluntary power may be stated to advantage. The powerful sensations of relish and taste, concurring with the spontaneity of the tongue (probably the most moveable and independent member of the whole system), and prompting a continuing movement, would be the beginning of a connexion, soon ripened, between the contact of a morsel of food and the definite acts of pressing it to the palate, and moving it about. The infant is unable to masticate: a morsel put into its mouth at first usually tumbles out. But if there occur spontaneous movements of the tongue, mouth, or jaw, giving birth to a strong relish, these movements are sustained, and begin to be associated with the sensations; so that after a time there grows up a firm connexion. The favouring circumstances are these:— the sensations are powerful; and the movements are remarkable for various and isolated spontaneity: the tongue and the mouth are the organs of all others prone to detached and isolated exertions.

The operation of a sour or bitter taste presents the case from the other side. The primary effect is to suspend the action of the organs; the mere infant can do no more. The spitting out of a nauseous morsel is a complex and a later acquisition.

The voluntary command of the lower extremity of the alimentary canal is wanting in infancy, and must be preceded by an artificial sensibility in favour of the retention of the excreta.

The pleasurable and painful sensations of Smell come into relationship with the inhalation and exhalation of air by the nostrils. The initiatory coincidence is not with the action of the lungs alone, but with the closure of the mouth also. Such coincidences are necessarily rare, and all acquirements that pre-suppose them are tardy. The act of sniffing is probably not attained before the third or fourth year, and often then by the help of instruction. It would be interesting to ascertain the period of this acquirement in the dog.

The sensations of Touch serving as antecedents in volition are numerous and important. The greater number, however, are of the class of intermediate sensibilities, as in the industrial arts; smoothing a surface, for example. The two great ultimate sensibilities of Touch, are the pleasure of the soft and warm contact, and the pain of pungent irritation of the skin. Both these are operative as volitional guides and stimuli, and, in both, connexions with definite movements, unformed at first, arise in the course of our voluntary education.

In the human infant, and in the infancy of the lower animals, the feeling of the warm contact with the mother is unquestionably a great power; the transition from the absence to the presence of the state is second only to the stimulus of nourishment; the rise of vital activity corresponding to it is, in all likelihood, very great. Whatever movements tend to bring on or heighten this state, may expect to be encouraged by the consequent elation of tone. Now, these movements are part of the locomotive group, which spontaneity brings into frequent play: and coincidences will readily arise between them and the attained delight of contact; the young quadruped succeeds by locomotion, the infant by thrusting out its limbs at first, and afterwards by more difficult movements, as turning in bed. If there were any one definite movement that on all occasions determined the transition from the cold naked state to the warm touch, a very few spontaneous concurrences with that movement would cement an effectual connexion. There is, however, scarcely any movement of this kind, suitable to all positions. One or two modes of attaining warmth are tolerably uniform, and therefore soon acquired; as bringing the limbs close to the body. A somewhat complicated adjustment is needed in most circumstances, involving the external perception of the eye—namely, moving up to the warm body of the mother: the young quadruped learns the lesson in a short time; the bird is even more precocious; while the human infant is very backward, and occupies weeks or months in the acquisition.

The pungent and painful sensations of Touch include the case already touched on, the retraction of any part from the shock of pain. This remedy being a simple and nearly uniform action, of a kind ready to occur in the course of spontaneity, we may expect to find it associated with the painful feeling at a comparatively early date. So early do we find it, that we are apt to regard it as an instinct. The same class of sensations includes the discipline of the whip. As an acutely painful feeling, the smart of the whip has two conflicting effects; it irritates the nerves, causing spasmodic movements, and it depresses vital power on the whole. If the stimulation of the smart predominates in a vigorous animal, the effect of the whip would be to increase activity in general; hence if the animal is running, its speed is quickened. If the crushing effect of the pain predominates, the existing movements are arrested. Such are the primitive tendencies of an acute smart; and even in the educated animal, the application of the whip is best understood if in harmony with these. To quicken a laggard, the acute prick, not severe, is the most directly efficacious course; to quiet down a too active or prancing steed, a shock amounting to depression of power is more useful; the curb has this kind of efficacy. To make the animal fall into a particular pace, the whip is used with the effect of stimulating movements, in the hope that a variation may occur, and not merely an increase of degree: if the desired movement arise, the torment ceases; the animal being supposed to connect mentally the movement with the cessation. A certain age must be attained before a horse will answer to discipline by changing its movements under the whip, and abiding by the one that brings immunity. It must have passed several stages beyond the instinctive situation to arrive at this point. An interval has elapsed, during which the animal has learnt consciously to seek an escape from pain; in point of fact to generalize its experiences of particular pains and particular movements of relief, and to connect *any pain* with movements and the hope of relief. A certain progress, both physical and intellectual, is requisite to this consummation.

The pleasures and pains of Sound have little peculiarity. If a pleasant sound is heard, some movements will be found favourable to the effect, others adverse; the first are likely to be sustained, the others arrested. An animal, with the power of locomotion, runs away from a painful sound; the retreat being guided by the relief from the pain. A child learns to become still under a pleasant sound; there is a felt increase in the pleasure from the fixed attitude, and a felt diminution from restlessness.

In Sight, we have a remarkable example of sensations uniformly influenced by movements. The pleasure of light is very strong; at all events, the attraction of the eye for a light is great. Indeed, this is a case where the stimulus given to the active members appears to exceed the pleasure of the sensation; the eye is apt to remain fixed on a light even when the feeling has passed into pain, being a kind of aberration from the proper course of the will. Now, when the infant, gazing on a flame, is deprived of the sensation, by the motion of the light to one side, being at first unable to follow, for want of an established connection between the departing sensation and the requisite turn of the head, it must wait on random spontaneity for a lucky hit. Should a chance movement of the head tend to recover the flame, that movement will be sustained by the power of the stimulation; movements that lose the light would not be sustained, but rather arrested. And, inasmuch as the same movement always suits the same case—the taking of the light to one side, being a definite optical effect, and the motion of the head for regaining it being always uniform—the ground is clear for an early and rapid association between the two facts, the optical experience and the muscular movement. The situation is a very general one, applying to every kind of interesting spectacle, and involving a comprehensive volitional aptitude, the command of the visual organs at the instigation of visual pleasures. I have supposed the rotation of the head to be the first attained means of recovering objects shifted away from direct vision; but the movements of the eyes themselves will sooner or later come into play. It is evident enough, however, from the observation of children, that the power of recovering a visible thing is not arrived at during the first months.

This example is instructive in various ways. The connexion of a pleasurable stimulus with heightened power has been hitherto assumed as not restricted to muscular movement; but as comprising, in undefined proportions, both muscular power and the organic functions. The acute smart, in its first or enlivening stage, may be affirmed with certainty to increase muscular energy, and to diminish the healthy vital functions. Perhaps the pungent stimulus of light is mainly expended on muscular augmentation; which alone is of service in the forming of the will.

Connected with sight is another case of great interest, the adjustment of the eye to changes of distance. The guiding sensation in this case is the *distinctness* of the image; the infant must be aware of the difference between confused and clear vision, and must derive pleasure in passing from the one to the other. Under any theory of vision, Berkeleian or other, some time must elapse ere this difference be felt; everything at the outset being confused. As soon as the sense of a clear image is attained, the child may enter on the course of connecting the spontaneity of the adjusting muscles with the agreeable experience; as in other cases, a confirming association may be expected to follow soon, the movements concerned being few and uniform.

The foregoing review of the Sensations comprises several of the Appetites—Exercise, Repose, and Hunger. The feelings of approaching Sleep are very powerful, but the state is one that provides for itself, by pure physical sequence, without special education. The resistance offered when one is prevented from going to sleep, or is reluctantly awakened, is not a primitive manifestation; the child only manifests discomfort by the appropriate emotional expressions.

3. The second step in the growth of the Will is the uniting of movements with intermediate Ends.

This supposes that a sensation, in itself indifferent, can awaken interest, by being the constant antecedent of some pleasure. Thus the sight of the mother's breast is indifferent as mere visual sensation; but very soon allies itself in the infant mind with the gratification of being fed. This is a case of the contiguous transfer of a feeling, and is exemplified in all our powerful sensations and feelings. The lower animals are excited to their utmost activity by the sight of their food or their prey; they are sufficiently intellectual to have a recollection of their own feelings, and to have that awakened by some associated object. Granting the possession of these transferred sensibilities, which make the acquirement of what is only a means, as exciting to the activities as the final end, the process of connecting these with the movements for attaining them is precisely the same as before. Thus the act of lifting a morsel to the mouth is urged in obedience to an intermediate end, and is urged with a degree of energy proportioned to the acquired force of that end. The infant is, after a time, excited to warm manifestations by the mere approach of a spoonful to its mouth. There is an ideal fruition in the very sight of the spoon coming nearer, with a corresponding elation of tone and energy; and when the young probationer is attempting the act for itself, there is a support given to successful movements, and a tendency to sink under obvious failure. The carrying of a morsel to the mouth is one of those definite and uniform movements so favourable to the process of volitional growth. It is, nevertheless, comparatively late, owing no doubt to the length of time occupied in the preparatory associations.

4. Movements that have become allied with definite sensations, are thereby brought out, and made ready for new alliances.

Spontaneity is supposed to be the earliest mode of bringing forward movements to be connected with feelings; but when a number of connexions have been once formed, the connected movements are of more frequent occurrence, and are discovered to have new influences over the feelings. Locomotion, at first spontaneous, is rapidly allied with the animal's wants, and, being called out on the corresponding occasions, may coincide with new gratifications. Connected, in the early stages, with the search for food, it may be passed on to the alliance with shelter, with companionship, with safety, and other agreeables. Introductions are constantly made to new connexions, thus overcoming the initial difficulty of obtaining the necessary coincidences.

5. Volition is enlarged, and made *general*, by various acquirements; and first, the Word of Command.

Instead of proceeding by detailed or piece-meal associations with ends, or with pleasures and pains, the individual takes a higher step by forming connexions between all possible modes of movement, and a certain series of marks or indications, through which the entire activity of the system may be amenable to control.

The first of these methods is the Word of Command. In the discipline and training, both of animals and of human beings, names are applied to the different actions, and, eventually, become the medium of evoking them. The horse is made to hear the word for halting, and at the same time is drawn in with the bridle; in no very great number of repetitions, the word alone suffices to cause the act. So in infants. By uttering names in connexion with their various movements, a means is given of evoking these movements at pleasure. The child is told to open its mouth; at first it does not know what is wished; some other means must be used for bringing on the movement, which movement is then coupled in the mind with the name. The primordial urgency of pleasure and pain,—the one to promote, the other to arrest movement,—is the motive power at the outset; and a name may become suggestive of these urgencies to the recollection, rendering them operative in the ideal form. The dog made to halt in the chase, by a word, is mentally referred by the word to the deterring pain of the whip. Also, in children, pain and pleasure, the first associates with actions, can have their motive force transferred to language, which is henceforth a distinct power in singling out desired movements.

6. Another instrumentality for extending volition is Imitation.

It has often been alleged, and is perhaps commonly believed, that Imitation is instinctive. The fact is otherwise. There is no ability to imitate in the new-born infant; the power is a late and slow acquisition, and one especially favourable for testing the general theory of the growth of will. Imitation (of what is seen) implies a bond of connexion between the sight of a movement executed by another person, and the impulse to move the same organ in ourselves; as in learning to dance. For vocal imitation, the links are between sensations in the ear, and movements of the chest, larynx, and mouth. The acquirement of articulate speech may be observed to take place thus. Some spontaneous articulation is necessary to begin with; the sound impresses the ear, and possibly communicates an agreeable stimulus, the tendency of which would be to sustain the vocal exertion. At all events, there is the commencement of an association between an articulating effort or movement, and an effect on the ear. Every repetition strengthens the growing bond; and the progress is accelerated when other persons catch up, and continue the sound. The attempt may now be made to invert the order, to make the articulating exertion arise at the instigation of the sound heard. This will not succeed at first; an associa-

IMITATION.

tion must be very firm in order to operate in the inverted order. But on some chance occasion, after repeated urgency, the spontaneity comes round, and it being preceded by the characteristic sensation, the associating link is strengthened according to the imitative order; and very soon the adhesion is complete. This process is gone through with several other articulations, and in the meantime, the voice becomes more ready to burst out at the hearing of articulate sounds, so that the trials are multiplied; the correcting power being the felt coincidence with the sound proposed for imitation. The child told to say *ta*, will perhaps say *na*, *ma*; at this period, however, it understands the tones of dissatisfaction expressed by others, if not aware of the discrepancy between its own performance and the model. After a time, it will become alive to the success of the coincidence. The primordial stimuli of pleasure and pain, are still the agency at work; spontaneity must precede; association in time completes the connexion; and an entirely new and distinct means is gained for determining specific actions.

The imitation of Pitch, the groundwork of the art of singing, goes through the same routine. A note spontaneously uttered impresses the ear with its pitch; and an association is commenced between the special tension of the vocal muscles and that sensation; which association goes on strengthening until the sound heard brings on the muscular effect. How rapid and complete this acquirement shall be, depends on the endowment of the ear, and on other circumstances already described.

The imitation of Movements at sight comprises a large part of our early voluntary education. The course is still the same. Movements from natural spontaneity,—of the arms, hands, fingers, and other visible parts,—must occur and be seen; the active muscular impulses are united with the visible or ocular appearances; eventually, the appearances (as manifested by others) can evoke the active impulses. If any pleasure attends the feeling of successful coincidence, or if any pain is made to go along with the insufficient reproduction of the model, there is an appeal to the fundamental motives, for continuing the successful, and abandoning the unsuccessful acts. The child is urged to clap hands; some movements are made, but not the proper ones; the depression of ill-success leads to their cessation. Perhaps no others take their place on that occasion; at another time, a more successful attempt is made, and the coincidence is agreeable; the bent is sustained, and an associating lesson given, under the stimulus (so favourable to contiguous adhesion) of a burst of the elation of success.

The volitional links, constituted in the acquirements of Imitation, are very numerous. They should have to be reckoned by hundreds, if not by thousands. A certain amount of Imitativeness belongs to animals. The young of many species are guided by the old in their early attempts. The characteristic of gregariousness follows the imitative power; there could be no community of action without this aptitude.

7. A farther extension of the voluntary acquirements leads to the power of Acting upon the Wish to move.

We can rise up, stretch forth the hand, sound a note, from the mere wish to perform these acts, without the consideration of any ultimate end of pleasure sought or pain avoided. Not that such movements occur without some reference to the final ends of human action. We do not go through the process called wishing, unless instigated by some motive, that is, in the last resort, some pleasure or pain. Moreover, we very seldom perform movement merely for the sake of moving; we may show our ability to any one denying it, and then the motive is either the pleasure of power or the pain of humiliation—both highly efficacious as springs of action. Most usually when we move to a wish, it is the wish to gain some end, the action being the means; as when thirsty, and passing a spring of water, we will or wish to perform the movements for drinking.

The link of association formed in order to confer voluntary power in this particular form, is the link between our *idea* of the movement and the movement itself; between the idea of raising the hand, and the act of raising it, there being a motive or urgency towards some end. The growth of this link is a step in advance of the imitative acquirement, and precisely in the same direction; imitation supposes a connexion between a movement and the *sight* of that movement performed by another person, as the drill-master; acting from a wish to move is to perform the movement on the thought, *idea*, or recollection or the appearance of the movement; the guiding circumstance is the coincidence of the actual movement as seen with the ideal picture of it; when we raise the hand to a certain height, we know that we have conformed to the idea given in our wish.

MOVEMENT TO THE IDEA OF THE EFFECT. 337

This further acquisition, the following out of imitation, involves a large stock of ideal representations of all possible movements, gained during our own performance of these movements, and our seeing others perform them. We have ideas of opening and closing the hand, spreading the fingers, grasping and letting loose; of putting the arms in all postures, and through varying degrees of rapidity. In acquiring those ideas we acquire also the links or connexions between them and the actual putting forth of the movements themselves; and but for these acquired links, voluntary power in its most familiar exercise would be entirely wanting. We have ideas also of the motions of our legs and feet; we form the wish to give a kick, and the power to fulfil the wish implies a link of association between the idea of the action, as a visible phenomenon, and the definite muscular stimuli for bringing the movement to pass. If no observation had ever been bestowed on the lower extremities, so as to arrive at this piece of education, the wish formed would be incompetent to create the act, notwithstanding the existence of a motive.

8. Voluntary power is consummated by the association of movements with the idea of the Effect to be produced.

When we direct our steps across the street to a certain house, the antecedent in the mind is the idea of our entering that house. When we stir the fire, the antecedent is the idea of producing the appearance of a blazing mass, together with the sensation of warmth. When we carry the hand to the mouth, it is by virtue of a connexion between the movements and the idea of satisfying hunger and thirst. In writing, the idea of certain things to be expressed is connected directly with the required movements of the hand.

Here we have a still more advanced class of associations. In accordance with the usual course of our progressive acquirements, intermediate links disappear, and a bridge is formed directly between what were the beginning and the end of a chain. The thing that we are bent on doing is what properly engages our attention; success in that is the pleasurable motive, failure the painful motive; exertion is continued until we succeed; and an association is formed between the actions producing the end and the end itself. We come to a shut door; the idea in the mind accompanied with the state of feeling that makes the motive,—a present want, prospective relief,—is the idea of that door open. Instead of thinking first of the movement of the hand in the act of opening, and proceeding from that to the action itself, we are carried at once from the idea of the open door to execute the movement of turning the handle.

The examples recently dwelt on have been chiefly movements guided by Sight and ideas of sight. It is scarcely necessary to do more than allude to the case of Hearing. Vocal Imitation is the association of sounds heard with movements of the organs of voice. Vocalizing to a Wish involves a sufficient adhesion between a vocal exertion and the *idea* or recollection of the sound so produced, as when a musician pitches a note and commences an air; or when a speaker gives utterance to words. These adhesions enter into the education of the individual in singing and in speaking, and are necessarily very numerous in a cultivated man or woman. Lastly, these associations are bridged over, and a link formed at once between movements of the voice and the idea of some end to be gained by its instrumentality; as in raising the voice to the shrill point for calling some one distant; or as when, without having in mind the idea of the words 'right face,' the officer of a company gives the word of command merely on the conception of the effect intended.

CHAPTER III.

CONTROL OF FEELINGS AND THOUGHTS.

1. As our voluntary actions consist in putting forth muscular power, the control of Feeling and of Thought is through the muscles.

Hitherto we have seen, in the operation of the will, the exerting of definite, select, and, it may be, combined movements for the gaining of ends. We have spoken only of *muscular* intervention in the attainment of our wishes. We have not even entertained as questions, whether the blood can circulate more or less rapidly, or the digestion accommodate itself, in obedience to pleasure and pain. In an emotional wave, there is a participation of organic change. A shock of pain deranges the organic functions; pleasure, by the Law of Conservation, is accompanied with organic, no less than with

VOLUNTARY CONTROL OPERATES THROUGH MUSCLES.

muscular, vigour. So far as concerns the fundamental link expressed by this law, there might be an association of organic, as well as of muscular, changes with states of pleasure and with states of pain; and often to the same good purpose: the augmentation of respiratory or of digestive vigour would directly heighten pleasure and abate pain. Notwithstanding all which facts, the muscular energies are alone selected for those definite associations with states of feeling which constitute the will. The power of movement stands alone in possessing the flexibility, the isolation, the independence, necessary for entering into the multifarious unions above detailed; and when we speak of voluntary control, we mean a control of the muscles. An explanation has, therefore, to be furnished of the stretching out of this control to feeling and to thought, which are phenomena more than muscular.

CONTROL OF THE FEELINGS.

2. The physical accompaniments of a feeling are (1) diffused nerve currents, (2) organic changes, and (3) muscular movements. The intervention of the will being restricted to movements, the voluntary control of the feelings hinges on the muscular accompaniments.

Muscular diffusion being only one of three elements, we have to learn from experience whether it plays a leading, or only a subordinate part. There are various alternative suppositions. The movements may be so essential, that their arrest is the cessation of the conscious state. Or the case may be that the other manifestations are checked by the refusal of the muscles to concur. Lastly, the movements may be requisite to the full play of the feeling, but not to its existing in a less degree, or in a modified form.

Referring to the arbitration of experience, we find such facts as these. First, In a comparatively feeble excitement, the outward suppression leads, not immediately, but very soon, to the cessation of the feeling. There is at the outset a struggle, but the refusal of the muscular vent seems to be the extinction of the other effects. The feeling does not cease at once with the suppression of the movements, showing that it can subsist without these; but the stoppage of the movement being followed soon by the decay of the feeling, we infer that the other accompaniments, and especially the nerve currents, are checked and gradually extinguished under the muscular arrest. A shock of surprise, for example, if not very powerful, can soon be quieted by repressing all the movements of expression. It is to be observed, however, that this is an emotion peculiarly muscular in its diffusion; the remark being far less true of the emotions that strongly affect the organic functions, as fear, tenderness, and pains generally.

Secondly, In strong feelings, the muscular repression appears not merely to fail, but to augment the consciousness of the feeling, as if the nervous currents were intensified by resistance. A certain impetus has been given, and must find a vent, and, if restrained outwardly, it seems to be more violent inwardly. We are familiar with such sayings as the mind 'preying upon itself,' for want of objective display, the need of an outlet to the surcharged emotions, the venting of joy, or grief, and the like.

The analogy of the weaker feelings makes it probable that, even with the stronger, muscular resistance would ultimately quell the interior currents of the brain, together with the mental excitement. The difficulty is to find a motive sufficient to overcome the stimulus of a strong emotion. It may seem better to give way at once than to make an ineffectual resistance. A burst of anger might be suppressed by a strong muscular effort; but the motive must be either powerful in itself, or aided by a habit of control.

Thirdly, There is a certain tendency in the muscular expression of a feeling to induce the feeling, through the connexion established, either naturally or by association, between this and the other portions of the physical circles of effects (SYMPATHY, § 2). This supposes that there is no intense preoccupation of the brain and mind; we could not force hilarious joy upon a depressed system. Besides, it may be our wish merely to counterfeit, before others, an emotion that we do not wish to feel, as happens more or less with the player on the stage.

3. The voluntary command of the muscles, as attained in the manner already described, is adequate to suppress their movements under emotion.

When the will has reached the summit of general command, as indicated in the preceding chapter, it is fit for any mode of exertion that can be represented to the mind; the mere visible idea of the movement to be effected will single out the reality. The mature volition is thus competent to whatever efforts may be necessary for directing any of the

EDUCATION IN THE SUPPRESSION OF FEELINGS.

muscles to move, or for restraining their movement; all which is applicable to the present case.

But long prior to this consummation, an education for suppressing the feelings, or at least the manifestation of them, is usually entered on. It is desired, for example, to cause a child to restrain inordinate crying, at an age when few voluntary links have been forged, and when recourse must be had to the primitive starting point of all volition. In the very early stages, the absence of definite connexions between the pleasurable feeling and the suppression,. and between the painful feeling and the indulgence, will lead to a great many fruitless attempts, as in all the beginnings of volition. A few successful coincidences will go far to fill up the blankness of the union between the motive impulses and the feelings in the special case; and the progress may then be rapid. The remaining difficulty will be the violence of the emotional wave, which may go beyond the motive power of available pleasure or admissible pain, even although the link of connexion between these and the definite impulses is sufficiently plain. This, however, is the difficulty all through life, in the control of the more intense paroxysms of emotion, and has nothing to do with the immaturity of the volitional links between pleasurable or painful motives and the actions suggested for securing the pleasure and banishing the pain.

The case is precisely analogous to the breaking in of colts, or the training of young dogs; the want of determinate connexions gives much trouble in the commencing stages; and as the deficiency is made up, the education proceeds apace.

COMMAND OF THE THOUGHTS.

4. It has been already considered (COMPOUND ASSOCIATION, § 8) in what way the will can influence the train of thoughts. The effect is due to the control of Attention.

We cannot, by mere will, command one set of ideas to arise rather than another, or make up for a feeble bond of adhesion; the forces of association are independent of volition. But the will can control some of the conditions of intellectual recovery: one of which is the directing of the attention to one thing present rather than to another. In solving a geometrical problem, it is necessary to recall various theorems previously learnt; for that purpose, the attention is kept fixed upon the diagrammatic construction representing the problem, and is turned away from all other things; in which attitude, the ideas suggested by contiguity and by similarity, are geometrical ideas more or less allied to the case in hand.

The case now supposed is an exercise of voluntary attention upon the muscles that guide the exercise of vision. The turning the eyes upon one part of the field of view, and not upon another, is a mode of voluntary control in no respect peculiar.

5. The command of the Attention passes beyond the senses to the ideas or thoughts. Of various objects coming into recollection, we can ponder upon one to the neglect of the rest. The will has power over muscular movements in *idea*.

It is a fact, that we can concentrate mental, no less than bodily, attention. When memory brings before us a string of facts, we can detain one and let the rest drop out of mind. Reviving our knowledge of a place, we are not obliged to go over the whole of it at an equal rate; we are able, and are usually disposed, to dwell upon some features, and thereby to stop the current of farther resuscitation.

In all this, the will seems to transcend the usual limits assigned to it, namely, the prompting of the voluntary muscles. Indeed, the fact would be wholly anomalous and inexplicable, but for the local identity of actual and of ideal movements (CONTIGUITY, § 11); and even with that local identity, it is only from experience that we could be aware that voluntary control could enter the sphere of the ideal. When we are tracing a mountain in recollection, we are, in everything but the muscular contractions of the eye or the head, repeating the same currents, and re-animating the same nervous tracks, as in the survey of the actual mountain; and, on the spur of a motive, we detain the mental gaze upon the top, the sides, the contour, the vegetation, exactly as in the real presence.

6. This part of voluntary control has its stages of growth, like the rest; and enters as an all-important element into our intellectual or thinking aptitudes.

Two courses may be assigned for the acquisition of this higher control. It may follow, at some distance, the command of the corresponding actual movements; or it may have to pass through an independent route, beginning with spontancity, and guided by the influence of pleasure and pain, under the Law of Conservation. In all probability, the first supposition is the correct one. We seem gradually to contract the power of mental concentration, after having attained the command of the senses,—the ability to direct the eye wherever we please, or to listen to one sound to the disregard of others. Having the full outward command, a certain share abides with us, when we pass from realities to ideas, from the sight of a building to the thought of it. The ability thus possessed is doubtless strengthened by exercise in the special domain of the ideal; a wide difference exists between the man that has seldom put forth the power of mental concentration, and him that has been in the constant practice of it.

Howsoever attained, the use of this power in intellectual production is great and conspicuous. Profuse reproduction, the result of observation and retentiveness, is of little avail for any valuable purpose, whether scientific, artistic, or practical, unless there be a power of selection, detention, and control, on the spur of the end to be achieved. By such power of fixing attention, both on actual objects, and on the ideas arising by mental suggestion, we can make up for natural deficiencies, and, both in acquirements and in production, can pass over more highly gifted, but less resolute competitors. When the motives are naturally strong, and fortified by habit, we do not allow the attention, either bodily or mental, to wander, or to follow the lead of chance reproduction, as in a dream or reverie; our definite purpose, whether to lay up a store of words, to master a principle, to solve a problem, to polish a work of taste, to construct a mechanical device, or to reconcile a clash of other men's wills, keeps the mind fixed upon whatever likely thoughts arise, and withdraws us at once from what is seen to have no bearing on the work.

When what is meant by 'plodding industry,' 'steadiness,' 'application,' 'patience,' is opposed to natural brilliancy, facility, or abundance of ideas, it is, in other words, force of will displayed in mental concentration, as against the forces of mere intellectual reproduction; two distinct parts of our constitution, following different laws, and unequally manifested in different individuals.

7. The voluntary command of the Thoughts has been formerly shown to enter into Constructive Association.

In the illustrations under the preceding head, 'constructiveness' has been involved; but it deserves a more special mention. The distinguishing feature of the process is a voluntary selection, adaptation, and combination, to suit some end; the motive force of this end is the active stimulus, and the agreement with it, the guide or touchstone of all suggestions. In verbal constructiveness, for example, a certain meaning is to be conveyed to another person; a number of words spring up by memory, related to that meaning, but demanding to be selected, arranged, qualified, in order to suit it exactly. The revival of past trains of language through contiguity and similarity, or a combination of contiguities and similarities, provides the separate elements; the will puts them together, under the sense of suitability; so long as that sense is dissatisfied, selection and adjustment must go on; when the satisfying point is reached, the constructive efforts cease.

8. The command of the Thoughts is an adjunct in the control of the Feelings.

The command over the thoughts is an exceedingly powerful adjunct in the control of the Feelings; being probably more efficacious than the voluntary sway of the muscular manifestations. Our emotions are more or less associated with objects, circumstances, and occasions, and spring up when these are present either in reality, or in idea; affection is awakened at the sight or thought of what is lovely, or endeared to us; fear is apt to arise when perils are brought to view. In this connexion lies the power of the orator and the poet to stir up the emotions of men. Now, we may ourselves, by force of will, entertain one class of thoughts, and disregard or banish another class. When a person has roused our anger by an injury, we can turn our thoughts upon the same person's conduct on other occasions, when of a nature to inspire love, admiration, or esteem; the consequence of such a diversion of the ideas will be to suppress the angry feeling by its opposite.

A fit of hilarious levity is difficult to quench by mere voluntary suppression of the muscular movements; the more so that the diaphragm is a muscle not so well under command as the muscles of the limbs. A more powerful instrument in such a case would be the turning of the thoughts upon some serious or indifferent matter; and especially a painful or depressing subject. Persons guilty of levity during a religious address are usually reminded of the terrors of the unknown world.

COMMAND OF THE FEELINGS THROUGH THE THOUGHTS.

The conquering of one strong feeling by exciting another, was designated by Thomas Chalmers, 'the expulsive power of a new affection,' and was much descanted on by him as an instrumentality of moral improvement. When a wrong taste was to be combated, he recommended the process of displacing it by the culture of something higher and better; as in substituting for the excitement of the theatre, or the alehouse, intellectual and other attractions.

Without the assistance of a new emotion, we may subdue or modify a present feeling, by carrying the attention away from all the thoughts or trains of ideas that cluster about it, and give it support. If we have strength of motive enough for diverting the mind from the thoughts of an alarming danger to some entirely different subject, the state of terror will subside.

The command of the thoughts requisite for such diversions is a high and uncommon gift or attainment, one of the most distinguishing examples of force of will, or of power of motive. There is a limit to the control thus exercised; no amount of stimulus will so change the current of ideas as to make joy at once supervene upon a shock of depression. Still, by a not unattainable strength of motive, and the assistance of habit, one can so far restrain the outbursts of emotion, as to make some approach to equanimity of life.

9. The reciprocal case—the power of the Feelings to command the Thoughts—is partly of the nature of Will, partly independent of the will.

When under a pleasurable feeling, we cling to all the thoughts, images, and recollections that chime in with, and sustain it—as in a fit of affection, of self-complacency, or of revenge—the case is one of volition pure and simple. By the direct operation of the fundamental power of self-conservation, every activity bringing pleasure is maintained and increased; and the exercise of attention, whether upon the things of sense or upon the stream of thought, is included in the principle. So, on the obverse side, a painful feeling ought to banish all the objects and ideas that tend to cherish it, just as we should remove a hot iron or a stinging nettle from the naked foot; and this, too, happens to a great extent: a self-complacent man banishes from his mind all the incidents that discord with his pretensions; an engrossed lover will not entertain the thought of obstacles and inevitable separation. In both these cases, the law of the will is fairly and strictly exemplified. And if there were no other influence at work, if the feelings had no other mode of operating, we should find ourselves always detaining thoughts, according as they give us pleasure, and turning our back upon such as produce pain, with an energy corresponding to the pain.

But we have formerly remarked, and must presently notice still more particularly, that the feelings have another property, the property of detaining every idea in alliance with them, whether pleasurable or painful, in proportion to their intensity; so that states of excitement, both painful and neutral, cause thoughts and images to persist in the mind by a power apart from the proper course of the will. A disgusting spectacle cannot be at once banished from the recollection, merely because it gives pain; if the will were the only power in the case, the object would be discarded and forgotten with promptitude. But the very fact that it has caused an intense or strong feeling gives it a persistence, in spite of the will. So any powerful shock, characterized neither by pleasure nor by pain, detains the mind upon the cause of it for a considerable time, and engrains it as a durable recollection, not because the shock was pleasurable, but merely because it was strong. The natural course of the will is pursued at the same time; it co-operates in the detention of the pleasurable, and in reducing the persistence of the painful; but it is not the sole or the dominant condition in either.

CHAPTER IV.

MOTIVES, OR ENDS.

1. From the nature or definition of Will, pure and proper, the Motives, or Ends of action, are our Pleasures and Pains.

In the Feelings, as formerly laid out, if the enumeration be complete, there ought to be found all the ultimate motive or ends of human action. The pleasures and pains of the various Senses (with the Muscular feelings), and of the Emotions,—embracing our whole susceptibility to happiness or misery,—are, in the last resort, the stimulants of our activity, the objects of pursuit and avoidance. The actual presence of any one of the list of pleasures, set forth under the different departments of Feelings, urges to action for its continuance; the presence of any one of the included pains is a signal to action for its abatement. The final classification of Motives, therefore, is the classification of pleasurable and painful feelings.

If we were to recapitulate what has been gone over, under the Senses and the Emotions, we should refer to the pleasures of Muscular Exercise and Repose, and the pains of Fatigue and of Restrained action; the great variety of pleasurable and painful susceptibilities connected with Organic Life—including such powerful solicitations as Thirst, and Hunger, and the whole catalogue of painful Diseases, with the reactionary condition named Health; the numerous stimulations, pleasurable and painful, of the Five Senses—Tastes, Colours, Touches, Sounds, Sights; the long array of the Special Emotions, containing potent charms and dread aversions—Novelty, Liberty, Tender and Sexual Emotion, Self-complacency and Approbation, with their opposites; the elation of Power and the depression of Impotence and Littleness, the Interest of Plot and Pursuit, the attractions of Knowledge, and the variegated excitements of Fine Art.

2. The elementary pleasures and pains incite us to action, when only in *prospect;* which implies an ideal persistence approaching to the power of actuality.

The property of intellectual or ideal retention belongs more or less to all the feelings of the mind; and has been usually adverted to in the description of each. The pain of over-fatigue is remembered after the occasion, and has a power to deter from the repetition of the actual state.

The circumstances regulating the ideal persistence of pleasures and pains, so as to give them an efficacy as motives, are principally these:—

(1) Their mere Strength, or Degree. It is a law of our intellectual nature that, other things being the same, the more vivid the present consciousness, the more it will persist or be remembered. This applies to pleasures, to pains, and to neutral excitement. A strong pleasure is better remembered than a weak; a greater pain is employed in punishment, because a less, being insufficiently remembered, is ineffectual to deter from crime. Our labours are directed, in the first place, to the causes of our great pleasures and our great pains, be-

cause these are more tenaciously held in the memory, and less liable to be overborne by the pressure of the actual. The acute sensual pleasures, affection, praise, power, æsthetic charm, are strongly worked for, because strongly felt, and strongly remembered; the more intense pains of disease, privation, disgrace, have an abiding efficacy because of their strength.

(2) *Continuance and Repetition.* The longer a pleasure is continued, and the oftener it is repeated, the better is it retained in absence as a motive to the will. It is the same with emotional states as it is with intellectual—with pain as with language, iteration gives intellectual persistence. A single attack of acute pain does not leave the intense precautionary motive generated by a series of attacks. Age and experience acquire moral wisdom, as well as intellectual; strength of motive as well as extent and clearness of intellectual vision. After repeated failures, we give up a chase, in spite of its allurements; not merely because our hopes are weakened, but also because our recollection is strengthened, by the repetition. Pleasures seldom tasted may not take their proper rank with us, in our habitual pursuits; we do not work for them in proportion to what we should actually gain by their fruition.

It necessarily happens that distance of time allows the memory of pleasure and pain to fade into imbecility of motive. A pleasure long past is deprived of its ideal enticement; a pain of old date has lost its volitional sting.

(3) *Intellectual Rank.* The feelings have a natural scale of intellectual persistency, commencing from the organic or physical sensibilities, and rising to the higher senses, and the more refined emotions. The sensations of hearing and sight; the pleasures of tender feeling, of complacency, of intellect, of Fine Art; the pains of grief and of remorse,—are in their nature more abiding as motives than muscular exercise, or occasional indigestion.

(4) *Special Endowment for the memory of Pleasure and Pain.* It is a fact that some minds are constituted by nature more retentive of pleasures and pains than others; just as there are differences in the memory for language or for spectacle. A superior degree of prudence, under circumstances in other respects the same, is resolvable into this fact. No one is unmoved by a present delight, or a present suffering; but when the reality is vanished, the recollection will be stronger in one man than in another—that is, will be more powerful to cope with the new and present urgencies that

put to the proof our memory given motives. The pains of incautious living are, in some minds, blotted out as soon as they are past; in others, they are retained with almost undiminished force. Both Prudence, and the Power of Sympathy with others, presuppose the tenacious memory for pleasures and pains; in other words, they are fully accounted for by assuming that speciality. Virtue, although not Knowledge, as Sokrates maintained, reposes on a property allied to Intellect, a mode of our Retentiveness, the subject matter being, not the intellectual elements commonly recognized, but pleasures and pains.

It is not easy to refer this special mode of Retentiveness to any local endowment, as we connect the memory for colour with a great development of the optical sensibility. Most probably, the power is allied to the Subjectivity of the character, the tendency to dwell upon subject states, as opposed to the engrossment of objectivity.

Prudential forethought and precaution in special things may be best referred to the greater strength and repetition of the feelings; as when a man is careful of his substance and not of his reputation; or the converse. On whatever subjects we feel most acutely, we best remember our feelings, and yield to them as motives of pursuit and avoidance. It is unnecessary to invoke, for such differences, a general retentiveness for pleasures and pains.

(5) In the effective recollection of feelings, for the purposes of the will, we are aided by collateral associations. Any strong pleasure gives impressiveness to all the acts and sensations that concurred with it; and these having their own independent persistency, as actions or as object states, aid in recovering the pleasure. Every one remembers the spot, and the occupation of the moment, when some joyful news was communicated. The patient in a surgical operation retains mentally the indelible stamp of the room and the surgeon's preparations. One part of the complex experience, so impressed, buoys up the rest.

It is scarcely necessary to add that the motive power of a feeling of *recent* occurrence partakes of the effectiveness of the actuality.

3. We direct our labours to many things that, though only of the nature of Means, attain by association all the force of our ultimate ends of pursuit. Such are Money, Bodily Strength, Knowledge, Formalities, and Virtues.

17

When any one object is constantly associated with a primary end of life, it acquires in our mind all the importance of the end; fields, and springs of water, are prized with the avidity belonging to the necessities of life. The great comprehensive means, termed wealth or Money, when its powers are understood, is aimed at according to the sum of the gratifications that it can bring, and of the pains that it can ward off, to ourselves and to the sharers in our sympathies. Such at least is the ideal of a well-balanced mind; for few persons follow this or any other end, mediate or ultimate, according to its precise value.

We have seen that a memory unfaithful to pleasure and pain misguides us in our voluntary pursuit of ends; not merely allowing the present to lord it over the future, but evincing partiality or preference as between things equally absent and ideal. The intervention of the associated ends leads to new disturbances in our estimate, and in the corresponding pursuit. The case of Money exemplifies these disturbing causes. In it, we have the curious fact of a means converted into a final end.

When anything has long been an object of solicitude from its bearing on the ultimate susceptibilities of the mind, the pleasure of its attainment corresponds to its influence on those susceptibilities. Without proceeding to realize the purchasable delights of money, we have already a thrill of enjoyment in the acquisition of it; the more so if we have felt such pains as physical privation, toil, impotence, indignity, tastes forbidden, with the aggravation of multiplied fears. The sense of being delivered from all this incubus, is a rebound, delightful in itself, before proceeding to convert the means into the final ends. Many *ideal* pains are banished at once by the possession of the instrument unused. There arises in minds prone to the exaggeration of fear, a reluctance to part with this wonderful sense of protection; which alone would suggest the keeping, rather than the spending, of money. When we add the feeling of superiority over others attaching to the possession and the *possible* employment of money, and farther the growth of a species of affection towards what has long occupied the energies, and given thrills of delight, we shall understand the process of inversion whereby a means becomes a final end. We should also take into account, in the case of money, its definite and numerical character, giving a charm to the arithmetical mind, and enabling the possesser to form a precise estimate of his gains and his total.

Similar observations apply to the other associated ends. Health is nothing in itself; it is a great deal as a means to happiness. To this extent, and no farther, the rational mind will pursue it; we should only be losers, if, in seeking health, we surrendered the things that make life agreeable. The prevailing error, however, is the other way. The retentiveness for the pains and discomforts of ill-health, and for the enjoyments thereby forfeited, is not good enough in the mass of men; and needs to be re-inforced by inculcation and reflection.

Like Money, Knowledge is liable to become an end in itself. Principally valuable as guidance in the various operations of life, as removing the stumbling blocks, and the terrors of ignorance, it contracts in some minds an independent charm, and gathers round it so many pleasing associations as to be a satisfying end of pursuit. The knowledge of many Languages is an immense toil and an incumbrance; but the sense of the end to be served gives them a value, which some minds feel in an exaggerated degree.

The Formalities of Law, of Business, and of Science are indispensable as means, worthless as ends. Not unfrequently, persons become enamoured of them to such an extent as to sacrifice the real ends on their account. The explanation is much the same as already given for the love of money.

Justice and Truth are generally held to be ends in themselves; but when we enquire more minutely into their bearings, we find that their importance is sufficiently justified by their instrumentality to other ends. If Justice were perfectly indifferent to human happiness, no nation would maintain Judges and Law Courts; and if Truth were of no more service than falsehood, Science would be unknown. But as both these qualities are entwined with human welfare at every turning it being impossible for the human race to exist without some regard to them, we cannot wonder that they attract our solicitude, and that we have a lively satisfaction in contemplating their triumph. The emotion of terror attaches us strongly, perhaps even in an exaggerated degree, to the Security conferred by Justice, among other good social arrangements; and we sometimes cling to a mere figment because it once represented this great attribute.

4. The Motives to the Will are swayed and biassed by the Persistence of Ideas.

Allusion has repeatedly been made to the intellectual property of all feelings, whereby they persist in the mind, and give persistence to the ideas and objects related to them. According to the degree of the excitement, and irrespective of its *quality*—as pleasure, pain, or neutral feeling—is the hold that it takes of the present consciousness, and imparts to the thoughts allied with it. The germ of the property is seen in the stimulation of the senses, more particularly sight, as when we involuntarily keep the eye fixed upon a light, even painfully intense. The infatuation of the moth is the crowning instance of the power of sensation, as such, to detain and control the movements; for although the distant flame may not be painfully intense, the singed body ought to neutralize any pleasure that the light can give.

A pleasurable feeling, besides moving the will, detains the thoughts, not simply as pleasure, but as excitement. This would be all right, if every such state were purely and solely pleasurable. But when we examine closely our very best pleasures, we find that, in all of them, more or less, the drops of pure delight are mingled with a quantity of mere excitement. Any great pleasure is sure to leave behind it an enduring state of neutral feeling, the pleasurable part of the wave subsiding long before the general tremor has ceased. But while there is excitement, there is detention and occupation of mind, and the exclusion of unrelated subjects and ideas. In an agreeable marvel, there is a small burst of genuine pleasure, but a still wider and more lasting state of excitement.

Hence our pleasurable emotions are all liable to detain the mind unduly, as regards our proper gratification. Thus, the pleasures of the tender emotion, if at all strong, are surrounded with an atmosphere of still stronger excitement; and the objects of our affection are apt to persist in the mind beyond the degree of the pleasure they give us, although in some proportion to that pleasure. The mind of the mother is arrested and held partly by the strong pleasures of maternity, and partly by the 'Fixed Idea' consequent on the still greater amount of agitation that she passes through. In the sexual feelings, there is the like mixture of pleasure and fixed idea, carrying the mind beyond the estimate of pleasure and pain, to the state named 'passion.' The pleasures of Power and Ambition are liable to the same inflammatory and passionate mixture. A man may be highly susceptible to the delights of power, without being passionately so, if he is moved solely by the strict value of that pleasure, and not by the engrossing power of the excitement so apt to invest any real pleasure. The gratification of revenge is a real pleasure, but the allied excitement is something still stronger; the *idea* of the revenge possesses the mind so strongly, that, to act it out, we will sacrifice more than the value of the pleasure accruing from it. In this passion especially, our happiness would often lie in forgetting the whole circumstances; but under excitement, the balancing of good and evil is impossible. We must execute whatever thought the mind at that moment, in the heat of feeling, exclusively entertains.

The operation is seen in still bolder relief in the painful feelings. As already remarked, the proper action of the will, having regard to our greatest good, would banish the thought of a disgust, or a blow, or a discord; but the excitement engendered is a force to detain the disagreeable subject. We are often haunted for life by some great and painful shock persisting in the memory in virtue of its intensity.

The extreme instance of irrational and morbid persistence is shown in Fear. It is the nature of that passion to take an excessive hold of the intellectual trains; everything that has ever been accompanied with the perturbation of fear has contracted an undue persistence, baffling and paralyzing the operation of the will. Our greatest pleasures are liable to plunge us into fears; the pleasurable emotions above named, as for example the maternal feeling, have their moments of serious alarm and their protracted states of solicitude.

The rational pursuit of ends is thus liable to many thwartings. The imperfect recollection of pleasures and pains, the tendency to substitute the means for the ends, the undue persistence of objects through emotion—are all against us. To these circumstances, we must add some others. First, our insufficient experience of good and evil, especially in early years, disqualifies us from judging of the comparative value of different objects of pursuit; the youthful predilections for this or that profession must needs be founded on a very inexact estimate. In the second place, many kinds of good and evil are only *probable* in their advent; such as the attainment of an office, the success of an enterprise, good or ill health. This introduces a totally new consideration to complicate the operation of our motives. The *beau idéal* of rationality consists in pursuing all objects with reference to the probability of their attainment; but probability is liable to the fluctuating estimates of hope and fear; states that are governed partly by the intelligence and partly by the feelings.

In the last place, our Habits are often opposed to the rational estimate of good or evil. Not merely what we term bad habits, which are irrational impulses confirmed by repetition, but conduct at first well calculated for our interests may, through change of circumstances, operate against our happiness on the whole; just as laws, originally good, may be continued when they have become noxious. The habit of saving may deprive us, in old age, of essential comforts; the habit of deference to others may prove hostile to our comfort when we come to a position of command.

These various considerations are of special importance in preparing the way for the great ethical question as to the existence of *disinterested* motives in the human mind.

CHAPTER V.

THE CONFLICT OF MOTIVES.

1. WHEN two pleasures concur, the result is a greater pleasure; when a pleasure concurs with a pain, the greater will neutralize the less, leaving a surplus.

As mere emotions, concurring pleasure and pain neutralize each other; and in this way, pain is frequently stifled before acting as a motive to the will. To procure an assuaging pleasure is a way of dealing with a pain, no less effectual than removing the cause by voluntary exertions. In one class of minds, the pains of life are met by tenderness, grief, sorrow, sympathy, by venting them in language, and by other emotional manifestations; and not by measures of prevention or extirpation. Such minds are the profusely emotional; and are in marked contrast with another class, the active or volitional, whose peculiarity it is to take active proceedings to cut off the sources of the evil.

2. The natural Spontaneity of the system may come into conflict with the proper Motives to the Will.

Spontaneity is a power all through life. The times of renewed vigour, after rest and nourishment, are times when the system is disposed to active exertion; when this is refused, there ensues a conflict. The young, being most exuberant in activity, burst out incontinently at those moments, unless withheld by very powerful motives. This is one of the impulses that require a severe discipline, in the shape of strong counter-motives. The force of the spontaneity and the force of the counter-motives are then measured against each other, and we call the one that succeeds stronger, having no other criterion of comparative strength.

When the activity is unduly stimulated, as by drugs, by pungent sensations, or by quick movements, it is so much the greater a power, and needs a greater motive to curb it. We see this in the restlessness of children in their violent sports; the natural activity is heightened by stimulation, and made harder to resist; quiescence is doubly repugnant.

A periodical tendency to action, the result of habit, would operate in the same way; as this is sometimes in opposition to the other motives, there is conflict, and the successful side is called the stronger.

3. Exhaustion, and natural inaction of the powers, are a bar to the influence of Motives.

This is the same fact in obverse. When the system is exhausted or physically indisposed,—its spontaneity and available energy past,—a more than ordinary motive is required to bring on exertion. The jaded horse needs more spurring. The exhausted mountain guide can be got to proceed only by the promise of an extra fee. Napoleon took his men across the Alps by plying them with the rattle of the drums when everything else failed.

4. In the conflicts of Opposing Volitions, properly so called, we may consider first the case of two Motives in the Actual.

Two actual pains or pleasures sometimes incite in opposite ways. An animal may be fatigued and also hungry; the one state prompting to rest, the other to exertion. We judge of the stronger motive by the result. A person may feel the pain of indoor confinement, but may decline the disagreeable alternative of cold and wet. In company, we may be solicited by spectacle, by music, by conversation; one gains the day, and is pronounced the greater pleasure, or at least the stronger motive.

One might continue, without end, to cite these conflicts of actual sensation or emotion, appending the uniform conclusion that the upshot is the test of the stronger motive. The instruction derivable from each observation of this kind is a fact in the character of the person, or the animal, observed; we find out the preferences, or comparative susceptibility of different persons, or of the same person at different times.

We are to presume, in the absence of any indications to the contrary, that the stronger motive in the shape of actual and present sensation or emotion, is the greater pleasure, or the smaller pain. Pleasure and pain, in the actual or real experience, are to be held as identical with motive power. If a man is laid hold of and detained by music, we must suppose that he is pleased to that extent. The disturbances and anomalies of the will scarcely begin to tell in the actual feeling. Any one crossing the street direct, through dirty pools, is inferred to have less pain from being splashed than from being delayed.

This remark is of importance in furnishing us with a clue to the pleasures and pains of other beings. The voluntary preferences of individuals, when two actual pleasures or pains are weighed together, show which is the greater in their case. An object that weighs as nothing in stimulating the will for attainment, is to be held as giving no pleasure; if, on the other hand, it never moves to aversion or avoidance, it is not a source of pain. The pleasures and pains of men and of animals are indicated with considerable fidelity by their voluntary conduct, and especially when the comparison is made upon the present or the actual experience. We have few means of judging of the feelings of the lower animals; they have but a narrow range of emotional expression; and we are driven mainly to the study of their actions in pursuit or avoidance. We can see that a dog relishes a meal, and runs from a whipping. The lower we descend, the more do we lose the criterion of emotional expression, and depend upon the preference of action. There may be a certain ambiguity even in this test; the influence of light, for example, works to the extent of fascination, and so may other feelings. Probably this is an exceptional case; at all events, if the test of the will is invalid, we have nothing beyond it to appeal to.

There are certain allowances that we can easily make in the application of the will as a test of strength of feeling. We should observe the influence of a motive under all variety of states, as to vigour, rest, nourishment, so as to eliminate difference in the active organs. We should weigh each motive against every other, and thus check our estimate by cross comparisons; in this way, we can establish for each individual a scale of preferences, and obtain a diagnosis of emotional character.

The comparison of one person with another requires an estimate to be made of the active disposition as a whole, or the proneness to active exertion generally. This may be gathered from the spontaneity, from the disposition to act for the sake of acting, and from all cases where we have an independent clue to the strength of a motive, as pleasure or pain. Two persons may be equally pained by an acute ailment; while the one bestirs himself for relief and the other remains idle. If we except a greater proneness in some organs than in others, as vocal exuberance combined with general sluggishness, the active disposition is a single fact, a unity or totality; the feelings are many and unequal. One statement will give the volitional character as a whole; the estimates of the motives are as numerous as our distinct sensibilities.

5. When the conflict is between the Actual and the Ideal, the result depends on the more or less vivid recollection of pleasure and pain.

This opens up a much wider sphere of conflict. Our voluntary determinations are most frequently the preference of an actual feeling to an ideal one, or the converse. We refuse a pleasurable relish, because of subsequent organic pains abiding in the recollection. An ideal motive owes its power not to the strength of the original feeling alone, but to that coupled with all the circumstances tending to make it persist in the memory. A young man and an old may be equally pained by an overdose of alcohol, but the elder has the best recollection of the pain, while the younger has the farther disadvantage of a keener present delight. Yet, when the natural endowment favours the retentiveness of pain and pleasure, we shall find youth temperate, and age a victim to present allurement. In this class of examples, the conditions are various and often perplexing. Suppose the case of a thief by profession, whose prospects in life are infamy and penal servitude. There are the following alternative explanations of his choice. His mental peculiarities may be assumed to be, the usual liking for the common enjoyments of life; an aversion to industry; a small ideal estimate of the yet unexperienced pains of punishment; and perhaps, also, a sanguine temperament that under-estimates the probabilities of capture. Suppose him to pass through a first imprisonment. A new and powerful motive is now introduced, an ideal repugnance, which ought to have great strength, if the punishment has told upon him. Should he not be reformed by the experience, we must assume the motives already stated at a still higher figure. We must also suppose, what is probably true of the criminal class generally, a low retentiveness for good and evil—the analytic expression of Imprudence; perhaps the most radically incurable of all natural defects.

The theory of Prison Discipline is based on such considerations as the following. In short imprisonments, the pains should be acute, so as to abide in the memory, and engender an intense repugnance. Loss of liberty, solitude and seclusion, regular work, and unstimulating food can be borne, for a short period, if there is little sense of the indignity and shame of going to jail. A brief confinement is the mild corrective suited to a first offence; which failing, there is needed an advance in severity. Recourse should next be had to the acute inflictions; which are principally whipping and muscular pains. The muscular pains are administered in various forms; as the tread wheel, the crank, extra drill, shot drill, and a newly devised punishment, introduced into the Scotch prisons, and said to be very deterring—the guard bed. With a view to increase the impressiveness of these severe applications, they should not be continued daily, but remitted for a few days; the mind having leisure in the interval to contemplate alike the past and the future, while the body is refreshed for the new infliction.

Long imprisonment and penal servitude are made deterring chiefly through the deprivation of liberty; to which are added, the withdrawing of the subject from the means of crime, and the inuring to a life of labour. Perhaps the defect of the system is the too even tenor of life, which does not impress the imagination of the depraved class with sufficient force. Occasional acute inflictions, would very much deepen the salutary dread of the condition; and are not uncalled for in the case of hardened criminals. The convict's yearly or half-yearly anti-holiday, would impart additional horror and gloom to his solitary reflections, and might have a greater influence on the minds of the beginners in crime.

6. The Intermediate Ends—Money, Health, Knowledge, Power, Society, Justice, &c.—enter, as motives, into conflict with the ultimate ends, Actual or Ideal, and with one another.

It has been seen what circumstances govern the motive force of the intermediate ends; the value of the ultimate pleasures and pains involved being only one, although the properly rational, estimate of their worth. These ends have all a certain motive power in every intelligent mind, sometimes too little and sometimes too great. When present ease and gratification is confronted with prospective wealth, or knowledge, or position, we see which is the stronger. Great relish for actual ease and pleasure; great repugnance to money-getting exertion; a feeble memory for the pleasures that money can purchase, or the pains it can relieve; the absence of occasions of fear and solicitude in connexion with penury; no affectionate interest contracted with wealth, through the pursuit of it—would constitute a character too little moved to the acquisition of money fortune, as a reversed state of the motives might lead to an excessive pursuit.

It is a rule, easily explicable on the principles laid down, that intermediate ends,—Wealth, Health, Knowledge, &c.—are too weak in early life, while in advancing years, they become too strong, in fact superseding the final ends. One reason of this last effect is that the ultimate pleasures of sense count for less in later life, while ideal gratifications, original or acquired, count for more; money and knowledge, having contracted a factitious interest of the ideal kind, are still sought for that, when the primary interests have ceased; and the more so, that the active pursuit in their service, has become a habit, and a necessity.

7. The Persistence of Ideas, through emotional excitement, counts in the conflict of Motives, and constitutes a class of Impassioned or Exaggerated Ends.

Undue persistence of ideas is most strongly exemplified in Fear. Any evil consequence that has been able to rouse our alarms, acquires an excessive fixity of tenure, and overweighs in the conflict of motives. This has been seen to be one of the exaggerating conditions of avarice. So, from having been a witness of revolutions, a susceptible mind takes on a morbid dread of anarchy and a revulsion to change. The care of health may assume the character of a morbid fixed idea, curtailing liberty and enjoyment to an absurd degree. The apprehensions of maternal feeling are apt to be exaggerated.

Vanity, Dignity, love of Power, are often found in the impassioned form, in weak minds. The extreme case of the fixed idea in general, and of the morbid predominance of these ideas in particular, occurs in the insane.

Sympathy, in its pure and fundamental character, is the possession of an idea, followed out irrespective of pleasure or pain, although these are more or less attached to its usual exercise. In the conflict of motives, this principle of action plays an important part; its predominance is the foremost motive to virtuous conduct. It subsists upon a vivid perception of the pain or misery of others; a perception more or less acute by nature or by education, and susceptible of being inflamed by oratory. The sympathies of individuals are generally partial or select; powerful to some modes of misery and inert to others. The conflicts of sympathy are with the purely egotistic pleasures of each individual; these last, when unnaturally strong, as in the child, are unequally met by the sympathetic impulses.

CHAPTER VI.

DELIBERATION.—RESOLUTION.—EFFORT.

1. In the prolonged weighing of motives, termed DELIBERATION, the suspense is a voluntary act, prompted by the remembered pains of acting too quickly.

Among our painful experiences, is the evil effect of acting hastily on the first motive that arises. At an early stage of education, we gratify hunger with whatever looks like food; we give to him that asketh, and believe whatever any one tells us. After a little time, we discover that the fruit of such impulses is often bad; that other motives, such as might change our conduct, would arise to our minds if we refrained from immediate action, and gave time to the intellect to suggest them. A deterring motive of the Intermediate class is thus created, and at its instigation, we fall into the attitude called Deliberation, which consists in pausing, waiting, ruminating, till other considerations rise to the view, and are confronted with one another, and with the first impulse.

We have, in this case, a conflict between some present impulse, some pleasure or pain, actual or ideal, that has risen before the mind, and the highly intellectual or ideal pain con-

EVIL OF PRECIPITATE ACTION.

stituted by former experience of the pains of immediately giving way to a motive stimulus. The deliberating impulse is the creature of education, growing with repeated examples of mischief, and at last triumphant in all conflicts with hasty promptings.

The same experience that induces delay, to give time for all the motives that arise, farther urges us not to protract the suspense too long. We know what amount of deliberation will ordinarily suffice to get out both sides of a case; to allow less and to allow more are mischievous, and the prospect of the mischief deters from the one and from the other. Most people defer answering an important letter, for at least one day; perhaps the case is so complicated that more time is required; which being given, the evils of protracting the decision come into play; action then ensues on the side where strength of impulse prevails.

Another source of evil is the undue impressiveness of the motive last suggested. Every consideration occurring to the mind is strongest at the moment of being first presented; if we act at that moment, we are apt to give too much weight to the new and too little to the old. Aware, by experience, of this danger also, we hold back till every motive has cooled down, as it were, from the first heat, and until all are nearly on an equal footing. In proportion as we are impressed, by experience, with this evil, does it abide with us, as a deterring motive, leading to voluntary suspense. A sudden thought, bursting on the view, has something of the dangerous predominance of an actual pleasure or pain; we are, however, taught the painful consequences thence arising; and if our memory for evil is adequate and just, we bridle in the mistaken activity that we are impelled to.

When opposing motives are numerous, it is a matter of real difficulty for the coolest mind to estimate them correctly. As an artificial help in such an emergency, Franklin, in a letter to Priestley, recommends the writing them down in two columns, so as to balance them piecemeal. When one, on one side, is felt to be about equal to one or two on the other, these are struck out, the complication being to that extent lessened. The repetition of this neutralizing and deleting process leaves the opposing sides at last so much reduced, that the comparison is safe and easy.

Another artificial precaution of some value in deliberating on a complicated matter, consists in keeping the deliberation open for a length of time, say a month, and recording the impression of every day. At the end of the time, the decisions on each side being summed up, the majority would testify, in all probability, to the strongest on the whole. The lapse of time would allow all considerations within our reach to come forward and have their weight, while the matter would be viewed under a considerable variety of circumstances and of mental temper.

A farther difficulty also suggested to the man of experience and reflection, and influencing the deliberative process, is the inability to judge of untried situations. What one has gone through needs only to be fairly remembered; but what is absolutely strange demands a careful constructive operation. Although the young cannot be made to see this, it comes home to advancing years. The sense of the resulting mistakes is a prompting of the nature of Ideal pain, to take the precautions of interrogating others, and referring to our own experience in the situations most nearly analogous. Choosing a profession, entering into a partnership, emigrating to another country, contracting the matrimonial tie, are all more or less haphazard in their consequences; they are less so, according as the individual has been taught by good and ill fortune how to deliberate.

2. The Deliberative process is in conformity with the theory of the Will, contained in the previous chapters.

In Deliberation, there is no suspension of the action of motives, but merely the addition of a new motive, the ideal evil of hasty action. Every pleasure or pain bearing on the occasion has its full weight, in accordance with the circumstances already described; and the action is always strictly the result of the total of motives.

It is in the deliberative situation that we are supposed to exert that mysterious power called the 'freedom' of the will, 'free choice,' 'moral liberty.' The only real fact underlying these expressions is the circumstance that we seldom act out a present motive. One may feel hunger, but may not follow out the prompting on the instant. Each human being has a large reserve, a permanent stock of motive power, being the totalized ends of life; a total that operates along with every actual stimulation, and quashes a great many passing motives. This reservoir of ideal ends is sometimes spoken of as the 'self' or 'ego' of the individual, the grand controlling principle; when it has full course we are said to be 'free;' when it is baffled by some transitory impulse or passion, we are said to be 'enslaved.' Now, Deliberation has the effect of bringing us under the sway of our interests on the whole, but does not thereby make us act without a motive. There is no intervening entity to determine whether the motive shall bring forth the act; a motive may be arrested, but only through the might of a stronger.

In metaphysical theory, it is often taken for granted that deliberation, or choice, is the type, representative, or essential feature of the Will. This is not the fact. The most general and essential attribute of the will, is to act at once on a motive, as when one seeks shelter from a shower; it is an exception, although of frequent occurrence, to stop and deliberate, that is, to suspend action, until an intellectual process has time given to it, to bring forward ideal motives which may possibly conflict with the actual, and change the result.

3. When the action suggested by a motive, or a concurrence of motives, cannot immediately commence, the intervening attitude is called RESOLUTION.

Besides the deliberate suspense, necessary for avoiding the known evils of precipitate volition, there may be a farther arrest of action. Many of our voluntary decisions are come to, before the time for acting commences. We deliberate to-day, what shall be done to-morrow, or next week, or next year. A name is required to indicate this situation of having ceased to deliberate without having begun to act. We call it RESOLUTION. If action followed at once on motive, there would be neither Deliberation nor Resolution; if it followed after such adequate comparison and balancing of motives, as experience testifies to be enough for precaution against haste, there would be no Resolution.

The state thus denominated is not a state of absolute quiescence or indifference. There is an activity engendered at once, the preliminary to the proper action; an attitude of waiting and watching the time and circumstances for commencing the course decreed. We are moved by health and pleasure to contrive a holiday; we know that to rush off at once under these very strong motives would probably entail misery. We suspend and deliberate; after allowing sufficient space for all motives to assemble and be heard, the result is in favour of the first suggestion. The interval that still divides us from the actual movement, is the interval of resolution, or preliminary volition.

In the state of resolution, we are liable to changes of

motive, inducing us to abandon the course resolved on. We have not, perhaps, at the time of ceasing to deliberate, had the motives fully before us; we may not have counted sufficiently with the toil and opposition and inconveniences that we should encounter, all which may come to the view afterwards, and reverse our decision. Hence we often abandon our resolutions either before action commences, or after commencing and grappling with the real difficulties. All this only shows that the deliberative process had been too hurriedly concluded. Irresolution is a sign either of want of deliberation, or of undue susceptibility to a present and actual motive. The resolute man is he that, in the first place, allows an ample deliberative suspense, and, in the second place, is under the power of the permanent or ideal motives, which is what we mean by steadiness of purpose.

We make resolutions for our whole lives, which necessarily run many risks of being broken. It is not merely through insufficient deliberation and infirmity of purpose, that we depart from such resolutions, but also from the occurrence of new motives, better insight, and altered circumstances.

We exist from day to day under a host of resolutions. Few of our actions are either *pro re nata*, or the result of a deliberation at once executed. We go forth every morning to fulfil 'engagements,' that is, carry out resolutions. The creature of impulse is he that does not retain the permanent motives embodied in his engagements or resolutions, but gives way to the spur of the occasion, as when the boy sent on an errand, loiters to play marbles.

For the same reason as above stated, with regard to deliberation, namely, familiarity of occurrence, we are apt to consider resolution as, not an incident, but an essential of the Will. In both cases, it is the *fallacia accidentis*, setting up an occasional property as the main property of a thing. The typical will neither deliberates nor resolves, but passes, without interval, from a motive state to an action. The superior intelligence of the higher beings induces upon this primitive link a series of artificial suspenses, not exceptions to the general law of the will, but complications of it; and the complicated modes are so common, and moreover so prominent and noticeable, that we fancy at last, that they are necessary to the very existence—a part, if not the whole essence, of will.

4. If, with a strong motive, there is weakness or insufficiency of the active organs, we have the peculiar consciousness, named EFFORT.

When we are moved to an exertion that we are fully equal to, we have a muscular feeling that is pleasurable or else indifferent; in either case, we say that the act costs no effort. As we approach the limits of our strength, the feeling gradually inclines to pain. The interval between easy performance and total inability, is marked by the presence of this familiar experience; the greater the pain, the greater is said to be the effort. As all pain is a motive to desist from whatever exercise is causing it, we should not continue to act, but for the pressure of some still stronger motive. In such cases, there is the necessity for an increasing stimulus, as the pain of the action increases. The state of effort, therefore, may be described as a muscular pain joined to the pain of a conflict of motives. On occasion of excessive exercise, and during spasm, we may have the organic pain of muscle besides.

5. The consciousness of Effort, like Deliberation and Resolution, is an accident, and not an essential, of the Will.

It is the nature of a voluntary act to be accompanied with consciousness. The feeling that constitutes the motive is one form; to which is added the consciousness of active exertion, which varies with the condition of the organs as compared with the demand made upon them; one of its phases being the state of effort. We are not entitled to include, in the essence of Will, the consciousness of Effort, any more than we can include the delight of exercise when the organs are fresh.*

* It has been maintained (Herschell's Astronomy, chap. viii.), that the consciousness of effort accompanying voluntary action is the proof that *mind* is the real source of voluntary power, and, by analogy, the source of all the powers of nature—as gravity and all other prime movers. This doctrine is liable to very strong objections.

First, As now stated, the consciousness of effort does not accompany all voluntary actions, but only that class where the active power is not fully equal to the work.

Secondly, Although some kind of consciousness accompanies voluntary power, there are also present a series of physical changes, and a physical expenditure, corresponding in amount to the work to be done. A certain amount of food, digested, assimilated, and consumed, is demanded for every voluntary exertion, and in greater quantity as the exertion is greater. In a deficiency of food, or in an exhausted condition

CHAPTER VII.

DESIRE.

1. DESIRE is the state of mind where there is a motive to act—some pleasure or pain, actual or ideal—without the ability. It is thus another of the states of interval, or suspense, between motive and execution.

When a pleasure prompts us to work for its continuance or increase, and when we at once follow the prompting, there is no place for desire. So with pain. Going out into the open air, we encounter a painful chill; we turn back and put on extra clothing; the pain has induced a remedy by the primordial stimulus of the will, guided by our acquired aptitudes. Walking at a distance from home, the air suddenly cools to the chilling point. We have no remedy at hand. The condition thus arising, a motive without the power of acting, is Desire.

2. In Desire, there is the presence of some motive, a pleasure or a pain, and a state of conflict, in itself painful.

The motive may be some present pleasure, which urges to action for its continuance or increase. It may be some pleasure conceived in idea, with a prompting to attain it in the reality, as the pleasure of a summer tour. It may be a present pain moving us to obtain mitigation or relief; or a

---

of the active members, the most intense consciousness, whether of effort or any other mode, is unable to bring forth voluntary or mechanical energy. With abundance of food, and good material conditions of the system, force will be exerted with or without the antecedent of consciousness.

Thirdly, The animal frame is the constant theatre of mechanical movements that are entirely withdrawn from consciousness. Such are the movements of the lungs, the heart, and the intestines; these the consciousness neither helps nor retards.

Fourthly, When voluntary actions become habitual, they are less and less associated with consciousness: approaching to the condition of the reflex or automatic actions last noticed.

Thus, whenever mind is a source of power, it is in conjunction with a material expenditure, such as would give rise to mechanical or other energy without the concurrence of mind; while, of the animal forces themselves, a considerable portion is entirely dissociated from mind or consciousness.

pending but future pain, ideally conceived, with a spur to prevent its becoming actual. So far as the motive itself is concerned, we may be under either pleasure or pain. But in so far as there is inability to obey the dictates of the motive, there is a pain of the nature of conflict; which must attach to every form of desire, although in certain cases neutralized by pleasurable accompaniments.

3. There are various modes of escape from the conflict, and unrest, of Desire.

The first is *forced quiescence;* to which are given the familiar names—endurance, resignation, fortitude, patience, contentment.

This is a voluntary exertion prompted by the pain of the conflict. It means the putting forth of a volition to restrain the motive force of desire, to deprive the state of its volitional urgency. If the motive is a present pleasure, the will can oppose the urgency to add to it, and so bring on the condition of serene and satisfying enjoyments; if a present pain, the restraint of the motive urgency ends in the state called endurance, patience, resignation; a remarkable form of consciousness, where pain, by a neutralizing volition, is reduced to the state of a feeling possessed of only emotional and intellectual characteristics.

The self-restraint, implied under endurance, coerces all the movements and inward springs of movement, that, but for such coercion, would be exerted with a view to relief, even although fruitless. The same volition may likewise suppress the diffusive manifestations and gesticulative outburst of strong feeling. Both are comprised in the renowned endurance of the old Spartan, or of the Indian under torture. As a remedial operation, such a vigorous suppressive effort, in the case of physical pain, can directly do little but save the muscular organs from exhaustion; indirectly it will stamp the pain on the memory by leaving the present consciousness to taste its utmost bitterness; so that the present endurance in that form may be favourable to future precaution. When the pain is ideal or imaginary, or the result of artificial stimulation, as when one frets at not having the good fortune of others around, the forced quiescence eventually works a cure. Also, in the case of pleasure craving for increase, the suppressive volition is of admirable efficacy; it takes away the marring ingredient from a real delight, which is then enjoyed in purity. In these two last instances, we can understand the value of contentment, a forced state of mind prompted by the conflict of desire, and, by repetition, confirmed into a habitual frame of mind, favourable to happiness.

Seeing that Desire may be viewed as so much pain, we may, as in the case of any other pain, assuage it by the application of pleasure. When children are seized with longings that cannot be gratified, they may be soothed by something agreeable. They may also be deterred from pursuing the vain illusion by the threat of pain.

Another resource common to desire with other pains, is a diversion of the thoughts, by some new object; a mode especially applicable to the ideal pains, and vain illusions of unbridled fancy. Change of scene, of circumstances, of companions, if not disagreeable, can effect a diversion of morbid intellectual trains, by intellectual forces.

4. A second outlet for Desire is *ideal or imaginary action*.

If we are prevented from acting under the stimulus of our feelings, we may at least indulge in ideal acting. One confined to bed desires to be abroad with the crowd, and, unable to realize the fact, resorts, in imagination, to favourite haunts and pursuits. There is in such an exercise a certain amount of ideal gratification, which, in peculiar and assignable circumstances, may partly atone for the want of the actual.

With the bodily pains and pleasures, imagined activity entirely fails. The setting out in thought on the search of food is nothing to the hungry man; the idea of breaking out of prison must often occur to the immured convict, but without alleviating the misery of confinement.

It is different with the higher senses and emotions, whose ideal persistence is so great as to approximate to the grateful tone of the reality. We may have a desire to visit or re-visit Switzerland; being prohibited from the reality, we may indulge in an ideal tour, which is not altogether devoid of satisfaction. If we are helped, in the effort of conception, by some vivid describer of the scenes and the life of the country, the imagined journey will give us considerable pleasure. The gratification afforded by the literature of imagination testifies to the possibility of such a mode of delight. There would still survive a certain amount of desire, from the known inferiority of the imagined to the real; but a discipline of suppression might overcome that remaining conflict, and leave us in the possession of whatever enjoyment could spring from ideal scenes and activity.

DESIRE LEADS TO IDEAL ACTION.

In this way, pleasing sights and sounds, forbidden to the senses, may still have a charm in imagination; and the ideal pursuit of them would enhance the pleasure. Still more are the pleasures of affection, complacency, power, revenge, knowledge, fit to be the subject of ideal longings and pursuit. These emotions can all be to some extent indulged in absence, so as to make us feel something of their warmth and elation. It is not in vain, therefore, that we sustain an ideal pursuit in favour of some object of love, some future of renown, some goal of accomplishment, some inaccessible height of moral excellence. The day-dreamer, whose ideal emotions are well supported, by the means formerly described, has moments of great enjoyment, although still liable to the pains of conflict, and to the equally painful exhaustion following on ideal excitement.

If a pleasure in memory or in imagination were as good as the reality, there would be no pursuit either actual or ideal, and no desire. Or if the reality had some painful experiences enough to do away with the superiority of the actual, we should be free from the urgency of motives to the will. Many occasions of pleasure exemplify one or other of these two positions; evenings in society, public entertainments, dignified pursuits, and the like. We may have a pleasure in thinking of places where we have formerly been, with a total absence of desire to return.

The spur of an ideal pleasure consists, partly in the perennial tendency of pleasure to seek for increase, and partly in the pain arising from a consciousness of the inferiority of the ideal to the actual. This pain is at its maximum in regard to the pleasures of organic life and of the inferior senses; and at its minimum in the pleasures termed elevating and refined.

5. The Provocatives of Desire are, in the first place, the actual *wants* or *deficiencies of the system*, and secondly, the *experience of pleasure*.

The first class correspond with the Appetites, and with those artificial cravings of the system generated by physical habits. We pass through a round of natural wants, for food, exercise, &c., and when each finds its gratification at hand, there is no room for desire. An interval or delay brings on the state of craving or longing, with the alternative outlets now described.

If we set aside the Appetites, the main provocative of

Desire is the experience of pleasure. When any pleasure has once been tasted, the recollection is afterwards a motive to regain it. The infant has no craving but for the breast; desire comes in with new pleasures. It is from enjoying the actual, that we come to desire the pleasures of sound, of spectacle, and of all the higher emotions. Sexuality is founded on an appetite, but the other pleasing emotions are brought, by a course of experience, to the longing pitch. Intense as is the feeling of maternity, no animal or human being preconceives it. The emotions of wonder, of complacency, of ambition, of revenge, of curiosity, of fine art, must be gratified in order to be evoked as permanent longings. Experience is necessary to temptation in this class of delights. A being solitary from birth would have no craving for society.

Even as regards Appetite, experience gives a definite aim to the longings, directing them upon the objects known as the means of their gratification. We crave for certain things that have always satisfied hunger, and for a known place suited to repose. This easy transition, effected by association, misled Butler into supposing that our appetites are not selfish; they do not go direct to the removal of pain and the bestowal of pleasure, but centre in a number of special objects.

A higher complication arises when we contemplate the appearances of enjoyment in others, and are led to crave for participation. We must still have a basis of personal knowledge; but when out of a very narrow experience of the good things of life, we venture to conceive the happiness of the children of fortune, our estimate is likely to be erroneous, and to be biassed by the feelings that control the imagination. How this bias works, is explained by the analysis of the ideal or imaginative faculty (Book II., chap. iv., § 15).

6. As all our pleasures and pains have the volitional property, that is, incite to action, so they all give birth to desire; from which circumstance, some feelings carry the fact of Desire in their names. Such are Avarice, Ambition, Curiosity.

This has very generally led to the including of Desire, as a phenomenon, in the classification of the feelings. In every desire, there is a pleasure or pain, but the fact itself is properly an aspect of volition or the Will.

7. As in actual volition, so in Desire, we may have the disturbing effect of the Fixed Idea.

Nothing is more common than a persistent idea giving origin to the conflicts, and the day dreams, and all the outgoings of Desire. The examples already given of the fixed idea in the motives of the will, have their prolongation and expansion in ideal longings, when pursuit is impossible. Such are the day-dreams of wealth, ambition, affection, future happiness.

8. Desire is incorrectly represented as a constant and necessary prelude of volition.

Like Deliberation and Resolution, the state of Desire has now been shown to be a transformation of the will proper, undergone in circumstances where the act does not immediately follow the motive. There remains a farther example of the same peculiarity, forming the subject of the next chapter.

CHAPTER VIII.

BELIEF.

1. The mental state termed BELIEF, while involving the Intellect and the Feelings, is, in its essential import, related to Activity, or the Will.

In believing that the sun will rise to-morrow, that next winter will be cold, that alcohol stimulates, that such a one is to be trusted, that Turkey is ill-governed, that free trade increases the wealth of nations, that human life is full of vicissitudes,—in what state of mind are we? a state purely intellectual, or intellectual and something besides? In all these affirmations there is an intellectual conception, but so there is in many things that we do not believe. We may understand the meaning of a proposition, we may conceive it with the utmost vividness, and yet not believe it. We may have an exact intellectual comprehension of the statement that the moon is only one hundred miles distant from the earth; but without any accompanying belief.

It is next to be seen, if a feeling, or emotion, added to the intellectual conception, will amount to the believing state. Suppose us to conceive and contemplate the approaching summer as beautiful and genial beyond all the summers of the century, we should have much pleasure in this contemplation, but the pleasure (although, as will be seen, a predisposing cause) does not constitute the belief. There is, thus, nothing either in Intellect or in Feeling, to impart the essence of Belief.

In the practice of every day life, we are accustomed to test men's belief by action, 'faith by works.' If a politician declares free trade to be good, and yet will not allow it to be acted on (there being no extraneous barriers in the way), people say he does not believe his own assertion. A general affirming that he was stronger and better entrenched than the enemy, and yet acting as if he were weaker, would be held as believing not what he affirmed, but what he acted on. A capitalist that withdraws his money from foreign governments, and invests it at a smaller interest in the English funds, is treated as having lost faith or confidence in the stability of the foreign powers. Any one pretending to believe in a future life of rewards and punishments, and acting precisely as if there were no such life, is justly set down as destitute of belief in the doctrine.

2. The relation of Belief to Activity is expressed by saying, that *what we believe we act upon*.

The instances above given, point to this and to no other conclusion. The difference between mere conceiving or imagining, with or without strong feeling, and belief, is acting, or being prepared to act, when the occasion arises. The belief that a sovereign is worth twenty shillings, is shown by the readiness to take the sovereign in exchange for the shillings; the belief that a sovereign is light is shown by refusing to take it as the equivalent of twenty shillings.

The definition will be best elucidated by the apparent exceptions.

(1) We often have a genuine belief, and yet do not act upon it. One may have the conviction strongly that abstinence from stimulants would favour health and happiness, and yet go on taking stimulants. And there are many parallels in the conduct of human beings. The case, however, is no real exception. Belief is a motive, or an inducement to act, but it may be overpowered by a stronger motive—a present pleasure, or relief from a present pain. We are inclined to act where we believe, but not always with an omnipotent strength of impulse. Belief is an active state, with different degrees of force; it is said to be strong or to be weak. It is

BELIEF GROUNDED IN ACTION. 373

strong when it carries us against a powerful counter impulse, weak when overpowered by an impulse not strong. Yet if it ever induces us to act at all, if it vanquishes the smallest resistance, it is belief. The believer in a future life may do very little in consequence of that belief; he may never act in the face of a strong opposition; but if he does anything at all that he would not otherwise do, if he incurs the smallest present sacrifice, he is admitted to have a real, though feeble, belief.

(2) The second apparent exception is furnished by the cases where we believe things that we never can have any occasion to act upon. Some philosophers of the present day believe that the sun is radiating away his heat, and will in some inconceivably long period cool down far below zero of Fahrenheit. Any fact more completely out of the active sphere of those philosophers could not be suggested to the human mind. It is the same with the alleged past history of the universe, sidereal and geological. An astronomer has many decided convictions in connexion with the remote nebulæ of the firmament. Even 'the long past events of human history, the exploits of Epaminondas, and the invasion of Britain by the Romans, are beyond our sphere of action, and are yet believed by us. And as regards the still existing arrangements of things, many men that will never cross the Sahara desert, believe what is told of its surface, of its burning days and chilling nights.

It is not hard to trace a reference to action in every one of these beliefs. Take the last-named first. When we believe the testimony of travellers as to the Sahara, we view that testimony as the same in kind with what we are accustomed to act upon. A traveller in Africa has also passed through France, and has perhaps told us many things respecting that country, and we have acted on his information. He has also told us of Sahara, and we have fallen into the same mental attitude in this case, although we may not have the same occasion to act it out. We express the attitude by saying, that *if* we went to Africa, we would do certain things in consequence of the information.

As regards the past, we believe history in two ways. The first use is analogous to what has been stated, namely, when we put the testimony to historical events on the same footing as the testimony that we now act upon. Another way, is when we form theories or doctrines of human affairs, reposing in part on those past events, and carry these doctrines into operation in our present practice.

The belief in sidereal phenomena immeasurably remote in space and in time, is a recognition of the *scientific method* employed upon these phenomena. The navigator sails the seas upon the faith of observations of the same nature as those applied to the distant stars and nebulæ. If an astronomer propounded doctrines as to the nebulæ, founded upon observations of a kind that would not be trusted in navigation or in the prediction of eclipses, we should be in a perceptibly different state of mind respecting such doctrines, and that state of mind is not improperly styled disbelief.

(3) In many notorious instances our belief is determined by the strength of our feelings, which may be alleged as a proof that it is grounded on the emotional part of our nature. The fact is admitted, but not the inference. It will be afterwards seen in what ways the feelings operate upon the belief, without themselves constituting the state of believing.

(4) Very frequently, belief is engendered by a purely intellectual process. Thus, when a proposition in geometry is first propounded to us, we may understand its purport without believing it; but, by going through a chain of reasoning or demonstration, an operation wholly of the intellect, we pass into a state of entire conviction. So with the thousands of cases where we are led into belief by mere argument, proof, or intellectual enlightenment; in all which, there is the appearance of an intellectual origin of belief.

The same conclusion is suggested by another set of facts, namely, our believing from the testimony of our senses, or personal experience; for perception by the senses is admitted to be a function of the intellect. It is by such an operation that we believe in gravity, in the connexion of sunrise with light and heat, and so on.

So, when we receive and adjudicate on the testimony of others, we are performing a function strictly intellectual.

Led seemingly by such facts as these, metaphysicians have been almost, if not altogether, unanimous in enrolling Belief among the intellectual powers. Nevertheless, it may be affirmed, that intellect alone will not constitute Belief, any more than it will constitute Volition. The reasonings of the Geometer do not create the state of belief, they merely bring affirmations under an already-formed belief, the belief in the axioms of the science. Unless that belief can be shown to be an intellectual product, the faith in demonstrative truth is not based in intellect. The precise function of our intelligence in believing will be shown in what follows.

3. Belief is a growth or development of the Will, under the pursuit of *intermediate* ends.

When a voluntary action at once brings a pleasure or dismisses a pain, as in masticating food in the mouth, we experience the primitive course of the will; there is an absence alike of deliberation, of resolution, of desire, and of belief. By a fiction, one might maintain that we are believing that the mouthful of food is pleasant, just as one might say that we choose, desire, and resolve to masticate and swallow the bolus; but in point of fact, such designations would never have come into existence had all volition been of this primordial type. It is the occurrence of a middle or intermediate state between the motive and the felt gratification that makes these various phases to appear.

Belief is shown when we are performing intermediate or associated actions. When we put forth the hand to seize an orange, peel it, and bring it to the mouth, we perform a number of actions, in themselves barren and unprofitable, and stimulated by a pleasure to follow, which pleasure at present exists as the ideal motive. In this situation, there is a fact or phenomenon, not expressed by any of the other names for what fills the void of a suspended volition; there may be present deliberation, resolution, and desire; yet something still remains. For example, in taking these steps to enjoy the sweetness of the orange juices, we may have passed through the phase of Desire; previous experience of the pleasure has given us an idea of it, accompanied by longing for perfect fruition. We may also have passed through a Deliberation and a Resolution. But what is not yet expressed, is our assuming that the actions now entered on will bring the state desired, and our maintaining a degree of voluntary exertion as energetic as if the pleasure were actually tasted. When we act for an intermediate end, as strongly as we should for the actual end, we are in a very peculiar situation, not implied in desire, however strong, nor in deliberation, nor in resolution, and deserving to be signalized by a name. The principal designation is Belief; the synonymes are faith, trust, credit, credence, confidence, assurance, security, reliance, certainty, dependence, anticipation, expectation.

The state is known to vary in degree. Having formed a desire, and having, if need be, deliberated and resolved, we may pursue the intermediate ends, either with all the energy that the ultimate consciousness would prompt, or, what is very common, with less than that energy; perhaps with three-fourths, with one-half, or with one-fourth the amount. This difference need have no connexion with the intensity of desire, or with the processes of deliberation or of resolution; it relates to a fact that has a separate standing in the mind; and the circumstances affecting it call for a special investigation.

4. Belief always contains an intellectual element; there being, in its least developed form, an Association of Means and End.

The very fact of working for an intermediate end, with the view to some remote or final end, implies an intellectual conception of both, and the association of the one with the other. The lamb running to its ewe mother for milk and warmth, has an intellectual train fixed in its mind—an idea of warmth and repletion associated with the idea or characteristic picture of its mother. All the actions of human beings for remote ends are based on the mental trains connecting the intermediate with the final.

We may properly describe these trains as a knowledge of natural facts, or of the order of the world, which all creatures that can do one thing for the sake of another, must possess to some degree. Every animal with a home, and able to leave it and to return, knows a little geography. The more extensive this knowledge, the greater the *power* of gaining ends. The stag knowing ten different pools to drink from, is so much better provided than when it knew but one.

Experience of nature, therefore, laid up in the memory, must enter into every situation where we exert belief. Nay, more. Such experience is, properly speaking, the *just ground of believing*, the condition in whose absence there ought to be no belief; and the greater the experience, the greater should be the believing energy. But if we find, in point of fact, that belief does not accord with experience, we must admit that there is some other spring of confidence than the natural conjunctions or successions, repeated before the view, and fixed in the mind by the force of contiguous association.

5. The mental foundations of Belief are to be sought (1) in our Activity, (2) in the Intellectual Associations of our Experience, and (3) in the Feelings.

It is here affirmed, not only that Belief in its essence is an active state, but that its foremost generating cause is the Activity of the system, to which are added influences Intellectual and Emotional.

(1) The Spontaneity of the moving organs is a source of action, the system being fresh, and there being no hindrance. Secondly, the additional Pleasure of Exercise is a farther prompting to activity. Thirdly, the Memory of this pleasure is a motive to begin acting with a view to the fruition of it; the operation of the will being enlarged by an intellectual bond. These three facts sum up the active tendency of volition; the two first are impulses of pure activity; the third is supported by the retentive function of the intellect.

Under these forces, one or more, we commence action, and, so long as there is no check, we continue till overtaken by exhaustion. We have no hesitation, doubt, or uncertainty; while yet ignorant of what belief means, we act precisely like a person in the highest state of confidence. Belief can do no more than produce unhesitating action, and we are already placed at this point.

Suppose now that we experience a check, as when our activity brings us pain. This is an arrest upon our present movements; and the memory of it has also a certain deterring effect. We do not again proceed in that track with the full force of our spontaneous and volitional urgencies; there is an element of repugnance that weakens, if it does not destroy, the active tendency. The young animal at first roams everywhere; in some one track it falls into a snare, and with difficulty escapes; it avoids that route in future; but as regards all others, it goes on as before. The primitive tendency to move freely in every direction is here broken in upon by a hostile experience; with respect to which there is in future an anticipation of danger, a state of belief in coming evil. Repeated experiences would confirm this deviation from the rule of immunity; but before any experience, the rule was proceeded on.

We can now understand what there is instinctive in the act of believing, and can account for the natural or primitive credulity of the mind. The mere disposition to act, growing out of our active endowments, carries belief with it; experience enlightening the intellect, does not create this active disposition, but merely causes it to be increased by the memory of attained fruition. A stronger natural spontaneity would make a stronger belief, experience remaining the same. Whatever course is entered on is believed in, until a check arise; a repeated check neutralizes the spontaneous and voluntary agency, destroying alike action and belief.

The phenomena of credulity and mistaken beliefs are in accordance with the active origin of the state. We strongly believe that whatever has been in the past will always be in the future, exactly as we have found it in an unbroken experience, however small; that is, we are disposed to act in any direction where we have never been checked. It does not need a long-continued iteration, amounting to indissoluble association, to generate a belief: a single instance under a motive to act is enough. The infant soon shows a belief in the mother's breasts; and if it could speculate on the future, it would believe in being fed in that manner to all eternity. The belief begins to be broken through when it gets spoon meat; and the anticipation is now partitioned, but still energetic in holding that the future will resemble the past in the precise manner already experienced.

There is thus generated, from the department of our Activity, a tendency, so wide as to be an important law of the mind, to proceed upon any unbroken experience with the whole energy of our active nature, and, accordingly, to believe, with a vigour corresponding to our natural activity, that what is uncontradicted is universal and eternal. Experience adds the force of habit to the inborn energy, and hence the tenacity of all early beliefs. Human nature everywhere believes that its own experience is the measure of all men's experience everywhere and in every time. Each one of us believes at first that every other person is made, and feels, like ourselves; and it takes a long education to abate the sweeping generalization, which in no one is ever entirely overcome. If belief were generated by the growth of an intellectual bond of experienced conjunctions, we should not form any judgment as to other men's feelings, until old enough to perform a difficult scientific operation of analogical reasoning; we should say absolutely nothing about the distant, the past, and the future, where our experience is null: we might believe that the water from a known well slakes our thirst, but we should not believe that the same water would slake the thirst of other persons who had not tried it, nor that any other water would slake our own thirst. It is the active energy of the mind that makes the 'anticipation of nature' so severely commented on by Bacon, as the parent of all error. This anticipation, corrected and reduced to the standard of experience, is the belief in the uniformity of nature.

We labour under a natural inability or disqualification to

conceive anything different from our most limited experience; but there is no necessity that we should still persist in assuming that what is absolutely unknown is exactly like what we know. Such intrinsic forwardness is not a quality of the intellect, it is the incontinence of our active nature. As we act first and feel afterwards; so we believe first and prove afterwards; not to be contradicted is to us sufficient proof. The impetus to generalize is born of our activity, and we are fortunate if we ever learn to apply to it the corrections of subsequent experience. An ordinary person, by no means unintelligent or uncultivated, happening to know one Frenchman, would unhesitatingly attribute to the whole French nation the mental peculiarities of that one individual. As regards many of our convictions, the strength is in the inverse ratio of the believer's experience.

6. (2) The second source of Belief is Intellectual Association.

The frequent experience of a succession leaves a firm association of the several steps, and the one suggests readily all the rest. This enters into belief, and augments in some degree the active tendency to proceed in a certain course. The successive acts of plucking an apple, putting it in the mouth, and chewing it, are followed by an agreeable sensation: and the whole train is by repetition firmly fixed in the mind. The main source of the energy shown in these intermediate acts is still the activity—partly spontaneous, partly volitional under the ideal motive of the sweetness. Yet the facility of passing intellectually from one step to another, through the strength of the association, counts as an addition to the strength of the impetus that carries us along through the series of acts. On a principle already expounded, the idea of an act has a certain efficacy in realizing it; and a secure association, bringing on the ideas, would help to bring on the actions. It may be safely maintained, however, that no mere association of ideas would set the activity in motion, or constitute the active disposition, called belief. A very strong association between 'apple' and 'sweetness,' generated by hearing the words often joined together (as from the 'dulce pomum' of the Latin Grammar), would make the one word suggest the other, and the corresponding ideas likewise suggest each other; but the taking action upon them still requires an active bent of the organs, growing out of the causes of our activity—spontaneity and a motive; and, until these are brought into play, there is no action and no active disposition, or belief.

When we have been disciplined to consult observation and experience before making affirmations respecting things distant in place or time, instead of generalizing haphazard, we import very extensive intellectual operations into the settlement of our beliefs; but these intellectual processes do not constitute the attitude of believing. They are set agoing by motives to the will—by the failures and checks encountered in proceeding on too narrow grounds; and when we have attained the improved knowledge, we follow it out into practice by virtue of voluntary determinations, whose course has been cleared by the higher flight of intelligence; yet there is nothing in mere intellect that would make us act, or contemplate action, and therefore nothing that makes us believe.

It is illustrative and interesting to note who are the *decided* characters in life—the men prompt and unhesitating in action on all occasions. They are men distinguished, not for intelligence, but for the active endowment; a profuse spontaneity lending itself to motives few and strong. Intelligence in excess paralyzes action, reducing it in quantity, although no doubt improving it in *quality*—in successful adaptation to ends.

7. (3) The third source or foundation of Belief is the Feelings.

We have already taken account of the influence of the Feelings in generating belief, and we need only to re-state in summary the manner of the operation.

We may first recall the two tests of belief—(1) the energy of pursuit of the intermediate ends, the final end not being in the grasp, and (2) the elation of mind through the mere prospect of the final end (when that is something agreeable). In both these aspects, belief is affected by feeling.

If the final end is a pleasure, and strongly realized in idea, the energy of pursuit is proportionably strong, and the conviction is strong, as shown by the obstacles surmounted not merely in the shape of resistance, but in the shape of total want of evidence. An object intensely desired is followed out with excessive credulity as to the chances of attainment.

There is another mode of strengthening the believing attitude by pleasure. Irrespective of the contemplation of the end, which is necessarily pleasure (whether direct, or indirect, as relief from pain), there may be other causes of pleasure operating at the moment to impart elation or buoyancy of tone. Such elation strengthens the believing temper, with respect to whatever is in hand. A traveller in quest of new regions is subject to alternations of confidence according to the states of mind that he passes through, from whatever cause. He is more sanguine when he is refreshed and vigorous, when the day is balmy, or the scenery cheerful, there being no real accession of evidence through any of these circumstances.

That a higher mood of enjoyment should be a higher mood of belief is evident on both aspects of belief. In the first place, whatever action is present is more vigorously pursued, with which vigour of pursuit the state of confidence is implicated. And, in the second place, as regards the cheering ideal foretaste of the final end, anything that improves the elation of tone has the very same effect as the improved prospect of the end would have, such improved prospect meaning a stronger belief. What we want from a strong assurance is mental comfort, and if the comfort arises concurrently with the belief, we have the thing wished, and the belief is for the moment made up by an adventitious or accidental mixture.

In some forms of Belief, as in Religion, the cheering circumstance is the prominent fact. Such belief is valued as a tonic to the mind, like any form of pleasure; the belief and the elation are convertible facts. Hence, when the belief is feeble, any accession of a joyful mood will be seen to strengthen the belief, while the opposite state will be supposed to weaken it; the fact being that the two influences conspire together, and we may, if we please, put both to the account of one, especially if the source of the other is hidden or unseen.

The cultivation of these last named beliefs is purely emotional, and consists in strengthening the associations of feeling in the mind; the case is in all respects identical with the growth of an affection. With any strong affection, there is implicated a corresponding strength of belief.

Mere strength of excitement, of the neutral kind, will control belief as it controls the will, by the force of the persisting idea. Whatever end very much inflames the mind, will be impressed according to the strength of the excitement, and irrespective of the pleasure or the pain of it, and, in determining to action, will constitute belief in whatever appears as the intermediate instrument. A very slight and casual association will be taken up and assumed as a cause. The mother having lost a child will conceive a repugnance to a certain thing associated in her mind with the child's death; she will keep aloof from that thing with the whole force of her will to save her other children; which is tantamount to believing in a connexion of cause and effect between the two facts. The influence of the feelings thus serves to confirm an intellectual link, perhaps only once experienced, into a strong association, such as a great many counter experiences may not be able to dissolve.

Lastly, the power of the feelings to command the presence of one class of thoughts, and banish all of a hostile kind from the view, necessarily operates in belief as in action. A fright fastens the thoughts upon the circumstances of alarm, and renders one unable to hold in the view such as could neutralize the terror. There are considerations within reach that would prevent us believing in the worst, but they cannot make their appearance; the well-timed reminder of them by the agency of a friend, is then an invaluable substitute for the paralyzed operation of our own intelligence.

8. The Belief in the order of the World, or the course of Nature, varies in character, in different persons, according to the relative predominance of the three causes enumerated.

All belief implicates the order of the world; or the connexion between one thing and another thing, such that the one can be employed as a means to secure the other as an end. We believe that a rushing stream is a prime mover; that vegetation needs rain and sunshine; that animals are produced from their own kind; that the body is strengthened by exercise.

The chief source of belief is unobstructed activity. A single experiment is enough to constitute belief; what we have done successfully once, we are ready to do again, without the smallest hesitation. Repetition may strengthen the tendency, but five repetitions do not give five times the conviction of one; it would be nearer the mark to say, that, apart from our educated tests of truth, fifty repetitions might perhaps double the strength of conviction of the first. We are all faith at the outset; we become sceptics by experience, that is, by encountering checks and exceptions. We begin with unbounded credulity, and are gradually educated into a more limited reliance.

Our belief in the physical laws is our primitive spontaneity *contracted* to the bounds of experience. Of this kind, is our faith in gravity, heat, light, and so on. Our trials are greatly simplified by the guidance of those that have gone before us.

As regards the more ordinary phenomena, we soon fall into the right channels of acting; an animal learns in a short time from what height it can jump with safety.

The long catalogue of perverted, extravagant, erratic beliefs, can in most instances be accounted for by some unusual degree of feeling, whether pleasure, pain, or mere excitement. We are hard to convince that anything we like can do us any mischief; this is strength of pleasurable feeling, operating through desire, and barring out from the thoughts the hostile experience. We believe in the wisdom and other merits of the persons that we love or admire; another of the many instances of the power of feeling. We have at first unlimited faith in testimony; whatever is told us is presumed, as a matter of course, to be true, just as what we find on a first trial, is expected to hold always. Experience has to limit this sweeping confidence; and if likings and dislikings are kept under, and remembered facts are alone trusted to, we acquire what is called a rational belief in testimony, namely, a belief proportioned to the absence of contradictory facts.

Our belief is influenced by our fellow beings in obvious ways. Sympathy and Imitation make us adopt the actions and the feelings of those about us; and the effect of society does not stop here, but goes the length of compulsion. By these combined influences, we are educated in all beliefs that transcend our own experience, and swayed even in what falls under our observation.

A mere intellectual statement, often repeated, disposes us to credence, but does not amount to the state of belief, till we have occasion to take some action upon it; and the real force of the state arises when our action receives some confirmation. We are in a very loose state of mind as regards many floating doctrines, such as the recondite assertions of science, and the higher mysteries of the supernatural. Should we make a single experiment for ourselves, and find it accord with what has been affirmed, we are at once elevated into confidence, perhaps even beyond the actual truth; the untutored mind knowing nothing of the repetitions and precautions necessary to establish a fact.

The superstitious beliefs of unenlightened ages,—astrology, alchemy, witchcraft,—and the perversions of scientific truth in early philosophy from the various strong emotions, are all explicable upon the influence of feeling in the originators, with the subsequent addition of authority and imitation.

9. Belief is opposed, not by Disbelief, but by DOUBT.

As mental attitudes, Belief and Disbelief are the same. We cannot believe one thing without disbelieving some other thing; if we believe that the sun is risen, we must disbelieve that he is below the horizon.

When we are unable to obtain a conviction, one way or other, we are said to *doubt*, to be in a state of uncertainty, or suspense. If the thing concerns us little, we are indifferent to this absence of the means of conviction. The condition of doubt is manifested in its true character, as a distressing experience, when we are obliged to act and are yet uncertain as to the course. The connexion of means and end does not command our belief or assurance; there are opposing suggestions or appearances, more or less evenly balanced; or there is nothing to go upon in either way. Hence we are in danger of being baulked in our ends; and, in addition, have all the vacillation of a conflict. In matters of great import, doubt is the name for unspeakable misery.

Doubt and Fear, although distinguishable, run very closely together. Doubt, in its painful and distressing form, is precisely the state of Fear. A cause of fear deepens the condition of doubt; circumstances of doubt will intensify fear. The same temperament is victorious alike over doubt and fear; the active disposition has been seen to be a spring of courage.

10. The opposing designations HOPE and DESPONDENCY signify phases of Belief.

Hope expresses belief in its cheering or elating aspect, being the confidence in future good, the belief that some agreeable end is more or less certain in its arrival. It farther denotes something less than total or complete assurance, or rather it is considered as ranging in compass from the smallest degree of confidence that can have any elating effect, up to the highest point when prospect is on a level with possession. Hence, in expressing hope, we usually append an epithet of degree; we have good hopes of a prosperous commercial year, we have faint hopes of the next harvest.

The opposite of Hope is not Fear, but Despondency, the belief in coming evil, a condition of mind the more depressing as the belief is stronger. An army over-matched is despondent; that is, believes in impending defeat. The state of Fear very readily supervenes; but there may be despondency, with the absence of fear proper. The extreme of Despondency is Despair.

When the hope or the despondency can be based on certain evidence, or on probable evidence as entertained by a highly disciplined judgment, they are comparatively little affected by extraneous agencies of elation or depression. But in matters of probable evidence, and in minds of little stability, the state of hope or despondency fluctuates with the influences that raise or depress the general tone. Every thing already said, of Belief in general, is true of belief under the name of Hope.

CHAPTER IX.

THE MORAL HABITS.

1. THE Moral Habits are the acquirements relating to Feelings and Volitions.

Besides the intellectual acquirements properly so called, as Language, Science, &c., we have a series of growths consisting in the increase or diminution of the feelings, and in modifications of the strength of the will, whereby some motives gain and others lose in practical efficacy. We speak of habits of Courage, Fortitude, Command of Temper, meaning that those qualities have attained, through education, a degree not attaching to them naturally.

2. The Moral Acquirements come under the general conditions of Retentiveness.

In heightening, or in detracting from, the natural strength of feelings and volitions, we are aided by all the circumstances enumerated in regard to the attainments of the intellect.

In the first place, a certain *repetition* is necessary, greater or less according to the change that has to be affected, and to the absence of other favouring circumstances. The moral education seldom reaches maturity till a late period of life.

In the second place, the mind may be more or less *concentrated* on the acquisition. Apart from the amount of repetition, moral progress depends greatly on the bent of the learner towards the special acquisition. If we are striving *con amore* to attain any important habitude, such as the Command of the Attention, the currents of the brain are exclusively set in this one direction, instead of being divided with other engrossments. A less efficient, although still a powerful, stimulus, is the application of pain.

In the third place, individuals differ in the power of Retentiveness or Adhesiveness, as a whole; rendering them apt as learners generally.

There are also local endowments leading to a special retentiveness in matters of knowledge; as when the good natural ear brings about rapid musical attainments. It might be over-refining to attempt to carry this supposition into the domain of the feelings.

3. The conditions special to the Moral Acquirements are, first, an Initiative, and, secondly, a Gradual Exposure in cases of conflict.

As a large and important branch of moral acquisition consists in strengthening one power to overcome another, it is of great advantage to have an uninterrupted series of successes: which can only be secured by strongly backing at first the motive to be strengthened, and by never giving it too much to do. Defeats should be avoided, especially in the early stages.

4. We may begin the detail by adverting to the voluntary control of Sense and Appetite.

We have seen, in the conflict of Motives, the sensations and the appetites resisted by ideal considerations, that is, by good and evil in the distance. Now, this control depends, at first, on the relative strength of Appetite and of the Memory of good and evil; eventually, however, repeated action in one way, either in indulging or in thwarting the appetite, brings into play Retentiveness, or habit, as an additional force on the prevailing side.

Take, as an example, the endurance of cold, for purposes of healthy stimulation, as in habitual cold bathing and exposure to weather. There is a conflict of volition between present sensation, and good and evil in the distance. The ideal motive may be at first too weak, and may need strengthening; for which end, it is desired to superadd the force of habit. The commencement demands an Initiative. Some cause from without should induce the regular and systematic exposure of the body to cold water and cold air. At the early stages, there may be felt a revulsion at the process. Repetition, if steady, has a twofold effect; it lowers the painful sensibility, and increases the tendency to perform the actions as the appointed time comes round. Now, with a view to the more speedy attainment of these two ends, there should never be any intermission, or giving way; and the shock encountered should not be of such an extreme kind, as would make an insurmountable aversion. Hence, an adequate initiative should concur with a graduation of the exposure; with these two conditions, the progress of the habit is steady and sure. The subject of the experiment can, after a time, be left to the ordinary motives; the moral education being complete.

A parallel illustration applies to the whole department of Temperance or control of Appetite.

Under the present head, we may notice the Command of the Attention, as against the diversions and solicitations of outward things. The infant is at the mercy of every sight and every sound, and has no power of consecutive attention, unless under some one sensation stronger than any of the rest. Early education has to reclaim the wandering and volatile gaze. The child is set to a short lesson, in the first instance, under a sufficient pressure from without to maintain the attention during that time, and in spite of casual diversions. The demand for concentration is increased slowly, never exceeding what the combined force of the initiative and the acquired bent can achieve.

Belonging to various situations and occupations is the habit of becoming indifferent to noise and to the distraction of spectacle, as in the bustle of towns and places of business. The ability to seclude the attention in the midst of noise may be acquired, if the conditions can be complied with. There must be to commence with some power sufficient to divert the mind from the noise for certain periods of time; during every such period a lesson is taken, and, by sufficient repetition, the power of indifference may become complete for all circumstances. The inuring process, while succeeding in most instances, entirely fails in some; the reason being that the sensitiveness cannot by any influence be sufficiently overcome to make a beginning. If these susceptible minds, instead of being at once immersed in the uproar, could be subjected to a steadily increasing noise, they might be hardened at last.

5. Culture applied to the Special Emotions may embrace (1) the Emotional susceptibility on the whole, and (2) the Emotions singly.

THE MORAL HABITS.

(1) There is in each person a certain Emotional constitution, or natural proneness to Emotion generally; shown in the amount of emotional fervour and display. This may be increased or diminished by cultivation, at the expense of the two other departments of the mind. By sympathy, stimulation, and encouragement, by occupying the mind with emotional exercises, the department acquires more than its natural dimensions, while Volition and Intellect are proportionably shrivelled. If, besides the positive encouragement of the emotional side, there are positive discouragements to exerting Will and Intelligence, the work of re-adjustment will go on still faster.

There are nations whose character is highly emotional in comparison with others; at the head of the scale in Europe, we may place the Italians, after which come the French, Germans, English. An English child domesticated in Rome or Florence, would contract something of the Italian fervour; an Italian child, reared in the north of Scotland, would be rendered more volitional or intellectual, and less emotional.

The leading displays of Emotion generally are, the susceptibility to Amusement, great Sociability, devotion to Fine Art, the warmer modes of Religious sentiment, and an emotional colouring impressed on scientific doctrines.

(2) Any single emotion may be made more or less copious. Much important discipline is involved in the encouragement or repression of individual emotions.

For example, the pleasure of Liberty, with the pain of Constraint, needs to be surmounted in many ways, being opposed to Industry, to Obedience or submission, and to the checks and obstructions of one's lot. No better example can be given of the power of habituation; while the manner of attaining it is in full accordance with the general rules. The dislike to restraints may be completely overcome, and with it the pleasurable rebound of liberty. When this is the case, we shall find that the initiative has been all-powerful to secure unbroken submission. In every well-ordered mind, there are numerous instances of restraints, at first painful, now utterly indifferent; scarcely any pleasure would be felt in breaking out from them. The old soldier has contracted a punctuality and an obedience, so thorough as to be mechanical; he neither feels the pang of constraint, nor would he rejoice in being set free from the obligation.

We have, in the case of Terror, a valuable illustration of the imperative nature of a gradual habituation. With a view to impart a certain degree of courage to a timid constitution, it is above all things necessary to avoid a severe fright. A gentle and graduated exposure to occasions of alarm might do much to establish courage by habit, all other circumstances being favourable; a single giving way is a serious loss of ground.

The developments of the Tender Feeling include an extensive course of habituation. Irrespective of the associations that connect it with special objects, constituting the affections, the indulgence of tender feeling increases the power of the emotion as a whole.

The Emotion of Self-tenderness, or Self-complacency, being a special direction of the general feeling, is amenable to culture or restraint. The initiative in the case must be the individual's own volition, it being impracticable for others to control, otherwise than by example or moral suasion, an emotion that works unseen.

The Emotion of Approbation, Praise, Glory, may be repressed by control, and its repression rendered habitual. It is a part of every one's experience to share in unmerited reproaches: and public men more especially have to contract a settled indifference to abuse. This is one of the cases where the system adjusts itself by the operation of Relativity. As praise and censure are felt in their highest force only while fresh, they are dependent on the occurrence of new occasions.

It is almost, if not altogether, a contradictory aim to become indifferent to blame, while fostering the pleasure of praise. We may acquire by habit a certain amount of indifference to other men's opinions, favourable or unfavourable, surrendering the pleasure as well as surmounting the pain. There is another course somewhat less sweeping: namely, to acquire a settled disesteem, or contempt, of certain individuals, whose censure thereby loses its force; while we retain a susceptibility to the opinion of others disposed to praise more than to blame us.

The Emotion of Power, being in its unbridled gratification so mischievous, is subjected to control on moral grounds. To attain habits of moderation in regard to this craving, a man must be himself impressed with the evils of it, so as to put forth a commanding volition, and thereby initiate a habitual coercion.

The outbursts of Irascibility have to be checked by voluntary control confirmed into habit. The education of the young comprises this department. The value of the initiative is fully manifested in this case. External influence, according to an ideal mixture of firmness and conciliation, is most happily employed in restraining the childish ebullitions of temper, so as to mature an early habit of coolness and suppression. It is more difficult to reach the deep-seated pleasure of malevolence than to check the incontinent paroxysms most usually identified with irascibility. A man may be exacting, jealous, revengeful, without showing fits of ill temper.

The department of Plot-interest may be pandered to by incontinent amusement, or restrained by self-command and by early discipline. A great indulgence in the amusements described under this head is a test of the Emotional nature as a whole.

The Emotions of Intellect are cherished or suppressed by the same causes as the intellect itself.

On the cultivation of Taste there is nothing new to be said. The transformation of a human being, born with a deficient sensibility, into an artistic nature, expresses perhaps the very utmost stretch that culture can effect, every circumstance being supposed favourable. There must be a great starving down of the predominating elements of the character, to bring forward this single feature from its low, to a high, estate.

The Moral Feelings exemplify in the most interesting case of all, the same general considerations. When the elements of the moral sentiment are known, the manner of its development and its confirmation into habit are sufficiently plain; but the importance of the subject deserves a separate chapter.

6. Certain Habits may be specified under the Activity or the Will.

(1) In connexion with the active organs, we contract habits of invigoration and endurance, as the result of practice. Whatever organ is steadily employed—the arm, the hand, the voice—attains greater strength and persistence, provided the habituation is gradual, and the demands never too great. Still, we must not forget, that such a strengthening process, if carried far, will usurp so much of the nutrition of the system, as seriously to impair other functions either bodily or mental. As regards physical expenditure, the intellect is our most costly function.

To evolve a larger quantity of spontaneous action than belongs to the constitution by nature, is one of the possible

CONTROL OF THE INTELLECTUAL TRAINS. 391

ways of re-distributing the powers of the system. A languid, inactive temperament may be spurred up to greater energy, by surrendering some other point of superiority; as when a man whose *forte* is intelligence enters the army, or other active profession.

(2) The habit of Endurance, as connected with Desire, might be advantageously dwelt upon. There are instances, where endurance is made habitual, under an outward initiative, as in apprenticeship to work. In other cases, it is the will's own resolution, under motives of good and evil. If a certain degree of steadiness can be maintained in bearing up against any endurable pain, the reward will follow in abatement of the effort or struggle.

7. The voluntary control of the Intellectual trains may pass into Habit.

There are two special modes of voluntary control of the trains of thought, and, in both, practice leads to habit.

(1) Mental concentration, as against digressions, wanderings, reveries, may be commanded by motive; and, if initiated adequately and maintained persistently, may acquire the ease that habituation gives.

(2) The power of dismissing a subject from the mind is an exercise of will in opposition to intellectual persistence, and is difficult according as that persistence is inflamed by feeling. At first a severe or impracticable effort, it is eventually commanded by men trained to intellectual professions, and is essential to the despatch of multifarious business.

It is important to repeat, that many of the acquisitions, detailed in this chapter, are vast changes, amounting almost to a reconstruction of the human character; and that, to render them possible, the conditions of plastic growth must be present in an unusually favourable degree. Bodily health and nourishment, exemption from fatigues, worry and harassment, absence of heavy drafts upon the plastic power by other acquisitions, together with the special conditions more particularly urged in this chapter, must conspire with a constitutional endowment of Retentiveness, to operate these great moral revolutions.

CHAPTER X.

PRUDENCE.—DUTY.—MORAL INABILITY.

1. HUMAN Pursuit, as a whole, is divided, for important practical reasons, into two great departments.

The first embraces the highest and most comprehensive regard to Self; and is designated PRUDENCE, Self-Love, the search after Happiness. It is opposed or thwarted mainly by the urgency of present good or evil, and by fixed ideas.

Happiness is made up of the total of our pleasures, diminished by the total of our pains; and the endeavour after it resolves itself into seeking the one and avoiding the other. There is a complicated mixture of good and evil always in the distance, and even in the absence of moral weakness, we should find the problem of our greatest happiness on the whole, one of considerable perplexity.

The influences on the side of Prudence are these:—

(1) The natural aptitude, so often alluded to, for remembering good and evil, by which the future interests are powerfully represented in the conflict with present or actual pleasure and pain.

(2) The influences brought to bear upon the mind, especially in early years, in the way of authority, example, warning, instruction; all which, if happily administered, may both supply motives and build up habits, such as to counteract the strong solicitations of present appetite or emotion.

(3) The acquired knowledge, referring to the good and evil consequences of action. A full acquaintance with the laws of our own bodies and minds, with the ongoings of society, and with the order of nature generally, counts on the side of prudence by making us aware of the less obvious tendencies of conduct.

(4) The floating opinion of those around us, the public inculcation of virtuous conduct, and the whole literature of moral suasion, backed by the display of approved examples, go a great way to form the prudential character of the mature individual.

Although the proper function of public opinion is to mould us to *duty*, as contrasted with mere prudence, yet in no country, has society refrained from both teaching and even compelling prudential conduct, according to approved standards.

(5) The reflections of the individual mind, frequently and earnestly turned upon what is best in the long run, are a powerful adjunct to the building up of a prudential character. The more we allow ourselves to dwell upon past errors, the more we increase their deterring force in the future. Moreover, a certain deliberative habit is necessary to carrying out wisely any end of pursuit, and most of all the pursuit of the end that includes and reconciles so many ends.

2. The second department of pursuit comprises the regard to others, and is named DUTY. It is warred against not only by the forces inimical to Prudence, but also occasionally by Prudence itself.

That, in the pursuit of our happiness, we shall not infringe on the happiness of others, is Duty, in its most imperative form. How far we shall make positive contributions to the good of our fellows is less definitely settled.

The following are the prominent influences in favour of Duty.

I.—The Sympathetic part of our nature has already been pointed out as the chief fountain of disinterested action. By virtue of sympathy, we are restrained from hurting other sentient beings; and the stronger the sympathy, the greater the restraint. In many instances, we abandon pleasures, and incur pains, rather than give pain to some one that has engaged our sympathy.

Sympathy is, in its foundation, a natural endowment, very feebly manifested in the lower races. It differs greatly among individuals of the same race; and may be much improved by education. Its main condition is the giving heed or attention to the feelings of others, instead of being wholly and at all times absorbed with what concerns ourselves alone; and this attention may be prompted by instructors and confirmed into habit.

II.—No amount of sympathy ever yet manifested by human beings would be enough to protect one man from another. The largest part of the check consists in the application of Prudential or self-regarding motives.

(1) Punishment, or the deliberate infliction of pain, in the

name of the collective mass of beings making a society, is the foremost incentive to Duty, considered as abstinence from injuring others. Not only is this the chief deterring instrument, it is also the means of settling and defining what duty is. Society prescribes the acts that are held to be injurious, and does not leave the point to the option of the individual citizen. Our own sympathies might take a different direction, inducing us to abstain from what the society enjoins, and do what society forbids ; but we are not permitted to exercise our own discretion in the matter. Hence duty is the line chalked out by public authority, or law, and indicated by penalty or punishment.

The penalties of law are thus of a two-fold importance in the matter of duty ; they both teach and enforce it. The frequent practice of abstaining from punishable acts generates the most important of all our active states, the aversion to whatever is forbidden in this form. Such aversion is Conscience in its most general type.

(2) The sense of our personal interest in establishing a systematic abstinence from injury on the part of one man to another, is a strong motive of the prudential kind. A very little reflection teaches us that unless each person consents of his own accord to abstain from molesting his neighbour, he is not safe himself; and that the best thing for all is a mutual understanding, or compact of non-interference, observed by each. No society can exist unless a considerable majority of its members are disposed to enter into, and to observe, such a compact. Punishment could not be applied to a whole community ; it is practicable only when the majority are voluntary in their own obedience, and strong enough to coerce the breakers of the compact.

It may be fairly doubted whether the most enlightened prudence would be enough of itself to maintain social obedience. At all events, self-love will do little or nothing for improving the condition of society ; to the pure self-seeker, posterity weighs as nothing. Nor would self-love easily allow of that temporary expenditure that is repaid by the affection of others ; a certain amount of natural generosity is necessary to reap this kind of gratification.

The average constitution of civilized man is a certain mixture of the prudential and the sympathetic; both elements are present, and neither is very powerful. Individuals are to be found prudential in the extreme, with little sympathy, and sympathetic in the extreme with little prudence; but an ordinary man has a moderate share of both. The performance of duty is secured in part by the self-regarding motives, and in part by the sympathetic or generous impulses, which prompt a certain amount of abstinence from injury and of self-sacrifice.

3. The supporting adjuncts of prudence are also applicable to strengthening the motives of Duty.

The arts of moral discipline and moral suasion, in other words, the means of inculcating the conduct prescribed by society as binding on all citizens, are numerous and well known. Early inculcation, and example, together with the use of punishment; the force of the public sentiment concurring with the power of the magistrate; the systematic reminders of the religious and moral teacher; the insinuating lessons of polite literature; and, not least, the mind's own habits of reflection upon duty;—are efficacious in bringing forward both the sympathetic and the self-regarding motives to abstain from the conduct forbidden by the social authority.

4. MORAL INABILITY expresses the insufficiency of ordinary motives, but not of all motives.

The child that cannot resist the temptation of sweets, the confirmed drunkard, the incorrigible thief, are spoken of as labouring under moral inability to comply with the behests of prudence and of duty. The meaning is, that the motives on one side are not adequately encountered by motives on the other side. It is not implied that motives might not be found strong enough to change the conduct in all cases. Still less is it implied that the link of uniform causation in the case of motive and action is irregular and uncertain.

There are states of mind, wherein all motives lose their power. An inability to remember or realize the consequences of actions; or a morbid delusion such as to pervert the trains of thought, will render a human being no longer amenable to the strongest motives; the inability then ceases to be moral. This is the state of insanity, and irresponsibility.

There is a middle condition between the sane and the properly insane, where motives have not lost their force, but where the severest sanctions of society, although present to the mind, are unequal to the passion of the moment. Such passionate fits may occur, under extraordinary circumstances, to persons accounted sane and responsible for their actions; if they occur to any one frequently, and under slight provocation, they constitute a degree of moral inability verging on the irresponsible.

In criminal procedure, a man is accounted responsible, if motives still continue to have power over him. There is no other general rule. It is requisite, in order to sustain the plea of irresponsibility or insanity, that the accused should not only be, but appear to the world generally to be, beyond the influence of motives.

CHAPTER XI.

LIBERTY AND NECESSITY.

1. THE exposition of the Will has proceeded on the Uniformity of Sequence between motive and action.

Throughout the foregoing chapters, it is either openly affirmed or tacitly supposed, that the same motive, in the same circumstances, will be followed by the same action. The uniformity of sequence, admitted to prevail in the physical world, is held to exist in the mental world, although the terms of the sequence are of a different character, as involving states of the subjective consciousness. Without this assumption, the whole superstructure of the theory of volition would be the baseless fabric of a vision. In so far as that theory has appeared to tally with the known facts and experience of human conduct, it vouches for the existence of law in the department of voluntary action.

Apart from the speculations and inductions of mental science, the practice of mankind, in the furtherance of their interests, assumes the principle of uniformity. No one ever supposes, either that human actions arise without motive, or that the same motives operate differently in the same circumstances. Hunger always impels to the search for food; tender feeling seeks objects of affection; anger leads to acts of revenge. If there be any interruption to these sequences, it is not put down to failure of the motives, but to the co-existence of others more powerful.

The operations of trade, of government, of human intercourse generally, would be impracticable without a reign of law in the actions of human beings. The master has to assume that wages will secure service; the sovereign power would have no basis but for the deterring operation of punishment. Such a thing as *character*, or the prediction of a man's future conduct from the past, would be unknown. We could no more subsist upon uncertainty in the moral world, than we could live on a planet where gravitation was liable to fits of intermission.

If it be true that by the side of all mental phenomena there runs a line of physical causation, the interruption of the mental sequences would imply irregularity in the physical. The two worlds must stand or fall together.

The prediction of human conduct is not less sure than the prediction of physical phenomena. The training of the mind is subject to no more uncertainty than the training of the body. The difficulty in both cases is the same, the complication and obscurity of the agents at work; and there are many instances where the mental is the more predicable of the two.

The universality of the law of causation has been denied both in ancient and in modern times; but the denial has not been restricted to the domain of mind. Sokrates divided knowledge into the *divine* and the *human*. Under the *divine*, he ranked Astronomy and Physical Philosophy generally, a department that was beyond the reach of human study, and reserved by the gods for their own special control, it being a profanity on the part of human beings to enquire by what laws, or on what principles, the department was regulated. The only course permitted was to approach the deities, and to ascertain their will and pleasure, by oracles and sacrifices. The *human* department included the peculiarly Sokratic enquiries respecting just and unjust, honourable and base, piety and impiety, sobriety, temperance, courage, the government of a state, and such like matters; on all these things, it was proper and imperative to make observations and enquiries, and to be guided in our conduct by the conclusions of our own intelligence.

A modern doctrine, qualifying the law of universal causation, is seen in the theory of a particular providence expounded by Thomas Chalmers and others. It is maintained that the Deity, while observing a strict regularity in all the phenomena that are

19

patent and understood, as the motions of the planets, the flow of the tides, the descent of rivers, may in the unexplained mysteries introduce deviations, as in the vicissitudes of the weather, the recovery of a sick man, or in turning the scale of a complicated deliberation of the mind.

In such theories, it is to be observed, that the exception to law is not confined to the mental world, but embraces, to an equal, if not to a greater, extent, the physical world.

2. The perplexity of the question of Free-will is mainly owing to the inaptness of the terms to express the facts.

The idea of 'freedom' as attaching to the human will appears as early as the writings of the Stoics. The virtuous man was said to be *free*, and the vicious man a *slave;* the intention of the metaphor being not to explain voluntary action, but to attach an elevating and ennobling attribute to virtue. Sokrates had used the same figure to contrast the inquirers into what he considered the proper departments of human study (justice, piety, &c.), with those that knew nothing of such subjects.

The epithets 'free' and 'slave,' as applied the one to the virtuous, the other to the vicious man, occur largely in the writings of Philo Judæus, through whom they probably extended to Christian Theology. As regards appropriateness in everything but the associations of dignity and indignity, no metaphors could have been more unhappy. So far as the idea of subjection is concerned, the virtuous man is the greater slave of the two; the more virtuous he is, the more he submits himself to authority and restraints of every description; while the thoroughly vicious man emancipates himself from every obligation, and is only rendered a slave at last when his fellows will tolerate him no longer. The true type of freedom is an unpunished villain, or a successful usurper.

The modern doctrine of Free-will, as opposed to Necessity, first assumed prominence and importance in connexion with the theory of Original Sin, and the Predestinarian views of St. Augustin. In a later age, it was disputed between Arminians and Calvinists.

The capital objection to Free-will, is the unsuitability, irrelevance, or impropriety of the metaphor 'freedom' in the question of the sequence of motive and act in volition. The proper meaning of 'free' is the absence of external compulsion; every sentient being, under a motive to act, and not interfered with by any other being, is to all intents free; the fox impelled by hunger, and proceeding unmolested to a poultry yard, is a free agent. Free trade, free soil, free press, have all intelligible significations; but the question whether, without any reference to outward compulsion, a man in following the bent of his own motives, is free, or is necessitated by his motives, has no relevance. If necessity means that every time a wish arises in the mind, it is gratified without fail; that there is no bar whatever to the realizing of every conceived pleasure, and the extinction of every nascent pain; such necessity is also the acme of freedom. The unfaltering sequence of motive and act, of desire and fulfilment, may be called necessity, but it is also perfect bliss; what we term freedom is but a means to such a consummation.

The speciality of voluntary action, as compared with the powers of the inanimate world, is that the antecedent and the consequent are conscious or mental states (coupled of course with bodily states). When a sentient creature is conscious of a pleasure or pain, real or ideal, and follows that up with a conscious exercise of its muscles, we have the fact of volition; a fact very different from the motion of running water, or of a shooting star, and requiring to be described in phraseology embodying mental facts as well as physical. But neither 'freedom' nor 'necessity' is the word for expressing what happens. There are always present two distinct phenomena, which have to be represented for what they are, a phenomenon of mind conjoined with a fact of body. The two phenomena are successive in time; the feeling first, the movement second. Our mental life contains a great many of these successions—pleasures followed by actions, and pains followed by actions. Not unfrequently two, three, or four feelings occur together, conspiring or conflicting with one another; and then the action is not what was wont to follow one feeling by itself, but is a resultant of the several feelings. Practically, this is a puzzle to the spectator, who cannot make due allowances for the plurality of impulses; but it makes no more difference to the phenomenon, than the difference between a stone falling perpendicular under the one force of the earth's gravity, and the moon impelled by a concurrence of forces calculable only by high mathematics.

We do not convert mental sequences into pure material laws, by calling them sequences, and maintaining them (on evidence of fact) to be uniform in their working. Even, if we did make this blundering conversion, the remedy would not lie in the use of the word 'free.' We might with equal appropriateness describe the stone as free to fall, the moon as free to deviate under solar disturbance; for the stone might be restrained, and the moon somehow compelled to keep to an ellipse. Such phraseology would be obviously unmeaning and absurd, but not a whit more so, than in the application to the mental sequence of voluntary action.*

3. On the doctrine of the uniform sequence of motive and action, meanings can be assigned to the several terms —Choice, Deliberation, Self-Determination, Moral Agency, Responsibility.

These terms are supposed to involve, more or less, the Liberty of the Will, and to be inexplicable on any other theory. They may all be explained, however, without the mysticism of Free-will.

Choice. When a person chooses one thing out of several presented, the choice is said to involve liberty or freedom. The simple fact is that each one of the objects has a certain attraction; while that fixed upon is presumed to have the greatest attraction of any. There are three dishes before one

* As it may seem an unlikely and overstrained hypothesis to represent men of the highest enlightenment as entangled in a mere verbal inaccuracy, a few parallel cases may be presented to the student.

The Eleatic Zeno endeavoured to demonstrate the impossibility of motion. He said that a body must move either in the place where it is, or in the place where it is not; but in neither case is motion possible; for on the first supposition the body leaves its place, and the second is absurd. Here is a plain fact contradicted by what has seemed to many an unanswerable demonstration. The real answer is that the language contradicts itself; motion is incompatible with the phrase *in* a place; the fact is properly expressed by *change of place.* Introduce this definition and the puzzle is at an end; retain the incompatible expression *in* a place, and there is an insoluble mystery. By a similar ingenuity in quibbling upon the word Infinite, the same philosopher reasoned that if Achilles and a Tortoise were to begin a race, Achilles would never beat the tortoise.

In the Philebus of Plato, there is a mystical theory wrought up through the application of the terms 'true' and 'false' to pleasures and pains. Truth and falsehood are properties belonging only to affirmations or beliefs; their employment to qualify pleasure and pain can only produce the nonsensical or absurd. As well might a pleasure be called round or square, wet or dry.

Many absurd questions have arisen through misapplying the attributes of the Extended or Object World, to the Subject Mind. If we were to ask how many pure spirits could stand on the point of a needle, or be contained in a cubical space, we should be guilty of the fallacy of irrelevant predication. The schoolmen debated whether the mind was in every part of the body, or only in the whole; the question is insoluble, because unreal. It is not an intelligible proposition, but a jargon.

at table; the one partaken of is what the individual likes best on the whole. This is the entire signification of choice. *Liberty* of choice has no meaning or application, unless with reference to some prohibition from without; the child who is not allowed to eat but of one dish, has no liberty of choice. In the absence of prohibition, the decision follows the strongest motive; being in fact the only test of strength of motive on the whole. One may choose the dish that gives least present gratification, but if so, there must be some other motive of good or evil in the distance. Any supposition of our acting without adequate motive leads at once to a self-contradiction; for we always judge of strength of motive by the action that prevails.

Deliberation. This word has already been explained at length, on the Motive theory of the Will. There is nothing implied under it that would countenance the employment of the unfortunate metaphor 'freedom.' When we are subjected to two opposing motives, several things may happen. We may decide at once, which shows that one is stronger than the other; we come upon three branching roads, and follow the one on the right, showing a decided preponderance of motive in that direction. This is simple choice without deliberative suspense. The second possibility is suspended action. This shows either that the motives are equally balanced, causing indecision, or that the deliberative veto is in exercise, whose motive is the experienced evils of hasty action in cases of distracting motives. After a time, the veto is withdrawn, the judgment being satisfied that sufficient comparison of opposing solicitations has been allowed; action ensues, and testifies which motive has in the end proved the strongest.

There is no relevant application of the term 'freedom' in any part of this process, unless on the supposition of being driven into action, by a power from without. A traveller with a brigand's pistol at his ear has no liberty of deliberation, or of anything else. An assembly surrounded with an armed force has lost its freedom. A mind exempt from all such compulsion is under the play of various motives, and at last decides; some one or more of the motives is thereby demonstrated superior to the others.

Self-determination. There is supposed to be implied in this word some peculiarity not fully expressed by the sequence of motive and action. A certain entity called 'self,' irresolvable into motive, is believed to interfere in voluntary action.

But, as with the other terms, self-determination has no intelligible meaning, except as opposed to compulsion from without. If a man's conduct follows the motives of his own mind, instead of being dictated by another man, he possesses self-determination in the proper sense of the word. It is not requisite that he should act otherwise than from sufficient motives, in order to be self-determined. 'Self,' in the matter of action, is only the sum of the feelings, pleasurable and painful, actual and ideal, that impel the conduct, together with the various activities impelled.

Self-determination may be used to indicate an important difference in our motives, the difference between the *permanent* interests and the *temporary* solicitations. He that submits to the first class is considered to be more particularly self-determined, than he that gives way to the temporary and passing motives. The distinction is real and important, and has been fully accounted for in the exposition of the Will. To neutralize, by internal resources, the fleeting actualities of pleasure and pain, is a great display of moral power, but has no bearing upon the supposed 'freedom' of the will. It is a fact of character, exactly expressed by the acquired strength of the ideal motives, which strength is shown by the fact of superiority to the present and the actual. Rigorous constancy is the glory of the character; the higher the constancy, the predictability, of the agent, the higher the excellence attained.

The collective 'I' or 'self' can be nothing different from the Feelings, Actions, and Intelligence of the individual; unless, indeed, the threefold classification of the mind be incomplete. But so long as human conduct can be accounted for by assigning certain Sensibilities to pleasure and pain, an Active machinery, and an Intelligence, we need not assume anything else to make up the 'I' or 'self.' When 'I' walk in the fields, there is nothing but a certain motive, founded in my feelings, operating upon my active organs; the sequence of these two portions of self gives the whole fact. The mode of expression 'I walk' does not alter the nature of the phenomenon.

Self-determination may put on an appearance of evading or contradicting the sequence of the will; as when a man departs from his usual line of conduct in order to puzzle or mystify spectators. It is, however, very obvious that the suspension of the person's usual conduct is still not without motive; there is a sufficiency of motive in the feelings of pride or satisfaction, in baulking the curiosity, or in overthrowing the calculations, of other persons.

The word 'Spontaneity' is a synonym for self-determination, but comes no nearer to a justification of the absurd metaphor. We have seen one important meaning of the word, in the doctrine of the inherent activity of the animal system, as contrasted with the activity stimulated by sense. The more common meaning is the same as above described, and has a tacit reference to the absence of compulsion, or even of suggestion or prompting, from without. The witness of a crime, in giving information without being summoned, acts spontaneously.

Moral Agency. The word 'moral' is ambiguous. As opposed to physical or material, it means mental, belonging to mind; in which signification, a moral agent is a voluntary agent, a being whose actions are impelled by its feelings.

It is no part of moral agency, in this sense, that there should be any suspension of the usual course of motives; it is necessary only that the individual being should feel pleasure and pain, and act with reference to those feelings. Every creature possessing mind is a moral agent.

In the second meaning, moral is opposed to immoral, or wrong, and is the same as 'right.' This is a much narrower signification. When Moral Philosophy is restricted to mean Ethical philosophy, or Duty, 'Moral' means appertaining to right and wrong, to duty, morality.

In this sense, a moral agent is one that acts according to right or duty, or else one whose actions are made amenable to a standard of right and wrong. The brutes are not moral agents in this signification, although they are in the preceding; no more are children, or the insane.

The circumstances that explain moral agency, in the narrower and more dignified application of the word, appear best in connexion with the word next to be commented on.

Responsibility, Accountability. A moral agent is usually said to be a responsible or accountable agent. The word responsibility is, properly speaking, figurative; by what is called 'metonymy,' the fact intended to be expressed is denoted by one of the adjuncts. A whole train of circumstances is supposed, of which only one is named. There are assumed (1) Law, or Authority, (2) actual or possible Disobedience, (3) an Accusation brought against the person disobeying, (4) the *Answer* to this accusation, and (5) the infliction of Punishment, in case the answer is deemed insufficient to purge the accusation.

It is hard at a first glance to see what connexion a supposed freedom of action has to do with any part of this process. According to the motive theory of the will, all is plain and straightforward. Assume the existence of Law, and everything follows by a natural course. To ensure obedience to law there must be some pain inflicted on the disobedient, sufficient, and no more sufficient, to deter from disobedience. Whoever is placed under the law, is liable to the penalty of disobeying it; but in all countries, ever so little civilized, certain forms are gone through to ensure the guilt of every one accused of disobedience, to which the words Responsibility, Accountability, are strictly applicable; after these forms are satisfied, and the guilt established, the penalty is inflicted.

Endless puzzles are foisted into a very simple process, the moment the word 'freedom' is mentioned. It is said, that it would not be right to punish a man unless he were a free agent; a truism, if by freedom, is meant only the absence of outward compulsion; in any other sense, a piece of absurdity. If it is expedient to place restrictions upon the conduct of sentient beings, and if the threatening of pain operates to arrest such conduct, the case for punishment is made out. We must justify the institution of Law, to begin with, and the tendency of pain to prevent the actions that bring it on, in the next place. The first postulate is Human Society; the second is the connexion (which must be uniform) between pain and action for avoiding it. Granting these two postulates, Punishability (carrying with it, in a well constituted society, Responsibility), is amply vindicated.

Whatever be the view taken of the ends of Punishment, it supposes the theory of the will as here contended for, namely, a uniform connexion between motive and act. Unless pain, present or prospective, impels human beings to avoid whatever brings it, and to perform whatever delivers from it, punishment has no relevance, whether the end be the benefit of the society, or the benefit of the offender, or both together.*

---

* The question has been debated, 'Is a man responsible for his Belief;' in other words, Is society justified in punishing men for their opinions? The two criteria of punishability will indicate the solution. In the first place, ought there to be Laws declaring that all citizens shall believe certain things? Secondly, will pains and penalties influence a man's belief, in the same way that they can influence actions? The answer to the first question, is another question, 'Shall there be Toleration of all opinions?' The answer to the second is, that penalties are

Another factitious difficulty originated in relation to punishment is the argument of the Owenites, 'that a man's actions are the result of his character, and he is not the author of his character: instead of punishing criminals, therefore, society should give them a better education.' The answer to which is, that society should do its best to educate all citizens to do right; but what if this education consists mainly in Punishment? Withdraw the power of punishing, and there is left no conceivable instrument of moral education. It is true that a good moral discipline is not wholly made up of punishment; the wise and benevolent parent does something, by the methods of allurement and kindness, to form the virtuous dispositions of the child. Still, we may ask, was ever any human being educated to the sense of right and wrong without the dread of pain accompanying forbidden actions? It may be affirmed, with safety, that punishment, or retribubution in some form, is one-half of the motive power to virtue in the very best of human beings, while it is more than three-fourths in the mass of mankind.

Another awkward form of expression connected with the subject is, that 'we can improve our character if we will.' This seems a contradiction to the motive theory of the Will, which makes man, as it were, the creature of circumstances. There is in the language, however, merely an example of the snares that we may get ourselves into, through seizing a question by the wrong end. Our character is improvable, when there are present to our minds motives to improve it; it is not improvable without such motives. No character is ever improved without an apposite train of motives—either the punishment renounced by the Owenite, or certain feelings of another kind, such as affections, sympathies, lofty ideals, and so on. To present these motives to the mind of any one is to employ the engines of improvement. To say to a man, you can improve if you will, is to employ a nonsensical formula; under cover of which, however, may lie some genuine motive power. For the speaker is, at the same time, intimating his own strong wish that his hearer should improve; he is presenting to the hearer's mind the IDEA of improvement: and probably, along with that, a number of fortifying considerations all of the nature of proper motives.

able to control beliefs, with a slight qualification. They can put a stop to the *profession* of any opinion; and in matters of doubtful speculation, they can so dispose the course of education and enquiry, that the mass of mankind shall firmly believe whatever the State dictates.

The word 'will,' in such expressions as the above, is a fiction thrust into the phenomenon of volition, like the word 'power' in cause and effect generally. To express causation we need only name one thing, the antecedent, or cause, and another thing, the effect; a flying cannon shot is a cause, the tumbling down of a wall is the effect. But people sometimes allow themselves the use of the additional word 'power' to complete as they suppose the statement; the cannon ball in motion has the 'power' to batter walls; a pure expletive, or pleonasm, whose tendency is to create a mystical or fictitious agency, in addition to the real agent, the moving ball.

To say we can be virtuous if we like, is about the worst way of expressing the simple fact, namely, that virtuous acts and a virtuous character are the consequence of certain appropriate motives or antecedents. Whoever wishes to make another person virtuous can proceed direct to the mark by supplying the known antecedents, not omitting penalties; whoever wishes to make himself virtuous, has, in the very act of wishing, a present motive, which will go a certain way to produce the effect.

The use of the phrase 'you can if you will,' besides acting as a cover for real motives, is a sort of appeal to the pride or dignity of a human being, and in that circumstance, may not be without some Rhetorical efficiency; insinuated praise is an oratorical weapon. As Rhetoric, the language may have some justification; the disaster is that the Rhetoric should be taken for good science and logic. The whole series of phrases connected with Will, Freedom, Choice, Deliberation, Self-Determination, Power to act if we will, are contrived to foster in us a feeling of artificial importance and dignity, by assimilating the too humble sequence of motive and act to the illustrious functions of the Judge, the Sovereign, the Umpire.

HISTORY OF THE FREE-WILL CONTROVERSY.

PLATO makes the distinction of voluntary and involuntary (ἑκούσιος and ἀκούσιος); but he does not ask whether the will is self-determined or whether it is necessitated.

ARISTOTLE'S doctrine of the Voluntary and Involuntary, as contained in the Nicomachean Ethics, Book III., is fully given in the abstract of that work (ETHICAL SYSTEMS, Aristotle). The misleading terms—Liberty and Necessity—had not in his time found their way into the subject; and he discusses the motives to the will from a practical and inductive point of view.

The STOICS and EPICUREANS, like Aristotle, can hardly be regarded as contributing to the history of the proper Free-will

FREE-WILL CONTROVERSY—THE FATHERS.

controversy, and their views are best given in connexion with their ethical doctrines (ETHICAL SYSTEMS, The Stoics, and The Epicureans).

From PLOTINUS we learn how the problem of freedom was understood by the NEO-PLATONISTS. Will ($\theta \acute{\epsilon} \lambda \eta \sigma \iota \varsigma$) is not a faculty of the soul, but its essential attribute. It is not the same thing as liberty. Voluntary action ($\tau \grave{o}$ $\acute{\epsilon} \kappa o \acute{v} \sigma \iota o \nu$) is power to act accompanied by a consciousness of what is done. Liberty is when the power to act is not impeded by any external restraint. Thus killing a man unconsciously is a free act, but not voluntary. Liberty in man consists in being able to live a pure and perfect life, conformably to the nature of the soul. The nature of every creature tends necessarily towards its good; whatever diverts it from this end is involuntary; whatever leads it thither is voluntary. Freedom is thus made to consist in independence of external causes. Plotinus does not therefore touch the peculiar problem of the will, whether the will is necessarily determined by motives; but merely expands the popular notion that freedom is to follow persistently what is good, and slavery to follow what is bad. We speak of slaves to sin, more rarely of slaves to holiness; yet, from the point of view of necessity, both expressions are equally correct, or equally incorrect.

The Christian Apologists of the second century insist strongly on what they call the freedom of the will. In opposition to the fatalism of the Stoics, and the apathy of the Epicureans, they laid great stress upon man's power to judge and act for himself. JUSTIN MARTYR (A.D. 150) attacks the Stoical doctrine of Fate. It is opposed to their own moral teaching, and overlooks the power of the demons. It is by free choice that men do right or wrong, and it is by the power of the demons that earnest men, like Sokrates, suffer, while Sardanapalus and Epicurus live in abundance and glory. The Stoics maintained that all things took place according to the necessity of Fate. Justin pointed out the dilemma in which this doctrine held them. If everything be derived from fate, wickedness is, and so God or fate is the cause of sin. The alternative is, that there is no real difference between virtue and vice, which is contrary to all sound sense and reason.

TERTULLIAN (160-220) in his paper against Marcion, vindicates the freedom of the will. Could not God have prevented the entrance of sin? And if he could, why did he not? Tertullian answers that evil arose, not from God, but from man. Man was left free to choose good or evil, life or death. But should not God have withheld this fatal gift? Nay, in bestowing liberty, was he not responsible for the consequent fall? Tertullian answers very rhetorically, what could be better than to make man in the image of God? It would be strange if man, the lord of others, should himself be a slave. This argument illustrates the use that the theory of free-will has been put to by theologians. It has been regarded as a door of escape from the awful dilemma that, in all ages, staggers piety, and strikes reason dumb: If God was willing that evil should be, he is not good; if he was unwilling, then he is not Almighty. This imports into the discussion an apparently insoluble contradiction, and necessarily leads to bewilderment and mystery. Admitting that our volitions are subject to the law of causation, it is possible and easy to vindicate human justice; it is possible even, to a certain extent, to vindicate divine justice. For since we are imperfect and in need of moral discipline, we must see that punishment is eminently calculated to effect our improvement. Why we were not made perfect at once, why the pursuit of happiness should be so arduous—it belongs not to any theory of the will to explain.

ST. AUGUSTIN, Bishop of Hippo (353-429), is as warm as Tertullian on the other side. He is the author of a complete scheme of Predestination that continued with little variation to the close of the theological discussion of Free Will. His views underwent several changes in the course of his life, but the shape they finally took remains identified with the doctrine of Predestination. The foundation of his views was his theory of grace and faith. He affirmed the total inability of man to accomplish any good works. Good works, the smallest as well as the greatest, come wholly from God. Grace attracts the corrupt will of man, and with an irresistible necessity awakens him to the need of redemption and to faith. This grace is bestowed not for merit, but of God's free gift. The will is determined and controlled by the agency of God, in consequence of what he has foreordained. The Elect were chosen, not because it was foreseen that they would believe and become holy (as most of the earlier fathers held), but in order that they might be made holy. Augustin thus clearly distinguishes his doctrine from that of mere foreknowledge. He holds that some were chosen to eternal life, and others were predestined to everlasting punishment. 'Whom he teaches, he teaches of his mercy; whom he does not teach, he does not teach because of judgment.' This doctrine seems to make God unjust. He foreordains that a man shall sin, and for this sin consigns him to eternal torments. Augustin's solution of the difficulty turns upon the doctrine of original sin. In Adam all men sinned, and rendered themselves justly liable to endless punishment. Adam's sin was the sin of every one of us. But Adam had free-will; it was in his own power to fix his destiny; he chose evil and death, and by his choice we all are irrevocably committed. God is not therefore the cause of that sin and consequent ruin; he cannot be accused of injustice in leaving us in the state to which we have *constructively*, as lawyers would say, brought ourselves. The origin of evil is thus placed in the free-will of Adam, not in the decree of God. As this reasoning, even if conclusive, seems more fitted to silence than to convince, Augustin feels the necessity of advancing a step farther. In his tract on Grace and Free-will, he observes, that God moves men's hearts towards good works of his mercy; towards bad, according to their deserts, by a judgment in part made known, in part mysterious, but always just. He does not elect men according to any merit they possess, but according to a hidden judgment. Let not injustice be attributed to God, who is the fountain of wisdom and justice. When he permits men to be seduced or hardened, believe that it is on account of their demerits; in those whom he mercifully saves, behold the grace of God rendering good for evil.

While Augustin's doctrine of Predestination seems to have left no place for free-will, we yet find warnings that in defending grace, free-will must not be given up, nor in defending free-will must grace be given up. It seems difficult to attribute any meaning to free-will in such passages. How is the existence of irresistible grace compatible with free self-determination! Again, he tells us that by the fall man lost both himself and his free will; that the will is truly free, when it is not the slave of vice or sin. Also, free-will is given to man, so that punishment for sin, both by divine and human law, is just. Neander observes that Augustin has confounded the conception of freedom, as a certain stage of moral development, and freedom from the determination of motives—a faculty possessed by all rational minds. Mozley says, after carefully examining the language of Augustin, that free-will means, with him, mere voluntary action, such as is admitted by all necessitarians; that the will (except perhaps Adam's) has no self-determining power, but is determined to evil and to good respectively, by original sin and by grace.

AQUINAS. Aquinas is a follower of Augustin in the doctrines of original sin, irresistible grace, and predestination. 'Præscientia meritorum non est causa vel ratio prædestinationis.' The doctrines of the church were to the schoolmen, what the acts of the legislature are to lawyers. They were subjects of deduction and argument, but not themselves to be questioned. But there is endless opportunity for ingenious interpretation in reconciling the doctrines with truth, or the laws with justice. It is, therefore, interesting to observe how Aquinas endeavoured to evade the consequences of a doctrine that he was not permitted to deny.

(1) In the first place, the number of the reprobate was made as small as possible, as though that would lighten the difficulty. Perhaps, he says, the angels that did not fall with Satan, were more numerous than all the damned—men and devils together.

(2) The difference between eternal happiness and misery *perhaps* amounts merely to degrees of good. According to Aquinas, there are two kinds of happiness; one is natural, and attainable by mere human effort; the other is spiritual. There is a corresponding distinction in virtue. There is a goodness in the world sufficient to attain natural happiness, as well as grace to attain spiritual happiness. Those kinds of goodness have their source respectively in Reason, and in God. The difference between those conditions is not one of good and evil, but of higher and lower good. Aquinas does not venture, further than by hints, to apply this theory of happiness to predestination and reprobation, except in one case. In favour of infants dying in original sin, he endea-

vours, by an ingenious feat of interpretation, to extract the sting from eternal punishment.

(3) Infants dying in original sin, are under the divine wrath due to that sin. However hard this conclusion may seem, it is unavoidable; infants are condemned not for actual, but for constructive, sin. But Augustin had said that the punishment of infants in hell was the mildest possible—*omnium esse mitissimam*. Aquinas then asks, if it was a *sensible* (or corporeal) punishment? No, for then it would not be the mildest possible. Did it involve affliction of soul? No, for that could arise only either from *culpa* or from *pœna*. If it arose from *culpa*, that implied the presence of an accusing conscience, and it would not be the mildest. Nor could it arise from *pœna*, which implied actual sin, or a will in opposition to the will of God. What then was the punishment of infants? It was the want of Divine Vision—the object that the supernatural faculties sought. 'In the other goods to which nature tends upon her own principles, those condemned for original sin will sustain no detriment.' The only difficulty now was a saying of St. Chrysostom's, that the loss of Divine Vision was the severest part of the punishment of the damned. Aquinas answers, that it is no pain to a well-ordered mind to want what its nature is not adapted to, provided the want does not arise from any fault of its own. The infants will rejoice in their lot, not repining because they are not angels. This reasoning, though confined by Aquinas to the case of infants, yet applies logically to the good, moral man, whose fault is substantially (unless a very technical view of sin be adopted) the sin of our first parents.*

CALVIN popularized the predestinarian views of St. Augustin. He accepts them in all their rigour, excluding every softening modification. He rejects the subtlety of Thomas Aquinas, that God predestinates man to glory, according to his merit, inasmuch as he decreed to bestow upon him the grace by which he merits glory. He held that God foreordained some to heaven, and others to hell, not for any merit or demerit, but simply because it was his will so to do. The fall of Adam was not to be attributed to free will, but to the divine decree.

The opponent of Augustin was PELAGIUS, who claimed for man complete freedom of self-determination and ascribed to God only

* Mozley's *Augustinian Doctrine of Predestination*, p. 302. We may subjoin some distinctions taken in regard to Freedom and Necessity. Peter Lombard says that three kinds of liberty must be discriminated:— (1) Freedom from necessity, which is possessed by God, since he cannot be coerced, and which, in man, is not affected by the fall; (2) freedom from sin, which was lost by the fall; (3) freedom from misery. Thomas Aquinas marks the following kinds of necessity:—(1) Natural, Absolute, or Intrinsic Necessity—that which cannot but be—is either *material* (*e.g. quod omne compositum ex contrariis necesse est corrumpi*) or *formal* (*e.g.* that the angles in a triangle are equal to two right angles). (2) Extrinsic Necessity is either of *means to ends* (as that food is necessary to life), or of *compulsion*, which last alone excludes will. Aquinas makes much of the

foreknowledge of what men, '*per liberae voluntatis arbitrium*,' would elect to do. After the time of Calvin, at the beginning of the 17th century, this view was again strongly advocated by ARMINIUS in Holland; and thenceforth the opposed tenets, in the *theological* phase of the question, have passed under the names of Calvinism and Arminianism.

The *philosophical* aspect begins to be more exclusively considered with the names that follow.

HOBBES. Hobbes's opinion on the Free-will controversy is given very clearly and concisely in a short tract on 'Liberty and Necessity,' written in answer to another by Bishop Bramhall. He gives first his opinion, under several heads, and afterwards assigns his reasons.

(1) When it occurs to a man to do or not to do a certain action, and he has no time, or no occasion, to *deliberate*, 'the doing it or abstaining *necessarily* follow the *present* thought he hath of the *good* or *evil* consequence thereof to himself.' In anger, the action follows the idea of revenge, in fear that of escape. Such actions are voluntary; for a voluntary action is one that follows immediately the *last appetite* (Hobbes's phrase for volition). *Rash* actions are strictly voluntary, and therefore punishable, 'For no action of a man can be said to be without deliberation, though never so sudden, because it is supposed he had time to deliberate all the precedent time of his life, whether he should do that kind of action or not.'

(2) *Deliberation* means considering whether it would be better to do the action or abstain, by imagining the consequences of it, both good and evil. This alternate imagination of good and evil consequences is the same as alternate *hope* and *fear*, or alternate appetite to do or quit the action.

(3) In deliberation, that is, the succession of contrary *appetites*, the last is the *Will*, and immediately precedes the doing of the action. All the appetites, prior to the last, are mere *intentions* or *inclinations*.

(4) An action is voluntary, if done upon deliberation, that is, upon choice and election. The meaning of *free*, as applied to a voluntary agent, is that he has not made an end of deliberating.

(5) '*Liberty* is the absence of all the impediments to action that are not contained in the nature of the agent.' [This means free-

difference between *judicium* and *ratio*. Brutes have not freedom; the sheep avoids a wolf, not *ex collatione quadam rationis*, but by natural instinct. But man has *ratio*, and *ratio* in contingent matters is concerned with opposites, and is not bound to follow any one. Inasmuch as man has *ratio*, he is not tied to one course. Will is related to free-will as *intellectus* is to *ratio*. *Intellectus* involves a mere apprehension of anything, as where principles are known of themselves without any *collatio;* but to reason is *devenire ex uno in cognitionem alterius*. In like manner, will (*velle*) is simply the desire of anything for its own sake; free-will (*eligere*) is the desire of anything as a means to an end. The end is related to the means, as a principle is to the conclusion dependent upon it.

dom from compulsion; Hobbes does not allow necessity to be a true contrast to freedom.]

(6) Nothing begins from itself. Hence, when an appetite or will arises, the cause is not the will itself, but something else, not in one's own disposing. The will is the necessary cause of voluntary actions, other things (than the will itself) are the cause of the will, therefore all voluntary actions have necessary causes, in other words, are necessitated.

(7) A *sufficient* or *necessary* cause is that which alone produces the effect. This is merely an identical proposition, to show that whatever is produced, is produced necessarily. The cause being given, the effect necessarily follows.

(8) The ordinary definition of a free agent, as that which, 'when all things are present which are needful to produce the effect, can nevertheless not produce it,' is contradictory and nonsensical.

For the truth of the five first positions, Hobbes appeals to every one's reflection and experience. The sixth position is, that nothing can begin *without a cause*. Now, there must be some special reason why a thing begins, when it does begin, rather than sooner or later; or else the thing must be eternal. The seventh point is, that events have *necessary* causes, if they have *sufficient* causes, that is, in fact, if they have causes at all. From these principles, it follows that there is no *freedom from necessity*. He adds, as an *argumentum ad hominem* to the bishop, that if necessity be denied, the decrees and prescience of God will be left without foundation.

DESCARTES, in his Fourth Meditation, gives a definition of Will and Freedom. 'The power of will consists only in this, that we are able to do or not to do the same thing, or rather in this alone, that in pursuing or shunning what is proposed to us by the understanding, we so act that we are not conscious of being determined to a particular action by any external force.' Freedom does not require indifference towards each of two courses, but is greater as we are more inclined towards truth or goodness. Indifference, not moving for want of a reason, is the lowest grade of liberty, and manifests a lack of knowledge rather than perfection of will.

In itself, Freedom is the same in man as in God, but it is exercised under different conditions. The will of God must have been indifferent from all eternity, as there was no antecedent idea of truth or good to determine it. It was from his almighty power that truth and good first arose. But man is differently situated: goodness has been established by God, and towards it the will cannot but tend. We are most free when the perfect knowledge of an object drives us to pursue it.

In answer to Hobbes, Descartes adduces the evidence of consciousness. However difficult it may be to reconcile foreordination with liberty, we have an internal feeling that the voluntary and the free are the same. This seems to indicate an anxiety to establish the internal fact, while otherwise willing to give up a liberty of indifference.

Theologically, he maintains a stringent theory of Providence. The perfection of God required that the least thought in us should have been pre-determined from all eternity. The decrees of God are unchangeable, and prayer has an efficacy only because the prayer is decreed together with the answer.

LOCKE was led in his chapter on Power (although it formed no part of his original plan), to investigate the nature of the will. He purposely avoided the metaphysical controversies regarding predestination and providence, refusing to deal with any supposed 'consequences,' and rigorously confining himself to the question— What is the nature of the liberty possessed by men? The opinion of so acute and impartial a mind upon the bare facts of the case, must be taken as a near approach to the testimony of consciousness. Like Aristotle, he draws the distinction between voluntary and involuntary, but does not separate the voluntary from the *freely* voluntary.* He recognizes a meaning in liberty as opposed to coercion, but not as opposed to necessity. He defines freedom as 'our being able to act or not to act, according as we shall choose or will.' This is the very definition contended for by Hobbes, and afterwards expressly adopted by the necessitarian Collins.

In Book II., Chap. XXI., he discusses the idea of Power. He enters at length into the nature of Will, and handles first the doctrine of Free-will, and next the motives to the will. As regards Freedom, he endeavours to extricate the question from the confused modes of expressing it. The true question is not whether the will is free, but whether the man is free. Liberty is the power to do or to forbear doing any particular action, according to the preference or direction of one's own mind.† A man is free, if his actions follow his mental motives—pleasures and pains; he is not free, when anything external to him forbids the actions so moved. Volition is an act of the mind exerting the dominion it takes itself to have over any part of the man, but is an operation better understood by any one's self-reflection, than by all the words employed to describe it. It is not to be confounded with desire; we may will to produce an effect that we do not desire.

With reference to the motive power, Locke resolves it into the *uneasiness* of the state of Desire. Hunger, thirst, and sex, are modes of uneasiness. When good determines the will, it operates first by creating a sense of uneasiness from the want of it. We find that the greatest prospects of good, as the joys of heaven,

---

* B. II. Chap. XXI., § 11.

† Locke asks the further question— whether a man is as free to will, as he is free to do what he wills. Of two courses, is he free to will whichever he pleases? This question involves an absurdity. They that make a question of it must suppose one will to determine the acts of another, and another to determine that; and so on *in infinitum.*

have a comparatively feeble motive power; while a bodily pain, violent love, passion, or revenge, can keep the will steady and intent. In a conflict, the will is urged by the greatest present uneasiness.

Looking at the innumerable solicitations to the will, and the way that our desires rise and fall by the working of our thoughts, Locke adds another condition of our Liberty of willing—namely, the power of suspending the prosecution of a desire, to give opportunity to examine all the consequences of the act: it is not a fault, but a perfection in our nature, to act on the final result of a fair examination. The constant determination towards our own happiness is no abridgment of liberty. A man could not be free, if his will were determined by anything but his own desire, guided by his own judgment.

SPINOZA denied free-will, because it was inconsistent with the nature of God, and with the laws to which human actions are subject. In a certain sense, God has freedom, as acting from a necessity inherent in his nature. But man has not even this freedom; his actions are determined by God. There is nothing really contingent. Contingency, free determination, disorder, chance, lie only in our ignorance.

The supposed *consciousness* of freedom arises from a forgetfulness of the causes that dispose us to will and desire. Volitions are the varying appetites of the soul. When there is a conflict of passions, men hardly know what they wish; but, in the absence of passion, the least impulse one way or another determines them. A volition implies memory, but memory is not in our power, so then volition cannot be. In dreams we make decisions as if awake, with the same consciousness of freedom; are those fantastic decisions to be considered free? Those who fancy that their soul decides freely, dream with their eyes open. Another explanation is that the undetermined will is the universal will abstracted from particular volitions. Although every actual volition has a cause, yet this abstract will is thought of as undetermined, for determinism is no part of the conception of volition.

God is not the author of evil, because evil is nothing positive. Everything that is, is perfect. Any imperfection arises from our habit of forming abstract ideas, and judging of things thereby as if they were all susceptible of the perfection that belongs to the definition, and were imperfect in so far as they fell short of it. But the good and the bad are not on an equality, although they both express in their way the will of God. The good have more perfection in being more closely allied to God.

The necessity of evil does not render punishment unjust. The wicked, although necessarily wicked, are none the less on that account to be feared and destroyed. A wicked man may be excusable, but this does not affect the treatment he must receive; a man bitten by a mad dog is not blameworthy, but people have a right to put him to death.

COLLINS has explained and defended the necessitarian doctrine in 'A Philosophical Enquiry concerning Human Liberty.' He accepts Locke's definition of liberty as 'a power in man to do as he wills or pleases.' His thesis is that every action is determined by the preceding causes. (1) *Experience* is not in favour of liberty. Many patrons of liberty have defined it in such a way as not to contradict necessity, or have conceded so much as to leave themselves no ground to stand upon. On the other hand, experience testifies that we are necessary agents, that our volitions are determined by causes; and even the supporters of free-will acknowledge that we do not prefer the worse, in other words, do not follow the weaker motive. (2) Whatever has a beginning has a cause, and every cause is a necessary cause. The doctrine of free-will is, therefore, a contradiction of the law of causality. (3) Liberty is an imperfection, and necessity an advantage and perfection. It is no perfection to be able to choose one out of two or more indifferent things. Angels are more perfect than men, because they are necessarily determined to prefer good to evil. (4) The decrees of God are necessary causes of events. Foreordination and liberty are mutually subversive. (5) If man were not a necessary agent, determined by pleasure and pain, there would be no foundation for rewards and punishment.

LEIBNITZ. 1. *The Nature of Liberty and Necessity.* Necessity is of two kinds—hypothetical and absolute. Hypothetical necessity is that laid upon future contingents by God's foreknowledge. This does not derogate from liberty. God's choice of the present from among possible worlds did not change, but only *actualized*, the free natures of his creatures. There is another distinction. Logical, Metaphysical, or Mathematical necessity depends upon the law of *Identity* or *Contradiction*; while moral necessity depends on the law of *Sufficient Reason*, and is simply the mind choosing the best, or following the strongest inclination. The principle of sufficient Reason affirms that every event has certain conditions, constituting the reason why it exists. God's perfect nature requires that he should not act without reason, nor prefer a weaker reason to a stronger. This necessity is compatible with freedom in God; so also in us. Motives do not impose upon us any absolute necessity, more than upon him. Without an inclination to good, choice would be mere blind chance. In things absolutely indifferent, there can be no choice, election, or will; since choice must be founded on some reason or principle. A will, acting without any motive, is a fiction, chimerical and self-contradictory.

2. *Necessity and Fatalism.* To the objection that necessity is identical with Fatalism, Leibnitz answers by distinguishing three kinds of fatalism. There is a Mahommedan fatalism, which supposes that if the effect is pre-determined, it happens without the cause. The fatalism of the Stoics taught men to be quiescent, for they were powerless to resist the course of things. There is a third kind of fatalism accepted by all Christians, admitting a certain destiny of things regulated by the providence of God.

3. *The influence of motives.* Leibnitz compared the will to a balance, and motives to the weights in the scales. This simile was taken from Bayle to illustrate the inactivity of the will, when under the pressure of equal motives, and of its action when one preponderated. Clarke objected to it on the ground that a balance is passive, while men are active beings. Leibnitz answered that the principle of sufficient reason was common to both agents and patients. He admits, however, that, strictly speaking, motives do not act on the mind as weights in a balance; they are rather dispositions in virtue of which the mind acts. To say that the mind can prefer a weak motive to a strong one, implies that it has other dispositions than motives, by virtue of which it can accept or reject the motives; whereas motives include all dispositions to act. The fear of a great pain weighs down the expectation of a pleasure. In the conflict of two passions, the stronger is victorious, unless the other is aided by reason or by some concurring passion. But generally a conflict of motives involves more than two; so that a better comparison than the balance would be, a force tending in many directions, and acting in the line of least resistance. Air compressed in a glass receiver, finds its way out where the glass is weakest.

SAMUEL CLARKE affirmed the existence of a power of self-motion or self-determination, which, in all animate agents, is spontaneity, in moral agents, is liberty. It is a great error to regard the mind as passive, like a balance. 'A free agent, when there is more than one perfectly reasonable way of acting, has still within itself, by virtue of its self-motive principle, a power of acting; and it may have strong reasons not to forbear acting, when yet there may be no possible reason for preferring one way to another.' Leibnitz pointed out the contradiction here, for if the mind has good reasons, there is no indifference. A man never has a sufficient reason for acting, when he has not a sufficient reason to act in a definite manner. No action can be general or abstracted from its circumstances, but must always be executed in some particular manner.

Clarke stakes the whole controversy upon the existence of this self-moving faculty. If man has not this power, then every human action is produced by some extrinsic cause; either the motive, or some subtle matter, or some other being. If it be a motive, then either abstract notions (*i.e.* motives) have a real subsistence (*i.e.* are substances), or else what is not a substance can put a body in motion. It is unnecessary to follow him in the other alternatives.

With reference to the action of motives, Clarke says the question is not whether a good or wise being cannot do evil or act unwisely, but whether the immediate physical cause of action be some sufficient reason acting on the agent, or the agent himself. This theory of self-motion has been severely criticized by Sir W. Hamilton. Clarke's definition, he observes, amounts only to the liberty of spontaneity, and not to liberty from necessity. Now, ' the *greatest spontaneity* is the *greatest necessity.*'

JONATHAN EDWARDS vindicates the doctrine of philosophical necessity in his work on the 'Freedom of the Will' (1754) in the interest of Calvinistic theology. His treatise, however, consists almost exclusively of philosophical arguments.

1. Edwards's own view. The will is that by which the mind chooses anything; and we are so constituted that on the mind choosing or wishing a movement of the body, the movement follows. The Will is determined by the strongest motive, and the strongest motive is the greatest apparent good. [By motive, he means the whole of what acts on the will.] Necessity is only a full and fixed connection between things; moral necessity is simply the fixed connexion between motives and volitions. Liberty is a power to do as one pleases; it is opposed to constraint and restraint. The other meanings ascribed to liberty are: (1) a Self-determining power, whereby the will causes its own volitions; (2) Indifference, or that, previous to volition, the mind is in equilibrium; (3) Contingence, the denial of any fixed connection between motives and volitions. These conceptions of liberty he proceeds to refute.

2. *Self-determination* is inconsistent and inconceivable. If the will determines its own acts, it doubtless does so in the same way in which it produces bodily movements—by acts of volition. Hence every free volition is preceded by a prior volition; and if this prior volition be free, it must be preceded by a prior volition, and so on *in infinitum*. Hence arises a contradiction. The first act of a series cannot be free, for it must have another before it; if the first act is not free, none of the subsequent acts can be free. It may be urged in reply, that there is no prior act determining a free volition, but that the act of determining is the same with the act of willing. The effect of this reply is, that the free volition is determined by nothing; it is entirely uncaused. Instead, therefore, of saying the will is self-determined, the proper expression would be *indetermined*. Indeterminism thus affirms that our volitions do not arise from any causes. It therefore contradicts the law of causality. Cause is sometimes defined as that which has a positive efficiency to produce an effect; but, in this sense, the absence of the sun would not be the cause of the fall of dew. A cause is the reason or ground why an event happens so and not otherwise; it is an antecedent firmly conjoined with its consequent. In this sense, everything that begins to be, must have a cause. This is a dictate of common sense, and the basis of all reasoning on things past, present, and to come. If things may exist without a cause, there is no possible proof for the existence of God. Nay more, we could be sure of nothing but what was present to our consciousness.

Indeterminism is sometimes made to depend on the active nature of the soul. Material events may require causes, but volitions do not depend on causes, or rather (for the sake of verbally saving causality) the soul is the cause of its volitions. Edwards answers, that this may explain why the soul acts at all, but not why it acts in a particular manner. And, unless the soul produce diverse acts, it cannot produce diverse effects, otherwise the same cause, in the same circumstances, would produce different effects at different times. In order, however, to demonstrate the futility of the argument drawn from the activity of the soul, it is necessary to examine carefully the notions of *Action* and *Passion*. It is said, by Dr. Clarke, that a necessary agent is a self-contradiction. Action excludes a moving cause, because to be an effect is to be passive. This is to build a demonstration on an arbitrary definition of a word. Edwards sums up the contradictions involved in the notion of activity as follows:—' To their notion of action, these things are essential—viz., That it should be necessary, and not necessary; that it should be from a cause, and no cause; that it should be the fruit of choice or design, and not the fruit of choice or design; that it should be the beginning of motion or exertion, and yet consequent on previous exertion; that it should be before it is; that it should spring immediately out of indifference, and yet be the effect of preponderation; that it should be self-originated, and also have its original from something else.' Absurd and inconsistent with itself, this metaphysical idea of action is entirely different from the common notion. The usual meaning of action is bodily movement: less strictly, heat is said to act upon wax. According to usage, action never means self-determination. Action may have a cause other than the agent, as easily as life may have a cause other than the living being. The same thing may be both cause and effect in respect of different objects. Metaphysicians have changed the meaning of the words 'action' and 'necessity,' but keep up the old attributes in spite of the new and distinct application of the term.

3. *Liberty of Indifference.* The will is alleged to be able to choose between two things equally attractive to the mind. But there never is such a perfect equality. Suppose I wish to touch any one spot on a chess-board, I generally accomplish it by some such steps as the following:—I make first a general resolution to touch some one, then determine to select one by chance—to touch what is nearest or most in the eye at some moment, and lastly I fix upon some one selected under those conditions. But at no step is there any equilibrium of motives. Among several objects, some one will catch the eye; ideas are not equally strong in the mind at one moment, or if so, they do not long continue. It must be kept distinctly in view, that what the will is more immediately concerned with, is not the *objects*, but the *acts* to be done concerning them. The objects may appear equal, but among the acts to be done affecting them, one may be decidedly preferable.

If indifference is regarded as essential to liberty, several absurd consequences follow. Indifference is often sinful. It is a state in which a man is as ready to choose, as to avoid, sin. It is destroyed by the presence of any habitual bias, and such bias can be neither virtuous nor vicious. The nearer habits of virtue are to infallibility, the less are they free and praiseworthy. Indifference is inconsistent with regarding any disposition or quality of mind as either virtuous or vicious. So in proportion to the strength of a motive, liberty is destroyed. Hence moral suasion is opposed to freedom. Finally, a choice without motive, and for no end, can have neither prudence nor wisdom in it.

4. *Contingence* is involved in liberty. But this cannot be, for no event happens without a cause. Hence events are *necessarily* connected with their causes, by which, however, Edwards means only that they invariably follow their causes. His definition of cause is correct; his only error was in retaining the word 'necessity' with its irrelevant and misleading associations.

5. *The influence of motives.* It is generally allowed that no volition takes place without a motive; but the mind, it is alleged, has the power of complying with the motive or not. This is a plain contradiction. How can the mind determine what motives shall influence it, and yet the motives be the ground or reason of its determination? Again, it is urged that volition does not follow the strongest motive. If not, then it must follow the weaker, that is, *pro tanto*, it acts without any motive. This is to contradict the law of cause and effect, and was, Edwards conceived, a perfect *reductio ad absurdum*. He did not anticipate that any one would impugn the universality of cause and effect.

6. *Foreknowledge.* The great point that Edwards sought to establish was that prescience involved as much necessity as predestination, and that, therefore, the extreme position of the Calvinists was as tenable as any that could be taken up by a theist. In the first place, it is evident from Scripture that God has a certain foreknowledge of the voluntary actions of men. Now, if volitions were contingent events, they could not be foreknown, because nothing can be known without evidence, and for a contingent event no evidence can be produced. A contingent event is not self-evident, and it cannot be evident from its connexion with any other event, for connexion destroys contingence. Nor is it an admissible supposition that God may have ways of knowing that we cannot conceive of. For it is a contradiction to suppose an event known as certain, and, at the same time, as uncertain. Another evasion is, that knowledge can have no influence on the thing known. Granted, but prescience may *prove* that an event is certain, without being the *cause* of its certainty. Certainty of knowledge does not make an infallible connexion between things, but it pre-supposes such a connexion. Again, it is said that with God there is no distinction of *before* and *after*; time is with him an eternal *now*. Edwards admits that there is no succession in God's knowledge, but observes that knowledge, whether before or after, implies the certainty of the thing known. If an event is known by him as certain, then it will most assuredly happen.

7. *Is liberty essential to morality?* The essence of virtue is supposed to consist, not in the *nature* of the acts of the will, but in their *cause*. But it is more consistent with common opinion to

regard moral evil as a deformity in the nature of certain dispositions and volitions. Ingratitude is hateful, not on account of the badness of its cause, but on account of its inherent deformity. It is true that our bodily movements are not in themselves either virtuous or vicious, but only the volitions and dispositions that produce them. This relation is erroneously supposed to exist between our volitions and some inner determining volitions. But mankind do not refer praise and blame to any occult causes of the will; they blame a man who does as he pleases, and who pleases to do wrong. When they ascribe an action to a man, they mean merely that the action is voluntary, not that it is self-determined. Their only conception of freedom is freedom from compulsion or restraint. They praise a man for his amiability, the gift of nature, as much as if it were the result of severe discipline. The will of God is necessarily good, but it is nevertheless praiseworthy. Although necessity is, therefore, perfectly compatible with praise and blame, it is nevertheless easy to understand how the opposite opinion should be generally entertained. Constraint is the proper and original meaning of necessity. Now, constraint is totally inconsistent with punishment and reward. Hence arises a strong association between blamelessness and necessity. When the word necessity is taken up by philosophers as the equivalent for certainty of connexion, the associated idea of blamelessness is carried insensibly and unwarily into the new meaning. But Edwards did not draw the obvious inference, that the word 'necessity' should be discarded from the controversy.

8. *Practical Consequences.* (1) Does the doctrine of necessity render efforts towards an end nugatory? This could only be said, if the doctrine affirmed, either that the event might follow without the means, or that the event might not follow, although the means was used. Does the doctrine of necessity effect any such rupture between means and ends? On the contrary, the certainty of the connexion between means and ends is the doctrine itself. (2) Does necessity lead to atheism and licentiousness? Edwards retorts on Liberty the charge of Atheism. How can the existence of God be proved without the principle that every change must have a cause? And how can it be maintained that every change has a cause, when the entire realm of volition is emancipated from causation? As to the charge of licentiousness, Edwards points to the exemplary conduct of the Calvinists, in contrast to the looseness that often coexists with Arminian doctrines.

PRICE, contending with Priestley, followed the view brought forward by Dr. Clarke. He defined liberty as a power of self-motion, and took up the following positions. (1) All animals possess spontaneity, and therefore liberty. (2) Liberty does not admit of degrees; between acting and not acting there is no middle course. (3) This liberty is possible. There must be somewhere a power of beginning motion, and we are conscious of such a power in ourselves. (4) In our volitions, we are not acted upon. (5) Liberty does not exclude the operation of motives. The power of self-determination can never be excited without some view or design. But it is an intolerable absurdity to make our motives or ends the *physical* causes of action. Our ideas may be the occasion of our acting, but are certainly not mechanical efficients.

PRIESTLEY, in his controversy with Price, maintained the following positions:—

1. He denied that our consciousness is in favour of freedom. All we believe is that we have power to do what we will or please. To will without a motive, or contrary to the influence of all the motives presented to the mind, is what no man can be conscious of. The mind cannot choose without some inclination or preference for the thing chosen. To deny this, is to deny that every change must have a cause.

2. *Philosophical necessity* is consistent with accountability. Punishment has an improving effect both on our own future conduct, and on the conduct of others; this is the meaning of justness of punishment. To say that one is praiseworthy means that he is actuated by good principles, and is therefore an object of love, and a fit person to be made happy.

3. *Permission of Evil.* As regards God, there is no distinction between permitting and appointing evil. In the case of man, the difference is great, for his power of interference and control is limited. In creating any man, God must foresee and accept all the consequences. Whatever reasons can be produced to show why God permits evil, will be available to justify his appointing it.

4. *Remorse and Pardon.* Priestley admits that it sounds harsh, but affirms it nevertheless to be true, that ' in all those crimes men reproach themselves with, God is the agent; and that they are no more agents than a sword.' Actions may be referred to the persons themselves as secondary causes, but they must also be traced to the first cause. Mankind at first necessarily refer their actions to themselves, a conviction that becomes deeply rooted, before they begin to regard themselves as instruments in the hands of a superior agent. Self-applause and self-reproach have their origin in the narrower view, and cease when we refer our actions to the first great cause. The necessitarian believing that, strictly speaking, nothing goes wrong *(whatever is, is right)*, cannot accuse himself of wrong doing. He has, therefore, nothing to do with repentance, confession, or pardon. This state of feeling, however, is a high and rare attainment; when the necessitarian mechanically refers his actions to himself, he will no doubt feel as others.

This admission by Priestley that remorse is inconsistent with necessity, has been turned to great account by Reid; but although the statement is very unguarded, it contains a portion of the truth. We may look upon a person's conduct in two aspects—in its effects, or in its causes. In its effects, it may be very hostile to human happiness, or the reverse. From this point of view, resentment and approbation are the spontaneous response of feeling; punishment and reward are clearly appropriate. On the other hand, we may confine our attention to the causes of the man's conduct—his circumstances, education, and opinions. In several ways, this tends to discourage angry feeling, and to arouse sympathy and pity. In the first place, we are looking away from the *effects* of the conduct, and the considerations that justify and require punishment; in the next place, we may reflect that, in like circumstances, we might not have done better ourselves; then, the conduct may have resulted from a weak moral nature, in which case we are always more ready to pity than to punish; and, lastly, since we are at the scientific point of view, there is strongly suggested the conception of resistless sequence—a notion strictly applicable to many material phenomena, but incorrect as to human actions.

5. Priestley considered that materialism, to which he subscribed, involved the doctrine of necessity.

REID has devoted a large part of his work on *The Active Powers*, to the discussion of the Liberty of Moral Agents.

I.—*The Nature of Liberty*. He defines liberty to be a power over the determinations of one's Will. Necessity is when the will follows something involuntary in the state of mind, or something external. Moral liberty does not apply to all voluntary actions; many such are done by instinct or habit, without reflection, and so without will. It is a power not enjoyed in infancy, but only in riper years. It extends as far as we are accountable; in short, freedom is the *sine qua non* of praise or blame. In order still farther to clear up the conception of liberty, Reid devotes two chapters to explain the notion of cause. Everything that changes must either change itself, or be changed by some other being. In the one case, it has active power, in the other case it is acted upon or passive. His definition of cause is,—that which has power to produce an effect. *We* are efficient causes in *our deliberate and voluntary* actions. We cannot will deliberately without believing that the thing willed is in our power [we may, if we merely expect the effect to follow]. We have a conviction of power to produce motion in our own bodies. To be an efficient cause is to be a free agent; a necessary agent is a contradiction in terms. In thus identifying freedom with power, Reid follows Clarke and Price, exposing himself to the refutation of Jonathan Edwards, not to mention the criticism of Sir W. Hamilton.

II.—*Arguments in Support of Free-will*. 1. We have by our constitution, a natural conviction or belief, that we act freely. The existence of such a belief is admitted by some fatalists themselves [Hamilton mentions Hommel, and also Lord Kames, who, however, withdrew the incautious admission]. The very notion of active power must arise from our constitution. We see events, but we see no potency nor chain linking one to the other, and therefore the notion of cause is not derived from external objects. Yet it is an unshaken conviction of the mind that every event has a cause that had power to produce it. (1) We are conscious of exercising power to produce some effect, and this implies a belief that we have power to produce the desired effect. [It, in truth, only

implies a belief that the effect will certainly happen, if we wish it.]
(2) Can any one blame himself for yielding to necessity? Remorse implies a conviction that we could have done better. Reid further explains what he means by the actions that are in our power. We have no conception of power that is not directed by the will. But there are many things that depend on our will that are not in our power. Madmen, idiots, infants, people in a violent rage, have not the power of self-government. Likewise, the violence of a motive, or an inveterate habit, diminishes liberty.

2. Liberty is involved in accountability. To be accountable, a man must understand the law by which he is bound, and his obligations to obey it; and he must have power to do what he is accountable for. So far as man's power over himself extends, so far is he accountable. Hence violent passion limits responsibility. It is said that to constitute an action criminal, it need only be voluntary. Reid says, more is necessary, namely, moral liberty. For (1) the actions of brutes are voluntary, but not criminal. (2) So are the actions of young children. (3) Madmen have understanding and will, but no moral liberty, and hence are not criminal. (4) An irresistible motive palliates or takes away guilt.

3. Man's power over his volitions is proved by the fact that he can prosecute a series of means towards an end. A plan of conduct requires understanding to contrive and power to execute it. Now, if each volition in the series was produced not by the man himself, but by some cause acting necessarily upon him, there is no evidence that he contrived the plan. The cause that directed the determinations, must have understood the plan, and intended the execution of it. Motives could not have done it, for they have not understanding to conceive a plan.

III.—*Refutation of the Argument for Necessity.* 1. The influence of motives. (1) Reid allows that motives influence to action, but they do not act. Upon this, Sir W. Hamilton remarks that if motives influence to action, they co-operate in producing a certain effect upon the agent. They are thus, on Reid's own view, causes, and efficient causes. It is of no consequence in the argument, whether motives be said to determine a man to act, or to influence (that is to determine) him to determine himself to act. (2) Reid goes on to say that it is the glory of rational beings to act according to the best motives. God can do everything; it is his praise that he does only what is best. But according to Hamilton, this is just one of the insoluble contradictions in the question. If we attribute to the Deity the power of moral evil, we detract from his essential goodness; and if, on the other hand, we deny him this power, we detract from his omnipotence. (3) Is there a motive in every action? Reid thinks not. Many trifling actions are done without any conscious motive. Stewart disagrees with Reid in this remark; and Hamilton observes:— 'Can we conceive any act of which there was not a sufficient cause, or concourse of causes, why the man performed it and no other? If not, call this cause, or these concauses, the *motive*, and there is no longer a dispute.' (4) It cannot be proved that when there is a motive on one side only, that motive must determine the action. Is there no such thing as wilfulness, caprice, or obstinacy? But 'Are not those all tendencies, and fatal tendencies, to act or not to act?' (5) Does the strongest motive prevail? If the test of the strongest motive is that it prevails, then the proposition is identical. The determination is made by the man, and not by the motive. 'But was the man determined by no motive to that determination? Was his specific volition to this or to that without a cause? On the supposition that the sum of influences (motives, dispositions, tendencies) to volition A, is equal to 12, and the sum of influences to counter volition B, equal to 8, can we conceive that the determination of volition A should not be necessary? We can only conceive the volition B to be determined by supposing that the man *creates* (calls from non-existence into existence) a certain supplement of influences. But this creation as actual, or in itself, is inconceivable, and even to conceive the possibility of this inconceivable act, we must suppose some cause by which the man is determined to exert it. We thus, in *thought*, never escape determination and necessity.' (6) It is very weak reasoning to infer from our power of predicting men's actions that they are necessarily determined by motives. Liberty is a power that men use according to their character. The wise use it wisely, the foolish, foolishly. (7) The doctrine of liberty does not render rewards and punishments of no effect. With wise men they will have their due effect, but not always with the foolish and vicious.

2. *The principle of sufficient Reason.* Reid makes a long criticism of this principle, as enounced by Leibnitz; but all reference to that may be omitted, since in so far as it applies to the present question, the principle is identical with the law of cause and effect. Reid's answer is that the man is the cause of action, but this evasion, as we have seen, has been refuted by Hamilton.

3. Every determination of the mind is foreseen by God, it is therefore necessary. This necessity may result in three ways: (1) a thing cannot be foreknown without being certain, or certain without being necessary. But there is no rule of reasoning from which it may be inferred that because an event necessarily shall be, therefore its production must be necessary. Its being certain does not determine whether it shall be freely or necessarily produced. (2) An event must be necessary because it is foreseen. Not so, for knowledge has no effect upon the thing known. God foresees his own future actions, but his foresight does not make them necessary. (3) No free action can be foreseen. This would prevent God foreseeing his own actions. Reid admits that there is no knowledge of future contingent actions in man. The prescience of God must therefore differ, not only in degree but in kind from our knowledge. Although we have no such knowledge, God may have. There is also a great analogy between the prescience of future contingents and the memory of past contin-

gents. Hamilton refutes this assertion. A past contingent is a contradiction, in becoming past it forthwith becomes necessary—it cannot but be. 'Now, so far is it from being true, as Reid soon after says, that every "argument to prove the impossibility of prescience (as the knowledge of future contingents) proves, with equal force, the impossibility of memory" (as the knowledge of past contingents), that the possibility of a memory of events *as contingent* was, I believe, never imagined by any philosopher—nor, in reality, is it by Reid himself. And, in fact, one of the most insoluble objections to the possibility of a free agency, arises (on the admission that all future events are foreseen by God) from the analogy of prescience to memory, it being impossible for the human mind to reconcile the supposition that an event may or may not occur, and the supposition that one of these alternatives has been foreseen as certain.'

Sir W. Hamilton occupies a peculiar position in regard to the present question. He demolishes all the chief popular arguments in favour of liberty, and rests the defence on his own Law of the Conditioned. At the same time, he attributes an exaggerated importance to Free-will, as being not only the foundation of morality, but the only doctrine from which we can legitimately infer the existence of God. The phenomena that require a deity for their explanation are exclusively mental: the phenomena of matter, taken by themselves, would ground even an argument to his negation. Fate or necessity might account for the material world; it is only because man is a free intelligence that a creator must be supposed endowed with free intelligence.

Hamilton admits, what is shown by Edwards, that the conception of an undetermined will is inconceivable. He thus disposes of the argument that the *person* is the cause of his volitions. 'But is the person an *original undetermined* cause of the determination of his will? If he be not, then is he not a *free* agent, and the scheme of Necessity is admitted. If he be, in the first place, it is impossible to *conceive* the possibility of this; and, in the second, if the fact, though inconceivable, be allowed, it is impossible to see how a *cause, undetermined by any motive*, can be a *rational, moral, and accountable cause.* There is no conceivable medium between *Fatalism* and *Casualism*: and the contradictory schemes of Liberty and Necessity themselves are inconceivable. For, as we cannot compass in thought an *undetermined cause,—an absolute commencement*—the fundamental hypothesis of the one; so we can as little think *an infinite series of determined causes—of relative commencements,*—the fundamental hypothesis of the other. The champions of the opposite doctrines are thus at once resistless in assault, and impotent in defence. The doctrine of Moral Liberty cannot be made conceivable, for we can only conceive the determined and the relative. As already stated, all that can be done is to show, (1) That, for the *fact* of Liberty, we have, immediately or mediately, the evidence of consciousness; and (2), that there are, among the phenomena of mind, many facts which we *must* admit as actual, but of whose possibility we are wholly unable to form any notion.' Again, 'A determination by motives cannot, to our understanding, escape from necessitation. Nay, were we even to admit as true, what we cannot think as possible, still the doctrine of a motiveless volition would be only casualism; and the free acts of an indifferent, are, morally and rationally, as worthless as the preordered passion of a determined, will.'

From his own point of view, Hamilton is free to expose the inconsistency of those who accept the law of causality, and yet make the will an exception. If causality and freedom are equally positive dictates of consciousness, there can be no ground for subordinating one of these dictates to the other. But by regarding causality as an impotence of thought, Hamilton thinks he can bring forward consciousness in favour of liberty. This fact of freedom is given either as an undoubted datum of consciousness, or as involved in an uncompromising law of duty.

In the last clause there is a reference to KANT's doctrine of Freedom. This will be stated in its proper connexion with his Ethical doctrine. [ETHICAL SYSTEMS.]

J. S. MILL, in his Examination of Sir W. Hamilton's Philosophy, has given a chapter to the Freedom of the Will. His polemic is chiefly against the theory of Sir W. Hamilton, whose attempt to create a prejudice in favour of his own peculiar views, by representing them as affording the only solid argument in support of the existence of God, Mr. Mill characterizes as 'not only repugnant to all the rules of philosophizing, but a grave offence against the morality of philosophic enquiry.' Both Hamilton and Mill are agreed upon the question at issue—namely, whether our volitions are emancipated from causation altogether. Both reject the evasion that 'I' am the cause.

1. *The evidence of experience.** Mr. Mill begins by conceding to Hamilton the inconceivability of an absolute commencement and an infinite regress. This double inconceivability applies, not only to volitions, but to all other events. Why then do we in regard to all events, except volitions, accept the alternative of regress? Because the causation-hypothesis is established by experience. But there is the same evidence in the case of our volitions. The antecedents are desires, aversions, habits, dispositions, and outward circumstances. The connexion between those antecedents and volitions is proved by every one's experience of themselves, by our observation of others, by our predicting their actions, and by the results of statistics. Where prediction is uncertain, it is because of the imperfection of our knowledge; we can predict more accurately the conduct of men,

---

* The evidence of experience is admitted by Mr. Mansel to be in favour of necessity:—' Were it not for the direct testimony of my own consciousness to my own freedom, I could regard human actions only as necessary links in the endless chain of phenomenal cause and effect.' Mansel's *Metaphysics*, p. 168.

than the changes of the weather. Hence a volition follows its moral causes, as a physical event follows its physical causes. Whether it *must* do so, Mr. Mill professes himself to be ignorant, and therefore condemns the use of the word necessity, but he knows that it always *does*.

2. *The testimony of Consciousness.* The evidence that decided Sir W. Hamilton was consciousness. We are either directly conscious of freedom, or indirectly through moral obligation. Mr. Mill examines first, whether we are conscious of free will, whether before decision, we are conscious of being able to decide either way. Properly speaking, this is a fact we cannot possibly be conscious of, as we are conscious only of what *is*, not of what *will be*. We know we can do a thing only by doing it. The belief in freedom must, therefore, be an interpretation of past experience. This internal feeling of freedom implies that we could have decided the other way; but, the truth is, not unless we preferred that way. When we imagine ourselves acting differently from what we did, we think of a change in the antecedents, as by knowing something that we did not know. Mr. Mill therefore altogether disputes the assertion that we are conscious of being able to act in opposition to the strongest present desire or aversion.

3. *Accountability.* Mr. Mill then examines whether moral responsibility involves freedom from causation. Responsibility means either that we expect to be punished for certain acts, or that we should deserve punishment for those acts. The first alternative may be thrown out of account. The question then is, whether free-will is involved in the justness of punishment. In this discussion, Mr. Mill assumes no particular theory of morals; it is enough that a difference between right and wrong be admitted, and a natural preference for the right. Whoever does wrong becomes a natural object of active dislike, and perhaps of punishment. The liability of the wrong-doer to be thus called to account has probably much to do with the feeling of being accountable. Oriental despots and persons of a superior caste show not the least feeling of accountability to their inferiors. Moreover, if there were a race of men, as mischievous as lions and tigers, we should treat them precisely as we treat wild beasts, although they acted necessarily; so that the most stringent form of fatalism is not inconsistent with putting a high value on goodness, nor with the existence of approbation and penalties. The real question, however, is—Would the punishment be just? Is it just to punish a man for what he cannot help? Certainly it is, if punishment is the only means by which he can be enabled to help it. Punishment is inflicted as a means towards an end, but if there is no efficacy in the means to procure the end, that is to say, if our volitions are not determined by motives, then punishment is without justification. If an end is justifiable, the sole and necessary means to that end must be justifiable. Now, the Necessitarian Theory proceeds upon two ends,—the benefit of the offender himself, and the protection of others. To punish a child

for its benefit is no more unjust than to administer medicine. In the defence of just rights, punishment must also be just. The feeling of accountability is then nothing more than the knowledge that punishment will be just. Nor is this a *petitio principii*. Mr. Mill considers himself entitled to assume the reality of moral distinctions, such reality not depending on any theory of the will. If this account should not be considered sufficient, how can we justify the punishment of crimes committed in obedience to a perverted conscience? Ravaillac and Balthasar Gérard regarded themselves as heroic martyrs. No person capable of being operated upon by the fear of punishment, will ever feel punishment for wrong-doing to be unjust.

4. *Necessity is not Fatalism.* The doctrine of Necessity is clearly distinguishable from Fatalism. Pure fatalism holds that our actions do not depend on our desires. A superior power overrides our wishes, and bends us according to its will. Modified fatalism proceeds upon the determination of our will by motives, but holds that our character is made *for* us and not by us, so that we are not responsible for our actions, and should in vain attempt to alter them. The true doctrine of causation holds that in so far as our character is amenable to moral discipline, we can improve it, if we desire. According to Mr. Mansel, such a theory of moral causation is really fatalism. Yet Kant held that the capability of predicting our actions does not destroy freedom: it is only in the formation of our character that we are free; and he almost admits that our actions necessarily follow from our character. But, in truth, the volitions tending to improve our character are as capable of being predicted as any voluntary actions. And necessity means only this possibility of being foreseen, so that we are no more free in the formation of our character, than in our subsequent volitions.

5. *The influence of Motives.* Mr. Mansel, following Reid, has denied that the strongest motive prevails, since there is no test of the strength of a motive but its ultimate prevalence. But (1) the strongest motive means the motive strongest in relation to pleasure and pain. (2) Even if the test referred to was the will, the proposition would still not be unmeaning. We say of two weights in a pair of scales, that the heavier will lift the other up; although we mean by the heavier only the weight that will lift the other up. This proposition implies that in most cases there is a heavier, and that this is always the same one, not one or the other, as it may happen. So also if there be motives uniformly followed by certain volitions, the free-will theory is not saved.

APPENDIX.

A.—*History of Nominalism and Realism*, p. **181.**

THE controversy respecting Universals first obtained its place in philosophy from the colloquies of Sokrates, and the writings and teachings of Plato. We need not here touch upon their predecessors Parmenides and Heracleitus, who, in a confused and unsytematic manner, approached this question from opposite sides, and whose speculations worked much upon the mind of Plato in determining both his aggressive dialectic, and his constructive theories. Parmenides of Elea, improving upon the ruder conceptions of Xenophanes, was the first to give emphatic proclamation to the celebrated Eleatic doctrine, Absolute *Ens* as opposed to Relative *Fientia* : *i.e.*, the Cogitable, which Parmenides conceived as the One and All of reality, Ἐν καὶ Πᾶν, enduring and unchangeable, of which the negative was unmeaning; and the Sensible or Perceivable, which was in perpetual change, succession, and multiplicity, without either unity, or reality, or endurance. To the last of these two departments Heracleitus assigned especial prominence. In place of the permanent underlying Ens, which he did not recognize, he substituted a cogitable process of *change*, or generalized concept of what was common to all the successive phases of change—a perpetual stream of generation and destruction, or implication of contraries, in which everything appeared only that it might disappear, without endurance or uniformity. In this doctrine of Heracleitus, the world of sense and particulars could not be the object either of certain knowledge or even of correct probable opinion; in that of Parmenides, it was recognized as an object of probable opinion, though not of certain knowledge. But in both doctrines, as well as in the theories of Democritus, it was degraded, and presented as incapable of yielding satisfaction to the search of a philosophizing mind, which could find neither truth nor reality except in the world of Concepts and Cogitata.

Besides the two theories above-mentioned, there were current in the Hellenic world, before the maturity of Sokrates, several other veins of speculation about the Cosmos, totally divergent one from the other, and by that very divergence sometimes stimulating curiosity, sometimes discouraging all study, as though the problems were hopeless. But Parmenides and Heracleitus, together with the arithmetical and geometrical hypotheses of the Pythagoreans, are expressly noticed by Aristotle as having specially contributed to form the philosophy of Plato.

Neither Parmenides, nor Heracleitus, nor the Pythagoreans, were Dialecticians. They gave out their own thoughts in their own way, with little or no regard to dissentients. They did not cultivate the art of argumentative attack or defence, nor the correct application and diversified confrontation of universal terms, which are the great instruments of that art. It was Zeno, the disciple of Parmenides, that first employed Dialectic in support of his master's theory, or rather against the counter theories of opponents. He showed, by arguments memorable for their subtlety, that the hypothesis of an Absolute, composed of *Entia Plura Discontinua*, led to consequences even more absurd than those that opponents deduced from the Parmenidean hypothesis of *Ens Unum Continuum*. The Dialectic, thus inaugurated by Zeno, reached still higher perfection in the colloquies of Sokrates; who not only employed a new method, but also introduced new topics of debate —ethical, political, and social matters instead of physics and the Cosmos.

The peculiar originality of Sokrates is well known: a man who wrote nothing, but passed his life in indiscriminate colloquy with every one; who professed to have no knowledge himself, but interrogated others on matters that they talked about familiarly and professed to know well; whose colloquies generally ended by puzzling the respondents, and by proving to themselves that they neither knew nor could explain even matters that they had begun by affirming confidently as too clear to need explanation. Aristotle tells us[*] that Sokrates was the first that set himself expressly and methodically to scrutinize the definitions of general or universal terms, and to confront them, not merely with each other, but also, by a sort of inductive process, with many particular cases that were, or appeared to be, included under them. And both Xenophon and Plato give us abundant examples of the terms to which Socrates applied his interrogatories:—What is the Holy? What is the Unholy? What is the Beautiful or Honourable? What is the Ugly or Base? What is Justice—Injustice—Temperance—Madness—Courage—Cowardice—A City—A man fit for civil life? What is the Command of Men? What is the character fit for commanding men? Such are the specimens, furnished by a hearer,[†] of the universal terms whereon the interrogatories of Sokrates bore. All of them were terms spoken and heard familiarly by citizens in the market-place, as if each understood them perfectly; but when Sokrates, professing his own ignorance, put questions asking for solutions of difficulties that perplexed his own mind, the answers showed that these

---

[*] Metaphysics, A. 987, b. 2; M. 1078, b. 18.
[†] Xenophon Memorab. I. 1, 16; IV. 6, 1-13.

difficulties were equally insoluble by respondents, who had never thought of them before. The confident persuasion of knowledge, with which the colloquy began, stood exposed as a false persuasion without any basis of reality. Such illusory semblance of knowledge was proclaimed by Sokrates to be the chronic, though unconscious, intellectual condition of his contemporaries. How he undertook, as the mission of a long life, to expose it, is impressively set forth in the Platonic Apology.

It was thus by Sokrates that the meaning of universal terms and universal propositions, and the relation of each respectively to particular terms and particular propositions, were first made a subject of express enquiry and analytical interrogation. His influence was powerful in imparting the same dialectic impulse to several companions: but most of all to Plato: who not only enlarged and amplified the range of Sokratic enquiry, but also brought the meaning of universal terms into something like system and theory, as a portion of the conditions of trustworthy science. Plato was the first to affirm the doctrine afterwards called REALISM, as the fundamental postulate of all true and proved cognition. He affirmed it boldly, and in its most extended sense, though he also produces (according to his frequent practice) many powerful arguments and unsolved objections against it. It was he (to use the striking phrase of Milton [*]) that first imported into the schools the portent of Realism. The doctrine has been since opposed, confuted, curtailed, transformed, diversified in many ways: but it has maintained its place in logical speculation, and has remained, under one phraseology or another, the creed of various philosophers, from that time down to the present.

The following account of the problems of Realism was handed down to the speculations of the mediæval philosophers, by Porhpyry (between 270-300 A.D.), in his Introduction to the treatise of Aristotle on the Categories. After informing Chrysaorius that he will prepare for him a concise statement of the doctrines of the old philosophers respecting Genus, Differentia, Species, Proprium, Accidens — 'abstaining from the deeper enquiries, but giving suitable development to the more simple,'—Porphyry thus proceeds—'For example, I shall decline discussing, in respect to Genera and Species—(1) Whether they have a substantive existence, or reside merely in naked mental conceptions; (2) Whether, assuming them to have substantive existence, they are bodies or incorporeals; (3) Whether their substantive existence is in and along with the objects of sense, or apart and separable. Upon this task I shall not enter, since it is of the greatest depth, and requires another larger investigation; but shall try at once to show you how the ancients (especially

---

[*] See the Latin verses—De Ideâ Platonicâ quemadmodum Aristoteles intellexit—
'At tu, perenne ruris Academi decus,
Hæc monstra si tu primus induxti scholis,' &c.

the Peripatetics), with a view to logical discourse, dealt with the topics now propounded.' *

Before Porphyry, all these three problems had been largely debated, first by Plato, next by Aristotle against Plato, again by the Stoics against both, and lastly by Plotinus and the Neo-Platonists as conciliators of Plato with Aristotle. After Porphyry, problems the same, or similar, continued to stand in the foreground of speculation, until the authority of Aristotle became discredited at all points by the influences of the sixteenth and seventeenth centuries. But in order to find the beginning of them, as questions provoking curiosity and opening dissentient points of view to inventive dialecticians, we must go back to the age and the dialogues of Plato.

The real Sokrates (*i.e.*, as he is described by Xenophon) inculcated in his conversation steady reverence for the invisible, as apart from and overriding the phenomena of sensible experience: but he interpreted the term in a religious sense, as signifying the agency of the personal gods, employed to produce effects beneficial or injurious to mankind.† He also puts forth his dialectic acuteness to prepare consistent and tenable definitions of familiar general terms (of which instances have already been given), at least so far as to make others feel, for the first time, that they did not understand these 'terms, though they had been always talking like persons that *did* understand. But the Platonic Sokrates (*i.e.*, as spokesman in the dialogues of Plato) enlarges both these discussions materially. Plato recognizes, not simply the invisible persons or gods, but also a separate world of invisible, impersonal entities or objects: one of which he postulates as the objective reality, though only a cogitable reality, correlating with each *general term*. These Entia he considers to be not merely distinct realities, but the only true and knowable realities: they are eternal and unchangeable, manifested by the fact that particulars partake in them, and imparting a partial show of stability to the indeterminate flux of particulars: and unless such separate Universal Entia be supposed, there is nothing whereon cognition can fasten, and consequently there can be no cognition at all.‡ These are the substantive, self-existent Ideas or Forms that Plato first presented to the philosophical world: sometimes with logical acuteness, oftener still with rich poetical and imaginative colouring. They constitute the main body and characteristic of the hypothesis of Realism.

But though the main hypothesis is the same, the accessories and manner of presentation differ materially among its different advocates. In these respects, indeed, Plato differs not only from others, but also from himself. Systematic teaching or exposition is not his purpose, nor does he ever give opinions in

* Porphyry—Introd. in Categor. init.
† Xenophon Memorabil. I. 4, 9-17; IV. 3, 14.
‡ Aristotel. Metaphys. I. 6, p. 987. b. 5; XIII. 4, p. 1078, b. 15.

his own name. We have from him an aggregate of detached dialogues, in many of which this same hypothesis is brought under discussion. But in each dialogue, the spokesmen approach it from a different side: while in others (distinguished by various critics as the Sokratic dialogues), it does not come under discussion at all; Plato being content to remain upon the Sokratic platform, and to debate the meaning of general terms without postulating in correlation with them an objective reality, apart from their respective particulars.

At the close of the Platonic dialogue called KRATYLUS, Sokrates is introduced as presenting the hypothesis of self-existent, eternal, unchangeable Ideas (exactly in the way that Aristotle ascribes to Plato) as the counter-proposition to the theory of universal flux and change announced by Heracleitus. Particulars are ever changing (it is here argued) and are thus out of the reach of cognition; but unless the Universal Ideas above them, such as the Self-beautiful, the Self-good, &c., be admitted as unchangeable objective realities, there can be nothing either nameable or knowable: cognition becomes impossible.

In the TIMAEUS, Plato describes the construction of the Cosmos by a divine Architect, and the model followed by the latter in his work. The distinction is here again brought out, and announced as capital, between the permanent, unalterable *Entia*, and the transient, ever-fluctuating, *Fientia*, which come and go, but never really *are*. *Entia* are apprehended by the cogitant or intelligent soul of the Kosmos, *Fientia* by the sentient or percipient soul; the cosmical soul as a whole, in order to suffice for both these tasks, is made up of diverse component elements—*Idem*, correlating with the first of the two—*Diversum*, correlating with the second—and Idem implicated with Diversum, corresponding to both in conjunction. The Divine Architect is described as constructing a Cosmos, composed both of soul and body, upon the pattern of the grand pre-existent Idea—Auto-zoon or the Self-animal: which included in itself as a genus the four distinct species—celestial (gods, visible and invisible), terrestrial, aerial, and aquatic.

The main point that Plato here insists upon is, the eternal and unchangeable reality of the cogitable objects called Ideas, prior both in time and in logical order to the transient objects of sight and touch, and serving as an exemplar to which these latter are made to approximate imperfectly. He assumes such priority, without proof, in the case of the Idea of Animal; but when he touches upon the four elements—Fire, Air, Water, Earth—he hesitates to make the same assumption, and thinks himself required to give a reason for it. The reason that he assigns (announced distinctly as his own) is as follows: If intellection (cogitation, Νοῦς), and true opinion, are two genera distinct from each other, there must clearly exist Forms or Ideas imperceptible to our senses, and apprehended only by cogitation or intellection: But if, as some persons think, true opinion is noway different

APPENDIX—NOMINALISM AND REALISM.

from intellection, then we must admit all the objects perceived by our senses as firm realities. Now, the fact is (he proceeds to say) that true opinion is not identical with intellection, but quite distinct, separate, and unlike to it. Intellection is communicated by teaching, through true reasoning, and is unshakeable by persuasion; true opinion is communicated by persuasion and removed by counter-persuasion, without true reasoning. True opinion may belong to any man; but intellection is the privilege only of gods and of a small section of mankind. Accordingly, since the two are distinct, the objects correlating with each of them must also be distinct from each other. There must exist, first, primary, eternal, unchangeable Forms, apprehended by intellect or cogitation, but imperceptible by sense; and, secondly, resemblances of these bearing the same name, generated and destroyed each in some place, and apprehended first by sense, afterwards by opinion. Thirdly, there must be the place wherein such resemblances are generated; a place itself imperceptible by sense, yet postulated, as a receptacle indispensable for them, by a dreamy and spurious kind of computation.

We see here that the proof given by Plato, in support of the existence of Forms as the primary realities, is essentially *psychological*: resting upon the fact that there is a distinct mental energy or faculty called Intellection (apart from sense and opinion), which must have its distinct objective correlate; and upon the farther fact, that Intellection is the high prerogative of the gods, shared only by a few chosen men. This last point of the case is more largely and emphatically brought out in the PHÆDRUS, where Sokrates delivers a highly poetical effusion respecting the partial inter-communion of the human soul with these eternal intellectual Realia. To contemplate them is the constant privilege of the gods; to do so is also the aspiration of the immortal soul of man generally, in the pre-existent state, prior to incorporation with the human body; though only in a few cases is such aspiration realized. Even those few human souls, that have succeeded in getting sight of the intellectual Ideas (essences without colour, figure, or tactile properties), lose all recollection of them when first entering into partnership with a human body; but are enabled gradually to recall them, by combining repeated impressions and experience of their resemblances in the world of sense. The revival of these divine elements is an inspiration of the nature of madness—though it is a variety of madness as much better than uninspired human reason as other varieties are worse. The soul, becoming insensible to ordinary pursuits, contracts a passionate devotion to these Universal Ideas, and to that dialectic communion especially with some pregnant youthful mind, that brings them into clear separate contemplation, disengaged from the limits and confusion of sense.

Here philosophy is represented as the special inspiration of a few, whose souls during the period of pre-existence have sufficiently caught sight of the Universal Ideas or Essences; so that these last, though overlaid and buried when the soul is first plunged in a body, are yet revivable afterwards under favourable circumstances, through their imperfect copies in the world of sense: especially by the sight of personal beauty in an ingenuous and aspiring youth, in which case the visible copy makes nearest approach to the perfection of the Universal Idea or Type. At the same time, Plato again presents to us the Cogitable Universals as the only objects of true cognition—the Sensible Particulars being objects merely of opinion.

In the PHÆDON, Sokrates advances the same doctrine, that the perceptions of sense are full of error and confusion, and can at best suggest nothing higher than opinion; that true cognition can never be attained except when the Cogitant Mind disengages itself from the body and comes into direct contemplation of the Universal Entia, objects eternal and always the same—The Self-beautiful, Self-good, Self-just, Self-great, Healthy, Strong, &c., all which objects are invisible, and can be apprehended only by the cogitation or intellect. It is this cogitable Universal that is alone real; Sensible Particulars are not real, nor lasting, nor trustworthy. None but a few philosophers, however, can attain such pure mental energy during this life; nor even they, fully and perfectly. But they will attain it fully after death, (their souls being immortal), if their lives have been passed in sober philosophical training. And their souls enjoyed it before birth, during the period of pre-existence: having acquired, before junction with the body, the knowledge of these Universals, which are forgotten during childhood, but recalled in the way of *reminiscence*, by sensible perceptions that make a distant approach to them. Thus, according to the Phædon and some other dialogues, all learning is merely reminiscence; the mind is brought back, by the laws of association, to the knowledge of Universal Realities that it had possessed in its state of pre-existence. Particulars of sense participate in these Universals to a certain extent, or resemble them imperfectly; and they are therefore called by the same name.

In the REPUBLIC, we have a repetition and copious illustration of this antithesis between the world of Universals or Cogitabilia, which are the only unchangeable realities, and the only objects of knowledge,—and the world of Sensible Particulars, which are transitory and confused shadows of these Universals, and are objects of opinion only. Full and Real *Ens* is knowable, *Non-Ens* is altogether unknowable; what is midway between the two is matter of opinion, and in such midway are the particulars of sense.* Respecting these last, no truth is attainable; whenever you affirm a proposition respecting any of them, you may with equal truth affirm the contrary at the same time. Nowhere is the contrast between the Universals or Real Ideas (among which the Idea of Good is the highest, predominant over all the rest), and the unreal Particulars, or Percepta of sense, more forcibly in-

---

* Plato Republ. V. p. 477-478.

sisted upon than in the Republic. Even the celestial bodies and their movements, being among these Percepta of sense, are ranked among phantoms interesting but useless to observe; they are the best of all Percepta, but they fall very short of the perfection that the mental eye contemplates in the Ideal — in the true Figures and Numbers, in the Real Velocity and the Real Slowness. In the simile commencing the seventh book of the Republic, Plato compares mankind to prisoners in a cave, chained in one particular attitude, so as to behold only an ever-varying multiplicity of shadows, projected, through the opening of the cave, upon the wall before them, by certain unseen Realities behind. The philosopher is one among a few, who by training or inspiration, have been enabled to face about from this original attitude, and to contemplate with his mind the real unchangeable Universals, instead of having his eye fixed upon their particular manifestations, at once shadowy and transient. By such mental revolution he comes round from the perceivable to the cogitable, from opinion to knowledge.

The distinction between these two is farther argued in the elaborate dialogue called THEÆTETUS, where Sokrates, trying to explain what Knowledge or Cognition is, refutes three proposed explanations; and shows, to his own satisfaction, that it is not sensible perception, that it is not true opinion, that it is not true opinion coupled with rational explanation. But he confesses himself unable to show what Knowledge or Cognition is, though he continues to announce it as correlating with realities Cogitable and Universal only.*

In the passages above noticed, and in many others besides, we find Plato drawing a capital distinction between Universals eternal and unchangeable — (each of them a Unit as well as a Universal),† which he affirms to be the only Real Entia—and Particulars transient and variable, which are not Entia at all, but are always coming or going; the Universals being objects of cogitation and of a psychological fact called Cognition, which he declares to be infallible; and the Particulars being objects of sense, and of another psychological fact radically different, called Opinion, which he pronounces to be fallible and misleading. Plato holds, moreover, that the Particulars, though generically distinct and separate from the Universals, have nevertheless a certain communion or participation with them, by virtue of which they become half-existent and half-cognizable, but never attain to full reality or cognizability.

This is the first statement of the theory of complete and un-

* Plato Theætêt., p. 173, 176, 186. Grote's Plato, vol. II. ch. 26, p. 370-395.
† Plato Philêbus, p. 15, A—B, ἑνάδων μονάδας, μίαν ἑκάστην οὖσαν ἀεὶ τὴν αὐτὴν, &c., Republic X., p. 596, A. The phrase of Milton—Unus et Universus—expresses this idea:—

'Sed quamlibet natura sit communior,
Tamen scorsus extat ad modum unius,' &c.

FIRST STATEMENT OF REALISM.

qualified Realism, which came to be known in the Middle Ages under the phrase *Universalia ante rem* or *extra rem*, and to be distinguished from the two counter theories *Universalia in re* (Aristotelian), and *Universalia post rem* (Nominalism). Indeed, the Platonic theory goes even farther than the phrase *Universalia ante rem*, which recognizes the particular as a reality, though posterior and derivative, for Plato attenuates it into phantom and shadow. The problem was now clearly set out in philosophy— What are the objects correlating with Universal terms, and with Particular terms? What is the relation between the two? Plato first gave to the world the solution called Realism, which lasted so long after his time. We shall presently find Aristotle taking issue with him on both the affirmations included in his theory.

But though Plato first introduced this theory into philosophy, he was neither blind to the objections against it, nor disposed to conceal them. His mind was at once poetically constructive and dialectically destructive; to both these impulses the theory furnished ample scope, while the form of his compositions (separate dialogues, with no mention of his own name) rendered it easy to give expression either to one or the other. Before Aristotle arose to take issue with him, we shall find him taking issue with himself, especially in the dialogues called Sophistes and Parmenides, not to mention the Philêbus, wherein he breaks down the unity even of his sovereign Idea, which in the Republic governs the Cogitable World—the Idea of Good.*

Both in the Sophistes and in the Parmenides, the leading disputant introduced by Plato is not Sokrates, but Parmenides and another person (unnamed) of the Eleatic school. In both dialogues objections are taken against the Realistic theory elsewhere propounded by Plato, though the objections adduced in the one are quite distinct from those noticed in the other. In the SOPHISTES, the Eleatic reasoner impugns successfully the theories of two classes of philosophers, one the opposite of the other; first, the Materialists, who recognized no *Entia* except the *Percepta* of Sense; next, the Realistic Idealists, who refused to recognize these last as real *Entia*, or as anything more than transient and mutable Generata or *Fientia*, while they confined the title of Entia to the Forms, cogitable, incorporeal, eternal, immutable, neither acting on anything, nor acted upon by anything. These persons are called in the Sophistes 'Friends of Forms,' and their theory is exactly what we have already cited out of so many other dialogues of Plato, drawing the marked line of separation between Entia and Fientia; between the Immutable, which alone is real and cognizable, and the Mutable, neither real nor cognizable. The Eleate in the Sophistes controverts this Platonic theory, and maintains—that among the Universal Entia there are included items mutable as well as immutable; that both are real

---

* Plato Philêbus, p. 65-66; see Grote's Plato, vol. II. ch. 30, p. 584-585.

and both cognizable; that *Non-Ens* (instead of being set in glaring contrast with Ens, as the totally incogitable against the infallibly cognizable)* is one among the multiplicity of Real Forms, meaning only what is different from *Ens*, and therefore cognizable not less than *Ens*; that *Percepta* and *Cogitata* are alike real, yet both only relatively real, correlating with minds percipient and cogitant. Thus, the reasoning in the Sophistes, while it sets aside the doctrine of *Universalia ante rem*, does not mark out any other relation between Universals and Particulars (neither *in re* nor *post rem*). It discusses chiefly the intercommunion or reciprocal exclusion of Universals with respect to each other; and, upon this point, far from representing them as Objects of infallible Cognition as contrasted with Opinion, it enrolls both Opinion and Discourse among the Universals themselves, and declares both of them to be readily combinable with *Non-Ens* and Falsehood. So that we have here error and fallibility recognized in the region of Universals, as well as in that of Particulars.

But it is principally in the dialogue PARMENIDES that Plato discusses with dialectical acuteness the relation of Universals to their Particulars; putting aside the intercommunion (affirmed in the Sophistes) or reciprocal exclusion between one Universal and another, as an hypothesis at least supremely difficult to vindicate, if at all admissible.† In the dialogue, Sokrates is introduced in the unusual character of a youthful and ardent aspirant in philosophy, defending the Platonic theory of Ideas, as we have seen it proclaimed in the Republic and in Timæus. The veteran Parmenides appears as the opponent to cross-examine him; and not only impugns the theory by several interrogatories which Sokrates cannot answer, but also intimates that there remain behind other objections equally serious requiring answer. Yet at the same time he declares that unless the theory be admitted, and unless *Universalia ante rem* can be sustained as existent, there is no trustworthy cognition attainable, nor any end to be served by philosophical debate. Moreover, Parmenides warns Sokrates that before he can acquire a mental condition competent to defend the theory, he must go through numerous preliminary dialectical exercises; following out both the affirmative and the negative hypotheses in respect to a great variety of Universalia severally. To illustrate the course prescribed, Parmenides gives a long specimen of this dialectic in handling his own doctrine of *Ens Unum*. He takes first the hypothesis *Si Unum Est*—next, the hypothesis *Si Unum non est*; and he deduces from each, by ingenious subtleties, double and contradictory conclusions. These he sums up at the end, challenging Sokrates to solve the puzzles before affirming his thesis.

Apart from these antinomies at the close of the dialogue, the

---

* Plato Republic, V., 478-479.

† Plato Parmenid. p. 129 E; with Stallbaum's Prolegomena to that Dialogue, p. 38-42.

cross-examination of Sokrates by Parmenides, in the middle of it, brings out forcibly against the Realistic theory objections such as those urged against it by the Nominalists of the Middle Ages. In the first place, we find that Plato conceived the theory itself differently from Porphyry and the philosophers that wrote subsequently to the Peripatetic criticism. Porphyry and his successors put the question, Whether Genera and Species had a separate existence, apart from the individuals composing them? Now, the world of Forms (the Cogitable or Ideal world as opposed to the Sensible), is not here conceived by Plato as peopled in the first instance by Genera and Species. Its first tenants are *attributes*, and attributes distinctly *relative*—Likeness, One and Many, Justice, Beauty, Goodness, &c. Sokrates, being asked by Parmenides whether he admits Forms corresponding with these names, answers unhesitatingly in the affirmative. He is next asked whether he admits Forms corresponding to the names Man, Fire, Water, &c., and instead of replying in the affirmative, intimates that he does not feel sure. Lastly, the question is put whether there are Forms corresponding to the names of mean objects—mud, hair, dirt, &c. At first he answers emphatically in the negative, and treats the affirmative as preposterous; there exists no cogitable hair, &c., but only the object of sense that we so denominate. Yet, on second thoughts, he is not without misgiving that there may be Forms even of these; though the supposition is so repulsive to him that he shakes it off as much as he can. Upon this last expression of sentiment Parmenides comments, ascribing it to the juvenility of Sokrates, and intimating that when Sokrates has become more deeply imbued with philosophy, he will cease to set aside any of these objects as unworthy.

Here we see that in the theory of Realism as conceived by Sokrates, the Self-Existent Universals are not Genera and Species as such, but Attributes (not Second Substances or Essences, but Accidents or Attributes, *e.g.*, Quality, Quantity, Relation, &c., to use the language afterwards introduced by the Aristotelian Categories); that no Genera or Species are admitted except with hesitation; and that the mean and undignified among them are scarcely admissible at all. This sentiment of dignity, associated with the *Universalia ante rem*, and the emotional necessity for tracing back particulars to an august and respected origin—is to be noted as a marked and lasting feature of the Realistic creed; and it even passed on to the *Universalia in re* as afterwards affirmed by Aristotle. Parmenides here takes exception to it (and so does Plato elsewhere*) as inconsistent with faithful adherence to scientific analogy.

Parmenides then proceeds (interrogating Sokrates) first to state what the Realistic theory is (Universals apart from Particulars—Particulars apart from Universals, yet having some participation in them, and named after them), next to bring out the

---

* Plato Sophist. 227 A. Politikus, p. 266 D.

difficulties attaching to it. The Universal or Form (he argues,) cannot be entire in each of its many separate particulars; nor yet is it divisible, so that a part can be in one particular, and a part in another. For take the Forms *Great, Equal, Small*; Equal magnitudes are equal because they partake in the Form of equality. But how can a part of the Form Equality, less than the whole Form, cause the magnitudes to be equal? How can the Form Smallness have any parts less than itself, or how can it be greater than anything?

The Form cannot be divided, nor can it co-exist undivided in each separate particular; accordingly, particulars can have no participation in it at all.

Again, you assume a Form of Greatness, because you see many particular objects, each of which appears to you great; this being the point of resemblance between them. But if you compare the Form of Greatness with any or all of the particular great objects, you will perceive a resemblance between them; this will require you to assume a higher Form, and so on upward, without limit.

Sokrates, thus embarrassed, starts the hypothesis that perhaps each of these Forms may be a cogitation, and nothing more, existing only within the mind. How? rejoins Parmenides. Can there be a cogitation of nothing at all? Must not each cogitation have a real *cogitatum* correlating with it—in this case, the one Form that is identical throughout many particulars? If you say that particulars partake in the Form, and that each Form is nothing but a cogitation, does not this imply that each particular is itself cogitant?

Again, Sokrates urges that the Forms are constant, unalterable, stationary in nature; that particulars resemble them, and participate in them only so far as to resemble them. But (rejoins Parmenides) if particulars resemble the Form, the Form must resemble them; accordingly, you must admit another and higher Form, as the point of resemblance between the Form and its particulars; and so on, upwards.

And farther (continues Parmenides), even admitting these Universal Forms as self-existent, how can we know anything about them? Forms can correlate only with Forms, Particulars only with Particulars. Thus, if I, an individual man, am master, I correlate with another individual man, who is my servant, and he on his side with me. But the Form of mastership, the universal self-existent master, must correlate with the Form of servantship, the universal servant. The correlation does not subsist between members of the two different worlds, but between different members of the same world respectively. Thus the Form of Cognition correlates with the Form of Truth; and the Form of each variety of Cognition, with the Form of the corresponding variety of Truth. But we, as individual subjects, do not possess in ourselves the Form of Cognition; our Cognition is our own, correlating with such truth as belongs to it and to ourselves. Our Cognition cannot reach to the Form of Truth, nor therefore to any other

Form; we can know nothing of the Self-good, Self-beautiful, Self-just, &c., even supposing such Forms to exist.

These acute and subtle arguments are nowhere answered by Plato. They remain as unsolved difficulties, embarrassing the Realistic theory; they are reinforced by farther difficulties no less grave, included in the dialectic Antinomies of Parmenides at the close of the dialogue, and by an unknown number of others indicated as producible, though not actually produced. Yet still Plato, with full consciousness of these difficulties, asserts unequivocally, that unless the Realistic theory can be sustained, philosophical research is fruitless, and truth cannot be reached. We see thus that the author of the theory has also left on record some of the most forcible arguments against it. It appears from Aristotle (though we do not learn the fact from the Platonic dialogues), that Plato, in his later years, symbolized the Ideas or Forms under the denomination of Ideal Numbers, generated by implication of The One with what he called The Great and Little, or the Indeterminate Dyad. This last, however, is not the programme wherein the Realistic theory stands opposed to Nominalism.

But the dialogue Parmenides, though full of acuteness on the negative side, not only furnishes no counter-theory, but asserts continued allegiance to the Realistic theory, which passed as Plato's doctrine to his successors. To impugn, forcibly and even unanswerably, a theory at once so sweeping and so little fortified by positive reasons, was what many dialecticians of the age could do. But to do this, and at the same time to construct a counter-theory, was a task requiring higher powers of mind. One, however, of Plato's disciples and successors was found adequate to the task—ARISTOTLE.

The Realistic Ontology of Plato is founded (as Aristotle himself remarks) upon *mistrust* and *contempt* of perception of *sense*, as bearing entirely on the flux of particulars, which never stand still so as to become objects of knowledge. All reality, and all cognoscibility, were supposed to reside in the separate world of Cogitable Universals *(extra rem* or *ante rem)*, of which, in some confused manner, particulars were supposed to partake. The Universal, apart from its particulars, was clearly and fully knowable, furnishing propositions constantly and infallibly true: the Universal, as manifested in its particulars, was never fully knowable, nor could ever become the subject of propositions, except such as were sometimes true and sometimes false.

Against this separation of the Universal from its Particulars, Aristotle entered a strong protest: as well as against the subsidiary hypothesis of a participation of the latter in the former: which participation, when the two had been declared separate, appeared to him not only untenable and uncertified, but unintelligible. His arguments are interesting, as being among the earliest objections known to us against Realism.

1. Realism is a useless multiplication of existences, serving no purpose. Wherever a number of particulars—be they sub-

stances eternal or perishable—be they substances, qualities, or relations—bear the same name, and thus have a Universal *in re* predicable of them in common—in every such case Plato assumes a Universal *extra rem*, or a separate self-existent Form; which explains nothing, and merely doubles the total to be summed up.*

2. Plato's arguments in support of Realism are either inconclusive, or prove too much. Wherever there is cognition (he argues), there must exist an eternal and unchangeable object of cognition, apart from particulars, which are changeable and perishable. No, replies Aristotle: cognition does not require the *Universalia extra rem*: for the *Universalia in re*, the constant predicate of all the particulars, is sufficient as an object of cognition. Moreover, if the argument were admitted, it would prove that there existed separate Forms or Universals of mere negations—for many of the constant predicates are altogether negative. Again, if Self-Existent Universals are to be assumed corresponding to all our cogitations, we must assume Universals of extinct particulars, and even of fictitious particulars, such as Hippocentaurs or Chimeras: for of these, too, we have phantasms or concepts in our minds.†

3. The most subtle disputants on this matter include *Relata*, among the Universals Ideas or Forms. This is absurd, because these do not constitute any Genus by themselves. These disputants have also urged against the Realistic theory that powerful and unsolved objection, entitled *The Third Man*.‡

4. The supporters of these Self-Existent Universals trace them to two *principia*—The One, and the Indeterminate Dyad; which they affirm to be prior in existence even to the Universals themselves. But this can never be granted: for in the first place, the Idea of Number must be logically prior to the Idea of the Dyad; but the Idea of Number is relative, and the Relative can never be prior to the Absolute or Self-Existent.

5. If we grant that wherever there is one constant predicate belonging to many particulars, or wherever there is stable and trustworthy cognition, in all such cases a Self-Existent Universal correlate *extra rem* is to be assumed, we shall find that this applies not merely to Substances or Essences, but also to the other Categories—Quality, Quantity, Relation, &c. But hereby we exclude the possibility of participation in them by Particulars:

* Aristot. Metaph. A. 990, a. 34; M. 1079, a. 2. Here we have the first appearance of the argument that William of Ockham, the Nominalist, put in the foreground of his case against Realism—'Entia non sunt multiplicanda præter necessitatem,' &c.

† Aristot. Metaphys. A. 990, b. 14; Scholia, p. 565, b. 10, Brandit.

‡ Aristot. Metaph. A. 990, b. 15, οἱ ἀκριβέστεροι τῶν λόγων. Both the points here noticed appear in the Parmenides of Plato.

The objection called *The Third Man*, is expressed by saying, that if there be a Form of man, resembling individual men, you must farther postulate some higher Form, marking the point of resemblance between the two: and so on higher, without end.

since from such participation the Particular derives its Substance or Essence alone, not its accidental predicates. Thus the Self-Existent Universal Dyad is eternal: but a particular pair, which derives its essential property of doubleness from partaking in this Universal Dyad, does not at the same time partake of eternity, unless by accident. Accordingly, there are no Universal Ideas, except of Substances or Essences: the common name, when applied to the world of sense and to that of cogitation, signifies the same thing—substance or essence. It is unmeaning to talk of anything else as signified—any other predicate common to many. Well then, if the Form of the Universals, and the Form of those particulars that participate in the Universals, be the same, we shall have something common to both the one and the other, so that the objection called *The Third Man* will become applicable, and a higher Form must be postulated. But if the Form of the Universals and the Form of the participating particulars, be not identical, then the same name, as signifying both, will be used equivocally; just as if you applied the same denomination *Man* to Kallias and to a piece of wood, without any common property to warrant it.

6. But the greatest difficulty of all is to understand how these Cogitable Universals, not being causes of any change or movement, contribute in any way to the objects of sense, either to the eternal or to the perishable: or how they assist us towards the knowledge thereof, being not in them, and therefore not their substance or essence: or how they stand in any real relation to their participants, being not immanent therein. Particulars certainly do not proceed from these Universals, in any intelligible sense. To say that the Universals are archetypes, and that particulars partake in them, is unmeaning, and mere poetic metaphor. For where is the working force to mould them in conformity with the Universals? Any one thing may *be* like, or may *become* like, to any other particular thing, by accident; or without any regular antecedent cause to produce such assimilation. The same particular substance, moreover, will have not one Universal archetype only, but several. Thus, the same individual man will have not only the Self-animal and the Self-biped, but also the Self-man, as Archetype. Then again, there will be Universal Archetypes, not merely for particular sensible objects, but also for Universals themselves: thus the Genus will be an archetype for its various species: so that the same which is now archetype, will, under other circumstances, be copy.

7. Furthermore, it seems impossible that what is Substance or Essence can be separate from that whereof it is the Substance or Essence. How then can the Universals, if they be the Essences of Sensible things, have any existence apart from those Sensible things? Plato tells us in the Phædon, that the Forms or Universals are the causes why particulars both exist at all, and come into such or such modes of existence. But even if we assume Universals as existing, still the Particulars participant therein will not come into being, unless there be some efficient cause to

produce movement; moreover, many other things come into being, though there be no Universals correlating therewith, *e.g.*, a house, or a ring. The same causes that were sufficient to bring these last into being, will be sufficient to bring all particulars into being, without assuming any Universals *extra rem* at all.

8. Again, if the Universals or Forms are Numbers, how can they ever be causes? Even if we suppose Particulars to be Numbers also, how can one set of Numbers be causes to the others? There can be no such causal influence, even if one set be eternal, and the other perishable.*

Out of the many objections raised by Aristotle against Plato, we have selected such as bore principally upon the theory of Realism: that is, upon the theory of *Universalia ante rem* or *extra rem*—self-existent, archetypal, cogitable substances, in which Particulars faintly participated. The objections are not superior in acuteness, and they are decidedly inferior, in clearness of enunciation, to those that Plato himself produces in the Parmenides. Moreover, several of them are founded upon Aristotle's point of view, and would have failed to convince Plato. The great merit of Aristotle is, that he went beyond the negative of the Parmenides, asserted this new point of view of his own, and formulated it into a counter-theory. He rejected altogether the separate and exclusive reality which Plato had claimed for his Absolutes of the Cogitable world, as well as the derivative and unreal semblance that alone Plato accorded to the sensible world. Without denying the distinction of the two, as conceivable and nameable, he maintained that truth and cognition required that they should be looked at in implication with each other. And he went even a step farther, in antithesis to Plato, by reversing the order of the two. Instead of considering the Cogitable Universals alone as real and complete in themselves, and the Sensible Particulars as degenerate and confused semblances of them, he placed complete reality in the sensible particulars alone,† and treated the cogitable universals as contributory appendages thereto; some being essential,

---

* Aristot. Metaph., A. 991, b. 13. Several other objections are made by Aristotle against that variety of the Platonic theory whereby the Ideas were commuted into Ideal numbers. These objections do not belong to the controversy of Realism against Nominalism.

† Aristotle takes pains to vindicate against both Plato and the Heracleiteans the dignity of the Sensible World. They that depreciate sensible objects as perpetually changing, unstable, and unknowable, make the mistake (he observes) of confining their attention to the sublunary interior of the Cosmos, where, indeed, generation and destruction largely prevail. But this is only a small portion of the entire Cosmos. In the largest portion—the visible, celestial, superlunary regions—there is no generation or destruction at all, nothing but permanence and uniformity. In appreciating the sensible world (Aristotle says), philosophers ought to pardon the shortcomings of the smaller portion on account of the excellencies of the larger; and not condemn both together on account of the smaller—(Metaphys., Γ. 1010, *a*. 32).

others non-essential, but all of them relative, and none of them independent integers. His philosophy was a complete revolution as compared with Parmenides and Plato; a revolution, too, the more calculated to last, because he embodied it in an elaborate and original theory of Logic, Metaphysics, and Ontology. He was the first philosopher that, besides recognizing the equivocal character of those general terms whereon speculative debate chiefly turns, endeavoured methodically to set out and compare the different meanings of each term, and their relations to each other.

However much the Ontology of Aristotle may fail to satisfy modern exigencies, still, as compared with the Platonic Realism, it was a considerable improvement. Instead of adopting Ens as a self-explaining term, contrasted with the Generated and Perishable (the doctrine of Plato in the Republic, Phædon, and Timæus), he discriminates several distinct meanings of Ens; a discrimination not always usefully pursued, but tending in the main towards a better theory. The distinction between Ens potential, and Ens actual, does not belong directly to the question between Realism and Nominalism, yet it is a portion of that philosophical revolution wrought by Aristotle against Plato—displacement of the seat of reality, and transfer of it from the Cogitable Universal to the Sensible Particular. The direct enunciation of this change is contained in his distinction of Ens into Fundamental and Concomitant (συμβεβηκός), and his still greater refinement on the same principle by enumerating the ten varieties of Ens called Categories or Predicaments.* He will not allow Ens (nor Unum) to be a Genus, partible into Species; he recognizes it only as a word of many analogous meanings, *one of them principal and fundamental*, the rest derivative and subordinate thereto, each in its own manner. Aristotle thus establishes a graduated scale of Entia, each having its own value and position, and its own mode of connexion with the common centre. That common centre, Aristotle declared to be of necessity some individual object —*Hoc Aliquid*, That Man, This Horse, &c. This was the common Subject, to which all the other Entia belonged as predicates, and without which none of them had any reality. We here fall into the language of Logic, the first theory of which we owe to Aristotle. His ontological classification was adapted to that theory.

As we are here concerned only with the different ways of conceiving the relation between the Particular and the Universal, we are not called on to criticise the well known decuple enumeration of Categories or Predicaments given by Aristotle, both in his Treatise called by that name and elsewhere. For our purpose it

* In enumerating the ten Categories, Aristotle takes his departure from the proposition—*Homo currit—Homo vincit*. He assumes a particular individual as Subject: and he distributes, under ten general heads, all the information that can be asked or given about that Subject—all the predicates that can be affirmed or denied thereof.

is enough to point out that the particular sensible *Hoc Aliquid* is declared to be the ultimate subject, to which all Universals attach, as determinants or accompaniments; and that if this condition be wanting, the unattached Universal cannot rank among complete Entia. The Subject or *First Substance*, which can never become a predicate, is established as the indispensable ultimate subject for all predicates; if that disappears, all predicates disappear along with it. The Particular thus becomes the keystone of the arch whereon all Universals rest. Aristotle is indeed careful to point out a gradation in these predicates; some are essential to the subject, and thus approach so near to the First Substance that he calls them *Second Substances;* others, and the most in number, are not thus essential; these last are *Concomitants* or *Accidents,* and some of them fall so much short of complete Entity that he

These ten κατηγορίαι—γένη τῶν κατηγοριῶν, sometimes simply τά γενη —σχήματα τῶν κατηγοριῶν—*Prædicamenta* in Latin—are as follows:—
1. Οὐσία—*Substantia*—Substance.
2. Ποσὸν—*Quantum*—Quantity.
3. Ποιὸν—*Quale*—Quality.
4. Πρός τι—*Ad aliquid*—Relation.
5. Ποῦ—*Ubi*—Location.
6. Πότε—*Quando*—Period of Time.
7. Κεῖσθαι—*Jacēre*—Attitude, Posture.
8. Ἔχειν—*Habēre*—Equipment, Appurtenances, Property.
9. Ποιεῖν—*Facere*—Active occupation.
10. Πάσχειν—*Pati*—Passive occupation.

1. The first Category, Substance, is distributed into Prima and Secunda. Prima, which is Substance *par excellence,* can only serve as a Subject in propositions, and can never be a Predicate. It is indispensable as a substratum for predicates; though alone and without some of them, it is a mere unmeaning term. Substantia Secunda describes the Species or Genus that includes the First. Respecting an unknown Subject—Kallias—you ask, What is Kallias? Answer is made by declaring the Second Substance, the Species he belongs to—Kallias is a man.

2. *Quantum*—How large is he? To this question answer is made under the same Category—He is six feet high, as thin as Kinesias, &c.

3. *Quale*—What manner of man is he? Answer the third Category —He is fair, flat-nosed, muscular, &c.

4. *Relata*—What are the relations that he stands in? He is father, master, director, &c.

5. *Ubi*—Where is he? In his house, in the market-place, &c.

6. *Quando*—Of what point of time do you speak? Yesterday, last year, now, &c.

7. *Jacēre*—In what attitude or posture is he? He is lying down, standing upright, kneeling, &c.

8. *Habēre*—What has he in the way of clothing, equipment, arms, property? He has boots, sword and shield, an axe, a house, &c.

9. *Facere*—In what is he actively occupied? He is speaking, writing, fencing, cutting wood, &c.

10. *Pati*—In what is he passively occupied? He is being beaten, reproved, rubbed, having his hair cut, &c.

describes them as near to Non-Entia.* But all of them, essential or unessential, are alike constituents or appendages of the First Substance or Particular Subject, and have no reality in any other character. We thus have the counter-theory of Aristotle against the Platonic Realism. Instead of separate Universal substances, containing in themselves full reality, and forfeiting much of that reality when they faded down into the shadowy copies called Particulars, he inverts the Platonic order, announces full reality to be the privilege of the Particular Sensible, and confines the function of the Universal to that of a Predicate, in or along with the Particular. There is no doctrine that he protests against more frequently, than the ascribing of separate reality to the Universal. The tendency to do this, he signalizes as a natural but unfortunate

Such is the list of Categories, or decuple classification of predicates, drawn up by Aristotle, seemingly from the comparison of many different propositions. He himself says, that there are various predicates that might be referred to more than one of the several heads; and he does not consider this as an objection to the classification. The fourth class—*Relata*—ought to be considered as including them all; the first Category is the common and indispensable Correlate to all the others. Aristotle's conception of relation is too narrow, and tied down by grammatical conjunctions of words. Yet it must be said, that the objections to his classification on this ground, are applicable also to the improved classifications of modern times, which dismiss the six last heads, and retain only the four first—Substance, Quantity, Quality, Relation. Of these four, the three first properly rank under the more general head of Relata.

Among all the ten heads of the Aristotelian scheme, the two that have been usually considered as most incongruous, and least entitled to their places, are, No. 7 and 8—*Jacēre* and *Habēre*. They are doubtless peculiarities; and they may fairly be considered as revealing the first projection of the scheme in Aristotle's mind. He began by conceiving an individual man as the Subject, and he tried to classify the various predicates applicable in reply to questions respecting the same. Now, in this point of view, the seventh and eighth Categories will be found important; referring to facts constantly varying, and often desirable to know; moreover not fit to rank under any of the other general heads, except under Relata, which comprises them as well as all the rest. But Aristotle afterwards proceeded to stretch the application of the scheme, so as to comprehend philosophy generally, and other subjects of Predication besides the individual man. Here undoubtedly the seventh and eighth heads appear narrow and trivial. Aristotle probably would never have introduced them, had such enlarged purpose been present to his mind from the beginning. Probably, too, he was not insensible to the perfection of the number Ten.

* Aristot. Metaph., E. 1026, b. 21. φαίνεται γὰρ τὸ συμβεβηκὸς ἐγγύς τι τοῦ μὴ ὄντος.
There cannot be a stronger illustration of the difference between the Platonic and the Aristotelian point of view, than the fact that Plato applies the same designation to all particular objects of sense—that they are only mid-way between Entia and Non-Entia. (Republic, v. 478-479.)

illusion, lessening the beneficial efficacy of universal demonstrative reasoning.* And he declares it to be a corollary, from this view of the Particular as indispensable subject, along with the Universal as its predicate:—That the first principles of demonstration in all the separate theoretical sciences, must be obtained by induction from particulars: first by impressions of sense preserved in the memory; then by multiplied remembrances enlarged into one experience; lastly, by many experiences generalized into one principle by the Noûs.†

While Aristotle thus declares Induction to be the source from whence demonstration in these separate sciences draws its first principles, we must at the same time acknowledge that his manner of treating science is not always conformable to this declaration, and that he often seems to forget Induction altogether. This is the case not only in his First Philosophy, or Metaphysics, but also in his Physics. He there professes to trace out what he calls beginnings, causes, elements, &c., and he analyzes most of the highest generalities. Yet still these analytical enquiries (whatever be their value) are usually, if not always, kept in subordination to the counter-theory that he had set up against the Platonic Realism. Complete reality resides (he constantly repeats) only in the particular sensible substances and sensible facts or movements that compose the aggregate Cosmos; which is not generated, but eternal, both as to substance and as to movement. If these sensible substances disappear, nothing remains. The beginnings and causes exist only relatively to these particulars. Form, Matter, Privation, are not real Beings, antecedent to the Cosmos, and pre-existent generators of the substances constituting the Cosmos; they are logical fragments or factors, obtained by mental analysis and comparison, assisting to methodize our philosophical point of view or conception of those substances; but incapable of being understood, and having no value of their own apart from the substances. Some such logical analysis (that of Aristotle or some other) is an indispensable condition even of the most strictly inductive philosophy.

There are some portions of the writings of Aristotle (especially the third book *De Animâ* and the twelfth book of the *Metaphysica*) where he appears to lose sight of the limit here indicated; but with few exceptions, we find him constantly remembering, and often repeating, the great truth formulated in his Categories—that full or substantive reality resides only in the *Hoc Aliquid*, with its predicates implicated with it—and that even the highest of these predicates (Second Substances) have no reality apart from some one of their particulars. We must recollect that though Aristotle

---

* Aristot. Analyt. Poster., I., p. 85, a. 31, b. 19.
† See the concluding chapter of the Analytica Posteriora.

A similar doctrine is stated by Plato in the Phædon (p. 96 B.), as one among the intellectual phases that Sokrates had passed through in the course of his life, without continuing in them.

denies to the predicates a *separate* reality, he recognizes in them an *adjective* reality, as accompaniments and determinants: he contemplates all the ten Categories as distinct varieties of existence.* This is sufficient as a basis for abstraction, whereby we can name them and reason upon them as distinct objects of thought or points of view, although none of them come into reality except as implicated with a sensible particular. Of such reasoning Aristotle's First Philosophy chiefly consists; and he introduces peculiar phrases to describe this distinction of reason, between two different points of view, where the real object spoken of is one and the same. The frequency of the occasions taken to point out that distinction, mark his anxiety to keep the First Philosophy in harmony with the theory of reality announced in his Categories.

The Categories of Aristotle appear to have become more widely known than any other part of his philosophy. They were much discussed by the sects coming after him; and even when not adopted, were present to speculative minds as a scheme to be amended.† Most of the arguments turned upon the nine later Categories; it was debated whether these were properly enumerated and discriminated, and whether the enumeration as a whole was exhaustive.

With these details, however, the question between Realism and its counter-theory (whether Conceptualism or Nominalism) is not materially concerned. The standard against Realism was raised by Aristotle in the First Category, when he proclaimed the Hoc Aliquid to be the only complete Ens, and the Universal to exist only along with it as a predicate, being nothing in itself apart; and when he enumerated *Quality* as one among the predicates, and nothing beyond. In the Platonic Realism (Phædon, Timæus, Parmenides) what Aristotle called Quality was the highest and most incontestable among all Substances -- the Good, the Beautiful, the Just, &c.; what Aristotle called Second Substance was also Substance in the Platonic Realism, though not so incontestably; but what Aristotle called First Substance was in the Platonic Realism no Substance at all, but only one among a multitude of confused and transient shadows. It is in the First and Third Categories that the capital antithesis of Aristotle against the Platonic Realism is contained. As far as that antithesis is concerned, it matters little whether the aggregate of predicates be subdivided under nine general heads (Categories) or under three.

In the century succeeding Aristotle, the STOIC philosophers altered his Categories, and drew up a new list of their own, containing only four distinct heads instead of ten. We have no record or explanation of the Stoic Categories from any of their

* Aristot. Metaphys., Δ. 1017, a. 24. ὁσαχῶς γὰρ λέγεται (τὰ σχήματα τῆς κατηγορίας) τοσαυταχῶς τὸ εἶναι σημαίνει.
† This is the just remark of Trendelenburg—Kategorienlehre—p. 217.

authors; so that we are compelled to accept the list on secondary authority, from the comments of critics, mostly opponents. But, as far as we can make out, they retained in their First Category the capital feature of Aristotle's First Category; the primacy of the First Substance or Hoc Aliquid, and its exclusive privilege of imparting reality to all the other Categories. Indeed, the Stoics seem not only to have retained this characteristic, but to have exaggerated it. They did not recognize so close an approach of the Universal to the Particular, as is implied by giving to it a second place in the same Category, and calling it Second Substance. The First Category of the Stoics (Something or Subject) included only particular substances; all Universals were by them ranked in the other Categories, being regarded as negations of substances, and designated by the term *Non-Somethings—Non-Substances.**

The Neo-Platonist PLOTINUS, in the third century after the Christian era, agreed with the Stoics (though looking from the opposite point of view) in disapproving Aristotle's arrangement of Second Substance in the same Category with First Substance.† He criticises at some length both the Aristotelian list of Categories, and the Stoic list; but he falls back into the Platonic and even the Parmenidean point of view. His capital distinction is between Cogitables and Sensibles. The Cogitabilia are in his view the most real; (*i.e.* the Aristotelian Second Substance is more real than the First;) among them the highest, Unum or Bonum, is the grand fountain and sovereign of all the rest. Plotinus thus departed altogether from the Aristotelian Categories, and revived the Platonic or Parmenidean Realism; yet not without some Aristotelian modifications. But it is remarkable that in this departure his devoted friend and scholar PORPHYRY did not follow him. Porphyry not only composed an Introduction to the Categories of Aristotle, but also vindicated them at great length, in a separate commentary, against the censures of Plotinus: Dexippus, Jamblichus, and Simplicius, followed in the same track.‡ Still, though Porphyry stood forward both as admirer and champion of the Aristotelian Categories, he did not consider that the question raised by the First Category of Aristotle against the Platonic Realism was finally decided. This is sufficiently proved by the three problems cited above out of the Introduction of Porphyry; where he proclaims it to be a deep and difficult inquiry, whether Genera and Species had not a real substantive existence apart from the individuals composing them. Aristotle, both in the Categories and in many other places, had declared his opinion distinctly in the negative, against Plato: but Porphyry had not made up his mind between

---

* Prantl—Gesch. der Logik. Vol. I. sect. vi. p. 420. οὗτινα τὰ κοινὰ παρ' αὐτοῖς λέγεται, &c.

† Plotinus. Ennead. VI. 1, 2.

‡ Simplicius. Schol. in Aristotel. Categ.—p. 40 a-b. Brandis.

SCOTUS ERIGENA.

the two, though he insists, in language very Aristotelian, on the distinction between First and Second Substance.* Through the translations and manuals of Boëthius and others, the Categories of Aristotle were transmitted to the Latin Churchmen, and continued to be read even through the darkest ages, when the Analytica and the Topica were unknown or neglected. The Aristotelian discrimination between First and Second Substance was thus always kept in sight, and Boëthius treated it much in the same manner as Porphyry had done before him.† Alcuin, Rhabanus Maurus, and Eric of Auxerre,‡ in the eighth and ninth centuries, repeated what they found in Boëthius, and upheld the Aristotelian tradition unimpaired. But SCOTUS ERIGENA (d. 880 A.D.) took an entirely opposite view, and reverted to the Platonic traditions, though with a large admixture of Aristotelian ideas. He was a Christian Platonist, blending the transcendentalism of Plato and Plotinus with theological dogmatic influences (derived from the Pseudo-Dionysius Areopagita and others) and verging somewhat even towards Pantheism. Scotus Erigena revived the doctrine of Cogitable *Universalia extra rem* and *ante rem*. He declared express opposition to the arrangement of the First Aristotelian Category, whereby the individual was put first, in the character of subject; the Universal second, in the character only of predicate; complete reality belonging to the two in conjunction. Scotus maintained that the Cogitable or Incorporeal Universal was the first, the true and complete real; from whence the sensible individuals were secondary, incomplete, multiple, derivatives.|| But though he thus adopts and enforces the Platonic theory of Universalia *ante rem* and *extra rem*, he does not think himself obliged to deny that Universalia may be *in re* also.

The contradiction of the Aristotelian traditions, so far as concerns the First Category, thus proclaimed by Scotus Erigena, appears to have provoked considerable opposition among his immediate successors. Nevertheless, he also obtained partizans. Remigius of Auxerre and others not only defended the Platonic Realism, but carried it as far as Plato himself had done; affirming that not only Universal Substances, but also Universal Accidents, had a real separate existence, apart from and anterior to individuals.§ The controversy for and against the Platonic Realism was thus distinctly launched in the schools of the middle ages.

* Prantl—Geschichte der Logik. Vol. I., sect. 11, p. 634, n. 69. Upon this account, Prantl finds Porphyry guilty of 'empiricism in its extreme crudeness'—'jene äusserste Rohheit des Empirismus.'

† Prantl—Geschichte der Logik. Vol. I., sect. 12, p. 685; Vol. II., sect. 1, p. 4-7. Trendelenburg—Kategorienlehre, p. 245.

‡ Ueberweg — Geschichte der Philosophie der patristischen und scholastischen Zeit, sect. 21, p. 115, ed. 2nd.

|| Prantl—Gesch. der Logik. Vol. II., ch. 13, p. 29-35.

§ Ueberweg—Geschicht der Philos., sect. 21, p. 113. Prantl—Gesch. der Logik, Vol. II., ch. 13, 44, 45-47.

It was upheld both as a philosophical revival, and as theologically orthodox, entitled to supersede the traditional counter-theory of Aristotle.

It has been stated above, that it was through Porphyry's *Isagoge* (in the translation of Boëthius) that the schoolmen became acquainted with the ancient dispute as to the nature of Universals. Of Plato's doctrines, except in a translation of part of the Timæus, they had for a long time only second-hand knowledge, chiefly through St. Augustin; of Aristotle, they knew down to the middle of the twelfth century, only the Categories and the *De Interpretatione* in translation, and not, until the beginning of the thirteenth, others besides the logical works. Down to about this time, logic or dialectic being the whole of philosophy, the question as to Universals almost excluded every other; and, even later, when the field of philosophy became much wider, it never lost the first place as long as scholasticism remained dominant.

Rather more than two centuries after the death of Scotus Erigena (about the end of the eleventh), the question was eagerly disputed, in its bearings upon the theological dogma of the Trinity, between ROSCELLIN, a canon of Compiègne, and ANSELM, Archbishop of Canterbury. Anselm maintained that all individual men were *in specie homo unus*, and formed a real unity; so too, although every person in the Godhead was perfect God, they were but one God. To this realistic doctrine, Roscellin (of whom very little is known), founding upon some of his immediate precursors, opposed a theory different from the Aristotelian. Maintaining with Aristotle, and even more strongly than Aristotle, that the individual particulars were the only real entities, he declared that, in genera and species, the individuals were held together only subjectively by means of a general name, bestowed upon them for their points of similarity. The Universals were neither *ante rem* (with Plato), nor *in re* (with Aristotle), but *post rem;* and in themselves were nothing at all beyond *voces* or *nomina*. Roscellin appears to have carried out the theory consistently, and not merely with reference to the special theological question. So far as that was concerned, he was not afraid to pronounce that the three persons were three individual Gods; and thereupon, his theology being condemned by an ecclesiastical council, the theory became suspect, and so remained until the late period of scholasticism. Its supporters were called by the name *vocales* or *nominales*, Nominalists; and it was at the same period of excited feeling that the name *realis*, Realist, was first used to designate the upholders of the ancient doctrine, as held either in the Platonic or the Aristotelian form.

To what lengths the discussion of the question was carried in the century that elapsed from the time of Anselm and Roscellin till the beginning of the second period of scholasticism, may be seen in a list drawn up by Prantl (Gesch. d. Log. II., pp. 118-21) of not less than thirteen distinct opinions, or shades of opinion, held by different schoolmen. Of these, the most distinguished was ABAELARD (1079-1142), who took up a position between the extremes of Realism and Nominalism. On the one hand, he denied the independent existence of Universals, and inclined rather to the Aristotelian view of their immanence *in rebus;* on the other, he inveighed against the nominalism of Roscellin, and pronounced that the Universals were not mere *voces*, but *sermones* or predications. Yet it is a mistake to describe him as a *Conceptualist*, the name conferred upon such as, agreeing with the Nominalists in regard to the purely subjective character *(post rem)* of the Universals, differed from these in ascribing to the mind the power of fashioning a Concept or notion correspondent to the general name.

In the 13th century, when Scholasticism reached its highest development, the supremacy of Aristotle was firmly established. We find accordingly in THOMAS AQUINAS (1226-74) a supporter of the Aristotelian doctrine of the Universals as immanent *in re;* but, at the same time, he declared that the intellect, by abstracting the *essential* attributes (quiddities) of things from their *accidental* attributes, forms Universals *post rem;* and, although he utterly rejected the Platonic assumption of ideas as real—the only truly real—*entia*, he yet maintained that the ideas or thoughts of things in the Divine mind, antecedent to creation, were *Universalia ante rem.*

His great rival in the next generation, DUNS SCOTUS (d. 1309), admitting the Universals in the same three-fold sense, determined the various related questions in a way peculiar to himself. Especially in regard to the question of the relation of the universal to the singular or individual, was he at war with his predecessors. Thomas had declared that in the individual, composed of form and matter *(materia signata)*, the *form* was the Universal, or element common to all the individuals; what marked off one individual from another—the so-called *principle of individuation*—was the *matter*, *e.g.* in Sokrates, *hæc caro, hæc ossa.* But as matter bore the character of defect or imperfection, Scotus complained that this was to represent the individual as made imperfect in being individualized, whereas it was the *ultima realitas*, the most truly perfect form of Existence. The principle of individuation must be something positive, and not, like matter, negative. The *quidditas*, or universal, must be supplemented by a *hæcceitas* to make it singular or individual; Sokrates was made individual by the addition of *Sokratitas* to his specific and generic characteristics as man and animal.

The next name is of the greatest importance. WILLIAM of OCKHAM (d. 1347), an Englishman and pupil of Duns Scotus, revived the nominalistic doctrine that had been so long discredited amongst the leading schoolmen and frowned upon by the Church. From him, if not earlier, is to be dated the period of the downfall of Scholasticism; severance beginning to be made of reason from faith, and philosophy being no longer prosecuted in the sole interest of theological dogma.

Universals (genera, species, and the like) were, he held, nothing real *extra animam*, but were only *in mente*. Calling everything that existed in or out of the mind a singular or individual, he asked how a term *(terminus)* like *homo* could be predicated of a number of individuals. The answers of every form of Realism, that of Duns Scotus included, led to absurdity; the Realists all began with the universal, and sought to explain from it the individual, whereas they ought to begin with the singular, which alone really exists, and ascend to the explanation of the universal. The true doctrine was that the universals were not at all in things, but in the mind; and in the proposition *homo est risibilis*, the term *homo* stood not for any universal man, but for the real individual man, who alone could laugh. As to the mode of existence of the universals in the mind, he contented himself with enumerating various opinions that were or might be held, without deciding for one in particular. But he was ever ready with the warning: *Entia non sunt multiplicanda præter necessitatem*. Though he was not a nominalist pure and simple,—in refusing to regard the universals as mere words or names and nothing more—it would be committing him to more than he has committed himself to, if we should call him, with some, a Conceptualist.

From the time of William of Ockham, the nominalistic doctrine, in some shape or other, remained triumphant in the schools. Formerly suspected and condemned, and revived by a determined opponent of the papal see, it yet became so firmly established as a philosophical tenet, that it was accepted by the most orthodox theologians; and, in the last days of scholasticism, it was actually Realism that became the suspicious doctrine. In fact, with philosophy growing more and more independent, and entering upon discussions that had no reference to religious dogma, it became possible for the later schoolmen to be Nominalists in regard to the question of Universals, while they were at the same time devout believers in the region of faith. It was when the question thus became an open one, that Realism, as a theory of Universals, fell into discredit: as a tendency of the human mind, Realism remained active as before, and upon the extension of the field of philosophy at the beginning of the modern period, it occupied new strongholds, from which it has not yet been dislodged.

Since the age of Descartes, Nominalism or Conceptualism has been professed by the great majority of thinkers; but the question has been allowed to sink into the second rank. In its stead, the discussion of the Origin of Knowledge,—in or before experience,—has risen into importance. When it was regarded as philosophically settled that Universals had no subsistence apart from the mind, it was a natural transition to pass to the consideration of their origin. But here, as in the question of perception, there has, during the whole modern period, been too little disposition to turn to account the results of the long mediæval struggle. In the question of Innate Ideas the old question is directly involved.

HOBBES is one of the few in later times to whom the question had lost none of its significance, and he is besides remarkable as perhaps the most outspoken representative of extreme Nominalism. His view cannot be better or more shortly given than in his own words : ' Of names, some are *common* to many things, as a *man*, a *tree;* others *proper* to one thing, as he *that writ the Iliad, Homer, this man, that man.* And a common name, being the name of many things severally taken, but not collectively of all together (as man is not the name of all mankind, but of every one, as of Peter, John, and the rest severally), is therefore called an *universal name;* and therefore this word *universal* is never the name of anything existent in nature, nor of any idea or phantasm formed in the mind, but always the name of some word or name ; so that when *a living creature, a stone, a spirit,* or any other thing, is said to be *universal,* it is not to be understood that any man, stone, &c., ever was or can be universal, but only that these words, *living creature, stone,* &c., are *universal names,* that is, names common to many things ; and the conceptions answering to them in our mind, are the images and phantasms of several living creatures or other things. And, therefore, for the understanding of the extent of an universal name, we need no other faculty but that of our imagination, by which we remember that such names bring sometimes one thing, sometimes another, into our mind.' (Hobbes, *De Corpore*, c. 2, § 10.)

LOCKE's view of Abstraction is contained in the Third Book of his Essay. In Chap. III., ' Of General Terms,' he asks (§ 6), ' how general words came to be made, seeing that all existing things are particular.' He replies, ' Words become general by being made the signs of general *ideas;* and Ideas become general, by separating from them the circumstances of Time and Place, and any other ideas that may determine them to this or that particular existence.' He goes on to say :—Children know nothing but particulars ; at first they know, for example, a small number of persons ; as their experience grows they become acquainted with a greater number, and discern their agreements ; they then frame an idea to comprise these points of agreement, which is to them the meaning of the general term ' man ;' they leave out of the Idea what is peculiar to Peter, James, and Mary, and retain what is common. The same process is repeated for still higher generalities, as ' animal.' A general is nothing but the power of representing so many particulars. Essences and Species are only other names for these abstract ideas. The sorting of things under names is the workmanship of the understanding, taking occasion *from the similitude it observes among them,* to make abstract general ideas; and to set them up in the mind as Patterns or Forms, to which they are found to agree. That the generalities are mere ideas, or mental products, and not real existences, is shown by the different composition of complex ideas in different minds; the idea of Covetousness in one man is not what it is in another.

Locke is thus substantially a Nominalist, but does not go deep into the psychological nature of general ideas. He remarks justly that the general idea proceeds upon similitude, designating the agreements of things, and leaving out the differences; but he does not affirm that the mental notion is still a notion of one or more particulars. That he does not see the bearings of a thoroughgoing Nominalism, is evident from his making little use of it, in arguing against Innate Ideas.

BERKELEY's Nominalism is notorious and pronounced, and was in reality the wedge that split up, in his mind, the received theory of Perception. In the well-known passage in the Introduction to his 'Principles of Human Knowledge,' he quotes the conceptualist doctrine,—as implying that the mind can form an idea of colour in the abstract by sinking every individual colour, and of motion in the abstract without conceiving a body moved, or the figure, direction, and velocity of the motion,—and comments upon the doctrine in these terms:—'Whether others have this wonderful faculty of abstracting their ideas, they best can tell. For myself, I find, indeed, I have a faculty of imagining, or representing to myself the ideas of those particular things I have perceived, and of variously compounding and dividing them. I can imagine a man with two heads, or the upper part of a man joined to the body of a horse. I can consider the hand, the eye, the nose, each by itself abstracted or separated from the rest of the body. But then, whatever hand or eye I imagine, it must have some particular shape and colour. Likewise, the idea of man that I frame to myself, must be either of a white, or a black, or a tawny; a straight, or a crooked, a tall, or a low, or a middle-sized man. I cannot by any effort of thought conceive the abstract idea above described. And it is equally impossible to form the abstract idea of motion distinct from the body moving, and which is neither swift nor slow, curvilinear nor rectilinear; and the like may be said of all other abstract general ideas whatsoever. To be plain, I own myself able to abstract in one sense, as when I consider some particular parts or qualities separated from others, with which though they are united in some object, yet it is possible they may really exist without them. But I deny that I can abstract one from another, or conceive separately, those qualities which it is impossible should exist separated; or that I can frame a general notion by abstracting from particulars in the manner aforesaid, which two last are the proper acceptations of abstractions.'

Berkeley recognizes in particular objects a power of *representing* a class; as when the geometer demonstrates a proposition upon a particular triangle, and infers it for all triangles. In this way, he says, the particular *may become general,* by standing for a whole class. The expression is incautious on his part; a *general particular* is an anomaly and a contradiction.

HUME follows Berkeley's Nominalism with avidity and admiration, and inadvertently ascribes to Berkeley the authorship of the doctrine. 'A very material question,' he says, 'has been started concerning abstract or general ideas, whether they be general or particular in the mind's conception of them. A great philosopher (Dr. Berkeley) has disputed the received opinion in this particular, and has asserted that all general ideas are nothing but particular ones annexed to a certain term, which gives them a more extensive signification, and makes them recall upon occasion other individuals which are similar to them. As I look upon this to be one of the greatest and most valuable discoveries that has been made of late years in the republic of letters, I shall here endeavour to confirm it by some arguments, which I hope will put it beyond all doubt and controversy.'

He states his view thus:—' All general ideas are nothing but particular ones annexed to a certain term, which gives them a more extensive signification, and makes them recall upon occasion other individuals which are similar to them [488]. A particular idea becomes general by being annexed to a general term, that is, to a term which, from a customary conjunction, has a relation to many other particular ideas, and readily recalls them in the imagination. Abstract ideas are therefore in themselves individual, however they may become general in their representation. The image in the mind is only that of a particular object, though the application of it in our reasoning be the same as if it was universal.'

REID (INTELLECTUAL POWERS—Essay on Abstraction) contends for the mind's power of forming general conceptions. He starts from the faculties of discerning difference and agreement; by these we are enabled to form classes, the names of which are *general names*. Such general names may be presumed to be the signs of general conceptions. We are able to form distinct conceptions of the separate attributes of anything, as length, breadth, figure, and so on. Indeed, our knowledge of a thing consists of the knowledge of those attributes; we know nothing of the essence of an individual apart from these. We can conceive a triangle, not merely as an individual, with its attributes of size, place, and time, but to the exclusion of these individualizing attributes. Attributes, inseparable in nature, may yet be disjoined in our conception. The general names of attributes are applicable to many individuals in the same sense, which cannot be if there are no general conceptions.

Reid refers to the history of the question of Realism and Nominalism. He dwells chiefly on the views of Berkeley and of Hume, declaring them to be no other than the opinions of the Nominalists and of Hobbes. On the whole, he confesses his ignorance of the 'manner how we conceive universals,' admitting, at the same time, that it cannot be by images of them, for there can be no image of a universal. In fact, Reid's position coincides very nearly with Conceptualism.

DUGALD STEWART avows himself on the side of Nominalism, and deduces from the doctrine what he considers important consequences. There are two ways of seizing hold of general truths; either by fixing the attention on one individual in such a manner, that our reasoning may involve no circumstances but what are common to the whole genus,—or, (laying aside entirely the consideration of things), by means of general terms. In either case, our conclusions must be general. The first method is exemplified in the diagrams of Geometry; the second in the symbols of Algebra.

The Abstract Idea is nothing more than the quality or qualities wherein different individuals resemble one another. Abstraction is the power of attending to the resembling attributes, and neglecting the points of difference.

Although Stewart is thus an avowed nominalist, he yet failed to see the incompatibility between his doctrine and the theory of innate ideas, or the origin he assigns to such notions as 'causation, time, number, truth, certainty, probability, extension;' which relate, he says, to things bearing no resemblance either to any of the sensible qualities of matter, or to any continuous mental operation. In short, we can have no idea of cause, apart altogether from causation in the concrete, as given us by perception through sense.

THOMAS BROWN expresses the generalizing process thus: There is, in the first place, the perception of two or more objects; in the second place, the feeling or notion [better *consciousness*] of their resemblance; and, lastly, the expression of this common relative feeling by a name, afterwards used as a general name for all those objects, the perception of which is followed by the same common feeling of resemblance. Brown thus approaches to the main position of Nominalism, the affirmation of Resemblance among particular objects; but he lays himself open to criticism by his mode of expressing this fact of resemblance; he calls it 'a feeling,' 'a general notion,' 'a common relative feeling,' 'a common feeling of relation:' all which are awkward and confused modes of stating that we perceive or discern the likeness of the particulars in question. The term 'feeling' is inappropriate as giving an emotional character to an intellectual fact.

In criticising Berkeley's handling of geometrical demonstration, Brown maintains that we have still a general notion, or 'relative feeling,' of the circumstances of agreement of particular things; without which general notion of a line, or a triangle, he thinks the demonstrations impossible and absurd. He says it is the very nature of a general notion not to be particular: for who can paint or particularize a mere relation? This is, on Brown's part, the vague mode of affirming that a general word designates certain particulars, together with the fact of their resemblance. As to the difficulty connected with mathematical demonstration, the remark may be made, that if the use of the general word 'triangle' *implies* the resemblance of a given figure to a great number of other figures, then so far as that resemblance goes, what is proved of one is proved of all; and no fictitious triangle in the abstract is required. The affirmation of resemblance carries with it the 'parity of reasoning' assigned as the mode of geometrical proof.

HAMILTON regards the whole controversy of Nominalism and Conceptualism as 'founded on the ambiguity of the terms employed. The opposite parties are substantially at one. Had our British philosophers been aware of the Leibnitzian distinction of Intuitive and Symbolical Knowledge; and had we, like the Germans, different terms, like *Begriff* and *Anschauung*, to denote different kinds of thought, there would have been as little difference of opinion in regard to the nature of general notions in this country as in the Empire. With us, Idea, Notion, Conception, &c., are confounded, or applied by different philosophers in different senses. I must put the reader on his guard against Dr. Thomas Brown's speculations on this subject. His own doctrine of universals, in so far as it is peculiar, is self-contradictory; and nothing can be more erroneous than his statement of the doctrine held by others, especially by the Nominalists.'

In some parts of his writings, Hamilton expresses the Nominalistic view with great exactness; while in others, and in his Logical system generally, he admits a form of Conceptualism. (See passages quoted in Mill's Hamilton, chap. XVII.) He considers that there are thoughts such as 'cannot be represented in the imagination, as *the thought suggested by a general term*' (Edition of Reid, p. 360). He also holds that we have *a priori* abstract ideas of Space and Time, a view difficult to reconcile with Nominalism.

JAMES MILL introduced some novelty into the mode of describing the idea corresponding to a general term. Suppose, he says, the word *foot* has been associated in the mind of a child with one foot only, it will in that case call up the idea of that one, and not of the other. Suppose next, that the same name 'foot' begins to be applied to the child's other foot. The sound is now associated not constantly with one thing, but sometimes with one thing, and sometimes with another. The consequence is that it calls up *sometimes the one and sometimes the other*. Again, the word 'man' is first applied to an individual; at first, therefore, it calls to mind that individual; it is then applied to another and another, and thus acquires the power of calling up any one or more of a large number indifferently. The result is that the word becomes associated with the idea of a *crowd*, a complex and indistinct idea. Thus the word 'man' is not a word having a very simple idea, as was the opinion of the Realists; nor a word having no idea at all, as was the view of the Nominalists; but a word calling up an indefinite number of ideas, by the power of association, and forming them into one very complex, and indistinct, but not therefore unintelligible, idea.

In this mode of stating the nature of the general idea, the author has brought into view one part of the operation, not previously laid stress upon; the fact that the general name brings to mind the particulars as a *host*, which is an important part of the case. In making general affirmations, we must be perpetually running over the particulars, to see that our generality conflicts with none of them; this constitutes the arduousness of general or abstract reasoning. Still, exception has been taken to the phrase 'a complex and indistinct idea' applied to the association with a general name; and a more guarded expression is desirable. The author's meaning is, first, that the name recalls not one individual, but many, and secondly, that a certain indistinctness belongs to our conception of the crowd. Both statements, with some explanation, are true. We do recall a number of individuals, in a rapid series; we can hardly be said to have them all before us at a glance; that would happen only if we had actually seen an assembled host; we pass from one to the others by rapid transitions. In the second place, as a consequence of the rapidity of the transitions, and of our examining the individuals only with reference to one point, we may be said to have an indistinct, or partial image of each; it being the tendency of the mind, in rapid thinking, to economize attention, by neglecting all the aspects of an object not relevant at the time. In speaking of what is common to birds, say 'feathers,' we glance hurriedly at a number of individuals, but we do not unfold to view the full individuality of each. The more complex a thing is, the greater the number of separate glances requisite to comprehend it, both at first and in the memory; we may therefore stop short at a partial view, but this is not to be confounded with an abstract idea in the meaning of Conceptualism.

SAMUEL BAILEY (Letters on the Human Mind, Vols. I., II.) has examined with great care the doctrine of general terms, being of opinion 'that a complete mastery of this part of mental philosophy furnishes a key for most of the difficulties besetting the subject, and throws a powerful light on all speculation whatsoever.' He makes full use of the nominalistic theory in refuting Innate Ideas.

According to him, there is no essential difference between what passes in the mind when *proper* names are heard, and when *general* names are heard. The peculiar feature, in the case of general names, may be stated to be, that there is possibly and frequently, but not necessarily, a greater range in the mental representations called up by any single appellation; still there is nothing but an individual image, or a group or a succession of individual images or representations passing through the mind. It must be obvious, on reflection, that this is, in truth, the only possible effect of general terms. We rank individual objects under a common name, on account of their resemblance to each other in one or more respects; and when we use such an appellation, the utmost that the nature of the case allows us to do, whether the name has been imposed by ourselves or others, is to recall to our own minds, or to those of our hearers, the whole of the single objects thus classed together. This is an extreme case, which, no doubt, may happen; but the result is usually far short of such a complete ideal muster, and we recall only a very inconsiderable part, or even sometimes only one, of the objects covered by the general term. It also appears that, if the ideas thus raised up are sometimes vague and indefinite, the same qualities frequently characterize the ideas raised up by proper names, and attend even the perception of external objects.

B.—*The Origin of Knowledge—Experience and Intuition,* p. 188.

The dialogues of PLATO present a number of different views of the nature and origin of knowledge. One of the most characteristic, the doctrine of *Reminiscence*, as set forth in the Phædrus, Phædon, and Menon, supposes the soul in a pre-existent state to have lived in the contemplation of the Eternal Ideas, and, when joined to a body, to have brought away slumbering recollections of them, revivable by the impressions of sense; all cognition, but especially the true, consists in such awakening of the mind's ancient knowledge lying dormant. This is a highly poetical presentation of the later doctrine of Innate Ideas. In the Republic, with the same fundamental conception of the origin of knowledge, he distinguishes its different grades: *Cognition* of Intelligibles is opposed to *Opinion* of Sensibles, and again each of them includes a higher and lower form—Cognition is *Nous* or *Dianoia* as it is direct or indirect, and Opinion may be *Belief* or mere *Conjecture*. The most explicit discussion of the question, What is knowledge? is in the Theætetus. There, while at the end he does not pretend to have given any settlement, in the course of the argument against the reduction of knowledge to sense-perception, he advances a peculiar theory. When the mind perceives sensible qualities like hardness, heat, sweetness, &c., it perceives them not *with*, but *through*, the senses. This at birth and equally in all: but some few, by going over and comparing simple impressions of sense, come to be able to apprehend, besides existence (essence and substance), sameness, difference, likeness, unlikeness, good, and evil, &c., where the apprehension is by the mind, of itself alone, and without any aid of bodily organs. This is a remarkable view, because, as has been observed, he supposes these cognitions to be developed only out of the review and comparison of facts of sense, and only by a select few—two points wherein he is at variance with the common supporters of native mental intuitions (See Grote's Plato II., p. 370, *seq.*).

We shall next advert to ARISTOTLE's opinions in regard to the existence of a class of primary or self-evident truths, claiming a right to be believed on the authority of Common Sense, without either warrant or limit from experience.

Sir William Hamilton (in his Dissertations on Reid, Appendix, p. 771-773) enrolls Aristotle with confidence among the philosophers that have vindicated the authority of Common Sense, as accrediting certain universal truths, independent of experience, and imposing a necessity of belief, such as experience never can impose. Yet, of all the Aristotelian passages cited by Sir W.

Hamilton to establish this position, only one (that from the Nicomachean Ethics, X., 2, p. 772, marked *f.* by Hamilton) has any real force; and that is countervailed by numerous others that he leaves unnoticed, as well as by the marked general tenor of Aristotle's writings.

In regard to Aristotle, there are two points to be examined—
1. What position does he take up in respect to the authority of Common Sense?
2. What doctrine does he lay down about the first *principia* or beginnings of scientific reasoning—the ἀρχαὶ συλλογιστικαι?

I.-That Aristotle did not regard Cause, Substance, Time, &c., as Intuitions, is shown by the subtle and elaborate reasonings that he employs to explain them, and by the censure that he bestows on the erroneous explanations and shortcomings of others. Indeed, in regard to Causality, when we read the great and perplexing diversity of meaning which Aristotle (and Plato before him in the Phædon) recognizes as belonging to this term, we cannot but be surprised to find modern philosophers treating it as enunciating a simple and intuitive idea. But as to Common Sense—taking the term as above explained, and as it is usually understood by those that have no particular theory to support—Aristotle takes up a position at once distinct and instructive; a position (to use the phraseology of Kant) not dogmatical, but critical. He constantly notices and reports the affirmations of Common Sense; he speaks of it with respect, and assigns to it a qualified value, partly as helping us to survey the subject on all sides, partly as a happy confirmation, where it coincides with what has been proved otherwise; but he does not appeal to it as authority in itself trustworthy or imperative.

Common Sense belongs to the region of opinion. Now, the distinction between matters of Opinion on the one hand, and matters of Science or Cognition on the other, is a marked and characteristic feature of Aristotle's philosophy. He sets, in pointed antithesis, DEMONSTRATION, or the method of Science—which divides itself into special subjects, each having some special *principia* of its own, then proceeds by legitimate steps of deductive reasoning from such *principia*, and arrives at conclusions sometimes universally true, always true for the most part—against RHETORIC and DIALECTIC, which deal with and discuss opinions upon all subjects, comparing opposite arguments, and landing in results more or less probable. Contrasting these two as separate lines of intellectual procedure, Aristotle lays down a theory of both. He recognizes the last as being to a great degree the common and spontaneous growth of society; while the first is from the beginning special, not merely as to subject, but as to persons—implying teacher and learner.

Rhetoric and Dialectic are treated by Aristotle as analogous processes. Of the matter of opinion and belief, with which both of them deal, he distinguishes three varieties:—1. Opinions or beliefs entertained by all. 2. By the majority. 3. By a minority of superior men, or by one man in respect to a science wherein he has acquired renown. It is these opinions or beliefs that the rhetorician or the dialectician attack and defend; bringing out all the arguments available for or against each.

The Aristotelian treatise on Rhetoric opens with the following words:—'Rhetoric is the counterpart of Dialectic; for both of them deal with such matters as do not fall within any special science, but belong in a certain way to the common knowledge of all. Hence every individual has his share of both, greater or less; for every one can, up to a certain point, both examine others and stand examination from others; every one tries to defend himself and to accuse others.'* To the same purpose Aristotle speaks about Dialectics, in the beginning of the Topica :—' The Dialectic Syllogism (he says) takes its premises from matters of opinion: that is, from matters that seem good to (or are believed by) all, or the majority, or the wise; either all the wise, or most of them, or the most celebrated.'— Aristotle distinguishes these matters of common opinion or belief, from three distinct other matters. 1. From matters that are not really such, but only in appearance; in which the smallest attention suffices to detect the false pretence of probability, while no one except a contentious Sophist ever thinks of advancing them. On the contrary, the real matters of common belief are never thus palpably false, but have always something deeper than a superficial show. 2. From the first truths or *principia*, upon which scientific demonstration proceeds. 3. From the paralogisms, or fallacious assumptions (ψευδογραφήματα), liable to occur in each particular science.

Now, what Aristotle here designates and defines as 'matters of common opinion and belief' (τὰ ἔνδοξα), includes all that is usually meant, and properly meant, by Common Sense; 'what is believed by all men or by most men.' But Aristotle does not claim any warrant or authority for the truth of these beliefs, on the ground of their being deliverances of Common Sense, and accepted (by all or by the majority) always as indisputable, often as self-evident. On the contrary, he ranks them as mere probabilities, some in a greater, some in a less degree; as matters whereon something may be said both *pro* and *con*, and whereon the full force of argument on both sides ought to be brought out, notwithstanding the supposed self-evidence in the minds of unscientific believers. Though, however, he encourages this dialectic discussion on both sides, as useful and instructive, he never affirms that it can, by itself, lead to certain scientific conclusions, or to anything more than strong probability on a balance of the countervailing considerations. The language that he uses in speaking of these deliverances of common sense is measured and just. After distinguishing the real common opinion from the fallacious simu-

* Aristot. Rhetor. I. 1. Compare Sophist. Elench., p. 172, a. 36.

lations of common opinion set up (according to him) by some pretenders, he declares, that in all cases of common opinion there is always something more than a mere superficial appearance of truth. In other words, wherever any opinion is really held by a large public, it always deserves the scrutiny of the philosopher, to ascertain how far it is erroneous, and, if it be erroneous, by what appearances of reason it has been enabled so far to prevail.

Again, at the beginning of the Topica (in which books he gives both a theory and precepts of dialectical debate), Aristotle specifies four different ends to be served by that treatise. It will be useful (he says)—

1. For our own practice in the work of debate. If we acquire a method and system, we shall find it easier to conduct a debate on any new subject, whenever such debate may arise.

2. For our daily intercourse with the ordinary public. When we have made for ourselves a full collection of the opinions held by the Many, we shall carry on our conversation with them out of their own doctrines, and not out of doctrines foreign to their minds; we shall thus be able to bring them round on any matter where we think them in error.

3. For the sciences belonging to philosophy. By discussing the difficulties on both sides, we shall more easily discriminate truth and falsehood in each separate scientific question.

4. For the first and highest among the *principia* of each particular science. These, since they are the first and highest of all, cannot be discussed out of *principia* special and peculiar to any separate science; but must be discussed through the opinions commonly received on the subject-matter of each. This is the main province of Dialectic: which, being essentially testing and critical, is connected by some threads with the *principia* of all the various scientific researches.

We see thus that Aristotle's language about Common Opinion or Common Sense is very guarded: that, instead of citing it as an authority, he carefully discriminates it from Science, and places it decidedly on a level lower than science, in respect of evidence: yet that he recognizes it as essential to be studied by the scientific man, with full confrontation of all the reasonings both for and against every opinion; not merely because such study will enable the scientific man to study and converse intelligibly and efficaciously with the vulgar; but also because it will sharpen his discernment for the truths of his own science; and because it furnishes the only materials for testing and limiting the first *principia* of that science.

II.—We will next advert to the judgment of Aristotle respecting these *principia* of science; how he supposes them to be acquired and verified. He discriminates various special sciences (geometry, arithmetic, astronomy, &c.), each of which has its own appropriate matter, and special *principia* from which it takes its departure. But there are also certain *principia* common to them all: and these he considers to fall under the cognizance of one grand comprehensive science, which includes all the rest: First Philosophy or Ontology—the science of Ens in its most general sense, *quatenus* Ens; while each of the separate Sciences confines itself to one exclusive department of Ens. The geometer does not debate nor prove the first *principia* of his own science: neither those that it has in common with other sciences, nor those peculiar to itself. He takes these for granted, and demonstrates the consequences that logically follow from them. It belongs to the First Philosopher to discuss the *principia* of all. Accordingly, the province of the First Philosopher is all-comprehensive, co-extensive with all the sciences. So also is the province of the Dialectician alike all-comprehensive. Thus far the two agree; but they differ as to method and purpose. The Dialectician seeks to enforce, confront, and value all the different reasons *pro* and *con*, consistent and inconsistent: the First Philosopher performs this too, or supposes it to be performed by others —but proceeds farther: namely, to determine certain axioms that may be trusted as sure grounds (along with certain other *principia*) for demonstrative conclusions in science.

Aristotle describes in his Analytica the process of demonstration, and the conditions required to render it valid. But what is the point of departure for this process? Aristotle declares that there cannot be a regress without end, demonstrating one conclusion from certain premises, then demonstrating those premises from others, and so on. You must arrive ultimately at some premises that are themselves undemonstrable, but that may be trusted as ground from whence to start in demonstrating conclusions. All demonstration is carried on through a middle term, which links together the two terms of the conclusion, though itself does not appear in the conclusion. Those undemonstrable propositions, from which demonstration begins, must be known without a middle term—that is, *immediately* known; they must be known in themselves—that is, not through any other propositions; they must be better known than the conclusions derived from them; they must be propositions first and most knowable. But these two last epithets (Aristotle often repeats) have two meanings: First and most knowable *by nature* or *absolutely*, are the most universal propositions: first and most knowable *to us*, are those propositions declaring the particular facts of sense. These two meanings designate truths correlative to each other, but at opposite ends of the intellectual line of march.

Of these undemonstrable *principia*, indispensable as the grounds of all demonstration, some are peculiar to each separate science, others are common to several or to all sciences. These common principles were called Axioms, in the mathematics, even in the time of Aristotle. Sometimes indeed he designates them as Axioms, without any special reference to mathematics: though he also uses the same name to denote other propositions, not of the like fundamental character. Now, how do we come to know these undemonstrable Axioms and other immediate propositions or *principia*, since we do not know them by demonstration? This is the second question to be answered, in appreciating Aristotle's views about the Philosophy of Common Sense.

He is very explicit in his way of answering this question. He pronounces it absurd to suppose that these immediate *principia* are innate or congenital,—in other words, that we possess them from the beginning, and yet that we remain for a long time without any consciousness of possessing them, seeing that they are the most accurate of all our *cognita*. What we possess at the beginning (Aristotle says) is only a mental power of inferior accuracy and dignity. We, as well as all other animals, begin with a congenital discriminative power called sensible perception. With many animals, the data of perception are transient, and soon disappear altogether, so that the cognition of such animals consists in nothing but successive acts of sensible perception. With us, on the contrary, as with some other animals, the data of perception are preserved by memory; accordingly our cognitions include both perceptions and remembrances. Farthermore, we are distinguished even from the better animals by this difference—that with us, but not with them, a rational order of thought grows out of such data of perception, when multiplied and long preserved. And thus, out of perception grows memory: out of memory of the same matter often repeated, grows experience—since many remembrances of the same thing constitute one numerical experience. Out of such experience, a farther consequence arises—That what is one and the same, in all the particulars, (the Universal or the one alongside of the many) becomes fixed or rests steadily within the mind. Herein lies the *principium* of Art, in reference to Agenda, or Facienda—of Science, in reference to Entia.

Thus these cognitive *principia* are not original and determinate possessions of the mind—nor do they spring from any other mental possessions of a higher cognitive order, but simply from data of sensible perception: which data are like runaway soldiers in a panic—first one stops his flight and halts, then a second follows the example, afterwards a third and fourth, until at length an orderly array is obtained. Our minds are so constituted as to render this possible. If a single individual impression is thus detained, it will presently acquire the character of a Universal in the mind: for though we perceive the particular, our perception is of the universal (*i.e.*, when we perceive Kallias, our perception is of man generally, not of the man Kallias). Again, the fixture of these lowest Universals in the mind will bring in those of the next highest order; until at length the Summa Genera and the absolute Universals acquire a steady establishment therein. Thus, from this or that particular animal, we shall rise as high as Animal Universally: and so on from Animal upwards.

We thus see clearly (Aristotle says)—That only by Induction can we come to know the first *principia* of demonstration: for it is by this process that sensible perception engraves the Universal on our minds.* We begin by the *notiora nobis* (Particulars), and ascend to the *notiora naturâ* or *simpliciter* (Universals). Some among our mental habits that are conversant with truth, are also capable of falsehood (such as Opinion and Reasoning): others are not so capable, but embrace uniformly truth, and nothing but truth—such are Science and Intellect (Νοῦς). Intellect is the only source more accurate than Science. Now, the *principia* of Demonstration are more accurate than the Demonstrations themselves—yet they cannot (as we have already observed) be the objects of Science. They must therefore be the object of what is more accurate than Science: namely, of Intellect. Intellect and the objects of Intellect will thus be the *principia* of Science and of the objects of Science. But these principles are not intuitive data or revelations. They are acquisitions gradually made : and there is a regular road whereby we travel up to them, quite distinct from the road whereby we travel down from them to scientific conclusions.

The chapter just indicated in the Analytica Posteriora, attesting the growth of those universals that form the *principia* of demonstration out of the particulars of sense, may be illustrated by a similar statement in the first book of the Metaphysica. Here, after stating that sensible perception is common to all animals, he distinguishes the lowest among animals, who have this alone ; then, a class next above them, who have it along with phantasy and memory, and some of whom are intelligent (like bees), yet still cannot learn, from being destitute of hearing ; farther, another class, one stage higher, who hear, and therefore can be taught something, yet arrive only at a scanty sum of experience ; lastly, still higher, the class men, who possess a large stock of phantasy, memory, and experience, fructifying into science and art.†
Experience (Aristotle says) is of particular facts ; art and science

* Aristot. Anal. Post. II., p. 100, b. 2, δῆλον δὴ ὅτι ἡμῖν τὰ πρῶτα ἐπαγωγῇ γνωρίζειν ἀναγκαῖον· καὶ γὰρ καὶ αἴσθησις οὕτω τὸ καθόλου ἐμποιεῖ; also Anal. Post. I., p. 81, b. 3, c. 18,—upon which passage, Waitz, in his note, explains as follows (p. 347) : 'Sententia nostri loci hæc est. Universales propositiones omnes inductione comparantur, quum etiam in iis, quæ a sensibus maxime aliena videntur, et quæ (ut mathematica, τὰ ἐξ ἀφαιρέσεως) cogitatione separantur a materia quacum conjuncta sunt, inductione probentur ea quæ de genere (*e.g.* de linea, de corpore mathematico) ad quod demonstratio pertineat prædicentur καθ' αὑτά et cum ejus natura conjuncta sint. Inductio autem iis nititur quæ sensibus percipiuntur : nam res singulares sentiuntur, scientia vero rerum singularium non datur sine inductione, non datur inductio sine sensu.'

† Aristot. Metaphys. A. I. 980, a. 25, b. 27, φρόνιμα μὲν ἄνευ τοῦ μανθάνειν, ὅσα μὴ δύναται τῶν ψόφων ἀκούειν, οἷον μέλιττα, καὶ εἴ τι τοιοῦτον ἄλλο γένος ζώων ἔστιν.
We remark here the line that he draws between the intelligence of bees, depending altogether upon sense, memory, and experience—and the higher intelligence which is superadded by the use of language ; when it becomes possible to teach and learn, and when general conceptions can be brought into view through appropriate names.

are of universals. Art is attained, when out of many conceptions of experience there arises one universal persuasion respecting phenomena similar to each other. We may know that Kallias, sick of a certain disease—that Sokrates, likewise sick of it—that A, B, C, and other individuals besides,—have been cured by a given remedy; but this persuasion respecting ever so many individual cases, is mere matter of experience. When, however, we proceed to generalize these cases, and then affirm that the remedy cures all persons suffering under the same disease, circumscribed by specific marks—fever or biliousness—this is art or science. One man may know the particular cases empirically, without having generalized them into a doctrine; another may have learnt the general doctrine, with little or no knowledge of the particular cases. Of these two, the last is the wiser and more philosophical man; but the first may be the more effective and successful as a practitioner.

In the passage above noticed, Aristotle draws the line of intellectual distinction between man and the lower animals. If he had considered that it was the prerogative of man to possess a stock of intuitive general truths, ready-made, and independent of experience, this was the occasion for saying so. He says the exact contrary. No modern psychologist could proclaim more fully than Aristotle here does, the derivation of all general concepts and general propositions from the phenomena of sense, through the successive stages of memory, association, comparison, abstraction. No one could give a more explicit acknowledgment of Induction from particulars of sense, as the process whereby we reach ultimately those propositions of the highest universality, as well as of the highest certainty; from whence, by legitimate deductive syllogism, we descend to demonstrate various conclusions. There is nothing in Aristotle about generalities originally inherent in the mind, connate although dormant at first and unknown, until they are evoked or elicited by the senses: nothing to countenance that nice distinction eulogized so emphatically by Hamilton (p. 772, a. note): 'Cognitio nostra amoris à mente primam originem, à Sensibus exordium habet primum.' In Aristotle's view, the Senses furnish both *originem* and *exordium:* the successive stages of mental procedure, whereby we rise from sense to universal propositions, are multiplied and gradual, without any break. He even goes so far as to say that 'we have sensible perception of the Universal.' His language undoubtedly calls for much criticism here. We shall only say that it discountenances altogether the doctrine that represents the Mind or Intellect as an original source of First or Universal Truths peculiar to itself. That opinion is mentioned by Aristotle, but mentioned only to be rejected. He denies that the mind possesses any such ready-made stores, latent until elicited into consciousness. Moreover, it is remarkable that the ground whereon he denies it, is much the same as that whereon the advocates of intuitions affirm it—viz., the supreme accuracy of these axioms. Aristotle cannot believe

ARISTOTLE OPPOSED TO INTUITIVE COGNITIONS. 41

that the mind includes cognitions of such value, without being conscious thereof. Nor will he grant that the mind possesses any native and inherent power of originating these inestimable *principia*.* He declares that they are generated in the mind only by the slow process of induction, as above described; beginning from the perceptive power (common to man with animals), together with that first stage of the intelligence (judging or discriminative) which he combines or identifies with perception, considering it to be alike congenital. From this humble basis, men can rise to the highest grades of cognition, though animals cannot. We even become competent (Aristotle says) to have sensible perception of the Universal: in the man Kallias, we see *man;* in the ox feeding near us, we see *animal*.

It must be remembered that when Aristotle, in this analysis of cognition, speaks of Induction, he means induction completely and accurately performed; just as, when he talks of Demonstration, he intends a good and legitimate demonstration; and just as (to use his own illustration in the Nicomachean Ethics), when he reasons upon a harper, or other professional artist, he always tacitly implies a good and accomplished artist. Induction, thus understood, and Demonstration, he considers to be the two processes for obtaining scientific faith or conviction; both of them being alike cogent and necessary, but Induction even more so than Demonstration; because if the *principia* furnished by the former were not necessary, neither could the conclusions deduced from them by the latter be necessary. Induction may thus stand alone without demonstration, but demonstration pre-supposes and postulates induction. Accordingly, when Aristotle proceeds to specify those functions of mind wherewith the inductive *principia* and the demonstrated conclusions correlate, he refers both of them to functions wherein (according to him) the mind is unerring and infallible—Intellect (Νοῦς) and Science. But, between these two, he ranks Intellect as the higher, and he refers the inductive *principia* to Intellect. He does not mean that Intellect (Νοῦς) generates or produces these principles. On the contrary, he distinctly negatives such a supposition, and declares that no generative force of this high order resides in the Intellect : while he tells us, with equal distinctness, that they are generated from a lower source—sensible perception,

---

* Aristot. Anal. Post. II. 19, p. 99, b. 26, εἰ δὴ ἔχομεν αὐτὰς, ἄτοπον συμβαίνει γὰρ ἀκριβεστέρας ἔχοντας γνώσεις ἀποδείξεως λανθάνειν — φανερὸν τοίνον ὅτι οὔτ᾽ ἔχειν οἷον τε, οὔτ᾽ ἀγνοοῦσι καὶ μηδεμίαν ἔχουσιν ἕξιν ἐγγίνεσθαι. ἀνάγκη ἄρα ἔχειν μέν τινα δύναμιν, μὴ τοιαύτην δ᾽ ἔχειν ἢ ἔσται τούτων τιμωτέρα κατ᾽ ἀκρίβειαν. See Metaphys. A. 993, a. 1.

Some modern psychologists, who admit that general propositions of a lower degree of universality are raised from induction and sense, contend that propositions of the highest universality are not so raised, but are the intuitive offspring of the intellect. Aristotle does not countenance such a doctrine : he says (Metaphys. A. 2,982, a. 22) that these truths furthest removed from sense are the most difficult to know of all. If they were intuitions, they would be the common possession of the race.

and through the gradual upward march of the inductive process. To say that they originate from sense through Induction, and nevertheless to refer them to Intellect (Νοῦς) as their subjective correlate—are not positions inconsistent with each other, in the view of Aristotle. He expressly distinguishes the two points, as requiring to be separately dealt with. By referring the *principia* to Intellect (Νοῦς), he does not intend to indicate their generating source, but their evidentiary value and dignity when generated and matured. They possess, in his view, the maximum of dignity, certainty, cogency, and necessity, because it is from them that even Demonstration derives the necessity of its conclusions; accordingly (pursuant to the inclination of the ancient philosophers for presuming affinity and commensurate dignity between the Cognitum and the Cognoscens), they belong as objective correlates to the most unerring cognitive function—the Intellect (Νοῦς). It is the Intellect that grasps these principles, and applies them to their legitimate purpose of scientific demonstration; hence, Aristotle calls Intellect not only the *principium* of Science, but the *principium principii*.

In the Analytica, from which we have hitherto cited, Aristotle explains the structure of the syllogism and the process of demonstration. He has in view mainly (though not exclusively) the more exact sciences, arithmetic, geometry, astronomy, &c. But he expressly tells us that all departments of inquiry are not capable of this exactness; that some come nearer to it than others; that we must be careful to require no more exactness from each than the subject admits; and that the method adopted by us must be such as will attain the admissible maximum of exactness. Now, each subject has some *principia*, and among them definitions, peculiar to itself; though there are also some *principia* common to all, and essential to the march of each. In some departments of study (Aristotle says) we get our view of *principia* or first principles by induction; in others, by sensible perception; in others again, by habitual action in a certain way; and by various other processes also. In each, it is important to look for first principles in the way naturally appropriate to the matter before us; for this is more than half of the whole work; upon right first principles will mainly depend the value of our conclusions. For what concerns Ethics, Aristotle tells us that the first principles are acquired through a course of well directed habitual action; and that they will be acquired easily, as well as certainly, if such a course be enforced on youth from the beginning. In the beginning of the Physica, he starts from that antithesis, so often found in his writings, between what is more knowable to us, and what is more knowable absolutely or by nature. The natural march of knowledge is to ascend from the first of these two termini (particulars of sense) upward to the second or opposite*—and then to descend downward by demonstration or deduction. The fact of motion he

---

* See also Aristot. Metaphys. Z. p. 1029, b. 1-14.

proves (against Melissus and Parmenides) by an express appeal to induction, as sufficient and conclusive evidence. In physical science (he says), the final appeal must be to the things and facts perceived by sense. In the treatise De Cælo, he lays it down that the *principia* must be homogeneous with the matters they belong to: the *principia* of perceivable matters must be themselves perceivable; those of eternal matters must be eternal; those of perishable matters perishable.

The treatises composing the Organon stand apart among Aristotle's works. In them he undertakes (for the first time in the history of mankind) the systematic study of significant propositions enunciative of truth and falsehood. He analyzes their constituent elements; he specifies the conditions determining the consistency or inconsistency of such propositions one with another; he teaches to arrange the propositions in such ways as to detect and dismiss the inconsistent, keeping our hold of the consistent. Here the signification of terms and propositions is never out of sight: the facts and realities of nature are regarded as so signified. Now, all language becomes significant only through the convention of mankind, according to Aristotle's express declaration; it is used by speakers to communicate what they mean, to hearers that understand them. We see thus that in these treatises the subjective point of view is brought into the foreground; the enunciation of what we see, remember, believe, disbelieve, doubt, anticipate, &c. It is not meant that the objective point of view is eliminated, but that it is taken in implication with, and in dependence upon, the subjective. Neither the one nor the other is dropped or hidden. It is under this double and conjoint point of view that Aristotle, in the Organon, presents to us, not only the processes of demonstration and confutation, but also the fundamental *principia* or axioms thereof; which axioms in the Analytica Posteriora (as we have already seen) he expressly declares to originate from the data of sense, and to be raised and generalized by induction.

Such is the way that Aristotle represents the fundamental principles of syllogistic demonstration, when he deals with them as portions of logic. But we also find him dealing with them as portions of Ontology or First Philosophy (this being his manner of characterizing his own treatise, now commonly known as the *Metaphysica*). To that science he decides, after some preliminary debate, that the task of formulating and defending the axioms belongs, because the application of these axioms is quite universal, for all grades and varieties of Entia. Ontology treats of Ens in its largest sense, with all its properties *quatenus Ens,* including Unum, Multa, Idem, Diversum, Posterius, Prius, Genus, Species, Totum, Partes, &c. Now, Ontology is with Aristotle a purely objective science; that is, a science wherein the subjective is dropt out of sight, and no account taken of it,—or wherein (to state the same fact in the language of relativity) the believing and reasoning subject is supposed constant. Ontology is the most comprehensive among all the objective sciences. Each of these sciences singles out a certain portion of it for special study. In treating the logical axioms as portions of Ontology, Aristotle undertakes to show their objective value; and this purpose, while it carries him away from the point of view that we remarked as prevailing in the Organon, at the same time brings him into conflict with various theories, all of them in his time more or less current. Several philosophers—Heracleitus, Anaxagoras, Democritus, Protagoras, had propounded theories which Aristotle here impugns. We do not mean that these philosophers expressly denied his fundamental axioms (which they probably never distinctly stated to themselves, and which Aristotle was the first to formulate), but their theories were to a certain extent inconsistent with these axioms, and were regarded by Aristotle as wholly inconsistent.

The two axioms announced in the Metaphysica, and vindicated by Aristotle, are—

1. The Maxim of Contradiction—It is impossible for the same thing to be and not to be; It is impossible for the same to belong and not to belong to the same, at the same time and in the same sense. This is the statement of the Maxim as a formula of Ontology. Announced as a formula of Logic, it would stand thus— The same proposition cannot be both true and false at the same time; You cannot both believe and disbelieve the same proposition at the same time; You cannot believe, at the same time, propositions contrary or contradictory. These last-mentioned formulæ are the logical ways of stating the axiom. They present it in reference to the believing or disbelieving (affirming or denying) Subject, distinctly brought to view along with the matter believed; not exclusively in reference to the matter believed, to the omission of the believer.

2. The Maxim of Excluded Middle—A given attribute either does belong, or does not belong to a subject (*i.e.*, provided that it has any relation to the subject at all); there is no medium, no real condition intermediate between the two. This is the Ontological Formula; and it will stand thus, when translated into Logic—Between a proposition and its contradictory opposite there is no tenable halting ground. If you disbelieve the one, you must pass at once to the belief of the other; you cannot at the same time disbelieve the other.

These two maxims thus teach—the first, that we cannot at the same time *believe* both a proposition and its contradictory opposite; the second, that we cannot at the same time *disbelieve* them both.*

---

* We have here discussed these two maxims chiefly in reference to Aristotle's manner of presenting them, and to the conceptions of his predecessors and contemporaries. An excellent view of the Maxims themselves, in their true meaning and value, will be found in Mr. John Stuart Mill's Examination of the Philosophy of Sir Wm. Hamilton, chap. xxi. p. 462-479.

MAXIM OF CONTRADICTION.   45

Now, Heracleitus, in his theory (a theory propounded much before the time of Protagoras and the persons called Sophists), denied all permanence or durability in nature, and recognized nothing except perpetual movement and change. He denied both durable substances and durable attributes; he considered nothing to be lasting except the universal law or principle of change—the ever-renewed junction or co-existence of contraries, and the perpetual transition of one contrary into the other. This view of the facts of nature was adopted by several other physical philosophers besides.* Indeed it lay at the bottom of Plato's new coinage—Rational Types or Forms, at once universal and real. The maxim of Contradiction is intended by Aristotle to controvert Heracleitus, and to uphold durable substances with definite attributes.

Again, the theory of Anaxagoras denied all simple bodies (excepting Noûs) and all definite attributes. He held that everything was mingled with everything else, though there might be some one or other predominant constituent. In all the changes visible throughout nature, there was no generation of anything new, but only the coming into prominence of some constituent that had before been comparatively latent. According to this theory, you could neither wholly affirm, nor wholly deny, any attribute of its subject. Both affirmation and denial were untrue: the real relation between the two was something half-way between affirmation and denial. The maxim of Excluded Middle is maintained by Aristotle as a doctrine in opposition to this theory of Anaxagoras.†

Both the two above-mentioned theories are objective. A third, that of Protagoras—*Homo Mensura*—brings forward prominently the subjective, and is quite distinct from either. Aristotle does indeed treat the Protagorean theory as substantially identical with that of Heracleitus, and as standing or falling therewith. This seems a mistake; the theory of Protagoras is as much opposed to Heracleitus as to Aristotle.

We have now to see how Aristotle sustains these two Axioms (which he calls 'the firmest of all truths and the most assuredly known') against theories opposed to them. In the first place, he repeats here what he had declared in the Analytica Posteriora —that they cannot be directly demonstrated, though they are themselves the *principia* of all demonstration. Some persons indeed thought that these Axioms were demonstrable; but this is an error, proceeding (he says) from complete ignorance of analytical theory. How, then, are these axioms to be proved against Heracleitus? Aristotle had told us in the Analytica that axioms were derived from particulars of sense by Induction, and apprehended or approved by the Noûς. He does not repeat that observation here; but he intimates that there is only one process

---

* See Grote's Plato—vol. I., ch. 1, p. 28-33.
† Grote—Plato, &c.—ch. 1, p. 49-57.

APPENDIX—ORIGIN OF KNOWLEDGE.

available for defending them, and that process amounts to an appeal to Induction. You can give no ontological reason in support of the axioms, except what will be condemned as a *petitio principii;* you must take them in their logical aspect, as enunciated in significant propositions. You must require the Heracleitean adversary to answer some question affirmatively, in terms significant both to himself and to others, and in a proposition declaring his belief on the point. If he will not do this, you can hold no discussion with him : he might as well be deaf and dumb : he is no better than a plant (to use Aristotle's own comparison). If he does it, he has bound himself to something determinate : first, the signification of the terms is a fact, excluding what is contrary or contradictory ; next, in declaring his belief, he at the same time declares that he does not believe in the contrary or contradictory, and is so understood by the hearers. We may grant what his theory affirms—that the subject of a proposition is continually under some change or movement; yet the identity designated by its name is still maintained,* and many true predications respecting it remain true in spite of its partial change. The argument in defence of the maxim of Contradiction is, that it is a postulate implied in all the particular statements, as to matters of daily experience, that a man understands and acts upon when heard from his neighbours ; a postulate such that, if you deny it, no speech is either significant or trustworthy to inform and guide those who hear it. If the speaker both affirms and denies the same fact at once, no information is conveyed, nor can the hearer act upon the words. Thus, in the Acharnenses of Aristophanes, Dikaeopolis knocks at the door of Euripides, and inquires whether the poet is within ; Kephisophon, the attendant, answers — 'Euripides is within and not within.' This answer is unintelligible ; Dikaeopolis cannot act upon it ; until Kephisophon explains that 'not within' is intended metaphorically. Then, again, all the actions in detail of a man's life are founded upon his own belief of some facts and disbelief of other facts ; he goes to Megara, believing that the person whom he desires to see is at Megara, and at the same time disbelieving the contrary : he acts upon his belief, both as to what is good and what is not good, in the way of pursuit and avoidance. You may cite innumerable examples both of speech and action in the detail of life, which the Heracleitean must go through like other persons ; and when, if he proceeded upon his own theory, he could neither give nor receive information by speech, nor ground any action upon the beliefs which he declares to co-exist in his own mind. Accordingly, the Heracleitean Kratylus (so Aristotle says) renounced the use of affirmative speech, and simply pointed with his finger.†

* This argument is given by Aristotle, Metaph. Γ. 1010, a. 6-24, contrasting change κατὰ τὸ ποσὸν and change κατὰ τὸ ποιόν.

† Aristot. Metaph. Γ. 1010, a. 13. Compare Plato Theætet. p. 179-180, about the aversion of the Heracleiteans for clear issues and propositions.

MAXIM OF EXCLUDED MIDDLE.

The maxim of Contradiction is thus seen to be only the general expression of a postulate implied in all such particular speeches as communicate real information. It is proved by a very copious and diversified Induction, from matters of experience familiar to every individual person. It is not less true in regard to propositions affirming changes, motions, or events, than in regard to those declaring durable states or attributes.

In the long pleading of Aristotle on behalf of the maxim of Contradiction against the Heracleiteans, the portion of it that appeals to Induction is the really forcible portion : conforming as it does to what he had laid down in the Analytica Posteriora about the inductive origin of the *principia* of demonstration. He employs, however, besides, several other dialectical arguments, built, more or less, upon theories of his own, and therefore not likely to weigh much with an Heracleitean theorist; who—arguing as he did that (because neither subject nor predicate were ever unchanged or stable for two moments together) no true proposition could be framed but was at the same time false, and that contraries were in perpetual co-existence,—could not by any general reasoning be involved in greater contradiction and inconsistency than he at once openly proclaimed.* It can only be shown that such a doctrine cannot be reconciled with the necessities of daily speech, as practised by himself, as well as by others. We read indeed one ingenious argument whereby Aristotle adopts this belief in the co-existence of Contraries, but explains it in a manner of his own, through his much employed distinction between potential and actual existence. Two contraries cannot co-exist (he says) in actuality : but they both may and do co-exist, in different senses —one or both of them being potential. This, however, is a theory totally different from that of Heracleitus : coincident only in words and in seeming. It does indeed eliminate the contradiction : but that very contradiction formed the characteristic feature and keystone of the Heracleitean theory. The case against this last theory is, that it is at variance with psychological facts, by incorrectly assuming the co-existence of contradictory beliefs in the mind : and that it conflicts both with postulates implied in the daily colloquy of detail between man and man, and with the volitional preferences that determine individual action. All of these are founded on a belief in the regular sequence of our sensations, and in the at least temporary durability of combined potential aggregates of sensations, which we enunciate in the language of definite attributes belonging to definite substances. This language, the common

---

* This is stated by Aristotle himself (Metaph. Γ. 1011 a. 15) οἱ δ' ἐν τῷ λόγῳ τὴν βίαν μόνον ζητοῦντες ἀδύνατον ζητοῦσιν· ἐναντία γαρ εἰπεῖν ἀξιοῦσιν, εὐθὺς ἐναντία λέγοντες. He here indeed applies this observation immediately to the Protagoreans, against whom it does not tell— instead of the Heracleiteans, against whom it does tell. Indeed, the whole of the reasoning in this part of the Metaphysica, is directed indiscriminately and in the same words against Protagoreans and Heracleiteans.

medium of communication among non-theorizing men, is accepted as a basis, and is generalized and regularized, in the logical theories of Aristotle.

The doctrine here mentioned is vindicated by Aristotle, not only against Heracleitus, by asserting the Maxim of Contradiction, but also against Anaxagoras, by asserting the Maxim of Excluded Middle. Here we have the second *principium* of demonstration, which, if it required to be defended at all, can only be defended (like the first) by a process of Induction. Aristotle adduces several arguments in support of it, some of which involve an appeal to induction, though not broadly or openly avowed; but others of them assume what adversaries, and Anaxagoras especially, were not likely to grant. We must remember that both Anaxagoras and Heracleitus propounded their theories as portions of physical philosophy or of Ontology; and that in their time no such logical principles and distinctions as those that Aristotle lays down in the Organon, had yet been made known or pressed upon their attention. Now, Aristotle, while professing to defend these Axioms as data of Ontology, forgets that they deal with the logical aspect of Ontology, as formulated in methodical propositions. His view of the Axioms cannot be properly appreciated without a classification of propositions, such as neither Heracleitus nor Anaxagoras found existing or originated for themselves. Aristotle has taught us—what Heracleitus and Anaxagoras had not been taught—to distinguish separate propositions as universal, particular and singular; and to distinguish pairs of propositions as contrary, sub-contrary, and contradictory. To take the simplest case, that of a singular proposition, in regard to which the distinction between contrary and contradictory has no application—such as the answer (cited above) of Kephisophon about Euripides. Here Aristotle would justly contend that the two propositions—*Euripides is within*—*Euripides is not within*—could not be either both of them true, or both of them false: that is, that we could neither believe both, nor disbelieve both. If Kephisophon had answered, Euripides is neither within, nor not within, Dikaeopolis would have found himself as much at a loss with the two negatives as he was with the two affirmatives. In regard to singular propositions, neither the doctrine of Heracleitus (to believe both affirmation and negation) nor that of Anaxagoras (to disbelieve both) is admissible. But when in place of singular propositions, we take either universal or particular propositions, the rule to follow is no longer so simple and peremptory. The universal affirmative and the universal negative are *contrary*; the particular affirmative and the particular negative are *sub-contrary*; the universal affirmative and the particular negative, or the universal negative and the particular affirmative, are *contradictory*. It is now noted in all manuals of Logic, that of two contrary propositions, both cannot be true, but both may be false; that of two sub-contraries, both may be true, but both cannot be false; and that, of two contradictories, one must be true and the other false.

THE SCHOOLMEN. In the mediæval period the question as to the Origin of Knowledge was thrown into the shade by the question as to the nature, and mode of existence, of Universals. Nevertheless, the different sides were each supported. On the one hand, the extreme experience-hypothesis was reduced to the formula often quoted since, *Nihil est in intellectu quod non prius fuerit in sensu;* on the other, we can see by the argument of Aquinas against the theory of knowledge *per species—omnium intelligibilium rationes, animæ naturaliter inditas,* that some did not shrink from the extreme statement of the opposed view.

It was at the close of the scholastic period, when the question of the universals was considered as settled against Realism (henceforth driven to assume masked forms) and their subjective character, whether in the sense of Nominalism or Conceptualism, was held to be established, that the problem of the Origin of such general ideas *before* or *in* experience, started into full importance. During the whole course of modern thought it has held a first place among philosophical questions.

DESCARTES heads the modern movement in philosophy, and in him we must look for the terms wherein the question was anew propounded. First, however, it is well, even if it were not in his case necessary, to indicate shortly his *general* philosophical position.

1. Proceeding on the analogy of mathematics, he began by seeking a principle, or principles, of indubitable certainty, whereon to rear a universal system of knowledge unimpeachable at every point:—There is, he declared, not a single thing that I am not able to doubt or call in question, save the fact of my own doubting. But doubting is thinking, and in thinking is implied being or existing: *I am, I exist,* is, therefore, a proposition necessarily true every time I pronounce or conceive it; *Cogito ergo sum* or *Ego sum res cogitans* is to me the one thing absolutely and for ever certain. And not only do I thus know *that* I am, but, at the same time, *what* I am—*a thinking being.* Although as yet nothing more, this I know with perfect *clearness* and *distinctness.*

2. Next he sought how to pass beyond this primal certainty— the simple consciousness of self as a thinking being:—I find in me an idea of perfection, or of an all-perfect being called God. Like everything else, such an idea must have its cause, for I apprehend, again with perfect clearness and distinctness, that, out of nothing, nothing can come. Now, as every cause must involve at least as much reality as there is in the effect, an imperfect being like myself cannot be the cause of such an idea of perfection. Wherefore it must be derived from a higher source, from such an all-powerful and perfect being as it portends, who has stamped it as his mark upon my mind: not to say that already in the very idea of such a perfect being the attribute of existence is implied as necessary to his perfection. Besides self, therefore, I now know that God exists, and that he must be the real cause of my own existence.

3. In the *Veracity* of God, in this way proved to exist, he now

APPENDIX—ORIGIN OF KNOWLEDGE.

found a guarantee of the existence of other beings, and of a material universe :—Formerly, no mere thought of mine sufficed to prove the existence of other beings or external things; for anything I knew, I dreamed, or was the victim of a constant deception. But now that I know an all-perfect God to exist, I can be certain that everything is as he has constituted me to apprehend it, when, that is to say, the apprehension is perfectly *clear* and *distinct*. Thus, clearly and distinctly apprehending Bodies to be real external substances, *i.e.*, independent existences with real attributes of Figure, Size, and Motion, modes of one universal and inseparable property—Extension, I can be sure that they *are* such. Qualities of colour, sound, heat, &c., on the other hand, I can be equally sure do not, as such, belong to the extended objects, because, when clearly and distinctly apprehended, they are seen to be only varieties of motion in these.

4. The whole nature of Mind being thus understood, from the beginning, as expressed by the one attribute *Thought* (construed, however, as *Thinking Substance*), and the whole nature of Body, at the end, as summed up in the one attribute *Extension* (*Extended Substance*), he found in the union of Mind and Body in man—in man only, for he regarded the lower animals as mere *automata*—an explanation of all such phenomena of appetite, bodily feeling, and sensation (colour, sound, &c., just alluded to) as can be referred neither to Mind nor to Body, taken simply and apart.

Such are the main positions of Descartes. His doctrine of Intuition, in so far as it is developed, may now be presented in the following statements :—

1. His general method, styled Deduction, whether used in rearing the whole edifice of philosophy or applied to special problems, requires the positing of certain indemonstrable and self-evident truths, in regard to which he himself employs the term *Intuition*.

2. First among such intuitive principles, and apprehended with a *clearness* and *distinctness*, to the level of which every other truth should be raised, is the certainty of *Cogito ergo sum*. Another, which stands him in even better stead, is *Ex nihilo nihil fit*. Still other examples are: What is done cannot be undone; It is impossible that the same thing can at once be and not be. Such truths are 'eternal,' although in some men they may be obscured by prejudice.

3. Amongst Ideas he distinguishes (1) Innate, (2) Adventitious, (3) Factitious or Imaginary. The Innate, *e.g.*, the idea of self as existent, of God, &c., are so named because they neither come adventitiously by way of sense, nor have the character of voluntary products or fictions of the mind. The idea of God he describes as like 'the workman's mark left imprinted on his work.' But, at other times, he argues, like many of his successors, for little more than innate faculties or modes of thinking, instead of thoughts; pre-dispositions to conceive, instead of ready-made eptions.

4. In the *Knowledge* of an object by sense-perception, there is more than a mere passive impression. What is real and constant in any object, as a piece of wax, under all conditions of sensible change —that it is a Substance, with attributes of Extension, Mobility, &c.—is perceived only *intellectually*, by direct *mental inspection* or *intuition*. To know such attributes implies the *conceiving* of an infinite possibility of variations of each, something quite beyond the scope of Sense, or of Imagination which waits on sense.

Before passing to Locke—the next great name in the general history of Intuition, it is necessary to take some account of others of his predecessors.

In the Cartesian school itself, as in Malebranche, the discussion of the question was too much complicated with the special difficulty of finding a theory of perception or knowledge to bridge the chasm fixed by Descartes between mind and matter, to permit of its being followed out here. But ARNAULD in the *Port Royal Logic*, Chapter I., has a short and simple statement, which, as it must have been known to Locke, may be briefly noticed.

1. As to the *nature* of Ideas, he emphasizes the same distinction between Image and Idea, Imagination and Pure Intellection or Conception, made by Descartes. Things can be clearly and distinctly conceived, whereof there is no adequate imagination, *e.g.*, a chiliogon; and others, of which there is no imagination possible at all, *e.g.*, Thought, Affirmation, God. This remembered, no more exact account can be given of what an Idea is, there being nothing more clear and simple to explain it by: 'It is everything that is in our mind when we can say with truth that we can conceive a thing, in whatsoever way it may be conceived.'

2. As to the *Origin* of Ideas, he contests the opinion of 'a philosopher of repute' (Gassendi), that all knowledge begins from sense, the rest being an affair of Composition, or Amplification and Diminution, or Accommodation and Analogy. [Gassendi, the contemporary and rival of Descartes, rejected the Innate theory most strenuously, and with an explicitness justifying the inference that, apart from Descartes' influence, it was a commonplace in the philosophy of the time: Locke's relation to him has often been remarked.] To this, Arnauld, in substance, objects, (1) that it is not true at all of certain ideas, and (2) that it is not properly true of any. First, The simple ideas of Being and Thought (involved in the proposition *Cogito ergo sum*) never entered by any sense, and are not compounded from sensible images; and the same is true of the idea of God: the mind has the faculty of forming such ideas for itself, and they cannot, without manifest absurdity, be referred to sense. In the next place, all that the impression on the sense effects, when it is this that does happen to arouse the mind, is to give the mind an 'occasion' to form one idea rather than another; and the idea has very rarely any resemblance to what takes place in the sense and in the brain.

In England, views in strong antithesis to Locke, were advanced by Cudworth, founding not upon Descartes, but upon the ancients; and, at a still earlier date (even than Descartes), by Lord Herbert of Cherbury.

CUDWORTH'S views, as explicitly set forth in the treatise on *Eternal and Immutable Morality*, were kept back from publication until after Locke's death. It will suffice, therefore, simply to remark (1) that (independently of Cartesian influence) he distinguishes between Sense and Fancy on the one hand and Intellection or the Innate Cognoscitive Power of the Soul on the other; (2) that he defines this power as a faculty the mind has of raising from within itself Intelligible Ideas and Conceptions of things, Intelligible Reasons of things *(Rationes)*, &c.—*e.g.*, Verity, Falsity, Cause, Effect, Genus, Species, Nullity, Contingency, Impossibility, Justice, Duty, 'Nothing can be and not be at the same time' (both as proposition and in every one of its words), &c.; (3) that he understands by knowledge of particular things the bringing and comprehending of them under such *Rationes*, and finds that 'scientific knowledge is best acquired by the soul's abstraction from the outward objects of sense, that it may the better attend to its own inward notions and ideas.'

LORD HERBERT OF CHERBURY, in his book '*De Veritate*' (1624) maintains the doctrine of Innate Ideas, under the name of *Natural Instincts*. Instinct is the first of our faculties brought into play, as *Discursus* (the understanding) is the last; the senses, both external and internal, coming between them. It is the speciality of Instinct to work *naturaliter (i.e.* without *Discursus)*; in the same way as minerals and vegetables have a faculty of self-preservation. *Notitiæ Communes* (nearly equivalent to First Principles) are the product of Natural Instinct. They are sacred principles, against which it is unlawful to contend, and are guaranteed by nature itself. If it be a common notion that Nature does nothing in vain, it is the same as if Nature herself spake—'I do nothing in vain.' The truth of Common notions is perceived *immediately*, at first sight, so presenting a contrast to the slow and uncertain steps of the Discursive faculty.

How, then, are those notions to be discovered? It is by 'our method,' which Herbert announces with great emphasis. There is no Philosophy or Religion so benighted but has its own special truth, mingled, it may be, with error; and the pure metal can be extracted from the ore by 'our method.' The great criterion, as he never wearies of repeating, is *universality*: what is accepted by all men must be true, and can arise from no source except natural instinct. Universal consent is to be gathered from laws, religions, philosophies, and books. Thus Religion is a common notion, for there is no nation or age without religion. The next thing to be considered is—what points are universally agreed to. This can be ascertained only by actually bringing together and sifting all religions. If this method (which is the only sure one) be considered too laborious, Herbert points out the easier mode of self-examination; if you examine your faculties, you will find God

CHARACTERS OF COMMON NOTIONS.

and Virtue given as eternal and universal truths. Every truth is attested by some faculty, error by none.

But in this introspection, the distinction must be borne in mind between *veritas rei*, of which the *principium* is without the mind, and *veritas intellectus*, which depends on the mind alone; in fine, between propositions always and everywhere true, and propositions true only here and now. [This seems to be an approach, in everything except the name, to the criterion of *necessity* afterwards brought forward by Leibnitz.] The mind is not a *tabula rasa*, but rather a *closed* book, that opens on the presentation of objects. Until called forth by objects, the common notions are latent. It is folly to suppose that they are brought in with the objects; they exist independently, being placed in us by nature. Nor is it any real difficulty that we do not understand *how* those notions are elicited; as little do we understand how touch, or taste, or smell is produced.

All common notions are not independent of *Discursus*, but such as are may be determined by the following characters. (1) *Priority*. Instinct precedes *Discursus*, and as already observed, is in animals the faculty of self-preservation. In a house built with regularity, beauty of symmetry is observed by natural instinct, long before reason comes in with its estimate of the proportions of the parts. (2) *Independence*. When a common notion has been obtained by observation, it may be deducible from some prior truth. Thus 'Man is an animal' depends for its truth upon the ultimate principle, that whatever affects our faculties in the same manner, is the same so far as we are concerned. Only the ultimate or underived truths are attributed to Natural Instinct. (3) *Universality* (excepting idiots and madmen). (4) *Certainty*. Those principles possess the highest authority, and, if understood, cannot be denied. (5) *Paramount Utility (Necessitas)*. Without common notions, there would be no principle of self-preservation: they are therefore essential to the existence of the race or the individual. (6) *Immediacy*. The truth of them is seen, *nulla interposita mora*.

JOHN LOCKE. Locke discusses the subject of innate speculative principles in his Essay on the Human Understanding, B. I., chaps. 2, 4. Innate principles are a class of notions stamped on the mind, which the soul brings into the world with it. Are there any such? Certainly not, if it is shown how men may reach all the knowledge they have without such ideas. For it would be absurd to say that colour was innate in a man that had eyes. Locke's refutation paves the way for the fundamental principle of his psychology, that all our knowledge and ideas arise from sense and reflection.

1. The first argument for innate ideas is that certain principles are admitted as true *universally*. To this Locke answers, that the argument breaks down, (1) if any other way can be pointed out whereby this universal assent may be attained. (2) There are no principles universally admitted. Take two that have a high title

APPENDIX—ORIGIN OF KNOWLEDGE.

to be considered innate : 'whatever is, is,' and 'it is impossible for the same thing to be and not to be.' These propositions are to a great part of mankind wholly unknown. They are unknown to children and idiots, and so they are not universally accepted. It would be a contradiction to say, that those propositions are imprinted on the mind, without the mind being conscious of them. That an idea is in the understanding, can only mean that it is understood. Hence, if there were innate ideas, they ought to be present in children and in idiots, as well as in others.

2. To avoid those exceptions, the universality is affirmed with qualifications ; it is said that all men assent to those principles when they come to the use of reason. This can only mean either that the time of discovering those native inscriptions is when men come to the use of reason, or that reason assists in the discovery of them. (1) If reason discovered those principles, that would not prove them innate ; for by reason we discover many truths that are not innate. Reason, as the faculty of deducing one truth from another, plainly cannot lead to innate principles. Reason should no more be necessary to decipher those native inscriptions, than to make our eyes perceive visible objects. (2) The coming to the use of reason is not the time of first knowing those maxims. How many instances have we of the exercise of reason by children before they learn that 'whatever is, is' ! Many illiterate people and savages, long after they come to the use of reason, are altogether ignorant of maxims so general. Those truths are never known before the use of reason, but may possibly be assented to some time after during a man's life ; and the same may be said of all other knowable truths. (3) If coming to the use of reason were the time of discovering the alleged innate notions, it would not prove them innate. For why should a notion be innate because it is first known when an entirely distinct faculty of the mind begins to exert itself ? It would be as good an argument, (and as near the truth) to say that those maxims were first assented to when men came to the use of speech.

3. Another form of the argument is, that as soon as the propositions are heard, and their terms understood, they are assented to. Maxims that the mind, without any teaching and at the very first proposal, assents to, are surely innate. (1) But assent at first hearing is characteristic of a multitude of truths ; such as, 'one and two are equal to three,' 'two bodies cannot be in the same place,' 'white is not black,' 'a square is not a circle,' &c. To every one of these, every man in his wits must assent at first hearing. And since no proposition can be innate, unless the ideas composing it be innate, then our ideas of colours, tastes, sounds, &c., will be innate. Nor can it be said that those propositions about concrete objects are drawn as consequences from the more general innate propositions, since the concrete judgments are known long before the abstract form. (2) Moreover, the argument of assent at first hearing supposes that those maxims may be unknown till proposed. For if they were ingrained in

OBJECTIONS TO INNATE IDEAS.

the mind, why need they be proposed in order to gain assent? Does proposing make them clearer? Then the teaching of men is better than the impression of nature, an opinion not favourable to the authority of innate truths. (3) It is sometimes said that the mind has an implicit knowledge of those principles, but not an explicit, before the first hearing. The only meaning that can be assigned to implicit or virtual knowledge, is that the mind is capable of knowing those principles. This is equally true of all knowledge, whether innate or not. (4) The argument of assent on first hearing is on the false supposition of no preceding teaching. Now, the words, and the meanings of the words, expressing the innate ideas, have been learned. And not only so, but the ideas that enter into the propositions are also acquired. If, then, we take out of a proposition the ideas in it and the words, what remains innate? A child assents to the proposition, 'an apple is not fire,' before it understands the terms of the maxim, 'it is impossible for the same thing to be and not to be,' and consequently before it can assent to the more general proposition. In conclusion Locke sums up: if there were innate ideas, they would be found in all men; there are no ideas found in all men, hence there are no innate ideas. He adds some further considerations by way of supporting this conclusion.

4. Those maxims are not the first known, for children do not know them. How explain such ignorance of notions, imprinted on the mind in indelible characters, to be the foundation of all acquired knowledge? Children distinguish between the nurse and the cat, without the aid of the maxim, that the same thing cannot be and not be—for that is a maxim wholly unknown to them. If children brought any truths into the world with them, such truths ought to appear early, whereas, being made up of abstract terms, they appear late.

5. Innate ideas appear least where what is innate shows itself clearest. Children, savages, illiterate people, being the least corrupted by custom or borrowed opinions, ought to exhibit those innate notions—the endowments of nature—with purity and distinctness. But those are the very persons most destitute of universal principles of knowledge. General maxims are best known in the schools and academies, where they help debate, but do little to advance knowledge.

6. In chap. 4, Locke examines some alleged innate ideas. As a proposition is made up of ideas, the doctrine of innate maxims will be decisively refuted, if it be shown that there are no innate ideas. Thus, in the maxim, 'it is impossible for the same thing to be and not to be,' Locke asks whether the notions of impossibility and identity be innate. He illustrates the difficulties involved in the conception of identity. Is a man, made as he is of body and soul, the same man when his body is changed? Were Euphorbus and Pythagoras, who had the same soul, the same man, though they lived ages asunder? And was the cock, that shared the soul with them, the same also? In what sense shall

we be the same men, when raised at the resurrection, that we are now? The notion of identity is far from being clear or distinct; can it then be the subject of undoubted and innate truth? Again take the maxim, 'the whole is bigger than a part.' This has a fair title to be considered innate. But whole and part have no meaning, except as applied to number and extension. If the maxim be innate, number and extension must also be innate. [Locke stopped here, thinking the point too clear for argument. But Kant afterwards adopted the paradox, and upheld the *à priori* character of Space as the corner-stone of his metaphysical construction.] In like manner, Locke examines whether the ideas of *Worship* and *God* are innate. In respect of the idea of God, he argues the subject at great length, applying most of the considerations that tell against innate ideas generally. He also discusses whether *Substance* be an innate idea. This idea, he observes, we have neither by sensation nor by reflection, and nature might with advantage have given it to us. For substance is a most confused notion, and is only a something of which we have no distinct positive idea, but which we take to be the substratum of our ideas.

SHAFTESBURY, in England, attempted to turn the edge of Locke's objections by declaring (but before Locke, the same had been affirmed) that all that was contended for was better expressed by the words *Connate* or *Connatural* than by the word *innate*: it was true the mind had no knowledge antecedent to experience, but it was so constituted or predisposed as inevitably to develop, *with* experience, ideas and truths not explained thereby.

In Germany, LEIBNITZ set up an elaborate defence of the Innate Theory, and is commonly represented as having made a distinct advance in the discussion of the question by the exceptions he took to the criticism of Locke. These are reducible to two. (1) He charges Locke with neglecting the difference between mere *truths of fact* or *positive truths* that may be arrived at by way of Inductive Experience, and *necessary truths*, or *truths of demonstration*, not to be proved except from principles implanted in the mind. (2) He charges Locke farther, with not seeing that innate knowledge is saved on simply making the unavoidable assumption that the intellect and its faculties are there from the first : ' the mind is innate to itself :' ' nihil est in intellectu quod non fuerit in sensu, *nisi ipse intellectus*.' His detailed objections are to be found in his posthumous work, *Nouveaux Essais sur l'entendement humain*.

A passage in a letter of Leibnitz's to a friend, gives a good idea of the position he took up against Locke. He there says : ' In Locke there are various particular truths not badly set forth; but on the main point he is far from being right, and he has not caught the nature of the Mind and of Truth. If he had properly considered the difference between necessary truths, *i.e.* those which are known by Demonstration, and the truths that we arrive at to a certain degree by Induction, he would have seen that necessary truths can be proved only from principles implanted in the mind

NECESSARY TRUTHS AND TRUTHS OF FACT. 57

—the so-called innate ideas; because the senses tell indeed what happens, but not what necessarily happens. He has also failed to observe that the notions of the Existent, of Substance, Identity, the True and Good, are innate to our mind for the reason that it is innate to itself, and within itself comprehends them all. Nihil est in intellectu quod non fuerit in sensu, *nisi ipse intellectus*.'

The *Nouveaux Essais* is a dialogue, continued through four books, corresponding to the books of Locke's essay, between Theophilus (Leibnitz himself) and Philalethes, a disciple of Locke. In Book I., Theophilus, after announcing that he has taken a new step in philosophy, and reached a point of view from which he can reconcile the discrepant views of former thinkers, declares that he goes beyond Descartes in accepting an innate idea of God; for rather all our thoughts and actions may be said to come from the depths of the soul itself without possibility of their being given by the senses. He will not, however, go into the demonstration of that at present, but content himself with making clear, on the common system, that there are ideas and principles that do not come from the senses, but are found within the mind, unformed by us, although the senses give us occasion to apprehend them. Locke, with all his power, failed to see the difference between *necessary truths*, whose source is in the understanding, and *truths of fact* drawn from sense, experience, and confused perceptions. The certitude of innate principles (such as, Every thing that is, is ; It is impossible that a thing should be and not be at the same time) is not to be based on the fact of universal consent, which can only be an index to, and never a demonstration of, them : it comes only from what is in us. Even though unknown, they are not therefore not innate, for they are recognized as soon as understood. In the mind there is always an infinity of cognitions that are not consciously apprehended ; and so the fact of their not being always apprehended makes nothing against the existence of (1) the pure ideas (opposed to the phantasms of sense) and (2) necessary truths of reason (in contrast to truths of fact) asserted to be graven on the mind. That the necessary truths of Arithmetic and Geometry exist thus *virtually* in the mind appears from the established possibility of drawing them forth out of a wholly untutored mind. But, in fine, the position to stand by is the difference that there is between necessary and eternal truths and mere truths of experience. ' The mind is able to know the one and the other, but of the first it is the source; and whatever number of particular experiences there may be of a universal truth, there can be no perpetual assurance of it, except its necessity is known by reason.' Elsewhere he mentions as things that the senses cannot give; ' Substance, the One, the Same, Cause, Perception, Reasoning ;' but otherwise merely repeats in different language statements like the above.

When Philalethes suggests that the *ready* consent of the mind to certain truths is sufficiently explained by the general faculty of knowing, Theophilus replies as follows : ' Very true ; but it is this particular relation of the human mind to these truths that renders the exercise of the faculty easy and natural with respect to them, and causes them to be called innate. It is no naked faculty, consisting in the mere possibility of understanding them: there is a disposition, an aptitude, a preformation, determining our mind and making it possible that they should be drawn forth from it. Just as there is a difference between the figures given to stone or marble indifferently, and those that its veins mark out already or are disposed to mark out if the workman takes advantage of them.' Farther on, to the objection that there is a difficulty in conceiving a truth to be in the mind, if the mind has never thought of it, he adds: 'It is as if one said that there is difficulty in conceiving veins to be in the marble before they are discovered.' In these sentences Leibnitz's theory is nearly completed.

After Leibnitz has next to be noticed KANT; but his contribution to the history of the present question, as before in the case of Descartes, cannot be viewed apart from his general philosophical position. Although his whole system, on the speculative side at least, may be described as a theory of the Origin of Knowledge, it cannot be properly understood without some preliminary reference to other lines of thought.

1. Kant found himself unable to subscribe to the metaphysical *dogmatism* of the school of Wolff (joining on to Leibnitz) that presumed to settle everything without any question of the mind's ability to pronounce at once and finally. This on the one hand: on the other he was startled by the *scepticism* of Hume (joining on through Berkeley to Locke) with its summary assertion of the impotence of human thought. As between the two, he conceived the idea of instituting *a critical inquiry into the foundations and limits of the mind's faculty of knowledge;* in his famous work, 'The Critique of the Pure Reason' (1781).

2. As here implied in the word 'pure' used of Reason, or the general faculty of knowing, he contended for the inherence in the mind, before all experience, of certain principles of knowledge, which he called *à priori;* and thus far was at one with former supporters of Innate Notions. Farther, with Leibnitz in particular, he agreed in taking *necessity* and *universality* as the marks or criteria of cognitions never to be attained to or explained by experience. Cognitions universally and necessarily true, and these not merely *analytic* or verbal (where the predicate only sets forth the implication of the subject), but *synthetic* or real (in which there is an extension of knowledge) he found, as he thought, existing in abundance: in Mathematics such, for instance, as $7+5=12$; Two straight lines cannot enclose a space, &c.; in Pure Physics, The quantity of matter in nature is constant, Action and Reaction in nature are equal; while the whole of traditional Metaphysics was made up of such. Criticism of the foundations and limits of human knowledge took with him, then, the special shape of an inquiry into the *conditions of the possibility of synthetic cognitions à priori.*

FORMS OF INTUITION.

3. In the peculiar solution that he gave of the old question of Innate Knowledge put into this new form, there can be traced the influence Hume had upon him from the opposite camp. Hume had meanwhile analyzed Causality into mere custom of sequence among the impressions of sense, and upon the untrustworthiness of such a purely subjective notion had based his general scepticism. Kant taking his stand upon the body of established mathematical truth (synthetic at the same time as necessary), rejected the sceptical conclusion; but accepting the subjective origin of the notion of Causality, proceeded to place all the native *à priori*, or non-empirical elements of knowledge in certain *subjective or mental 'Forms' destined to enfold, while requiring to be supplemented by the 'Matter' of Experience.*

4. The mind, therefore, in Kant's view, has no sort of knowledge antecedent to and independent of experience, as many philosophers have more or less boldly asserted: it has, before experience, nothing except the 'forms' as the moulds into which the empirical elements that come primarily by way of sense are made to run; and unless this 'matter' of experience is supplied, there is no knowledge of any kind possible. But when the 'matter' is provided, and the 'forms' are applied to their true and appropriate 'matter'—there are, as will be seen, cases wherein this does, and others wherein it does not take place—the mind is then not bound down to its particular experiences, but can really conceive and utter universal and necessary (synthetic) truths that no mere experience could ever give.

The detailed exposition of Kant's theory falls under three heads.

I.—*Transcendental Æsthetic.* The impressions of sense are (passively) *received* as empirical 'matter' into certain pure or *à priori* 'forms,' distinguished by the special name of 'Forms of Intuition.'

1. The data of the *internal* sense (joy, pain, &c.) fall into, or are received as, a series or succession, in *Time:* the data of the *external* senses are received, directly, as lying outside of us and by the side of each other, in *Space;* indirectly, in their influence upon our internal state, as a succession in *Time.*

2. As forms, Space and Time are of non-empirical origin; they cannot be thought away, as everything can that has been acquired. They are forms of *intuition*, in having nothing of the character of abstracted *concepts*.

3. If they were not *à priori*, there would be no foundation possible for the established (synthetic *à priori*) truths of Mathematics and Geometry resting upon the intuition of Space, nor for Arithmetic, which, consisting of the repetition or succession of units, rests upon the intuition of Time.

4. How are we enabled actually to construct the pure science of Mathematics, made up of synthetic truths *à priori*, is thus to be explained. Because the subjective forms of space or Time are mixed up with all our sense-perceptions (intuitions), and only such *phenomena* in Space and Time (not Things-in-themselves

or *noumena*) are ever open to our intuitive apprehension, we may pronounce freely *à priori* in all that relates to determinations of Space and Time, provided it is understood of *phenomena*, constituted by the very addition of these mental forms.

II.—*Transcendental Logic—Analytic.* Phenomena (constituted out of the 'matter' of sense as ordered in the Forms of Intuition) themselves in turn become 'matter,' which the mind, as *spontaneously* active, combines and orders in the process of Judgment, under certain 'forms,' distinguished by the special name of 'Categories of the Understanding.'

1. These are twelve in number, and discoverable from the common analysis of judgments in logic.

a. Three categories of QUANTITY: *Unity, Plurality, Universality* (as involved in Singular, Particular, Universal judgments respectively).

b. Three of QUALITY: *Reality, Negation, Limitation* (in Positive, Negative, Infinite judgments).

c. Three of RELATION: *Substantiality, Causality, Community* or *Reciprocal action* (in Categorical, Hypothetical, Disjunctive judgments).

d. Three of MODALITY: *Possibility, Existence, Necessity* (in Problematic, Assertory, Apodeictic judgments).

2. Until a synthesis of intuitions (perceptions) takes place under some one of these pure or *à priori* concepts, there is no Knowledge, or, in the proper meaning of the word, Experience. The fact of such a synthesis makes all the difference between the mere perception of a particular sequence in the subjective consciousness, *e.g.* my having the sense of weight in supporting a body, and the objective experience, true for all, The body is heavy.

3. The reason, now, why we can farther say that no possible experience will not come under the Categories, as in saying that effects *must* have a cause—or, which is the same thing, why we are enabled to utter synthetic judgments *à priori*, objectively valid, regarding nature—is this, that without the Categories (forms of the spontaneous activity of the pure *ego*) there cannot be any experience at all; experience, actual or possible, *is* phenomena bound together in the Categories.

4. But, if we can extend our knowledge beyond actual experience because experience is constituted by the Categories of the Understanding, the extension is only to be *possible* objects of experience, which are phenomena in Time and Space; never to Things-in-themselves or Noumena, of which there can be no sensible (intuitive) apprehension.

[Kant makes this apparent chiefly by the consideration, under the head of 'Schematism of the pure concepts of the Understanding,' of the conditions under which sensible phenomena can be subsumed under the Categories. But we must here forego the exposition of this, and of the system of 'Principles of the pure understanding' or (synthetic *à priori*) Rules for the objective use of the Categories, that follows. These, including (1) 'Axioms of Intuition,' (2) 'Anticipations of Perception,' (3) 'Analogies of Experience'—Amid all changes of phenomena, Substance abides the same, All change obeys the law of Cause and Effect, Substances co-existing in space act and re-act upon each other; (4) 'Postulates of Empirical Thought'—are the *à priori* construction that the mind is able to make of a Pure Science, or Metaphysic, of Nature.

III.—*Transcendental Logic—Dialectic.* Besides the Categories of the Understanding, there are certain other forms of the thinking faculty, according to which the mind seeks to bring its knowledge to higher unities: these are distinguished by the special name of 'Ideas of the Reason' [Reason to be taken here in a narrow sense as opposed to Sense and Understanding].

1. The Ideas of the Reason are three in number: (*a*) The (psychological) idea of the *Soul*, as a thinking substance, immaterial, simple and indestructible; (*b*) The (cosmological) idea of the *World*, as a system or connected whole of phenomena; (*c*) The (theological) idea of *God*, as supreme condition of the possibility of all things, the being of beings.

2. These Ideas of the Reason applied to our Cognitions have a true *regulative* function, being a constant spur towards bringing our relative intellectual experience to the higher unity of the absolute or unconditioned: but they are not *constitutive* principles, giving any real advance of knowledge, for truly objective knowledge is only of phenomena as possible objects of experience.

3. Nevertheless, by a law of our mental nature, we cannot avoid ascribing an illusory objective reality to these Ideas, making thus a 'transcendent' application of the Categories to objects there can never be any possible experience of ('transcendent of experience' *versus* 'immanent to experience'): and by this 'natural dialectic of the Reason,' we become involved in a maze of deception or 'transcendental show,' as seen in the Paralogisms regarding the metaphysical nature of the soul, the Antinomies or contradictory and mutually destructive assertions regarding the universe, and the sophistical arguments for the existence of God—that make up Metaphysics.

(The acknowledged powerlessness of the *Speculative* Reason to find conditions for the validity of the synthetic judgments *à priori* of Metaphysics—to prove theoretically the existence of the soul, God, &c., Kant overcame by setting forth Immortality, Free-will, and God, as postulates of the *Practical* Reason or Moral Faculty; and the Ideas of the Reason then became of use in helping the mind to conceive assumptions that were *morally* necessary.)

Besides rousing Kant in Germany to undertake his *critical* inquiries, the general philosophical scepticism of Hume, evoked in Scotland a protest of a different kind, in the *believing* Common-sense doctrine of Reid. But of Reid's views there was a singular anticipation made by the Jesuit Père Buffier in 1724, in an attempt to refute another and earlier sceptical doctrine, developed out of the fundamental principle of Cartesianism.

FATHER BUFFIER. Buffier anticipated Reid, both in the doctrine of Common Sense, and in the easy way of bringing truths to it. He describes Common Sense as 'that disposition or quality which Nature has placed in all men, or evidently in the far greater number of them, in order to enable them all, when they have arrived at the age and use of reason, to form a common and uniform judgment with respect to objects different from the internal sentiment of their own perception, and which judgment is not the consequence of any anterior principle.' With respect to at least some first principles, men in general are as good philosophers as Descartes or Locke, for all that they have to decide is a matter of fact, namely, whether they cannot help making a particular judgment. But Buffier does not exclude Philosophy altogether; on the contrary, he gives some marks or tests whereby the dictates of common sense may be scientifically ascertained. (1) First principles are so clear that, 'if we attempt to defend or attack them, it cannot be done but by propositions which manifestly are neither more clear nor more certain. (2) They are so universally received amongst men, in all times and countries, and by all degrees of capacity, that those who attack them are, comparatively to the rest of mankind, manifestly less than one to a hundred, or even a thousand.' (3) However they may be discredited by speculation, all men, even such as disavow them, must act in their conduct as if they were true.

The truths that Buffier considers to belong to common sense are scattered through his book on 'First Truths.' The basis of all knowledge is 'the interior sense we each of us have of our own existence, and what we feel within ourselves.' Every attempt to prove this truth only makes it darker. In like manner, the idea of unity (personality) is a first truth. Our identity follows from our unity or indivisibility. In opposition to Malebranche, who asserts that mind cannot act upon body, Buffier maintains as a first truth, that *my soul produces motions in my body.*

Among first truths are included the following:—(1) 'There are other beings and other men in the world besides me. (2) There is in them something that is called truth, wisdom, prudence; and this something is not merely arbitrary. (3) There is in me something that I call intelligence or mind, and something which is not that intelligence or mind, and which is named *body;* so that each possesses properties different from the other. (4) What is generally said and thought by men in all ages and countries, is true. (5) All men have not combined to deceive and impose upon me. (6) All that I see, in which is found order, and a permanent, uniform, and constant order, must have an intelligence for its cause.'

What may hold the place of first truths in the testimony of the senses? Buffier's answer shows great laxity in the selection of first truths. (1) 'They (the senses) always give a faithful report of things as they appear to them. (2) What appears to them is almost always conformable to the truth in matters proper for men in general to know, unless some rational cause of doubt presents itself. (3) It will be easy to discern when the evidence of the senses is doubtful, by the reflections we shall point out.' Another first truth is that a thing may be impossible although we see no contradiction in it. Again, the validity of testimony in certain cases, is a first truth; there are circumstances wherein no rational man could reject the testimony of other men. Also the free agency of man is a first truth; free will is 'the disposition a man feels within himself, of his capacity to act or not to act, to choose or not to choose a thing, at the same moment.'

Dr. Thomas Reid. The word Sense, as used by Philosophers, from Locke to Hutcheson, has signified a means of furnishing our minds with ideas, without including judgment, which is the perception of agreement or disagreement of our ideas. But, in common language, Sense always implies judgment. Common Sense is the degree of judgment common to men that we can converse and transact business with, or call to account for their conduct. 'To judge of First Principles requires no more than a sound mind free from prejudice, and a distinct conception of the question. The learned and the unlearned, the philosopher and the day-labourer, are upon a level, and will pass the same judgment, when they are not misled by some bias.' A man is not now moved by the subtle arguments of Zeno against motion, though, perhaps, he knows not how to answer them.

Although First Principles are self-evident, and not to be proved by any arguments, still a certain kind of reasoning may be applied in their support. (1) To show that the principle rejected stands upon the same footing with others that are admitted. (2) As in Mathematics, the *reductio ad absurdum* may be employed. (3) The consent of ages and nations, of the learned and unlearned, ought to have great authority with regard to first principles, where every man is a competent judge. (4) Opinions that appear so early in the mind, that they cannot be the effect of education or of false reasoning, have a good claim to be considered as first principles.

Reid asks whether the decisions of Common Sense can be brought into a code such as all reasonable men shall acquiesce in. He acknowledges the difficulty of the task, and does not profess that his own enumeration is perfectly satisfactory. His classification proceeds on the distinction between necessary and contingent truths. That a cone is the third part of a cylinder, of the same base and height, is a necessary truth. It does not depend upon the will and power of any being. That the Sun is the centre of the planetary system is a contingent truth; it depends on the power and will of the Being that made the planets.

I.—*Principles of Contingent Truth.* (1) Everything that I am conscious of exists. The irresistible conviction we have of the reality of what we are conscious of, is not the effect of reasoning; it is immediate and intuitive, and therefore a first principle. (2) The thoughts that I am conscious of, are the thoughts of a being that I call *myself*, my *mind*, my *person*. (3) Those things did really happen that I distinctly remember. (4) Our own personal identity and continued existence, as far back as we remember anything distinctly. (5) Those things do really exist that we distinctly perceive by our senses, and are what we perceive them to be. [This is Dr. Reid's theory of the external world elevated to the dignity of a first principle.] (6) We have some degree of power over our actions and the determinations of our will. The origin of our idea of power is not easily assigned. Power is not an object of sense or consciousness. We see events as successive, but not the power whereby they are produced. We are conscious of the operations of our minds; but power is not an operation of mind. It is, however, implied in every act of volition, and in all deliberation and resolution. Likewise, when we approve or disapprove, we believe that men have power to do or not to do. (7) The natural faculties, whereby we distinguish truth from error, are not fallacious. (8) Our fellow-men with whom we converse are possessed of life and intelligence. (9) Certain features of the countenance, sounds of the voice, and gestures of the body, indicate certain thoughts and dispositions of mind. The signification of those things we do not learn by experience, but by a kind of natural perception. Children, almost as soon as born, may be frightened by an angry or threatening tone of voice. (10) There is a certain regard due to human testimony in matters of fact, and even to human authority in matters of opinion. (11) There are many events depending on the will of man, possessing a self-evident probability, greater or less, according to circumstances. In men of sound mind, we expect a certain degree of regularity in their conduct. (12) In the phenomena of nature, what is to be, will probably be like what has been in similar circumstances. Hume has shown that this principle is not grounded on reason, and has not the intuitive evidence of mathematical axioms.

II.—*Principles of Necessary Truth*. In regard to those, Reid thinks it enough to divide them into classes, and to mention some by way of specimen in each class.

1. Grammatical Principles. (1) Every adjective in a sentence must belong to some substantive expressed or understood. (2) Every complete sentence must have a verb.

2. Logical Principles. (1) Any contexture of words, that does not make a proposition, is neither true nor false. (2) Every proposition is either true or false. (3) No proposition can be both true and false at the same time. (4) Reasoning in a circle proves nothing. (5) Whatever may be truly affirmed of a genus, may be truly affirmed of all its species, and of all the individuals belonging to that species.

3. The Mathematical Axioms.

4. The Principles of Taste. Setting aside the tastes acquired by habit and fashion, there is a natural taste, that is partly animal and partly rational. Rational taste is the pleasure of

contemplating what is conceived as excellent in its kind. This taste may be true or false, according as it is founded on true or false judgment. If it may be true or false, it must have first principles. Natural taste is the pleasure or disgust arising from certain objects before we are capable of perceiving any excellence or defect in them.

5. First Principles in Morals. (1) An unjust action has more demerit than an ungenerous one. (2) A generous action has more merit than a merely just one. (3) No man ought to be blamed for what it was not in his power to hinder. (4) We ought not to do to others what we should think unjust or unfair to be done to us in like circumstances. [By endeavouring to make the golden rule more precise, Reid has converted it into an identical proposition.]

6. Metaphysical Principles. (1) The qualities that we perceive by our senses must have a subject (which we call body), and the thoughts we are conscious of must have a subject (which we call mind). The distinction between sensible qualities, and the substance to which they belong, is not the invention of philosophers, but is found in the structure of all languages. (2) Whatever begins to exist must have a cause. (3) Design and intelligence in the cause may be inferred with certainty, from marks or signs of them in the effect.

7. We may refer to some of the necessary truths regarding Matter. (1) All bodies must consist of parts. (2) Two bodies cannot occupy the same place at the same time. (3) The same body cannot be in different places at the same time. (4) A body cannot be moved from one place to another without passing through intermediate space.

We may add also some of the First Principles connected with the Senses. (1) A certain sensation of touch suggests to the mind the conception of hardness, and creates the belief of its existence. (2) The notion of extension is suggested by feelings of touch, but is not given us by any sense. (3) It is by instinct we know the part of our body affected by particular pains.

DUGALD STEWART. The chief point wherein Stewart departs from Reid in the treatment of the Fundamental Laws of Belief (as he prefers to call the dictates of Common Sense), is in regard to Mathematical demonstration.

1. *Mathematical Axioms.* On this subject Stewart follows Locke in preference to Reid. Locke observes that, although the axioms are appealed to in proof of particular cases, yet they are only verbal generalizations of what, in particular instances, has been already acknowledged as true. Also many of the maxims are mere verbal propositions, explaining only the meaning of words. Stewart quotes Dr. Campbell to the effect that all axioms in Arithmetic and Geometry are identical propositions—reducible to the maxim 'whatever is, is.' That one and four make five means that five is the name of one added to four. To this doctrine Stewart adheres so far as Arithmetic is concerned. In Algebra

and Arithmetic, 'All our investigations amount to nothing more, than to a comparison of different expressions of the same thing. But the axioms of Euclid are not definitions, they are universal propositions applicable to an infinite variety of instances. Reid said that the axioms are necessary truths; and so the conclusions drawn from them were necessary. But, as was observed by Locke, it is impossible to deduce from the axioms a single inference. The axioms cannot be compared with the first Principles of Natural Philosophy, such as the laws of motion, from which the subordinate truths of that science are derived. The principles of Mathematics are, not the axioms, but the definitions. 'Yet although nothing is deduced from the axioms, they are nevertheless implied and taken for granted in all our reasonings; without them we could not advance a step.' [In a note Stewart observes that by the Axioms he does not mean all those prefixed to Euclid, which include the definition of parallel lines. He considers it a reproach to Mathematics that the so-called Axiom regarding parallel lines has not been made the subject of demonstration.]

2. *Mathematical Demonstration.* Demonstrative evidence, the characteristic of mathematics, has arrested universal attention, but has not been satisfactorily explained. The true account of mathematical demonstration seems to be—that it flows from the *definitions*. In other sciences, the propositions we attempt to prove express facts real or supposed; in mathematics, the propositions assert merely a connexion between certain suppositions and certain consequences. The whole object is to trace the consequences flowing from an assumed hypothesis. In the same manner, we might devise arbitrary definitions about moral or political ideas, and deduce from them a science as certain as geometry. The science of mechanics is an actual instance, 'in which, from arbitrary hypotheses concerning physical laws, the consequences are traced which would follow, if such was really the order of nature.' In the same way, a code of law might consist of rules strictly deduced from certain principles, with much of the method and all the certainty of geometry. The reasoning of the mathematician is true only of his hypothetical circle; if applied to a figure described on paper, it would fail, because all the radii could not be proved to be exactly equal. The peculiar certainty of mathematics thus rests upon the definitions, which are hypotheses and not descriptions of facts.

Stewart considers that the certainty of arithmetic is likewise derived from hypotheses or definitions. That $2 + 2 = 4$, and $3 + 2 = 5$, are definitions analogous to those in Euclid, and forming the material of all the complicated results in the science. But he objects to the theory of Leibnitz, that all mathematical truths are identical propositions. The plausibility of this theory arises from the fact, that the geometrical notions of equality and of coincidence are the same; all the propositions ultimately resting upon an imaginary application of one triangle to another. As superimposed figures occupy the same space, it was easy to slide into the belief that identity and equality were convertible terms. Hence it is said, all mathematical propositions are reducible to the form, $a = a$. But this form does not truly render the meaning of the proposition, $2 + 2 = 4$.

3. The other Laws of Belief resemble the axioms of Geometry in two respects: 1st, they do not enlarge our knowledge; and secondly, they are implied or involved in all our reasonings. Stewart advances two objections to the phrase—principles of common sense: it designates, as principles, laws of belief from which no inference can be deduced; and secondly, it refers the origin of these laws to common sense, a phraseology that he considers unfit for the logician, and unwarranted by ordinary usage.

Stewart defends the alleged instinctive power of interpreting certain expressions of the countenance, certain gestures of the body, and certain tones of the voice. This had been resolved by Priestley into associated experiences: but, for the other opinion, Stewart offers two reasons: (1) Children understand the meaning of smiles and frowns long before they could remark the connexion between a passion and its expression. (2) We are more *affected* by natural signs than by artificial ones. One is more affected by the facial expression of hatred than by the word *hatred*.

Another instinct adduced by Stewart, is what he calls the law of Sympathetic Imitation. This is contrasted with the intentional imitation of a scholar; it depends 'on the mimical powers connected with our *bodily frame*.' If we see a man laughing or sad, we have a tendency to take on the expression of those states. So yawning is contagious. 'Even when we *conceive* in solitude the expression of any passion, the effect of the conception is visible in our own appearance.' Also, we imitate instinctively the tones and accents of our companions. As we advance in years, this propensity to imitation grows weaker.

Sir W. Hamilton. I.—*Common Sense*. All reasoning comes at last to principles that cannot be proved, but are the basis of all proof. Such primary facts rest upon consciousness. To what extent, then, is consciousness an infallible authority? What we are actually conscious of, it is impossible for scepticism to doubt; but the dicta of consciousness, as evidence of facts beyond their own existence, may without self-contradiction be disputed. Thus, the reality of our perceptions of solidity and extension is beyond controversy; but the reality of an external world, evidenced by these, may be doubted. Common Sense consists of all the original data of Consciousness.

'The argument from Common Sense is one strictly philosophical and scientific.' The decision is not refused to the judgment of philosophers and accorded to the verdict of the vulgar. The problem of philosophy, and a difficult one, is to discover the elementary feelings or beliefs. This task cannot be taken out of the hands of philosophers. Sometimes the purport of the doctrine of Common Sense has been misunderstood, and it has been regarded as an appeal to 'the undeveloped beliefs of the unreflecting many.' Into this error fell Beattie, Oswald, and, in his earlier work, even Reid. But Hamilton alleges that Reid improves in his subsequent works, and that his treatment of Casualty with reference to the criterion of necessity, shows that he did not contemplate any uncritical appeal to Common Sense.

The criteria of the principles of Common Sense are these:— 1. *Incomprehensibility* [an inapt word for expressing that they are fundamental and not to be explained by reference to anything else]. 2. *Simplicity* [another name for the same fact]. 3. *Necessity*, and *Absolute Universality*. 4. *Certainty* [what is both necessary and universal must be certain. Hence in reality the four criteria consist of (1) the defining attribute of the principles, namely, that they are ultimate principles, and (2) the usually assigned attributes—Necessity and Universality].

Hamilton assigns historically three epochs in the meaning of Necessity:—(1) In the Aristotelian epoch, it was chiefly, if not exclusively, objective. (2) By Leibnitz, it was considered primarily as subjective. (3) By Hamilton himself, Necessity is farther developed into the two forms, *positive* and *negative* necessity; the application appears under the next head.

II.—*The Law of the Conditioned.* Necessity may be the result either of a power *(positive)*, or of an impotency *(negative)* of the mind. In Perception, I cannot but think that I, and something different from me, exist. Existence is thus a native cognition, for it is a condition of thinking that all that I am conscious of exists. Other positive notions are the Logical Principles, the intuitions of Space and Time, &c. But there are negative cognitions the result of an impotence of our faculties. Hence the Law of the Conditioned, which is expressed thus:—' All that is conceivable in thought lies between two extremes, which, as contradictory of each other, cannot both be true, but of which, as mutual contradictories, one must.' Thus Space must be bounded or not bounded, but we are unable to conceive either alternative. We cannot conceive space as a whole, beyond which there is no further space. Neither can we conceive space as without limits. Let us imagine space never so large, we yet fall infinitely short of infinite space. But finite and infinite space are contradictories; therefore, although we are unable to conceive either alternative, one must be true and the other false. The conception of Time illustrates the same law. Starting from the present, we cannot think past time as bounded, as beginning to be. On the other hand, we cannot conceive time going backwards without end; eternity is too big for our imagination. Yet time had either a beginning or it had not. Thus 'the conditioned or the thinkable lies between two extremes or poles; and these extremes or poles are each of them unconditioned, each of them inconceivable, each of them exclusive or contradictory of the other.'

The chief applications of the Law of the Conditioned are to the Principles of Causality and Substance. Take first Causality.

Causality is the law of the Conditioned applied to a thing thought as existing in time. No object can be known unless thought as existent; and in time. Thinking the object, we cannot think it not to exist. This will be admitted of the present, but possibly denied of the past and future, under the belief that we can think annihilation or creation. But we cannot conceive an atom taken from the sum of existing objects. No more can we conceive creation. For what is creation? 'It is not the springing of nothing into something. Far from it :—it is conceived, and is by us conceivable, merely as the evolution of a new form of existence, by the fiat of the Deity.' We are therefore unable to annihilate in thought any object; we cannot conceive its absolute commencement. Given an object we know that as a phenomenon it began to be, but we must think it as existing previously in its elements. If then the object existed before in a different form, this is only to say that it had causes. Thus the law of the conditioned shows us that every phenomenon must have *some* causes, but what those causes are must be learned from experience. Granting his theory of Causality, Hamilton thinks that he is armed with a philosophical defence of the freedom of the will. He points out the contradictions of his predecessors, who held that *every* change had a cause, but excepted the changes of volition. If our moral consciousness give us freedom, and our intellectual consciousness give us universal causation, it follows that our faculty of knowledge is self contradictory. By regarding Causality as founded on an impotence of the mind, Hamilton thinks that such a negative judgment cannot prevail against the positive testimony of consciousness.

Hamilton has not applied the law of the Conditioned, with much detail, to the principle of Substance. The problem is— Why must I suppose that every known phenomenon is related to an unknown substance? We cannot think a phenomenon without a substance, nor a substance without a phenomenon. Take an object; strip it of all its qualities; and try to think the residuary substance. It is unthinkable. In the same way, try to think a quality as a quality, and nothing more. It is unthinkable, except as a phenomenon of something that does not appear; as, in short, the accident of a substance. This is the law of Substance and Phenomenon, and is merely an instance of the law of the conditioned.

JOHN STUART MILL. Mr. Mill's views on necessary truths are contained in his Logic, Book II., chaps. 5—7. He begins by asking why, if the foundation of all science is Induction, a peculiar certainty is ascribed to the sciences that are almost entirely deductive. The character of certainty and necessity attributed to mathematical truths is an illusion; and depends upon ascribing them to purely imaginary objects. There exist no points without magnitude; no lines without breadth, nor perfectly straight. In answer to this, it is said that the points and lines exist in our conceptions merely; but the ideal lines and figures are copies of actual lines and figures. Now a point is the *minimum visibile*. A geometrical line is inconceivable. Mr. Mill agrees with Dugald Stewart in regarding geometry as built upon hypotheses. The definitions of geometry are generalizations, obviously easy, of the properties of lines and figures. The conclusions of geometry are necessary, only as implicated in the suppositions from which they are evolved. The suppositions themselves merely approximate (though practically with sufficient accuracy) to the actual truth. That axioms as well as definitions must be admitted among the first principles, has been shewn by Whewell in his polemic against Stewart. Two axioms must be postulated: that two straight lines cannot inclose a space, and some property of parallel lines not involved in their definition. Regarding the foundation of the axioms, two views are held; one that they are experimental truths resting on observation; the other that they are *à priori* truths. The chief arguments in support of the *à priori* theory are the following:—

I.—In the first place, if our belief that two straight lines cannot enclose a space, were derived from the senses, we could know the truth of the proposition only by seeing or feeling the straight lines; whereas it is seen to be true by merely thinking of them. By simply thinking of a stone thrown into the water, we could not conclude that it would go to the bottom. On the contrary, if I could be made to conceive a straight line without having seen one, I should at once know that two such lines cannot enclose a space. Moreover, the senses cannot assure us that, if two straight lines were prolonged to infinity, they would continue for ever to diverge.

The answer to these arguments is found in the capacity of geometrical forms for being painted in the imagination with a distinctness equal to reality. This enables us to make mental pictures of all combinations of lines and angles so closely resembling the realities, as to be as fit subjects of geometrical experimentation as the realities themselves. If, then, by mere thinking we satisfy ourselves of the truth of an axiom, it is because we know that the imaginary lines perfectly represent the real ones, and that we may conclude from them to real ones, as we may from one real line to another. Thus, although we cannot follow two diverging lines by the eye to infinity, yet we know that, if they begin to converge, it must be at a finite distance; thither we can follow them in imagination, and satisfy ourselves that if the lines begin to approach, they will not be straight, but curved.

II.—The second argument is, that the axioms are conceived as universally and necessarily true. Experience cannot give to any proposition the character of necessity. The meaning of a necessary truth, as explained by Dr. Whewell, is a proposition the negation of which is not only false but inconceivable. The test of a necessary truth is the inconceivableness of the counter proposition. The power of conceiving depends very much on our constant experience, and familiar habits of thought. When two things have often been seen and thought of together, and never in any instance seen or thought of separately, there is an increasing difficulty (which may in the end become insuperable) of conceiving the two things apart. Thus, the existence of antipodes was denied, because men could not conceive gravity acting upwards as well as downwards. The Cartesians rejected the law of gravitation, because they could not conceive a body acting where it was not. The inconceivability will be strongest where the experience is oldest and most familiar, and where nothing ever occurs to shake our conviction, or even to suggest an exception. It is thus, from the effect of constant association, that we are unable to conceive the reverse of the axioms. We have not even an analogy to help us to conceive two straight lines enclosing a space. Nay, when we imagine two straight lines, in order to conceive them enclosing a space, we repeat the very experiment that establishes the contrary. For it has been shown that imaginary lines serve as well for proving geometrical truths as lines in actual objects.

Dr. Whewell has illustrated in his own person the tendency of habitual association to make an experimental truth appear necessary. He continually asserts that propositions, known to have been discovered by genius and labour, appear, when once established, so self-evident, that, but for historical proof, we should believe that they would be recognized as necessarily true. He says, that the first law of motion might have been known to be true independently of experience, and that, at some future time, chemists may possibly come to see that the law of chemical combination in definite proportions is a necessary truth.

The logical basis of Arithmetic and Algebra. In Chapter VI., Mr. Mill examines the nature of arithmetic and algebra. The first theory that he examines is founded upon extreme Nominalism. It asserts that all the propositions in arithmetic are merely verbal, and that its processes are but the ringing of changes on a few expressions. But how, if the processes of arithmetic are mere substitutions of one expression of fact for another, does the fact itself come out changed? It is no doubt the peculiarity of arithmetic and algebra that they are the crowning example of symbolical thinking—that is, reasoning by signs, without carrying along with us the ideas represented by the signs. Algebra represents all numbers without distinction, investigating their modes of combination. Since, then, algebra is true, not merely of lines and angles like geometry, but of all things in nature, it is no wonder that the symbols should not excite in our minds ideas of any particular thing.

Mr. Mill denies that the definitions of the several numbers express only the meaning of words; like the so-called definitions of Geometry, they likewise involve an observed matter of fact.

Arithmetic is based upon inductions, and these are of two kinds: first, the definitions (improperly so called) of the numbers, and, secondly, the axioms—The sums of equals are equal; The differences of equals are equal. The inductions are strictly true of all objects, although a hypothetical element may be involved; the unit of the numbers must be the same or equal. One pound added to one pound will not make two pounds, if one pound be troy and the other avoirdupois. Mathematical certainty is certainty of inference or implication. Conclusions are true hypothetically; how far the hypothesis is true is left for separate consideration. It is of course practicable to arrive at new conclusions from assumed facts, as well as from observed facts; Descartes' theory of vortices being a pertinent example.

Criticism of Spencer's Theory. Mr. Spencer agrees with Mr. Mill in regarding the axioms as 'simply our earliest inductions from experience,' but he holds that inconceivableness is the ultimate test of all belief. And for two reasons. A belief held by all persons at all times ought to rank as a primitive truth. Secondly, the test of universal or invariable belief, is our inability to conceive the alleged truth as false. I believe that I feel cold, because I cannot conceive that I am not. So far Mr. Spencer. agrees with the intuitive school, but he differs from that school in holding the fallibility of the test of inconceivableness. It is itself an infallible test, but is liable to erroneous application; and occasional failure is incident to all tests. Mr. Spencer's doctrine, therefore, does not erect the curable, but only the incurable limitations of the conceptive faculty into laws of the outward universe.

Mr. Spencer's arguments for the test of inconceivableness are two in number. (1) Every invariable belief represents the aggregate of all past experience. The inconceivableness of a thing implies that it is wholly at variance with all that is inscribed on the register of human experience. Mr. Mill answers, even if this test of inconceivableness represents our experience, why resort to it when we can go at once to experience itself? Uniformity of experience is itself far from being universally a criterion of truth; and inconceivableness is still farther from being a test of uniformity of experience. (2) Whether inconceivability be good evidence or bad, no stronger evidence is to be obtained. In Mr. Spencer's use of the word 'inconceivable,' there is an ambiguity whence has been derived much of the plausibility of his argument. Inconceivableness may signify inability to get rid of an *idea*, or inability to get rid of a *belief*. It was in the second sense, not in the first, that antipodes were inconceivable. It is in the first sense that we cannot conceive an end to space. In Mr. Spencer's argument, inconceivable really means unbelievable. 'When Mr. Spencer says that while looking at the sun a man cannot conceive that he is looking into darkness, he means a man cannot *believe* that he is doing so.' Now, many have disbelieved the externality of matter, even although they may have been unable to *imagine* tangible objects as mere states of consciousness. One may be unable to get rid of the idea of externality, and nevertheless regard it as an illusion. Thus we believe that the earth moves, and not the sun, although we constantly conceive the sun as rising and setting, and the earth as motionless. Whether then we mean by inconceivable ness, inability to get rid of an idea or inability to get rid of a belief, Mr. Spencer's argument fails to be convincing.

HENRY L. MANSEL. Mr. Mansel has examined the subject of Intuition in his Prolegomena Logica, Chap. III.—VI., and in his Metaphysics. He takes up four kinds of necessity: mathematical, metaphysical, logical, and moral. He, to a great degree, follows Kant and Sir W. Hamilton.

I.—MATHEMATICAL NECESSITY. Mr. Mansel adopts the criterion of Necessity, enounced by Leibnitz. Whatever truths we must admit as everywhere and always necessary, must arise, not from observation, but from the constitution of the mind. Attempts have indeed been made to explain this necessity by a constant association of ideas, but associations, however frequent and uniform, fail to produce a higher conviction than one of mere physical necessity.

1. *The Axioms of Geometry.* The axioms of Geometry contain both analytical and synthetical judgments, (the distinction corresponding to Mill's verbal and real propositions).*

It is upon the synthetical judgments that the dispute turns. Are those axioms *à priori*, or derived from experience? Mr. Mansel says that Mr. Mill's argument contradicts the direct evidence of consciousness, and, however powerful as an *argumentum ad hominem* against Dr. Whewell, fails to meet the real question at issue. 'What is required is to account, not for the necessity of geometrical axioms as *truths* relating to objects without the mind, but as *thoughts* relating to objects within.' 'Why must I invest imaginary objects with attributes not contained in the definition of them? I can imagine the sun remaining continually fixed in the meridian, or a stone sinking 99 times and floating the 100th; and yet my experience of the contrary is as invariable as my experience of the geometrical properties of bodies.' Why then do we attribute a higher necessity to the axioms of Geometry? The answer is taken direct from Kant. It is because space is itself an *à priori* notion, not derived from without, but part of the original furniture of the mind. The author here draws a distinction between the part played by imagination in empirical and in necessary judgments. In empirical judgments, its value depends upon the fidelity of its adherency to the original. Geometrical truths, on the other hand, are absolutely true of the objects of imagination, but only nearly true of real objects. The reason is, that the truths of physical science depend on experience alone, but geometry relates to the figures of that *à priori* space, which is the indispensable condition of all experience.

2. *Arithmetic.* Arithmetic is richly, as geometry is scantily,

* Analytical judgments are: 'The whole is greater than its part;' 'If equals be added to equals, the sums are equal;' 'Things that are equal to the same are equal to each other.' Synthetical judgments are: 'A straight line is the shortest distance between two points;' 'Two straight lines which, being met by a third, make the interior angles less than two right angles, will meet, if produced.'

supplied with *à priori* principles. 'It is not by reasoning we learn that two and two make four, nor from this proposition can we in any way deduce that four and two make six.' We must have recourse in each separate case to the senses or the imagination, and, by presenting to the one or to the other a number of individual objects corresponding to each term separately, *envisage* the resulting sum.*

No number is capable of definition. Six cannot be defined as 5 + 1. In this view of Arithmetic, Mansel remarks that he differs from Leibnitz, Hegel, and Mill. [It is not proper to put Mill along with Leibnitz in this connexion.]

II.—METAPHYSICAL NECESSITY. Metaphysics, as well as Mathematics, has been regarded as possessed of Synthetical judgments. Two are selected for examination, the Principles of Substance and Causality.

1. *The Principle of Substance* is that all objects of perception are qualities that exist in some subject to which they belong. Reid said a ball has colour and figure, but it is not colour and figure; it is something that has colour and figure,—it is a substance. Berkeley thought it more consonant even with common sense to reject this imperceptible support of perceived attributes. Hume observed that, as we are conscious of nothing but impressions and ideas, we may as well throw away the barren figment of Mind. In opposition to this, Reid appealed to the Principle of Substance as a dictate of common sense. But are we conscious of substance? Reid and Stewart have again and again conceded that we are not; they have consequently abandoned the only position from which a successful attack could be made on either Berkeley or Hume. Mr. Mansel therefore, after Maine de Biran, affirms that we are immediately conscious of *Self* as substance. The one intuited substance is myself, in the form of a power conscious of itself. The notion of substance, thus derived, may be applied to other conscious beings, but not farther. In regard to physical phenomena, we have no *positive* notion of substance other than the phenomena themselves. Mr. Mansel is thus unable to prove substance against Berkeley, but he nevertheless complains that Berkeley denied, instead of merely doubting, the existence of matter. In conclusion, it is not a necessary truth that all sensible qualities belong to a subject. 'Nor is it correct to call it a fundamental law of human belief; if by that expression is meant anything more than an assertion of the universal tendency of men to liken other things to themselves, and to speak of them under forms of expression adapted to such likeness, far beyond the point where the parallel fails.'

* In a note, Mr. Mansel adds, 'The real point at issue is not whether 4 and 2 + 2 are at bottom identical—so that *both being given*, an analysis of each will ultimately show their correspondence; but whether the former notion, definition and all, is contained in the latter. In other words, whether a man who has never learned to count beyond two, could obtain 3, 4, 5, and all higher numbers, by mere dissection of the numbers which he possesses already.'

2. *The Principle of Causality.*—Whatever begins to exist must take place in consequence of some cause. Hume and Brown regard cause as mere invariable sequence. This theory of causation confounds two facts. That every event must have some antecedent or other, is one thing; that this particular event must have this particular antecedent, is a very different thing. The uniformity of nature is only a law of things, an observed fact, the contradictory of which is at any time conceivable. This portion of the principle of causation is not a necessary truth. But that every event must have some antecedent or other is a necessary truth. For we must think every event as occurring in time, and therefore as related to some antecedent in time. Thus far Mr. Mansel adopts the theory of Sir W. Hamilton.

The analysis that resolves causation into mere temporal antecedents is, however, imperfect. To complete the notion of cause, we must add the idea of *productive power*. Reid was unable to meet Hume's theory of causation, as he was unable to meet his theory of substance, and in both cases for the same reason. He denied a consciousness of mind as distinguished from its states and operations. Hume showed that volition had no power to move a limb, for paralysis might supervene, and the supposed power of volition would be destroyed. Mr. Mansel seeks for an intuition of power. 'The intuition of Power is not immediately given in the action of matter upon matter; nor yet can it be given in the action of matter upon mind, nor in that of mind upon matter; for to this day we are utterly ignorant how matter and mind operate upon each other.' Where, then, is such an intuition to be found? *In mind as determining its own modifications.* 'In every act of volition, I am fully conscious that it is in my power to form the resolution or to abstain; and this constitutes the presentative consciousness of free will and of power.' The idea of power is thus a relation between ourselves and our volitions (not our movements). Can any similar relation exist between the heat of fire and the melting of wax? It cannot be said that there is; and thus Causality, as applied to matter, is a negative notion. The only positive meaning of cause is either some antecedent or an invariable antecedent. Mr. Mansel (in this respect following Hamilton) draws attention to the fact that by breaking through the objective necessity of Causality, a door is opened for the admission of free-will.

III.—LOGICAL NECESSITY consists of the three laws of thought, the well-known principles of Identity, Contradiction, and Excluded Middle. The discussion of those laws, however, falls more within the province of logic.

IV.—MORAL NECESSITY. Moral judgments are necessary, as, *e.g.*, ingratitude and treachery must at all times be worthy of condemnation. (For the theory of duty, see ETHICAL SYSTEMS, Mansel.)

C.—On Happiness.

The highest application of the facts and laws of the mind is to Human Happiness. The doctrines relative to the Feelings have the most direct bearing on this end. It may be useful to resume briefly the various considerations bearing upon Happiness, and to compare them with the maxims that have grown up in the experience of mankind. We shall thus also supply an indispensable chapter of Ethics.

Happiness being defined the surplus of pleasure over pain, its pursuit must lie in accumulating things agreeable, and in warding off the opposites. The susceptibilities of the mind to enjoyment should be gratified to the utmost, and the susceptibilities to suffering should be spared to the utmost. It is impossible to contest this general conclusion, without altering the signification of the word. Still, the practical carrying out of the maxim, under all the complications of the human system, bodily and mental, demands many adjustments and reservations.

If the enumeration of Muscular Feelings, Sensations, and Emotions be complete, it contains all our pleasures and pains. It is unnecessary to repeat the list in detail. On the side of PLEASURE, we have, as leading elements:—Muscular Exercise, Rest after exercise; Healthy Organic Sensibility in general, and Alimentary Sensations in particular; Sweet Tastes and Odours; Soft and Warm Touches; Melody and Harmony in Sound; Cheerful Light and Coloured Spectacle; the Sexual feelings; Liberty after constraint; Novelty and Wonder; the warm Tender Emotions; Sexual, Maternal and Paternal Love, Friendship, Admiration, Esteem, and Sociability in general; Self-complacency and Praise; Power, Influence, Command; Revenge; the Interest of Plot and Pursuit; the charms of Knowledge and Intellectual exertion; the cycle of the Fine Arts, culminating in Music, Painting, and Poetry, with which we couple the enjoyment of Natural Beauty; the satisfaction attainable through Sympathy and the Moral Sentiment. In such an array, we seem to have all, or nearly all, the ultimate gratifications of human nature. They may spread themselves by association on allied objects, and especially on the means or instrumentality for procuring them, as Health, Wealth, Knowledge, Power, Dignified Position, Virtue, Society, Country, Life.

The PAINS are mostly implied in the negation of the pleasures Muscular fatigue, Organic derangements and diseases, Cold, Hunger, ill Tastes and Odours; Skin lacerations; Discords in Sound; Darkness, Gloom, and excessive glare of Light; ungratified Sexual Appetite; Restraint after Freedom; Monotony; Fear in all its manifestations; privation in the Affections, Sorrow; Self-humiliation and Shame; Impotence and Servitude; disappointed Revenge; baulked Pursuit or Plot; Intellectual Contradictions and Obscurity; the Æsthetically Ugly; Harrowed Sympathies; an evil Conscience.

As summed up in groups or aggregates, we have the pains or evils of Ill Health, Poverty, Toil, Ignorance, Meanness and Impotence, Isolation, and general Obstruction, Death.

Looking at human nature on the whole, we may single out as pleasures of the first order, Maternal love, Sexual love, Paternal love, Friendship, Complacency and Approbation, Power and Liberty newly achieved, Relishes, Stimulants, Warmth after chillness, and the higher delights of the ordinary Senses. In the absence of any considerable pains, a small selection of these gratifications, regularly supplied, would make up a joyful existence.

There are various practically important distinctions among our pleasures. In the first place, a certain number are *primary* susceptibilities of the human constitution; as the organic pleasures, the simpler gratifications of the five senses, the appetite of sex, and the elementary emotions. Others are *cultivated* or acquired, or are incidental to a high mental cultivation; as the higher susceptibilities to Fine Art, the affections and tender associations, the pleasures of knowledge. While cultivation may thus enlarge the sphere of pleasure, it necessarily creates new susceptibilities to pain; the absence or negation of those qualities rendered artificially agreeable must needs be painful.

Another distinction of importance is between the pleasures that appear as *appetite*, and those that are *desired* only in consequence of gratification. The natural appetites are well known; to refuse the objects of these is to inflict suffering. Other pleasures, if unstimulated, are unfelt: the rustic, inexperienced in the excitement of cities, has no painful longings for their pleasures; not through the want of susceptibility, but from there being no craving for such things prior to actual tasting. Human beings cannot be contented without the gratification of natural appetites; as to the privation of other pleasures, mere ignorance is bliss.

While it is a property of pleasure generally to prompt to effort and to desire without limit, there are certain circumstances that neutralize this tendency. One of these is the occurrence of pain at a certain stage, as when appetite palls by exhausted irritability. Another mode of quenching the insatiability of the pleasurable is found in the soothing tendency of the massive pleasures; a gentle and diffused stimulus is quieting and soporific. These constitute an important exception to the law of pleasure, and give birth to our serene and satisfying enjoyments, as warmth, affection, and the forms of beauty suggestive of repose. But Fine Art also contains, and glories in, ways of stimulating unbounded desire, under the name of the Ideal.

A farther mode of classifying pleasures is into—(1) those that are productive of pleasure to others, as the sympathies and benevolent affections, and all the pleasurable associations with virtuous conduct; (2) the gratifications that all may share in, as most of the Fine Art pleasures; (3) those that are in their nature attainable by all, but are consumed by the user, as many material agencies—food, space, house furniture, and, with a certain qualification, love, which, in the actual, is limited in quantity; (4) pleasures where a single person is gratified at the expense of others, as in power, dignity, and fame. The one extreme is identified with the harmony and mutual sympathy of human beings, the other with rivalry and mutual hostility.

The leading circumstance of Happiness—the accumulation of whatever can yield pleasure and remove pain—is qualified, in the first place, by the Law of RELATIVITY, as formerly explained. The operation of this law has a number of pregnant consequences, more or less taken into account in men's practice.

1. Absolute and entire Novelty of Sensation is necessary to the highest zest of any pleasure. A newly attained delight—a mother's first child, a first love, is beyond what can ever be realized again.

2. Every pleasure must be remitted in order to maintain its efficacy. Only for a certain limited time can the thrill of any delight be maintained; the stimulus then requires to be withdrawn for a period corresponding to the intensity of the effect.

3. In order to maintain a considerable flow of delight, each person must possess a variety of sources of pleasure; and the more that these differ in kind, or the more complete the alternation, the greater the happiness. It is hopeless to attain much enjoyment by playing upon any single string, however acute may be its thrill.

4. The reaction from pain is a source of great delight; as in restoration to health, the dispersing of a deep gloom or melancholy, the recovery from panic, the quenching of a long-repressed appetite. It is not true, however, that all pleasure demands to be preceded by pain; mere remission is enough to dispose us for the gratification of food, exercise, music, or society. The distinction between the two kinds of pleasures is an important one; the last are our best and purest delights, although the first may by virtue of previous suffering be very intense.

5. Alternation is of great avail in lightening the pains of toil. When exhausted by one kind of work, we may yet be capable of some other, until such time as the system generally is worn out. The change, however, must be real: as in passing from mental work to bodily exertion; from reflection to expression; from abstract speculation to business; from science to fine art; from isolated action to co-operation with others.

6. The same emotion may be prolonged in its resonance by mere change of subject. The elation of the sublime is renewed in passing from one vast prospect to another, as in journeying through Alpine scenery.

7. The extension of our Happiness depends upon the acquiring of tastes, or susceptibilities of delight, in addition to what we have by nature. This will be again alluded to among the bearings of education on happiness.

The relations of Happiness to HEALTH are of great importance, but somewhat complicated in the statement.

Health must be defined as not simply the absence of physical pain, or derangement, but also a certain amount of vigour both for action and for sensibility. The healthy condition is not in itself a pleasure, except in the moments of recovery from illness, or of invigoration after depression.

It is manifestly essential that each one should have vigour sufficient to bear up against all unavoidable labours and burdens; without this, life must be a perpetual sense of oppression.

There is a still closer connexion between health and happiness, in the fact that certain physical functions of the nerves, and of some other special organs, are expressly allied to our sensibility. The human system has many sides, and many functions; and of the mental manifestations, there are three distinct departments, corresponding to the divisions of the mind. Now, happiness is not the immediate result of either Volition or Intelligence, but of *Feeling*, or the Emotional side of our being. A natural endowment for emotion, and great vigour and freshness in the organs concerned in emotion,—partly the Brain, and partly the Digestion, and the Secreting processes formerly shown to be related to feeling—make the physical basis of susceptibility to pleasure; hence the conservation of all these functions is the kind of health that directly bears on happiness.

It is well known that there are great differences in diseases, as respects their influence on the tone of enjoyment. Certain forms of nervous derangement, indigestion in most of its varieties, enfeebled circulation, are immediate sources of mental depression; on the other hand, the brain may be far on the road to paralysis, the heart may be in a state of degeneration, the lungs may be forming tubercles, the kidney affected with a mortal disease, while as yet but little diminution has taken place in the aptitude for enjoyment. In the one class of ailments, happiness is impaired almost from the first; in the other, the loss appears in shortened life. In the first case, there is a self-correcting reminder; in the second, a fatal sense of security, which as yet mankind have never learned to surmount by an effort of the reason.

As a general rule, hardly any employment of one's means and resources is so advantageous as the maintenance of a high state of vigour, both in the body in general, and in the organs of emotional sensibility in particular. Better to surrender many objects of pleasure, than to impair the organs of pleasure; few stimulants in a highly conditioned system are preferable to a greater number in an exhausted state of the sensibility. The rule may not be without exceptions; a less degree of health, coupled with one's supreme gratification, is more desirable than the very highest degree without that. One may be happier in the town, although healthier in the country. But, on the whole, the tendency is to undervalue the element of physical freshness in our pursuits, not to see that the loss of physical tone, consequent on the excess of toil, is a chief cause of our disappointment in attaining the objects of our toil. The man that has made his fortune, and sacrificed his zest for enjoyment, is an unsuccessful man.

The problem of health necessarily involves all the special precautions against the known injuries and ailments. It involves the still more comprehensive purpose expressed generally by the proportioning of Expenditure to means of Support;—that is to say, the limitation of exhausting agencies—labour, irregularities, excesses; and the husbanding of sustaining and renovating agencies—nutrition, air, regimen, and all the hygienic resources. It is farther desirable that the economical adjustment of waste and supply should be commenced from our earliest years, and not, as usually happens, after a conscious reduction of vigour has roused the individual to a sense of imminent danger. There is a known proportion of labour, rest, nourishment, and exciting pleasure, suited to the average constitution, and compatible with the full duration of life; on this each one is safe to proceed at the outset, until the specialities of constitution are known. Any one presuming by virtue of youthful vigour and the absence of immediate bad consequences, to abridge the usual allowance of food, of sleep, of rest, of bodily exercise, and not at the same time owning any counterbalancing sources of renovation, is perilling life or happiness.

The special bearings of ACTIVITY and Occupation on Happiness, have been almost exhausted under the emotion of Plot-interest and Pursuit. Irrespective of the necessity of productive labour or industry, a great deal is constantly said respecting occupation as such, with a view to happiness. Some of our pleasures are pleasures of Activity, as bodily and mental exercise in the fresh condition of the system, and the putting forth of special energies and endowments; these are enhanced either by yielding valuable products, or by gratifying the pride of superiority to others. But the all-important feature of occupation is the anæsthetic tendency of pursuit, already dwelt upon. Whatever may be the number or variety of our passive enjoyments, we cannot fill the day with these; the greatest compass of emotional susceptibility would be exhausted by a succession of pleasurable stimulants, with uninterrupted self-consciousness. The alternation of the object-regards with the subject-states is indispensable to avoiding the ennui of too much conscious excitement; and this is most readily supplied in the engrossment of pursuit. By spending the larger part of the day in the indifferentism of a routine occupation, we are prepared, during the remainder, to burst out into flashes of keen self-consciousness. The fewer our pleasures, the more needful for us to have a deadening occupation to fill the time, to banish self-consciousness when it could only be painful.

The explanation of the use of Activity to happiness implies the limitation. If the susceptibility to pleasure—the emotional temperament—be highly developed, and the sources of pleasure numerous and unexhausting, the portion of life deadened by

KNOWLEDGE.

occupation and pursuit may be proportionally contracted, to give scope to the wakened sensibilities—the full consciousness of enjoyment.

Happiness is materially affected by KNOWLEDGE, or an acquaintance with the course of nature and of humanity. The characteristic of knowledge is accuracy, certainty, precision; its highest form is expressed by Science.

That a knowledge of the order of nature is requisite for extracting the good, and neutralizing the evil, agencies is plain enough. But the wide compass of the knowable cannot be overtaken by one mind; there is a division of labour; each department having its experts, relied on by the rest of the community. What kind and amount of knowledge it is advisable for all to possess, with a view to happiness, may not be easily agreed upon. The following considerations are offered on this point.

1. The acquisition of knowledge in any considerable amount, or to any great degree of precision, is toilsome, costly, and unpalatable to the mass of mankind; so that to dispense with it makes a clear gain, provided the want is fraught with no serious results. By favourable accidents of situation—such as a lot with few complications and risks, a ready access to skilled advisers, an aptitude for enduring the commoner hazards, a surplus of worldly means to remedy blunders, and general good fortune,—a small amount of acquired knowledge may answer all the ends of life. Ignorance implies large dependence on others, and on the accidents of things; and, according to circumstances, is blissful or tragic in its issues.

2. On the supposition that one is willing to pay the cost of acquisition, for the greater command and certainty of the means of happiness, the subjects directly applicable to the end appear to be these. In the first place, there should be a familiarity with our Bodily Constitution; a knowledge still more requisite when as parents, guardians, teachers, we have the control of the lives of others. In the next place, the elements of Physical and Chemical science, besides their direct bearing on the physiology of the human frame, have many collateral applications in everyday life, as in matters relating to cleanliness, warmth, clothing, purity of the air, cookery, &c. In the third place, some knowledge of the Mind, whether attained by observation, by theory, or by both conjoined, is of value in appreciating character and dispositions, and in the guidance and management of those about us. Fourthly, knowledge of the course of Affairs in the world generally, arrived at by observation and by historical and political studies, is essential to the guidance of our footsteps in the society we live in. Fifthly, whatever studies lead to an accurate estimate of Evidence, are of the highest import; their application extending much beyond our own happiness. A large number of our decisions must be made upon evidence that is only Probable; and to find out where the preponderance lies needs either practical or scientific training. The aptitude for judging according to the

reasons of things, if it were more widely possessed, would be seen to ramify in endless ameliorations of the lot of humanity. Besides the success that would attend expectations so based, it is in the nature of such reasonings to command *agreement* among different minds, and thereby conduce to harmonious co-operation, where at present the rule is distraction and discord.

The poetical and romantic pictures, cherished for the sake of our aspirations and ideals, are directly opposed to the conditions of the knowledge now depicted, and add to our difficulties, both in attaining it, and in putting it in practice. Yet, as these ideals, although they should be moderately indulged in, cannot be expelled from human life, it is a point of some moment, to know what is their exact bias, and to make allowance for that, when we have to quit fancy for the domain of fact. Now, the exaggerating tendencies of artistic embellishment, to be guarded against, relate mainly to the possibilities of happiness; giving an overstrained account of what human nature can do, and can enjoy. The romancist uniformly oversteps the limitations of the human faculties, and throws out lures to make us attempt too much; an exact knowledge of the physical and the mental laws, and of that crowning aspect of them, the general law called Correlation or Persistence of Force, is the best counteractive.

3. In knowledge of the kind now specified, lies the means of conquering the happiness-destroyer, Fear. For the sake of this great victory, Epicurus thought the sacrifice of religion not too much. No other source of courage is comparable to knowledge; it teaches what fears are baseless, without sapping the wise precautions against evil.

4. When the attainment of such knowledge as is now specified, is a special liking or individual taste, the concurrence is one fortunate for happiness to self, and a power of good for all around. Each highly-cultivated intelligence, combining exactness with extent of acquirement, is a luminous body thrown out on the dark ways of human life.

The bearings upon Happiness, of EDUCATION or Training, in its widest compass, are next to be noted, the special department of high intellectual culture having been now sufficiently adverted to.

1. Whatever training and instructions can do to fit us for our necessary avocations and labours, adds to our happiness. The pains of labour are alleviated by a good early training to the work. The horseman that has been habituated to the saddle from childhood, is not only more efficient, but more at ease than the late learner. Pitt's training in oratory under his father, contributed alike to his greatness, and to his enjoyment of the exercise of speaking.

2. A training to inevitable restraints, if commenced from early years, and sustained without intermission, triumphs over all uneasiness. Such is the submission of the soldier born in the army, and the habituation of the priest to his artificial mode of life.

It is on this principle, that the child carefully trained to prudential and moral restraints, and so secured against the relapses of the neglected offspring of vice and poverty, is placed, by that fact alone, on a vantage ground of happiness.

3. The amusements and amenities of life are only enjoyed to the full after special training. Even our games, sports, and pastimes, must be the subject of instruction; while the exercise and enjoyment of the Fine Arts—Music, Painting, Elocution— involve the cost of special masters. What are termed accomplishments are artificial and refined pleasures; they are a pure addition to the sum of enjoyment, and have no other meaning.

A very large mass of human pleasure is mixed up with our sociability; and much of our education consists in fitting us for intercourse with others; the end being to reduce the friction of uncultivated minds associating together, and to increase the pleasures of co-operation, sympathy, and affection.

An acquaintance with foreign languages may be classed among the means of pleasure. For people generally, they are the luxuries of education. The ancient tongues introduce us to a large fund of novel impressions; the languages of our contemporaries open an additional field of fresh and varied interest. It may be doubted, however, if the cost of the acquirement is repaid, in the majority of cases, by the advantage.

(4) Tastes may be formed and strengthened by education, and every taste that there are means to gratify, is a part of happiness. An instructor, or a companion, may foster in us a taste for plants, for conchology, for antiquities; the meaning of which is that these several objects find a greater response of joyful feeling. Whether such an acquirement is desirable on the whole depends on circumstances; the education thus bestowed must occupy a space in one's life, and may possibly exclude some more valuable acquisition.

Education with a view to the maximum of happiness is a very different thing from education to greatness, or the maximum of efficiency for some important function. For happiness, tastes and accomplishments should be widely extended; even if there be one leading taste, it should not be exclusive; the law of relativity forbids the highest enjoyment to the monopoly of the mind with a single subject. Yet such monopoly is the condition of the greatest vigour of the faculties for some one end. The man that towers in science, in art, in statesmanship, in business, needs to be so engrossed with his subject, as to be excluded from variety of interests; he may have the reward of his greatness in moments of triumphant superiority, but he is liable to periods of protracted ennui.

As there is a natural constitution fitted for happiness, so there is an education possessing a like fitness.

There can be no very great happiness without paying regard to INDIVIDUALITY. The ideal state is the gratification of each taste, and the exercise of each faculty, in exact proportion to their degree of prominence. If the natural sociability be great, the opportunities should correspond; if little, there should be an exemption from society. Many persons have some one prevailing bent, which being gratified makes happiness in itself, and which being refused leaves a blank not to be otherwise filled up. Sokrates declared that he would rather die than give up his vocation of cross-questioning. Faraday was miserable till he was placed in Davy's laboratory. Human beings differ so much, that the very same lot may be felicity to one and wretchedness to another.

The individuality that is not to be satisfied without a disproportionate share of worldly advantages being put out of the account, the most important circumstance is a fitting Occupation. To ascertain betimes the most decided bent and aptitude of each person, and to find a career suited to that, is the prime requisite of a fortunate lot. Next to a harmonizing avocation is the choice of Recreations and tastes, which may infuse gladness into the hours of leisure, the holiday weeks, and the years of retirement. This, well thought of, and prepared for, by early choice, by education and fostering, will make oases in the desert waste of an unattractive profession.

The existence of unsatisfied DESIRE is, so far as it goes, unhappiness. An effort of judgment must pronounce whether we should endeavour to suppress a desire impracticable, or retain it either as a goal of pursuit or as an ideal longing. Forced contentment is the result of the first alternative; activity in actual, or in imaginary pursuit, is the second.

If an object is attainable by efforts not out of proportion to its value, we naturally pursue it. Contentment in the midst of wretchedness, squalor, poverty, is no virtue.

The indulgence in Ideals is a nicer question. Without giving some scope to our longings for higher fortunes and greater excellence, we should feel that we were cribbed, cabined, and confined; while such longings are liable to unfit us for seizing the actual. One of the most prudent and systematic of livers, Andrew Combe, pled for a moderate indulgence in fiction; there is neither possibility nor propriety in excluding poetry and romance from the class of open pleasures. Ideals are a kind of *stimulation*, and the wisest will always differ as to the limits of their employment; although there can be little doubt as to which is the safe side.

We are next to consider the relation of Happiness to WEALTH, or worldly abundance and advantages. At first sight, this would seem a simple matter. Not merely the terms of the definition of happiness, but all the conditions now considered, suppose a certain amount of worldly means; health, knowledge, education, individuality, are not to be obtained except at some expense; and are attainable in higher degrees according to the resources at our disposal. The general rule is apparently what is expressed in the remark of Sydney Smith, that he was a happier man for every additional guinea that came to him. Such at least is the deliberate judgment of the great mass of mankind, and the guiding principle of nearly all their labours; some may be industrious from other motives, but the general multitude labour for money. And scarcely any limit is admitted to the pursuit; it would seem as if, at no pitch of pecuniary fortune, farther acquisition were considered futile.

Some of the consequences of this principle in its naked and unqualified aspect are undoubtedly grave and unpalatable to contemplate. Whoever would wish to believe in something like equality among human beings, must revolt at a doctrine which proportions enjoyment to wealth, and assigns to the millions of mankind a lot incompatible with any tolerable share of happiness. Moreover, the prize offered to cupidity, in the statement of such a principle, cannot but seem dangerous to the safety of possessions, and the order of society. Accordingly, moralists in every age have sought to invalidate the doctrine, by a counter statement of evils attaching to the possession of great riches. With some truth, a vast amount of exaggeration and rhetoric has been infused into the attack on opulence. That the rich are not perfectly happy is a fact, that they are not happier than the poor is an untenable position. Wealth multiplies the pleasures and alleviates the pains of life; and if it brings any evils peculiar to itself, it also brings remedies.

The most obvious temptation of wealth, coupled with idleness, is to immoderate indulgences. Another is the aiming at too many excitements, which necessarily entails troubles in management, as well as expenditure. A certain aptitude for business is necessary to smooth the possession and enjoyment of wealth; there may be individuals so devoid of this turn as to feel acutely the disadvantages; but, in their case, poverty is equally hopeless. To observe the limitations of the human powers, both in labour and in enjoyment, is not as yet the virtue of any class, while it is practicable only to a certain grade of abundance.

There are vices of the rich that mar their happiness; but most of them are also vices of the poor. So there are virtues of the poor favourable to happiness; all which are equally possible, and still more fruitful, to the rich. That prime requisite, Health, is very imperfectly secured in the lowest grades even of respectable citizenship. The public registers have demonstrated that mortality and disease diminish at every rise in the scale of wealth. The difference in the means of Knowledge and Education is no less strongly in favour of the superior happiness of the rich.

The relationship of Happiness to VIRTUE, or Duty, is difficult to state with impartiality and precision. Here too we encounter the fervid views of the oratorical moralist, sanctified by the usage of all countries. It has been often laid down, that happiness, full and complete, is found in duty and in nothing else.

In order to see whether this assertion admits of being verified, it is necessary to approach the question from the other end. We must begin with the clear and undeniable fact, that duty, or virtue, is a sacrifice or surrender of something agreeable, from a regard to the interests of others; as when we pay our share of public burdens, and restrain our desires for what is not our own. It is the essential of such acts to be painful; although, under certain circumstances, they may become agreeable. It would be a self-contradiction to maintain that acts of virtue are, from their very nature, and at all times, delightful; virtue in that case would not be virtue; being swallowed up in pleasure, it would be viewed simply as pleasure, and often disapproved of, as excessive and tending to vice.

We have already seen, under what limitations benevolence is a source of pleasure [p. 244]; the main condition being reciprocation, in some form or other. There is nothing necessarily self-rewarding either in benevolence or in duty. As regards duty, the principle of reciprocation also applies; when our abstaining from injury to other persons insures their abstaining from injury to us, we have the full value of our self-denial. It is the endeavour of society to secure this kind of reciprocity, and not only so, but to make each one's abstinence indispensable to their immunity. Virtue then becomes happiness, not by nature, but by institution. If a man can reap the advantages of society without paying the cost, he is happy in his vice, and would be less happy in his virtue.

It is one of the effects of moral training to create revulsion of feeling to whatever society deems wrong; vice is clothed with painful associations, and virtue is the only road compatible with happiness. Such essentially is Conscience. The person trained to a high intensity of these feelings is unable to take delight in things really delightful, if they are forbidden by conscience, echoing society.

The only remaining circumstance that spoils the happiness of doing wrong is the existence of a certain amount of sympathy, or natural disinterestedness, in each one's constitution. The effect of sympathy is to make one shrink from the infliction of obvious pain, and to neutralize, in some degree, the pleasure of following out a natural bent at the expense of misery to others.

But for these three circumstances,—sure retribution, the associations of moral training, and a fund of natural sympathy—the neglect of duty would, to all appearance, be the direct road to happiness. If we look to the facts, and not to what we wish and endeavour to bring about, we find that the happiest man is not the man of highest virtues, but he that can obtain social reciprocity and immunity, at a moderate outlay. To realize the greatest happiness of virtue, we should be careful to conform to the standard of the time, neither rising above nor falling beneath it; we should make our virtues apparent and showy, and perform them at the least sacrifice to ourselves: we should have our associations with duty, as well as our natural sympathies, only in a moderate degree of strength.

It is thus in vain to identify virtue with prudence, that is, with happiness. Duty is in part, and only in part, coincident with enjoyment. To form men to the highest virtues, we must appeal to other motives than their happiness, to the sources of disinterested conduct so often alluded to. It will then appear that very great virtue is often opposed to happiness; the applause bestowed on the sublimely virtuous man is by way of making good a deficiency.

The happiness of RELIGION, in its relation to a future life, is not comparable to any of the enjoyments of this life. But as experienced through the sensibilities of our common nature, it may be not improperly brought into the comparison. The religious affections grow up like any others: they are more or less favoured by natural constitution, cherished by exercise, and echoed from all venerated objects and symbols. The religious fears are overcome by the same laws of our being as any other fears. The resulting happiness is the predominance of the affections over the fears. The pleasures of devotion have their fixed amount, in each individual, like the pleasures of knowledge or of fine art.

The securing of Happiness in any considerable degree, supposes METHOD, or a plan of life, well conceived, and steadily adhered to. This is only to apply to the crowning end, what is necessary in the subordinate pursuits of Health, Wealth, or Knowledge. Each one must choose what pleasures to follow out, what desires to suppress, what training to undergo, so as on the whole to make the most of one's individual lot. Misconceptions of ends, ignorance of means, succumbing to passing impulses, are fatal to success in all pursuits; the victim of such weaknessess loses the game, or must be saved by some other power.

It has to be admitted, however, that the stretch of energy requisite to compass so large an end, costs a great deal to the system; it is a heavy per centage deducted from the realized happiness. There are not a few instances where enjoyment is attained without any plan at all, the accidents being favourable; just as many persons have health, or wealth, without a thought of one or other; being all the happier that thought can be dispensed with.

Some individualities are so unfitted for prudential foresight, that they must either come under the sway of others or be left to the accidents. A being of a higher order, looking before and after, will desire a plan, and endeavour to abide by it. Forming an estimate of life as a whole, such a being has a settled tone of mind corresponding to that, not being much elated nor much depressed, by the fluctuations on one side or the other. If attainable by the individual, this settled and balanced estimate is worthy of the highest endeavours. It might be artificially aided, by diary or record, which would recall to mind, more forcibly than the best memory, the tenor of life in the long run, to quell the exaggerations of the passing moods.

D.—*Classifications of the Mind.*

THE INTELLECTUAL POWERS.

1. THOMAS AQUINAS.

First, Powers preceding the Intellect.

I.—VEGETATIVE. 1. *Nutrition;* 2. *Growth;* 3. *Generation.*

II.—EXTERNAL SENSES (five in number).

III.—INTERNAL SENSES. 1. *Common Sense* (the sense that compares and distinguishes the objects of the several senses); 2. *Imagination;* 3. *Æstimativa* (discerning in objects what is not revealed by the senses, as the enmity of the wolf to the sheep); 4. *Memory* (including Reminiscence).

Secondly, The Intellect—comprising, 1. *Memory* (the retention or conservation of *species*); 2. *Reason;* 3. *Intelligentia* (properly an act of the intellect); 4. both *practical* and *speculative* Reason; 5. *Conscience.*

2. HERBERT OF CHERBURY.

His classification is mixed, and we give it as it stands, including Emotions as well as Intellect.

I.—NATURAL INSTINCT (explained under the history of Intuition, Appendix B).

II.—INTERNAL SENSE. 1. *Incorporeal* (having no physical antecedents, as joy, love, hope, trust); 2. *Corporeal*, arising from the *humores* (hunger, thirst, lust, melancholy, &c.); 3. *Objective* feelings *(ab objectis invecti)*, including certain pleasures and pains derived from external objects; 4. *Mixed Sense.*

III.—EXTERNAL SENSES, not confined absurdly to five; for there are as many senses as there are *differentiæ* in the objects of sense.

IV.—DISCURSUS, which is the faculty of intellect proper.

3. GASSENDI.

I.—SENSE.

II.—PHANTASY.

III.—INTELLECT. 1. *Apprehension of God* or Spirits; 2. *Reflection;* and 3. *Reasoning.*

4. THOMAS REID.

1. *External Senses;* 2. *Memory;* 3. *Conception* or Simple Apprehension; 4. *Abstraction* (Nominalism and Realism); 5. *Judgment* (First Truths); 6. *Reasoning* (Demonstration and Probable Reasoning); 7. *Taste.*

5. DUGALD STEWART.

1. *Consciousness;* 2. *External Perception;* 3. *Attention;* 4. *Conception;* 5. *Abstraction;* 6. *Association of Ideas;* 7. *Memory;* 8. *Imagination;* 9. *Reasoning* (taking up Logic).

6. THOMAS BROWN.

I.—EXTERNAL AFFECTIONS. 1. *Sensation;* 2. *Organic States.*

II.—INTERNAL AFFECTIONS. 1. *Intellectual States.* (1) Simple

THE INTELLECTUAL POWERS.—THE EMOTIONS.

Suggestion (the laws of Association); and (2) *Relative Suggestion* (Comparison, Resemblance). 2. *The Emotions* (given in detail afterwards).

7. SIR W. HAMILTON.

Sir W. Hamilton enumerates six faculties:—1. *Presentative* (the Senses and Self-consciousness); 2. *Conservative* (mere retention in the memory); 3. *Reproductive* (depends on the Laws of Association); 4. *Elaborative* (Abstraction and Reasoning); 5. *Representative* (Imagination); 6. *Regulative* (the faculty of *à priori* truths).

8. SAMUEL BAILEY.

I.—DISCERNING. 1. *Through the Senses;* 2. Not through the Senses (*Introspection*).

II.—CONCEIVING, having ideas or mental representations. 1. Conceiving *without individual recognition;* 2. Conceiving *with individual recognition;* 3. *Imagining,* or conceiving under new combinations.

III.—BELIEVING, 1. *On evidence,* and 2. *without evidence.*

IV.—REASONING, 1. *Contingent,* and 2. *Demonstrative.*

9. HERBERT SPENCER.

Mr. Spencer defines *cognitions* as the *relations* subsisting among our feelings, and classifies them as follows; 1. *Presentative* cognitions (localizing sensations); 2. *Presentative-representative,* perception of the whole from a part (as when the sight of an orange brings to mind all its other attributes); 3. *Representative;* including all acts of recollection: 4. *Re-representative,* the higher abstractions formed by symbols, as in Mathematics.

10. For the sake of comparison, we may add the classification adopted in the present volume. I.—THE ANTECEDENTS OF THE INTELLECT. 1. *Muscularity,* and 2. The *Senses.* II.—THE INTELLECT. 1. *Discrimination,* or the sense of difference; 2. *Similarity,* or the sense of agreement; and 3. *Retentiveness.*

THE EMOTIONS.

1. REID.

His Active Powers are divided into three parts:—

I.—MECHANICAL PRINCIPLES OF ACTION. 1. *Instinct;* 2. *Habit.*

II.—ANIMAL PRINCIPLES. 1. *Appetites;* 2. *Desires* (Power, Esteem, Knowledge); 3. *Affections* (Benevolent and Malevolent; Passion, Disposition, Opinion).

III.—RATIONAL PRINCIPLES. 1. *Self-love;* 2. *Duty.*

2. DUGALD STEWART.

I.—INSTINCTIVE PRINCIPLES OF ACTION. 1. *Appetites;* 2. *Desires* (Knowledge, Society, Esteem, Power, Superiority); 3. *Affections* (Benevolent and Malevolent).

II.—RATIONAL AND GOVERNING PRINCIPLES OF ACTION. 1. *Prudence;* 2. *Moral Faculty;* 3. *Decency,* or a regard to character; 4. *Sympathy;* 5. the *Ridiculous;* 6. *Taste.*

3. THOMAS BROWN.

I.—IMMEDIATE, excited by present objects. 1. *Cheerfulness* and *Melancholy;* 2. *Wonder;* 3. *Languor;* 4. *Beauty;* 5. *Sublimity;* 6. the *Ludicrous;* 7. *Moral feeling;* 8. *Love* and *Hate;* 9. *Sympathy;* 10. *Pride* and *Humility.*

II.—RETROSPECTIVE. 1. *Anger;* 2. *Gratitude;* 3. *Simple Regret* and *Gladness;* 4. *Remorse* and its opposite.

III.—PROSPECTIVE. 1. The *Desires* (Continued Existence, Pleasure, Action, Society, Knowledge, Power, Affection, Glory, the Happiness of others, Evil to others); 2. *Fears;* 3. *Hope;* 4. *Expectation;* 5. *Anticipation.*

4. SIR W. HAMILTON.

Sir W. Hamilton has, first, Sensations (the five senses and organic sensations) and, secondly, the Sentiments or internal feelings. These are divided as follows: I.—THE CONTEMPLATIVE, subdivided into, 1. Those of the subsidiary faculties, including (1) those of *self-consciousness* (Tedium and its opposite), and (2) those of *Imagination* (Order, Symmetry, Unity in Variety); 2. Those of the *Elaborative* Faculty (Wit, the pleasures of Truth and Science, and the gratification of adapting Means to Ends). *Beauty* and *Sublimity* arise from the joint energy of the Imagination and the Understanding.

II.—THE PRACTICAL feelings relate to, 1. *Self-Preservation* (Hunger and Thirst, Loathing, Sorrow, Bodily pain, Anxiety, Repose, &c.); 2. *The Enjoyment of our Existence;* 3. *The Preservation of the Species;* 4. Our Tendency towards *Development* and *Perfection;* and 5. The *Moral Law.*

5. HERBERT SPENCER.

Mr. Spencer's classification runs parallel to his arrangement of the intellectual powers. 1. *Presentative feelings,* ordinarily called Sensations; 2. *Presentative-representative feelings,* including the simple emotions, as Terror; 3. *Representative feelings,* such as those roused by a descriptive poet; 4. *Re-representative feelings,* such as Property, Justice.

6. KANT.

I.—SENSUOUS, coming through—1. *Sense* (Tedium, Contentment), or 2. *Imagination* (Taste).

II.—INTELLECTUAL, from 1. the *Concepts* of the Understanding; and 2. the *Ideas* of the Reason. He takes the *Affections* and *Passions* under the Will.

7. HERBART.

Herbart, and his followers Waitz and Nahlowsky. *First,* Feelings Proper. I.—FORMAL. 1. The *general or elementary* feelings (Oppression and Relief, Exertion and Ease, Seeking and Finding, Success and Defeat, Harmony and Contrast, Power and Weakness); 2. the *Special or complicated* feelings (Expectation, Astonishment, Doubt, &c.).

II.—QUALITATIVE. 1. Feelings of *Sense;* 2. higher or *Intellectual* feelings (Truth and Probability); the Æsthetic; the Moral; the Religious.

THE LAWS OF ASSOCIATION. 91

Secondly, Complex Emotional States. I. THOSE INVOLVING CONATION (Desire or Aversion). 1. *Sympathetic* feeling; 2. *Love*, both Sensual and Ideal.

II.—STATES RESTING ON AN ORGANIC FOUNDATION. 1. The *Disposition* or mood of mind, tone, or general hilarity; 2. the *Affections*.

8. SCHLEIDLER.

I.—SENSE-FEELING. 1. Connected with *bodily existence* (Health, Depression, Hunger, &c.); 2. *Organic* (feelings of Special Sense); 3. *Inner Sense* (Temper or high spirits).

II.—FEELINGS CONNECTED WITH IDEAS. 1. Ideas from *Sense* (Disgust, Sympathy with pain); 2. from *Imagination* (Hope and Fear); 3. from *Understanding* (Shame, Reproach, &c.); 4. the *lower Æsthetic feelings* (Physical Beauty).

III.—INTELLECTUAL FEELINGS. 1. *From acquiring Knowledge;* pain of idleness; 2. *from Intellectual exercise* (Novelty, System, Order, Symmetry, Harmony and Rhythm, Simple and Complex, Wit and Humour, Comic and Ridiculous).

IV.—RATIONAL FEELINGS. 1. *Truth feelings;* 2. *the Higher Æsthetic;* 3. *Moral feelings;* 4. *Sympathetic feelings;* 5. *Religious feelings.*

THE LAWS OF ASSOCIATION.

We subjoin a brief note to illustrate the Principles of Association, as they have been stated by various authors.

1. Aristotle had grasped the fact of association, holding that 'every mental movement is determined to arise as the sequel of a certain other.' He mentions *Similarity, Contrariety, Coadjacency* or *Contiguity*, but gives no detailed exposition of them.

2. Ludovicus Vives. 'Quae simul sunt a Phantasia comprehensa, si alterutrum occurrat, solet secum alterum representare.' Hamilton's Reid, pp. 896 n, 898 n, 908 n.

3. Hobbes gives the law of *Contiguity*. What causes the coherence of ideas is 'their first coherence or consequence at that time when they are produced by sense.' A special instance of this orderly succession, is Cause and Effect.

4. Locke, in a short chapter, exemplifies the effect of Association in creating prejudice, antipathies, and obstacles to truth, but he does not gather up his illustrations under any generalized statement of associating principles.

5. Hume enumerates *Resemblance, Contiguity*, and *Cause* and *Effect;* and he resolves *Contrast* into Causation and Resemblance.

6. Gerard, in his 'Essay on Genius,' states two kinds of principles of Association—Simple and Compound. Of the Simple, there are three:—1. *Resemblance*, whenever perceptions 'at all resemble, one of them being present to the mind, will naturally transport it to the conception of the other'; 2. *Contrariety;* 3. *Vicinity*, '.the conception of any object naturally carries the thoughts to the idea of another object, which was connected

with it either in place or time.' The Compound embrace (1) Co-existent qualities; (2) Cause and Effect; (3) Order.

7. Beattie has—1. *Resemblance*, 'one event or story leads us to think of another that is like it'; 2. *Contrariety;* 3. *Contiguity or Vicinity*, 'when the idea occurs of any place with which we are acquainted, we are apt to pass, by an easy and quick transition, to those of the adjoining places, of the persons who live there, &c.'; 4. *Cause and Effect.* [The statements of Gerard and Beattie are very imperfect.]

8. Hartley has only *Contiguity*, which he expresses thus, 'Sensations are associated when their impressions are either made precisely at the same instant of time, or in the contiguous successive instants.' Association is thus synchronous or successive.

9. James Mill follows Hartley's statement. 'Our ideas spring up or exist in the order in which the sensations existed, of which they are the copies.' He properly objects to making causation a distinct principle, but is unsuccessful in his attempt to resolve Resemblance into Contiguity. *Contrast* arises generally from a *vivid conjunction.*

10. Dugald Stewart (herein following Reid) observes that the causes of Association are so diverse that they can hardly be reduced to a few heads, but enumerates as obvious modes of connection, *Resemblance* (including *Analogy)*, *Contrariety*, *Vicinity* in time and place; he adds as less obvious modes, *Cause* and *Effect*, *Means* and *Ends*, *Premises* and *Conclusions*.

11. Thomas Brown mentions *Contiguity*, *Resemblance* (including *Analogy)*, and *Contrast*, but thinks they may be reduced to one expression; all Suggestion (his word for Association) may depend on prior co-existence, or on immediate proximity of feelings (not of objects).

12. Sir W. Hamilton gives the following as *general laws* of mental succession. I.—The Law of *Associability* or *Possible Co-suggestion:*—All thoughts of the same mental subjects are associable, or capable of suggesting each other. II.—The Law of *Repetition* or *Direct Remembrance:*—Thoughts co-identical in modification, but differing in time, tend to suggest each other. III.—The Law of *Redintegration*, of *Indirect Resemblance*, or of *Reminiscence:*—Thoughts once co-identical in time, are, however different as mental modes, again suggestive of each other, and that in the mutual order which they originally held.

His *Special Laws* are those:—1. The Law of *Similars;*—Things—thoughts resembling each other (be the resemblance simple or analogical) are mutually suggestive. Since resembling modifications are, *to us*, in their resembling points, *identical*, they call up each other according to the Law of Repetition. 2. The Law of *Contrast*. 3. The Law of *Coadjacency*, embracing Cause and Effect, Whole and Parts, Substance and Attribute, Sign and Signified.

E.—*Meanings of certain Terms.*

CONSCIOUSNESS. This may be considered the leading term of Mental Science; all the most subtle distinctions and the most debated questions are unavoidably connected with it. The employment of the word in this treatise has been, as far as possible, consistent with the views maintained as to the fundamental nature of Perception and Knowledge.

Some advantage may be gained by a brief review of the various significations of the term. In popular language, two or three gradations of meaning may be traced. In one class of applications, consciousness is mental life, as opposed to torpor or insensibility; the loss of consciousness is mental extinction for the time; while, on the other hand, a more than ordinary wakefulness and excitement is a heightened form of consciousness. In a second class of meanings, the subjective state, as opposed to the objective, is more particularly intended; when a person is said to be morbidly or excessively conscious, there is indicated an excessive attention to the feelings and the thoughts, and a slender amount of occupation with outward things. It is this meaning that determined Reid and Stewart to apply the name to the distinctive faculty of the mental philosopher, in cognizing operations of the mind.

If, as is generally maintained, the second meaning be too narrow, there is no alternative but to abide by the first or more comprehensive meaning. In this case, the term is the widest in mental philosophy; nay more, if consciousness is the only possible criterion of existence, it is the widest term in the vocabulary of mankind. The sum of all consciousnesses is the sum of all existences.

Consciousness, then, is divided into the two great departments —the OBJECT consciousness, and the SUBJECT consciousness; the greatest transition, or antithesis, within the compass of our being. When putting forth energy, as in muscular exertion, and in the activity of the senses, we are objectively conscious; in pleasure or pain, and in memory, we are subjectively conscious.

Great as is the contrast of the two modes of activity, there are designations that mix and confound them; the chief of these is the term 'Sensation,' next to be adverted to.

A singular position, in the matter of Consciousness, has been taken up by Sir W. Hamilton, and by the Germans almost universally; namely, that Consciousness as a whole, is based on the knowing or intellectual consciousness, or is possible, only through knowledge. We feel only as we *know* that we feel; we are pleased only as we know that we are pleased. It is not the intensity of a feeling that makes the feeling; but the operation of cognizing or knowing the state of feeling.

It must be granted that we cannot have any feeling without

having some knowledge of it; it is the nature of mental excitement to leave some trace of itself in the memory. Farther, any strong emotion calls attention to itself; it may also, however, lead attention away to the object cause, and diminish the subjective consciousness. On any view, the knowledge or attention, although an accompaniment of the state, is not its foundation. If this were so, the increase of the cognitive act would be the increase of the feeling; whereas the fact is the reverse; the less that we are occupied in the properly intellectual function, the more are we possessed with the feeling proper.

It is most accordant with the facts, to regard Feeling as a distinct conscious element, whether cognized or not, whether much or little attended to in the way of discrimination, agreement, or memory. The three functions of the mind are so interwoven and implicated that it is scarcely, if it all, possible to find any one absolutely alone in its exercise; we cannot be all Feeling, without any share of an intellectual element; we cannot be all Will, without either feeling or intellect. The nearest approach to isolation is in the objective consciousness, which, in the moment of its highest engrossment, is an exclusively Intellectual occupation.

SENSATION. The concurrence of various contrasting phenomena in the fact expressed by Sensation, renders this word often ambiguous.

1. In Sensation, there is a combination of physical facts, with a mental fact. Thus, in sight, the physical processes are known to be—the action of light on the retina, a series of nerve currents, and certain outgoing influences to muscles and viscera; while the mental phenomenon is the feeling, or subject state accompanying these. The word is properly applicable, and should be confined in its application, to the strictly mental fact.

2. In the great contrast of the object and the subject consciousness, the word Sensation is applied to both the one and the other. This is owing to the repeated transitions between the two in actual sensation. In looking at a beautiful prospect, the mind passes, by fits and starts, from the one attitude to the other; while engrossed with the extent, figure, distance, and even with the colours of the scene, the attitude is objective; when conscious of the pleasure, the attitude is subjective. Now, the word Sensation applies to both attitudes; unless when put in contrast to Perception, which, in its reference, is purely objective. In this last case, Sensation is limited to the pleasurable or painful accompaniment of the state.

The contrast of Sensation and Perception is thus the contrast between the sensitive and the cognitive, intellectual, or knowledge-giving functions. Hence Perception is applied to the knowledge obtained both directly and indirectly through the exercise of the Senses; the one is called immediate perception, and the other mediate, or acquired perception.

It is with reference to this contrast, that Hamilton enunciates his law of the universe relative of Sensation and Perception; the meaning of which is that the more the mind is subjectively engaged, the less the objective attention, and conversely.

3. In Sensation, past experiences are inextricably woven with a present impression; a circumstance tending to confuse the boundary line between Sense and Intellect. When we look at a tree, the present consciousness is not the bare result of the present stimulation, but that combined with a sum total of past impressions. In short, the mind's retentiveness overlays all present effects; and what seems sensation is an actual stimulation mixed with memory.

Farther, as in Sensation we must be conscious of Agreement and of Difference, which are also intellectual functions, it is clear that there cannot be such a thing as Sensation (in the cognitive meaning) without processes of the Intellect. Hence the question as to the origin of our Ideas in Sense, is charged with ambiguity; yet many of the arguments in favour of Innate Ideas are founded on the supposition that the experience of the Senses excludes such intellectual elements as Likeness, Unlikeness, Equality and Proportion; whereas it is impossible to exclude such attributes from the perceptive process.

PRESENTATION and REPRESENTATION. These words are made, by some metaphysicians, the starting point in the exposition of the mind. The phenomena indicated by them have been fully recognized in the present work, although under other names.

'Presentation' and 'Intuition' are applied to signify the cognition of an object present to the view, in all its circumstantials, and definite relationships in space, and in time: it is the full present actuality of sensation. In looking at a circle drawn on paper before us, the mental cognition is in the highest degree individual or concrete; it is a *presentation*, or *intuition*. But when, after seeing many circles, we form an abstract or general conception of a circle, embodied although that may be in an individual, we are said to possess a *representation*, or to be in a state of *representative* consciousness. So far, the distinction coincides with the distinction between the concrete, in its extreme form of present individuality, and the general or abstract.

The distinction equally holds in subjective cognitions. An actual fit of anger is presentative; the reflecting on it, when past, is representative. The one is an *intuition*, the other a *thought*.

The Presentative or Intuitive knowledge is also termed *Immediate;* the Representative is *Mediate;* the one is known in itself, the other through something else. The individual circle looked at is known by an immediate act; the general property is known mediately through some concrete circle or circles. Sensation is thus contrasted with Perception; the sensation is what is actually felt; the perception is the additional something that is suggested. Colour is sensation; distance (in the Berkeleian view) is perception, representation, or thought.

Hamilton applies the distinction, as already seen (p. 208), in distinguishing the theories of External Perception. His own view is Presentationism; he holds that the consciousness of external reality is *immediate* like the consciousness of colour, touch, or resistance.

Presentation thus corresponds to Sensation in the third meaning above given; a mode of consciousness, however, which is supposable only, and not a matter of fact. What we believe to be a present sensation is, in reality, a complicated product of past and present impressions, a resultant of numerous shocks of difference and of agreement.

PERSONAL IDENTITY. Much controversy has been raised on the question as to our personal or continual identity. Some of the difficulty arises from the ambiguity of the words Sameness, or Identity. There are degrees of sameness; we call two trees the same, merely because they are of one species. The sort of identity, or amount of sameness, intended, under personal identity, is when we call an individual tree the same throughout its whole existence, from germination to final decay. A human body is called the same, or identical, through its whole life, in spite of important diversities; for not only are the actual particles repeatedly changed, but the plan, or arrangement, of those particles is greatly altered in the different stages. A block of marble, a statue, a building, retain a much higher identity, than a plant or animal.

In living beings, therefore, unbroken continuity is the feature of the sameness. The English nation is called the same nation down from the Saxon times. The identity of the United States of America would probably be counted from the date of the Independence, which shows that an unbroken political system is the idea that we form of national identity.

It is, however, in the mind, or subjective life, that the question of sameness is most subtle and perplexed. There are different modes of expressing the identity of a being endowed with mind. One is the notion of a persistent *substance* distinct from, and underlying all the passing moods of consciousness—of feeling, thought, and will; a permanent thread, holding together the variable and shifting manifestations that make our mental life. Of such a substance there can be no proof offered; it is purely hypothetical, but the hypothesis has been found satisfactory to many, and has been considered as self-evident or intuitively certain. Berkeley, in repudiating a substratum of matter, maintained this hypothetical groundwork of mind. Hume declined both entities; resolving matter and mind alike into the sequence of conscious states.

Locke expressed the fact of identity as the ' consciousness of present and past actions in the person to whom they belong.' Person ' is a thinking, intelligent being, that has reason and reflection, and can consider itself as itself, the same thinking being, in different times and places; which it does only by that consciousness which is inseparable from thinking.' ' For, since consciousness always accompanies thinking, and is what makes every one to be what each calls ' self,' and thereby distinguishes self from all other thinking beings; in this alone consists personal identity'—Essay, Book II., chap. 27).

Locke has been attacked on various grounds. First, by Butler and others, for holding that consciousness *makes* self; the objectors holding the view first stated, that the personality is something prior to and apart from the consciousness, as truth precedes and is distinct from the knowledge of it. Reid considers it very strange that personal identity should be confounded with the evidence that we have of our personal identity, that is, with consciousness. We must be the same, before we are known to be the same. Self is one thing; the cognizance of self another thing.

In the second place, Locke's view has been supposed to lead to the absurdity that a man may be, and not be, at the same time, the person that did a particular action, namely, something that has entirely passed out of his consciousness. Consciousness is fugitive: personality is enduring and consecutive. This objection might have been fenced by introducing the *potential* or *possible* consciousness along with the actual. Any experience that has ever entered into our mental personality retains a link, stronger or feebler, with the present, and is within the possibility of being reproduced.

Another criticism is that consciousness is confounded with memory. Locke, however, understood consciousness in a large meaning, as containing the memory of the past, as well as the cognizance of the actual or present. Yet he ought to have adverted to the distinction between present and remembered states, as vital in this question. The best metaphysicians agree that the question at issue involves the nature of our *belief in memory* (see, among others, Brown, Lect. XIII.). We have certain states that we call present, actual, immediate, as in the consciousness of a present light, sound, or taste. We have another class of experiences when these effects are no longer supported in the actual, but remembered, or retained in the ideal; with them is involved the belief that they are not merely what they are now, but are also the remains or products of former states of the kind termed actual; that they somehow represent an experience in past time, as well as constitute an experience in present time.

This memory and belief of the past is not fully exhausted by its mere contrast with the present; there is farther contained in it, the orderly sequence or succession of our mental states. Each item of the past is viewed as preceding some things also past, and as succeeding others. The total past is an orderly retrospect or record, wherein everything has a definite place.

Thus the fact of unbroken succession enters into identity in the mental personality, as well as into the identity of a plant, or animal, a society, or a nation. The mind, however, is self-recording, and preserves its history from an early date; the identity prior to each one's earliest recollection of self, is only objective, like a tree; the parents and others are the testimony to the succession of the individual in the years of mental incompetency.

The Belief in Memory may probably be regarded as standing at one remove from an ultimate law of the mind, namely, the law that connects Belief with our Spontaneous and Voluntary Activity (p. 337).

Full recollection of anything assigns it its point in the stream or succession. This is the difference between memory and imagination: both are ideal as opposed to present actuality: they are faculties of the concrete as opposed to abstraction; but memory can, and imagination cannot, find a determinate place for its objects in the continuous record of the mental life.

SUBSTANCE. This word may be viewed, says Hamilton, either as derived from 'subsistendo,' what subsists by itself, or from 'substando,' what subsists in its accidents, being the basis of qualities or attributes. The two derivations come to the same thing.

Common language has always set forth the contrast of substance and quality or attribute. But as everything that we know or can conceive may be termed a quality, or attribute, if all qualities are supposed withdrawn, there is nothing left to stand for substance. Gold has the qualities of weight, hardness, ductility, colour, &c.; what then is the substance 'gold'? Matter has the property 'Inertia;' what is the substance?

One way out of the difficulty is to postulate an unknown, and unknowable entity, underlying, and in some mysterious way holding together, the various attributes. We are said to be driven by an intuitive and irresistible tendency, to make this assumption; which intuition is held to justify us in such an extreme measure. There is an unknowable substance matter, the subject of the attribute inertia, and of all the special modes of the different kinds of matter—gold, marble, water, oxygen, and the rest. The same hypothetical unknown entity, is expressed in another antithesis— the *noumenon* as against the phenomenon; what *is*, in contrast to what *appears*.

Another way out of the difficulty is to regard the common language as itself unguarded and inaccurate, and as demanding qualification and adjustment. Instead of treating all the energies of a thing as attributes predicable of an unknown essence, a distinction is made between the fundamental, constant, inerasible attributes, and those that are variable, fluctuating, or separable. Thus, as regards 'matter,' the property 'inertia' is fundamental and irremovable; the properties—colour, transparency, hardness, elasticity, oxidation, &c., are variable and fluctuating. 'Inertia' would then be the 'substance' of matter in general; this, together with a certain specific gravity, colour, ductility, &c., would be the substance of gold. Such a rendering comes much nearer to the popular apprehension of substance, than the impalpable and unknown entity. A thing is substantial that resists, as a stone wall; a piece of gauze, a column of smoke, a ghost, are called unsubstantial; they have little or no resisting power.

In this view, substance corresponds with the defining property of each object: what is also called in Aristotelian, and likewise in common language, the Essence.

The Substance of Body, or matter generally, would thus be what is common to all Body—Inertia.

With respect to Mind, the question of Substance is the question of Personal Identity in another shape. The same theorists that assume a persistent unknown something as underlying all consciousness, with a view to Personal Identity, would call this entity, the Substance of Mind, and the known functions of Mind, its qualities or attributes. According to the other view, the Substance of Mind is the three fundamental and defining attributes; those powers or functions, which, being present, constitute mind, and in whose absence we do not apply the name. They are Feeling, Volition, and Intellect; these may vary in degree to an indefinite extent, but in some degree they must be conjoined in everything that we call mind.

A second mode of justifying the current antithesis of substance and quality, without assuming an inconceivable entity, is to call the *total* of any concrete, the Substance, and each one of its properties mentioned singly, a Quality, or attribute. Of the total conjunction of powers, called gold,—weight, hardness, colour, &c., are the qualities in the detail.

It has been previously seen in what acceptations Substance was used by Aristotle. Locke regards the idea of Substance as a complex idea, the aggregate of the ideas of the distinctive attributes. Of substance in general, he allows an obscure, vague, indistinct idea, growing out of the relationship of supporter and support, a general relative notion. If we call any qualities modes or accidents, we imply a correlative subject or substratum, of which they are modes or accidents.

Reid says:—'To me, nothing seems more absurd than that there should be extension without anything extended, or motion without anything moved; yet I cannot give reasons for my opinion, because it seems to me self-evident, and an immediate dictate of my nature.' Hamilton considers that his Law of the Conditioned is applicable to explain Substance and Accident. We are compelled, he says, to pass beyond what appears the phenomenal to an existence absolute, unknown, and incomprehensible. But this compulsion is not itself an ultimate fact of mind; it grows out of the principle of the Conditioned, from which also springs our belief of the law of Cause. (Reid, p. 935).

It has been made a question, whether Space and Time are Substances. Cudworth, Newton, and Clarke, held that they are attributes, and imply a substance, which must be God.

According to Fichte:—'Attributes synthetically united give substance, and substance analyzed gives attributes; a continued substratum, or supporter of attributes, is an impossible conception.'

CLASSICS IN PSYCHOLOGY
AN ARNO PRESS COLLECTION

Angell, James Rowland. **Psychology: On Introductory Study of the Structure and Function of Human Consciousness.** 4th edition. 1908

Bain, Alexander. **Mental Science.** 1868

Baldwin, James Mark. **Social and Ethical Interpretations in Mental Development.** 2nd edition. 1899

Bechterev, Vladimir Michailovitch. **General Principles of Human Reflexology.** [1932]

Binet, Alfred and Th[éodore] Simon. **The Development of Intelligence in Children.** 1916

Bogardus, Emory S. **Fundamentals of Social Psychology.** 1924

Buytendijk, F. J. J. **The Mind of the Dog.** 1936

Ebbinghaus, Hermann. **Psychology: An Elementary Text-Book.** 1908

Goddard, Henry Herbert. **The Kallikak Family.** 1931

Hobhouse, L[eonard] T. **Mind in Evolution.** 1915

Holt, Edwin B. **The Concept of Consciousness.** 1914

Külpe, Oswald. **Outlines of Psychology.** 1895

Ladd-Franklin, Christine. **Colour and Colour Theories.** 1929

Lectures Delivered at the 20th Anniversary Celebration of Clark University. (Reprinted from *The American Journal of Psychology*, Vol. 21, Nos. 2 and 3). 1910

Lipps, Theodor. **Psychological Studies.** 2nd edition. 1926

Loeb, Jacques. **Comparative Physiology of the Brain and Comparative Psychology.** 1900

Lotze, Hermann. **Outlines of Psychology.** [1885]

McDougall, William. **The Group Mind.** 2nd edition. 1920

Meier, Norman C., editor. **Studies in the Psychology of Art: Volume III.** 1939

Morgan, C. Lloyd. **Habit and Instinct.** 1896

Münsterberg, Hugo. **Psychology and Industrial Efficiency.** 1913

Murchison, Carl, editor. **Psychologies of 1930.** 1930

Piéron, Henri. **Thought and the Brain.** 1927

Pillsbury, W[alter] B[owers]. **Attention.** 1908

[Poffenberger, A. T., editor]. **James McKeen Cattell: Man of Science.** 1947

Preyer, W[illiam] **The Mind of the Child: Parts I and II.** 1890/1889

The Psychology of Skill: Three Studies. 1973

Reymert, Martin L., editor. **Feelings and Emotions: The Wittenberg Symposium.** 1928

Ribot, Th[éodule Armand]. **Essay on the Creative Imagination.** 1906

Roback, A[braham] A[aron]. **The Psychology of Character.** 1927

I. M. Sechenov: Biographical Sketch and Essays. (Reprinted from *Selected Works* by I. Sechenov). 1935

Sherrington, Charles. **The Integrative Action of the Nervous System.** 2nd edition. 1947

Spearman, C[harles]. **The Nature of 'Intelligence' and the Principles of Cognition.** 1923

Thorndike, Edward L. **Education: A First Book.** 1912

Thorndike, Edward L., E. O. Bregman, M. V. Cobb, et al. **The Measurement of Intelligence.** [1927]

Titchener, Edward Bradford. **Lectures on the Elementary Psychology of Feeling and Attention.** 1908

Titchener, Edward Bradford. **Lectures on the Experimental Psychology of the Thought-Processes.** 1909

Washburn, Margaret Floy. **Movement and Mental Imagery.** 1916

Whipple, Guy Montrose. **Manual of Mental and Physical Tests: Parts I and II.** 2nd edition. 1914/1915

Woodworth, Robert Sessions. **Dynamic Psychology.** 1918

Wundt, Wilhelm. **An Introduction to Psychology.** 1912

Yerkes, Robert M. **The Dancing Mouse** and **The Mind of a Gorilla.** 1907/1926